TIBETAN RENAISSANCE

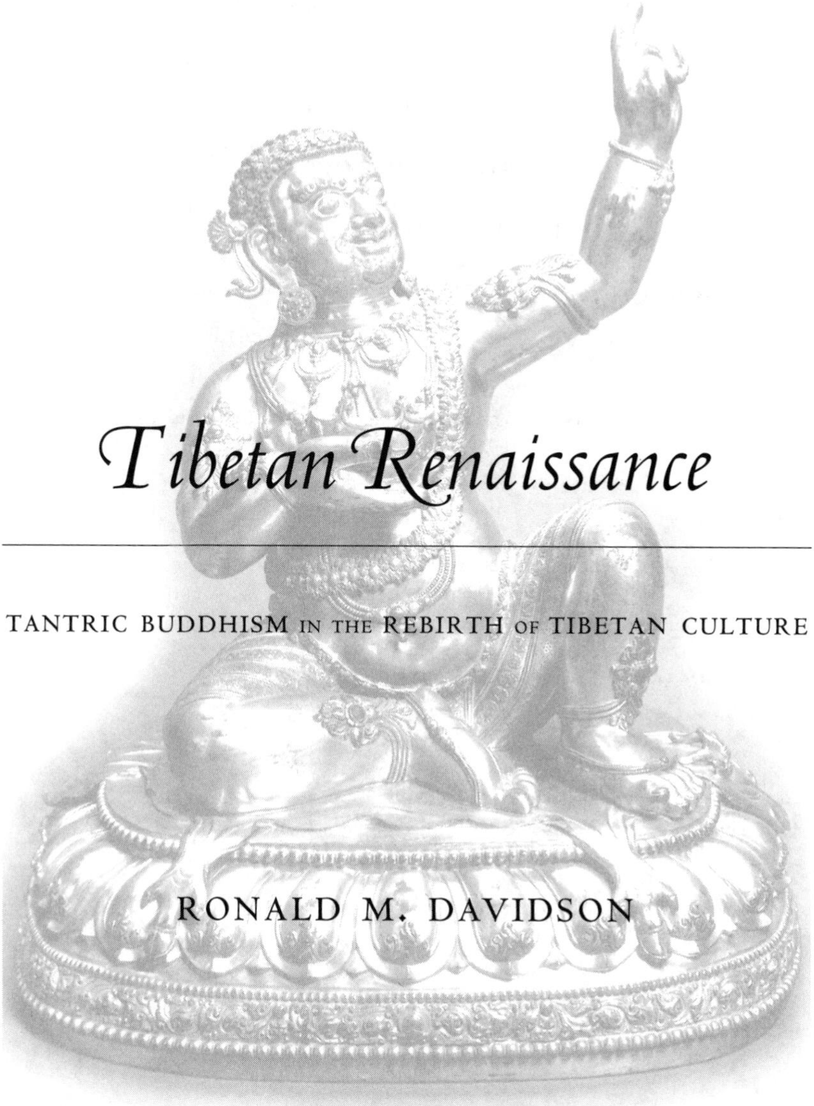

Tibetan Renaissance

TANTRIC BUDDHISM IN THE REBIRTH OF TIBETAN CULTURE

RONALD M. DAVIDSON

COLUMBIA UNIVERSITY PRESS / NEW YORK

[redacted]

The publication of this volume was assisted with grants from the College of Arts and Sciences, Fairfield University, and the Department of Religious Studies, Fairfield University.

COLUMBIA UNIVERSITY PRESS
Publishers Since 1893
New York Chichester, West Sussex

Library of Congress Cataloging-in-Publication Data
Davidson, Ronald M., 1950-
Tibetan renaissance : Tantric Buddhism in the rebirth of Tibetan culture / Ronald M. Davidson.
p. cm.
Includes bibliographical references and index.
ISBN 0-231-13470-3 (cloth) — ISBN 0-231-13471-1 (pbk.)
1. Buddhism—China—Tibet. 2. Tantric Buddhism—China—Tibet.
I. Title.
BQ7612.D38 2004
294.3—dc22 2004056154

∞
Columbia University Press books are printed on permanent and durable acid-free paper.
Printed in the United States of America

c 10 9 8 7 6 5 4 3 2 1

Contents

Preface

This book seeks to recognize one of the most remarkable achievements in human history: the rebirth and reformation of Tibetan culture, approximately a century after the catastrophic collapse and fragmentation of the Tibetan empire in the mid ninth century. Somewhat overlooked in both traditional and modern accounts of the phenomenon is the simple fact that Tibetans employed the vocabulary, texts and rituals of one of the least likely candidates for the promotion of cultural stability—Indian tantric Buddhism—to accomplish much of this feat. Based on their study and translation of the most esoteric of yogic instructions and Buddhist scriptures in the final phase of Indian Buddhism, Tibetans reorganized their social and religious horizon to accommodate the evolving institutions of clan-based esoteric lineages and religious orders. Over time, they refined their implementation of tantric ideals until Tibet became known as the field of activity for the Buddhas and bodhisattvas. As a result, Tibet eventually displaced India itself as the perceived source for ideal Buddhist study and practice, becoming the goal of devout Buddhist pilgrims from much of Eurasia, and the reference point for all viable esoteric Buddhism.

However, this work could not have seen the light of day without the willing participation of my Tibetan teachers and friends, preeminently Ngor Thar-rtse mkhan-po bSod-nams rgya-mtsho (Hiroshi Sonami) who read with me so many of the Sakya texts used and translated here. His generosity of spirit was only equaled by his insistence that I consider translating into English many of the works we read together, through our eleven years of association from 1976 until his untimely death on November 22, 1987. We both knew that such an idea went against the grain of the culture of secrecy nurtured by the Sakya order for so many centuries, but Thar-rtse mkhan-po also believed that for Tibetan Buddhism to prosper in diaspora, it must redefine itself in unforeseen ways. Even while we differed on the validity of sources and the methodology of historical representation, we agreed that the Sakya tradition was just as glorious as it has been proclaimed. The subsequent approval I received in 1996 from H.H. Sakya Trinzen, the head of the Sakya order, for the publication of my translation of the *Root Text of the *Mārgaphala* (Appendix 2) was more than anything else a vindication of Ngor Thar-rtse mkhan-po's vision of the future.

The other person most influential in the development of this work is my friend and colleague, David Germano, of the University of Virginia. Almost from the moment we met, David and I have been mutually supportive of each other's work. He, however, has consistently made time for my manuscripts and provided a venue for their assessment. Those of us who teach at predominantly undergraduate institutions do not have the asset of vetting our writings with graduate classes, and David has consistently provided this for me. He has used versions of this book in his graduate classes at UVA for many years, inviting me down to tangle with his graduate students and their insistent questioning of all received scholarship, even the unpublished kind. I treasure his willingness to make room for my sometimes impenetrable prose and odd jottings about the two or three centuries of Tibetan Buddhism that we both believe was extraordinary in every sense of the word.

Many other friends, colleagues and institutions deserve more gratitude than I can muster on these pages. Matthew Kapstein has been a source of inspiration and a reference point since we first met in 1971. Janet Gyatso and I have shared observations about Tibetan and Buddhist life since even before our graduate days at Berkeley. Dr. Cyrus Stearns very graciously shared both his own translation of the *Root Text of the *Mārgaphala* and his criticism of my rendering, thus saving me from many errors, great and small. David Jackson has often been a supportive presence, even when we disagreed about Sakya directions. Bryan Cuevas kindly read the entire manuscript and made many helpful suggestions. My friends Stephen Goodman and Kenneth Eastman both have known me longer than I would care to admit and deserve my thanks for many kindnesses. Roberto Vitali, Dan Martin, David S. Ruegg, Samten Karmay and Per Kværne have been consistent sources of encouragement and constant standards of good scholarship. Jan-Ulrich Sobisch made possible my obtainment of parts of the *Phag mo gru pa bka' 'bum*, and Leonard van der Kuijp provided me photocopies of manuscripts he had secured in China. My supporters at Fairfield University also deserve my gratitude: Academic Vice President Orin Grossman, Dean Timothy Snyder, John Thiel, Paul Lakeland, Frank Hannafey, and all my colleagues in the Department of Religious Studies.

In India, Dr. Banarsi Lal has been more helpful that I can express, from his reaching out to me in 1983 through our association in 1996–97 and on, until the present. Professor Samdhong Rinpoche, the Central Institute of Higher Tibetan Studies and Sampurnanand Sanskrit University deserve my thanks for their providing an institutional home during various research periods. This research was supported by grants from the American Institute of Indian Studies, the Council for the International Exchange of Scholars' Senior Fulbright Research Fellowship, the United States Information Service, the College of Arts and Sciences at Fairfield University, Fairfield University's Faculty Research Committee, and my colleagues at the Department of Religious Studies.

Moreover, I must certainly thank Wendy Lochner of Columbia University Press for undertaking the publication of this difficult, lengthy and complex manuscript. She has encouraged my work in our discussions together, and Columbia's editorial staff—Leslie Kriesel, Suzanne Ryan and Margaret Yamashita—have been exemplary in their attention to the requirements of this project. For their patience and perseverance I am eternally grateful.

Finally, I wish to express my gratitude to my wife, Dr. Katherine Schwab, who has taught me that not all the world revolves around texts and languages, but who has been supportive in my frenzies of writing and publishing these last several years. Her kindness and grace have afforded me the luxury to be seized by the gods of scholarly endeavor, however meager the outcome. As always, the errors that no doubt afflict this work of history and interpretation can in no way be imputed to the many remarkable teachers, friends and colleagues I have had the good fortune to know, but these errors instead remain mine alone.

Ronald M. Davidson

FAIRFIELD, CONNECTICUT

Maps, Figures, and Tables

MAPS

FIGURES

TABLES

Pronunciation Guide

The correct orthographic transcription of Tibetan words renders a mass of consonants that defy pronunciation by ordinary mortals not initiated into the conventions of silent letters, vowel shifts, tonal modifications, and the host of other adjustments required for their comprehension. Following the lead of my other colleagues, I have used a spelling method similar to that employed by Toni Huber in some of his publications but adjusted to the pronunciation as I experienced it, primarily when studying with Tsang lamas. This usage principally introduces the vowel "é," which is pronounced as "ay," as in the English word "day." I also have used an umlaut to nasalize vowels—for example, Khön, the clan name—and to separate vowels read in succession, as in Deü, in an attempt to encourage the pronunciation of each vowel. Each of these choices is dissatisfactory in some measure but yield a result better than that of many of the alternatives. As the saying goes, "For each lama his own doctrine and for each valley its own dialect." So even though I have heard an eminent teacher's name pronounced "Potowa," my own teachers generally said "Potoba." For the cognoscenti, an orthographic guide translating my transcription into the standard Wylie system is included at the end of this volume, and the correct Tibetan orthography has been used in all the notes. The Sanskrit words were romanized according to the now standard transcription method, and the few Chinese words were transcribed using the *pinyin* system.

Introduction

> We are happy to have heard that the Prince-Bodhisattva's noble figure is well and that his august activity extends everywhere. We, the righteous recipients of your generosity, are also well. You have looked on all with your great gracious love and have extensively acted with the intent to benefit generally both the kingdom and the Buddha's doctrine. But especially you have included even lowly persons like us into your inner circle (lit., heart's maṇḍala). Therefore, your speech has been like a stream of nectar. Moreover, as we have found the finer things, complete in all requisites, come into our possession by the power of your intention to invest us with them, our happiness has naturally increased.
>
> —Pakpa's letter to Khubilai, ca. 1255–59[1]

The widespread perception of Tibet is that of a traditional theocracy in which a priest-king presided until recently over a large monastic populace and received international acclaim as the icon of the true Buddhist religion. But what of Tibet before these factors took place? It may seem surprising that Tibet achieved its religious distinction while emerging from a catastrophic collapse of culture and by forming a civilization that institutionalized the position of Buddhism in a manner not seen before. Chögyel Pakpa, part of whose obsequious letter to Khubilai Khan is translated above, represents the Tibetan paradox of a Buddhist monk in political office. He stands as an emblem of Tibetan historical unfoldment, a sign of a civilization that effected a successful transition from utter disarray to Pan-Asian acclaim for its Buddhist accomplishments.

Pakpa was the inheritor of a lineage of Buddhist practice that stretched from the Mongol court of the Yuan dynasty, back through the halls of Sakya Monastery in southern Central Tibet, on into the dim recesses of the Indian development of esoteric, or tantric, Buddhism. Pakpa's institutional base, Sakya

Monastery, was founded in 1073 C.E. and became the fountainhead of several esoteric practices, most notably one known as the Path and Fruit (**mārga-phala*: *Lamdré*) system. Yet Pakpa's position as the agent of several secretive systems of tantric Buddhism was dependent on the dedicated activity of several generations of Tibetans and Indians beginning in the late tenth and early eleventh century. For some three hundred years, from approximately 950 to 1250, Buddhist monks and yogins paved the way for the ultimate victory of the esoteric religion throughout much of Asia. During this period they had taken forms of Buddhism that had survived on the periphery of Indian institutional life and turned them into the centerpieces of groups sponsoring a religious revival. In the process, Tibetans fashioned events almost without parallel in human history: the composition and codification of the Tibetan canon and the creation of Tibetan institutional religious life.

This book is about the renaissance period in Tibetan history, a period after the vigor of the Tibetan imperium (ca. 650–850) and following the dark time of Tibetan social unrest (ca. 850–950). Most particularly, this book is about the place of late Indian esoteric Buddhism as a focal point for the cultural reintegration of the remnants of Tibetan civilization into the larger Asian universe. From the tenth to the twelfth century, Tibetans used the evolving literature and practices of later esoteric Buddhism as iconic forms and points of reference to reconstruct institutions, found monasteries, and reorganize the political realities of the four horns of Central Tibet. The status of the newly translated scriptures as the most secret and most efficacious of religious methods—the sexiest, if you will—assured them the preeminent position, so that translators specializing in this literature achieved the de facto aristocratic status that some could not obtain by birth. The most notorious of these Tibetan translators acted in the capacity of feudal lords, actualizing through their behavior the metaphor embedded in the ritual life of the esoteric system: becoming the sanctified lord of a spiritual state. The process that ultimately led to the Dalai Lama's theocracy began with these tenth- to twelfth-century personalities, whose monastic status was sometimes lost and their vows compromised in the exercise of power and dominion.

Four themes play out in the movement of Tibetan religious and cultural life during its renaissance. First, Tibetans knit together their fragmented culture by using the textual and ritual tools provided by Buddhist religious systems, especially the late esoteric, yoga-based systems of Indian tantric Buddhism. This is most curious, for late tantric Buddhism was a local form in India, not a unifier of Pan-Indian Buddhist identity in the way it eventually became in Tibet. Second, during their cultural reemergence, Tibetans wrestled with the process of translating enormous amounts of material into an evolving literary language. This astonishing accomplishment brought them new knowledge and access to the ideology of Indian civilization and eventually caused them to textualize their culture, yielding multiple textual communities. Third, Central Tibetans promoted their new Buddhist culture so successfully, and on such an elaborate scale, that by the twelfth century they had managed to displace India as the preferred source of international Buddhist ideology. In this, they were assisted by the declining security situation in India, which was plagued by Islamic incursions from the eleventh through the thirteenth century. Finally, Tibetan lamas employed the new ritual and ideological forms to establish a narrative of the religiopolitical authority of the Buddhist monk, so that monks could eventually replace the old royal line as the legitimate rulers of Central Tibet.

In all of this, the old Tibetan aristocratic clans, which constituted much of the authoritative Buddhist clergy, were a principal driving force. All Tibetans at this time—and at all other times as well—had to pursue their individual or common agendas on the social grid fashioned by the clan structure, as opposed to those without landed family corporate support. Paradoxically, Tibet's aristocratic clans had been problematic during the imperium and had contributed to social instability during the early period of fragmentation. During the renaissance, though, they served as the primary foci for stable institution building. This is particularly true of the Tibet of our study: the four horns of Central Tibet. This area encompasses the provinces of Ü and Tsang, and so "Tibet" in this book principally refers to that domain (map 1). This was the region in which the great clans of the renaissance period established their estates and employed religion for multiple, sometimes conflicting, ends. This was the area from which the recognized sects or denominations of Tibetan Buddhism were to arise, to build institutions, to find success, and to achieve legitimacy. This was the territory in which the great ritual and literary developments of Tibetan religion in the renaissance period took place.

There are several paradoxes throughout this byzantine process, not the least of which concerned the tantric sources for the movement, as these consisted predominantly of the *mahāyoga* or *yoginī-tantra* scriptures, instructions, and rituals. Since the renaissance period, Tibetans have configured their culture around a series of closely related texts espousing forms of Buddhist yoga. By doing this, they achieved a common discourse that they could not have obtained solely from their surviving Buddhist or indigenous Tibetan religious systems. However, this new series of religious reference points—with its ideology of personal empowerment, antinomian conduct, and internal yogic meditation—threatened to overwhelm the emerging fragile civilization. Ultimately, the aristocratic clans, both those left over from the old royal dynasty

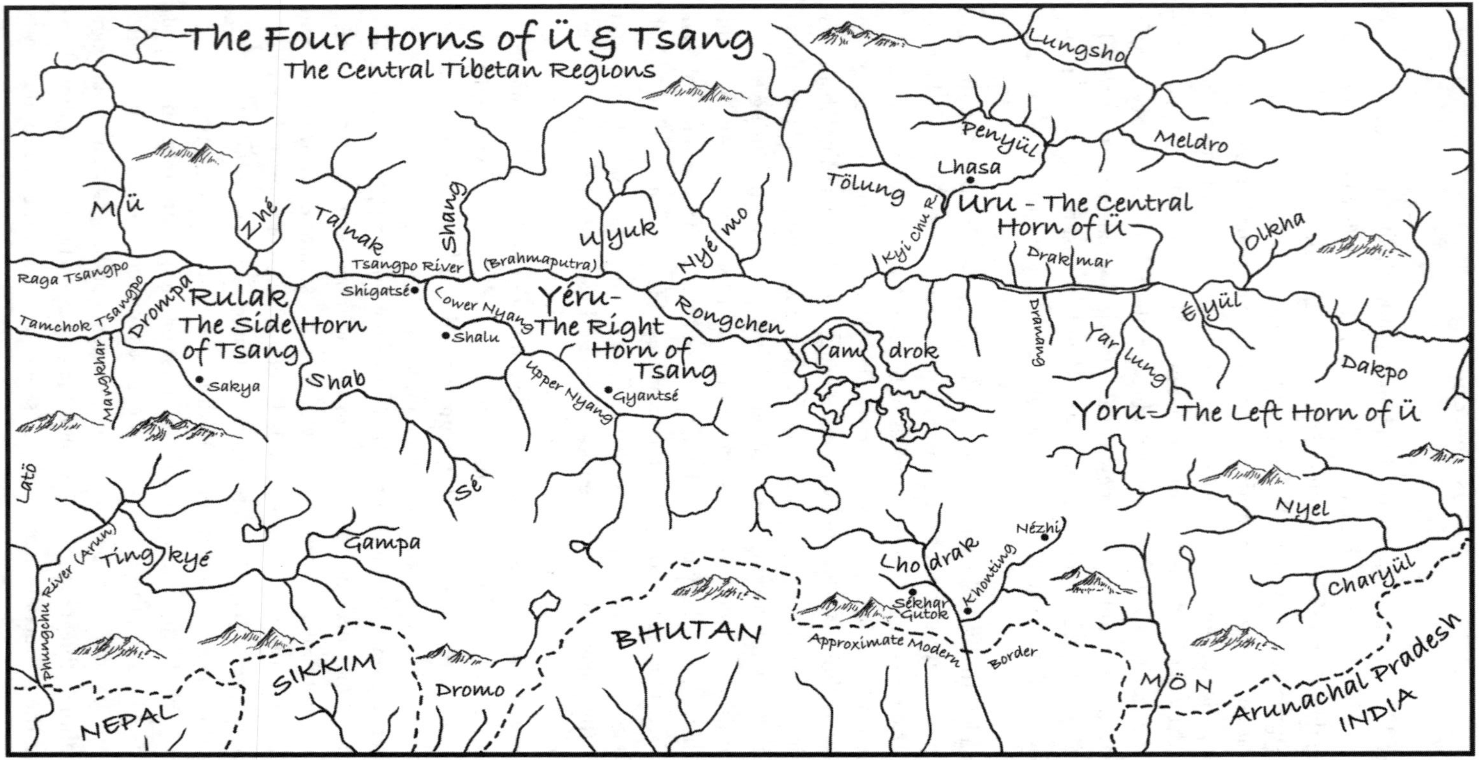

MAP 1 The Four Horns of Tibet with Major Regions in Ü-Tsang.

and some newer aristocratic groups, took control of much of this renaissance movement, even though Buddhism in Tibet never came exclusively under the dominion of the aristocracy. The great clans' reassertion of control began a dispute between those clans and individuals representing the old royal dynastic religiosity and those adopting the new persuasion. The Khön clan, the founders of Sakya Monastery, became one of the mediating forces in this conflict, for they simultaneously represented the legacy of the old empire even while they actively supported the new movement. Their capacity to embody both worlds and the dynamics of their institutional and ritual systems were so successful that they eventually attracted the attention and sought the patronage of Chinggis Khan's Mongol grandsons.

Even as desensitized to outstanding ability as postmodern societies seem, it is easy to see that the accomplishment of the Tibetan monks and scholars was extraordinary. Tibetans had come out of the dark ages of the collapse of the Tibetan empire into the dawn of a new period of cultural and religious efflorescence. Indeed, Tibetan historical literature describes this period using the metaphor of a fire's reignition from a few embers left by its previous flame. As a consequence, Tibetans made a cultural pilgrimage from internecine wars and clan feuds to a period of intellectual and spiritual vigor. The position of those who dedicated their lives to translating the esoteric Buddhist system into the fertile valley of Tibetan religious life contributed in ways that they themselves seemed to understand only partially. In the course of events, these saints and scholars managed to formulate a new and stable religious life for the Tibetan people, one that both took into account the previous efforts of Tibetan clerics and kings and forged a new kind of Buddhist dimension. The catalyst for all of these was the ritual and the yogic literature that had evolved in India from the eighth to the eleventh century and its privileging of the rough, rural, and tribal realities of India's regional centers and local traditions, in some ways analogous to the Tibetans' own situation.

It is one of the accidents of Tibetan religious history that the story of the several dozen preeminent intellectuals of this period remains obscure. Largely ignored as humans in the aftermath of their achievement, they have become enshrined as images of Tibetan religious life, with the narratives of their real lives lying in dust on monastery bookshelves. These rigorous scholars, most of them Buddhist monks, struggled through almost unimaginable difficulties and turned the obscure doctrines and rituals of esoteric Buddhism into living institutions in their country. By doing so, they embedded the meditative, ritual, and conceptual models of Indian esoterism into the newly emergent revival of the Tibetan language, and they also resurrected the old lexicons and nomenclature to meet the challenge of the leading edge of Buddhist life. The ensuing textual legacy caused the Tibetans to reassess themselves so that the source of legitimacy and authority would thereafter be defined by reference to Buddhist texts.

Many of these same textual specialists were equally self-absorbed, with visions of personal grandeur and exhibiting an aggressive posture within their society. Some had come from modest backgrounds, the sons of yak herders or nomads driving pungent bovines at altitudes that freeze the blood on the highest grasslands of the world. Others represented the greater and lesser clans, whose authority drew on mythic systems, familial alliances, and landed resources. Some of the esoteric translators also were consumed with ambition, and they used their linguistic and literary training to assume aristocratic dominion over the areas that fell under the control of their newly constructed establishments. The result was the continuing fragmentation of Tibet, with zones of personal or corporate dominion transformed from political estates into religious fiefdoms. Moreover, the same systems of ritual, yoga, and meditation that so assisted the reemergence of Tibetan public life also embodied the Indian feudal world in its models and vocabulary. This was an imagined universe that could not admit of direct political unification, even though it was stable in its regional affirmation.

PAKPA AND THE MONGOL ENDGAME

In this world of religious princes and aristocratic translators, the young monk Pakpa became both pawn and promoter in the rise of the Mongol dynasty and its interest in Central Tibet, which began in the 1230s. His position marks the installation of esoteric Buddhism and the Sakya order as an imperial ideological force on the Eurasian continent. Sometimes obsequious, sometimes formal, Pakpa's relationship with the cruel imperial conqueror Khubilai Khan is one of the enigmas in the history of Central Asia. Brought before Mongol leaders around 1246 C.E., Pakpa arrived with his younger brother in the encampment of Köden Khan as hostages accompanying their uncle Sakya Paṇḍita. Pakpa was just over ten years of age and had to comprehend his imprisonment as a representative of both his uncle and the Tibetan people at large. In response to the threat of immanent invasion, Sakya Paṇḍita was forced to spend his last days in the entourage of these Mongol princes who strove with one another to secure the legacy of their grandfather, Chinggis. Together, Sakya Paṇḍita and Pakpa managed to rein in the destructive potential of the greatest military machine the world had ever seen, so that Central Tibet, in particular, was spared the ravages that other civilizations suffered, sometimes to their annihilation. After Sakya Paṇḍita's success at diverting a full-scale Mongol invasion of Tibet, Pakpa was to watch his uncle die as yet another hostage of Köden Khan.[2] Then Pakpa took his place as the sanctified chattel swapped among the ruthless warlords of the Central Asian steppe, eventually coming to Khubilai's attention. Nonetheless, Pakpa's term in the Mongol hands turned out to become one of the most engaging success stories in history. He not only won his relative freedom, but as a Buddhist monk, Sakya Paṇḍita's successor, and Khubilai's spiritual confidant, he eventually obtained dominion over political Tibet for his clan and his order. Brought as a political prisoner in 1246, he was enthroned as Khubilai's national preceptor on January 9, 1261, and as imperial preceptor in 1269/70.[3]

Most historians ask one of two questions about Pakpa: what was his activity and influence in Khubilai's court, and what was his legacy in the hundred years of Mongolian rule over the Tibetan plateau? Both these questions are important, and both have been answered to a greater or lesser extent. According to some, Pakpa legitimated Khubilai as a "universal monarch" (*cakravartin*), or divine bodhisattva, and produced a religiopolitical theory of Mongol world domination.[4] Another explanation emphasizes the precedent that the Tangut rulers had established in their relations with the Tibetans. In a similar manner, Pakpa assisted Khubilai by sponsoring magical solutions to personal health or military success.[5] In addition, he supported grand public celebrations and successfully debated the Chinese Daoists to Khubilai's benefit.[6] Finally, he introduced into Tibet the Mongols' administrative systems: their census, taxation systems, and division into myriarchies, to name but a few.[7]

A question less frequently posed is nevertheless germane to the larger issue of the success of Tibetan Buddhism in the Pan-Asian social world: what was there about Sakya Paṇḍita and Pakpa that caused the Mongols to require their presence in the first place? Most of those few scholars posing this question are political and military historians, and accordingly, their answers have been political or military answers, with interpersonal or social reasons representing added value. In their view, Köden needed a representative of the Tibetan people to offer their surrender and to act as the Mongol's governing agent, despite the probability that the remnants of the old Tibetan royal family might have served them better.[8] Similarly, some propose that the secular involvement and political adroitness of Tibetan Buddhists were definitive, through either their maintenance of their own territory in Tibet or their capacity to mediate Mongol disputes.[9] Alternatively, we are assured that Pakpa represented a civilization with a similar legacy of nomadism and that his sect affirmed the tantric accommodation to indigenous shamanism, so that the Mongols sponsored Tibetan Buddhists over others for reasons of similarity.[10] The observation has been made that the Sakya tradition was familially based, indicating a system of longevity, which the Mongols were seeking in lieu of their normal method of subjugating a nation by suborning its feudal families.[11] Finally, some authors have indicated that Pakpa ingratiated himself with Chabi, Khubilai's empress, influencing her to manipulate her husband on Pakpa's behalf.[12]

Each of these explanations has helped us understand the orientation and values associated with Mongols in general and Khubilai in particular. Yet the overwhelming importance placed on exclusively functionalist explanations indicates that more than anything else, Pakpa became a useful cog in the Mongol administration and was rewarded with the gift of Tibet.[13] It seems appropriate to ask whether this assessment accurately identifies the role of the Tibetans among the grandsons of Chinggis Khan. Perhaps, instead, the received analysis reflects the predisposition of these authors to assess this role principally through the filters of Chinese political documents and the suppositions of the social sciences and political history. Indeed, one difficulty with the received explanation is that many of the religions present or available to the Mongol court—Nestorian and Catholic Christianity, Daoism, Manichaeism, Chinese Buddhism, Confucian ritualism, Mongol shamanism, and Sufic Islam—could have performed these tasks almost equally as well. It also is instructive to recall that Chinggis himself was motivated to patronize his own shamanistic tradition, specifically in the person of Teb Tnggri (Kököchü). Teb Tnggri was the source of the prophecy that Chinggis would become the world conqueror, and his position was essential to Chinggis' dominance, even though the two came to be mortal enemies in the struggle for power.[14] In fact, Teb Tnggri's prophecy was so important to the Mongol successors of the Great Khan that Khubilai's brother Hülegü—the Il-khan of Iran—began his letter to King Louis IX of France with a Latin translation of the shaman's pronouncement.[15] In principle at least, the political and social functions attributed to Pakpa appear to have been fulfilled equally well by shamans associated with Chinggis, whose need for them was not less than Khubilai's. When we also realize that Pakpa's neoconservative form of esoteric Buddhism was perhaps the least accommodating to actual shamanistic practice, the Mongol patronage is all the more curious.

We might also question a solely functionalist assessment in regard to the observation that Köden, Möngke, and Khubilai were not the only grandsons of Chinggis to patronize esoteric Buddhist masters from Tibet and India. As the Il-khan of Iran, Hülegü was the supporter of the Pagmo Drupa lineage of the Kagyüpa. The initial period of the Il-khans, in fact, was noted for its Buddhist missionary activity, with Buddhist temples and monasteries built in northern Iran from 1258 until the conversion of Ghazam to Shi'ism in 1295, after which all the existing Buddhist sites were destroyed.[16] Here we find little affirmation from Iranologists about the Mongols' social need to placate their populace or resolve domestic disputes.

It seems difficult, therefore, to follow the proposal that in this instance, Buddhism legitimated the Mongols' rule, for no Muslim population has ever perceived the Buddhist religion as legitimate. If anything, the Buddhist patronage of the period problematized the Il-khans' maintenance of power, but for forty years they brought masters from Tibet, India, and Kashmir. The fact that their support lasted only a few decades might be seen as vindicating the solely political nature of Buddhist patronage, but the Yuan involvement with Tibetan religion was almost as finite in duration. Buddhism did not spread widely among the Mongols until it was reintroduced by the third Dalai Lama, Sönam Gyamtso (1543–88).[17]

Moreover, while any discussion of the nature of religious conversion movements must take into account their sociopolitical functions, the nature and dynamic of the system that Pakpa offered surely must have affected the manner of its reception. Even so, most historians have not yet situated the attributes of Sakya or Kagyüpa forms of esoteric Buddhism in this history.[18] Indeed, much of the tantric literature—including some of the earliest materials—has been overlooked, and we may wonder whether some scholars have been excessively dismissive of the Tibetan and Mongol religious landscape.[19]

In reality, the Mongol patronage of Tibetan and Indian Buddhist masters was an important moment in the spread of arguably the most successful form of Buddhism to have matured in India.[20] Like Kumārajīva (344–411), monks other than Pakpa had been taken as spoils in military campaigns.[21] And like Fotudeng's fourth-century relationship with Shile, many Buddhist masters established a relationship with a warlord based on the presumption of supernormal ability.[22] However, it is instructive to recall that all the monks and yogins courted by Khubilai and his brothers represented a specific kind of Buddhism, the late tantric form found in the *mahāyoga* and *yoginī-tantras*.[23] Developed in an environment of Indian social and political fragmentation, this kind of Buddhism matured in the halls of great Indian monasteries, small retreat centers, and city temples. Coming to Tibet beginning in the late eighth century, this late tantric form of Buddhism provided political, artistic, linguistic, cultural, economic, and legal services and helped in the coalescence and reemergence of the Tibetan culture in an unprecedented manner. Its masters employed their Buddhist training in an exceptionally broad range of applications, so that late Indian esoteric Buddhism both served the needs of a variety of individuals or groups and developed sophisticated dynamics within these new populaces.

Given its source in the fragmented world of early medieval Indian religious life, esoteric Buddhism also tended to reinforce a social agenda that militated against long-term political unity. The Mongol grandsons of Chinggis were but one of many peoples who found themselves enraptured and ennobled by this Buddhist system, even while it eroded their ability to govern successfully. By the end of the Yuan dynasty (1368), the Mongolian court's practice of esoteric rituals had become a caricature of the rituals' ostensible purpose and contributed to the demise of the dynasty.[24] Even then, the esoteric system continued to prosper within Tibet, a society whose missionary activities broadcast the "most secret" of all Buddhist practices, with its monasteries and temples found from the Pacific coast of China to the states of eastern Europe.

HISTORICAL AGENTS IN THE RENAISSANCE

This book is concerned primarily with the lacunae in the story, the nature and activity of Buddhist representatives in the early Tibetan renaissance, the period in which the latest and most complex of all Indian Buddhist religious systems made its most dramatic transmission to another culture. By means of its adoption in Tibet, the roof of the world became perceived as the island of religion, the source of mystical spirituality. Consequently, by the end of the twelfth century, Central Tibet had assumed the position of the great successor of Indian esoteric Buddhism and had established itself as the locus of study for Tangut, Chinese, Nepalese, and even Indians themselves. Such exuberant developments did not come easily or without profound internal struggle, however.

Unfortunately, much of the history of that struggle has yet to be told, and the absence of a synthetic historical narrative has allowed both Tibetan annalists and their modern representatives to portray Tibet as if it became simply a subset of India, with Tibetan centers pale iterations of the larger Indian monasteries. The fallacy of this representation is immediately apparent from the surviving records, which depict Tibetan groups in both conflict and cooperation. In either case, the overwhelming majority of their decisions were grounded in Tibetan, not Indian, relationships and ideals. Based on my understanding of the documents, I have been able to trace a fairly large number of loosely associated actors, who may be grouped as follows:

First there were the Nyingma aristocrats—those like Nubchen and his sons, or Zurchen and Zurchung—who handed down the esoteric and related works from the old royal dynasty. They also composed new works whose drift was increasingly philosophical and whose message was embedded in Tibetan models of religious authority. The first *Old Tantric Canon* was probably assembled by members of the Zur clan, and we see analogous figures in the other Nyingma lineages of the continuously transmitted Holy Word (*bka' ma*).[25]

Second, there were the Bendé and associated quasi monks, who were like the modern Tibetan lay religious (*chos pa*): part clergy, part laity, and intermittently observing some monastic traditions. They and others, like the "Arhats with hair tufts," developed peculiar attributes of dress and coiffure, some of which appear similar to forms seen among the warrior monks (*dab dob*) in the big monasteries of modern Central Tibet. The Bendé were closely associated with the temples of the old royal dynasty that based their functioning on precedents from the dynastic period.

Third, there were the popular preachers, as Martin has termed them, like the five sons of the god Pehar, as well as Star King (Lu Kargyel) and related figures, who were understood as heterodox by some remnants of the imperial house. They and the religious group calling itself "absorbed in religious conduct" (*'ban 'dzi ba*) were featured in the proclamations and hagiographies associated with the kings of Gugé Purang in West Tibet.

Fourth, there were the crazy yogins (*smyong ba*), invoking the behavior of Mila Repa or other wandering tantrikas constructing a Tibetan version of Indian siddha behavior. Some were occasionally on a continuum with the popular preachers, and their songs had wide appeal. Others were more closely related to the Indian or Nepalese siddhas wandering in and out of Tibet, such as Padampa Sangyé or Gayādhara.

Fifth, there were the Eastern Vinaya monks, the most overlooked group from the tenth to the twelfth century, even though they occupied several hundred sites throughout the "four horns of Tibet" that defined the central provinces of Ü and Tsang. The Eastern Vinaya monks initially specialized in the old-fashioned Vinaya, Sūtra, and Abhidharma systems inherited from the royal dynasty, although they began to accommodate themselves to the Kadampa curriculum in the third quarter of the eleventh century. The Eastern Vinaya monks' closest associations were with the Kadampa monks at that time and some members of the Bendé, with whom they occasionally feuded. By the last half of the eleventh century, the Eastern Vinaya monks were contesting with one another as well, over the possession of temples and land. Indeed, the intermittent strife among the various groups of the Eastern Vinaya monks had catastrophic consequences for the major edifices in Central Tibet during the twelfth century.

Sixth, there were the Kadampa monks, who were at first relatively few with curiously little initial influence, for they never established an independent Vinaya system, and most of the Kadampa monks received ordination under the aegis of the Eastern Vinaya. They did, though, sow the seeds of the curriculum employed in the great Buddhist monasteries in North India. This curriculum became quite influential in the twelfth century, some decades after Atiśa's death, and the texts and syllabi became important markers of Tibetan intellectual development. Kadampa monks also generated popular preaching techniques through novel approaches to instructing the untutored in the Holy Dharma.

Seventh, there were the Treasure finders such as Nyang-rel, Chégom Nakpo, or analogous figures in the eleventh and twelfth centuries. Many were attached to or associated with the ancient temples and thus represented some of the Bendé, the "elders" (*gnas brtan*), and other quasi-monk figures, but other Treasure finders were aristocrats with independent domains of authority. The Treasure finders were inspired by, possessed by, or considered incarnations of any number of royal dynastic figures, but most particularly Trihsong Détsen, Vimalamitra, Bairotsana, and, increasingly during the twelfth century, Padmasambhava.

Eighth, there were some non-Kadampa Western Vinaya monks following the path of Rinchen Zangpo, but few were active in Central Tibet. The Western Vinaya had been brought to Tibet by the Indian missionary Dānaśīla during the time of Yéshé-Ö, but it remained in the Gugé Purang principality, and most Vinaya histories indicate that this Vinaya transmission had little influence elsewhere. Nonetheless, Tibetan Western Vinaya monk missives were occasionally influential, as in the case of the royal monk Shiwa-Ö's *Proclamation* of 1092 C.E.

Ninth, there were the translators of the new texts in Central Tibet from the time of Tsalana Yéshé Gyeltsen and Drokmi-lotsāwa onward. Their specialties were most frequently the tantras, and this was the great period of tantric translations, much as the royal dynasty was the great period of basic Mahāyāna *tripiṭaka* translations. Two chapters of this book are devoted to these translators, with Drokmi as their leader, exemplar, and sometimes antagonist.

Tenth, there were wandering Indians, Nepalese, Kashmiris, and the odd Singhalese, Khotanese, or Tangut monks and yogins. Some of them were tantrikas of various stripes, and others were ordained clergy. It would be a mistake to assume that any foreign group was in complete agreement with another foreign group at this time, and they occasionally were seen in conflict or disagreement about Buddhist goals and purposes. In any case, they represented a mobile, ever shifting source of authenticity with which Tibetans continually wrestled. This motley group also became more apparent as time progressed, largely because of the Tanguts' interest in Central Tibet in the twelfth century and the declining situation for the Buddhists in India.

Eleventh, there were occasionally glimpsed the elusive Bön-po priests (*gshen*). Sustaining a mythology of their descent from the legendary country of Tazik, Bön-po priests had conducted ancestral rituals for the old dynasty yet were persecuted at least once by the Buddhist emperor Trihsong Détsen in a wave of Buddhist popularity in the eighth century. Bön-po certainly played a role in the Treasure (Terma) movement, outlined in chapter 6, but there is an astonishing paucity of historical sources in the Bön literature that treat the renaissance period.[26] Of those that exist, most are so mythological that their utility is negligible. Buddhist hagiographical works occasionally mention Bön-po representatives but are so cursory as to be unhelpful.

Just to make matters more challenging, any assessment must take into account multiple membership in these aforementioned groups, depending on the local conditions. Thus, an individual might be an Eastern Vinaya monk, who at the same time studied both the Kadampa and Nyingma systems. The level of involvement in one or another group might change from place to place as well, so that the activity and organization of the Eastern Vinaya monks (perhaps the largest single group) was manifestly different in the Nyang valley of Tsang than it was in the Yarlung valley, or in Dranang, or Lhasa, Yerpa, or elsewhere. Thus we find that Sölnak Tangpoché, founded in 1017, was the early center of Vinaya, Mahāyāna Sūtra, and Yogācāra teaching in Yarlung, while Dranang became, under Drapa Ngönshé, an area increasingly concerned with the ancient system of tantric practice.

We also must be attentive to clan affiliation while recounting the narratives of these groups and individuals. The great clans of Central Tibet—most left over from the imperium, though some arose during the period of unrest—formed centers of gravity from which none entirely escaped. But they did not constitute a specific group dynamic, so that certain members of a clan (such as the Ché or the Ngok) were heavily invested in the new Treasure movement while others founded Eastern Vinaya temples or translated new documents. What the clans did was bring authority, organization, and resources to some of these groups. They also provided the mechanism for inheritance and legitimacy to stabilize the evolving sects of Central Tibetan Buddhism.

Finally, visible throughout this period but especially toward the end, are the neoconservatives, those who formed and propounded the new Buddhist orthodoxy. Unlike the agenda of indigenous Tibetan conservatives—who maintained the superiority of the older aristocratic clans and the authority of the indigenous gods and looked for the restoration of the monarchy and the resurrection of the imperium—the neoconservatives took as their standard of authenticity the feudalistic Buddhist monasteries in India. For these persons, the great Buddhist monasteries and their scholarly preceptors constituted the ideal for an orthodox curriculum, as well as an enlightened monastic and civil administration. For them, anything un-Indian was by definition un-Buddhist, so that all innovations in doctrine, ritual, behavior, or meditation instructions were, *prima facie*, illegitimate, simply because they could not be tied to an Indic text or Indian tradition. In certain cases, even this was not enough, for some of the neoconservatives castigated practices or ideas that were observably Indian but not part of the curriculum of selected great monasteries. Accordingly, Tibetans assailed Indian teachers like the notorious Red Ācārya or Padampa Sangyé for their lapses. Unlike the aforementioned groups, though, the neoconservatives were not a specific sociological formation but an ideological voice appropriated by selected individuals, although it is quite clear that this voice was strongest in West Tibet and the province of Tsang.

THE SAKYA PARADIGM AND THE PRESENT WORK

While this book takes the entire renaissance era as its field of investigation, its focus will be on the formative factors and development of the stable social and physical institutions in general and the Sakyapa systems in particular. Because it was so important to the eventual disposition of Tibet, the forms of esoteric Buddhism employed by the Sakyapa are of greater concern than the other interesting and vital developments, an unfortunate limitation but one necessitated by the wealth of available material and the energy of the period. This emphasis is especially true of the system that Khubilai himself began to study after his initiation into the Hevajra maṇḍala in 1263 C.E.[27] Known in Tibet as the Lamdré, or the "Path and Its Fruit," the chronicles of this meditative program is the subject of a monograph by Cyrus Stearns, whose learned work uses a tradition-based methodology.[28] Consequently, the attributes of critical history—the social factors, the ideological imperatives, and the attendant religious framework—remain in need of more consideration.[29]

Sometimes referred to as the "crest jewel" of the Sakya tantric practice, the Lamdré was ostensibly brought to Tibet in the 1040s by one of the more eccentric characters in Indian Buddhist history: Kāyastha Gayādhara. In Tibet, Gayādhara is reputed to have met the learned and avaricious Drokmi-lotsāwa, and for five fruitful years the two collaborated on various translations. Unfortunately, there is some question about Gayādhara's reputation, and so the possible Indian antecedents of the Lamdré should be examined, and the entire system placed in the context of the interaction between Tibetan religious representatives and their neighbors. This book argues that the Lamdré became much more than Gayādhara was said to have made it. Far from being simply a series of complex internal yogic meditations, the Lamdré also became an icon for the emerging power and authority of the Khön clan in southern Central Tibet. Along with the other esoteric traditions employed at Sakya, the Lamdré embodied the Khön claims to uniqueness and allowed the Khön to establish themselves as one of the most important aristocratic culture bearers of this medieval pre-Mongol period.

This book is divided into nine chapters and a conclusion. Chapter 1 examines the Indian background of ninth- and tenth-century Indian esoteric Buddhism. It summarizes the sociopolitical and religious conditions of early medieval India, surveys the tantric developments, and builds on my previous work dedicated to this period.[30] The chapter also presents early versions of the legends of the Indian siddhas Nāropā and Virūpa, for they were the two most important siddhas for renaissance Tibetans.

Chapter 2 reviews Tibet's political and social circumstances with the demise of the royal dynasty of the Yarlung kings, as well as the position of Relpachen, his assassination, and his brother's usurpation of the throne. The chapter then depicts the collapse of the empire through the succession dispute among the surviving princes' factions and the consequences for Tibetan governmental systems and clan affiliations. Tibet's slide into social disorder and the three insurrections are discussed in some detail, as well as the situation of religion as it was known at the end of the darkest time in the period of fragmentation.

Chapter 3 examines the reemergence of Buddhism in Central Tibet in the late tenth and eleventh centuries. We investigate the extraordinary activity of the early "men of Ü-Tsang" in order to show the rise of the Central Tibetan temple network as an essential precursor of the great translators. This chapter emphasizes this network and examines the conflicts between these monks and the Bendé and other quasi monks. We also consider the eventual influx of the Kadampa, whose renowned founder Atiśa did not come to Central Tibet until around 1046 C.E., many decades after the reintroduction of monastic Buddhism from the China-Tibetan border.

Chapter 4 turns the focus on the later translators, exploring their position as mediators between Tibet and South Asia. In the process, we look behind the motives and methods of translation into the process of textual production by Indians in Tibet. The lineal legitimacy of the translators also is examined, especially the classic instance of hagiographical invention by the legatees of Marpa. The translators' challenges to the representatives of the old royal dynastic religious systems (by this time called the "Ancient Ones" [Nyingma]) are discussed as well. Finally, we show the personalities and groups of the eleventh century to be entranced by an emerging cult of knowledge and gnosis.

Chapter 5 turns to the figure of Drokmi, among the earliest of the Central Tibetan esoteric translators and a larger-than-life personality. We explore his travels to Nepal and India and his encounter with Gayādhara, the eccentric and somewhat dubious Bengali saint. We look at Drokmi's activities through a translation and analysis of the earliest work on Drokmi, by Drakpa Gyeltsen (1148–1216). Drokmi's enclave at the cave residence of Mugulung, the background of Gayādhara, and Drokmi's literary legacy are discussed, and the root text of the Lamdré and the "eight subsidiary cycles of practice" are summarized. Finally, we examine Drokmi's translation oeuvre, showing the decisions and directions he took in selecting from the esoteric archive and translating it into Tibetan.

Chapter 6 is concerned with the Nyingma response to the new socioreligious situation: the ideology of Treasure texts (Terma). The chapter investigates early textual affirmations that "treasure" denoted the precious artifacts discovered in the ruins of the temples of the ancient empire. It moves on to a consideration of the position of the Tibetan emperors, their ancestral legacy, the importance of the old temples, guardian spirits, and the evolving culture of scriptural production in Tibet. Following this, we examine the defense of the Nyingma vision, whether Holy Word (*bka' ma*) or Terma as a response to the translators' and neoconservatives' challenges. The chapter concludes with a discussion of "awareness" (*rig pa*) as a Tibetan religious contribution, different from the gnostic emphasis of the newly translated scriptures.

Chapter 7 moves to the later eleventh century, when Tibetans had begun to systematize and organize the inheritance of a century of effort. We consider the popular religious message of the Kadampa and Kagyüpa as well as the new intellectual contributions in the area of Buddhist philosophy and in tantric theory. Padampa Sangyé and his mission in Tsang Province are proposed as a classic example of Indian religious fluidity. The Khön clan is presented as a paradigmatic instance of clan-based religious formation, beginning with its mythological inception as the descent of divinities, the real position of the Khön in the early imperium, and the stories of the Khön in the period of fragmentation. We look at the first real Khön personality, Khön Könchok Gyelpo, his training with Drokmi and others, and his founding of Sakya Monastery.

Chapter 8 shifts the frame of reference to the early twelfth century and discusses Central Tibetan religious confidence and the institutionalization of religious systems. The reason that the Kālacakra began to gain wide acceptance is considered, as well as the doctrinal developments in Mahāyānist philosophy by Chapa Chökyi Sengé, the temporary efflorescence of women's practice with Chö, and the tantric ideology of Gampopa. The balance of the chapter focuses on the first of the five Sakya masters, Sachen Kunga Nyingpo, his early life and his eventual literary career. He was guided by an important but understudied figure, Bari-lotsāwa, and Bari's training in Indian ritual and his contribution to Sakya construction are described. Sachen's literary career—particularly as it involves the Lamdré—is outlined in some detail. The chapter concludes with an analysis of the "short transmission," which was said to have been granted to Sachen Kunga Nyingpo by the siddha Virūpa.

Chapter 9 considers the latter half of the twelfth and very early thirteenth century. The chapter begins with the sense of both crisis and opportunity experienced by Central Tibetans at that time. We discuss Gampopa's successors, especially Lama Zhang, the first Karmapa, and Pagmo Drupa, and explore the problem behavior of "crazy" saints, particularly of the Zhiché and Chö traditions. The chapter also examines the growing sense of internationalization, with the influx of both Tangut and Indians at this time. Much of the chapter is devoted to the life and career of Sachen's two sons: Sönam Tsémo and Drakpa Gyeltsen. Pakpa's work among the Mongols—or any subsequent Sakya activity—would hardly have been possible without their agency. The two brothers, temperamentally very different from each other, are placed in the context of the middle twelfth through the early thirteenth century.

Finally, the conclusion recapitulates the manner in which Indian esoterism acted as a catalyst for the renaissance of Central Tibetan culture and institutional life, even while inhibiting the unification of political Tibet.

This work concludes with three appendices: a chart of probable Eastern Vinaya temples, an edition and translation of the central esoteric work of the Lamdré, and a table of concordance on the surviving early Lamdré commentaries to the fourteenth century.

The reader may wonder why the book avoids directly treating the two figures with whom I opened this introduction: Sakya Paṇḍita and Pakpa, the fourth and fifth of the "Five Great Ones" in the Sakya order. I have done this for two reasons. First, Sakya Paṇḍita's written work (as opposed to his missionary activity) almost exclusively encounters the other side of Tibetan Buddhism, representing scholasticism and its neoconservative presentation in the fields of monastic Buddhism. This material has been and continues to be explored by those better prepared than I to articulate the major concerns of this seminal figure in Tibetan intellectual history. Yet it was clearly the esoteric elements that became important to the Mongols and, even before this, the site of struggle between clans and social groups in eleventh- and twelfth-century Central Tibet and the overt attraction of the Tanguts to Tibetan Buddhism. Sakya Paṇḍita's uncle and major preceptor in the esoteric system was Drakpa Gyeltsen, who died only twenty-eight years before the Mongols intervened in his learned nephew's life. Given the narrowness of chronology, it may be presumed that the esoteric aspects of the Sakya system would have changed little in that period. Second, while Pakpa was almost exclusively concerned with esoterism (in the manner of his great-uncles and not his uncle), Pakpa lived most of his life in the orbit of the Mongol court and is best investigated in that context. However, the nature of esoteric Buddhism in the Tibetan renaissance and the central position that clans enjoyed in this extraordinary period beg clarification, and so I have elected to make them my focus.

RENAISSANCE AS A TROPE

Readers may find themselves wrestling with certain expectations about this book. Those studying Tibet have become accustomed to the declaration that the reintroduction of Buddhist and Indic culture into Tibet during and after the late tenth century C.E. was a renaissance of the Tibetan civilization. Yet there can be no doubt that the term "Renaissance" is a rubric replete with ideological and categorical associations. Perhaps this use stems from Petrarch's basic perception of the fourteenth century as the reemergence of civilization, freed from the shrouded night of the medieval ages, a perception that has held the historical imagination for some time.[31] Its only relief has been Filippo Villani's sense, from the beginning of the fifteenth century, of the revival of the classical culture, although this theme was foreshadowed by Petrarch.[32] Indeed, the acknowledgment of the revival of Hellenic learning was so strong that Theodore Beza, Calvin's Geneva successor, identified the flood of Greek scholars to Europe following the Ottoman conquest of Constantinople in 1453 as the watershed event of the period. Later historians pointed out that Greek learning was already coming into vogue with the cult of the classics inaugurated by Boccacio and was fueled by the study of Latin and Greek among Italian humanists, a study spread in the fifteenth century by means of Herr Gutenberg's amazing instrument of propagation.

Certainly, the Renaissance was a complex and multifaceted phenomenon. It involved sociopolitical events in the fragmentation of the state during the fourteenth century and the rise of guild economies in the noncapital cities. The decimation of the population from the Black Death and famine was augmented by wandering bands of armed men in western Europe, and the general sense of disintegration was exacerbated by the two and sometimes three popes, as well as the collapse of the Holy Roman Empire. Decentralization was also invested in the new cosmology of Copernicus, despite its suppression by the church and the discovery of the New World in 1492, which was also the year of the inauguration of the Spanish Inquisition and the expulsion of the Jews from Spain by Queen Isabella and King Ferdinand. More than any other quality, however, the Renaissance represents the rise of humanism, when Leonardo presciently seemed to engrave in European collective awareness the later haunting exclamation of Hamlet, "What a piece of work is man! How noble in reason! How infinite in faculties!" (act 2, scene 2), with a similar sense of human promise at least unfulfilled if not positively denied.

Clearly, facile comparisons with the European Renaissance must be eliminated if we are to understand the circumstances in Central Tibet from the last half of the tenth century C.E. to the Mongol involvement. Tibet enjoyed no holdover from Bactrian and Gandhāran Hellenism, and no Michelangelos or Salutatis were rearticulating their understanding of the Greek achievement. Humanism did not arise and precipitate the spread of allegorical literature or the curriculum of *studia humanitatis*. Printing, already employed widely in China from the eleventh century, did not influence Tibet until the thirteenth century; even then it was not used to establish textual scholarship in the foreign scriptural languages in the manner of Greek learning under Marcillio Ficino.

Decentralization was part of the problem of sociopolitical conflict in Tibet, not the cause for regional sophistication, and there were no mathematically based movements toward applied technical virtuosity, as in Leonardo's case. Indeed, the central image of the period—the "Renaissance man"—remained unknown in Asia, to my knowledge, although the hagiographers of occasional saints declare them to have "all knowledge." Both the indigenous culture and the monasteries of Buddhist India supported an estimation of artisans that assigned to them relatively low esteem, and we see no analogy to the sixteenth-century shift in artists' status in Europe that allowed for the urbane painter of the high Renaissance.[33] Thus, at this time Central Tibet produced no saints in laboratories, no humanist engineers, and no poetic mathematicians. To this day, most Tibetans remain unclear about the fundamentals of quantification and look at qualitative definitions as the *sine qua non* of all precise description.

Among the plethora of trajectories engaged during the Renaissance period, the Reformation is frequently listed, often as a necessary consequence of humanism and decentralization.[34] While there was a restoration of monastic Buddhism in Central Tibet in the late tenth and early eleventh century—stimulated in part by a state-sponsored reform movement in the western Tibetan kingdom of Gugé-Purang—from the historical vantage we might consider it both a new sociology (monastic Buddhism being absent) and a proliferation of potential modes of spirituality rather than a fragmentation of the monolithic institution of "the church." Indeed, this period displays its greatest commonality with the sociology of emerging religious movements elsewhere, as seen in the work of Stark and Bainbridge, and others.[35] If the movement also implied the development of pictorial representations of the great figures of Buddhism in the newly built or refurbished monasteries, the donative and narrative representations were predominantly Tibetan developments of the contemporary Indian, Newar, Kashmiri, and Central Asian styles. Such iconography was certainly not the explosive reengagement of lost classical standards of representation from nature, to be quickly exceeded by the artists of Lorenzo de Medici's Florence, through the emergence of patronage driven by international banking. Instead, throughout the twentieth century, Tibetan religious art remained formulaic, highly mannered, and little touched by issues of perspective, actual human anatomy, and direct observation from nature.

Yet if we are to take seriously our investigation of history, we must see that the presumption of gradualism afflicting humane letters since the time of the Enlightenment is particularly suspicious in the face of so much evidence to the contrary. Systems analysis instead invites us to investigate the leaps of complexity implied in the model of punctuated equilibrium developed by Stephen Jay Gould and Niles Eldredge to explain the biology of evolution.[36] Extending this biological paradigm to human cultures, we can see that civilizations appear to compress phenomenal development into an incredibly short span of time, a veritable burst of sociopolitical, economic, artistic, intellectual, literary, and spiritual activity. These bursts may be unprecedented, as in the case of the Athens of Pericles or the rise of the Qin dynasty. Alternatively, they may be focused through an ideology of the rebirth of a lost age, a formulation that drives the culture to much greater accomplishment than that previously experienced in the paradise lost. Both of these instances—new innovation and subsequent rebirth—may be further differentiated by the degree to which they rely on an exterior frame of reference to establish the standards of development. For example, from 645 to 794, Japan modeled four cities in imitation of Changan—Naniwakyō, Nagaokakyō, Nara, and Heiankyō—unprecedented for the Japanese but all constructed on the model of the Tang capital. During a similar period, 618 to 842, Tibetans developed their first unified civilization, which imported culture from China, India, Khotan, Persia, Kashmir, and other countries, but their ability to appropriate cultural models from several sources allowed them a latitude in decision making unavailable to the Japanese.

If the European Renaissance is the most dramatic example of the rebirth process in our own history, we should not ignore similar circumstances in Song-dynasty China or during the later diffusion (*phyi dar*) period of Tibet, which occurred almost simultaneously. In both the Chinese and the Tibetan instances, neglected literary and cultural expressions reemerged, with a narrative of recapturing the spirit of a lost age. Thus, the new translation period might be considered a rebirth of sociocultural life in Central Tibet, and if not *the* Renaissance, it constituted *a* renaissance of Tibetan society attempting to recapture the dynamism of the empire, even if its political realization remained outside Tibet's grasp.

Thus if Tibet was a special place in the world, the renaissance period was an extraordinary time. Making a painful transition from the fragmentation and fall of the royal dynasty, the coalescence of culture in the late tenth to the thirteenth century was facilitated by the doctrines, rituals, and practices of Buddhism, primarily late esoteric Buddhism. Tibet's proximity to India and the Tarim Basin served as a catalyst to the rebirth, and Tibetan scholars, sometimes at the cost of their lives, traveled to Nepal and India in search of the true Buddhism. There they studied in the great monasteries and the small retreat establishments of Buddhist masters, engaging both yogins and monks in their pursuit of the holy Dharma. They brought back not only books but also the literate culture of Indian monasteries, retreat sites, and study centers and used the new esoteric system to assist the renewal of the Tibetan civilization. The great aristocratic clans successfully integrated, domesticated, and institutionalized the Indian yogic systems found in some of the most outrageous religious documents ever composed. Nonetheless, within this extreme version of Buddhism, both the noble clans and the Tibetan commoners discovered the tools for cultural transformation.

I

Early Medieval India and the Esoteric Rhapsody

You have sent [the religious envoys] Era Aro, Mañjuśrī, and retinue, with the best of wealth—silver and gold—to seek the Holy Dharma of India, so that they might open a window to illuminate the deep darkness of Tibet.

As the veritable Buddhaguhya (one whose secret is the Buddha), it gladdens my heart that the Meridian of Royal Authority in the world, the one who has straightened the crooked ways of power within his administration, the Supreme Lord in an unbroken stream of divine manifestations, the Lord Trihsong Détsen should order thus:

"Ride the high plain of Dharma, human and divine!" So he informed Mañjuśrī and Murita not to regard the great diseases forming through the concentration of wind, bile, and phlegm in this heap of the blazing bejeweled body, or through the obstructions of 80,000 demons.

They have persevered, coming from such a high place to invite me there, but I am powerless to go. The Bodhisattva, Ārya Mañjuśrī himself admonished me, "If you go to Tibet, you will lose your life!" Even though I cannot make the journey, I am sending the meditative instruction, my *Yogāvātara*, in response to the King's presents.

—Buddhaguhya's *Bhoṭasvāmidāsalekha* 1.6–9[1]

Buddhaguhya's lament reflects the ambivalence of so many Indian monks to the call of the Tibetan civilization. In Indian Buddhists' eyes, Tibetans were remarkably primitive yet highly dedicated to the Buddhist cause. While Indian Buddhism was encountering setback after setback, the Tibetans appeared to represent a potent source for Buddhist support, and the flowering of Tibetan Buddhism after the eleventh century appears as much the result of Indic problems as the emergence of Tibetan possibilities. Like Sakya Paṇḍita's summons from Köden Khan almost five centuries later, Buddhaguhya's invitation was from a foreign leader, an imperial lord who was marginally civilized by the Asian standards of the day, to a monk who represented the esoteric dispensation. In each instance, the call for the Buddhist monk to become a member of the imperial entourage was motivated by a spectrum of values: a fascination with the charisma of Buddhist spirituality, a desire to appropriate the products of Indian civilization, a need for the sacralization of military authority, a feeling of incompleteness without a famous saint at one's beck and call, and a fear that this saint's gods may hold the key to omnipotence, to mention but a few. Such invitations themselves were dependent on Buddhaguhya's and Sakya Paṇḍita's public aura, a reputation for holiness and learning that the agents of the monarch would have discovered from the monks' contemporaries.

Whether we are speaking of the thirteenth-century Mongols or the fifth-century capture of the Kuchean monk Kumārajīva by the Chinese general Lüguang, the magnetism of Buddhist saintliness acted as a lodestone on the minds of Central Asian adventurers. The initial attraction of esoteric Buddhism to such imperial personalities represented the beginning of the dialogical process. Without the continual verification of its authority, power, utility, and ritual drama—or without the monks' capacity to speak directly to issues of spirituality, language, divinity, and hierarchy—the tantric Buddhist system would have become yet another curious footnote submerged in tomes dedicated to minor religious movements. As I will show, the tantric system was preeminently, perhaps uniquely, capable of this discourse and many other discourses supporting social, political, and cultural systems out of balance. Such capacities simply stem from tantric Buddhism's time and place of generation, for it was a response to fluid conditions in which Buddhist representatives were under extreme duress. Consequently, the Buddhist tantric system possessed adaptive strategies that allowed it to become the tradition of choice in disparate geographical and cultural zones and that permitted it to speak with authority across the centuries to the present. Indeed, it is paradoxical that the Tibetan emperors eventually looked at tantric Buddhism with much wariness and that the great period of the system's efflorescence in Tibet was not the result of the Tibetan imperium but of its collapse. With its capacity to validate locality and individual charisma, though, the esoteric system was very much at home in the sociocultural disarray that constituted postimperial Central Tibet.

This chapter discusses the Indian origin of esoteric Buddhism in general, with an emphasis on those texts and personalities that informed and supported the specific Tibetan iteration of the movement. Even though Tibetocentric and Sinocentric writers often ignore its Indianness, Indian esoteric Buddhism did not arise for the express purpose of converting the courts and appealing to the intelligentsia of Tibet, China, Japan, Burma, or elsewhere. Yet its success was so dramatic in these areas, and the eclipse of Buddhism in India was so complete, that the occlusion of its Indian origin appears to be a normative theme in works devoted to the subject. In reality, the Indian ground of esoteric Buddhism was as important as its time, which was the early medieval period (seventh to twelfth centuries). This chapter first sketches the sociopolitical realities of India in this era. Then it summarizes the Buddhist developments of that time and outlines its institutional esoterism, which presents a sacralization of the overlord as a medieval feudal ideal. The tradition of the "perfected" (*siddha*) is introduced as a new category of Buddhist saint, a Buddhist iteration of an older form of personality associated with the goal of dominion as the emperor of sorcerers (*vidyādharacakravartin*). We introduce tantric literature and its relationship to various forms of practice, showing the Tibetan selection of certain varieties over others. With respect to Tibetan renaissance systems, the ideal siddha was often either Nāropā or Virūpa, and their hagiographies are summarized, with an emphasis on the siddha themes and the historical context, especially as they explain the Tibetan categorization of their lineages as embodying either study (*bshad brgyud*) or practice (*sgrub brgyud*). Unfortunately, the first part of this chapter is a necessary revisitation of many of the ideas already described in greater detail in my previous work. Thus those readers familiar with that text could simply skip to where I consider esoteric literary categories in a somewhat different light.

SOCIOPOLITICAL INDIA IN THE MEDIEVAL PERIOD

The source of Buddhist esoterism was the specific time and place of early medieval India, the period after the final end of the Imperial Guptas around 550 C.E. and especially following the death of Harṣa in 647 C.E., with the subsequent demise of the Puṣyabhūti dynasty. This time was difficult for Indians in general, with changes in almost every parameter of Indian life. Northern India, heretofore dominant or at least equal to the south in India's military and political dynamics, became for the first time subordinate in the energy and exuberance of the new period. Instead, South India and its predominantly Śaiva kings assumed center place and took the initiative in so many ways. First and foremost, this meant that North India's polities were increasingly forced to submit to invidious raids on their territories, their wealth, and the safety of their cities. The most difficult military period was between the mid-seventh and mid-eighth century, when we gain little sense of the vitality of North India and instead see the overwhelming importance of the Pallavas, the Gaṅgās, and related kingdoms south of the Deccan plateau. By the mid-eighth century, India had settled on a rough tension among the major powers located in Kanauj (the Gurjara-Pratīhāras), Bengal (the Pālas), and the Kṛṣṇa River valley (the Rāṣṭrakūṭas). For the two centuries between 750 and 950, these three competed for authority, with the Rāṣṭrakūṭas dominant in nearly every sphere. Even when the Rāṣṭrakūṭas fell, it did not spell the resurgence of the north, for the Ghaznivid Muslims were poised to take their position as raiders from Afghanistan, and the Coḷas were developing their elegant civilization in the south. If the Pālas seemed to be out of the field of strife, it was only for a while, and the dynasty was finally overwhelmed by a realignment of power in favor of southern Bengal. Thus by the end of the twelfth century, just before the massive incursions of the Islamic Turks, the political situation in North India was again represented by a series of fragmented polities, from Bengal to Gujarat, from Kashmir all the way down to the Deccan plateau in the south. Only South India stood strong and relatively united.

These political realities obscure the nature of state-to-state relations, which proceeded along the lines that have been termed either sāmanta feudalism by Chattopadhyaya or the segmentary state, a model advanced by Stein.[2] Briefly, these descriptives mean that the larger states established a series of relations with the smaller, contiguous states. Within each of these polities, large or small, were analogous layers of bureaucracy. Thus each polity had a minister for war and peace, had primary generals, established formal ritual relationships with specific religious traditions, and so forth. Subordinate states established a taxation/commerce (tribute) relationship to their overlords (*rājādhirāja*), and the ruler of the lesser polity was frequently installed at a coronation ceremony (*abhiṣeka*) by the overlord or attended the overlord's own coronation. For the early medieval period, then, much of India established a series of ritual, commercial, and military relations among states, with the lesser states enjoying the protection and prerogatives and suffering the consequences of their involvement with the great princes. These smaller states would act as buffer or client states between the larger polities, so that an array (*maṇḍala*) of vassal countries stood around the overlord in all directions. But sometimes a smaller state would grow strong and would eclipse the larger polity, especially if the latter was having succession battles or if it had treated its vassals with cavalier impunity. Under these circumstances, vassals might temporarily bond together to attempt to overthrow the overlord, with the consequence that one of the previously subordinate states became the new great power in the area.

The economic consequences for North India during this period were devastating, especially for the larger metropolitan areas. They were frequently raided from the seventh century onward and suffered from a net population loss, not so much from an overall decline in the Indian population as from a consistent pattern of relocation as families and individuals became either political or economic refugees. With this decline of the previous metropolitan centers, the well-established trade systems and guilds became casualties of the period, in part because of the new international trade monopolies enjoyed by Islamic and Manichaean merchants beginning in the eighth century. The Rāṣṭrakūṭas, for example, found it in their best interest to support Islamic merchants, and 'Abbassid dhirams were the preferred currency of the realm in the south for almost two centuries. At the regional level, local lords also appropriated indigenous trading markets so as to accrue guild and temple wealth to maintain the expensive military campaigns, for either adventurism or defense of the state. As a result, the wealth of North India increasingly came into the hands of either their kings or the southern princes.

On the receiving end, the small regional centers became the target of much of the population's relocation. The early medieval period saw the rise and coalescence of many smaller states in places where none had previously existed or where only tribal groups had prospered. Indeed, many of these tribal groups became the sources of the new states, with the Gurjaras, Ābhīras, Śabaras, Gonds, Kirātas, and others forming new small countries in which the core population zones occupied traditional lands but were now engaged in land reclamation and concomitant deforestation. Between the core areas were peripheral zones where swidden agriculture and hunter-gatherer practices by tribal or semi-Hinduized peoples made affiliation difficult, so that the periphery remained a question in alliance and allegiance.

With the new populations in the regional centers came new aesthetics and the problem of new identities and gods. The aesthetics were based in the representations of autochthonous divinities and traditional decorative patterns and were inscribed in media, such as stone, that had not been worked by these people before, so that the workshops first placed in the metropolitan culture became relocated to a semirural environment. Not only artists but also Brahmans were actively courted by many of these small states for reasons of religious legitimacy and legal skills. Legitimacy of rule was often established through ritual means and by the new assumption of powers (inscriptions of decisions, royal prerogatives) that had been exercised by other rulers in similar positions. The Brahmans' legal skills were employed in their invocation of precedents established elsewhere to bring indigenous contracts and traditional agreements into the Pan-Indian legal framework. This effort entailed principally the placement of the group into the superstructure of caste (What caste is a Śabara king? What are their rites of passage?) and to place their gods in the pantheon recognized in the evolving corpus of Purāṇic literature.[3] In the process, tribal peoples—then as now—frequently found themselves displaced from their lands rather than included among landholders or demoted to a position far beneath the free power and authority they had previously enjoyed. Now with their sacred sites taken and their tribal lands under cultivation by Brahmans, tribal peoples all too often received much less than was their due.

The principal religious influences of the period stemmed from the Śaiva cultus supported by the predominantly Śaiva southern states. The indigenous gods and local spirits also were encountered by both new aggressive polities and concomitant displaced populations, as tribal regions outside previously Hindu areas become the targets of settlements. The result was an explosion of divinities, anthropomorphic and zoomorphic, some of which (particularly the many local goddesses) were simply identified as a form of this or that goddess or the Great Goddess (Mahādevī) herself. Interestingly, while the devotional phenomenon (*bhakti*) was gaining adherents all over India—again, mostly in the south—it was rather inconsequential in patterns understood by Buddhist authors. That is, writers from the seventh to the twelfth century generally did not recognize the importance of this new form of religious emotion.

Rather, Buddhists consistently represent Śaiva ascetics—along with the ordinary, or garden-variety Brahmans—as the principal antagonists to the Buddhadharma. Especially notable were the extreme groups among the Śaivas, those employing human bones or extraordinary behaviors (e.g., omophagy, scatophagy) as part of their ritual practices. A few groups (especially the Kaulas) engaged in ritual copulation, and the tribal peoples frequently offered human sacrifices to the goddesses of the earth or the locale. All these activities tended to impress Buddhist authors as objects of fascination, derision, imitation, or other responses. Among the most important of the Śaiva groups were the Kāpālikas, those ritually imitating the penance of Śiva-Bhairava following his decapitation of the creator Brahmā. Another important group was the Pāśupatas, whose courting of unmerited public condemnation (by imitating the behavior of dogs and cattle) and their virtuosity of song and dance (as strong contributors to the classical performing arts) made them the objects of public fascination and royal patronage.

Culturally, the medieval period was the real classical time for poetry, the arts, music, and dance. This was the great era of Hindu temple building, when some of the most magnificent structures were planned and executed. Even though this has been represented as a chaotic and dark period, which was true for some decades between the sixth and eighth centuries, it did not exhibit the cultural disintegration often portrayed as a hallmark of the medieval period. Instead, this was a time of shifting standards and new rules, some of which speak of intellectual and artistic excellence, while others inhibited the sense of civic responsibility that had appeared in the documents of previous ages. This was a time in which kings and priests were attributed divinity, thereby granting them a license and willfulness that some certainly abused. Most important, the institutions evolving in India at this time accepted disunity and discontinuity as given and natural conditions, so that topics the modern world might take for granted—such as equality, unity, and universality—were simply not part of the overall discourse of the civilization.

THE BUDDHIST EXPERIENCE AND INSTITUTIONAL ESOTERIC BUDDHISM

As a minority tradition in India at all times during its tenure on Indian soil, the fortunes of Buddhist institutions waxed and waned throughout its history. The early medieval period proved particularly difficult. With the increasing importance of South India, institutions of North Indian origin found themselves either accommodating the new direction or losing out to its force. Unfortunately, Buddhist communities followed the latter avenue, and their decline was accentuated by the economic and political environment, as well as by decisions made by Buddhist intellectuals.

Of first importance were the consequences of the loss of Buddhist patronage. Since its inception, Buddhist monks had been successful in aligning themselves with the great guilds of North India, especially the international trading guilds that took goods from India and returned with the products of China, Rome, Indonesia, and elsewhere. Monks traveled with these merchants, providing skilled linguistic, legal, and medical services in exchange for patronage at home and abroad. Monasteries lent money to Buddhist laymen involved in high-risk international commerce, undercutting the usurious interest rates demanded of the banking guilds on the subcontinent. For their part, trade guilds found their association with monks and monasteries useful, learning accounting and astrology from an honored institution that had no stake in caste but only a burning desire to spread the Teaching of the Teacher. The symbiosis between monastery and guild also was effective in countering the power of political agents and the hubris of the military, so that kings and warlords found that they needed both monasteries and guilds, even though each proved difficult to control. In this way, the Buddhists propagated their message through India and abroad in part with the assistance of guilds and in part through the strategy of services the monks provided.

Much of this changed with the collapse of the great trading guilds in the climate of increased adventurism after Harṣa's death in 647 C.E. The preference given to Arab seafarers by the Rāṣṭrakūṭas and the overwhelming success of Sogdian merchants in the Tarim Basin during and after the seventh century exacerbated the situation in India. There, petty local lords often managed trade for themselves and frequently found ways of increasing their profit by piracy or conspiracy with criminal gangs. As a consequence of the increase of refugees, military deserters, unpaid soldiers and other armed groups, law and order in India deteriorated as well. Even well-funded guilds like the southern Ayyāvoḷe groups carried weapons wherever they went and sometimes doubled as criminal corporations. Orders of militant sādhus, like some of the Pāśupatas, found employment as armed guards for caravans.

Because they were unable to come to terms with many of the southern kings and lords, Buddhist communities in the Kṛṣṇa River valley—a site of extraordinary Buddhist activity for almost a thousand years—slowly disappeared in the rising tide of militant Śaivism. As a consequence, many Buddhist communities contracted into larger, fortresslike monasteries in North India, West India, the far south, and especially the areas of royal patronage in the east. By the tenth century, Indian Buddhist monasteries were predominantly found in Orissa, Bengal, Bihar, Uttar Pradesh, along the west coast, and in a few smaller sites in Madhya Pradesh. Andhra was almost entirely lost, as well as most of the south, except for the communities in and around Nagapattinam, which relied on the connection with Śrī Laṅka and Indonesia for much of its vitality. Most of South India assumed an aura of menace in medieval Buddhist mythology, in which demonesses lie in wait to seize Buddhist monks and merchants or blood-drinking kings sacrifice travelers to angry goddesses.

Even in Bihar, Orissa, and Bengal, the Buddhist strongholds, problems with patronage continued to afflict the monasteries, so that they increasingly operated like the feudal lords that granted them both land and prerogatives. The greatest of the megamonasteries—such as Nālandā, Odantapuri, Somapuri, and Vikramaśīla—had entire sections of the countryside dedicated to their maintenance. They attracted monks from Central Asia, Southeast Asia, and East Asia by the power of their collective scholarship. With perhaps 2,500 to 3,000 monks engaged in study, meditation, and financial transactions in the largest of these, the great monasteries became both the best-organized force in their districts and important political institutions. They collected revenue and maintained police powers in these domains, so that some monks acted as the bureaucrats they had become in all but name. It is ironic that as Buddhist institutions grew scarcer and under greater regional duress, they grew larger and gained greater international attention.

Finally, the persistent problems of Brahmanical antagonism and a search for institutional stability appear to have afflicted Buddhist doctrinal self-representation. No longer would Buddhist thinkers produce the highly original and dynamic systems of Buddhist thought. Instead, two developments occurred in the seventh century that changed the way that Indian Buddhists promoted their philosophical discourse. The first was an extreme movement within the Madhyamaka school of thought, claiming that no Buddhist technical language of any variety was desirable. All statements, it claimed, would imply the contraposition and therefore be rendered absurd (*prasaṅga*) by their very formulation. At the same time, Buddhist intellectuals began to appropriate the language and agenda of Brahmanical epistemologists, so that the presumptive privileging of sensory experience over insight or gnosis was internalized by Buddhist thinkers and included in Buddhist curricula.

Unfortunately, these directions had many unforeseen consequences. In the case of the extreme Madhyamaka position, Buddhists began to appear as if they had nothing to say or at least that any statements verifying the fundamentals of the monastic regimen, or karma, or the Buddhist path were inherently problematic. While Nāgārjuna had warned against a misunderstanding of his position, this is certainly what occurred for those less attuned to the fine points of dialectical doctrine, with certain monks considering that virtue and the rules of order would now become negotiable. Conversely, with the epistemological development, it appeared that if Buddhist statements were not absurd, they were at least derivative from Brahmanical postulates. Although Buddhists in this latter venue had demonstrated that they could speak the language of medieval Indian philosophy, their relative neglect of a position specifically verifying Buddhist doctrine and philosophical architecture—self-contained and without recourse to Brahmanical assumptions—meant that others tended to see them as a subset of all the epistemologists in India instead of as distinct and radical. In both cases, such perceptions belonged to the reception of these developments in the Indian context in the seventh or eighth century and had different consequences in Tibet, especially from the late eleventh century onward.

These internal developments assisted the next phase: the ritual world of esoteric Buddhism. According to our evidence, the mature esoteric movement coalesced in the second half of the seventh century. Earlier texts discussed items like protective mantras and the organization of various sorts of iconographic arrangements into maṇḍalas, and even consecratory rites (*abhiṣeka*) and the occasional visualization of oneself as the Buddha. These discussions, however, were not integrated into a self-aware movement and did not necessarily work in cooperation, so that mantras might be specified in one part of a text and a visualization of a maṇḍala in another part, but without the requisite relationship. In the last part of the seventh century, though, we begin to see evidence of the increasingly cohesive integration of these and other elements under the broad metaphor of becoming the overlord of a circle of vassal states.

The metaphor was not grounded in the theoretical discussions of polity found in such Indian classical treatises as the *Arthaśāstra* but was a direct consequence of the sāmanta feudalism found in medieval India, most particularly from the seventh century onward.

The feudal system at that time mandated that the aspiring king be consecrated into the position of overlord by a ceremony in which he became divine by being invested in his person with a god or gods and took his place in the center of a maṇḍala of subordinate states. These subsidiary states acted as buffers encompassing the great state, which is why it was called a maṇḍala: a circle. Because each of the subordinate states was self-contained, a lesser state could assume the position of a great state and occupy the center of the maṇḍala. The vocabulary of early esoteric Buddhism, in fact, almost precisely mirrors the political terminology found in the inscriptions and documents of the seventh and eighth centuries. The Indians were quite aware of the parallels:

The monk obtains consecration (*abhiṣeka*) from his preceptor (*vajrācārya*) so that he takes pride in himself as a divinity (*devatābhimāna*) and will be given dominion over a circle of divinities (*maṇḍala*) of different families (*kula*). He comes into the company of yogins with spells (*mantrin*) so that he can employ their secret spells (*guhyamantra*). He is protected by Vajrapāṇi, the general of secrets (*guhyakādhipati*). He becomes authorized to engage in ritual behavior (*karma*), which varies from pacific (*śāntika*) to destructive (*abhicāraka*).	The prince obtains coronation (*abhiṣeka*) from his priest (*purohita*) so that he is recognized as composed of fragments of divinity (*devāṃśa*) and will be given dominion over a circle of vassals (*maṇḍala*) of different lineages (*kula*). He comes into the company of his counselors (*mantrin*) so that he can make use of their confidential counsel (*guhyamantra*). He is protected by the head of the army (*tantrādhipati*). He becomes authorized to engage in royal behavior (*rājakarma*), which varies from pacific (*śāntika*) to ritually destructive (*abhicāraka*).

The implications of this metaphorical imitation were worked out in detail through the seventh to tenth centuries, and over time the terminology of entire classes of scriptures became filled with the ideology of politicomilitary models. Some works, such as the *Mahākāla-tantra*, devoted whole chapters to the assumption of state power and how this might be effected. In such instances, the author essentially loses the metaphor and slips back into a position analogous to the final chapter of the *Arthaśāstra*, which specifies magical means when military adventurism is of no avail. Others works clearly state the metaphor as a metaphor ("Just as a *cakravartin* is coronated . . . so shall you") but still assume that the ritual actions (*tantrakarma*) will yield tangible sociopolitical benefits to the mantrin's patrons. Thus, the patronage presumption of so much of esoteric Buddhism is that the yogin will assume the metaphorical position of the overlord while providing esoteric services for actual monarchs.

The metaphor, however, does not mean that esoteric Buddhism may be reduced to a cynical attempt by faltering institutions to secure a position of sycophancy at the feet of murderous tyrants. Instead, it indicates that Buddhists consistently paid close attention to the popular models dominating public life, especially as such models became ubiquitous in the culture in which their institutions evolved. Because the monasteries had already emulated the great feudal holdings of the lords in every direction, the transition to seeing these as inherent in human experience was both swift and natural. This was analogous to the appropriation of a democratic structure by the early Samgha, based on similar structures in the political lives of the Śākyas and Licchavis. In each of these instances, we find a sacralization of the status quo, a redefinition of the organization of reality and space, so that Buddhist doctrine took the given culture as real rather than false. The act of sacralization, in fact, speaks of the fundamental action consistently represented in the esoteric scriptures: the transmutation of poison into nectar. In the way that the poisons of the personality—ignorance, desire, hatred—are transformed by the meditator into the nectar of forms of gnosis, in that same way the structure of reality may be transformed into a hierarchy of spirituality. Instead of the relationship between maṇḍalas of states being ruled by suspicion and duplicity, the maṇḍala of the meditator is a field of compassion and insight. Nevertheless, we cannot escape the fact that the roots of the system were feudal and that the maṇḍalas were political in nature and described fragmented communities responding to hierarchy and control. All this had consequences for the behavior of individuals and entire communities in Tibet.

THE PERFECTED: SIDDHAS AND THE MARGINS OF SOCIETY

While it is more familiar in the context of specifically medieval religious movements, the designation "perfected" (*siddha*) seems to have been employed first for a category of Jaina saint in the centuries before the common era. In this usage, siddhas are devoid of karma and exist eternally on an elevated plane at the summit of the universe.[4] For Jaina authors, the lack of karma means that the soul is not weighed down into the mundane, and this renders siddhas invisible to ordinary perceptions. Their refined bodies are almost human in form but shadowy and indistinct. Even though they are of unimaginable nature, such siddhas have not achieved the final liberation of the Jaina arhats.

Yet the recognizable precursors to Buddhist siddhas are found in Indian political texts and romantic literature, and the Jainas sometimes disparagingly referred to them as "worldly siddhas," for they were concerned with powers (*siddhi*). Instead of being indistinct, these siddhas were very visible and operated on the margins of society, in the twilight zone between the forest and the fields, a place of potency and magic. In this domain, siddhas were known for their various rites that attempted to coerce powerful beings into granting them status, longevity, magical feats, aerial flight, and other abilities. The literature of siddhas shows them to be obsessed with the powers and supernormal abilities attributed to an analogous class of individuals, the sorcerers (*vidyādhara*). The sorcerers owed their title to either the spells or knowledge (*vidyā*) that they wielded in their terrestrial or celestial realms.

The development of the siddha as a new form of Buddhist saint ultimately relied on the synthesis of a number of disparate factors: the perceived need for a new variety of saint, the encounter with tribal peoples and outcaste groups, the appropriation of Śaiva and Śākta practices and textual materials, the dislocation of populations from the great trading centers that had sustained Buddhism before and continued to sustain institutional esoteric Buddhism, and the integration into local or tribal-based emerging feudal systems, to name but a few. Buddhist siddhas represented a new social prototype that provided to regional centers and disenfranchised groups a model of autonomous power outside the artifice of caste Hinduism and offered sophisticated religious approval that did not require the abandonment of regional identity, as opposed to the depersonalization that Buddhist monks experienced in their great monasteries. Siddhas sang in songs composed in different languages or in idioms representative of the aesthetics and images employed and expected by these new groups. Siddhas affirmed the importance of local culture with tribal-related rituals, the naturalness of the jungle, the perimeter, the mountain, and the edge of the field; all these values were praised in Buddhist siddha literature. They used images and told stories that violated Brahmanical ideals and must have both shocked and delighted their audiences. Their concern for storytelling became canonical in the most extreme of Buddhist scriptures, the *yoginī-tantras*, and they freely played with language as children play with toys, sometimes irresponsibly, with potentially disastrous results.

The institutionalization of some siddha literature by the more conservative siddha and monastic community relied heavily on the most developed hermeneutical strategies that Buddhism has ever seen, all with limited success. In the process of domestication, these characters became almost as much literary events as human beings and became organized as literary personas with the numerical procedures (especially the numbers forty, fifty, and eighty to eighty-four and eighty-five) already evident in the village and regional political organizations. Thus the economic and political structures of Orissa, Bengal, Madhya Pradesh, Oḍiyāna, and the Koṅkana coast became the formulas by which siddhas were organized in the institutional literature. Through this institutionalization of noninstitutional esoterism, the tantric canon integrated ideas and behaviors derived from Śaiva, Śākta, Saura, Vaiṣṇava, regional divinities, and local cemetery siddha traditions, all on a catch-as-catch-can basis. Overall, the institutional domestication process took nearly four centuries—from the eighth through the eleventh—with some loose ends still visible.

Not only the spectrum of behavior but also (for some at least) the continuum of behavior extended from the description of siddhas in the *Arthaśāstra* to the Buddhist and Nāth siddhas throughout the medieval period and into the activity of sādhus today. As eccentric and sometimes criminal characters, siddhas were frequently the object of fascination as well as veneration, for they wrapped themselves in an aura of power and potency that had not been so successfully purveyed before. This spectrum of behavior—and of sacred languages—stemmed from the fact that siddhas came from a variety of backgrounds and did not have a Pan-Indic institutional structure to provide the relatively uniform socialization that the Buddhist monastery afforded the esoteric monks. Some siddhas, however, had come from an elite background and were well educated at the highest level but left the monastery, metropolis, or royal court to begin a new career of primitive association, free of the strictures incumbent on the resolutely status-conscious Indians. Others were from the lowest order and came to the siddha's life in a desperate move to make sense of the world that continued to unravel as the gods seemingly supported the capricious conduct of men with swords, power, and wealth. Siddhas from every level brought both strengths and weaknesses, so that the emerging culture of the perfected was constituted by a series of ritual engagements and personal skills, in which charisma and devotion played as important a part as intelligence and naturalness.

TANTRIC LITERATURE AND RITUAL

The tantric literature and ritual systems that became iconic during the Central Tibetan renaissance were drawn from a diverse background. Some were late-seventh- to early-ninth-century compositions and had spread to China and Japan as well as to Tibet and elsewhere, and the most acceptable scriptures had their genesis or editing in the monastic milieu. Especially important were tantras later classified into three categories: "ritual" (*kriyā-tantra*), "practical" (*caryā-tantra*), and "yogic" (*yoga-tantra*). These categories included such works as the *Susiddhikara*, the *Mahāvairocanābhisambodhi*, the *Sarvadurgatipariṣodhana*, and the *Sarvatathāgata-tattvasaṁgraha*, although many others were propagated under these tantric rubrics. These works and their proponents emphasized large maṇḍala systems and their imperial metaphor while downplaying the Indian intensions of eros and power implicit or explicit in both the metaphor and its supporting literature. The other ritual system promoted in these texts tended to emphasize a Buddhist form of the ancient Indian fire sacrifice (*homa*), for the purposes of the four tantric ritual goals: pacifying (diseases, enemies, emotions), augmenting (money, power, merit), controlling (opponents, gods, passions), and killing (enemies, gods, sense of self). In the courts of the kings of China, Tibet, Nanzhao, and elsewhere, official translations of esoteric scriptures tailored their systems to the needs of real potentates, thereby discouraging or forbidding the fissiparous elements of Indian Buddhism. Even then, the intermittent bans on restricted texts and practices were often incomplete or ineffectual, and some illicit works circulated, although they found no place in the imperial catalogs of approved scriptures.

However, there was something of a discontinuity between the spectrum of tantric systems available in India and the menu of those circulating beyond India's borders. Citations in both Indian Buddhist and non-Buddhist literature make clear that tantric practices and the attendant literature in India from the mid-eighth century onward represented a much greater variation than that found in the texts accepted into the restricted environments of court-supported Buddhism abroad or even those surreptitiously transmitted outside approved venues. Many of these illicit texts proclaimed themselves *mahāyoga-tantras* or *yoginī-tantras* and were eventually classified by some into the "highest yoga" category (*yogottara*), a fourth classification of ritual and literature floating above the ritual/practical/yogic categories mentioned previously. These four classes became most popular with Tibetans, who strongly resisted all other typologies, but Indian authors fielded a large variety of classifications, so that a unanimity of position regarding category structures remained as elusive in this as in almost all other areas of tantric Buddhism.[5]

In this regard, works might be classified into one or another category depending on how they were used. The *Mañjuśrīnāmasaṁgīti*, for example, was often reclassified according to the whim of the author and the vocabulary of his exegesis, sometimes considered a *yoga-tantra* but more often higher. This process was important, for all the proponents of different paths—Indians, Kashmiris, Nepalese, Tibetans—understood that the status of a master was to some degree dependent on the status of his system. Consequently, the placement of that system on an ascending scale of religious value marked the placement of the master on an ascending scale of social importance, although Indians seemed a bit more blasé than others about such classifications, since they tended to redefine their categories at a moment's notice. Yet the desire for status meant that complex disputes over seemingly trivial details were driven by the need for lineal and personal validation, on which depended recruitment, resource allocation, and institutional viability. This underlying process can be seen in the two cases of the attempted revival in Tibet of the "lower tantras" (i.e., *kriyā* to *yoga*) by Butön Rinchendrup (1290–1364) and Ngorchen Künga Zangpo (1382–1456).[6] Neither had much success, and they were limited by the logic of stratification: why should a meditator spend his time practicing the lower tantras when the higher ones were available, promised quicker liberation, and conferred greater worldly benefits on its proponents?

Among the most important of the tantric systems for renaissance Tibetans, three stand out: the Guhyasamāja, the Cakrasaṁvara, and the Hevajra. All three had multiple texts—root tantras, exegetical tantras, commentaries, practical manuals, and initiatory and consecration works—as well as multiple lineages in India and were widely accepted by the late tenth century. All three united the practices associated with generating a maṇḍala (the generation process: *utpattikrama*) and the psychosexual yogic practices (the completion process: *sampannakrama*) associated with the extreme siddhas. The former (*utpattikrama*) constituted a complex series of visualizations in which the world was dissolved and replaced by a perfect cosmopolis of Buddhist deities in an impenetrable citadel, with the meditator envisioning himself as the central divinity. The new world, a maṇḍala, was a spiritualized feudal environment with the meditator as the lord of the maṇḍala surrounded by a divine court of vassals representing different families (*kula*) in the different directions. Certainly, the form and vocabulary of the ritual emphasized the new birth (*utpatti*) of the deity, and the meditator was said to purify his birth by this means. In this, the self-visualization of the meditator as divine following his consecration (*abhiṣeka*) was a ritual application of the medieval doctrine that a newly coronated (*abhiṣikta*) king became divine by means of the rite.

The other ritual system emphasized in the *mahāyoga* and *yoginī-tantras* was the internal and psychosexual yogic meditations of the completion process (*sampannakrama*), which was allied with a new series of consecrations. In this case, the other coronation ceremonies were lumped together as the first, or pot, consecration (*kalaśābhiṣeka*). Beyond this one were added the secret consecration (*guyhābhiṣeka*), the insight-gnosis consecration (*prajñājñānābhiṣeka*), and the fourth consecration (*caturthābhiṣeka*). In India, the consecrations were performed physically, and the secret consecration involved the disciple bringing a female partner to the consecrating master, who copulated with the woman and the resulting ejaculate was consumed by the disciple. The insight-gnosis consecration required the disciple to copulate with the partner—designated the insight (*prajñā*) but also called the "ritual seal" (*karma-mudrā*)—under the tutelage of the master to receive an introduction to the gnosis arising from the ritual performance. Finally, the fourth consecration, which varied widely, most often represented the master's instruction to the disciple about the meaning of the secret and insight-gnosis consecrations. All of these involved the Indian mythology of the sacramental power of withholding or ingesting semen.

As the new systems became codified in the ninth century, the consecrations were said to provide access to the ritual or yogic practices. In this organization, the pot consecration authorized the generation process, the visualization of oneself in the maṇḍala. The secret consecration authenticated the yogic system of "self-consecration" (*svādhiṣṭhāna*). Here the yogin visualized his internal wheels (*cakra*), channels (*nāḍī*), and vital air (*vāyu*), with a flame arising from the navel wheel, going up the central channel, and causing the semen-related "thought of awakening" (*bodhicitta*) to drip down from the fontanel. This practice eventually became the source for the "psychic heat" (*gtum mo*) system widely employed by Tibetan "cotton-clad" saints, like the well-known Mila Repa. The insight-gnosis consecration authorized the yogin to perform the psychosexual practices of the "maṇḍala-wheel" yoga (*maṇḍalacakra*). In this, the yogin copulated with a partner, but instead of releasing the semen/*bodhicitta* into the vagina, it was visualized as being drawn upward to the fontanel through the channels and wheels. The visualized rise of the semen/*bodhicitta* was said to create a series of sensations of joy. Because of difficulties associated with either sexuality (i.e., celibacy) or finding an ideal partner (*karmamudrā*), this practice was sometimes carried out with a visualized consort (*jñānamudrā*) rather than with one of flesh and blood. Nonetheless, the process was still said to yield the ascending states of joy. Finally, the fourth consecration was given various attributes, but frequently it authorized the yogin to meditate on the absolute, often given the metaphor of the "great seal" (*mahāmudrā*).

With the completion process yogic practices, the yogin was said to encounter the transformation of the ordinary winds, channels, elements, fluids, and letters that constituted his subtle body (*vajrakāya*). In particular, the winds associated with the ordinary physiological activities, known as the "karmic winds" (*karmavāyu*), would be guided into the central channel and thereby transformed into the gnostic wind (*jñānavāyu*), so that the varieties and attributes of gnosis envisioned by Buddhists would become attained through these yogic practices. In addition, the two principal completion process practices were accompanied by a bewildering variety of yogas: dream yoga, illusory body, corpse reanimation, and so forth. Yet with respect to the primary goal—as a result of his pursuing the yogic postures, breathing exercises, sexual practices, visualizations, and the related complex disciplines that formed the completion process—the yogin was said to observe directly in a controlled manner the experiences of the dissolution of the elements, which unfold in an uncontrolled experience for those at the point of death.[7] In the same way that the generation process is said to purify birth, through the birth of the deity in the maṇḍala, the completion process is said to purify death, through the union of phenomenal appearance and emptiness.

Within this broad framework, the Guhyasamāja system was grounded in the ritual developments of the *yoga-tantra* materials, and many of its texts simply recognize their tradition as *yoga-tantra*, even though it was eventually classified as *mahāyoga-tantra* and this latter term was used in these same works as well. By the end of the eighth century, the basic text of the *Guhyasamāja-tantra* had already been completed in eighteen chapters, and various masters were developing systems and commentaries. During the ninth century, two schools of ritual became codified and widely accepted: the Jñānapāda school, named after the master Buddhajñānapāda, and the Ārya school, named after the lineage of masters from the eighth-century tantric Nāgārjuna, followed by the tantric Āryadeva and Candrakīrti. There were other traditions, to be sure, but these two were the most fruitful, in part because the Ārya school appropriated the identities of the well-known Madhyamaka authorities who had lived centuries before them, and in part because the masters of these two schools were very successful in their institutionalization, aligning themselves with Buddhist centers throughout North India and around Śrī Śaila in South India (map 2).

Like the other successful traditions, the Guhyasamāja system contributed to the Buddhist lexicon both a ritual organization and a technical vocabulary. In the surviving *Guhyasamāja-tantra*, the ritual of the generation process is divided into four sections—service (*sevā*), proximate accomplishment (*upasādhana*), accomplishment (*sādhana*), and great accomplishment (*mahāsādhana*)—although the last chapter of the tantra begins to extend these four to the completion process as well.[8] Based on this tantra, each of the two traditions formulated its own principal maṇḍala, with the Jñānapāda school articulating a maṇḍala employing Mañjuvajra as its central divinity and the Ārya school proposing a maṇḍala featuring Akṣobhyavajra and his retinue.[9] Why the distinction? Both divinities are found in the *Guhyasamāja-tantra*, but the traditions state that they embody the separate revelations of their founding masters.[10]

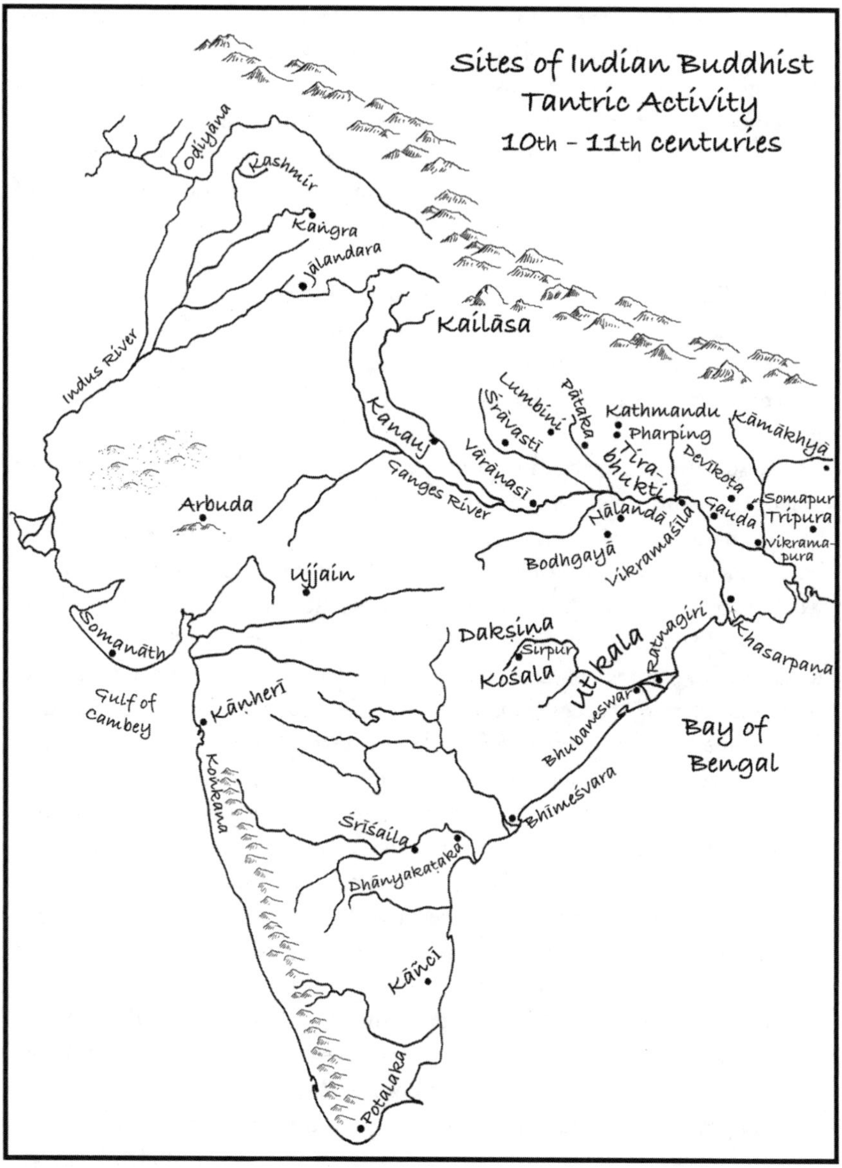

MAP 2 Sites of Indian Buddhist Tantric Activity, Tenth and Eleventh Centuries.

Buddhajñānapāda, for example, was said to have received the revelation from an emanation of the eternal Buddha Vajradhara, whereas Nāgārjuna's maṇḍala was ostensibly the result of his study of the practices with Saraha, although sometimes other figures are mentioned in the chaotic Nāgārjuna lore.[11]

In terms of vocabulary, the Ārya school's greatest contribution was the articulation of experience during the completion process on ascending grades of emptiness and light values.[12]

śūnya (emptiness)	āloka (light)
atiśūnya (exceeding emptiness)	ālokābhāsa (appearance of light)
mahāśūnya (great emptiness)	ālokopalabdhi (perception of light)
sarvaśūnya (universal emptiness)	prabhāsvara (clear light)

These levels of realization were developed through the five meditative practices (*pañcakrama*) delineated by the same school and embodied in the text by that name, the *Pañcakrama*. This profoundly influential work appears to have had at least two different authors, Nāgārjuna and Śākyamitra, which would support a model of community composition rather than individual inspiration.[13] In any event, the five consist of the processes of the "adamantine repetition" (*vajrajāpa*), of the "purity of all purity" (*sarvaśuddhiviśuddhi*), of the "self-consecration" (*svādhiṣṭhāna*), of the "realization of the highest secret bliss" (*paramarahasyasukhābhisambodhi*), and of the process of "union" (*yuganaddhakrama*). The Ārya school's vocabulary system, like the four grades of the generation process, proved to be remarkably influential and continues to this day to configure the manner in which Tibetans discuss this and related material.

For its part, the Cakrasaṁvara system represented a new attempt to bring a sense of place to the tantric table. The earliest form of the tantra had emerged by the late eighth century, and eventually at least three schools of practice coalesced: those attributed to Luhi, Ghaṇṭapāda, and Kāṇha. All three schools emphasized sacred geography, a movement initially developed through the Cakrasaṁvara maṇḍala and the myth of its origin. Adapted from a story articulated in such *yoga-tantra* works as the *Sarvatathāgata-tattvasaṁgraha*, Cakrasaṁvara proponents maintained that the eternal Buddha Vajradhara emanated a form, Heruka, to control Maheśvara (Śiva) and his twenty-four Bhairavas, along with their consorts. Maheśvara was eventually humiliated and destroyed, and Heruka took his place on top of Mount Sumeru, with the twenty-four Bhairavas controlling the twenty-four pilgrimage sites of India.[14] These twenty-four were given various values in a list for which we have several variations, but some form of the list was included in virtually every Cakrasaṁvara maṇḍala.

While the exact number of deities in individual maṇḍalas differed, each featured Cakrasaṁvara (as Heruka) in the center and three concentric rings of eight Bhairavas per ring progressing out from the center, representing the maṇḍalas of mind, speech, and body. A well-accepted version identifies the following twenty-four sites in the maṇḍala:

Four pīṭhas: uḍḍiyāna, jālandhara, pullīyamalaya, and arbuda.
Four upapīṭhas: godāvarī, rāmeśvara, devīkoṭa, and mālava.
Two kṣetras: kāmarūpa and oḍra; and two upakṣetras: triśākuni and kośala.
Two chandohas: kaliṅga and lampāka; and the two upacchandohas: kāñci and himālaya.
Two melāpakas: pretapuri and gṛhadevatā; and two upamelāpakas: saurāṣṭra and suvarṇadvīpa.
Two śmaśānas: nagara and sindhu; and the two upaśmaśānas: maru and kulatā.

Because of its interest in sacred geography, some Indian masters of the Cakrasaṁvara were well aware that sacred sites existed outside India as well as inside it, and the list includes Suvarṇadvīpa, a medieval kingdom variously located in Burma or Indonesia.[15] Some Tibetans eventually came to consider their country as Pretapuri ("city of ghosts," a melāpaka), combining indigenous legends of Tibetans' origins with the mythology of Indian sacred domains.[16] Curiously, the various manipulations of yoga that became attached to the Cakrasaṁvara system held less overall importance than the ideology of sacred geography, and the Cakrasaṁvara completion process became influenced first by the Ārya school's vocabulary and ordering of yoga and subsequently by the Hevajra-related nomenclature.

The succeeding chapters of this book often mention the *Hevajra-tantra*, which was composed in India later than the other two great tantras. The *Hevajra-tantra* is categorically a siddha production, probably from somewhere in eastern India (Bengal, Bihar, Assam, or Orissa) and was probably written during the late ninth or early tenth century. Also termed the *Dvikalpa* because of its two ritual sections (*kalpa*), the *Hevajra-tantra* was considered a section of the "great *Hevajra-tantra*" in 500,000 verses, and the identification of a received text as a smaller part of a vast mythic work was a common trope in esoteric writing. Like the *Guhyasamāja-tantra* and the *Cakrasaṁvara-tantra*, the *Hevajra-tantra* is a text at the center of a web of mutually referring and sometimes conflicting scriptures, commentaries, and ritual manuals. Most important for our purposes are two related scriptures, the *Saṁpuṭa-tantra* and the [*Ḍākinī*]-*Vajrapañjara-tantra*, both of which are considered to be the most significant of the many commentarial tantras. As will become evident, the *Hevajra-tantra* and its various lineages were profoundly influential for renaissance Central Tibetans. They represent a ritual and meditative tradition that became central to both the Sakyapa and the Kagyüpa orders, although the Sakyapa emphasized it more than any other.

The Sakyapa describe four lineages of the Hevajra generation process that they maintain—those of the siddhas Ḍombiheruka, Kāṇha, Saroruhavajra, and Kṛṣṇapaṇḍita—and these are representative, even if it is clear that there were many more available. Indeed, the works of the famous tantrika scholar Ratnākaraśānti were among the more influential, although some Tibetans questioned the great paṇḍita's spirituality.[17] At the heart of most lineages was the basic Hevajra maṇḍala, a form curiously old even if its Hevajra application was not. The maṇḍala features Hevajra, with his feminine partner Nairātmyā, surrounded by eight *ḍākinīs*, variously identified. We see analogous systems in India from the fifth century onward, largely in tribal sites and those dedicated to the seven or eight "mothers" (*mātṛkā*).[18] This is the same form that became iterated threefold in the Cakrasaṁvara maṇḍalas and is observable elsewhere in *yoginī-tantra* sources.

Beyond the generation process maṇḍalas, the Hevajra system was supremely influential in its espousing a fourfold gradation in the completion process, analogous to the Ārya school's model of Guhyasamāja practice but quite different from it in reality. The *Hevajra-tantra* indicates that four levels of ecstasy or orgasm occur during the psychosexual practices and are associated with the *bodhicitta* passing through various wheels/psychic centers. These four forms of bliss are also allied with four moments of realization, the four wheels, the bodies of the Buddha, and the like, in another hierarchy of experience.[19]

CONSECRATIONS	JOYS	MOMENTS	CAKRAS	BODY	SYLLABLE
ācārya	ānanda	vicitra	svabhāvikakāya	head	HAṂ
guhya	paramānanda	vipāka	sambhogakāya	throat	OṂ
prajñājñāna	viramānanda	vimarda	dharmakāya	heart	HŪṂ
caturtha	sahajānanda	vilakṣaṇa	nirmāṇakāya	navel	A

This table demonstrates that the joy (*ānanda*), supreme joy (*paramānanda*), absence of joy (*viramānanda*), and natural joy (*sahajānanda*) represent ascending levels of realization associated with the four moments: variety (*vicitra*), maturation (*vipāka*), eclipse (*vimarda*), and signlessness (*vilakṣaṇa*). We must note that the order of the joys and the moments, their meaning, and their association with the different cakras in the different psychic centers all were disputed by various masters, each with his preferred version. Moreover, the initial movement in this direction was probably begun by Guhyasamāja masters like Buddhajñānapāda and Padmavajra but was most successfully integrated into tantric scripture with the composition of the *Hevajra-tantra*. Thus, the Hevajra masters, like all tantric authors, brought to the table disparate materials and wedded them together with a vision of deity, emphasizing, in their case, the experiential realm of the completion process.

We will discuss other influential tantric traditions from time to time, and two deserve mention now. In some sense, they appear among the oldest and the youngest, although this means that they are separated by only four centuries at the most. At least as old as the *Guhyasamāja-tantra* are rituals and some form of a scripture dedicated to Yamāri/Yamāntaka/Vajrabhairava, taken collectively as the victor over the god of death (*yama*) and a manifestation of the bodhisattva Mañjuśrī. One lineage was brought to Central Tibet by Ralo Dorjé-drak (b. 1016), and his career is discussed in some detail in chapter 4. The Yamāri tradition is the source for many of the magical rites, especially killing rituals, employed in India, Nepal, and Tibet, and the Yamāri texts feature some of the most interesting vignettes of Indian rural ghost lore and sorcery.

On another scale entirely is the tantra of much fascination today, the *Kālacakra-tantra*. This work was reputedly first translated into Tibetan around 1027 C.E. by Gyijo Dawé Öser, and thus versions were available throughout the renaissance.[20] Surprisingly, however, the work was only marginally influential before the twelfth century but achieved great importance in the following centuries when it became the focus of the unorthodox positions of the Jonangpa order. Perhaps the *Kālacakra-tantra*'s initially tepid reception was a function of its atypical literary character. It is the only tantra of my acquaintance that indicates single authorship: it is well written and well organized, with five long chapters of similar length that work nicely together. Its inherent complexity and integrated organization meant that it needed to be approached with great effort and discipline, as it is necessary to know the content of each chapter in order to understand the grand architecture and specific application of the work as a whole. This differs from the highly idiosyncratic form of most tantras, which have many short chapters and contain multiple internal contradictions, styles, and authors. Apparently the *Kālacakra-tantra* was appropriate to the great syntheses and institutional developments of the thirteenth century, when the Mongols brought order and unity to Tibet, for the *Kālacakra* is the quintessential example of a unified, orderly vision. But because its influence was greatest outside the chronological frame of the present study, I have not emphasized it in a manner commensurate with its later importance.

NĀROPĀ THE LEGEND: THE GREAT PAṆḌITA GOES NATIVE

The aforementioned systems were predominantly composed by and transmitted through Buddhist siddhas, generally laymen but occasionally including monks or failed monks, and the stories of these figures can make very entertaining reading, which was one of their many purposes. Like other hagiographical forms, siddha narratives are syntheses of several factors—genres, expectations, prototypes, and so forth—all organized by a spectrum of patronage requirements and social forms. The social forms were distinct from the specific needs of the time and community, and the hagiographies represent consistently emerging sacred personas for their protagonists. Moreover, siddha hagiographies in particular are best examined individually in light of the yogic system in which they were generated, supported, and transmitted. But because my main emphasis is not India, these and other tasks must remain only partially fulfilled.

Here we may turn our attention from the siddha hagiographies' earliest sources in India to their further employment as media for religious transmission outside India's borders. The earlier, oral varieties required rearticulation with greater emphasis on certain values. In these instances, the hagiographies' literary construction was an important focus, since these works were preeminently literary events and could not be construed as history in any meaningful sense of the term, although they might contain much historical information. Finally, we should consider the relationship between the narratives and the concomitant ritual or meditative systems as far as these systems are explored or available to us, since the hagiographies frequently embody spiritual, psychological, or physiological experiences said to occur during the practice of these systems.

Arguably the most important of these eccentric personalities for the Central Tibetan renaissance is Nāropā. Like Saraha, another siddha popular with Tibetan chroniclers, Nāropā was a figure around whom so much hagiography has been wrapped that it scarcely seems possible to find room for a real person (figure 1). Chapter 4 looks at a contemporary record of Nāropā, which demonstrates that he was a Bengali lay guru interested in politics, religion, food, and the mild intoxicant betel and to have died in 1041/42 C.E. However, in the

FIGURE 1 Nāropā. After an early-thirteenth-century painting in the Alchi Sum-tsek

manner that Buddhists tend to do with their saints, Kagyüpa hagiographies depersonalize Nāropā, casting him in several preestablished molds. Because of their inattention to evidence, Tibetan hagiographers disagree on his location, family, early career, and the majority of other details. Many Tibetans incorrectly locate him in Kashmir, while others accurately place him in Bengal; some say he was a Brahman, others that he was a prince, and one Indian source—the version found in the compendium attributed to Abhayadattaśrī—indicates that he was from a low-caste family of liquor sellers (*śauṇḍika*).

One of the earliest sources is the thirteenth-century text of Gyel-tangpa Déchen Dorjé, whose thirty-three-verse homage and attendant prose commentary begins by portraying Nāropā's youth as virtually identical with the Buddha's.[21] In this narrative, Nāropā is born in Bengal, in a city named Nagara (i.e., "city"). He is born into the Śākya lineage, the son of king *Kuśalavarman, and comes into the world in the month that the Buddha was born (*vaiśākha*), as understood by Tibetans. Like Siddhārtha himself, Nāropā learns all the scriptures without being taught. He is married against his wishes and eventually renounces lay life and becomes the great abbot of Nālandā, called Abhayakīrti:[22]

In performance of the abbot's duties in that way,
He spread the doctrine and reversed all the serious problems.
He cut the hair of the tīrthikas and planted the banner of victory of religion.
Homage to Nāropā, the lord of the doctrine!

While thus doing his duties for the doctrine,
Jñānaḍākinī conferred a prophecy:
"Seek out Tillipa, who contemplates the essential meaning!"
Homage to Nāropā, who received this prophecy!

In response, Nāropā sang a song of renunciation and went seeking Tillipa.
The Nālandā monks all begged him to stay,
But he would not listen and sought the guru with faith.
Homage to Nāropā, with correct karmic connections!

While seeking the lord guru with devotion,
He persevered in his ascetic practices.
But a bodiless voice told him to meditate on Cakrasaṁvara instead of Hevajra.
Homage to Nāropā, who accomplished Cakrasaṁvara!

But Cakrasaṁvara himself told Nāropā that if Tillipa
Were not sought out or relied on, Nāropā would not obtain Buddhahood.
So with faith and devotion he sought the guru with the correct characteristics.
Homage to Nāropā, who seeks the guru!

Endeavoring in that way and seeking the guru,
When he was finally encountered, Nāropā did not recognize the guru,
So that he suffered with longing, faith, and devotion.
Homage to Nāropā, who purified his obscurations and met the guru face to face!

With the power of devotion he prayed to request the Dharma,
And the lord guru demonstrated the deep Dharma of symbols.

Understanding those symbols, Nāropā realized the reality of Dharma.
Homage to Nāropā, who was liberated by the Dharma of symbols!

So the lord guru Tillipa, who was the manifest Buddha (*nirmāṇakāya*),
In order to ripen Nāropā's stream of consciousness, conferred the four consecrations.
Recognizing the meaning of the consecrations, Nāropā sang an entire song.
Homage to Nāropā, who obtained the consecrations!

Impelled by faith and in accordance with the guru's directions,
Nāropā jumped from a fortress roof, was stabbed in the kidneys with a stake,
Leaped in the sandalwood fire, made a bridge in a swamp, and so forth.
Homage to Nāropā, who practiced the difficult path!

A king then heard of Nāropā's qualities in his practice,
And having witnessed Nāropā's power [and tantric gaze], he had faith and devotion.
The king offered his daughter, and through his practice Nāropā killed and revived beings.
Homage to Nāropā, who performed the sexual practice!

Then the king's chaplain *Kākavana
[Conceived ill will] toward the practice of the lord of yogins, Nāropā,
But saw that the result of his desire, anger, and so on would lead him to hell.
Homage to Nāropā, who leads beings to repentance and confession!

Then after that, directly in front of Nāropā,
The lord Tillipa flew up into the realm of space,
And sang a song, conferring all the Dharma in his advice.
Homage to Nāropā, who offered his own song out of devotion!

With his recognition of realization, he obtained the highest accomplishment.
Having that accomplishment, in accordance with his own qualities,
Having secured his prophecy, he peacefully remained in the state of nondifferentiation.
Homage to Nāropā, who succeeded by following the master's instructions!

In this narrative, Nāropā is stirred from his complacency as the abbot of the flagship monastery in late Buddhist India. Jñānaḍākinī appears and accuses him of not understanding the meaning of the sentences he is reading, a meaning that is understood by Tilopa/Tillipa/Telopa, however the great siddha's name may be spelled by an individual author. Against the wishes of its monks, Nāropā leaves his monastery to seek Telopa, who plays hide-and-seek with the great scholar. Nāropā is first examined to see if he understands nonverbal signs and then is given the initiations that authorize him to practice. Curiously, most of the hagiographies do not emphasize the yogic training he is said to have received from Telopa, for most have little to say about the yogic content or about the nature of the transmission between Telopa and Nāropā.[23] Instead, the hagiographers become invested in the narrative of guru devotion and the thirteen trials that are inflicted on Nāropā, who is portrayed in a religious sense as a latter-day Herakles. It is the trials themselves that afford Nāropā his training, and he achieves his goal through the practice of the difficult vow (*vratacaryā*), the total negation of social approval, and the total immersion in the life of the tantric yogin. If the nature of the trials varies according to the hagiographer, the individual episodes of the narrative become the site of the hagiographer's art, with each description increasing the suffering and torment that Nāropā experienced in his search for awakening. Finally the story ends, as do all siddha hagiographies, with the demonstration of siddhi, the siddha's magical power over the gods (the sun, river, etc. are gods) and the elements of reality.

The deemphasis on content in most of the narratives is all the more intriguing, as Telopa is said to have received four (or six) main transmissions. Although there is again some difference of opinion, one standard list may be related. From Nāgārjunapāda, Telopa received instruction in the *Guhyasamāja-tantra*, the *Catuḥpīṭha-tantra*, and the yogas of illusory body and consciousness transference; from Caryapāda, he received the *Mahāmāyā-tantra* and the dream yoga practices; from Lwabapa, he received all the mother (or *yoginī*) tantras, including the *Cakrasaṁvara*, and the yoga of clear light; and from Subhaginī, Telopa received the *Hevajra-tantra* and the yoga of psychic heat (*cāṇḍālī*).[24] Elsewhere, the narratives maintain that Telopa transmitted to Nāropā the completion process systems that eventually became identified as the "six instructions (or yogas) of Nāropā": psychic heat, illusory body, dream yoga, clear light, intermediate realm transference (*bar do*), and corpse reanimation.[25] All the authorities are adamant, moreover, that Telopa brought these yogic practices together first and that he did not, in fact, need such aids, for he was the manifestation (*nirmāṇakāya*) of the eternal Buddha Vajradhara, which is a clever career choice, indeed. Thus, Nāropā's involvement with Telopa is the face-to-face confrontation with the eternal awakened state in the unlikely form of an outcaste yogin with a predilection for fish.

VIRŪPA'S HAGIOGRAPHY: MR. UGLY COMES TO TOWN

Before considering the principal messages of Nāropā's hagiography, we will look at the hagiography of the siddha Virūpa for comparison, as both contain many similarities and many intriguing differences. The tradition records Nāropā's general period but not that for Virūpa, whose dates were discussed extensively in Tibet. By the fifteenth century, one Sakyapa scholar, Ngorchen Kunga Zangpo (1382–1456), concluded that Virūpa was identical with the abbot of the great monastery Nālandā, Dharmapāla, who was an important personage in the "proposal of consciousness" (*vijñānavāda*) system of Mahāyāna scholasticism.[26] Based on these ideas, Ngorchen leaped into the fantasy realm of Tibetan lineage lists and the old royal Tibetan chronology of mythic kings and divine descent, and deduced that Virūpa had lived about 1,020 years after the Buddha's nirvāṇa.[27] If we assume that Ngorchen was using Sakya Paṇḍita's chronology for the Buddha's life, then the founder's nirvāṇa would have been in 2134 B.C.E., and Virūpa would have lived around 1114 B.C.E. or so, a date centuries before most ancient Indian and modern estimates of the actual birth of Śākyamuni Buddha.[28] We will see that great antiquity is one of the important values of Tibetan religion, and imputing it into the lives of the saints becomes an essential tool for the affirmation of their sanctity and authority.

In Virūpa's case, the issue has resonance, for he was said to have left the monastery under a cloud even while achieving a high degree of liberation. He wandered throughout India, frequently involved in disputes with the Tīrthikas, a term that may indicate Śaiva or Śākta yogins, Brahmans, or others outside a Buddhist affiliation. Virūpa's narrative is constructed with nearly all the siddha formative factors and thereby represents a paradigmatic example of how siddha hagiographical literature combines Indian religiosity, Tibetan fascination, belletristic models, a curious conservatism, multiple points of literary departure, and the centrality of first-person verse narratives cast in the *dohā* form in the Apabhraṁśa language. Through the technique of a Buddhist *Pilgrim's Progress*, Virūpa's hagiography takes the reader through mythic sites and ritual combat, all with an ear to the humorous juxtaposition of the sacred and the absurd.

While we have little solid information about the Indian materials written about Virūpa, the Tibetan Virūpa texts, in contrast, are on much firmer ground, for Virūpa was the singular focus of the Sakyapa denomination, much as Nāropā was the object of fascination for the Kagyüpa. Accordingly, our earliest surviving Tibetan discussion of the life of Virūpa occurs in the work of Sachen Kunga Nyingpo (1092–1158), the first of the great lamas in the Sakyapa denomination of Tibetan Buddhism. As a paean to Virūpa, Sachen's work appears to be a supplication for realization and an entreaty to the teacher from afar (*bla ma rgyang 'bod*), which is a durable genre in Tibetan literature. Moreover, his paean became as important for Sachen's own hagiography as it is to Virūpa's and is worthy of a complete translation:

Panegyric to the Glorious Virūpa[29]

Homage to Virūpa!
A-la-la! The Lord Virūpa
From out of the spontaneous and without manifestation,[30]
In this way [to be related] the brilliance and luminosity
of your auspiciousness
is beyond conceptualization.
E-ma-ho! You have become auspicious for me!

Your splendor has eliminated all conceptualizations [in me],
So having expanded the internal wind of the three doors [of body,
speech, and mind] into the four joys [of the completion stage],
And having transformed my troubled karma into bliss and emptiness,
Thus purified, in view of recollecting your life a little, I will pay homage
to it!

Your auspiciousness is the conjunction of the benefit for self and others
that is supreme happiness and benefit for self and others.
Through knowledge and love, having taught the lucky disciple
The highest path, you set him into nirvana.
I bow with my head to the play of the highest immovable.

Born in this world into the kṣatriya (warrior) caste,
He renounced it and concluded the study of the five areas of expertise.
He was depended on, since he taught the curriculum to the different
levels in the Saṁgha.
I bow with my head to the renowned Sthavira Dharmapāla.

Being Vāgīśa [lord of speech], he was not bested in debate
About the texts of the Mahāyāna, which have the three trainings
as their object.

I bow with my head to the second omniscient one, the life tree
of the doctrine,
Indisputable on the surface of the earth.

Having satisfied all those assembled with the nectar of various vehicles
of the Dharma,
As the coming of the day satisfies the assembly of beings with the dew,
At night, he achieved liberation through accomplishment of the secret
practice.
Homage to him on the sixth Bodhisattva stage, chosen by Nairātmyā
herself!

In order to lead beings though the practice of the ascetic vow (*vratacaryā*),
By means of this inferior activity, he left the Saṁgha's sacred precincts
And headed for town, wandering everywhere[31] in the world.
I bow with my head to him renowned by all as Birwa.

He turned the Ganges back and tamed a misguided king.
Having seized the sun, he drank the wine in the whole area.
Uninebriated, he broke the lingam and tamed Caṇḍikā.
I bow with my head to him renowned as the lord of magicians.

In that way, at the conclusion of his displays of limitless power,
He tamed Kārttika in Saurāṣṭra.
I bow with my head to the play of nondual great bliss
Which encompasses the realm of space through nonreferential
compassion.

He articulated the profound path by means of the four aural streams
Which constitute the method for quickly realizing that exact reality
Of the very pure bliss and emptiness in all elements of existence.
I bow with my head to him, who ripens and liberates the fortunate
disciples.[32]

E-ma! Lord, I pray that you will seize me visibly
Again and again in that way,
Since I have not obtained liberation's stage,
The sphere of absolute perfection!

If you will just increase this stream of nectar,
A flood of those [yogic practices] arisen from

The power of your compassion—
I pray that you bring this goal to completion!

And even those who study as you did,
I pray that they create benefit for the dispensation,
That they are never separated from the two tantric processes,
And never become subject to the path's obstacles!

The internal wind of the completely pure three doors
Is expanded by the successive four joys.
Having dissolved the winds into the four essential movements,[33]
May the consecration of Vajradhara be obtained!

And this closely cherished place,
Has penetrated the earth (*Sa*) and sky with renown,
Pale (*kya*) like a water lily opening for the full moon,
May it play with the auspiciousness of virtue![34]

While it is not entirely clear from this panegyric, other hagiographies of Virūpa indicate that as the great Paṇḍita Dharmapāla, he was considered an accomplished scholar who had a tortured secret: he had failed at his Vajrayāna practice of reciting the mantra of Cakrasaṁvara. Giving up in despair, Dharmapāla threw his rosary in the monastic latrine, vowing to meditate no more. That night, Nairātmyā herself came to Dharmapāla's aid, by appearing to him and eventually initiating him on six successive nights so that he could attain the sixth stage of the bodhisattva (*abhimukhī bhūmi*: face-to-face).

The Sakyapas, for whom Virūpa is the eternal Buddha, maintain that Nairātmyā conferred on the new siddha a total of four realizations and a text. Drakpa Gyeltsen's (1148–1216) hagiography articulates the defining moment:[35]

[Four Aural Streams]:[36] *a.* In that manner, because the emanation body [Nairātmyā] completely bestowed on him the four consecrations, he experienced the "non-diminution of the river of consecration." *b.* Because there arose in him the realization of the first through the sixth levels of the bodhisattva, he experienced the "non-severance of the stream of benediction." *c.* Before, there had not arisen for him any certainty of feeling either the signs of success or the accomplishment of perfection. Indeed, since inauspicious signs arose, he had become depressed. Then, he thought, "Previously, unadorned by the pronouncement of the holy, I did not recognize (those negative indications) as being signs of the 'heat' of concentration; but now, since

I have correctly realized this, I have obtained the 'non-reversal of the thrust of instruction.'"[37] *d.* Finally, as he obtained the distinguished certainty that, as of that point, his realization and that of the completely perfected Buddha were equal, he gained the "ability to satisfy the concerns of the faith."

Nairātmyā also bestowed on Dharmapāla/Virūpa, we are told, the obscure yogic text of the *Mārga-phala system, discussed in chapters 5 and 8 and translated in appendix 2. The system takes its name *Mārga-phala (Tib.: Lamdré) from this work, for it discusses the relationship between the path (*lam*) and its fruit (*'bras bu*). This difficult text was to become the centerpiece of Sakyapa spirituality and its claim to superiority over all other traditions.

Thereafter, Dharmapāla takes up with women and wine, in the best siddha manner, so that he is asked to leave the monastery and is charged with being ecclesiastically deformed (*virūpa*), from which he takes his name and is the reason I translate it as Mr. Ugly. The rest of the hagiography describes Virūpa's performance of miracles, converting non-Buddhists (*tīrthikas*), destroying their images, and stopping their sanguinary rituals. Finally, Virūpa's aggressive combat with tīrthikas is brought to a halt by the intervention of Khasarpaṇa Avalokiteśvara, the deity inhabiting a popular Buddhist pilgrimage site in southern Bengal. We are assured that Virūpa eventually merged into a wall at the Śaiva site of Somanātha in Gujarat, where he became an ever-living statue and may be seen there today.[38]

Despite the lineal affirmation, there is little reason to believe that Virūpa was a great scholar prior to his inspiration, and the surviving works attributed to Virūpa reveal a siddha concerned with many of the same issues as were the other siddha singers of Apabhraṁśa songs: the evil of non-Buddhist practices, the importance of the guru, the fact that realization is beyond learning, and so forth. If the Virūpa of the Sakyapa hagiographies actually lived—and we have no reason to believe otherwise—we would expect to find him around the last quarter of the tenth century, probably not later and certainly not much earlier. This estimation is based on Virūpa's strong hagiographical association with two sites that had in fact relatively short life spans: Somanātha and Bhīmeśvara, the latter at the mouth of the Godāvarī River. Bhīmeśvara was probably built by either Chāḷukya Bhīma I (r. 892–921) or Dānārṇava (r. 971–73), while Somanātha was built by Mūlarāja I around 960 to 973 and desecrated or destroyed by Maḥmūd of Ghazna in 1026, to be reestablished at a later date. Assuming there was a Virūpa who went to these places and developed a system transmitted to Tibet in the second quarter of the eleventh century, he was probably a personage of the second half of the tenth century, most likely in its final quarter (975–1000).

Virūpa would have been a failed monk, probably not excessively learned, and given to hanging around with the wandering bards for whom composition in Apabhraṁśa was the norm. Indeed, the Sakyapas have preserved corrupted versions of an Apabhraṁśa hagiographical statement by a Birwa. He would have taken this derogatory name, Viruā/Birwa (Prakritic forms of the name Virūpa), as a badge of courage, although he was by no means the first, or, probably the last, to be so called; even some later Sakyapa authors maintained that Virūpa appeared three times.[39] The *Mārga-phala scholar Khyentsé Wangchuk (1524–68) noted that there must have been an earlier Virūpa who was the teacher of the female siddha Sukhasiddhi, a statement based on other hagiographies reporting this relationship.[40]

HAGIOGRAPHY, LINEAGE, AND TRANSMISSION

The hagiographies of the siddhas most responsible for the Kagyüpa and Sakyapa orders have explicit messages that were to be conveyed to their followers down through their respective lineages. First and foremost, the texts develop iconic forms through their narratives. In each case the prototype represents the subordinate stature of institutions, for no institution, we are assured, was superior to the real quest for illumination. Each of our siddhas is depicted as having begun as a great monastic scholar but ended up as a sādhu guru. Both had great success in the monastery prior to their real success as saints, and their awakening was in profound measure dependent on their abandoning the worldly trappings of the great Buddhist monasteries to shed the burdens of intellectual vitality and religious authority. This was done in order to assume the mantles of soteriological authenticity, for position and learning were deemed inauthentic per se by these traditions. Yet the message is in some sense more subtle than that, for both figures had to be able to abandon their positions, hard enough to win, before they could attain their exalted status as yogins and teachers. Thus, worldly religious success was a prerequisite to their achievement as siddhas.

In each case as well, the connection between the supreme guru and the divine realm is immediate—Telopa is Vajradhara himself; Nāropā is stirred from his complacency by Jñānaḍākinī; and Virūpa receives instruction directly from Nairātmyā, who confers the *Mārga-phala text on him as verification of her grace and authentication of his realization. Here, too, there are specific karmic elements that must ripen correctly and the correct deity must be propitiated, as each discovers. So, Nāropā begins his quest by meditating on Hevajra but is informed that he must abandon this contemplation and devote himself to

Cakrasaṁvara instead. The reverse is Virūpa's lot: starting out a failure at the Cakrasaṁvara system, he is informed by Hevajra's consort (Nairātmyā) that she is to be his focus. In each case, the tradition institutionalized this privileging of one tantra and its instructions over another, for the Sakyapa maintained the importance of Hevajra practices while still cultivating various Cakrasaṁvara lineages, and vice versa for the Kagyüpa.

The differences were important as well, and they are framed directly in the narrative. There is little doubt that the lack of an explicitly textual message in the overall Kagyüpa hagiographical story facilitated its concentration on personalities and yogic systems, with an indirect emphasis on the scriptural and textual basis for their practices. Instead, their primary focus has been devotion to the teacher, the performance of difficult tasks, and the practice of intense yogic exercises, to some degree unleavened by textual complications. It follows, therefore, that they have maintained a less restrained attitude toward alternative sources of spirituality, which was one factor that allowed them to participate in the Tibetan phenomenon of revealed treasure texts (*gter ma*) in a way that the Sakyapa followers did not. Conversely, the Sakyapa have emphasized the *Root of the Path and Its Fruit* (*Lam 'bras rtsa ba*: **Mārga-phala-mūla-śāstra*), the text that was said to have been bequeathed to Virūpa by Nairātmyā's divine presence, and this orientation has been a factor in the Sakyapa denomination's very conservative engagement with the Buddhist world outside its own lineages. However, the commonality between them must not be overlooked, for both the Sakyapa and the Kagyüpa have taken as the ultimate standard of spirituality the instructions in yogic systems—whether oral or written—rather than the tantric scriptures per se.

Whenever the hagiographical Virūpa lived, the *Mārga-phala masters generally maintain that he taught his two primary disciples differently, reflecting the different potential of each and the kind of instruction appropriate to his needs. This is an old Buddhist principle, certainly, and the emphasis on its application to Virūpa's disciples is in keeping with the fundamentals of esoteric transmission, wherein a master bestows specific teachings on individuals. The way that the *Mārga-phala/Lamdré lineage understands this principle follows its comprehension of the importance of the *Mārga-phala text, which was ostensibly the content transmitted by Nairātmyā to Virūpa.

We are assured that Ḍombiheruka obtained a version of the *Mārga-phala teaching without the benefit of having had the text transmitted to him. While the precise content that might have been transmitted in India remains unclear, Tibetan authors have alluded to three attributes of this alternative transmission.[41] First, we are informed that Ḍombiheruka's system really embodied a spectrum of Hevajra maṇḍalas, such as that found in his *Śrī-Hevajrasādhana*, maṇḍalas that eventually became the standard for much of the initiatory and practice manuals found in the lineages of the *Mārga-phala. Second, the emphasis on these maṇḍalas, rituals, and meditative systems was the outgrowth of their involvement with a scholastic level of textual analysis. The teaching of the *Hevajra-tantra*, the *Vajrapañjara*, the *Samputa*, and the other scriptural materials that were transmitted and taught with the Lamdré are said to be an outgrowth of the lineage begun by Ḍombiheruka but learned from Virūpa. Finally, the short teaching on the completion process, eventually appended with the other subsidiary practices to the *Pod Ser*, the *Yellow Book*, was sometimes included with this exegetical material. As a consequence of these parameters, this form of the *Mārga-phala/Lamdré is said to be the "rootless" Lamdré (*rtsa ba med pa'i lam 'bras*), for the lineage did not transmit the "root text" of the system. Curiously, though, because it became heavily involved in the scriptural systems, this lineage is also called the "explanatory lineage" of the Lamdré (*lam 'bras bshad brgyud*).[42]

Kāṇha, conversely, was the disciple to whom Virūpa is said to have transmitted the root text of the *Mārga-phala (figure 2). Kāṇha was said to have been one of the Śaiva yogins who were subdued by Virūpa, and there is circumstantial verification of this part of the narrative. In the compendium of old Bengali poetry that has come to be known as the *Songs of Action* (*Caryāgīti*), a Kāṇha sings of dressing as a Kāpālika yogin while being a Buddhist. Certainly, members of the extreme sect of Śaivism must have converted, even though it is not clear how commonly this happened. Apparently there have been several siddhas with the name Kāṇha/Kṛṣṇa, so that the identification of the old Bengali poet with Virūpa's disciple is potentially true but is by no means assured.

However the lineages of Ḍombiheruka and Kāṇha may be understood, it is important to comprehend that the tradition depicts through this lineal architecture the siddha legacy as being both textual and yogic. When the first explanations of the *Mārga-phala/Lamdré appeared in the early twelfth century, they already contained both the narratives of antinomian siddha activity and the more restrictive statements of the institutionalized scriptures. Since such statements included the esoteric rules of behavior—vows, rituals, confession texts, and the like—it is apparent that the Tibetan Lamdré per se unites the two major streams of the esoteric system in India. Thus, although it may be difficult to authenticate the hagiographical lineage as represented in the tradition, it is easy to see that the Lamdré in Tibet could not have arisen without a total engagement of the esoteric movement.

Finally, in conceiving of a dual lineal descent in this way, the Lamdré system, like all the tantric traditions, sought to construct the Ādiguru (first guru)

FIGURE 2 *Mārga-phala lineage painting. Clockwise from upper left: Vajradhara, Nairātmyā, Kāṇha, Virūpa. Tibet, second half of the fifteenth century. Color and gold paint on cloth, 57.5 x 50.2 cm. *© The Cleveland Museum of Art, 2004. Purchase from the J. H. Wade Fund, 1960.206*

as the grand ancestor of the supreme lineage, in this case Virūpa. Thus the tantric system simultaneously invokes and supplants the biological reality of physical kinship with a spiritual heritage or esoteric kinship. Here, esoteric kinship is defined as obtaining the consecration in a maṇḍala, so that one receives authority from the teacher (ācārya) and is born into the Buddha family. A verse popular from the eighth to the eleventh century is recited at the conclusion of both the Mahāyānist and Vajrayānist rites and, in the latter case, is repeated by the disciple following his consecration:

> Today my birth is fruitful and my life is profitable.
> Today I am born into the family of the Buddha,
> And I am properly the son of the Buddha.[43]

In this effort the Vajrayānist masters were working on Indian models of descent and authority, for kinship is the basis of caste and is at the center of all transmission of authority from one generation to another, whether in the case of Brahmans reciting the *Vedas* or in the coronation of a crown prince under the aegis of his father, which is the metaphor used in esoteric Buddhism.

Accordingly, those disciples being consecrated together were referred to as "vajra" brothers and sisters (*vajrabhātṛbhaginī*), denoting their sacred status, for the word "vajra" was often prefixed to a word as a sign that a mundane designation was being elevated to a sanctified Buddhist sense.[44] One of the more important rules of behavior was that they were to keep from fighting with one another, especially when gathered together in the tantric feast.[45] In this instance, one goal of the tantric feast was to break down caste identity and supplant it with a specifically tantric Buddhist affiliation, for food prohibitions remain (along with marriage and employment) a means for case enforcement. Accordingly, all were to eat together in the gathering of vajra-family members, for "there are no false conceptions towards these foods; the Brahman, the dog, and the outcaste all eat together, for they are each of the same nature."[46]

The redefinition of kinship along spiritual lines was partially effective, and although Indian tantric literature likes to feature those born into higher castes, caste was not a bar to tantric consecration so far as we can tell. It may well be that as it is for the modern Ramanandi sect, caste was an important factor in certain kinds of institutional decisions, namely, the caste of the guru, the caste of the disciple; who gets to become abbot; and so forth.[47] Even so, I have seen no evidence that a caste (*varṇa*), a birth group (*jāti*), a specific clan (*gotra*), or a local family (*kula*) ever obtained exclusive rights over institutional appointments or became the sole authority to perform rites and obtain disciples in Buddhist India. We have sufficient mention of various outcastes (Ḍombiheruka, Kukuri, Telopa) from whom the higher castes would receive consecration that the structure of tantric Buddhism was moderately effective in thwarting an excessive emphasis on caste, the dominant paradigm of Indian social life. This point is significant, for in Central Tibet, the social position of a lama's family became extremely important, and descent from the aristocratic clans eventually became closely aligned with obtaining authority over institutions. The dissimilar treatment of social background, in reality, became one of the important characteristics differentiating Tibetan religious institutions from Indian ones. This fact is even more paradoxical, for on the whole Tibetan society tends to be more egalitarian than Indian society. Certainly it became far more Buddhist, but the retention of clan identity was a thread running through most of Tibetan religious life, something Tibetans struggled with throughout the renaissance period.

CONCLUSION: EMERGING INDIAN RITUALS

Much of India's authority was based on its ability to continually develop and sustain both a complex ritual life and a profound philosophical system, two trajectories that remained in tension during the Central Tibetan renaissance. In a sense, tantric Buddhism is ritual trumping intellectual posturing, for the most popular siddhas, as we have seen, posed as learned monks abandoning their exalted positions for the life of the wandering saint, beholden to no one. These hagiographical narratives reinforce an ideological landscape clearly modeled on real figures making real contributions to Buddhist thought, although siddhas were probably the real poseurs. Nonetheless, their ability to capture the popular imagination of village bards and court sycophants meant that they brought to Buddhism a legitimacy somewhat eclipsed in the staid monastic world.

For Tibetans, the Indian tantric system's breadth of behavior gave them access to the products of Indian civilization—medicine, mathematics, grammar, astrology, philosophy, ritual, and religious imagination—while not requiring that they abandon their somewhat rough character. Of the many forms of Buddhism, only the tantras represented the fundamental identity of the religious and political spheres, and only the tantras afforded Tibetans carte blanche to indulge their fascination with rituals. Only the tantric system validated the indigenous gods as important in their own rights, and the maṇḍalas of the tantras proved expansive enough to integrate every little sprite and local demon somewhere in the spiritual landscape. The tantric system's greatest liability, a predilection for antinomian behavior based on nonfoundational ethics, remained the issue with which Tibetans were to wrestle for the next thousand years, as Indians had done in the centuries before.

This was more true for renaissance Central Tibetans than for others, like their Chinese and Japanese brethren, since yogins in the land of snows became especially fascinated with the yogic systems inscribed in the *mahāyoga-tantras* and the *yoginī-tantras*. Explicit psychosexual practices were described in their specific secretive instructional manuals (*upadeśa*) and supported by the narratives of wild siddhas in jungles or on the margins of polite society, struggling with non-Buddhists for supremacy. In these texts and stories, both aristocratic clansmen and ordinary Tibetans found the validation of natural human existence, of sexuality and sensory involvement, of place identity and corporate clan function. The values of the tantras, while not conducive to social stability within India, were turned to those ends in Ü-Tsang, which had experienced the height of power under the royal dynasty only to see it collapse into disaster in the mid-ninth century. The renaissance is really the story of the great Central Tibetan clans' employment of tantric and yogic documents to help their society, which was just emerging from a catastrophic collapse. That process of disintegration eventually led to the subsequent rebirth of Tibet.

2

The Demise of Dynasty and a Poorly Lit Path

In that way, a king from the devil's own family
Will exhaust the merit of the Tibetan people.
The Buddha's doctrine will entirely deteriorate. . . .
Having ruined the Jokhang temple, evil people will punish each other.
With perverse words, they will scold those of good conduct
And praise others indulging in sinful activity.
All the monasteries will become the homes of deer
And temples will be cattle pens.
Teachers will have to take on the burdens of maintenance workers
And monks will be sent to hunt animals for a living.
Alas! Those of the dark nature will spread far and wide.

—*The Pillar Testament of Songtsen Gampo*[1]

It seems so easy to see Tibet as an indelibly Buddhist country, but this pleasant illusion was constructed from the real work of generations of dedicated Tibetan Buddhists. The image is all the more extraordinary because over the course of several centuries, Tibet was a strongly militaristic empire, an empire that collapsed into a very difficult period of social and political chaos. Tibetan documents refer to this catastrophe as the beginning of the period of political fragmentation (*rgyal khrims sil bu'i dus*) or the manner of decline of the doctrine (*bstan pa'i bsnubs lugs*), the latter phrase invoking the mythos of the eventual eclipse of the Buddha's dispensation. Only after the period of social unrest was the Tibetan renaissance possible, for the culture's rebirth used many of the remnants of the dynasty to construct a new way of Buddhism, one that contributed to a social order with a markedly different dynamic, including a strong inhibition against political reunification. Consequently, even when a measure of religious and social stability was achieved, political unity remained elusive until the Mongol period.

This chapter examines the disintegration and collapse of the Tibetan imperial system in the mid-ninth century and the position that Buddhism played in contributing to the dynasty's demise. The paradox of Tibetan Buddhism is that some forms of the religion were complicit in unraveling the empire in the ninth century, much as some forms of Buddhism were central to the reemergence of Tibetan civilization in the tenth century. The chapter then traces what is known of the political situation during the time of fragmentation, including the division of the imperial house into two branches and the three revolts that afflicted Tibetans in both the northeast and in Central Tibet. The chapter also looks at the era through the later chronicle's perception of the decline of social and religious order, with the concomitant rise of heterodox practices. The position of the aristocratic clans, such as they are known, also is discussed. All these factors played a part in the later coalescence of Buddhist culture and civilization in tenth- and eleventh-century Central Tibet, which is considered the preeminent area of Tibet throughout the book.

GOOD INTENTIONS AT THE END OF THE EMPIRE

The best starting place for a discussion of the later diffusion is to understand what "Tibet" was in the ninth and tenth centuries. Our sources—mainly a later and incomplete mixture of royal lineage, history of the Dharma, and hagiography texts—exhibit the same hesitation about the period from the middle ninth century to the end of the tenth that Florentine Renaissance authors do about the era preceding their own. The age is seen as dark and fragmented, with meager evidence of positive activity. Although we have several lists of the imperial descendants' names, there is little evidence of their activities or interests for several decades beyond their presumed lineal maintenance and self-preservation. Later literature alludes to the existence of temples from the royal dynastic period in various states of disrepair, but the condition of the Tibetan people as a whole is uncertain. Lineage lists for the Sakyapa and Nyingma traditions trace individuals back through this period, but with a few notable exceptions, they remain only names, without verification or even hagiographical narratives. The almost complete lack of postdynastic royal inscriptions, the absence of chronologically confident textual materials, and the lack of almost any concrete references to Central Tibet in Chinese histories of the period all obscure the condition of Ü-Tsang.

One of the primary dicta of historical writing is that an absence of evidence is sometimes misleading, and the time of fragmentation is an example of this phenomenon. Because of a paucity of information, it comes as something of a shock to think of Central Tibet in the late ninth and most of the tenth century as a place where much must have been happening. Songtsen Gampo and his clan herded Tibet into Asian history by establishing a degree of unity among a large population base, one so dynamic that it could intimidate and control China's great Tang dynasty. Moreover, Songtsen Gampo's extraordinary performance was intermittently reenacted by his successors throughout the dynasty. Indeed, Beckwith showed that between 618 and 842, Tibet was one of the most fearsome armed states in Asia, certainly on a par with the later Tangut, Khitan, Uigur, and Mongol forces that dominated Asia from the twelfth to the fifteenth century.[2] When the royal dynasty collapsed, the population of Tibet probably did not experience some Malthusian catastrophe only to reemerge a century later. While the population base certainly may have experienced a net loss over some of this period, given the sparse settlement over vast geographical areas, it is doubtful that it was more than a small percentage, which must have left a relatively large population intact.

Little is known about the cultivation of Buddhism during the last half of the ninth to the end of the tenth century or what forms of religious praxis were observed. Most of the information from the royal dynasty indicates that Buddhism had been the doctrine of the court and specific clans among the aristocracy, so that the religion now survived in a fragmented form within limited principalities claiming royal descent.[3] A popular Buddhist awareness seems to have penetrated village and nomad life, but a majority of Tibetans probably kept practicing the forms of religion and culture that they did before the intrusion of court-sponsored Buddhist agendas. Certainly, tenuous suggestions from the dark period and the immediate aftermath show the gains made by the Buddhist literary language, which became the acceptable mode of diction to embody the mythos of clans and their lineages in the holdings of feudal princes.[4] It was primarily within these fragmented principalities, in fact, that the aristocracy kept alive the flame of Dharma and spread lay practices to the populace, for the clans invested in holdings appear to have been just the ground necessary for Buddhism to spring once more into life, like a fire from seemingly cold embers.

Our investigation of the dynasty's collapse in 842 C.E.—and into the period of fragmentation as a whole—has been remarkably facilitated by the publication of a wealth of documents in the last three decades in Tibet and in the West. These materials reveal an extraordinary range of variation in dates and activities ascribed to the principals. But as Tucci observed, because the history of Tibet has been subsumed under the history of Buddhism in Tibet, even these new materials say little about the events following the collapse of the royal dynasty.[5] Indeed, early Tibetan sources are sometimes little more than royal lineage lists, such as the one Hackin published from Dunhuang, and through much of the twelfth century, unadorned lists of the royal genealogy are the staple of historical writing in the political arena.[6]

Perhaps one reason for this paucity of discussion is an uneasiness on the part of religiously oriented writers, for it is clear that Buddhist activities assisted in the disintegration of the dynasty. Relpachen's strongly pro-Buddhist agenda was one cause of the Tibetan emperor's assassination around 840/41.[7] Relpachen is depicted declaring that his predecessors had espoused the three duties of the emperor: the construction of imperially sponsored temples, the maintenance of happiness for the Tibetan people, and the infliction of warfare on the enemies of imperial Tibet. Whereas the previous emperors had performed one or another duty, or perhaps two or even all three in succession, Relpachen was going to perform all three simultaneously: a recipe for deficit spending and bureaucratic jealousy.[8] Relpachen employed bureaus of scholars to put into place the orthographic changes to the Tibetan language that had been initiated by his predecessor Sénalek in 812 but that required the rewriting of vast quantities of manuscripts. This was a task that further entailed not only expenditures for paper and ink but also quantities of gold and silver for the letters of treasured collections.[9] In the process, Relpachen ordered the completion of the catalogs for three of the royal collections—those in the palaces of Denkar, Chimpu, and Pangtang—and the translation of new materials under the aegis of Indian masters.[10]

To this end, he inaugurated the construction or refurbishment of thirty imperially sponsored temples all over the realm. Some of these had been royally sponsored before then but were now converted by Relpachen to the new use.[11] Ten of these were in Central Tibet, where his predecessors had already developed the first great monastery of Samyé (ca. 780) as well as several dozen other temples. Twenty of Relpachen's temples, though, were founded in eastern or northeastern Tibet and became important sites for the eventual reemergence of Buddhism in the next century. The first consequence of this expansion of the Buddhist clerical order was the recruitment of large numbers of monks with the concomitant requirement for their maintenance, so that one monk would be assigned the support of seven families.

Relpachen was also noted for three great proclamations.[12] First, no Vinaya materials other than those of the Mūlasarvāstivāda would be translated, but the translation of all parts of this Vinaya would be completed. Second, no tantras at all would be translated.[13] Finally, all the weights and measures of the empire would be replaced by those used in Central India, so that everything from grain to gold would move to the new Indian standard. All three were intensifications of prior imperial policies, for Tibetan emperors had assiduously sought to maintain a uniformity of Buddhist practice, grounded in the recitation of Mahāyāna sūtra literature and dedicated to the maintenance of a celibate clergy, perhaps to avoid the development of charismatic aristocratic competitors. Tantric literature, particularly the more antinomian *mahāyoga-tantras*, were seen as destabilizing, and the earliest surviving *Testament of the Ba/Wa Clan* (*dBa' bzhed*) indicates that Relpachen's grandfather Trihsong Détsen also had entirely forbidden tantric translation.[14]

While the sociopolitical forms inherent in tantric maṇḍalas might seem tailored to royal use, in fact its distribution of power through a complex feudal system of quasi-independent vassals was problematic, and the tantric ritualization of Tibet during the renaissance later enacted and validated the emperors' fears of fissiparous forces. For their part, the Tibetan emperors tended to restrict the few esoteric displays to a cult of Vairocana, which had as much a sūtra component as a tantric one.[15] The tantric literature they actually supported was strongly institutional in design and doubtless was used for imperial purposes.[16] Consequently, the restrictions on the translation of tantric literature—although never entirely enforceable—meant that the dynasty was the period of the great sūtra translations, from languages like Chinese as well as Sanskrit. The use of Indian weights and measures was equally important, for Relpachen calculated that Central Tibet's economic fortune was most closely allied to the trans-Himalayan trade. Unfortunately, Relpachen discovered too late that the Tibetan emperor was not so powerful as the Buddha Vairocana after all, and he fell to an assassin's knife around 840/41.

Fueled with popular resentment against such breathtaking expenditures and sweeping changes of received culture, the last of the real emperors, Darma Trih Udum-tsen (i.e., Lang Darma, ca. 803–42), began a campaign against the entrenched power of the Buddhist clergy, and the received records depict his suppression in dramatic terms.[17] We are told that initially, for six months, Darma blandly supported Buddhist activities, but his ministers managed to get Ba Gyelpo Tagna, of the powerful Ba clan, appointed to an official position. Ba Gyelpo Tagna undertook a number of actions that contradicted the dispensation of the Buddha. As a result, there arose frost and hail in Lhasa, crop disease and famine, human epidemics and livestock epizootics. Seeing this, Darma turned his mind against the Dharma and became possessed by a demon, according to the religious view. During the next six and a half months, he appointed evil ministers who closed temples, burned books, defrocked monks, and caused the remaining religious to flee back to India or to Kham or Xining in northeast Tibet, on the borders of China.

Any critical assessment, though, of Darma's campaign against the clergy should be considered in light of the other anti-Buddhist campaign in contemporary Asia, the suppression of Buddhism under the Wuzong emperor. This Tang emperor's disfavor with the clergy also began in 841—the same time as Darma's persecution was inaugurated—and Wuzong's concluded with the full-fledged suppression of the religion in 845 and 846, ending only with Wuzong's death in 846.[18] Evidently, both these suppressions resulted from the combination of falling revenues from Buddhist-controlled estates, the decline of head taxes through the expansion of Buddhist ordination certificates, the erosion of aristocratic authority in the face of the Buddhist public persona, and the excessive expenditures on Buddhist ritual and monastic activities. In addition, in Tibet, the empire was not growing but static with a very large army and a paucity of new resources.

Although Darma may have been possessed by a demon from the monks' perspective, in fact his "suppression" was most likely an attempt to redress large capital expenditures on behalf of both the military and the clergy, faced as he was with a dwindling resource base and a declining sense of imperial authority and beset by challenges from both the pro-Buddhist and anti-Buddhist clans.[19] In the process, both the Buddhist and anti-Buddhist forces began to pursue their individual agendas (as they also did during the Wuzong suppression in China). The agendas quickly became associated with specific clan positions and hardened by mutual antagonism with little attempt at rapprochement, since the aristocratic families allied with either side could anticipate a loss of position and estates if defeated. Consequently, much of the destruction of religious sites doubtless was caused by the accelerating clan hostilities that Darma precipitated but that quickly exceeded his ability to control.

FRAGMENTATION: FLIGHT IN THE DARK, LIGHT IN THE TOMBS

In response, a Buddhist monk, the hermit Lhalung Pelgyi Dorjé of Yerpa—well socialized into the Mahāyānist ideology of killing a tyrant in order to save him—assassinated Darma while the emperor was reading the Néütang monolith inscription.[20] Pelgyi Dorjé escaped by a clever deception and fled into hiding.[21] This assassination came, however, at exactly the wrong point in the empire's history: the aristocracy was now polarized by the religious suppression; the treasury was strained; and Darma's succession was very unclear. Apparently, his junior queen Tsépongza gave birth to the royal heir, Namdé Ösung, in the old fortress of Yumbu Lhagang just before Darma's assassination, although there are other versions of their paternity, one claiming that Namdé Ösung was born after Darma had already died. At a later date, the elder queen Belpen Zama produced a son, Trihdé Yumten, somewhere in the Uru region around Lhasa.[22]

Between these two—Yumten and Ösung, with their respective clan factions—succession became an issue, especially as the rule of primogeniture had not been universally applied to the Tibetan royal house and Yumten's legitimacy was doubtful. Moreover, the sources seem to indicate that the young princes were the focus of the rivalry between the Dro and the Ba/Wa, with the Dro supporting Ösung and the Ba supporting Yumten.[23] A story circulated that Yumten was not the legitimate issue of Darma but the result of a plot by the Bel family to provide a boy to their barren daughter. According to this story, Yumten was said to be first shown as ostensibly a newborn, although he already had teeth. Nonetheless, he was accepted as a royal heir, based on the "firm insistence of the mother" (*yum kyi bka' brtan*). This story was accepted by such thirteenth- and fourteenth-century figures as Déü José but was discounted by Tsuglak Trengwa and others, and the earliest Tibetan sources do not mention it at all.[24] Petech pointed out that the Chinese reports of the Tibetan empire maintain that Darma had no issue and that a boy (whom Petech equates with Yumten) was placed on the throne by the queen's clan. But these Chinese sources are not uniformly reliable and seemed to know, for example, nothing about Darma's assassination.[25]

Our chronicles maintain that the problem of succession was the point over which the empire became divided, and the initial decision was that Yumten would take over the part of Tibet known as Uru (the central horn: on map 1, roughly eastern Central Tibet above the Tsangpo River) and that Ösung would control Yoru (the left horn: roughly eastern Central Tibet below the Tsangpo). These areas were uneven in resources, population, and land, so a low-level conflict between the two continued over the expansion of influence and dominion. We know that the two heirs operated independently, for documents from Dunhuang indicate that Ösung was sufficiently powerful to renew a grant to Buddhist clergy in 844 but that Yumten seemed to come into his own in the decades following Darma's assassination.[26] The Dunhuang letter from Yumten specifically rails against evil members of the Dro and Chog clans, and certainly there was every reason to question the allegiance of specific individuals, for Tibet was enmeshed in a series of revolts from around 845 to 910. These are designated in the surviving documents as the "three popular uprisings" (*kheng log gsum*), although they certainly drew from a variety of strata and lasted for almost seventy years.[27]

The first of the uprisings was actually a separatist attempt by an aristocrat, Lön Gungzher, who was a member of the Wa/Wé (~ Ba) clan and an administrator in Tibetan territory in the northeast, around Dunhuang.[28] Dunhuang was lost to the Chinese warlord Zhang Yichao in 848, perhaps partially as a result of Lön Gungzher's activities, so we have some indication that separatist movements began almost as soon as the center of the empire weakened. The royal dynasty began to contract in exactly those areas (like Dunhuang) that had been under Tibetan dominion for only a few decades, but the weakness of the Chinese empire at the close of the Tang was also evident, for the Tibetan language continued to be used in civil documents for several decades after the direct administration from Lhasa was but a dim memory.

Lön Gungzher became embroiled in a series of difficulties with the governor of the city of Shanzhou, a Tibetan named Zhang Bibi, a member of the Dro family who represented the pro-Chinese faction among the colonial governors.[29] Lön Gungzher was incensed with the murder of Darma and detected the involvement of the hated Dro clan. After much conflict, Lön Gungzher was victorious, but he personified the disintegrating sense of order, as he put to death all the males in the Shanzhou/Amdo area; plundered the prefectures of Kuo, Gua, Su, Hami, and Qocho; and was subdued by Zhang Yichao only in 851. Not one to abandon his goal, Lön Gungzher later attempted an insurrection against the Chinese and made his final appearance in Chinese politics as a severed head in a sack on its way to the Chinese capital Changan in 866.

Because the Chinese recorded mostly those troubles within their territorial interests in the Amdo region, we know less about insurrections of Tibetans operating in areas not immediately contiguous to China. However, preserved fragments of the *Great Chronicle* (*Lo rgyus chen mo*) of Khutön Tsöndrü Yungdrung (1011–75) reveal the tension between the houses of Yumten and Ösung, on one hand, and the great clans of Dro and Ba/Wé, on the other. The second of the insurrections may have taken place in 904, for that is the time the renowned Nyingma author Nubchen Sangyé Yéshé lost four of his six sons to the trouble and ultimately was forced to take refuge in Nepal, where he had gone six times earlier.[30] Greater problems apparently occurred after Ösung and Yumten died, and Ösung may have died during the third insurrection, for he was said to have been killed by one Tséroduk.[31] Ösung was the last of the Tibetan royal family to be buried at the royal necropolis in Chongyé, and (in the face of chronological uncertainty) Vitali proposes that his death date was 905.[32]

Ösung's son, Pel Khortsen, was not the most engaging character, even if he was forced into becoming the figurehead ruler as an adolescent while two powerful councilors apparently made the decisions.[33] The historian Déü José highlights Pel Khortsen's rash temper (*zhe gnag pa*) and foolish nature (*glen pa*), which were evident even in performing with a bad attitude the funerary rites for his father.[34] A popular saying of the day summed up the people's feelings about this difficult personality: "The Lord is the 'Wheel of Glory' (*dPal-'khor*); his Queen is the 'Wheel of Happiness' (*sKyid-'khor*); their conjugal relation is a Wheel of Trouble (*lan-'khor*)."[35] Eventually, the assaults of his enemies cost Pel Khortsen his life as well, and he died as a result of the troubles,

TABLE 1 Simplified Ösung Succession Through the Eleventh Century

Ösung (d. 905?)

Pel Khortsen (ca. 881–911)

Nyima-gön (r. ca. 911–50)	Trashi Tsekpa-pel (ca. 911–50)
Rigpa-gön/Trashi-gön/ Détsug-gön (ca. 950–57)	Peldé/Ödé/Kyidé (ca. 980–1000)
Khor-ré / Song-ngé (Yéshé-Ö, ca. 959–1024)	Pawa-désé / Trihdé / Trihchung / Nyagdé
Lha Dépo / Devarāja / Nāgarāja (ca. 996–1024)	Ökyi-bar
Ödé / Jangchub-Ö / Shiwa-Ö (r. ca. 1024–57)	Trihdé-bar / Yuchen and six more brothers
Tse-dé (r. ca. 1057–90)	Yutok / Joga and four more brothers
	Namdé / Joga / Tséde — Lha chenpo (r. 12th c.)

SOURCE: Derived from Hazod 2000b, p. 182, nn. 7, 8.

killed by Taktsé-nyak around 910.[36] His sons fled; Trih Kyidé Nyimagön, the elder, escaped to Purang, where he founded the house of the future kings of Gugé and Purang.[37] The three sons of Trih Kyidé Nyimagön, who were called the three "Gön" of Western Tibet, laid the foundation for the eventual reinfusion of Buddhism in that area under direction of Lha-lama Yéshé-Ö and his successors (table 1). The younger of Pel Khortsen's sons, Trashi Tsekpel, stayed on in Central Tibet and had three sons as well, called the three "Dé" of the Eastern section (i.e., Central Tibet being east of Gugé). These three men—Peldé, Ödé, and Kyidé—and their contention or competition with the descendants of Yumten, were instrumental in the reintroduction of Buddhist learning into some areas in Central Tibet.

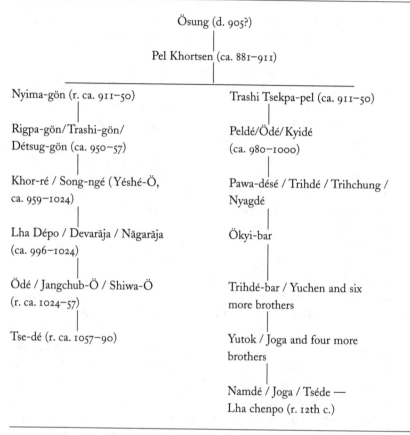

The Tibetan memory of this period's chaos comes predominantly from the *Great Chronicle*, and the fragments from that work by Khutön deliver a frightening lesson on the way in which weak institutions and religious rumors combined with personal ambition to assist the disintegration of Tibet.

> The sign [for insurrection] was the rising of a bird. Formerly it occurred in Kham, with Lön Gungzher as the ringleader. But even before that was the revolt in Uru (in Central Tibet), with Lopo Lojung-bé as the ringleader. Then the insurrection occurred in Tsang, with Og-am Khudöl Sumdruk as the ringleader. The cause was in response to the occlusion of nobility, and generally it was a result of excessive disparity between the power of the nobles and their servants. The Uru insurrection was a response to the conflict between the Dro and Bé clans. In Yuru the insurrection was by Zhangjé Séné, who killed Yuné, the latter having been made a chief. There were two wives of that lord [Yuné], one of whom was selected to be the consort [of Zhangjé Séné], and the other one—named Bepsa Wamo-shung—became jealous. At that time, Zhangjé Séné had his subjects constructing a canal at the foot of a hill (lit., a hill's neck). This powerful woman [Wamo-shung] said to all the workmen, "It is easier to struggle for (i.e., remove) the neck of a man, than the neck of a hill." When she said that, all felt defeated.[38]

Like so much of Tibetan life, aspects of these insurrections were driven by signs and prognostication, and the *Great Chronicle* names the divine architect (*phya mkhan*) and motivating force as Dranka Pelgyi Yönten, the monk-minister who had been unjustly killed during or shortly after Relpachen's reign.[39] He was envisioned riding an iron wolf and displaying signs for the insurrection, such as the blooming at dawn of *tarka* flowers where the rebels were to collect in secret.[40] The bird was interpreted as a spirit bird (*srin bya*), a destructive form assumed by a demonic figure known as Khölpo Sémong and directed by Dranka Pelgyi Yönten, who was taking his revenge on the clans of his killers.

The result was not simply the demise of a central government but the collapse of civil and social institutions as well. The early writers are poignant regarding the loss of identity and virtue resulting from the gathering violence. One noble "in a single day, aged by his grief, is said to have died. For both the lord and the servants have all exhausted the Swastika (diagram of eternal auspiciousness) of happiness and have fallen into the matrix of affliction."[41] Thus, no longer was Tibetan civil life ruled by the cosmic diagram ensuring them health and welfare, but now a malignant nexus was to place its mark on the development and disposition of events, and Tibetans could only suffer through the bad period that was just beginning. Déü José is even more heartbreaking:

> With the pent up evil of these troubled times, one exalted person would commit crimes against another exalted person. The edifice of nobility was occluded with the revolt of the Öbar vassals. A mother was unable to confide in her son; there was no agreement between advisor and minister, or father and uncle. The king's minister Nyak Tokpo was robbed and killed, and corpses seemed to rise from the barren snow.[42]

The twelfth-century mystic Nyang-rel, himself of the nobility, also described the total erosion of all social forms: "A son did not listen to his father, a servant did not acknowledge his lord, and the vassal did not hear the noble."[43] In language that explicitly acknowledges the importance of all hierarchy in this stratified society, the historians consistently depict the age as a collapse of the social orders that were held together by the ritual and linguistic forms, forms that were no longer being observed.

Accordingly, the authors acknowledge that the rule of law, known as the "golden yoke, the order of the king" (*rgyal khrims*), and the rule of religious obligations, known as the "silk protective cord, the order of the Dharma" (*chos khrims*), unraveled without any fail-safe system of checks or appeal to a court of last resort.[44] Indeed, the final insult to the old system was the robbing of the royal tombs by members of the aristocracy. Although his chronology reflects the questionable dating of the histories concerning this period, Tsuglak Treng-wa indicates the extent of the grave robbing:

> Nine years following the rebellions, in the fire-bird year, Shüpu, Taktsé and the others, the four conspired together and decided to open up the tombs, so that they generally dug them up. Nyak burrowed into Tön-kharda, Shüpu plundered the tomb with the lion on it, and Dreng Chökhu dug up the Trülgyel tomb [of Tüsong]. Then Ngozher Nyiwa seized it and stayed. Dro and Chog together took over Songtsen's tomb and remained.[45]

Elsewhere the same author notes that once Samyé and the temples of Lhasa had fallen into disrepair, the tombs were opened and the imperial treasury in the Trandruk Palace was plundered.[46]

In sum, the eclipse of order following the Tibetan royal dynasty lasted approximately a hundred years, with the traditional total sometimes said to be actually nine cycles of the twelve-year era, or 108 years.[47] The precision of this statement is belied by the lack of concerted record keeping, and so there is probably no better index of the dysfunctional character of this fractured culture. In an environment where records were consistently maintained as long as the institutions for archival support endured, the Tibetans appeared to have made little attempt to keep a chronicle of their tribulations, resulting in two entirely different macrochronologies of the period, termed the "long" and "short" chronologies.[48] Even the best of our later histories fail in their chronological reckonings during the early period of fragmentation, and we can piece together the period only through a variety of means. Part of the problem is the lack of corroborating evidence from Chinese sources, which should provide us a better understanding of the period, yet most discussions to date ignore the geopolitical realities.[49]

In fact, it cannot have been an accident that the Chinese, the Tibetan empire, and other Central Asian principals endured a series of calamities of almost exactly the same nature at almost precisely the same time and came out of them at almost exactly the same juncture. The Tibetan and Chinese suppressions of Buddhism were in the 840s. Their empires became unraveled in the 840s to 870s, exactly when the Uigur state collapsed in 840, and the fragmentation of their inner Asia colonies was the result. All around the borders of both empires, with the collapse of civil institutions and their replacement with military dictators, warlordism became the norm, and we have seen that the main adversary of the Tibetan warlord Lön Gungzher was Zhang Bibi, the Tibetan governor of the Chinese city of Shanzhou. In China, the formal chronology of the disintegration of the Tang in 907 masks the reality that the Tang government ceased to be a viable national entity after 875, having been weakened by the Pangxün mutiny (868–69) and the Huangchao rebellion of 875–84.[50] We cannot look to ninth-century destabilizing influences from either the west or south, for this was a period of relative institutional strength in both areas, with the 'Abbassids extending their control into Central Asia, and the Pālas and Gujara Pratīhāras still vital in North India. All our documents point to the Hexi area around Qinghai Lake, the Gansu corridor, and the intersection of western China and eastern Tibet as the loci of instability. We must conclude, then, that during this period the societies and economies of Central Tibet, China, and the Uigur states strongly influenced one another's development, and in their decline they had the cold comfort of shared misery for a little more than a century.

RELIGION ON AN UNEVEN PATH

In the face of this fragmented political and cultural environment, we must ask why the Central Tibetans would eventually look to a Buddhist revival during the second half of the tenth century as a desideratum. It appears that their support of Buddhism had much to do with the Tibetan perception of empire, their sense of its loss, and the consequent degradation of Tibetan life. Buddhist masters had clearly aligned themselves with the royal house and had lent international prestige to efforts toward unification. Empire building had become an extension of Buddhism's "magical" effect and mostly benign domestic influence in early Tibet, particularly while the empire was still strong. For those in the tenth century, left with the physical and cultural relics of the Buddhist temples and the remnants of the royal house in various locales, the empire at its height was a verification of the union of temporal authority and spirituality inherent in the figure of the bodhisattva/king. Urgyen Lingpa's fourteenth-century statement in the *Documentary Will of the King* (*rGyal po bka'i thang yig*) expresses very well the sentiment: "There are four means for the king's virtuous practice: the quality of a righteous tomb, his dwelling in a palace, his building of a house of divinity, and his erection of a properly calculated monolith. When these are consecrated, the people of his thousand district assemble."[51]

The image of kingship thus implies tombs, palaces, temples, and monoliths. Ösung, however, was the last of the kings interred in a tomb at the imperial necropolis in Chongyé. Only the kings of Gugé in West Tibet revived the tradition of erecting imperial monoliths, although at least one later imitation of the imperial form was erected in Central Tibet.[52] Nonetheless, the remains of the many small temples still standing in the population centers of the four horns of Tibet and around the northeast certainly reminded the remnants of the royal house in Central and West Tibet that the grandeur of conquest, the prestige of Chinese imperial brides, and the wealth of Central, South, and East Asian tributaries all were intimately wedded to the support of the monastic forms of Buddhism. The loss of empire seemed concomitant with the loss of monastic Buddhist practice, and while political unity might remain elusive, religious revival was an attainable goal.

In reality, some forms of Buddhism continued to be practiced, at least among or supported by the hereditary aristocracy and feudal lords, although it is clear that some popular forms had evolved with the retrenchment of the aristocracy in areas of strength. By the eleventh century, the systems of Buddhism surviving from the dynasty were termed Nyingma (*rnying ma*, old style), a designation represented in tension with the Sarma (*gsar ma*, new style) tantric and philosophical systems introduced beginning in the late tenth century.[53] Those practices and texts ostensibly handed down in a continuous lineage from the period of the early translations were named Kahma (*bka' ma*), the Holy Word, and the term was eventually used to distinguish them from the treasure texts, Terma, that were revealed during the renaissance.

The authoritative nature of some Kahma texts, however, was questionable, and the practices associated with them seemed too Tibetan, with language and ideas that were appropriate to Tibetan rather than Indian culture. This was certainly true of many of the Nyingma tantras, works that did not fit Indian models of tantric literature. Even though their titles contained the word *tantra*, the Nyingma tantras seem unconventional and are much more philosophical and abstract than their Indian prototypes, which tend to emphasize rituals, mantras, painting, the ingestion of unattractive substances, and materia medica.[54] By contrast, many Kahma tantras positively reveled in new philosophical ideas and meditative practices, culminating in the very diffuse doctrines of the Great Perfection (*rdzogs chen*). This term, said to be the translation of *paripūrṇa* in Devaputra's eleventh-century instructional list, was generally identified with Atiyoga, which in some hierarchies identifies the supreme yoga.[55] Based on the very Indian idea of soteriological stratigraphy, at least by the late tenth century, Nyingma writers had formulated a doctrine of nine vehicles: Śrāvakayāna, Pratyekabuddhayāna, Bodhisattvayāna, Kriyāyāna, Ubha[ya]yāna, Yogayāna, Mahāyogayāna, Anuyogayāna, and Atiyogayāna.

A basis for the last four terms had certainly existed in India, but not as separate vehicles and not in that order. In some of the tantras eventually classified as *mahāyoga*, the set of four terms—*yoga*, *anuyoga*, *atiyoga*, *mahāyoga*—is sometimes articulated as markers for specific visualizations in the generation process. Thus, the meditator engages in a process of purification and initial visualization of Vajrasattva (= *yoga*); he invokes the visualization of the main maṇḍala of the primary deity, for example, Guhyasamāja-Akṣobhyavajra (= *anuyoga*); he completes the external visualization and moves to the creation of an internal maṇḍala (= *atiyoga*); finally, the inner maṇḍala is blessed with mantras and further visualization (= *mahāyoga*).[56] But if these terms were employed in this manner in such texts, they may have been circulating elsewhere in another order. We do see the Nyingma arrangement (*yoga*, *mahāyoga*, *anuyoga*, *atiyoga*) represented in Devaputra's early-eleventh-century list as four aspects of yoga, but whether it was arranged in that way by him or by one of his Tibetan followers is uncertain.[57] Be that as it may, they were not identified in that list as vehicles, and the Sanskrit terms for the nine vehicles became somewhat artificial category markers in the hands of Nyingma authors, categories that were correspondingly filled with the new tantric scriptures.

Eleventh-century Nyingma writers indicated that they believed that seven Kahma lineages of tantric practice had survived the early period of fragmentation.[58] From Nyak Jñāna came practices of the Great Perfection Mental Class (*sems sde*) or Mental Position (*sems phyogs*) and the deity Dütsi; from Padmasambhava came the three cycles of Yamāntaka; from Ma Rinchen Chok came Vimala's *Net of Illusion* transmission; from Drokmi Pelgyi Yéshé came the Mothers' practices; from Langchung Pelgyi Sengé came Buddhaguhya's systems of Yoga and Mahāyoga; from Namké Nyingpo came Hūṁkara's Yangdak; and again from Padmasambhava came a second Yamāntaka system. Most of these eventually became associated with the Eight Pronouncements (*bka' brgyad*, a group of eight deities) and the Mental Class of Great Perfection precepts. Another series of transmissions brought the sūtra and exoteric works into the eleventh century.

Of these lineages, the overwhelming indications are that two ritual and meditative transmissions were important to Nyingma partisans during the renaissance. First were the complex rituals that tradition associated with the deities Vajrakīla, Yangdak Heruka, and the Mamo goddesses, the three groups most often cited among the Eight Pronouncement deities of the *mahāyoga* texts. Teachers with a background in one or more of these three will often be encountered in this book, and the Sakyapa, in particular, retained rituals from the first two. Second was the Mental Position of the Great Perfection (*rdzogs chen sems phyogs*), which was elaborated in multiple systems by multiple masters. By the mid-eleventh century, three developments stood out: the Nyang system (*myang lugs*), the Rong system (*rong lugs*), and the Kham system (*khams lugs*), and all these are represented by texts surviving from the thirteenth to sixteenth centuries; earlier works have not yet been located.[59]

The Kham system was said to have been codified and promoted by one of the more intriguing of the dark period's Nyingma authorities, Aro Yéshé Jungné.[60] Probably active in the second half of the tenth century, Aro's tradition was said by the author of the *Blue Annals* to unite teaching from the Chinese Chan master Heshang Moheyan with the practices associated with the Great Perfection.[61] Aro also is sometimes assigned his own Mental Position system (*A-ro lugs*), and a fourteenth-century work outlines a later understanding of his ideas.[62] The recent printing of Aro's most famous work, his *Method for Entering Mahāyānist Yoga* (*Theg pa chen po'i rnal 'byor 'jug pa'i thabs*) makes his assessment a bit easier. According to the fourteenth-century *Longchen Chöjung*, Aro's many writings are divided into six major sections: outer, inner, secret, on affliction, on literary categories, and the incarnation's instructions.[63] The *Method for Entering Mahāyānist Yoga*, the leading work in the outer section, is a relatively succinct pedagogical text for Mahāyānist instruction and follows the pattern of many similar Buddhist works. In four chapters, it outlines the nature of suffering, its cause in grasping after self, nirvāṇa as the highest bliss, and its accomplishment by the realization of nonself.[64] Little in this work can be convincingly related to the Northern Chan of Moheyan, although other works may have had a more direct relationship. Even among the orthodox, Aro's work was quite influential throughout the eleventh and twelfth centuries, and we find important thirteenth-century Kadampa authors among the Kham system's more representative authorities.[65]

Most instructive for understanding the social position of dynastic religious systems are the names in the Nyingma Kahma lineage lists. The majority of tantric traditions are dominated by members of aristocratic clans previously included in the imperial entourage until the end of Relpachen's reign: Sé, Dro, Ba, Nyak, Chim, Gö, Ché, Chog-ro, and so forth.[66] Often the lineages indicate that Nyingma lamas during the early period of fragmentation transmitted their teachings directly to their sons. Individual lineages eventually identified themselves by these aristocratic designations, and consequently the lineages of Vajrakīla are those employing the methods of Chim, Nanam, and so forth, with one given the ultimate aristocratic identity, the king's cycle of Vajrakīla (*rgyal po skor*).[67] Occasionally we discover individuals in the lineages who are not aristocratic, but this is rare and generally bracketed by others in the lineage who were more representative of the vested interests. For the members of the royal house and for those following in their fragmentary footsteps, Buddhism was very much a religion in aristocratic keeping, and they expanded on the received rituals and meditations, developing the new rites and literature that were eventually classified as Nyingma.

An understanding of specifically popular religion is much more difficult. Certainly it continued to employ the gods of the fields, possession of various classes of priests by mountain or local divinities, burned deodar branch offerings, and the consultation with local magicians (*lde'u*, *phywa mkhan*, etc.) for the purpose of prognostication, to name only a few important practices.[68] Concerns of ritual and community purity were paramount in this context, so that the subterranean Lu (*klu*) spirits, the field-inhabiting Sadak (*sa bdag*), and the Nyen living in trees and rocks were entreated to inhibit the spread of disease. As Karmay translates one ritual,

> With this essence from the forests of the mountains above,
> Incense with a pleasant fragrance and correctly prepared,
> Let us purify the gods above
> Let us also purify the Lu below
> as well as the Nyen in the middle.
> Let us purify our seats,
> Our clothes and objects,
> May everything be purified![69]

Likewise, the rites of passage sometimes required the movement of one's personal gods, as from the one house to another in the case of marriage, or the travel of the soul to the realm of the dead.[70]

Tibetan writers identified most of these practices as the "religion of humans" (*mi chos*), as distinguished from the religion of the gods (*lha chos*), which normatively indicated Buddhism. For its part, the Bon religion was sometimes included in the former, sometimes in the latter, and generally had a foot in both camps.[71] Most of what little we know about Bon during the ninth and early tenth centuries is limited to the rituals for the deceased (*dur bon*), prognostication, offerings to mountain spirits, and the other elements classified in the lower vehicles of the nine ways of Bon.[72] Their continuous investiture in these rites is one reason that it is sometimes classified as a "religion of humans." However, given their equal emphasis on an ideology of liberation, it is implausible that there was no soteriological ideology or Great Perfection tradition by the end of the tenth century among the five great clans that came to dominate Central Tibetan Bonpo identity: the Shen, Dru, Zhu, Pa, and Meü lineages.[73] The nature of Bonpo thought and practice becomes somewhat clear only in the eleventh and twelfth centuries, when the renaissance already was in full bloom.

At a more mundane level, practitioners of the religion of humans were concerned with the rules of society and stories about the spirits of the landscape. Most famously, Songtsen Gampo is noted as having issued sixteen rules that were classified as human religion and that primarily denoted ethical conduct.[74] All the oral literature, the epics of mythic kings like Gesar, the stories of heroes and villains, and the songs of praise to the deities of mountains and the locales, became understood as human religion.[75] The degree to which such practices were integrated with Buddhism in the early period is problematic, and the indications are tantalizingly slender. Yet by the late tenth century we begin to gain a sense of the spread of some sort of Buddhism into rural communities, perhaps especially concerned with reciting Buddhist texts during postmortem rituals but also extending to the blessing of crops and the protection from noxious spirits.

Somewhere between the aristocratic and rustic social levels were interesting groups serving in Central Tibet as the remnants of the Buddhist behaviors. The *Scholars' Festival* (*mKhas pa'i dga' ston*) includes a description drawn from Khutön's *Great Chronicle* depicting some of these personalities:

> Now because many of the ministers who destroyed the Dharma [during Darma's suppression] with various punishments had themselves died of disease, everyone agreed that it was retribution for destroying the Dharma. Accordingly, they set up the two Jowo statues in religious meetings dedicated to Maitreya, and made offerings. Then, taking as their own [signs] the symbols of the statues, [individuals] put on skirts tied with "collars" in a religious manner. They shaved part of their hair and tied up the rest in imi-

> tation of the statues' crowns. Then, saying that they were going to perform the three months of summer retreat, they stayed in temples and observed the five practices of the laity. Then, saying that they had performed the Vinaya practices of the summer retreat, they returned to town and took up married life. So then, there arose many who were called "Arhats with hair knots," and they began to serve as chaplains for the people. For services at the death of a middle-aged man, they would recite the one hundred thousand (verse version of the *Perfection of Insight*); for a boy, they recited the twenty thousand; for a child they recited the eight thousand. Two readers having great insight[76] while reading some commentary speculated on the future, saying that "this red-lettered text appears to summarize the meaning; this black-lettered one explains it in detail; and this little text investigates doubts." As a result of their pronouncements, little in the way of skill in explanation ensued. Mantrins in general did explain meditative systems without meditating but looked to the rituals of the Bonpo for examples, which they practiced. Singing texts [according to folk tunes], they studied village rituals. Since rites of sex and killing, as well as rituals of raising the undead (*vetāla*), had spread, some ritual murders occurred.[77]

While some people used the designation "Arhats with hair knots" (*dgra bcom gtsug phud can*), others called themselves elder Arhats (*gnas brtan dgra bcom*), elders (*gnas brtan*), religious (*ban de*), or "absorbed in religious conduct" (*'ban 'dzi ba*).[78] Many of these served as temple wardens or door keepers in the decades following the demise of the dynasty, although numerous temples were ultimately abandoned and fell into irredeemable disrepair, so that some of the imperially sponsored temples of the ninth century do not appear in the list of these revived in the tenth and eleventh centuries (see appendix 1), at least under their own names. The practices observed by these groups were those of the occasional monk, their Buddhist practices interspersed with liturgies for the dead, charismatic rituals, and attention to householders' duties.

Tibetan writers on the period also accuse members of these groups of a pattern of decline and illicit behavior, and their concerns were several. First, a highly visible section of the community left over from the early period—and for that reason now classified as old-style Buddhism, the Nyingma—was engaged in various disreputable activities, and the late-tenth-century Ordinance of Lha-lama Yéshé-Ö lists offensive acts carried out in the name of Dharma.[79] These included the ritualized slaughter of animals (and, we are to believe, possibly humans as well), the ritualized indulgence in sexual activity, and the claim that various unbalanced states of mind constituted the contemplation of emptiness. While the ordinance refers to a group called Ben-dziba (absorbed in religious conduct), the individuals were often known throughout Tibet as Ngakpas, or mantrins, a term denoting a specific variety of village lama. These individuals had some claims to formal aristocratic roots and were ritually involved in esoteric practice but with a weak awareness of the Buddhist intellectual or ethical matrix. There was little appeal on their part to the ideology of worldly propriety as the support for absolute understanding; instead, propriety itself might be directly assaulted, so that all conventions were by nature illusory.

Sometimes, as in the case of a certain Lu Kargyel (Star King), they may have represented themselves as alternatively Bonpo or Buddhist, depending on the requirements of the moment.[80] The *Pillar Testament* (*bKa' 'chems ka khol ma*) presents a devastating critique of Ngakpas granting consecration (*abhiṣeka*) without having received it, deceiving people by singing mantras as if they were songs, and offering sexual congress during *abhiṣeka* rituals for a fee, a form of ritualized prostitution.[81] Ritualized slaughter was conducted by those who declared that they had supernormal insight, and crowds of believers followed self-appointed teachers acting against the basic premises of Buddhist ideology. Thus, every sort of drooling schizophrenic could claim to be a fully enlightened siddha as he cut the head off yet another hapless beast in the name of liberation, a phenomenon still seen in certain Himalayan Buddhist communities.[82]

In the late tenth to early eleventh century, religious polemicists, whose position is revealed in the preceding quotation, certainly felt that the dynasty's collapse had resulted in the sudden efflorescence of illegitimate practices. These were sometimes represented as the "misunderstanding" of the esoteric scriptures, by taking tantric antinomian statements in as literal a manner as Indians had often done before them. Alternatively, local practices were sometimes appropriated by Buddhists with little regard to the standard controls over this enterprise, controls exhibited by Indian Buddhists in the past. The consequence was a general sense of a religious tradition out of control, with the monastic clothing and outward forms being maintained even while the actual behavior of Tibetan religious was slowly being accommodated to Tibetan village rites of blood sacrifice to mountain gods and to the marked Tibetan proclivity toward a greater sense of sexual license.

The fragmentation of power apparently served Buddhist missionary purposes in a peculiar manner: the investiture of the local fiefdoms with the court-based ideology and value systems. As the Lhasa court fragmented and power became transferred to the local centers, the systems attendant on the royal dynasty would have been transferred to the major population and aristocratic clans: art, ritual, oral literature, documentary preservation, connoisseurship of craft, and the like. Along with these, the image of the ruler supporting the Indic religion also must have been transferred and eventually acclaimed by popular consensus. This is seen, certainly, in the Tibetanization of literary composition, with the development of a large and growing esoteric literature composed by the regional aristocratic holders of esoteric Buddhist praxis, a literature considered in subsequent chapters.[83] The argument for a widespread domestication of Buddhism is also strong in view of the popular support required for the incredible number of small temples to be constructed so quickly with the missionary activity of the Eastern Vinaya monks in the late tenth and early eleventh century.

CLANS IN THE TENTH AND ELEVENTH CENTURIES

Through the period of fragmentation, the aristocratic clans and regional lords became the centers for both political power and religious authority, sometimes vested in the same person. Tibetan society was highly stratified, with the aristocracy (*sku drag* or *sger pa*) holding a variety of estates distributed throughout Tibet, some large and some very small.[84] Their relationship to the landed domains meant that when a clan managed to secure estates in a specific area, they often took the name of the geographical designation of their primary or first holdings as their clan designation. Thus many of the old aristocratic clans of the dynastic period began as local lords holding estates in Chim, Nup, Lé, Cha, and so on, and these became their clan names. Members of the same clan were identified as descending from a common divine ancestor, and as with aristocratic houses everywhere, they made marital alliances based on social status and perceived benefit. Later documents preserve a list of the clan holdings during the later days of the dynasty (table 2), but the geographical locations of some areas are obscure. Moreover, many of the more important clans in the late tenth and early eleventh century are not represented here. Others are known from Dunhuang documents and the records preserved later by Tibetan historians.[85]

A supplementary list indicates clan movement in the aftermath of the insurrections: the Dro and Chog-ro moved into the Drompa/Lhatsé area; the Nyang and Nang held the Drang-khar Ché-chen; the Shüpu and Nyiwa took over Cha-tsang gung-nang; the Khu and Nyak controlled Namo shampo; and the Tsé and other Shüpu occupied Po-gyü tsékhar.[86] In this we see that clan branches might have had holdings in a number of geographical areas, and the Dro, for example, possessed estates in locales as diverse as northeastern Tibet (Amdo) and Ladakh.

Even though these clans wielded enormous power, this does not mean that the clan structures were ossified into a caste system, for Tibetan social dynamics has generally supported limited mobility, with the ascension of new clans under special circumstances and the eventual eclipse of others.[87] Certainly, some

TABLE 2 Royal Dynastic Clan Domains

CIVIL AND MILITARY ADMINISTRATION

Uru: Nanam, Bé, Nön, and Shöbu clans
Yoru: Nyang, Chim, Yé, and So clans
Yéru: Khyungpo, Gö, Pa-tsap, and Langpa clans
Rulak: Dro ('Bro), Khyungpo, Namdé, and Chim clans

INDIVIDUAL ESTATES

Locale	*Clans*
Yarlung sog-kha	Khu, Nyak
Yamdrok nak-khim	Kuring dé-nga
Ching-nga, Ching-yül	Gö, Nup
Cha-uk sa-tsik	Drang-jé pa-nga
Dré (Brad) and Zhong-pa	Nanam
Drag-rum tö-mé	Chépong
Tsang tö-mé	Dro('Bro), Khyungpo
Lung-shö nampo	Dru ('Dru), Chuk-tsam
Pen-yül	Dro (sGro), Ma
Nyang-ro, Drompa	Dré, Ché
Shang, Lé	Chiri, Lé
Yung-wa ché-chung	Dranka
Zha-gé désum	Bé
Nam-ra, Chag-gong	Dring, Chag
Dam-shö karmo	Cha (Phya), Ra

SOURCE: *mKhas pa'i dga' ston*, pp. 186–91.

clans from the old dynasty such as the Khyungpo or the Nyö eventually survived into the modern period, but others did not, and many of modern Tibet's aristocratic houses were the result of a number of factors.[88] These factors included the accrual of extreme wealth through business endeavors, the recognition of an incarnate lama (especially the Dalai Lama) in an ordinary family, and the elevation of a person of exceptional ability for various reasons. In our case, as Tibet emerged from the period of darkness, both the old clans (Ngok, Chim, Ché, etc.) and the new clans (Marpa, etc.) became part of the renaissance process and demonstrated their capacity for development.

Moreover, marital arrangements appeared to be more fluid in the tenth and eleventh centuries than at some other times, when the system of aristocratic grades and concomitant marriage restrictions was more rigidly enforced.[89] Although aristocratic families in the renaissance generally chose their spouses from other aristocratic families, occasionally different lines of the same clan intermarried. There even were instances of an extraordinary commoner marrying an aristocrat's daughter, as in the case of Drokmi, the great translator. Clans sometimes divided into subsidiary houses and even changed their clan names. For example, a member of one branch of the Chim clan, an ancient noble house, changed its name to Zhang during the tenth century, although the reason for this change is not stated. In the imperial period, the designation Zhang was awarded to important ministers, generally because they provided daughters to members of the imperial house, and it may be that this person served in a ministerial capacity to one of the surviving branches of the dynasty.[90] Other clan branches adopted the subdesignation "corner" (*zur*), using a building metaphor for the subclan, just as we use a horticultural one (e.g., branch), and it may be that the well-authenticated Nyingma supporters, the Zur clan of Tsang Province, obtained their name in this manner.

The Zur clan also demonstrated another practice, adopting a young man, related or distant, to become the heir of the clan branch.[91] This form of adoption became an essential legal system supporting the later Tibetan aristocratic structure, and its evidence in the eleventh century indicates that it was probably an early tradition as well. Adoption was sometimes necessary in the case of a celibate landholding teacher who may have needed a clan heir to maintain his property following his demise, so that the temple buildings and any associated lands would not fall into dispute or be escheated by the local lord. While some ancient temples certainly became considered the property of a community obliged to contribute the fees (*khral tsho*) for its maintenance and the funds going to the overall organization, others were maintained as private property or part of an estate, and from time to time, these varieties became the objects of dispute. In such instances, members of an aristocratic house were able to sustain their titles by means of adoption.

Despite this information, we actually know very little about the structure or organization of the clans during the early period of fragmentation and the early renaissance. Their composition, specific marital arrangements, populations, specific distribution, and a host of other issues remain dim to our vision. Occasionally—as in the case of the Ché, the Nyang, the Nyak, the Khön, and the Lang clans—some meager records survive, but they are rare and often uninformative about the tenth and eleventh centuries.[92] Other clan documents we know by rumor, as, for instance, the family record of the Ngok clan, but so far they consist only of titles found in other sources.[93] It is clear, however, that by the end of the tenth century, some clans were expanding their holdings and areas of activity while others were not, and this effort at expansion most often spilled over into the area of religion.[94] The Ché and Ngok clans, for example, eventually became heavily invested in various Buddhist lineages, and this pattern of clan domination of religious affairs continued as a consistent theme throughout Tibet's history. As a consequence, we are constantly be drawn back into a discussion of clans, as the formation of stable Tibetan Buddhist institutions eventually depended on the great clans' full participation and sense of ownership of the process.

CONCLUSION: A CHANGE OF FORTUNE IN TIBET

In the intermittent chaos at the end of empire, Central Tibetans struggled to achieve a semblance of order, but at an important level they did not succeed. The pattern of insurrections, the looting of the royal tombs, the flight of monks (and, we may presume, other culture-bearing refugees), and the consistent decay of social mores depict an all-too-familiar process of a culture self-destructing. Buddhist monastic institutions, supportive of the Tibetan empire in all its manifestations, was also complicitous in its demise, for like many other religious groups in Asia, the Buddhists did not learn to restrain their desire for privilege and authority. Ever agile, however, Buddhists managed to find a more sustained placement among the populace in the post-imperial period than they did under the imperium itself. Extending themselves in the ritual sphere to postmortem rites, religious healing, magical systems, and the composition of Tibetan scriptures embodying a specifically Tibetan Buddhism, the religious aristocrats, temple wardens, and itinerant preachers made a place for themselves in a manner that we can but dimly perceive. All this came with a price, however: the loss of monastic Buddhism in Central Tibet. This meant that the monks—the international representatives of a Buddhist world order—would no longer recite texts, dispute points of doctrine, invite in eminent monks from other countries, and provide an antidote to Tibetan provincialism. This meant that those common-born Tibetans outside the aristocratic clans would no longer have an avenue for legitimacy, for they no longer had the vehicle of monastic office to validate their religious authority. For these and many other reasons, Tibetans eventually returned to the search for monastic vitality.

3

Renaissance and Reformation: The Eastern Vinaya Monks

> Now I will set forth the way in which the Holy Dharma sprang up from the embers,
> And the manner that the congregations spread.
> Thus Gongpa-sel, who has four titles, revived it
> During the time of the three princes:
> Ngadak Trihchung, Trihdé Göntsen, and [Tsalana] Yéshé Gyeltsen.
> Yes, the Buddha's dispensation is like waves in an ocean—peaks and valleys.
> Or like the rising and setting of the sun and moon—luminosity and dimness.
> Or like stairways—leading up and leading down.
> Or like the grain, high in summer but stubble in winter.
>
> —The scholar Déü (ca. 1260)[1]

Finally, we arrive at the Central Tibetan renaissance, which, as in the European period, is sometimes considered in conjunction with a reform movement. In Tibetan religious history, the activities of Tibetans and Indians at this time are collectively known as the "later spread" or "later translation" of the Dharma and are illustrated by the Tibetan metaphor of fire springing up from seemingly cold embers. The "later spread" is a Tibetan periodization, for it is commonplace to divide the Tibetan involvement with Indic and Buddhist civilizations into the earlier royal dynastic diffusion from the seventh to mid-ninth centuries (*snga dar*) and the later spread of the Dharma (*phyi dar*), beginning in the latter half of the tenth century. Sometimes this is understood as the early translation (*snga 'gyur*), as opposed to the new translation (*gsar 'gyur*) period, and this literary topos is observed throughout indigenous Tibetan literature, although it is contested in some venues.

The Central Tibetan renaissance in the tenth to thirteenth century was the result of several movements, not all of which have been given a balanced assessment in either indigenous Tibetan writings or modern scholarship. Preeminent among these trajectories was the reimportation of the Vinaya rule of Buddhist monasticism from the northeastern sections of the Tibetan cultural world, on the borders with China and Central Asia.

This chapter examines the reinvigoration of monasticism in the four horns of Tibet by a handful of Tibetans traveling to the surviving monastic centers in the northeast (Amdo). There they secured the *Mūlasarvāstivāda-vinaya* and other parts of the royal dynastic curriculum and returned to Ü-Tsang where they reintroduced the rituals and study even as they clashed with entrenched interests. The chapter also looks at the western Tibetan revival sponsored by the descendants of Ösung in the regions of Gugé and Purang, leading to the invitation of the celebrated Indian monk Atiśa and his founding of the Kadampa order. In contrast to the received wisdom, however, the chapter argues that the Kadampa order was only modestly influential in mid-eleventh-century Central Tibet. Indeed, the development of a vital and complex temple system under the supervision of the Central Tibetan monks Lumé, Lotön, and others had a commanding presence, despite the higher profile that Atiśa and the Kadampa order enjoyed in later literature. Nonetheless, neither the Eastern Vinaya nor the Kadampa groups—as monastic-based, normative Mahāyānist movements—by themselves proved sufficient to stimulate the great revival of Tibetan civilization, although that rebirth was dependent on both in various ways.

The question of the Tibetans' motivation to seek monastic Buddhism again at this time is difficult to determine. In part it appears to be an act of memory, in part a question of economic and political security, and in part dissatisfaction with the received traditions. In the first case, the Central Tibetans inherited four items from the dynasty: the memory of empire embedded in the stories of the period and persons of the surviving imperial lineage; the feeling of loss and horror enduring from the chaos of its fragmentation; the physical remains of the small temples, tombs, monoliths, and manuscript troves from the period; and the still evolving religious practices in the hands of individuals, representing either the great clans surviving through the period of fragmentation or the lay-religious quasi monks keeping the temples and performing their rites.

More than a century passed between the time of Darma's assassination and the Central Tibetan movement toward Buddhist monastic reintroduction, an effort retarded by the country's economic and political disarray. In Central Tibet, support for the clerics, their building programs, and collateral matériel would have been a drain on a purely village economy. At the aristocratic level, the intermittent power contests that this warring-states period imposed on the four horns of Tibet inhibited the development of investment in international trade, pan-national guilds, centers of manufacture, and so on. Many from the aristocracy, moreover, must have been concerned about their own fortunes in the shifting alliances between the remnants of Yumten's and Ösrung's successors. But political and economic problems seldom last forever, and we have tantalizing suggestions that the last half of the tenth century was a time of economic coalescence and the reemergence of some political stability.

Perhaps the most important motivation was a widespread and profound dissatisfaction with the received wisdom of the contemporary Buddhist congregations. Doubt about the authenticity of many Buddhist practices had clearly emerged by the late tenth century, along with a strong sense that the revival of Tibetan civilization depended in some essential manner on the temples' once again being occupied by real monks, not the keepers of the keys who practiced when the spirit moved them.[2] The feeling is expressed in several records showing that true Buddhism survived outside the four horns of Tibet, especially in the northeast, where Tibetans had formed a vibrant regional center. Grounded in the Buddhist practice surviving on the border between Tibet and China, the reimportation of the Vinaya into the heart of Tibet was a watershed moment in its religious history.

IN PURSUIT OF VIRTUE IN THE NORTHEAST

It is no coincidence that the period of the renaissance almost exactly mirrors a rebirth experienced in Central Asia and China generally and in the northeastern Tibetan Hexi and Liangzhou areas in particular. Certainly it was not from the south that Tibetans received their economic and cultural strength, for the later tenth century saw the Pratīhāras and the Pālas in North India only marginally survive the Rāṣṭrakūṭa collapse of 973 C.E. Conversely, in China, the reemergence of a central authority was instrumental in the development of one of the golden ages of China: the Song. Although the coalescence of the Northern Song is nominally identified as 960, the Song actually took until 979 to solidify control over North China, when Song Taizong overcame the Shato warlord of Beihan.[3] A degree of stability was established in the Hexi area between 982 and 1004 with the emergence of the Tangut state to the north and its triangular relationship with the Song and the Khitan.[4] Moreover, the Nanzhao kingdom, China's southwestern part-time allies, part-time antagonists, had given way to the sinicized Dali kingdom in 937.[5] The political strength of all these areas facilitated Tibet's economic development and allowed the growth of a class of culturally essential but nonproducing individuals: the Buddhist monks.

Tibet's better-developed economic base and greater sense of political stability in the late tenth century precipitated a resurgence of interest in the resurrection of the old temple complexes left over from the royal dynastic period. Drakpa Gyeltsen's *Royal Genealogy* maintains that while 108 temples had been founded during the regnal years of both Trihsong Détsen and Trihdé Songtsen, 1,008 temples were consecrated by Trihtsuk Détsen Relpachen, numbers that were evidently hyperbolic but still indicative of a continual Tibetan fascination with the emperors' religious constructions.[6] There is a more persuasive list of thirty important institutions where monastic instruction was nurtured under the aegis of Relpachen, and these and similar structures, along with Samyé, became the basis for Buddhist revitalization in Central Tibet.[7]

Although both Tibetan literature and modern discussions have tended to focus on the establishment of Samyé during the royal dynasty and the developments in West Tibet during the new translation period, several factors favored local institution building in the late tenth century, with the localized small temples and monasteries collectively constituting the single most important element in the first several centuries of Central Tibetan Buddhism. During the early period, these temples sent a dramatic message to Tibetans about the dedication of the royal house to the Indian religion. During the difficult times of the late ninth and early tenth century, they provided material evidence of the sacred sites' continuing to evoke the memories of the dynasty. During the tenth and eleventh centuries, together with Samyé, they provided a network of physical foci for the social and mercantile interaction of small traveling merchants and Tibetan religious.[8] The many temples also served as rallying points for local princes attempting to make themselves over in the mythic memory of the ancient kings. The importance of the temple network and its symbolic associations is recognized in later literature in the formula of the temples' geomantic influence. In this twelfth-century model, which has interesting psychosexual overtones, the temples constructed by the members of the dynasty acted as ritual daggers nailing down the cliff demoness of Tibet at various parts of her body.[9] Both the arrangement and narrative are curiously reminiscent of the *pīṭhas* in India built around locales where the dismembered body of Satī, the wife of Śiva, fell, and like the *pīṭhas*, the demon-taming temples reveal a sacred network intersecting an overarching mythology and local cultus. Historically, the interaction of local princes and the temple system set the stage for the reintroduction of monastic Buddhism into Ü-Tsang toward the end of the tenth century and provided the fundamental model of religious and political legitimacy for further temple construction throughout the Tibetan plateau.

The actual reintroduction of monastic Buddhism into Central Tibet was the result of the enduring political and cultural relationships between Tibetans in the northeast (Tsongkha/Hexi region) and in Central Tibet. The standard story is that in the midst of the destruction of Buddhism by Darma, three monks of the meditation center at Chuwori Gomdra, one of Relpachen's temples, noticed other monks behaving as if deranged. The other monks beat drums, changed their clothing, led dogs, and went hunting. Once informed of the fate of monks in Central Tibet, the three—Yo-gejung, Tsang Rapsel, and Mar Shākya Sengé—escaped to the West Tibetan regions and on to Central Asia (Hor).[10] Their living conditions were quite uncertain there, however, and when they heard of Darma's assassination, they elected to search elsewhere. With the help of a Central Asian Buddhist layman, Shākya Shérap, they took their donkey load of Vinaya and Abhidharma texts and made their way to the monastery of Anchung Namdzong, somewhere in the Tsongkha area. There they met a young Bonpo man who came to play a central role in the story. With the help of two Chinese monks—sometimes identified as Heshang Kawa and Heshang Genbak—the young man was ordained Géwasel (or Gongpa-sel) and resided in the monastery of Dentik, on the banks of the Yellow River close to the modern Chinese city of Xining. Young men from Central Tibet came to meet Géwasel, were ordained, and eventually returned to spread the Dharma in the heart of Tibet.

The events as they actually occurred were far more complex than this flat formulaic rendition. Our early sources mention a network of various temples that became the goal of monks and virtuous laymen fleeing the Buddhist suppression in Central Tibet. This goal should not come as a surprise, for twenty of the thirty teaching temples (*chos grwa*) constructed or supported by Relpachen were located in the eastern Tibetan areas of Kham or Amdo. Because both Anchung and Dentik were listed as centers for meditation (*sgom grwa*), it is not surprising that monks trained in one center should seek out others. Tibetan monks seeking safety and accommodation in the northeast would have conducted themselves in keeping with the normative practices of imperially supported clergy. Accordingly, Ka-ö Chog-drakpa, a Tibetan traveling all the way from Nepal, had heard of the disaster in the four horns of Tibet and brought to Amdo his donkey load of Abhidharma works.[11] Lhalung Rapjor-yang and Rongtön Sengé-drak came from Yerpa with many works of Vinaya and Abhidharma, and Rongtön had been himself a product of the teaching temples set up by Relpachen. Moreover, six disciples of Char Ratna and other followers of the great translators and Indian masters of the royal dynasty found themselves meeting in Amdo, having traveled the great distance by various means. Even Darma's assassin, Lhalung Pelgyi Dorjé, was said to have arrived there with quantities of Abhidharma and Vinaya texts.[12]

On a mission from the Buddha, these and other monks took over temples and contemplation caves in the Hexi area, in order to maintain the teaching traditions. Tsang Rapsel nurtured a small monastery at the cave of Khangsar Yaripuk. Ka-ö Chog-drakpa took over the temple of Pelsang Kharchak drilbu. Lhalung took the temple of Dashö-tsel, and Rongtön controlled the temple of Changtsa Jerong. Apparently these temples, of uncertain location, already existed but were underpopulated until the arrival of the refugees from Central Tibet in the ninth century. Anxious to preserve and to expand the precious ordination lineage that they represented, the refugee monks became proselytizers, and their ordination of Géwasel led to the further ordination of groups like the "six excellent men," mostly from eastern Tibetan aristocratic families, as well as many others.[13] The population became large enough, in fact, for two (or even three) separate Vinaya traditions eventually to emerge by the time the first candidates for ordination arrived from Central Tibet more than a century later.[14] The lineage maintained by Drum Yeshé Gyeltsen—which was the one eventually transmitted to monks from Central Tibet—was called the "monks' lineage" (*btsun brgyud*). In contrast, the ordination lineage transmitted by Nub Pelgyi Jangchub was termed the "teacher's lineage" (*mkhan brgyud*), and a fairly strong rivalry and tension grew between the two groups in Amdo.[15]

Early Tibetan chronicles indicate that tenth-century Central Tibetans looked to the northeast for a vibrant Vinaya tradition, and the intersection of political and religious activity represented there shows why Tibetan Buddhist monks in the area had such high visibility.[16] With the help of Chinese imperial and local sources, the complexity of the Tsongkha and Liangzhou region has come into better focus (map 3).[17] Certainly there was a powerful political and economic basis, for the Tibetan city of Xiliangfu (modern Wuwei) in the Liangzhou area in 998 alone had a population of 128,000, the majority actually Tibetans.[18] Liangzhou was also the center of the thriving Tibetan horse trade, going strong at least from 990. We have some measure of the wealth of the area by the tribute sent by one Panlezhi (perhaps 'Phan bla-rje in Tibetan), possibly of the Lang clan, who rose to power in 1001 and sent five thousand horses to the Song capital in Kaifeng in 1002 as tribute.[19] After Panlezhi's assassination by a rogue Tangut party in 1004, his youngest brother, Siduodu, was elected to govern Liangzhou and the city of Xiliangfu, but his official position was diminished, in part by the plague of 1006.[20]

The Tibetan district of Tsongkha (around modern Xining), to the south of Liangzhou and east of Lake Qinghai, produced another Tibetan leader. In

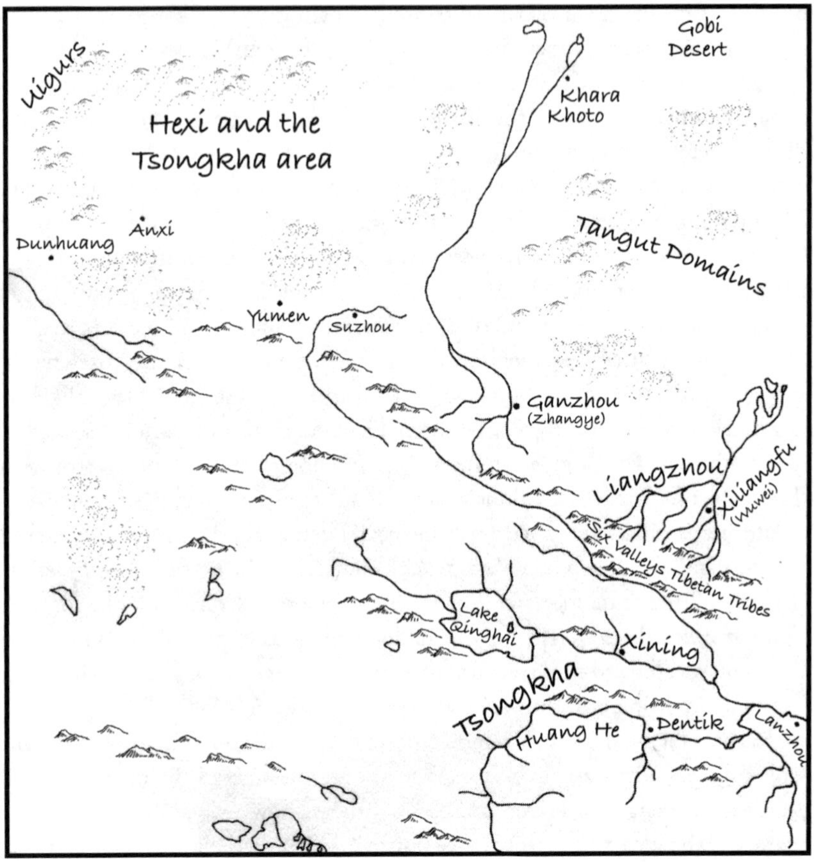

MAP 3 Hexi and the Tsongkha Area.

1008, a prince originally from West Tibet, whose name transcribed into Chinese is Qi Nanlu Wen Qianbu (997–1065)—perhaps Trih Namdé Tsenpo in Tibetan—was abducted from Tsongkha by the monk Lilicun with the assistance of a local strongman. Temporarily removed to Kuozhe in the northwest, he was enthroned as emperor (*btsan po*), and later he and Lilicun returned to Tsongkha. There he was given the designation prince (*rgyal sras*) by the people of the area, and its Chinese transcription, Jiaosile (or Gusile), was the title generally used in Chinese documents thereafter for Tibetan leaders following in his footsteps.[21] Later Tibetan lists of kingly descent (*rgyal rabs*) identify this house as scions of Ösung's great-grandson Ödé, one of the "three Dé of the eastern district" born to Trashi Tsekpel.[22] By 1014 Jiaosile was capable of assembling an army of 40,000 to 60,000 men to fight the Tangut incursions. Despite the fall of the Uigur Khanate to the Tanguts around 1028 and the Tibetan areas of Liangzhou in 1031, this local Tibetan lord managed to fend off the Tangut attack in 1035, assisted by the Tibetans who fled Liangzhou to join him. The success of the Tsongkha prince in repelling the Tanguts was recognized by the Song in 1041 with the imperial title of military commissioner of Hexi (*hexi chiedu shi*).[23] The Tangut belligerency ultimately turned in the favor of the Tibetans: Central Asian trade became routed through the Tsongkha area since the previous caravan routes became closed to merchants because of Tangut adventurism. The region experienced a fragile peace that was eventually broken by the Jurchen Tungus who conquered the Khitan, the Tangut, and all of northern China in the early twelfth century.

Amid this political and military activity, Buddhist monks consistently assumed leadership roles. Not only did Lilicun work with a Miaoquan chieftain to capture and enthrone Jiaosile, but Buddhist monks also played important political roles in the area. Both Siduodu and Jiaosile were frequently noted in the Chinese annals for their involvement with monks, and in 1008 Siduodu began sending three monks every three years to the Song capital to receive purple robes from the Chinese court. In the Gansu corridor, these robes not only marked imperial favor but also signaled the monks' success in exerting a pacific influence on the area's unruly groups of seminomadic peoples. As Iwasaki noted, when a monk received the purple robe, it "represented a reward for the services that he had rendered in controlling the Buddhist tribes."[24] Monks occasionally acted as the de facto or de jure heads of these tribes as well, for one of the eighteen leaders of the Six Valleys tribes around the city of Xiliangfu in 1007 might have been a monk, given his designation of "precious one" (*rin po che*), perhaps the earliest attestation of this as a religious title.[25]

While some of these monks may have been of Chinese or Uigur descent, at least as early as 1015, some recipients of the purple robe are specified as Tibetan, and Tibetan monks were involved in military campaigns on the Chinese borderlands as well. In 1054, the monk Cun-zhuige received simultaneously the purple robe and the title of army commander (*dujunqu*) for his assistance in pacifying Tibetan tribes.[26] Monasteries also were state supported, and Xiliangfu was noted as having a famous pagoda—perhaps the illustrious Kumārajīva Pagoda of the modern city of Wuwei—and several monasteries, one of which (Dayunsi) still stands today. These and many other monasteries probably represented the institutional bases in which Tibetans and other Buddhists maintained their literature, promulgated their rituals, and interacted with one another across ethnic lines. Even the traditional story relates that Géwasel needed the services of two Chinese monks to receive ordination at Dentik

Monastery, and it appears that the blend of cultures was close to that existing today in the Chinese-Tibetan borderlands. Accordingly, when Tibetans in Ü-Tsang began looking for sources of religiosity, their immediate attention was not drawn to the Gugé-Purang kingdom in the West, even though Ösung's descendants were moving toward a Buddhist revival. Instead, after hearing of the thriving monasteries, the many temples, the important monks in Tsongkha, they went there for the spark of their religious revival.

TO CENTRAL TIBET ON A MISSION FROM BUDDHA

The remnants of the house of Yumten represented the opportunity that Tibetans had been seeking, although the surviving members are depicted as somewhat reluctant supporters. By the late tenth century—despite questions about Yumten's legitimate paternity—his successors dominated many of the areas of Central Tibet most closely associated with the old dynasty (table 3).

The young men of Ü-Tsang—whether we count four, five, six, seven, ten, twelve, or thirteen (all these numbers are mentioned in the sources)—came to the northeast for their ordination in Tsongkha. Most sources make them the direct disciples of Géwasel, but this is highly unlikely and represents the Tibetan proclivity to associate famous religious figures with other famous figures. Even later Tibetan authors like Tséwang Norbu (1698–1755) were aware of the chronological difficulties and had to explain them away by proposing that some of these men had excessively long lives.[27] In all probability, there were multiple monastic generations between Géwasel and the group of men who eventually spread monastic Buddhism from the northeast.[28] They also certainly had many different teachers or preceptors, and several are found in the sources: Drum Yéshé Gyeltsen, Dro Mañjuśrī, Chog-ro Pelgyi Wangchuk, Drum Chinglakchen, and Tülwa Yéshé Gyeltsen.[29] Although we can have only modest confidence in this list, it certainly indicates the vitality of monastic practice, with the Drum clan taking a primary position in supporting the monks.

According to legend, the new Ü-Tsang monks were appointed by their teachers to various positions or careers according to their capabilities: Lumé Shérap Tsültrim (or Tsültrim Shérap), from Ü Shatsar, was appointed to maintain the Vinaya. Tsongtsün Shérap Sengé, since he was intelligent, was made professor (*bshad pa mkhan*). Lotön Dorjé Wangchuk, because of his great power, was appointed protector of the Dharma. Dring Yéshé Yönten, because he was bossy, was made the temple keeper. Ba Tsültrim Lotrö was appointed master meditator, and Sumpa Yéshé Lotrö was made bursar. Following his specification of these appointments, Déü José quips that, of course, even though they

TABLE 3 Simplified Yum-ten Succession Through the Eleventh Century

Yum-ten

Trihdé Gön-nyön

Rigpa-gön	Nyi-ö Pelgön
Trihdépo	Gönchö
Trih Öpo	Tsalana Yéshé Gyeltsen
Atsara / Trihdé Göntsen / Trihdé Göntsek	Ngadak Trihpa
Lha Détsen	Bodhi-rātsa (ca. 1050)
Gyelbu Yöndak / Lhatsün Tönpa	Gélo
Wangchuk-trih and four brothers	Gön-né
Tokpo	Trashi-gön / Ngönmo / Wangdé / Lha Kadampa

SOURCE: From Hazod 2000b, pp. 181–89, version I.

all had been appointed to these positions, nobody listened to the abbot (ostensibly Géwasel or Drum Yéshé Gyeltsen) who appointed them, and each did just what he liked.[30] Preparing themselves for the cold of the northern plains that they had to traverse to reach the four horns of Tibet, they had specially made cloaks (*ber nag*) and hats of a peculiar Bonpo style used in ritual (*zhwa 'ob*) but smeared with yellow matter in the four corners to identify it as Buddhist; this hat became a trademark of the various groups that grew out of the movement.[31]

Some sources tell an intriguing story about Lotön's individual initiative in precipitating their departure. According to this narrative, Lotön decided to go ahead first with a band of merchants to Central Tibet, to see whether they could find support for their common venture.

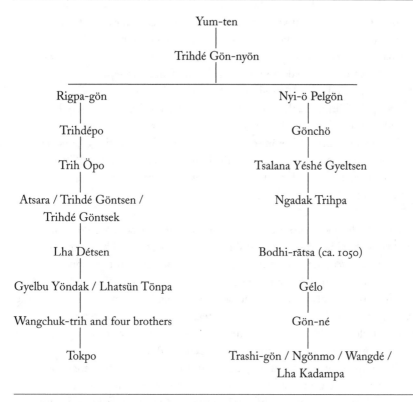

> Lotön said to the others, "You wait here. I'll go to Ü-Tsang and see if we are able to spread the Dharma or not. If we are able, then I'll stay there and you all come on up. If we're not able to spread religion, then I'll come on back down here." He then accompanied some merchants from Denma (in Kham) and they encountered good business in Sumtrang. When they indicated that they wanted to return [to eastern Tibet], he replied, "You guys have not even begun to get in on the good business yet!" So they went to Tsang. At Gurmo Rapkha [Lotön's hometown], was Lonak Tsuksen. Lotön said to him, "Your son should go stay in Ü after having been ordained." So the boy was sent and Lotön sent a letter [back to Dentik telling Lumé and the others to come]. And because the business [between eastern Tibet and Tsang] had been good, the Gurmo market came about. This market is also through the kindness of Lotön.[32]

If Lotön had gone to Ü-Tsang in advance of the others, it would explain the rapidity with which the Tsang establishments progressed. The accounts, however, partly contradict one another, for some maintain that the monks eventually went their own ways for different reasons. In any event, there is little doubt that the business relationships gradually increasing between Tsongkha and the reviving areas of Central Tibet began to recreate the historical symbiosis of the Buddhist clergy and traveling merchants, a symbiosis that has so well served Buddhist missionary efforts throughout Central Asian history.

By the time the band as a whole set out, Lumé and Lotön were considered the leaders of the group, and they continued to accrue support and company for some time. They evidently were corresponding with Trihdé Göntsen, in whom they decided to place their trust, and there is an early tradition that the young men had gone to Tsongkha for ordination at his instigation in the first place.[33] Whatever the real circumstances, both this royal lord and his cousin (or son or brother) Tsalana Yéshé Gyeltsen welcomed them back to Ü and provided them shelter and support. The sources give various dates for their arrival in Central Tibet, and although they differ widely, Dromtön's 978 and Khépa-déü's 988 probably bracket the correct period.[34] An early chronicle offers a graphic account of the devastating condition of Samyé (and, it is to be understood, the other royal temples) that these men encountered:[35]

> Then the ten men of Ü and Tsang arrived in Samyé. There, they were granted hospitality by Trihdé Göntsen, who asked them, "Who is your leader?" "Lumé is!" they replied. Then Trihdé Göntsen placed in Lumé's hand the whole bunch of rusty keys to the main temple, the U-tsé of Samyé. Lumé opened the door of the circumambulatory path (*'khor sa*) and saw it filled

> with brambles and fallen plaster.[36] Water from tree branches (coming in the windows) had smeared all the paintings. In the Drum Hall (*rnga khang*), a series of four of the pillars out of twelve—which occupy the middle and edges of the room—were cut down.[37] The remaining ones were desiccated [from rot] and tangled together.[38] In the intermediate circumambulatory path (*'khor sa bar pa*), [Lumé] saw it filled with the wealth of the temple endowment, complete with a fox's den in the middle. The statues of the U-tsé all had birds' nests in their hands and on their crowns. All the crowns were fetid with bird excreta. Lumé looked at the temple treasury. He then sealed all the doors with a magic rope guarding against snakes and demons. "This place is generally a swamp!" he said, and took all the keys back.[39] These he returned to the king and said, "I'm an abbot. And because abbots are defiled in the presence of temple treasuries, I will not take charge of this place!" He was then offered the Khamsum Sangkhang and still refused. The Butsel Serkhang-ling was offered to the two, Lotön and Tsongtsün Shérap Sengé, but they would not accept it. They replied, "There are many disciples to be converted elsewhere!" and departed for Tsang (their homes). Rakshi Tsültrim Jungné was offered Gégyé and afterward also entrusted Butsel. Then Lumé was offered Kachu (which he accepted for a while). Then he bade the others good-bye, saying, "Take the path to Uru and Yönru!"[40] Lumé then brought in many horse loads of goods in order to revive the U-tsé of Samyé, and he was finally successful in repairing its many problems.[41] He then entrusted the keys to Ba Tsültrim Lotrö and Rakshi Tsültrim Jungné.

Doubtless, the majority of older temples were in conditions similar to that of Samyé, with broken plaster and rotten rafters or beams. Thus the first priority for these men was the revival of these seats of spirituality that were so closely associated with the ancient emperors (figure 3). Consequently, Lumé's unwillingness to accept responsibility for the treasury of Samyé did not mean that he was unconcerned about this most prestigious monastery's eventual resuscitation, as the episode shows. Instead, the political aura of these temples—and the continual involvement of the remnants of the imperial house and the old aristocratic clans in the disposition and use of these temples—meant that anyone serving in the capacity of chaplain or resident lama would be unable to be independent of the system that continued the fragmentation of Tibetan culture. In fact, Lumé's attention to the Samyé central temple, the U-tsé, ran into political problems almost immediately, but from his own congregation. His initial efforts at its renovation were blocked by Ba Tsültrim Lotrö and Rakshi Tsültrim Jungné in a dispute over territory, so that Lumé requested the personal intervention of Trihdé Göntsen to grant him this authority.[42]

FIGURE 3 Samyé U-tsé temple. After a modern photograph

The temples and clans supporting the temples' reconstruction provided legitimacy for these new monks, so that other areas could respond to the opportunity and become the source for the formation of entirely new institutions. Accordingly, the temples became the starting point but not the end strategy for the missionaries, and they began the process of community formation and the institutionalization of their Vinaya systems. The congregations (*tsho/sde pa*) that they organized in Ü (the horns Uru and Yoru) and Tsang (the horns Yéru and Rulak) became the basis for the temples' revival and construction in the several areas.[43] These groups established some of the patterns for the stable revival of Buddhism in Central Tibet, and based on their successes, real monasteries began to be built by the next generation of missionaries. However, the fractiousness evinced right at the beginning, with the conflict over Lumé's desire to renovate Samyé, continued to be a hallmark of the Eastern Vinaya communities for the next two centuries.

While Lumé was occupied with taking care of Kachu, Samyé, and other royal dynastic sites in Ü, the two major monks from Tsang—Lotön Dorjé Wangchuk and Tsongtsün Shérap Sengé—departed for their homes, as the preceding story related.[44] Lotön founded Gyengong (997) in the Nyang-rong area close to the eventual site of Shalu and was responsible for the training of twenty-four scholarly disciples (*mkhan bu*).[45] He also is associated with various visions, such as one of the worldly *ḍākinī* Dorjé Raptenma on the road to Pelmo Pelta in Tsang, when this goddess spoke of her association with his future monastery.[46] And as he was laying out the temple foundations for Gyengong, he had a vision of four local feminine divinities (*dkar mo mched bzhi*) who offered him assistance, so that he knew this site was auspicious.[47] Lotön's eight primary disciples were the among the great missionaries of monasticism in eleventh-century Tsang.[48] While Sumtön Pakpa Gyeltsen took over the abbatial duties of Gyengong, Gya Shākya Zhönu constructed Tang in Latö-mar and became the abbot of Drompa-gyang. It was here that two famous monks who went to study in India, Tag-lo and Drokmi, were ordained. Between Gyengong and Tang, Gya Shākya Zhönu also founded the Büldok-lhak Lhakhang. Langtön Jampa constructed the temple of Ompuk and others at Tsangdram, Bumtang, Chagsa, Trihgong, Götön, Trölma, and elsewhere, so that his communities were divided into western and eastern branches.[49] Kyi Atsarya Yéshé Wangpo also was exemplary in his activity, with three temples in the Shang area: Shang Kharlung, Gyéré Langra, and Mushang-kyi Rokam. It was Chétön Shérap Jungné, however, who was destined to found the greatest monastery on this list: Shalu, which eventually became the home of many excellent scholars, from Butön Rinchendrup onward (table 4).[50]

Lotön's traveling companion, Tsongtsün Shérap Sengé, was just as busy. His home was in Shabkyi Go-nga, in the Shab valley, which he used as a base of operations, although the precise location of this village is still obscure. He himself established at least four centers, two to the west and two to the east. The ones in the east were in the Nyang valley, the temples of Né-nying and Né-sar, on either side of the later city of Gyantse; west of these were the temples of Kelkor and Gyenkor, whose location is now uncertain.[51] Tsongtsün's disciples continued his work and extended it by including other communities (said to be five) in a larger confederation. Batsün Lotrö Yönten was made the abbot of Tsi-lhakhang, and his disciple took charge of Kek Né-nying, becoming the source for the Western Ba group and Tsi-lhakhang becoming the source of the Eastern Ba group, with others in between.[52] Likewise, groups and communities associated with various other temples in the area were offered to Batsün by Yöl-togbep, Ra Lotrö Zangpo, Gya Tsülseng, Kongpo Yéjung, Marpa Dorjé Yéshé, Népo Drakpa Gyeltsen, and others, who remain for us only names on a rapidly growing list. The temples or monasteries they presented to Tsongtsün represent not only the individual missionary activity of the several disciples but also the reemergence of the monastic hierarchical structure that had been eclipsed during the period of fragmentation.

TABLE 4 The Eastern Vinaya Monks of Ü-Tsang

MONKS	PRINCIPAL DISCIPLES
Ü	
Lumé Shérap Tsültrim	Dru-mer Tsültrim Jungné, Zhang Nanam Dorjé-Wangchuk, Ngok Jangchub Jungné, Len Yéshé Shérap
Dring Yéshé Yönten	Ngok Lekpé Shérap, An Shākya-kyap, Ya-tsün Könchok Gyelwa, Tsur-tsün Gyelwa, Mar-tsün Gyelwa
Sumpa Yéshé Lotrö	
Batsün Lotrö Wangchuk	Tsültrim Jangchub
Rakshi Tsültrim Jungné	Chen-ngok Lotrö Gyelwa, Kawa Shākya Wangchuk
Tsang	
Lotön Dorjé Wangchuk	Sumtön Pakpa Gyeltsen, Gya Shākya Zhönu, Kyotön Shérap Dorjé, Langtön Jampa, Kyi Atsarya Yéshé Wangpo, Chétön Shérap Jungné, Zhutön Zhon-nu Tsöndru, Dhartön Shākya Lotrö
Tsongtsün Shérap Sengé	Batsün Lotrö Yönten

The greatest representative of this structure, though, must have been Lumé, for he united the strands of hierarchical patronage, the old edifices of the royal dynasty, and the importance of the Buddhist monastic discipline in Ü (map 4). In this he was successful, for Lumé, his disciples, and descendants are extensively represented in Tibetan historical literature on the period, far beyond their geographical or discrete lineal importance. It is clear that much of his time was initially spent renovating the U-tsé central temple of Samyé. In fact, the sources say that Lumé did not travel far beyond Ü, primarily restricting his movements to the intersection of Samyé, Kachu, and Yerpa. Yerpa, now called Drak Yerpa, is just east of Lhasa and also was affiliated with the royal dynasty. For his base of operations during the latter part of his life, Lumé used both Kachu, a temple northeast of Samyé, and Yerpa (ca. 1010) as his seats of instruction. He did, however, visit other areas, such as Drisiru, Lamo Chagdéü (perhaps the same as Dré Kyiru), Balam-né, Mora-gyel (1009), Mogar Drésa (1017, invited by Drum Barwa Jangchub), Tangchen, and Sera Pukpa.[53] While residing at Sera

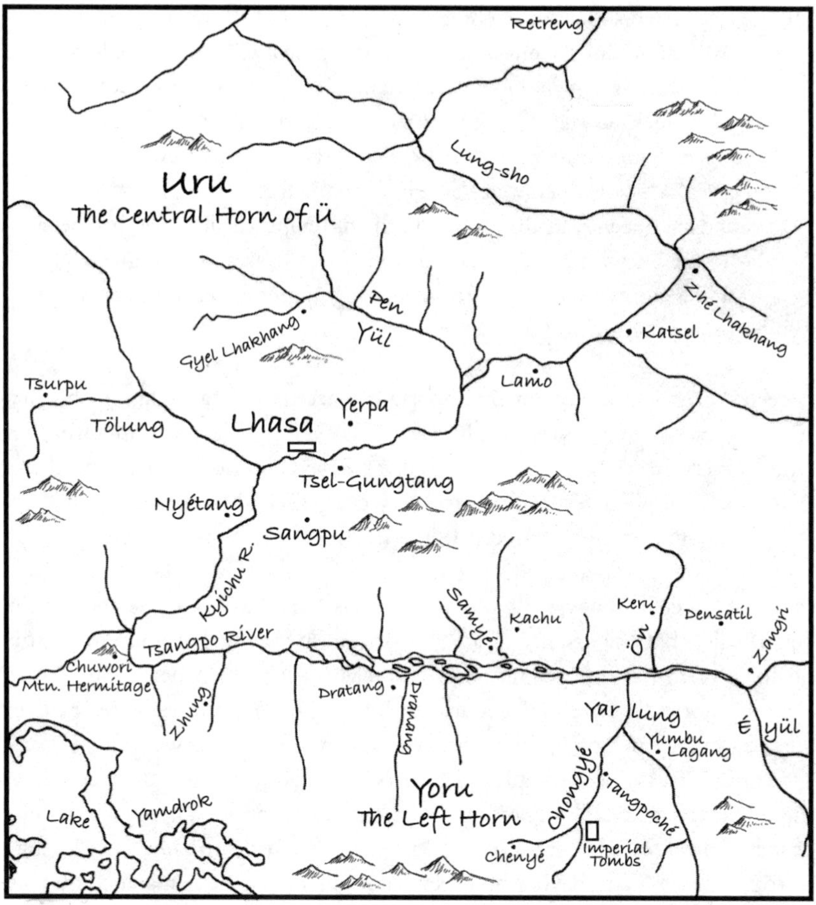

MAP 4 Uru and Northern Yoru.

Pukpa, Lumé died on the road going to Sölnak Tangpoché, a very important monastery (1017) constructed by one of his principal disciples, Dru-mer.[54] Both he and Dru-mer found their final resting place in the great stūpa Blazing Light (*mchod rten 'od 'bar*) in Tangpoché.

Lumé had four primary disciples, known as the "four pillars," one of the many instances in which important individuals are represented by metaphors of architecture and construction.[55] Sources indicate that the disciples were instructed mainly in Yerpa, perhaps after 1010, and given Tucci's description of the site as he found it in 1949, we can understand its attraction to Lumé and his followers (figure 4):[56]

> Yerpa appeared suddenly before my eyes at a bend of the road, a cascade of small white buildings along steep, green overgrown cliffs. One could have thought one was not in Tibet. Giant junipers and tufts of rhododendron topped a thick tangle of undergrowth, brushwood and grass victoriously fighting the hard barrenness of rocks. The cliffs were riddled with burrows and caves, some of which were so high up on the face of the abrupt hill that it would have been risky to climb up to them. Temples and chapels had been built in the bigger ones. We reached the place at dusk and were greeted by a warbling and twittering of birds conferring upon the hermitage an air of unexpected merriness.[57]

Indeed, Yerpa was an extremely important place in Tibetan religious history. Not only did Darma's assassin, Lha-lung Pelgyi Dorjé, set out from Yerpa, but almost every important teacher in the renaissance period spent time there. Atiśa, for example, later found Yerpa very congenial when he first went there in 1048 and evidently preferred it to the fractious atmosphere of Lhasa. Yerpa eventually was compared with Lhasa: if the capital city was the life tree (*srog shing*) of Tibet, Yerpa was the life tree of Lhasa, an allusion to the ancient Tibetan belief that the essence of a person or group may be harbored in a natural object. One pilgrimage guide to Yerpa relates a lengthy panegyric to Yerpa's virtues—normally unremarkable in pilgrimage guides—but these descriptives are occasionally picked up in normative Tibetan histories as well.[58]

Another of Lumé's disciples, Zhang Nanam Dorjé Wangchuk, was one of the few early monks' disciples who is given dates (976–1060), and he is supposed to have founded the Gyel-luk Lhékyi Lhakhang (or Gyel Lhakhang) in 1012, after already having built Rachak.[59] His is an early instance that we hear of a monk of Ü traveling to India for study—perhaps around the time of Drokmi, whom we consider in detail later—and according to tradition, Zhang Nanam both received the Vinaya from the monk/siddha Vajrāsana in India and taught it in India as well, possibly to other Tibetans. Zhang's disciples ordained some early Kadampa monks, and the famous Kadampa teacher Potoba (1031–1105) was said to have been in the abbatial succession at Gyel Lhakhang, which was one of three Buddhist centers torched by the Mongol army in 1239/40.[60] Lumé's other famous disciples included Ngok Jangchub Jungné, who took over Yerpa after his master's demise and built or assisted in the construction of a host of small temples, of which at least ten or more were completed.[61] Ngok was said to have taken over as the preceptor and teacher of new monks after Lumé, for when Lumé was active no one would have dared to serve in a position of preeminence. But Ngok did not have the same luck, and his charisma was not as successful in keeping the community together, for

FIGURE 4 Yerpa. After a photograph by Richardson

during his leadership the Eastern Vinaya groups formalized their separate identities.[62] Besides Ngok, there was Len Yéshé Shérap, who was actually from Yerpa, and Dru-mer Tsültrim Jungné, who was interred with his master. Both Len Yéshé Shérap and Dru-mer Tsültrim Jungné were also responsible for a few new or renovated temples, with many disciples extending their activities.

The method of these missionaries was, for many, to return to their hometowns after their ordination and training, hometowns where they had political and economic contacts from which they could build support. Whether they were given the keys to old temples from the royal dynasty or were granted land to build anew, in both instances they formed their patronage groups out of prior associations, strengthened by the ideology of religious revival, nostalgia for the old dynasty, and the promise of economic relations with other areas. Their groups of patrons and devotees evidently considered the revival of Buddhism to be a central issue in the reconstruction of Tibetan civilization, and eventually all the forms of Tibetan culture came to be seen as extending from the religious. Most Tibetan histories were quite aware of the country's militarily exposed position during the next centuries, for there was to be nothing like a unified political system until the domination of the Mongols in the thirteenth century. In fact, the golden yoke of the kingly law (*rgyal khrims*) continued to be fragmented (*sil bu*), even as the silk chord of the religious law (*chos khrims*) was growing in importance, and Khépa-déü noted that they relied on religion to protect Tibet, as a person relies on the blessing of a silk protection thread (*dar mdud*) to keep his life safe.[63] Thus, by the eleventh century, Central Tibetan monks were classed among the "important men" (*mi chen po*), and their efforts at spreading the message were understood as contributing to social cohesiveness and organization, a trend in Tibetan public life that continues to the present.[64]

I have provided here a small but representative selection of figures from the early accounts. The lists are mostly just that, names and little more, although we can piece together occasional geographical locations for the temples, the majority of which seemed not to have survived into the twentieth century. Other active figures of the period—Sumpa, Rakshi, Ba, Dring Yéshé Yönten, and so forth—were engaged in this missionary activity as well. In reality, the literature represents a dizzying process of temple construction and congregation formation in Ü and Tsang from the late tenth through the twelfth century, with several hundred sites or congregations developed under the aegis of representatives of their tradition.[65]

Appendix 1 lists 246 temples, caves, and residences possibly used by the Eastern Vinaya monks by the mid-eleventh century. This list is tentative, however, and should be approached with caution. We have no definite chronology for most of the temples, and I have simply limited the list to those temples built by the first generation of the Eastern Vinaya monks coming to Ü-Tsang and their immediate disciples. The problems with this list are manifold, beginning with the fact that the same temple may be given two different names (e.g., Lan pa rta 'bres = Lan pa'i pho brang), and two different temples often have very similar names and may be confused.[66] Also problematic is the fact that although many from the second generation of disciples certainly may have constructed their widening circle of temples by this time, their structures were not included on the list. Moreover, the list does not register temples under construction or even being completed in the mid-eleventh century, as evinced from Atiśa's hagiography, for the Bengali monk was called on to consecrate temples that he neither constructed nor controlled.[67] Thus we should regard appendix 1 as an approximation. The number of temples constructed by the time of Atiśa's arrival in Ü would have been between two hundred and three hundred or perhaps a few more.

As in the case of those structures for which we have photographs from before 1959, most of these temples were doubtless small, one- or two-story buildings, constructed with a single chapel and perhaps a second small hall—altogether very modest institutions (figure 5). Despite the exalted image of the Eastern Vinaya monks in Tibetan literature, that they revived the Vinaya in Ü-Tsang "up from the dying embers," we must neither exaggerate the edifices

FIGURE 5 Kachu. After a photograph by Richardson

they renovated and built nor underestimate the importance of their contribution. Many of these structures were not occupied all year round, and we have instances of monks closing their temples to go receive instruction or participate in rituals when an important monastery nearby sponsored a teacher or ritual event.

In addition, because most monks studied with several teachers, the exact affiliation of many of the temples is variously described, so that one source attributes a building to the Batsün group, while another affiliates it with Dring's congregation. Their relationships were, however, a point of honor and, sometimes, of contention, in part because of the economics of these institutions. Relationships were often supported by the flow of funds from subsidiary congregations to the main temple or monastery, such as Sölnak Tangpoché or another great temple. This funding was referred to as a "tax" (*khral*) or "monk tax" (*sham thabs khral*), although the term might better be understood in the period as something like obligatory professional dues. Whatever weak governmental structures may have existed, there is no sense that they had anything to do with the collection and distribution of such funds.[68] Certainly, assets were broadly collected at this time, and Sumpa Yéshé Lotrö is depicted in Atiśa's hagiography as suggesting that the funds collected from the monks of the four orders of Tibet should be donated to the Bengali teacher.[69]

Perhaps the best information about asset allocation is from Tsang Province, where Lotön was said to have eight and a half revenue groups contributing to his effort—three from his "upper" communities and five and a half from his "lower" communities, although there were more overall communities than these.[70] Similarly, Tsongtsün was said to have had nine funding groups contributing to his principal monastery of Ngoling. It is also certain that related communities assembled from time to time for various purposes, such as making monastic decisions about the placement of novice monks whose preceptors had died.[71] Unfortunately, almost everything else about these funding associations is unknown (quantity of funds, contractual relationships, etc.), except that later disciples following the path of the Eastern Vinaya continued the practice.[72]

The influence of the Eastern Vinaya tradition extended in part from the reality that Lumé, Lotön, and the others did not simply bring the Vinaya, as is the standard representation in both Tibetan and modern studies. The early documents make clear that the Vinaya was their most important contribution, with its preestablished institutional structure, system of relations, rules of order, procedures for the adjudication of disputes, and so forth. However, the new monks from the northeast also brought with them the curriculum of study that had been used in the ancient imperial temples. Preeminent was the study of the *Prajñāpāramitā* scriptures, but the investigation of the technical literature of Indian Buddhism also was emphasized. This especially meant learning the Abhidharma, probably the Mahāyānist Abhidharma found in the Yogācāra work of the *Abhidharmasamuccaya*, but some of the sources also indicate that the voluminous *Yogācāra-bhūmi* was studied.[73] This would not have been surprising, given the strong tradition of Yogācāra study that had flourished in Dunhuang during the Tibetan occupation, and the legacy of this scholastic scholarship doubtless influenced the curriculum brought to Central Tibet. As a result, Sölnak Tangpoché, one of Lumé's favored institutions, became the center of scholasticism and represented the revival of the imperial curriculum in the religious life of the Yarlung valley.[74] From the time of its construction (1017) through the late twelfth century, it was the center for the study of *Perfection of Insight* and the Madhyamaka treatises. Its abbots—like Khutön Tsöndru Yungdrung (1011–75)—eventually became leaders in the fusion of the old curriculum with the new Kadampa materials brought to Central Tibet in the mid- to late eleventh century.[75]

In contrast, a group of Eastern Vinaya monks were closely involved with both the older tantric systems from the earlier transmission of the Dharma and the later esoteric systems that began to arrive through the efforts of the eleventh-century translators. Preeminent among the Nyingma monastic tantrists was the eccentric Drapa Ngönshé (1012–90), a scion of one of the great aristocratic clans of the Tibetan imperium, the Chim.[76] He was a monk ordained by two monks in Lumé's line, Béso Kerwa and Yamshü Gyelwa-ö, and was noted for his understanding of Abhidharma (probably the *Abhidharmasamuccaya*), from which he got his name as "knower (*shes*) of Abhidharma" (*mngon pa*). Yet Drapa Ngönshé became central to the construction and development of the Eastern Vinaya cloisters maintaining tantric practice.[77] The two most important tantric centers for Eastern Vinaya teaching, Pukpoché and Dratang (1081), were directly connected to Drapa Ngönshé, his teacher Yamshü, and his disciples.[78] Drapa Ngönshé was so successful in enticing Eastern Vinaya monks to adopt the esoteric ritual system that he elicited the envy of Khutön, Lumé's disciple and abbot of the great monastery of Sölnak Tangpoché. We are told that Khutön took the expedient of resorting to black magic to destroy Drapa Ngönshé, but to no avail.[79]

Later in life, as happened to some of the eleventh-century tantric monks, Drapa Ngönshé gave up his robes, leaving the Dranang area by the Brahmaputra and moving southeast into Yarlung, where he founded the new center of Chenyé.[80] He certainly received both Nyingma and the newer teachings, the later primarily through Zangskar-lotsāwa, and the Nyingma tradition remembers him as both a master of the traditional system and a treasure finder of note.[81] Much later, Drapa became a figure of rather free association, like many of the eleventh-century personalities, and was credited for the discovery of the *Four Medical Tantras* in 1038, although there seems to be little historical basis for this assignment.

CONFLICT ON THE ROOF OF THE WORLD

The Eastern Vinaya monks certainly did not underestimate the power of the religious forms that had been flourishing in the four horns of Tibet in the absence of monastic Buddhism, forms that prospered in the citadels, the manor houses of nobles, and a few of the old temples. The surviving elements of the old order had several agendas that did not coincide with the new models of Dharma being brought in, and the old masters did not see the importance of this revival, since they had not concluded that religion was lost in any significant sense. Even while they maintained, for example, library materials associated with some of the old temples—materials initially hidden during Darma's suppression and brought out again—they were accused of misunderstanding them in the new climate. With their political connections, proven economic assets, and energetic building programs, the protagonists of the Eastern Vinaya in early-eleventh-century Central Tibet were destined to interact with the remnants of the older dispensation. Inevitably there arose friction between the new monks and the older established communities—the Arhats with hair knots, the Bendé, the Ngakpa, and temple guardians of various stripes—many of whom were well practiced in the Nyingma esoteric system.

The conflict between the new congregations and the older order sometimes played out in a characteristically Tibetan manner: the infliction of spells by one group on another. One story given in the two Déü chronicles is illustrative.

> At that time, Khyungpo Sengé Gyeltsen, Bé Gyelwa Lotrö, and Ngenlam Gyelwé Wangpo, the three mantrins (Ngakpa), fell in league with some monks. Formerly, the new congregations and the mantrins had exchanged homage to one another, but Lotsün and Batsün eliminated any possibility for paying homage [to mantrins]. So the three mantrins became unhappy and performed an act of evil sorcery. One night, they brought down three thunderbolts onto Lotsün, but because he slept beneath some scriptures, he did not perish.[82]

The sticking point in the episode is when Lotön Dorjé Wangchuk (here called Lotsün) and Batsün Lotrö (another of the "men from Ü-Tsang") interfered in the honorary practice of the new monks and the old school mantrins paying homage to one another. By the standards of Tibetan etiquette, different groups of religious should exchange elaborate greetings and establish hierarchy based on socially approved gradations of aristocracy, seniority, and spirituality. According to monastic Buddhist standards, however, all these mantrins are laity, and no monk can be allowed to subordinate himself to a layman, for the monk has left the world and thus is—by virtue of ordination—superior to all the untonsured. In response, the mantrins are depicted as resorting to the world of sorcery and magical retribution, but Lotön, the real culprit in their eyes, is saved by a text of the Buddha's word.

As the eleventh century drew on, the increased exposure of the eastern monks exacerbated such conflicts, and certainly not all were resolved by magical enterprise. The *Pillar Testament* (*bKa' 'chems ka khol ma*) reflects on events in the Lhasa area's earlier history, conveying a very poor picture of civil relations among the different religious communities in the eleventh century. The text—posing as the word of the first emperor Songtsen Gampo—uses the literary technique of prophecy to depict recent history, taking as the focal point the various congregations' relationships to the Avalokiteśvara Jowo image in the Jokhang in Lhasa:

> Then there will occur many monks in these groups, and the many bodhisattvas among them will make offerings and serve in worship of this [Jowo] image. They will [build and] maintain temples in every direction and will very correctly practice the holy comportment.
>
> But then there will be Bendé who are emanations of the devil's family. Disputing with the religious groups, they will defile them and drag them

> down. The Bendé will lay siege to Nézhi (in Lhodrak), raising embankments and fortifications. With spears they will impale monks and cast discus weapons at them. Then these Bendé will plunder the [monks'] temples, fighting with the chaplains over the offering vessels.[83]

There can be little doubt that such incidents actually happened, for Tibetans have intermittently resorted to violence to resolve conflicts of religious claims. Nor was the strife unidirectional, for the Eastern Vinaya monks were quite aggressive in their seizing of temples and disparagement of others' religious activities. Lotön is even accused of having poisoned in 1035 the most famous of early Bonpo treasure revealers, Shenchen Lugah, although the allegation is quite late and very problematic.[84] While it may be untrue, the allegation is indicative of the tension among competing factions in the tenth to eleventh centuries.

The conflict between these groups was really a conflict of values and models of religiosity. The lay mantrins represented the royal dynastic and indigenous Tibetan ideology of the unity of the sacred and secular; the gods and kings of Tibet were just as important as the Buddhas of India.[85] This kind of sage was grounded in the political and religious power inherited from his ancestral connection to aristocratic lines of descent from a clan divine in nature and emplaced in a specific valley, whose spirits were under his control. The mantrins saw their home temples as citadels of religion, and their duty to perform rites for the immediate communities of gods and men, over which they wielded both religious and temporal authority, for these two were understood as inseparable. They saw that while monks had fled Ü-Tsang when trouble began with Darma Trih Udum-tsen, the mantrins held their ground, maintaining the secret practices and protecting Central Tibet as chaos reigned.

Conversely, the monks represented theoretically egalitarian values, since a candidate from any background could obtain religious authority by ritual authentication (ordination) rather than by familial means. Although in fact most of the monks were from the ancient great clans of Central Tibet, their claims to religious authority came from their ordination and vows of celibacy, from their efforts to create stability and harmony in the revival of learning, and from the economic and institutional benefits that had accrued since the monks arrived. Without knowing that Indian Buddhism had already outlined an uneasy truce between esoteric lay and scholastic clerical communities, technically known as the "articulation of the necessity of the triple discipline" (*trisaṁvara*), many Tibetans were uninformed about the means for adjudicating the respective claims of lay and monastic representatives.[86] The ideology of the triple discipline eventually was introduced formally by Atiśa in the mid-eleventh century, but by then the translators' phenomenon was well under way.

WEST TIBET AND THE KADAMPA CONNECTION

Recent histories covering the Tibetan renaissance have emphasized the activity in the tenth and eleventh centuries of the monk-kings of West Tibet in the line of Ösung; the work of the earliest translator sponsored in their line, Rinchen Zangpo (958–1055); and especially the missionary enterprise of the Bengali monk Atiśa Dīpaṁkara Śrījñāna (983?-1054, figure 6).[87] According to these and many later Tibetan sources, Atiśa's coming to Tibet in 1042 was the threshold moment in the efflorescence of Buddhism and provided a stable foundation for monastic scholarship for the next thousand years. However, the circumstances of the West Tibetan connection to Central Tibet—and, accordingly, its influence on the ultimate disposition of Tibetan Buddhism—was more complex than has been generally acknowledged.

Because the lives of the men from West Tibet already have been well documented, I present here only a brief sketch of their activities and their impact, along with a revised estimate of their actual influence in Ü-Tsang in the eleventh century.[88]

According to the Tibetan documents, Lha lama Yéshé-Ö was aghast at the forms of Buddhism on display in the kingdom of Gugé, so he sent twenty-one intelligent young men to study in Kashmir sometime in the last quarter of the tenth century.[89] Because of the trip's rigors and the Tibetans' lack of immunity to Indian diseases, most of them perished, but the preeminent scholar Rinchen Zangpo was the foremost of the two that survived. Relying on the largess of the imperial household of Gugé-Purang, he and his immediate disciples constructed or were associated with the construction of many Buddhist temples in the western kingdom, and it is traditionally maintained that Rinchen Zangpo was responsible for 108 centers of Buddhist practice. One recent survey indicates that the total by the mid-eleventh century may have been something like three to four dozen between 992 and the time Atiśa left Gugé-Purang for Ü-Tsang in 1045 but that the pace continued to accelerate over this period.[90]

By the 1030s, it was decided that a famous scholar from eastern India should be invited, in contrast to most of the Indian monks, who previously had come from Kashmir.[91] The hagiographical texts maintain that Tibet was threatened by heterodox practices—especially those associated with the notorious Ācārya Marpo (Prajñāgupta) and the heretical blue-robed group (*nīlāmbara*)—but these figures may have come a bit later and were anachronistically projected back into the period.[92] Jangchub-Ö, Lha lama's monk-king successor, seems to have been very concerned with legitimacy in monastic life and certainly contemplated renovating Samyé, perhaps anxious that the growing movement in Central Tibet was appropriating all the royal dynastic sites.[93]

FIGURE 6 Atiśa and Dromtön. After a detail in a twelfth-century Kadampa painting

Accordingly, the well-known Buddhist monk Nagtso Tsültrim Gyelwa (b. 1012) was asked to convey Jangchub-Ö's invitation to Atiśa, who was then serving as the abbot of Vikramaśīla monastery, located in the modern state of Bihar. Nagtso left Tibet in 1037 and led a party of four other Tibetan scholars to Vikramaśīla, first stopping at the Mahābodhi temple in Bodhgayā to pay their respects to the seat of enlightenment. Arriving in Vikramaśīla, they encountered Nagtso's Tibetan teacher of Abhidharma in residence, Gya-lo Tsöndrü Sengé, and through him negotiated with Atiśa to come to Tibet.[94]

Evidently this took some time, and during the interval Nagtso went to see Nāropā in Phullahari and other teachers in Bengal and continued his studies at Vikramaśīla.[95] Finally, Gya-lo, Nagtso, and Atiśa left for Tibet, staying near Kathmandu for a year and founding Stham Vihāra on the model of Vikramaśīla.[96] Atiśa and Nagtso arrived in Purang in 1042 and stayed three years, during which time Atiśa met with Rinchen Zangpo, composed his famous *A Lamp for the Path*, and worked with Tibetans on the translation of several works. He was closest to Nagtso, and thereafter they stayed together for a year in Mangyül, by Nagtso's homeland. They finally decided to go to Central Tibet and arrived in Tsang Province in 1046, where they stayed for a year before going on to Samyé in 1047 and then on to the other horns of Tibet. Atiśa spent some years in Yerpa, trying to avoid Lhasa, although his disciples would go there for religious festivals, and he himself resided there for a time. The

Bengali monk established his greatest presence, however, in Nyétang (in the Kyichu valley), where he passed away in 1054. During this time, Atiśa became a minor celebrity in Central Tibet, and many of the important Tibetan lamas of the mid-eleventh century either hosted him or received his teachings at one time.

On the face of it, and as depicted by later Kadampa and Gelugpa authors, Atiśa seems to have been very influential in Central Tibet during his life, but a closer look shows why this was not the case in the mid-eleventh century. First, the majority of monks, even Kadampa monks explicitly following Atiśa's spiritual program, received their monastic vows and Vinaya training at the hands of the Eastern Vinaya monks. Every history of the Vinaya in Tibet states that Atiśa had no transmission of the Vinaya to Tibetans during his thirteen years in Tibet.[97] The reason for this was simple: he was a monk of the Lokottaravāda section of the *Mahāsāṁghika-vinaya*, and when he attempted to teach it in Nyétang, he was stopped by his Tibetan disciples, who were maintaining the old prohibition laid down by Relpachen and other kings against teaching any Vinaya other than the Mūlasarvāstivāda.[98]

Therefore when Atiśa traveled through Tibet, he seldom founded temples or institutions, and all those that he did found—such as the White Temple (Lha khang dkar po) in Mangyül in 1045/46—eventually became dependent on the Eastern Vinaya monks' prior relationships, networks, and organization. Atiśa certainly was called on to bless new temples, and he was asked to consecrate the Āryadeva temple and an ancient temple in Ü.[99] Such episodes confirm that most of the temples in which Atiśa taught were actually constructed by prior teachers and remained in their hands after Atiśa left. Thus, while Atiśa's lectures and rituals may occasionally have been well attended, when these monks left the temporary congregation, they simply returned to their hometowns. Sociologists like Stark and Bainbridge refer to this kind of involvement in emerging systems as "audience cults," which were the least stable of all groups, for when the master is gone, the relationship tends to evaporate as well.[100]

The absence of a structured Vinaya relationship meant that cloisters in Tibet rarely could have been organized along the lines that Atiśa would have approved for such centers as Stham Vihāra in Kathmandu. When Atiśa went to teach or translate at a temple or monastery, he was usually hosted by members of the Eastern Vinaya transmission. Indeed, without their patronage, it is unlikely that Atiśa would have been able to have much impact at all, for he was not always welcomed. Even Atiśa's lengthy hagiography frequently mentions hostility encountered by Atiśa and his entourage throughout the four horns of Tibet. Characteristically, Tibetans attributed this hostility to the machinations of Dranka Pelgyi Yönten, the spirit of the assassinated monk who was considered the specter instigating the rebellions of the period of fragmentation.[101]

The early textual record actually depicts Atiśa as something of a pawn in the hands of Tibetan teachers, acting according to their desires as he traveled through their domains and stayed in their temples. Atiśa had little choice in following their agendas, for important Tibetan monks of the period are referred to again and again as "Big Men." So, when he arrived in Tsang, Sumpa Yéshé Lotrö (who, if actually alive, must have been very old) reputedly invited Atiśa to come to Gyasar-gang, his institution.[102] In Ü, Lümé's disciple Khutön Tsöndrü Yungdrung was considered the Biggest Man. His invitation to the Bengali monk is significant in the hagiography for its recognition of Atiśa's value, and yet the hagiography also measures Atiśa by Tibetan standards.[103] Such invitations placed curricular burdens on Atiśa, as they frequently established the texts that he was to teach. When he stayed at Khutön's flagship monastery, Sölnak Tangpoché, for example, much of what he taught fit into the curriculum already developed in the Eastern Vinaya system, although Yogācāra and related treatises were amplified somewhat.[104] When he resided in Samyé, Atiśa was asked to maintain a similar teaching schedule.[105] Elsewhere, he complained that he was not allowed to teach either his beloved *Mahāsāṁghika-vinaya* or the songs of realization (*dohā*) that were so important in Bengal during this period.[106] When we compare his teaching schedule with the tantric texts that he and his Tibetan followers were translating at this time, we can appreciate the difference: while Atiśa was teaching the *Ratnagotravibhāga* in Sölnak Tangpoché, he and Dromtön were translating tantric ritual manuals—Cakrasaṁvara, Yamāntaka, and so forth.[107]

The restrictive Vinaya selection further affected Atiśa's followers. As the Kadampa masters began establishing their own monastic centers, they followed one or another lineages of the Eastern Vinaya tradition, even if the intellectual part of the curriculum was Kadampa in origin. Thus, the great Kadampa monasteries—like the new temple at Nyétang (1055), or Sangpu Néütok (1073) by Ngok Lekpé Shérap—were founded mainly in the Eastern Vinaya tradition. Only Retreng (1056/7), founded by Dromtön Gyelwé Jungné, seemed to be an exception. Consequently, Atiśa's hagiography needed to specify which group in the Eastern Vinaya it was that individual Kadampa monasteries followed after Atiśa's death, in part to emphasize Retreng's unique position:

> In that way, among the four monasteries founded in Ü as Residences (*gdan sa*) for Lord Atiśa, Nyétang, founded by Bangtön in O, was taken over by those of the Ba-Rak group. Drengyi Lhading in Yarlung at Sédu was occu-

> pied by the Lumé group. Ngoktönpa collecting the community together in Sangpu, erected the "Canopy the Size of a Door Cover" (*rgya phibs phya ra tsam cig*), which was appropriated by the Dring group. However, Retreng, since it was established with the counsel of both Géshé (Drom-)Tönpa and Neljorpa (Shérap Dorjé), in the northern site of Retreng was constructed the Eagle's Head (*khyung mgo can*).[108] Because, though, this is a great house based on the deep ideas of Géshé Tönpa, it did not fall into the company of any Tibetan sect—neither Ba-Rag, nor Lumé, nor the Dring group. So what was it? It was a small satellite of Vikramaśīla. It was the Residence of the Lord [Atiśa], the spiritual construction of Géshé Tönpa, the chief ancestor protecting the precious Kadampa teaching, and the Lord's primary *caitya* in all the realm of snow, from West Tibet to the Center.[109]

Although this is the Kadampa presentation, Drakpa Gyeltsen affirmed that in the twelfth century, while not exactly included in the major sectarian divisions of the Eastern Vinaya lineages, the Kadampa monasteries were closely tied to these groups. Retreng was affiliated with the Ba-Rak congregation; Nyé-tang was connected with the Ma congregation; and Sangpu was part of the Dring congregation.[110] The aggressiveness of the Eastern Vinaya monks is evident in the case of the old Nyétang temple, for with Atiśa's death we can see the struggle for control of that establishment. Members of the Ba-Rak group—those in the lineage of Batsün Lotrö and Rakshi Tsültrim Jungné were frequently amalgamated into a single organization—initially did not succeed in seizing the site, only to gain control of it at a later time.[111]

HISTORY AS THE VICTORY OF GREAT IDEAS AND GOOD ORGANIZATION

Thus, it should be understood that the initial impact of West Tibetan Buddhism on Ü-Tsang in the eleventh century was modest. The disciples of Rinchen Zangpo were almost entirely focused on the Gugé-Purang area, and the Kadampa monks were building few, albeit important, monasteries in Central Tibet, principally in those areas not already dominated by the Eastern Vinaya congregations. The 246 institutions listed in appendix 1 are in many ways indicative of this difference, for the Eastern Vinaya monks had insinuated themselves firmly into the social fabric of Ü-Tsang for more than half a century before Atiśa was even invited to Tibet, and each of their institutions was supported by networks of supply, allegiance, blood relationship, and authority. Consequently, despite their interest in spreading the Dharma to Central Tibet, the kings of Gugé-Purang were inessential to the revival of Buddhism in mid-eleventh-century Ü-Tsang.

Both the Kadampa connection and the authority of kings like Lha-lama and Jangchub-Ö have been accorded great significance throughout later Tibetan and secondary Western literature. Why such a skewed emphasis? I believe there are at least three reasons: the Tibetan privileging of the Ösung line with a consequent historical amnesia about the activities of Yumten's descendants, the importance of the Kadampa or Kadampa-related doctrinal and teaching systems in the late eleventh century onward, and the overwhelming rewriting of history after the founding of the New Kadampa lineage by Tsongkhapa in 1409.

The early histories indicate that the Tibetan revival came about through the agency and patronage of three members of the scattered royal house: Lha-lama Yéshé-Ö in Purang, Trihdé Göntsen of Uru, and Tsalana Yéshé Gyeltsen around Samyé.[112] As can be seen in the succession tables, two of these were in the Yumten lineage, with only Lha-lama Yéshé-Ö representing the Ösung line. Nonetheless, Tibetan literature depicts the descendants of Yumten as being not very interested in the new forms of the Buddhist religion per se. As Sönam Tsémo observed, "Even though, in these four horns of Central Tibet, [the later spread of the Dharma] was not incited by the command of some Dharma-protecting king, but out of the power of previous prayers . . . the doctrine spread out and expanded."[113] Although Lumé and his disciples were given access to royal dynastic sites, many writers indicate that this was done with royal acquiescence rather than with actual royal involvement. By contrast, not only were Lha-lama and his descendants represented as active patrons of orthodox monastic preceptors, but many also became monks themselves, being ordained and adopting the robes of the order. They issued several edicts verifying their interest in suppressing heterodox practices and cultivated the presence of exemplary monks who represented the Vinaya and Mahāyānist sūtra literature.

Contradicting this received representation, Petech showed that Tsalana Yéshé Gyeltsen was actively involved in translation efforts and apparently became a monk later in life, for at least one of the colophons to his translations confirms that he was Lha-tsün, a royal monk, in the same mold as Lha-lama Yéshé-Ö.[114] The sixteen translations on which he worked include one of the Guhyasamāja commentarial tantras, the *Vajrahṛdayālaṁkāra-tantra*, and many of the most important of the works were associated with the Jñānapāda school of Guhyasamāja practice, including seminal works by Buddhajñānapāda himself.[115] As most of these were translated in conjunction with Kamalaguhya/gupta—who had worked with Rinchen Zangpo sometime after 996—the translations were doubtless completed in the first quarter of the eleventh century and in Tibet itself, for we have no indication that the royal monk traveled to India.[116]

Despite this, Tibetan historians have invariably overlooked this level of involvement, and even works dedicated to Guhyasamāja history, such as the great 1634 chronicle of Amé-shep, attributes the introduction of the Jñānapāda school to Nyen-lotsāwa Darma-drak, although Rinchen Zangpo, Smṛti Jñānakīrti, and Nyö-lotsāwa Yönten-drak are also sometimes mentioned.[117] This curiosity is compounded by the fact that Tsalana Yéshé Gyeltsen's translations are influenced by the Nyingma terminology and are therefore some of the few places where the term "great perfection" (*rdzogs chen*) is located in writings widely accepted as canonical.[118] But even when Nyingma apologists defend the term by referring to these texts, they neglect Tsalana Yéshé Gyeltsen's agency in the discussion and obscure his position. This is in accord with the larger process of disavowing the Yumten line in political genealogies, in which as Hazod observed, "Even the origin from Yumten (Yum-brtan) sometimes is denied within the milieus of the ruling dynasties, and is replaced by an artificially constructed genealogy of Ösung ('Od-srungs)."[119] The Yumten line was said to be of improper ancestry (*rigs ma dag pa*) so that its descendants' legitimacy was questionable to the degree that they could not be traced to the Ösung line of descent. The same could be said of much of the religious activity in Central Tibet, for the real efforts of the Yumten lineage were occluded (except for a few colophons), and the later translators and the introduction from the West were accorded pride of place.

The observation that the Kadampa monks had a modest initial effect on Ü-Tsang must be understood as specific to the mid-eleventh century, for their influence on Tibetan monastic curriculum and values was a slow-growing vine. By 1076, with the royally sponsored convocation in Gugé, those who were interested in philosophical and doctrinal systems saw that they were beginning to come into their own, and the convocation was dominated by monks trained in scholastic epistemology and logic. Ultimately, it was the Kadampa order that organized and sustained this aspect of Tibetan intellectual life, which was based in large part on the translations by Ngok-lo Loden Shérap and other Kadampa scholars. Even though this turn to scholastic scholarship took several decades to mature, we shall see that already by the early twelfth century—little more than half a century after Atiśa's death—the Kadampa curriculum had become part of mainstream Buddhist study in Central Tibet, in a way it had not been previously.

Finally, the early documents regarding the history of Buddhism in Tibet show that Atiśa was not considered overwhelmingly important to the Tibetan renaissance, at least not until the late fourteenth century. Until that time, when the topic "up from the embers" is related in most Tibetan histories, the focus was on the vitality of the Eastern Vinaya monks, with Atiśa and the Kadampa as an afterthought, which is what they initially were.[120] By the fifteenth century, with Tsongkhapa's embrace of the Kadampa curriculum, Atiśa went from being perceived as an important Bengali teacher with modest consequences for Tibetan institutions to being proposed as the prescient physician who knew the panacea for Tibetans' spiritual illness, a St. John crying in the wilderness of Tibet, anticipating the triumph of the messiah Tsongkhapa. From the fifteenth century onward, the emphasis on Atiśa's contribution grew, and the histories of Tsongkhapa's movement almost always begin with the Bengali monk's overwhelming contribution to Tibetan spiritual life.[121]

CONCLUSION: A TRADITION UNDER THE IMPERIAL SHADOW

Tibetans inherited much from the ancient dynasty that had brought them to international fame and fortune, but the fragmented nature of Central Tibetan religious observances at the end of the tenth century led them to seek a more authentic form of Buddhist practice. The Mahāyānist-based curriculum and the Vinaya-based organization provided a sense of stability in a world that had already changed too fast. The Eastern Vinaya monks brought with them the living legacy of the early dissemination of the Dharma, with its emphasis on the study of the Mahāyānist sūtras, the *Mūlasarvāstivāda-vinaya*, the Sarvāstivāda Abhidharma, or Yogācāra works. Because of its rules of ordination, it allowed those who were not scions of the great clans to participate and still provided a sense of authority and control to the clan members who dominated its leadership. The Eastern Vinaya monks occupied a moral high ground, supporting both public order and ethical viability, which had been consistently threatened in Ü-Tsang. The immediacy of the local temples, distributed in every valley in the four horns of Tibet, meant that the establishment of civic virtue and religious value was effected through the strategy of monastic example. The monks and their lay followers became the neighborhood reference points for the Tibetan sense of self and for a life of virtue.

By the mid-eleventh century, individuals like Drapa Ngönshé had already begun to appropriate the practice of the ancient tantric system, and others like Ngok Lekpé Shérap became invested in the Kadampa curriculum, even while they retained the Eastern Vinaya lineage and organizational procedures. Ultimately, the Eastern Vinaya temple system, with its growing awareness of lineage, became the platform for the next development, the time of the great translators of the eleventh century. Indeed, more than anything else, the rebirth of Tibetan civilization was the result of Tibetan translators of Indian tantric literature, their charisma as the new religious representatives, and their authority augmented by Indian yogins, who themselves had a vested interest in highlighting the translators' accomplishments. The Mahāyānist curriculum—whether the older Eastern Vinaya or the newer Kadampa—had too many liabilities to become the lore of the land. It did not provide the magical authority for the protection of Tibet in the absence of a central government; it did not consecrate its holders with the metaphor of power and position that the tantric system did; it did not bequeath the great rituals of dominion and authority found in the tantras; it did not provide the ideology of interlocking community organization that is found in tantric maṇḍalas; and it did not transmit secret yogic systems claiming to confer Buddhahood in this very life. While all these attributes were present in the various older tantras, there were many reservations about their authenticity, and some of these questions are explored with the cult of the translators.

4

Translators as the New Aristocracy

When he said that he wanted to seek the Dharma in the southern land of Nepal, his mother and father asked him, "There's Dharma here in Tibet, why do you want to go to Nepal?"

—Hagiography of Ra-lotsāwa (b. 1016 C.E.)[1]

We encountered a Madhyadeśa text, and I listened to the explanation of the Indian Abbot, Śrī Sumatikīrti. Then I, the monk Drakpa Shérap, translated the text: But since the mind of the sacred ones is like the light of a full autumn moon, when my errors appear so illuminated, I pray that you are patient, as if I were your own son.

—Translators' colophon to **Catuḥkrama* of Kāṇha, translated ca. 1090 C.E.[2]

O, I'm Tibet's little cleric Dorjé-drak, and since I've concluded realization of the two processes [of tantra], whatever happened, good or bad, happy or sad, I've this kind of confidence, without regret:

I killed thirteen vajrins, most important Darma Dodé.
Even if I'm born in hell for this, I've no regret.
I took about five young ladies as my consorts, led by Öser Bumé. Even though lost in lust, I've no regret.

—Verses ascribed to Ra-lotsāwa[3]

Much of what we know about Buddhism in general, and Buddhist esoterism in particular, is a result of the incredible performance of Chinese and Tibetan translators of Indian literature over several centuries. We have seen that Tibetans formulated their study of Buddhism into an earlier diffusion (*snga dar*) and the later spread of the Dharma (*phyi dar*), otherwise understood as the early translation (*snga 'gyur*), as opposed to the new translation (*gsar 'gyur*), period. It is also sometimes claimed that the later translators followed in the footsteps of the earlier pioneers who, after all, invented the target language now called classical Tibetan.[4] In keeping with this position, the new translation scholars were well-educated drudges who were less inventive than their predecessors and sometimes relied on a word-for-word system of translation, analogous to the mechanical *verbum ad verbum* style employed by scholastic translators of Greek, like William of Moerbeke.[5] In contrast, the earlier translators employed the more sophisticated "spirit of the text" (*ad sententiam transferre*) style of Greek-to-Latin translation proposed by Manuel Chrysoloras when he arrived in Florence in 1397. According to this idea, the important breakthroughs in Tibetan translation practices belong to the earlier exponents rather than their subsequent followers.

As in most forms of received wisdom, there is some truth to these claims. Certainly, the glory of creating classical Tibetan is a triumph of the imperially sponsored translation bureaus. And we also can observe the undeniably mechanical style of the fourteenth-century translators, such as Butön or Shong Lotrö Tenpa.[6] Yet this analysis sometimes implies a secondary status to the new translation personalities and seldom considers the problems associated with the revival, even renaissance, of a culture that had been fragmented and would not ever again be politically or militarily what it once had been. Moreover, it is not commonly recognized that the sociologies of the translators during these two periods were entirely different, as were their motivations, the literature they translated, and the results they obtained. A lack of regard for the later scholars also does not acknowledge that the religious culture-bearers from the tenth to the twelfth century did what their predecessors did not do: they put together a high classical religious/literary culture centered in monasteries that did not succumb to the fissiparous forces of Tibetan civilization for a thousand years, a culture in which—whatever its faults—Tibetans became the focal point of literature, ritual, and philosophy for much of the Eurasian continent. No wonder that Tibetans have considered, and still consider, their later transmission translators to have been divinely inspired and uniquely qualified, depicting their achievement with the iconography of a two-headed cuckoo, a bird said to know perfectly both the source and the target languages.

Such accomplishments, however, do not happen in human societies without institution building and the concomitant self-interest. The translators of this period frequently acted in the de facto, and sometimes de jure, positions of feudal lords and were given their rights of dominion not necessarily by birth or their positions in the traditional social hierarchy but by their consecration as the new lords of the Dharma. Spending time in India and reinvigorating Tibetan intellectual and institutional life, they themselves became the objects of cultic activity, so we can confidently declare the early eleventh through the early twelfth century the period of the translators' religious supremacy. In their appropriation of power that had previously been the sole purview of the aristocracy, they and the Eastern Vinaya teachers became harbingers of the process by which Buddhist monks eventually supplanted the royal line as the power in the land.

This chapter presents some of the story of the tantric translators of the later diffusion, especially those who traveled to South Asia, for some translators, like Tsalana Yéshé Gyeltsen, appear never to have left home. For those who did, their challenges in studying Indian languages in Nepal and India, their personal sojourns over the Himalayas, and their new social status upon returning are the fundamental themes. Sometimes from modest backgrounds, the tantric translators (lotsāwa) of the new translation period (Sarma) are seen as intellectuals engaged in an endeavor that was often difficult, at times contentious, but nonetheless rewarding of their enterprise. The content of their studies was most frequently the yogic and ritual systems found in the *mahāyoga* and *yoginī-tantras*, associated instructional manuals (*upadeśa*), and analogous yogic texts. The value of their efforts was so evident that new works were, in some cases, produced by the interaction between an Indian Paṇḍita and a Tibetan translator, a phenomenon I term "gray" texts. Furthermore, the translators' contributions were so important that their legacy was seriously misrepresented by some of their followers, and Marpa is taken as an example of this process. Many translators, like Ralo Dorjé-drak, formed relationships to religious figures irrespective of their sectarian affiliation, whereas others, like Gö-lotsāwa Khukpa Lhétsé, launched a neoconservative assault on the literature of the older systems. All participated in the new thirst for knowledge, which was regarded as the salvation of the Tibetan civilization and the lamp that would illuminate the darkness in the "city of ghosts" (Pretapuri), as some Tibetans perceived their fragmented religious culture.

MANTRINS AND MOTIVATION FOR NEW TRANSLATIONS

Tibetan literature, by and large, rather blithely accepts the inevitability of this stage: the rise of the translator as a figure of personality, spirituality, and political power in the eleventh and twelfth centuries. If an author bothers to explain one of the most astonishing literary movements in human history, he usually describes the process as being needed to "resolve doubts."[7] Most do not take the explanation even that far, and we simply read that this or that lordly scion of the old imperium wished to bring back the Dharma to Tibet and sent young Tibetans to retrieve texts from India to be translated. Indians were invited, and the translation process began to be institutionalized on the economic and political bases that had been pioneered by Lumé, Lotön, and the rest. In West Tibet, we might have expected this to some degree, since Lhalama and his dynasty were exposed to the proximity of Kashmir and did not have the profusion of sites from the royal period with which to contend, with fewer library resources or the close contact with Tsongkha available farther east.[8] The decision to support translation in Gugé-Purang, therefore, might seem to have been more intuitive, whereas in Central Tibet it would appear less so, given that the monastic revival was well under way before any translators appeared in Ü-Tsang.

The issue of "doubts" was mainly a question of the clash of institutional cultures—and the problem of resolving their disparate claims—so that the twelfth-century *Pillar Testament* (*bKa' 'chems ka khol ma*) indicates that the translation movement really began because of trouble between the older vested religious interests and the new monks.[9] Resolving doubts in this context, therefore, cannot be simply a question of available information, for there can be little doubt that the primary problem in the four horns of Tibet in the early eleventh century was not an absence of information but the clamor of multiple voices. There were voices for the Vinaya, voices for the old esoteric system, and voices for philosophical discourse, all claiming that they should be given pride of place in the coalescence of the culture.

Accordingly, the problem of doubt that precipitated the movement toward renewed translation really came about because of the disparity between the aristocratic and royal standards of appropriate conduct, on the one hand, and the decidedly inappropriate behavior of individuals or groups in Tibet, on the other hand. The latter were sometimes esoteric lamas employing tantric texts that had been translated during the royal dynasty. In this case, such practices as sexual yoga or murderous assaults were sometimes castigated by those in authority as a "misunderstanding" of the esoteric scriptures. They claimed that individuals had interpreted certain antinomian statements in the tantras in a literal manner, even though this is exactly what some Indians had actually done before them. The result was a general sense of a religious tradition fragmented and out of control, with the monastic clothing and outward forms being maintained while the actual behaviors of Tibetan religious were slowly being accommodated to Tibetan village practices of blood sacrifice to mountain gods and the marked Tibetan proclivity to greater sexual license.

This situation may also suggest one other reason that Central Tibetans ultimately sought the Dharma in India: a sense of ritual closure. The documents show that the esoteric form of Buddhism was considered both the most prestigious and the most problematic. There was certainly a feeling that many Tibetans had transgressed the vow structure of the esoteric dispensation—either from ignorance or out of a sense of personal entitlement—and we see evolve an idea of community responsibility for this behavior as well. According to the normative texts on esoteric consecration, if one substantially transgresses the vows, one will be compelled to reestablish them by accepting the consecration once again.[10] Much of the writing about the period of fragmentation can be understood in this light. The period was a result of the transgression of vows by Darma, but his evil conduct was further compounded by the willful corruption of the true Dharma by various individuals who had maintained the esoteric system. Accordingly, the religious protectors did not protect Tibet, which became the field of vultures with the three insurrections, the opening of the tombs, and the loss of unification. The only possible course of conduct would be to send young men to India, to receive again the consecration of learning in the Buddhadharma, to bring back to Tibet the pure esoteric dispensation, and to resurrect the temples and monasteries with Indian consultants, not just Tibetans from the northeast.

As time went on, it became obvious that not all the texts used in aristocratic Nyingma ritual systems or philosophical libraries were authentic translations of one of the known sources for royal dynastic Buddhism. Some of the texts had certainly been augmented, transposed, pieced together, or wholly invented in Tibet, and the process appeared to accelerate during the late tenth to twelfth century, so that as the religious communities began to emerge, new texts with indigenous Tibetan ideas did as well. Since there has never been a positive language or affirmative model in Tibetan culture to authenticate indigenous Tibetan doctrinal or ritual developments, the authors of such texts had no recourse but to veil them in the cloak of legitimacy by providing them with the clothing of translated works. Yet Tibetan creativity in some instances neglected standard Indian guidelines for the practice of scriptural composition.[11] Consequently, the standard Buddhist appropriation of local practices was sometimes put into place in Tibet with little regard to the controls over this enterprise that had been exhibited by Buddhists in the past. Thus, the products of Nyingma textual efforts were often curious hybrids of sūtra and tantra. Without a competent cadre of experts trained in the language systems of the scriptural source cultures (Sanskrit, Chinese, Khotanese, or Apabhraṁśa), it was difficult—not to say impossible—to determine which works were Indian and which were not. Many of the apocryphal texts, for example, had been equipped with pseudo-Indic or pseudo-other language titles, and to the eye of the literate Tibetan unschooled in Indic languages, it all might as well have been Homeric Greek.

Unfortunately, the Tibetans' faith in Indians' capacity to resolve their doubts was sadly misplaced, for the Indic system happily tolerated the chaos of far more voices than these, and the supporting socioeconomic realities of the aging Pāla dynasty—under the long-lived Mahīpāla I (r. ca. 992–1042)—were entirely off the scale possible for petty rulers on the roof of the world. The multiplicity of claims and standards of behavior were sustainable only in the complex and highly diversified communities found in and around the large population centers of India and, to a lesser extent, in the mediating Himalayan kingdoms. Central Tibetans in the intermediate areas of Kashmir and Nepal, and even more in India itself, found such a cacophony of possibilities that any idea they might have had of finding the one true Dharma seemed hopeless. In India, they discovered even more directions in the practice of Buddhism than they expected, and the literature is replete with examples of Central Tibetan translators being surprised by the new directions evinced by the Indians they encountered, especially in the new yogic literature associated with Guhyasamāja, Cakrasaṁvara, Hevajra, Vajrabhairava, and similar systems. Even more disconcerting, when they returned home, the translators of the new esoteric material had contend with the fact that Indian esoterism had changed sufficiently to have created contentious issues with the representatives of the earlier traditions, all of whom were now categorized as Nyingma, the "Old (out-of-date) Guys." As the volume of translations increased, so did the problems, not only with the Nyingma representatives but also with individuals within the new translation camp as well, for not all the young men going to India returned with the best of Buddhist behavior in mind.

TRANS-HIMALAYAN CORONATION

These factors must be seen in light of the overwhelming sense of legitimacy that the act of translation brought to those who pursued it, and Tibetans continually depicted the translators as if they had become de facto gentry by means of their education in South Asia, coronated as Dharma kings. Tibetan writers tended to mark the end of the early period of religious diffusion not from the 841/42 suppression of Buddhism by Darma but from the transmission and translation of the Yamāntaka materials by Candrakīrti and Odren Lotrö Wangchuk.[12] Likewise, some identified the later diffusion (*phyi dar*) as simply the later translation period (*phyi 'gyur*), not with the "up from embers" temple organizations established by Lumé and Lotön.[13] Perhaps the preeminent measure of Tibetans' fascination with translation is illustrated by those authors who saw the later diffusion inaugurated by Smṛti Jñānakīrti.[14]

As Nyang-rel tells the story, a Nepalese named Pema Marutsé needed to obtain an expert in Dharma for Lha-lama in Gugé, and so he went to India. There he found Smṛti and Ācārya Phralaringba (a Newar?), but on the way back to Tibet, the Nepalese translator Pema Marutsé died. Undaunted, Smṛti and Phralaringba continued on but were captured by bandits and sold into slavery to a rebel lord named Shak-tsen, who occupied Tanak, just northwest of Shigatse.[15] In Tanak, the two Buddhist scholars spent their time tending sheep and doubtless ruminating on the nature of karma and cosmic irony. Eventually they were liberated when they were recognized by Len Tsültrim Nyingpo to be monks, and the two overqualified shepherds made their way to Kham.[16] There, Smṛti began his translation of various esoteric works and his study of Tibetan, which eventually yielded his grammatical description of the language.[17] Since our two lost Indian scholars tending sheep were evidently freed by the disciples of the Eastern Vinaya monks from Tsongkha, it is unclear why they would have been accorded the position of inaugurating the later diffusion of the Dharma, except for the inherent authority of translation as the *sine qua non* of medieval Tibetan religion.

It is all the more paradoxical that we know so little about the overwhelming majority of young Tibetan men who braved the rigors of an extraordinary trip to the subcontinent. Even if they were lucky enough to be sponsored by one or another lord descended from the great emperors, their impediments were daunting. They first had to travel to some intermediary point, usually Nepal or Kashmir, where they might find a group of merchants who were knowledgeable in both Tibetan and the vernacular of North India, medieval Apabhraṁśa or proto-Hindustani. There they learned to communicate in the language from which they would eventually study Sanskrit. Many failed at this point, for not everyone, however diligent or faithful, can fathom another language when the culture lacks even the most fundamental pedagogical method. Indeed, we have examples of individuals returning to Tibet after years in South Asia without having comprehended the rudiments of any Indic language.

Others may have failed from the poor treatment that Indians all too often provide visitors in their environment, although some Indians, to be sure, welcome the irregular traveler. Many other Indians, though, enjoy the ridicule of foreigners, and Xuanzang relates a tale that the large monastery at Bodhgayā, the Mahābodhyārāma, was founded because a Singhalese prince had so many bad experiences traveling to Buddhist pilgrimage sites in India.[18] Wherever he went, he was greeted with disdain and humiliation, all because he was from a "border country," the terminology Indians employed for those outside the population centers inhabited by caste Hindus. Consequently, the Mahābodhyārāma monastery was founded for traveling monks from Śrī Laṅka. Albīrūnī, writing about the same time as Drokmi and Marpa were in India, states that for Indians, "all their fanaticism is directed against those who do not belong to them—against all foreigners."[19] While Albīrūnī's perspective certainly may have been skewed—he was accompanying the Ghaznavid incursions—nonetheless his statements resonate with other observations. Tibetans, for their part, were from a border country, and to this day many Indians deprecate Tibetans for their differing sense of cleanliness, propriety, and descent. Accordingly, the occasional references to Tibetans being greeted with acclaim in India may have been isolated occurrences based on the ideology of Buddhist monasticism or Tibetans' attempts at self-justification, for who would want to tell the local tyrant in Tsang that his religious representative had been received as the outcaste that all Tibetans surely were?

India was also physically challenging for aspiring Tibetan translators. The majority of them who went to India probably died there, far from home, with one or another of India's extraordinary diseases: malaria, hepatitis, cholera, gastroenteritis, various forms of dermatitis leading to blood infections, encephalitis, and so forth. According to Yijing's record of Chinese pilgrims in the seventh century, the hazards of disease were matched only by the problems of banditry, imprisonment by local warlords, flood, fire, and famine.[20] Those Tibetans who survived also had to acclimate to wet weather in the summer, the only time Ü-Tsang is really pleasant, and to the hot season from late March to June. The change of diet, the lack of quantities of meat, the different nutriments, the problems associated with assimilating new sources of protein—these certainly assisted the extraordinary mortality rate of aspiring translators. Adding to this was the stress of adjusting to a different altitude, for the Tibetans' physiologies embodied their genetic strengths and weaknesses that had been developed at high altitude over many generations.

Once Tibetans became physically and culturally acclimated to India, they began the real work of absorbing their training in the doctrinal and ritual fundamentals of Buddhist culture. Some doubtless found this easier than others did, and the eleventh-century translators must have benefited from their predecessors, although it is not clear how much preparation they had before arriving in Kashmir, Nepal, or India. Those who left records indicated a minimal training: Marpa learned letters; Gö-lotsāwa Khukpa Lhétsé was impressed by the translators' affluence; but most appeared to be only slightly prepared to encounter the depth of Buddhist training. If he landed in a large monastery, a Tibetan was a negligible entity until he matured intellectually, and even then he would never have been considered on a par with Indian monks in the selection for positions of leadership. Although individual Tibetans may have been accorded esteem by individual Indian teachers, I know of no instance in which a Tibetan monk was placed at the helm of an Indian Buddhist monastery, however good his linguistic, meditative, or intellectual ability. Individual Tibetans were frequently received with applause, gifts, and important appointments in China, Mongolia, or Russia, but the Indians appear to have required greater efforts to consider foreigners on a par with themselves within the boundaries of India, however Indians may have comported themselves outside its borders. Although Central Asians, Tibetans, and Chinese regularly elevated Indians to positions of authority, it is doubtful that this process was ever reversed, whatever the anticaste rhetoric or internationalist sentiment of Indian Buddhism.

We also know little about the way in which Indian monasteries conducted their pedagogical business in the eleventh and twelfth centuries, and particularly whether any consideration was granted to foreigners. Few of the translators have left any discussion of the Indian monastic curricula, beyond a list of the titles and an indication that examinations were held and certificates issued. A student might begin with grammar, and the *Candravyākaraṇa* or the *Kalāpa* systems seemed popular.[21] For the Tibetans, though, the study would have been new, for early Tibetan writing on Sanskrit grammar was impoverished, and the received translations of Indian grammars into Tibetan stem only from the thirteenth century.[22]

After the initial study of the language, the old Buddhist mainstays of the Abhidharma and Vinaya were generally handled though the lens of Vasubandhu's *Abhidharmakośa* and Guṇaprabha's *Vinayasūtra*, rather than the requirement that the old texts of the Sarvāstivāda (*Jñānaprasthāna*, etc.) be learned or that the enormous *Mūlasarvāstivāda-vinaya* itself be mastered, except for specialists in each of these areas. Mahāyānist scriptural studies especially were marked by the rise of *Abhisamayālaṁkāra* exegesis—unknown to Xuanzang in the seventh century—and the continued instruction in the Jātaka and Avadāna narratives. Clearly, however, the curriculum of the larger monasteries changed from the emphasis on the "mere consciousness" treatises that Xuanzang had studied in Nālandā when he was there. By the time Tibetans arrived in Nālandā (or Vikramaśīla, Somapuri, or Odantapuri), the flagship monasteries had adopted the epistemological and scholastic manuals emphasizing the ideas of Dharmakīrti, Candrakīrti, and Bhāvaviveka: the *Pramāṇaviniścaya*, commentaries on the *Pramāṇavārtika* and the *Mūlamadhyamaka-kārikā*, independent Madhyamaka works like the *Satyadvayavibhaṅga*, and the all-inclusive work of Śāntideva. Advanced students might pursue other synthetic epistemologists, such as Śāntarakṣita, or study one of the controversies of the day; for example, could the awareness of the Buddha be understood as containing an element of cognition (*sākāravāda*) or not (*nirākāravāda*)?

Those Tibetans pursuing the study of tantrism might have been initially attracted to the professors of esoterism ensconced in these Bihari and Bengali institutions, and many Tibetans began their studies there. Others, however, found much more fertile ground in the smaller monasteries and regional temples in Kashmir, Bengal, and Nepal. The story of esoterism continued to emphasize regional variations and traditions, individual teachers and specific yogins, for these were the institutions supporting the advanced yogic systems of the completion process. Even if the great centers of learning may have had temples dedicated to tantric deities—there was a Cakrasaṁvara temple in Nālandā—or possessed Vajrayāna specialists of the order of Ratnākaraśānti, the centers of siddha spirituality remained at the margins. Nāropā was especially esteemed in his East Indian hermitage of Phullahari, and his disciples, such as Phamthingpa Vāgīśvarakīrti and his brother Bodhibhadra, were celebrated in their Pharping hermitage in the south of the Kathmandu valley. So many times, though, we learn that a Tibetan found his master through a chance encounter or in a jungle environment, although this "jungle" may have been a village outside the major supply routes.

Whether in a large affluent monastery or a small forest hermitage, many of the translators began working there, rendering the texts they were studying into Tibetan even as their instruction continued. The colophons to their translations sometimes allow us a glimpse of their lives: "We, the Paṇḍita Parahitaprabha and the Tibetan lotsāwa Zugah Dorjé, found an old manuscript in the *Amṛtodbhava-vihāra of Kashmir, so we translated it."[23] Similarly, we sometimes read about translations in Nepal, at sites not now so well known as they once were: "At the exceedingly famous great site (*mahāpīṭha*) of Nyéwé Tungchöpa(?) in the city of Kathmandu, Nepal, the scholar Jaitakarṇṇa and the Tibetan translator Shākyabhikṣu Nyima Gyeltsen Pel-zangpo translated this work."[24] Some translations, though, were clearly completed in the large monasteries in India, and may even have been initially revised there as well:

> The Magadhan Paṇḍita Ānandabhadra and the Tibetan translator Sétsa Sönam Gyeltsen translated, edited, and finalized this in accordance with a Magadhan text in front of the self-originated Viśuddha-stūpa to the south of the great city of Tirahati. Later, Tarpa-lotsāwa, the Sthavira Nyima Gyeltsen, correctly translated it according to the instruction he heard from the siddha Karṇaśrī in Śrī Nālandā-mahāvihāra.[25]

After Atiśa either founded the Stham Bihar or gave it the new name Vikramaśīla as a declaration of a formal relationship with his own Bihari institution, Tibetans sometimes represented themselves as translating in Vikramaśīla, although it is not clear that Mel-gyo, for example, ever visited the great monastery in Bihar: "The Indian Upādhyāya Mañjuśrī and the Tibetan translator Mel-gyo Lotrö Drakpa translated this, revised, and finalized this translation at the Mahāvihāra of Vikramaśīla."[26] We have no idea of the actual proportion of translations done in Kashmir, India, or Nepal, as opposed to Tibet, but it is clear that the majority of the translations were not finalized south of the Himalayas, for the conditions in India continued to worsen for Buddhist monks as the eleventh century progressed, and Indians seemed to become increasingly frequent visitors during the twelfth and thirteenth centuries.

Returning to their home base, these new translators seldom had the wealthy facilities available to royal dynastic translators or Chinese monks in their imperial court bureaus. The new translators also were not subjected to the restrictions of translation incumbent on those endowed with such imperial facilities. Many of the translators were lucky if they secured initial funding from the legacy of a noble house, which might include a place to live and a degree of legitimacy. If they also received assistance from an Indian Paṇḍita wandering through the area, so much the better, for most Tibetans would not have had access to much more than the minimal supplies of ink and paper and a manuscript copy of the *Mahāvyuttpati*. A few may have had a copy of Smṛti Jñānkīrti's grammar, and it is said that Rongzom's writings on grammar were composed for the benefit of Marpa Chökyi Lotrö, the famous Kagyüpa founder.[27] Most Tibetans made good-faith efforts in translation, but some of the translators—particularly in the thirteenth and fourteenth centuries—relied entirely on a mechanical word-for-word system, perhaps a result of the decline of the Indian institutions and the paucity of paṇḍitas.[28] This procedure often rendered their texts as little more than gibberish, and we can only pity their cadre of disciples who were forced to try to make sense of the word salad that resulted in such instances.

The translators also had textual problems, and anyone studying late Buddhist manuscript traditions can only stand in amazement at the successes of these Tibetan scholars in the face of the chaos of an Indian manuscript. The Tibetans encountered two problems. First was a change in scripts employed by the Indian scribes around the ninth century or so, the "*nāgarī* shift," in which the older *siddhamātṛkā*-based scripts derived from old Gupta Brahmī were phased out and replaced by a series of newer scripts. These newer scripts were fundamentally different from this time onward, especially in East India and Nepal, and Indians often had difficulty comprehending the older manuscripts and their complex ligatures. Only the *śāradā* script used in Kashmir during and after the ninth century retained some of the features of *siddhamātṛkā* that had been lost in many of the *nāgarī* scripts being developed in Bengal, Bihar and elsewhere.[29] Thus, a degree of continuity can be seen in the Kashmiri manuscripts, but this was of less value for the Tibetans in Ü-Tsang, especially those who had been trained in monasteries using the newer script.

In addition, manuscript facility remained an issue, since translators frequently employed manuscripts left by others or tried to use the old manuscript libraries first put together during the royal dynasty. Consequently, the manuscripts that might be encountered in these older sites remained closed books to many of the scholars who found them, Indian as well as Tibetan. This question was brought up by the eleventh-century Nyingma representatives, who were forced to encounter questions of their own legitimacy by decrying the lack of later Indian Paṇḍitas' ability to read the older scripts, so that questions of the authenticity of Nyingma texts remained more problematic than they were represented by their opponents.

The other issue regarding Indian manuscripts of the period was simply the carelessness and ineptitude of so many Indians scribes in transmitting their manuscripts. Albīrūnī commented around 1030 that

> the Indian scribes are careless, and do not take pains to produce correct and well-collated copies. In consequence, the highest results of the author's mental development are lost by their negligence, and his book becomes already in the first or second copy so full of faults that the text appears as something entirely new, which [no one] could any longer understand.[30]

Not only were Indian scribes inattentive to the business of copying, they often used the expedient of having a scholar recite a text, so that the copyist would take down the phonetic rendering of a Sanskrit text according to Bengali or Newar pronunciation, thereby creating further difficulties. Other Indians were notorious for "cooking" the manuscripts, that is, copies from an incomplete or damaged manuscript would be filled in with material that the scholars had themselves produced, rather than securing a second copy to collate with the first. These and other practices sometimes gave a willing and competent translator an incomprehensible set of palm leaves or a birch bark codex. At a later time, Kyobpa Pel-zangpo pleaded, "I could not find a Paṇḍita or secure a second manuscript, so may the learned be patient with those parts that are in error; this text should be edited and the erroneous sections corrected!"[31] Eleventh-century translators sometimes circumvented these difficulties by adopting the old royal dynastic translation as the basis for revision, a process cultivated by Atiśa and his followers in both Gugé and Central Tibet. This practice, though, only perpetuated uncertainty for some, as the differences in recensions over three to four centuries were such that the new Indian text was manifestly different from the version on which the previous translation was based.

THE CURIOUS CAREER OF RALO DORJÉ-DRAK

Whatever their difficulties, there can be little doubt that the authenticity of translation per se provided its protagonists with a sense of entitlement that could match the credentials enjoyed by the older aristocracy. The learned translators captured the imagination of Tibetans in a way that the earlier monks from Tsongkha had not. In their public personas, the translators evoked the religious dynamism of the royal dynasty, which could not be equaled in the secular political or military spheres. While local lords were geographically restricted in their authority, the translators could claim all of Tibet as their range in their propagation of the Dharma. Their influence in domains of religion—derived from their successful adventures in the grand monastic establishments of South Asia—was sufficient for them to attract disciples and resources away from the monks following in the footsteps of Lumé and Lotön. As experience in studying Sanskrit on the other side of the Himalayas became the standard against which all other forms of religiosity were measured, the aura of the lotsāwa (translator) spilled over into the civil affairs of Central Tibet, for Tibetans were generally loath to make the same hard divisions between the secular and the sacred that Indian monks often did in India. Whereas many of the eleventh-century translators did not seize the opportunities for political power as they were presented to them, it is clear that the most famous exercised varying degrees of political and economic authority and that virtually all doing so were translators of tantric Buddhist texts.

In this process, the translators clashed not only with other civil authorities but also with Nyingma religious representatives seeking similar domains, and even with other lotsāwa when their spheres of activity collided. This political collision was not necessarily because of disagreements over scriptural authenticity—Nyingma traditions in opposition to Sarma (new translation) systems—although sometimes it was. Instead, the basis for conflict was more often at the level of the individual personality, their sense of authority, and the friction of enormous egos, which were fed by the esoteric visualization of oneself as this or that royal divinity beyond the human realm. At times, the clash of old/new systems became the vehicle for their disagreements (and was certainly in the background), but this was occasional rather than central, and we find influential Sarma esoteric translators at loggerheads with one another as often as they were with the Nyingma masters.

Perhaps the most notorious of all the eleventh-century translators was Ralotsāwa Dorjé-drak, who enjoyed the reputation of being one of the seminal figures of the eleventh century. His hagiography, apparently a compilation of accounts, is one of the longest surviving narratives of the early Sarma translators and perhaps was compiled sometime in the thirteenth century or later. This scurrilous document, which has done as much for Ralo's reputation as Tsang-nyön's fifteenth-century *Biography of Mila Repa* (*Mi la rnam thar*) did for the cotton-clad saint, is analogous to the latter in its penchant for the fictive rendering of a saint's life. Even if Ralo's hagiography took great liberties with historical truth, there can be little doubt that it approximately renders the mix of worldly desire and religious conviction that was so well expressed in the lives of many eleventh-century Tibetan masters of the esoteric system.

Ralo probably was born in 1016, the son of Ratön Könchok Dorjé and his wife, Dorjé Peldzom, in the area of Nyénam-lang.[32] This valley extends along the Pochu River directly down into Nepal, in the modern county of Nyalam on the Nepalese border. Ralo was the middle of five sons, and his father was of the minor aristocracy and represented a long line of mantrins professing Nyingma practices for seven generations. His father performed practices of Yangdak Heruka and Dorjé Purpa (Vajrakīla), the two most important deities of the traditionally transmitted Holy Word (Kahma) systems among the Nyingma. Ralo received consecrations in these lineages by the age of eight, and his hagiographer provides many examples of supernormal experiences he was supposed to have had as a child, such as Pelden Lhamo's carrying him on a trip around Tibet when he was an infant of six months. Because Ralo survived these episodes, he was given the name Deathless Lightning-strike ('Chi-med rdo-rje-thogs). He was educated by his father in the various practices of a Himalayan community, and his quickness earned him a reputation for intelligence, so that some called him Embodied Insight (Shes-rab 'byung-gnas). Nonetheless, his childhood was marked by episodes of his extreme abusiveness, both verbal and physical, toward his elders.[33] Apparently his betrothal to a young lady in the area went sour, and he headed south to Nepal to learn more about the Dharma.[34] Around 1030, Ralo, a lad of fourteen, ended up on the road to the big city of Lalita-paṭṭana (Pāṭan) in Nepal's Kathmandu valley.

The Nepal that Ralo encountered was quite different from his valley in Tibet. As is frequently seen in contemporaneous Tibetan literature, the hagiography represents Pāṭan as a Buddhist pure land:

> The form of the valley was that of a lotus fully blossomed. It was auspicious and evoked feelings of delight. Many varieties of grain grew there, and waters of eight qualities cascaded. It was surrounded by fragrant ponds for bathing. It was a pure garden of medicine nurturing life. There were sites wondrous for being subdued by the feet of those engaging in righteous assembly, with herds of horses, elephants, and bullocks wandering without anxiety in meadows of different flowers. It was the residence of scholars and

> siddhas. Because it had so many charnel grounds where assembled heroes and *ḍākinīs*, it seemed the same as the miraculous island of Khecarī (*ḍākinīs*). In every direction, the city was surrounded by forests having trees of various kinds of fruit, sandalwood, fragrant aloe, and so forth. Resounding and filling them were cuckoos and parrots, and various small birds of exquisite call. In the midst of all this, was the great city with four wide boulevards and four great gates in the surrounding city wall. About 500,000 households resided there, the buildings all of even size, demonstrating a place of good harvest, and filled with people. On the elegant mansions, like the palace of the king, there were five hundred levels all with unlimited fabulous arrays of gems in crystal, jade, and ivory. Within the amazing diversity of shops distributed throughout the city squares were scattered on display the many goods produced by every country and region. Because all the people of the city enjoyed sufficiency and lacked mutual animosity, they all laughed and played many games with each other. Many girls played the lute (*vina*) or flute and enjoyed breaking out into song. In every direction were innumerable physical, vocal, and mental supports of the triple gem. Before them, a continual stream of good offerings were made, and done in a manner displaying good character. Wherever one goes, people display sincerity, and whomever one befriends, that person is trustworthy.[35]

Ralo's hagiography makes a King Balahasti the ruler of Pāṭan, but we have no record of a Nepalese king by this name, and we know that the eleventh century was a troubled period for Nepalese rulers, with fourteen monarchs accounted as having reigned sometime in this century. This is in the middle of the period sometimes called Ṭhakurī (879–1200), although other historians have suggested "transitional" as a designation. Neither term is really satisfactory, as apparently not all the royal houses were of the Ṭhakurī caste, and no period of history should be reduced to a transition between important periods.[36] In some ways, the Kathmandu valley of Ralo's acquaintance acted as a specific variation on the rise of Indic regional centers, analogous to Kashmir, Assam, Kaṅgra, Kumaon, and so forth.

We do know that in the last two decades of the tenth century, Guṇakāmadeva pulled together the fragmented political environment of Nepāla Maṇḍala (the Kathmandu valley) under a single rule, perhaps after having shared joint rule for a while.[37] After him, double rule was reinstated, probably with a king at one palace in Pāṭan and the other across the Bagmati River in Kathmandu. By the time Ralo arrived, Lakṣmīkāmadeva was the primary ruler of the Lalita-paṭṭana kingdom, perhaps having been in some form of power as early as 1010.[38] All the sources confirm that the city of Pāṭan itself was under the direct administration of Vijayadeva, who was in power about 1030 to 1037 and again from 1039 to 1048, or for most of the time that Ralo was in town.[39] The second period of Vijayadeva's reign was shared with Bhāskaradeva, in a similar arrangement as seen previously with Lakṣmīkāmadeva. This was the period in which Atiśa and Nagtso stayed in Kathmandu on their way to West Tibet. The fragile political climate is described by various sources that mention Lakṣmīkāmadeva performing ceremonies for the peace of the nation and indicate that around 1039/40 a war broke out in Bhaktapur. Stable political rule eluded the Nepalese for another century and a half, until a measure of it was realized in Arimalla's new dynasty, founded in 1200.

Ralo would have come to Nepal by one of the two extremely important trade routes that brought goods back and forth from the Tibetan plateau directly into the valley (map 5). The Tibet trade was sufficiently consequential to be mentioned in the 695 C.E. Lagantol inscription of the Licchavi king Śivadeva II, who included provision for corveé labor on the Tibet route when he granted a village for the support of Pāśupata ascetics.[40] Of the two routes, the eastern route was doubtless that followed by Ralo around 1030, for it comes down through Nyénam—and its well-established market at Tsongdü (modern Nyalam)—along the Pochu/Bhote Kosi River, over ridges probably to Chautara, across the Indrawati, and then passes down into the valley beside Sankhu. Maintaining a position north of the current Arniko Highway, the old trade route proceeds directly to Bodhnāth, turning south at the Chābhil stūpa, passing west of the probable site of the old Licchavi palace of Kailāsakūṭa—now a mound just north of Paśupatināth—and over the bridge to Pāṭan, bypassing Kathmandu altogether.

The western route to Tibet, conversely, goes up through Kathmandu, to the sometimes autonomous fiefdom of Navakoṭ. From there it joins the Trishuli/Kyirong-Tsangpo River climbing up through the Mangyül valley to Kyirong and on to Dzongkha, the hub of commerce in the area of Gungtang and an important stopping point between Kathmandu and the kingdom of Gugé. It was along this western route that Nagtso-lotsāwa brought Atiśa into West Tibet in 1042, having spent a year at Swayambhū-caitya, Navakoṭ, and Stham Bihār.[41] In traditional times, both Dzongkha and Nyalam were relatively easy to reach during the late spring and early fall, just before and after the monsoon rains caused landslides that made the trip dangerous. Ralo's hagiography indicated that the trip from Nyénam to Pāṭan took ten days, a reasonable time for the more than one-hundred-mile excursion.[42] Traditional traders would have provided both company and protection to Tibetans aspiring to religion, and although Ralo's hagiography insists that he first went

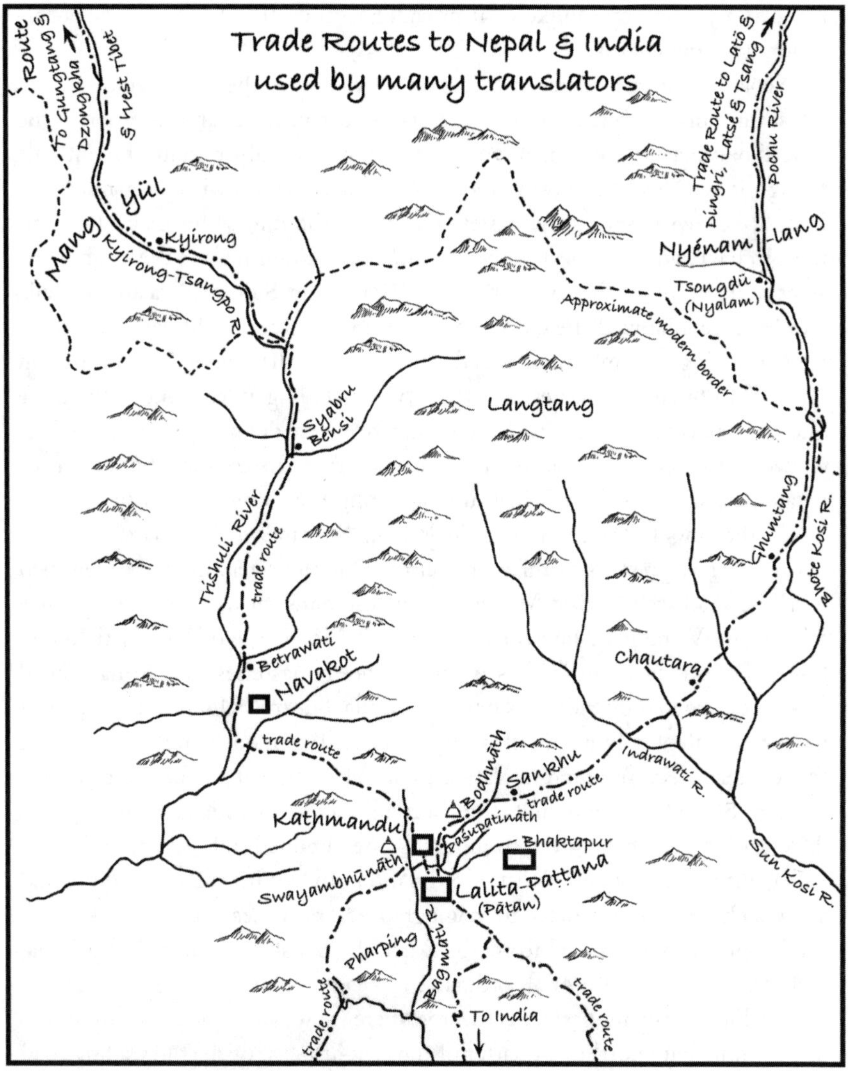

MAP 5 Trade Routes to Nepal and India Used by Many Translators.

alone as a young boy (unlikely), it provides several other instances of his collusion with merchants.[43]

Nepal had been a center of Buddhist activity since the Licchavi kings, and Aṁśuvarman's 607/8 C.E. Second Harigaon Stele provides an indication of the official patronage of five major and several minor Buddhist establishments, although it is difficult in most cases to match those names with known institutions.[44] Likewise, several monasteries listed in the king's chronicles for both the Licchavi and post-Licchavi periods are not yet identified.[45] We might consider more accurate the report that the Pāṭan King Siddhi Narasiṁha Malla (1618–61) reorganized the city monasteries into a group of fifteen, with three from outlying communities added to constitute the major monasteries in Pāṭan.[46] But many monasteries in the city—including at least one of the three said to be newly built by this Pāṭan monarch—were definitely older or not included in the report, so that the political rhetoric of its contents hinder an accurate assessment of Pāṭan's institutions during the eleventh century.

Confirming Ralo's monastery in Pāṭan, *Sūryatala-mahāvihāra (Ye-rang nyi-ma-steng), presents a similar problem.[47] This monastery might be identified with the Waṁ Bāhā (East Monastery), whose Sanskrit name is Sūryavarma-Saṁskarita-Vajrakīrti Mahāvihāra: the Great Monastery of Vajrakīrti Refurbished by Sūryavarman.[48] This is one of the monasteries said to have been newly constructed by Siddhi Narasiṁha Malla, but the colophon to a 1440/41 manuscript already indicates its prior existence. Two name similarities suggest this center as Ralo's home in Pāṭan. First, no other Pāṭan monastery of age contains Sūrya (= nyi-ma) in its title. Second, Ralo's monastic name was Dorjé-drak, said to have been given to him when he obtained full ordination in Nālandā, but the hagiography's list of ordination officials in Nālandā is quite odd and may have been concocted for hagiographical purposes.[49] Dorjé-drak, however, is probably translated from Vajrakīrti, the Sanskrit name of Waṁ Bāhā, and may be a reflection of an ordination lineage maintained there, at least in theory. Finally, the monastery is exactly where we would expect Ralo to find it: in the immediate northeast quarter of the city, just east of the old trading road he would have used after crossing the Bagmati River.

Just as curious is the person of Ralo's great master that he met there: Bhāro. The thirteenth-century hagiography gives no more information about the identity of this figure, but the colophon of several of Ralo's translations maintain that they were done by him in conjunction with Bharo Chagdum.[50] This last designation (*phyag rdum*) is the honorific form for *lag rdum*, the standard translation of the Sanskrit *kuṇḍa*, and when applied to people, normally these terms indicate a deformed limb, which is how it was translated into Tibetan. When identifying an object, however, a *kuṇḍa* is a fire pit or area (also called *agni-kuṇḍa*), specifically where *homa* fire rites were performed for the purposes of propitiation, initiation, or one of the tantric rituals.[51] This pit is employed for a variety of rituals in current Newar bāhā usage, and we may expect that in the eleventh century it was reserved for those few officials who were designated elders (*sthavira*) in the community and who had received advanced initiation.[52] The other part of the name, Bhāro, was a new political title given to important members of the merchant (*vaiśya*, *urāya* or similar) castes and marked the bearer as a minor aristocrat with a title attested primarily from the eleventh century onward.[53] These Newar nobles had a particular involvement with Buddhism, and in the mid-eleventh century Gasu Bhāro and his son Dhoga Bhāro were patrons to Buddhist masters.[54]

We might reasonably presume then that Ralo's master was named *Kuṇḍa Bhāro, for all the old documents have the Bhāro placed second in a name, and had been at one time the master of the homa-related esoteric ceremonies of his monastery, coming from a merchant family of means and having had political connections in the court of Vijayadeva, the ruler of Pāṭan. Bhāro was certainly a specialist in esoteric ritual and at one point confessed that he knew virtually nothing about Buddhist doctrine or monastic decorum; rather, he knew the rituals and meditations of Vajravārāhī and Vajrabhairava.[55] His monastery was certainly a lay-based institution, and Locke's intuition that this may have always been the principal nature of Newar esoteric centers certainly seems to apply in this early-eleventh-century case, for the presence of wives (*bhari*) and feminine family members is attested in the hagiography.[56] As primarily a householder center, the monastery would have appeared invitingly comfortable yet enticingly exotic to Ralo and would have given him a good mediating facility to study Indic materials and become exposed to Indic religious values without having to assume the identity of a Buddhist monk right away.

Ralo must have learned much from his master during his first visit to Pāṭan, for he was consecrated into the rituals for Vajravārāhī and Vajrabhairava this first time around. He also secured the support of an influential Newar merchant, one *Candrabhadra, whom he healed from a disease with rituals in the Vajravārāhī cycle, and Ralo received an appointment as the good merchant's ritual priest (*purohita*).[57] Conversely, Ralo also secured the enmity of a Śaivite magician named Pūṛnakāla, whom he encountered while circumambulating Swayambhūcaitya. According to the story, Pūṛnakāla encountered Ralo and claimed the Tibetan for his own disciple, an unlikely scenario given eleventh-century Śaivite emphasis on issues of caste. Ralo—ever the diplomat—is said to have replied that since he was a Buddhist, he could see no reason to become involved in Brahmanical learning, for "why would I dismount a horse to ride a donkey?"[58] The result of this interaction, we are told, is that Ralo and Pūṛnakāla became engaged in a magical war, which did not please *Kuṇḍa Bhāro. Still, the senior esoteric master provided Ralo with the various means to ward off the magic of his opponent: Ralo set a painting of Vajravārāhī on his bed in his place and hid in a jar while Pūṛnakāla's magical darts turned the painting into dust. The denouement of the contest occurred when Pūṛnakāla committed suicide, out of despair that he had not conquered the young Tibetan magus. The hagiography strongly suggests that this pattern of magical contest—perfected at the expense of the hapless Śaivite magician—was employed for all enemies of the true Dharma (i.e., all of Ralo's enemies), in Tibet as well as in Nepal and India.

Following his adventures, *Kuṇḍa Bhāro presented Ralo with a vajra and bell (*vajraghaṇṭa*) that had belonged to Padmavajra, along with his personal statue of Vajrabhairava and a copy of a text of magical instructions (*gdams ngag gi be bum*), thereby confirming the continuing importance of physical relics in Buddhist ritual lineages.[59] On the way home to Tibet, Ralo met one of his older brothers, Tentreü, who was coming to search for him, since Ralo's family had heard that the boy had been killed in a magical duel with a Tīrthika magician. Once the two of them returned, however, all was not well, for the family was in an ongoing dispute with those in another village over the fortunes of Ralo's betrothed. The hagiography presents Ralo as using his magic to secure the young lady's freedom, and the hagiographer easily glosses over the ethical questions about the application of force for familial ends by affirming that Ralo's family business was the Dharma and therefore justified the magical assault on the other clan.[60]

TANTRIC ACTION IN PRACTICE

The young master Ralo then began the activities that were to consume most of the rest of his life: teaching the new revelation of Vajrabhairava, engaging in magical contests, and securing the peace and prosperity of various areas of Tibet. Ralo apparently had few reservations about exhibiting a series of public presentations of this supposedly secret tradition and propagating the rituals far and wide, even though his master is depicted in several places as warning him against exactly this behavior.[61] While Newars continued to be highly secretive of their ritual life, Tibetans—certainly since the eleventh century—have, with some exceptions, been quite willing to temporize on this issue of the secret nature of the esoteric system. Ralo's antagonists seemed, for example, to know virtually everything about his ritual life, and their hostility to the public displays was a centerpiece of this antagonism.

Ralo's first priestly opponent brought these questions of ethics and publicity to the fore. Khön Shākya Lotrö of the Mugulung area of Tsang—an area examined later when discussing Drokmi's residence there—became jealous of Ralo's fame and success. Shākya Lotrö is depicted as a member of the Khön family in Tsang and was probably the real father of Khön Könchok Gyelpo, the eventual founder of Sakya Monastery. Conforming with what we know of the Khön clan, Shākya Lotrö is seen as a master of the Vajrakīla and Yangdak Heruka systems of ritual and meditation, both good Nyingma systems that Ralo's father himself had practiced. In an attempt to moderate Ralo's success, Khön Shākya Lotrö is said to have circulated the statement that the young translator "requested from the Tīrthika named Bhāro the [ritual of] an animal-headed Tīrthika god. With this accomplishment, he confuses all these people—just meeting him will lead you to hell!"[62] Ralo heard about this and wanted to depart Tibet for Nepal in order to avoid conflict.

Avalokiteśvara, however, intervened on behalf of the Tibetan people, indicating that even he, the Bodhisattva of compassion, needed to use rough means for a difficult clientele: "Especially in this island of darkness known as the country of Tibet—because people make all kinds of claims about the greatness of their teaching, personality, and doctrinal view, disparaging others—they accumulate bad karma: this is black magic (*abhicāra*) country!"[63] Thus commanded by the guardian of Tibet, Ralo was forced to engage his enemy. With the killing rites (*abhicāra*) of Vajrabhairava, he slew Khön Shākya Lotrö, and all saw Vajrabhairava, carrying the fifty-eight-divinity maṇḍala of Yangdak in a skull cap to indicate his superiority over the other god, merge with Ralo.[64] All the patrons and disciples of Shākya Lotrö planned revenge and assembled an army, but Ralo conjured up a great wind to blow them in all directions. Thereupon, we are told, the disciples of Khön Shākya Lotrö became Ralo's disciples, and his feudal subjects (*'bangs*) became Ralo's subjects as well.

Ralo's fame spread, and the hagiography relates that he spent much of his time renovating old temples in Dingri, Latö and elsewhere, much as the monks coming to Central Tibet from Tsongkha did. Ralo sponsored copies of the scriptures, had statues built or repaired, banned hunting and fishing wherever he went, restricted traffic on roads and rivers as protection from bandits, released prisoners languishing in the prisons of capricious Tibetan lords, and performed numerous acts of benefit.[65] At one point, though, he went to pay his respects to Langlap Jangchub Dorjé, an important master of the Nyingma system of Vajrakīla. But Langlap snubbed Ralo, with the same charge as before, that Vajrabhairava and Bhāro were Tīrthika products and did not represent an authentic Buddhist lineage at all. Again a test of magic ensued, but this time Ralo could not claim victory and barely escaped with his life, having to revive his disciples magically after Langlap sent down a rain of *vajrakīla*-like thunderbolts. The goddess Tārā appeared to Ralo and counseled him to return immediately to Nepal, for he needed more training under Bhāro to succeed against such a powerful foe. Accordingly, Ralo returned to Nepal and received the new teaching as well as more instruction from other masters in the valley, such as Phamthingpa, the Indian Vajrapāṇi, and Haḍu Karpo.[66] He visited the valley's pilgrimage sites and then departed in the company of a large group of merchants going from Pāṭan to India. There he was ordained at Nālandā, we are told, and studied extensively with Mañdzu-lingpa, a Nepalese who was the abbot of the monastery. Eventually, Ralo returned to Nepal and then went back to Tibet. Then he engaged Langlap Jangchub Dorjé again and finally bested him in magical combat.[67]

From then until his death, Ralo continued to teach the Vajrabhairava system to increasingly large audiences, killing his enemies in magical contests, reviving old temples (including Samyé), and eventually seducing young women. Toward the end of the hagiography, Ralo is challenged (as he had been by others) by Géshé Tréü-chok. "If," the good Géshé asked, "you hold the discipline of a *bhikṣu*, aren't you afraid that your pursuit of killing and sex (*sbyor sgrol*) will land you in hell?"[68] Ralo replied that he has been responsible for killing thirteen *vajradharas*, including Marpa's son Darma Dodé, and that he has taken five consorts, including the eleven-year-old daughter of Kongpo Agyel.[69] Even though that last little stunt landed him in prison and even though he risked being reborn in hell, he claimed he was unrepentant. Although 112 temples, including Samyé and Trandruk, were renovated at the expense of many starving to death, he was unrepentant. Nothing that was termed "perverted" by others caused him doubt because of his propitiation of Vajrabhairava. Tibetans have generally accepted Ralo's representation in literature, and the Nyingma apologist Sogdokpa credits Ralo with having murdered thirteen bodhisattvas and thirteen translators through Vajrabhairava *abhicāra* rituals.[70]

Much else could be said about the stories and hagiographical pronouncements in this remarkable piece of religious literature, but here some reflections might be proposed. First, in the case of Ralo, the tension between the newly translated material and the older ritual systems of Nyingma esoterism was only partly at issue. Certainly, Ralo's hagiography frequently depicts him as conflicting with those in positions of authority in the older systems, and he is shown sending a letter to Setön Sönam Öser—a master of the lion-headed Ḍākinī rites—claiming that the specific deities of Vajrakumāra (Kīla) and Yangdak Vajraheruka may be great but had no power over him.[71] Yet Ralo is also shown as fond of the tradition of Padmasambhava: he meditates in Padmasambhava's cave just outside Phamthing and receives visions; he reputedly discovers treasures buried by the Indian magus; and the claim for a treasure system attributed to Ralo would later be celebrated by the great Nyingma apologist Ratna Lingpa.[72] Fundamentally, then, Ralo is not seen denigrating the ancient system per se, and it would be curious if indeed he did, since his father and relatives evidently continued its practice. Likewise, Ralo is often seen in conflict with representatives of the new systems or monastics who questioned his ability to represent himself as a monk with several wives.

More interesting perhaps was the contest between Ralo and Gö-lotsāwa Khukpa Lhétsé, the translator of the *Guhyasamāja* and one of the more fractious personalities of the period.[73] Gö-lotsāwa's given name, Khukpa Lhétsé—which was not his monastic name—became the center of a discussion about his family history. The *Blue Annals* says that "Gö Khukpa" means that he was born in Tanak-pu, a village in the upper Tanak valley, from a union of members of the Gö clan.[74] The date given in the available sources is not certain, but he was a contemporary of Ralo and Zurchung Shérap Drakpa (1014–74).[75] We are told that since Gö-lotsāwa's mother was an emanation of the goddess Tārā, he was called Lhétsé, or protected by a divinity. The *Blue Annals'* author, Gölo Zhönu-pel, noted that only a fool would accept the idea that he was born (*btsas pa*) in a cattle pen (*lhas ra*).[76] Others maintained that, yes, both the learned translator's father and mother were from the aristocratic Gö clan but that they were brother and sister. Gö-lotsāwa was therefore born in a cattle pen because his mother and father were attempting to hide in shame the results of their incestuous union.[77]

Most sources agree that as a youth, Gö-lotsāwa first went to study with the famous Zurpoché, a highly regarded Nyingma master in Tsang, but received no instruction in the Dharma, which would seem to corroborate that there was some difficulty in Gö-lotsāwa's past. Next he went to Drokmi but learned very little at much expense, for Drokmi was obsessed with the need for funds. Finally, he joined forces with Gyijo Dawé Öser, who became a great translator in his own right. They traveled together and studied extensively in Nepal and India. Gö-lotsāwa was also said to have hosted Gayādhara on the Indian's second trip to Tibet.[78] Once he became established, Gö-lotsāwa's relationships with the Zur masters have been described as cordial. Gölo Zhönu-pel stated that Zurchung came to Tanak-pu to study the *Hevajra* with the great translator and that another time, the translator even prostrated himself to Zurchung.[79] Nonetheless, Gö-lotsāwa accused the Zur clan of fabricating scriptures, and his change of attitude may have been a result of seeing Nyingma scriptural composition at first hand.

The contest with Ralo began when Gö-lotsāwa is said to have cast aspersions on Ralo's teachers, in the now familiar pattern. The hagiographer also portrays Gö-lotsāwa as performing *abhicāra* rites against Ralo, rites drawn from Gö-lotsāwa's Guhyasamāja lineage. Ralo, of course, could not allow such activities to go unnoticed and replied with his own dark magic. At this point, three hundred villages in Tanak were drawn into the dispute, and seventy of them eventually marched against Ralo, challenging him with afflicting them in the thaumaturgical cross fire. He conquered these villagers with magic so that they vomited blood, and he rolled their armor and weapons into a ball.

In all of this, it is clear that Ralo's justification of his antinomian position was taken from a literal reading of sections of the *mahāyoga-tantras*, in which no evil is a sin for the awakened master. We should also recognize that for this time, Ralo was also thought to have continued the ordination of new monks, as if the practices of killing and sexual license had no effect on his maintenance of the monastic precepts. It is unclear if there was an Indian precedent for such a position, for the portrayal of Indian teachers who performed such acts—such as the transformation of Mahācārya Dharmapāla into the siddha Virūpa—involved the expulsion of the offender from the monastic enclave.

In contrast, their hagiographers depicted Ralo and others as having performed masterly religious activity that spilled over into the secular sphere, for good or ill. Although the exceeding of religious parameters and the wielding of temporal influence had been predominantly the prerogative of the landed gentry, the translators' religious training did grant them certain forms of legitimacy that their familial associations might not (and, in some cases, could not) provide, especially capital accrual and land tenure, but also the commandeering of resources for building projects. The defeat of Gö-lotsāwa demonstrates that lotsāwas exercised a degree of political authority over the valleys in which they settled, and the death of Khukpa Lhétsé left the village of Tanak-pu without a center of secular or religious authority. Translators set up their *densa* (*gdan sa*, seat of power), a word semantically related to terms of land in the *Old Tibetan Chronicle* (*skya sa*, *sngo sa*), to terms of royal gathering in available recensions of the *Pronouncement of the Ba Clan* (*mdun sa*), and most closely to the kings' throne of dominion (*rgyal sa*). Some of the esoteric translators ended their careers by renouncing their vows (Drokmi), fathering illegitimate children (Ralo), or establishing a nice little harem for themselves of willing female disciples (Marpa and Ralo), in this way emulating the behavior of the feudal gentry, who bequeathed estates principally through patriarchal primogeniture. Particularly as the lineages spread out and developed, many of the eleventh-century esoteric masters handed down their lines to their direct progeny or to members of their clan, thereby fusing clan and religion through the Buddhist rewriting of family documents to accompany the new practices.[80] Even without such documents, lineage was embedded in the ubiquitous metaphor of building construction—four pillars, eight planks, and so forth—indicating the centrality of categories of place. The result of these practices was that the eleventh- and twelfth-century Mantrayāna lineages were most frequently designated by clan names (Rong lugs, 'Khon lugs, rNgog lugs, lCe lugs, Rwa lugs, etc.) and only infrequently by personalities ('Brog lugs). Place-name designations (e.g., Sa lugs) are most often extensions of the *densa* (religious centers) as the places of dominion.

The astonishing ability of the eleventh-century translators (and other religious) to secure public acclaim despite their activities was possible only because of the Tibetan model of the convergence of religious and secular authority, and the use of the former to extend the latter.[81] An episode in Ralo's hagiography has a former monk, Pön Gyel-lé, confessing how he had made the transition from monk to local strongman:

> I first was a monk, and listened to the Dharma from many teachers. Later, through the influence of past evil karma, I was not capable of practicing Dharma but instead made many wars and disturbances for the sake of women. I killed many men and horses. Because it is the means required to take the office of local lord, I greatly robbed and beat many tenant farmers and others. With this sin of mine, it seems there is nowhere to go but hell, so may the lama seize me with his compassion![82]

This specifically Tibetan process was perhaps assisted by the laicization of Newar esoteric centers in which masters like *Kuṇḍa Bhāro were both ritual masters (*vajrācārya*) and titled aristocrats with landed estates in the Nepalese feudal hierarchy. Yet we have already seen that in Tsongkha the same pattern emerged: lamas became feudal princes in the Chinese service and gained recognition for their ability in battle. By the end of the twelfth century, this paradigm eventually matured into the model of the lama as fully empowered and was well represented by Lama Zhang's employment of monks and soldiers.[83]

THE MYSTERIOUS MASTER MARPA

The esoteric translators were thus sometimes involved in several levels of competition and potential conflict. On one hand, the esoteric model of superiority beyond the older Mahāyānist ideal of the bodhisattva had seemingly been accepted by the majority of Indians, Nepalese, and Tibetans. The frequent and sometimes strident claims made for the quick path of the Vajrayāna, promising the awakening of the Buddha in this very life, appeared to be verified by the visualization of the individual as the Buddha in the center of the maṇḍala. For Tibetans, the fact that this variety had been so widely accepted in North India provided yet another level of authenticity over and above their own insistent need for complex and evocative rituals. Individuals in the lineage of the old emperors of Tibet in the eleventh century found in the maṇḍala their own desire for control and centrality, so that the pictorial representation of the maṇḍalas of Vairocana or Mañjuśrī on their walls appeared to verify their claims to authority in the fragmented world of Tibetan real politik. Accordingly, the institutional form of Buddhist esoterism served the purposes for which it was so well designed: the sacralization of feudal authority.

On the other hand, the translators representing Buddhist esoterism often were trained directly within the siddha tradition, so they intuitively understood the limits of religiopolitical forms. In fact, their claims to authenticity seldom rested on the maṇḍalas found in the great tantras but relied instead on the siddha ideal of devotion to the instructions of the perfected master, who hands to the well-prepared disciple the intuitive knowledge of absolute reality through advanced yogic discipline. In this subculture, the master's lineal instructions were most often seen as circumventing the laborious scriptural materials, so that the yogin could directly penetrate reality without the impediment of protracted textual investigation and interpretation. The precious instructions, handed down in a fragile lineage from the primordial Buddha Vajradhara directly to the master of the translator's teacher (or similarly short lineage), thus became the touchstone for the authentic instructions yielding liberation. And if the lineage of oral instruction became the *sine qua non* of siddha esoterism, then for Tibetans—and probably Indians as well—the shorter the lineage was between Vajradhara and the Tibetan translator, the less corrupted the system must be. Little wonder that in the eleventh and twelfth centuries, the sites of struggle were as much issues of lineage and oral instructions as they were of the authentically Buddhist nature of this or that scripture.

In one case, the discontinuities between fabulous claims made and what little can be known of the actual nature of the translators' lives were apparent. Marpa-lotsāwa Chökyi Lotrö was certainly one of the great exemplars of the period, and his hagiographical association with the siddha Nāropā has become a monument of Tibetan fictionalization. Tsang-nyön Heruka's (1452–1507) early-sixteenth-century hagiography of Marpa portrays the great translator in a manner appropriate to the Kagyüpa proclivity to fictionalize almost every aspects of its lineage, but few of the elements have a historical background. Even the widely accepted *Blue Annals'* dates for Marpa, 1012 to 1097, are not those of earlier or contemporary sources and are almost certainly incorrect. While many sources provide no dates at all—merely specifying Marpa's age at various junctures in his life—other sources accept that he was born in a bird (*bya*) year, which could place his birth in 1009 or 1021, with the latter date the more likely because of his early association with Drokmi.[84] Marpa's father and mother are given several names, possibly meaning that none of them are correct, an impression bolstered by the early sources, which do not identify his parents by name.

It may be true, though, that Marpa's parents or grandparents emigrated from Maryül (Ladakh) to Lho-drak, where he was born.[85] Marpa is represented by the best sources as being an impossible personality: continually fighting with others, in love with drinking beer, and talking incessantly. One hagiography has Marpa's father think that either he will kill someone or someone will kill him. Consequently, his parents, who evidently were wealthy, spent some of their assets on his education, sending him far away at the age of eleven to study with Drokmi. However, Drokmi required great presents for any teaching, and after three years Marpa decided to go to Nepal on his own to learn directly from Nepalese and Indians. As a teenage boy, Marpa traveled with a senior scholar, Nyö-lotsāwa Yönten-drak, and the Nyö clan records of the latter's life provide a good counterpoint to Marpa's more fictionalized record.[86]

According to Nyö-lotsāwa's account, the sixteen-year-old Marpa joined the fifty-five-year-old scholar and more than twenty other youths going to study in Nepal. In fact, Marpa probably received much of his instruction in Pharping, where the two (or four) Phamtingpa brothers—who were Nāropā's disciples—taught (figure 7). After some time in Nepal, they went to India together and eventually parted company, Marpa heading to the west and Nyö-lotsāwa to the east. Nyö-lotsāwa met one Baliṁ Ācārya and studied with him the tantric syllabus of the period, including the *Hevajra*, *Cakrasaṁvara*, *Mahāmāyā*, *Guhyasamāja*, and other tantras, their rituals, and commentaries. By the common Kagyüpa reckoning, Marpa went to study with Nāropā in Kashmir and eventually worked with thirteen paṇḍitas, including the mythically eccentric Kukuripa, who lived with his canine sexual partner on the shores of a lake of boiling hemlock poison, a curious residential decision. By the Nyö reckoning, they were gone for seven years and seven months, but Kagyüpa authors sometimes inflate Marpa's period of study to decades and make him superior to Nyö-lotsāwa at every turn.[87] There seemed to have been much animosity on the part of Marpa's chroniclers, for they depict Nyö-lotsāwa as a jealous and destructive traveling companion, throwing Marpa's books into a river and engaging in deceit. But there is little reason to believe this fable, and for their part the Nyö clan records treat Marpa with dignity.[88]

Part of the problem that has dogged Marpa's record is the fact that Nāropā died around 1040–42 and that Marpa was supposed to have spent twelve or

FIGURE 7 Pharping. Photograph by the author

more years with Nāropā during his three trips to India.[89] Even with an early birthdate for Marpa, this length of contact is difficult to justify. Although some scholars have tried to resolve this dilemma, the approved response seems to be to ignore the inconsistency altogether.[90] Some Kagyüpa writers even resorted to the expedient of having Marpa meet Nāropā *after* the latter's death during the Tibetan's third trip to India.[91] The question is germane, considering the testimony of the eminent Nagtso, the Tibetan who shouldered much of the responsibility for inviting Atiśa and guiding him through West and Central Tibet. His story is found in a letter written by Drakpa Gyeltsen in response to three questions put to him by a teacher from Kham, Jangchub Sengé, who indicated that there was a controversy as to whether Marpa ever actually met Nāropā. Drakpa Gyeltsen's response is illuminating:[92]

> Now in answer to your question on whether or not Marpa ever met the Lord Nāropā, because these [Kagyüpa] traditions have no source text (*lung*), they entirely rely on a chronicle (*lo rgyus*) and are hard to understand beyond the chronicle's presentation. However, Nagtso-lotsāwa had this to say:
>
> > Because I went alone as an insignificant monk to invite the Lord Atiśa—and since he tarried for one year as a result of an opportunity in Magadha—

I thought that I would go see the Lord Nāropā, since his reputation was so great. I went east from Magadha for a month, as I had heard that the lord was staying in the monastery known as Phullahari. Very great merit arose from being able to go see him.

On the day I arrived, they said some feudal prince had come to pay homage. So I went to the spot, and a great throne had been erected. I sat right in front of it. The whole crowd started buzzing, "The lord is coming!" I looked and the lord was physically quite corpulent, with his white hair [stained with henna] bright red and a vermilion turban bound on top. He was being carried [on a palanquin] by four men and chewing betel leaf. I grabbed his feet and thought, "I should listen to his pronouncements!" Stronger and stronger people, though, pushed me farther and farther from his seat, and finally I was tossed out of the crowd. So, there I saw the lord's face but did not actually hear his voice.

Then, returning [to Magadha] Lord Atiśa and I—master and disciple—stayed in the Kathmandu Valley for a year [1041/42]. At that time we heard that Lord Nāropā had set down the burden of his body and his mind had passed to the celestial *ḍākinīs*, who accompanied him with divine cymbals. Even at the cremation site, there were many miraculous offerings, such as the sound of divine cymbals and a rain of flowers. Then we stayed for three years in Ngari in Western Tibet [1042–45]and then came east and stayed in Gungtang for a year [1045/6]. Again I came down east to Nyétang, since Lord Atiśa was teaching the Dharma. There Marpa Lotrö listened a few sessions and left.

People have said that having met Lord (Nāropā), he listened to the Dharma a long time. I heard the unimpeachable story through a direct source that Marpa did not say that. Marpa's own disciple, while he was at Pen-yül, was Tsangdar Dépa Yéshé. He said, "What others say about my teacher and Lord Nāropā meeting, he himself said, 'I never arrived there (Phullahari)!' My teacher [Marpa] heard all of his instructions from Nāropā's direct disciple Gaṅga Metrīpa." Now I myself heard this statement from one of Dépa Yéshé's own disciples.

[Drakpa Gyeltsen continues:] So, it is not certain that Marpa made these claims for himself. There is a song, said to be Marpa's which makes the claim [about meeting Nāropā], but Ngok Chökyi Dorjé, Mé-tsönpo Sönam Gyeltsen, etc., do not maintain this lyric. Instead, it was maintained by a yogin from Ngom-shö who spread it about. Many know it not to have been written by Marpa himself. Now while Mila Repa accepted the verse, according to Ngendzong Repa's testimony it does not appear that the song was written by Mila himself. Those who know it as not being Marpa's would counter anyone saying that it was his by pointing out the fact that the lyric is internally contradictory and was written by someone with no knowledge of India, since many errors concerning the country occur in it.

Thus it is clear that it is not Marpa's words (and that Marpa did not visit Nāropā).

Generally, lies and falsification reject both reason and scripture.
If everything commonly said is accomplished, just however,
Then there will be little attention to the well spoken [truth].
Since this is the evil time, the barbarian [Turk] king is victorious in Magadha.
He falsifies religion and spreads it [Islam] all over, vilifying true practitioners.
If you wish to meet excellent personalities, but cannot because of local misfortune,
Then if you practice the true Dharma correctly, you certainly will meet a real servant of the Lord of Sages [Śākyamuni].

If this is true, and Marpa principally studied with Newar and Indian disciples of Nāropā, it would answer many of the questions often asked about inconsistencies in the literature surrounding these figures.[93] For example, some of the colophons of Marpa's translations have them translated at Nāropā's retreat in Puṣpahari, in Kashmir, whereas others simply specify that P[h]ullahari was Nāropā's monastery.[94] Phullahari was Nāropā's retreat, but it was in East India (Bihar or Bengal), not in Kashmir, and whoever concocted the colophons was either unaware of that fact or attempted to gain credibility by transforming *pulla/phulla* (*phullā*: "in blossom") into *puṣpa* (simply "flower") and placing it in Kashmir. This association may have been the result of Nyö-lotsāwa's depiction of Marpa as having studied in the west, but the Nyö record also makes no mention of Nāropā.

Surrounded by Kashmiri Paṇḍitas in the late eleventh or early twelfth century, it was either inconceivable or uncomfortable to Kagyüpa authorities that Nāropā was probably Bengali. Tsuglak Trengwa attributes the source of the Kashmiri ascription to the *Instructions on Convergence and Transference* (*Sre 'pho'i zhal gdams*) of Ngok Chökyi Dorjé (1023–90) and acknowledges that it does not fit with the tradition of the Rechung's Oral Transmission (*Ras chung snyan rgyud*), which affirms the specifically Bengali location of Nāropā's hermitage.[95] It is clear that wherever Nāropā lived, the early Kagyüpa authors did know that Marpa's association with the Bengali siddha was tenuous, so it became important to identify the place of Marpa's study with the site of Nāropā's retreat.

These efforts were actually successful, and Gampopa accepted the identity of Nāropā's monastery as Puṣpahari in Kashmir, despite traces of an anomaly in the lineage with Thar-pa lam-tön (? *Mokṣamārga-panthaka) intervening between Nāropā and Marpa.[96] Various authorities' clumsy attempts at resolving the irresolvable simply demonstrate the probable veracity of Nagtso's observation about Marpa's career and highlight the efforts a lineage was willing to make in order to shorten the distance between the premier siddha Nāropā and the Kagyüpa translator of great merit, Marpa.

It may also be noted that there is implicit in Drakpa Gyeltsen's letter the expectation that a legitimate siddha lineage coming into Tibet will have three components: a song (*glu*), a story (*lo rgyus*), and a text (*lung*). This was true for the Sakya Lamdré as well and seems to be the standard observed in some other lineages. Drakpa Gyeltsen also appears to believe that a specific text was lacking for the special transmissions that the Kagyüpa obtained through Marpa, although the great translator certainly had many texts that he transmitted. Thus, for Drakpa Gyeltsen and perhaps others, the entirely oral nature of some of the instructions seems to have been a problem, and we again note the importance of physical realia to the affirmations of authenticity. Ralo's possession of Padmavajra's ritual implements and of *Kuṇḍa Bhāro's statue of Vajrabhairava, along with the text of the secret magical instructions, categorically demonstrate the authentic transmission of the Dharma. As we will see later, the fame of Sakya Monastery in Tsang was much facilitated by Bari-lotsāwa's assiduous relic collecting, and the trade in relics became important to establish a public persona for these specific sacred sites.

Whatever the source of his training, Marpa was very well received when he returned to Lho-drak, and he was offered his choice of land. He chose to live a bit upstream from the old site of Khon-ting, an ancient temple founded by the first emperor Songtsen Gampo and the locus of much of the religious revitalization through textual discoveries of treasure texts in the twelfth century. Marpa's fame and family position in Lho-drak ensured him a place at the political table, and he was made chieftain (*gtso bo*) of the area on his return. Ultimately, he built two residences, his principal home at Drowo-lung and a tower of nine stories for his sons. The tower, called the Nine-Storied Sons' Fortress (Sékhar Gutok, figure 8) is indicative of the unrest in late-eleventh-century Tibet, for fortified citadels were seldom constructed without necessity. Ultimately, Marpa was able to aggregate to himself a Mormon-like harem of nine sexual consorts and to father seven sons. Unfortunately, with the exception of his eldest, Darma Dodé, who died early (Ralo claimed responsibility for his death), the rest of his sons were not able to build on Marpa's religious empire. We are even treated to the unsavory image of one of Marpa's sons gambling

FIGURE 8 Sékhar Gutok. After a photograph by Richardson

away his father's bone relics in a game of chance; they were later collected by Ngok Dodé, who took responsibility for constructing Marpa's mausoleum. The Kagyüpa chroniclers acknowledge the unfortunate nature of Marpa's progeny by saying that Nāropā prophesied that Marpa's familial line would disappear like an illusory flower in the sky while his religious lineage would run like a river through the world, both of which proved to be true.[97]

GRAY TEXTS, NEW TRANSLATION APOCRYPHA, AND ZHAMA CHÖKYI GYELPO

From this vantage point, the later editorial efforts at constructing an artificial lineage appear curious and potentially counterproductive. But they were effective—as seen in the Kagyüpa case—for despite the evidence, the Tibetans were so invested in these translators that they eventually swept aside contrary indications. In reality, the willingness of Central Tibetans to provide carte blanche to Tibetan translators eventually permitted a rather dramatic redefinition of what constitutes an authentic Buddhist text. During the royal dynastic period, the great convocation called by Trihdé Songtsen attempted to establish policy for all translations, or at least imperially sponsored ones. Esoteric literature was first on the list of knotty problems, and the drift of the discussion was that because this literature was esoteric, it should not be revealed to just anyone, for this contradicted the texts themselves. Accordingly, only certain texts were allowed to be translated.[98] The discussion presumed that esoteric literature was found in the form of physical texts, spoken by the Buddha, and that the texts of the tantras were themselves the most esoteric, the most problematic, and therefore the most closely guarded.

All these presumptions were called into question in the new translation period. Perhaps the best examples of the systematic subversion of these categories were exactly the esoteric meditative directions (*upadeśa*: *gdams ngag*), said to be revealed by the gnostic *ḍākinīs*—one of the varieties of *ḍākinīs*—frequently in the (mythic) land of Oḍiyāna, and handed to a siddha, who brought these instructions to Tibet.[99] In the eleventh century, these directions functionally supplanted the tantric scriptures themselves yet did not claim to be the word of the or a Buddha, even though they were accorded the highest authority. Clearly, the text of the Lamdré, discussed in the next chapter, was of this variety. The myth of Virūpa presented this work as a formal text, handed from the goddess Nairātmyā to Virūpa, then to Kāṇha, and on down through the lineage to Gayādhara, who eventually transported it to Tibet as an oral text. Other esoteric works "translated" into Tibetan were far less well authenticated than even that, for many of these came to Tibet not as actual texts but as the insight revealed to a siddha, who transported it to Tibet and then articulated it to a translator, who rendered the insight into Tibetan. Works like these were thus very far from the normative model of an Indian text, a work understood in India, written in an Indic language, employed in India centers of Buddhist praxis, and then transported to Tibet so that it could be practiced on the roof of the world. We have no evidence, in reality, that many of these instructional "texts" ever existed in India. But their esoteric public aura became so overwhelming that great sums of money were gained from their transmission, and Drokmi (for one) tried to corner the market in teaching the Lamdré, not to mention other works.

I would like to deem these texts "gray," for they are neither definitely Indian nor identifiably Tibetan.[100] Unlike the some of the clearly apocryphal works written in the tenth and eleventh centuries during the period of fragmentation and used in the Nyingma tradition, the new translation quasi apocrypha cannot be so easily dismissed as solely Tibetan compositions. Rather, they appear to be the result of the collaboration of an Indian/Nepalese/Kashmiri siddha/scholar with a Tibetan having excellent training in Indic languages. In this instance, gray texts are formulated with the requirements of the specific Indian yogin and individual Tibetan in mind, so that each is well served in his needs by the "translations" of such "texts" that were probably only thematic issues in the minds of the South Asian paṇḍita before he crossed that final high pass into the Tibetan plateau. These texts, however, are not simply fabrications for personal gain or self-aggrandizement, although these factors are sometimes all too apparent. Rather, they represent the continual unfoldment of the Buddhist esoteric tradition in another sociogeographical environment, decidedly on a continuum with the composition of the tantras and esoteric instructional works in India itself. Whereas the tantras derive from the encounter of the normative Indic Buddhist tradition with regional factors—outcaste, tribal, and other groups—these gray texts are the encounter of that same tradition with a new region: Tibet. Thus, they are apocryphal in the sense that they are not what they represent themselves to be, but then very few Indian Buddhist scriptures or other compositions actually are precisely what they are represented to be. Conversely, these new works are authentic in that they demonstrate the method of continual composition under the specific circumstances of Buddhist insight embedded in both a time and a place.

Excellent examples of gray texts are those composed by the collaborative production of Padampa Sangyé Kamalaśīla and Zhama Chökyi Gyelpo in the latter part of the eleventh and the early twelfth century. They are good test cases for two reasons. First, there are several of them. Zhama-lotsāwa was responsible for many translations of siddha-related literature, in which the teachings and identity of siddhas are curious or clearly unlike known Indic models. Second, the Zhama translations were employed in the Zhiché lineages that sputtered on for a while, but without the great institution building of other traditions. His sister, Zhama Macik, became a notable figure in the history of the Lamdré and was representative of the position that Tibetan women sometimes could hold, in contrast to the greater difficulties experienced by Indian women. Yet the Zhama tradition of Lamdré did not become institutionalized in the way that the Khön clan did, so that by the sixteenth century it was merely a footnote in Lamdré history. Like his sister, Zhama-lotsāwa was not able to establish a long-lived system of practice based on the teachings received from the enigmatic Indian teacher. Indeed, in the standard hagiographies of Padampa Sangyé, Zhama-lotsāwa is only a footnote, if even that.[101] Consequently, there has been little investment in reorienting the hagiographical material, editing its colophons and the rest of the institutional procedure visible in the case of the ostensible relationship between Nāropā and Marpa.

Zhama-lotsāwa was responsible for fifteen translations of esoteric instructions and hagiographies that are consecutively included in the canon (To. 2439–53), and others are represented in an extracanonical collection.[102] None of the texts is long, but much the same could be said of so many of the works that have proved to be instrumental in the formation of eleventh- to twelfth-century Tibetan esoterica. Most interesting, however, is the claim of many of them to have been extracted directly from the Secret Treasury of the Ḍākinīs (*ḍākinī-guhyakośa*: *mkha' 'gro gsang mdzod*) by Padampa and transmitted to Zhama-lotsāwa, who translated them as is. For example, the colophon to the *Śrī-Vajraḍākinīgītā*:[103]

> The Sign of the Ḍākinī in Five Fascicles—In conference with the Chieftainess of the Element, it was given to Lord Dampa the Indian from its residence as a roll of paper in the Secret Treasury. Subsequently, one in attendance in Dingri, Zhama-lotsāwa translated it and entrusted it to the bodhisattva Kunga. This is the completion of the fourfold signs from the distinguished eight great songs.

While the Zhiché and Chö systems of Padampa are examined in later chapters, here the nexus of paṇḍita and lotsāwa are viewed in a different light. In these descriptions, many of the distinguishing characteristics—a roll of paper extracted from a hidden treasury, a secret guardian, a chosen reveler who is not the actual person writing down the material—appear to be on a continuum with the contemporary phenomenon of the Tibetan treasure tradition. Equally, we find certain anomalous forms in Zhama's texts; for example, the expansion of siddhas to a list of 381 personalities in one work appears to be the only text anywhere to include more than eighty-five names in a siddha list.[104]

Based on these and other instances, we must wonder whether some new translation personalities were composing new materials under the influence of Indic patterns, much as the older Nyingma system clearly did. Although no one text definitively demonstrates a larger movement toward Sarma apocrypha, collectively the drift is undeniable. The dozens of new translation materials that may be simply the product of the Indian/Tibetan nexus—including some of the more famous of the secret teachings transmitted to Tibetan translators by esoteric Indian masters—appear to have been credulously accepted by their initial representatives, even though their ultimate source was unclear or sometimes disputed. The creative process of translation here worked closely with the creative process of religious inspiration and imagination. Little wonder that the introduction of the great volume of esoteric materials during this period called for a response on many fronts.

THE INVENTION OF NEOCONSERVATIVE ORTHODOXY

If some of the later tradition appears willing to suspend critical reflection on the scriptures coming from India and elsewhere from the tenth to twelfth centuries, certain individuals actually operating in this time were not so credulous. We have seen that there were problems of behavior, viewed as from either Tibetan misunderstanding or the introduction of non-Buddhist practices into Tibet. Likewise, throughout this period specific authors tried to differentiate among textual materials that were actually Indian, actually Buddhist, and authentically in the tradition—a procedure that questioned the Indic bases of many works then circulating in Tibet. Predominantly because of later polemics, scholars are used to thinking of the challenge to textual authenticity as a function of the new, authentic, Indic esoteric scriptures challenging the received wisdom of the older apocryphal scriptures of the Nyingma, but this is certainly not always the case for the eleventh or twelfth century.[105] However, the proponents of the newer scriptures eventually were successful in using their own standards to judge the authority of the older system, and the displacement of many older scriptures from the accepted sphere of legitimacy resulted in the formation of two esoteric canons: the tantric section of the approved canon (*bKa' 'gyur*), on the one hand, and the *Old Tantric Canon* (*rNying ma rgyud 'bum*), on the other. Such a model, however, is largely represented through the lens of fourteenth- and fifteenth-century canonical discussions featuring such figures as Butön, Chomden Rigrel, and Ratna Lingpa. The nature of earlier scriptural polemics was a little more complex, and two statements of textual authenticity, both from the second half of the eleventh century, are the *Disputing Perverse Mantric Texts* (*sNgags log sun 'byin*) of Gö-lotsāwa Khukpa Lhétsé and the *Proclamation* (*bKa' shog*) of Podrang Shiwa-Ö.[106]

The *Disputing Perverse Mantric Texts* is the earliest surviving work to emphasize scripture to this degree, although a work of the same name and similar content attributed to Rinchen Zangpo has not yet been located. Rinchen Zangpo's text may have been allied with the position of the Gugé ruler Lhalama Yéshé-Ö, for Sogdokpa Lotrö Gyeltsen subsumes it as such in his defense of the Nyingma system during the late sixteenth or early seventeenth century.[107] As its name indicates, the *Disputing Perverse Mantric Texts* is a challenge to texts representing themselves as authentic scriptures of the Mantrayāna. Gö-lotsāwa opens with a presentation of the degeneration of time, following the Hindu scheme of the Kṛtya-, Treta-, Dvāpara-, and Kali-yugas, which had replaced the Buddhist eon system in Vajrayāna hermeneutics to justify a four-category system of the tantric canon. Gö-lotsāwa's point is that we should expect all sorts of false teachings during this age of degeneration. For example, a Tibetan chronology of the preaching of the Highest Yoga tantras—112 years after the Buddha's parinirvāṇa—is refuted as unknown in India.

After gliding through the early translation period, Gö-lotsāwa turns to the principal works of the Nyingma—the Holy Word (Kahma) transmissions of the Mahāyoga, Anuyoga, and mental class of Atiyoga (*mdo sgyu sems gsum*). According to Gö-lotsāwa, the royal dynastic translator Ma Rinchen-chok composed the *Guhyagarbha* (*gSang snying*) and other *Māyājāla* works of the Mahāyoga corpus. Pagor Bairotsana composed the five texts of the mental class of Atiyoga.[108] Nub Sangyé Rinchen composed the **Adbhūta* (*rMad du byung ba*) works which, when added to the previous five, brings the mental-class materials in the basic canon to eighteen.[109] Aro Yéshé Jungné conspired on the commentarial works of the mental class, and Darchen-pel fabricated the Anuyoga works. Sangyé Rinpoché composed some of the central works on the deities of the Eight Pronouncements (*bka' brgyad*), with other Tibetans filling in the texts on the Mothers (*ma mo*), and so forth. Their method involved a combination of using non-Buddhist sources and doctrines and mixing them together through these authors' own conceptions. The defining characteristic of Tibetan fabrications is that they are unknown to Indic Paṇḍitas when they are asked about these works.

There are some curiosities about this polemic attributed to Gö-lotsāwa. For example, the received versions make no reference to Treasure literature (Terma), which is to be of great concern to the later refutations of Chaglo Chöjé-pel and Butön.[110] This certainly does not mean that such literature did not exist at this time but that it appears not to be considered a separate category of apocrypha. Second, it is clear that Gö-lotsāwa does not condemn early translations per se, for he validates many of the renderings done during the royal dynastic period, questioning only those that did not satisfy his criterion that they be known to current Indians. It also is apparent that he condemned, as many of the later neo-conservatives did, authentically Indic works along with those certainly Tibetan in origin. The most celebrated example is the *Guhyagarbha*, which he ascribed to Ma Rinchen-chok.[111] A later Nyingma apologist, Sogdokpa, took great pains to point out that not only was a Sanskrit manuscript of this work from Samyé obtained by Chomden Rigrel but that a second manuscript was secured by Lowo-lotsāwa Pelden Jangchub from Stham Bihār in Kathmandu, the same institution founded by Atiśa. This second manuscript was ostensibly made the basis of another translation by one Maṇika Śrījñāna, and the Pukdrak canon preserves an alternative translation by Tarpa-lotsāwa.[112]

The other eleventh-century work, the *Proclamation* of Podrang Shiwa-Ö, Karmay dates to 1092.[113] This is an interesting work, for it narrows the category of authenticity. Not only are specifically Nyingma apocrypha cast aside, but works of excellent Indic pedigree are castigated as well. Shiwa-Ö, a royal prince of Gugé-Purang who took the monastic precepts in the manner of some of his predecessors, claimed that some of these materials were not conducive to liberation and identified all of them as "Tibetan in composition," even though it is clear that an Indian, the notorious red master (*atsarya dmar po*), promulgated many of them and six are said to be his compositions.[114] Actually, many of these were simply later *yoginī-tantras* or their offshoots, and some of the *Tilaka-tantras* or related texts were so included, such as the *Mahāmudrā-tilaka-tantra*, the *Rahasyānanda-tilaka*, the *Jñāna-garbha*, and the *Jñāna-tilaka*. Well-accepted standard works of esoteric practice, such as the *Pañcakrama*, also are identified as inauthentic. The most interesting titles among the "inauthentic texts" are ten works of diverse origin, all discussing aspects of Mahāmudrā, and were exactly the kinds of works with which Zhama and Marpa were concerned. All together, they provide us with a perspective on Shiwa-Ö, that he was less concerned with the standards applied by Gö-lotsāwa about the same time and considered that the works in question were deleterious to Tibetans' practice of the monastic path, so they should be eliminated. Shiwa-Ö concluded this section by warning that the coded language (*sandhyā-bhāṣā*) of the *Mother-tantras* (i.e., *yoginī-tantras*) was misunderstood by monks, who were breaking their vows as a result. Thus the continuing tension between the graphic language and antinomian practices of the siddha scriptures was especially problematic to this scion of the West Tibetan royal house.

Consequently, when the question of orthodoxy is considered, the neoconservative view really occupies one of two perspectives. On one hand, a work, teaching, or ritual is deemed authentic if it is Indian in origin, although this is sometimes difficult to determine. On the other hand, the work, teaching, or ritual may be considered inauthentic, irrespective of its origin. This latter instance was exemplified by Dromtön when he rather curtly requested Atiśa not to discuss the siddhas' *dohā* verses, for they might corrupt Tibetan morals, and the same argument is encountered almost half a century later with Shiwa-Ö. It is important to understand that the neoconservative position is not necessarily scholastic, although it was eventually adopted by the greatest of scholastics, Sakya Paṇḍita. Instead, it represents a greatly restricted image of the authentic Dharma, and this idealized perception might be held as much by tantric authorities as by scholastic professors. This very idea is only marginally Buddhist, however, for Indians had always kept to the ideal of a canon with indeterminate limits. This is the reason that they—unlike the Chinese and Tibetans—never once compiled a closed catalog of scriptures of the Buddha's word.[115] The neoconservative position was also not necessarily appropriated by Sarma translators, for many like Ralo or Drokmi formed alliances or pursued enemies based on personal rather than sectarian or literary lines.

THE CULT AND CULTURE OF KNOWLEDGE

Finally, in the eleventh century, Tibetans became obsessed with all forms of knowledge, which affected both the older school and the new dispensation. In the final analysis, the translators did not simply translate for purposes of self-presentation and personal aggrandizement, even if these elements were factors for some esoteric masters. Rather, once the political order—and its ability to pacify fractious elements—was stabilized, the translators' efforts were driven mainly by the overwhelming social value placed on the new forms of knowledge to which Tibetans were exposed. From the late tenth through the twelfth century, Tibetans longed for all things knowable in the wide world, as if the intellectual famine of the previous era required satiation, like some colossal dragon suddenly waking voracious from a lengthy repose. They devoured all forms of knowledge, seemingly for its own sake, importing experts in every variety of discipline available in India and Central Asia. Starting in the eleventh century, the four horns of Tibet seemed awash with masters helping translate texts on literature, art, medicine, hippology, polity, prosody, astrology, and a variety of other topics. Their success at this endeavor should be acknowledged, for until 1959, Tibet was widely considered the locus of esoteric knowledge, and Tibetans were uniquely successful all across Asia in promoting themselves as the sole stewards of secret understanding.

Esoteric studies were front and center in this process, the main—if sometimes indigestible—course for the knowledge-starved Tibetans. In this regard, the newly translated esoteric scriptures provided an all-embracing rubric of knowledge, a cognitive term (*jñāna*) in which knowledge became the sign for both cultural success and spiritual accomplishment. If we consider the number of scriptures included in the canon with *jñāna* in the title, we arrive at a total of twenty. It is astonishing to realize that the majority of them were only translated during a few decades in the middle of the eleventh century. If we take out the one short esoteric spell text (To. 522 *Jñānolkadhāraṇī*), the three versions of scriptures to Amitāyus (To. 674–76), and the three Mahāyāna sūtras with gnosis in the title translated during the early period (To. 100, 122, 131), then all the other works were translated by masters working in the early to middle eleventh century.[116] Of these, only the *Mañjuśrīnāmasaṁgīti* was translated at other times as well.[117] It is clear that something was afoot, and the process was driven by a degree of selectivity.

Rongzom Chözang's mid-eleventh-century claim (discussed in chapter 6) that Indians would compose texts according to topical popularity might even be considered here, for six short tantras having "gnosis" in their title were translated by Drokmi, who certainly could have used this material to his advantage. Such a process would still verify (and in fact authenticate) the Tibetans' overwhelming interest in the topic of knowledge, but the issue is somewhat muddied by the evidence that other short tantras of this variety remained untranslated in the Sarma period. The recent publication of the *Arising of Gnosis Scripture* (*Jñānodaya-tantra*) demonstrates that the archive was not exhausted, assuming that this work had already been composed in either India or Nepal, for it had not been translated into Tibetan so far as the editors could tell.[118] It is thus probable that the various works on gnosis, with which these translators seemed especially concerned, were actually selected and translated from a larger archive of texts on the topic, texts that were not pursued with the same alacrity either in the early period or at a later date.

Titles, certainly, do not make the work, and sometimes the relationship between the issues implied by the titles of esoteric texts and their actual contents is tenuous at best. Nonetheless, we should understand that such titles are merely the tip of the proverbial iceberg, for gnosis, awareness, and the various varieties of knowledge are often found in other esoteric works as well. Indeed, whole sections of tantras are dedicated to the topic of gnosis (*jñāna*)—or sometimes "innate" gnosis (*sahajajñāna*)—a fact apparent to readers of the *yoginī-tantras* in particular.[119] The relationship between this new class of literature and intuitions about gnosis/knowledge was sufficiently important in India for Ratnākaraśānti, Advayavajra, and other figures to feature the topic in their commentaries and treatises on the genre. Eventually this direction led to a chapter in the final great scripture of esoteric Buddhism in India, the *Kālacakra-tantra*, which, however, had little influence on Tibetan tantric intellectuals until the early part of the twelfth century.

While space prevents an extended discussion, the Buddhist term "gnosis" has attributes that differentiate it from that other great Buddhist cognitive term, "insight" (*prajñā*). Insight, most explicitly embodied in the scriptures of the Perfection of Insight (*Prajñāpāramitā*), could not satisfy the need for knowledge, since the primary orientation of these sacred works was that of deconstructing positive associations with the absolute, so that all elements of reality are understood as empty of their own nature. This direction may have been profitable during the stable period of the Gupta and Vākāṭaka hegemonies in South Asia, during which knowledge of the wider world seemed to gush into the very porous borders of India. But by the eleventh century in Tibet, these texts were closely associated with postmortem practices—reading the Perfection of Insight scriptures or making copies were among the most popular of Buddhist death rituals. Moreover, the contents of the Perfection of Insight scriptures did not seem to speak of the exciting world at large; it merely told the Tibetans what they already knew, that they did not understand the nature of reality.

Conversely, the esoteric tantras revealed previously unknown dimensions of the world—languages, medicine, the nature of the internal body, cosmology, new and mysterious scripts, unpronounceable words, astrological calculations, rituals for longevity and political dominion and sexual potency, to name but a few. This all was seemingly good utilitarian material, which was put in exciting language and promoted by the most sophisticated civilization available to Tibetans: India. Even better, it was organized under headings that promised both discrete knowledge and ultimate salvation (*jñāna*) for this term carried both associations in Indian Buddhism. A bodhisattva is supposed to accumulate knowledge (*jñānasambhāra*) on the early stages of the path, and the realization of the five forms of gnosis (*pañcajñāna*) is extolled as the secret of liberation, so that he would obtain the knowledge of all things in all modes (*sarvākārajñatā*). *Jñāna*, in fact, became so closely associated with forms of discrete knowledge that a controversy in the mid-eleventh century erupted as to whether there was *jñāna* at the level of the Buddha, what varieties were present, or whether he superseded its need. Writers from Rongzom on considered the emerging urgency of questions of gnoseology, discussing whether gnosis/knowledge could be both the means and the goal of religious life.[120] In all these discussions, there is little question why Tibetan were so fascinated: what could be more appealing to a culture feeling that it was emerging from a fractured darkness than to be greeted with a gift of knowledge?

CONCLUSION: THE TRANSLATOR AS PROMETHEUS

If the later spread of the Dharma represented the opportunity to import new systems of religiosity or practices of yoga—and translate the new "speech of the Buddha"—it also inaugurated a time fraught with difficulty and uncertainty. At this time, Central Tibetans were reviving ancient learning, reemerging from a time of psychological, if not physical, darkness, and reacquainting themselves with a world that once had seemed at their beck and call. They could have jettisoned the remnants of Indian Buddhism, adopted Chinese varieties, accepted Allah as the One God, or simply done nothing other than continued to fashion a few new ritual and visionary systems in service of the aristocracy. After all, Afghans and Central Asians had had Buddhism longer than the Tibetans had, and the Mongols had supported Buddhism for about 150 years, yet they all yielded in turn to the call or coercion of other religions.

There was no reason and every reason for Central Tibetans to seek out and reinvent Tibetan Buddhism.

The works of the tenth and eleventh centuries give the irresistible impression that Tibetans were searching for both empowerment and understanding. Individuals and clans sought to empower themselves in a world chaotic and potentially hostile, by seeking the identity of the microcosmic yoga and macrocosmic maṇḍala. The rituals procured and propitiated by Ralo, the emphasis on Newar magical formulas, the attention to yogic systems, and the continual significance of magic powers speak of a people seeking the chimera of control. For many Tibetans, the translation of the multiple killing rituals from their Indian masters, as well as the record of their use, was eloquent testimony to a category of Buddhists suspicious of their environment and wary of their fellow man. Likewise, the clear enactment of sexual yoga by select translators reinforced the drift from celibacy, and the resultant progeny among aristocratic clansmen—as in the case of Marpa's children—buttressed the Tibetan predisposition to unify religious, social, and political lines of descent, so that charisma, domain, authority, and dominion were seen as being on a continuum.

There was light at the end of that tunnel. In his acknowledgment of the profound influence that learning had on his age, Boccacio referred to the learned scholar as the second Prometheus, bringing a new fire to the civilization in defiance of the gods.[121] Certainly the translators were accorded analogous respect and honor, if they sometimes (like Prometheus) had to suffer the consequences of their hubris. While the tenth and eleventh centuries in Central Tibet were still far removed from the eloquent panegyric to learning found at the beginning of Butön's *History of the Dharma* (1322), we can understand the impact that the refined intellect and polished mind must have had on those holding merely political power.[122] Indeed, the gathering of translators and scholars in Toling in 1076 seemed like an event to herald a new age, as it was treated by the participants in their later descriptions.[123] They had succeeded where their predecessors had not: they had formed stable institutions already lasting a century and gaining acceptance amid the broader populace on a daily basis; they had developed the means to ensure that their values were embodied in these institutions; and they had developed a critique of indigenous composition so that the true Dharma of India would reign supreme.

In the process, they attempted to fashion a new textual culture in Ü-Tsang, one that held the literary standards of contemporary India as the paradigm for sanctity, elegance, and interpretation.[124] Indic works became the textual icons for the age, so that their patterns of introduction, exegesis, and recapitulation became the models for Tibetan imitation. From this, however, no single textual community formed in Tibet, since the entrenched Tibetan narratives, the rapid indigenous scriptural composition, the disparate lineages from India, and the common experience with the Eastern Vinaya curriculum all worked against uniformity in textual reference. Consequently, Tibetans never arrived at a common tantric syllabus and so did not succeed in establishing—beyond doubt or challenge—that one body of lore represented the supreme pinnacle of the Buddhist world. In this they stood alongside many other Buddhist cultures and in stark contrast to the European experience.

Perhaps the new emphasis on gnosis (*jñāna*) and self-awareness (*rang gi rig pa*) found in the literature evolving from the tenth to the twelfth century is a function of these trajectories. Although the new learning and its expanding cognitive potentials must have appeared in a peculiar way to be far superior to the previous times, Tibetans simply could not relinquish their glorious past. The drama of this time may even have blinded Tibetans to the simple reality that once developed, learning must be maintained. When reading over the hagiographies of the translators, one is struck time and again that the decision to institutionalize classical language studies, so clearly influential during the Italian Renaissance and beyond, was not to be reproduced by Tibetans within Tibet. Like the derivation of European civilization from the classical Greek and Roman worlds, the Tibetan horizon was dependent on the importation of religious and intellectual models from India, but evidently little attempt was made to institutionalize Sanskrit learning in Tibet. Even though Tibetans had the books in monastery repositories—Samyé, Ngor, Retreng, Sakya—and great archives and enclaves of scholars of Sanskrit Buddhism living in Nepal, the majority of Tibetan clerics simply elected to memorize the translations rather than either read the remnants of the originals or again dip into the ocean of Sanskrit literature. Except for the occasional eccentric individual who traveled to Nepal, Sanskrit study was effectively dead in Tibet by the late fourteenth century.

Yet the translators also sought out and employed their training in part for personal empowerment. For them, their intelligence and learning were tools to ends. The translators were the stars of the evolving culture of Central Tibet, and they knew it. At this juncture, any similarity between these figures and the great writers of the Italian Renaissance must be called into question. The tantric literature translators of eleventh-century Central Tibet all too often interpreted the Buddhist ideal of individual liberation as a personal license to be flaunted. Those who subscribed to this value had poorly internalized their lessons in the great monasteries of Magadha, Bengal, and Kashmir and instead emphasized the religion on the margins. Rather than applying themselves to the perfect accomplishment of gnosis, they turned to the goals already apparent in the worldview of politically and culturally fragmented Tibet: control, dominion, authority, power, and punishment. While there were many self-effacing scholars in the Tibetan Samgha—Nagtso-lotsāwa comes immediately to mind—most of them did not concentrate on the Mantrayāna but were specialists in epistemology or the bodhisattva path. Thus the tantric translators—preeminently Drokmi-lotsāwa and his peers—represented the real embodiment of the nonduality of this world (with all its dreams and challenges) and the absolute.

5

Drokmi: The Doyen of Central Tibetan Translators

Our minds have little experience in the ocean of Sanskrit language. So that beings, though, might obtain the eye of nonreferential gnosis, we have translated the maṇḍalas, mantras, rituals and mudrās, that others might come to be kings of the Vidyādharas.

Even though we have faith in this text and a desire to benefit others, since we made questionable translations and affirmed the work, may the *ḍākinīs* have patience with our errors, for we have not yet obtained the saintly path.

—Translators' colophon by Drokmi and Gayādhara to Durjayacandra's *Suparigraha-maṇḍalavidhi-sādhana*[1]

Not all the early translators were as emblematic of the tension between the royal dynastic lineages and the new translation systems as Gö-lotsāwa Khukpa Lhétsé. Many were simply not concerned with the polemical field and its consequences. Others refrained from becoming de facto or de jure feudal lords in their respective valleys, and most did not gain a reputation for excessive behavior. Nonetheless, most of the new translators held a common value: the form of the Buddhadharma being translated from current Indic sources was preferable to that which had remained in Tibet throughout the earlier period of fragmentation and occlusion. Moreover, they all had proved their intellectual—if not their spiritual—skills in the process of articulating the spectrum of Buddhist texts into the literary language of classical Tibetan, a language in many ways as foreign to native Tibetan speakers as it is to non-Tibetans.

Drokmi Shākya Yéshé, the primary translator of the *Hevajra-tantra* systems, was a master of this literary language (figure 9). As in the instances of

FIGURE 9 Drokmi-lotsāwa Shākya Yéshé.
After a detail of a sixteenth-century painting

most other Tibetan lotsāwas, he was required to spend long years in difficult conditions in India, studying with Indians who may not have cared for his Tibetan habits, and saddled with the expectations of the local princes who had sent him. He found it necessary to master at least two of the Indic literary languages and needed to spend great amounts of time in ritual and meditative studies, beyond the linguistic and philosophical backgrounds necessary. His pioneering activity in Bihar and Bengal was carried out after an acclimation period in Nepal, yet he found the Indic esoteric system sufficiently challenging that even after years in India, he continued his studies with excellent scholars at his home in Tsang. Drokmi was, in many was, an exemplary representative of the translation process, for in the period of his translation activity in Tibet he managed to produce accurate and even polished translations of some of the most influential of the esoteric scriptures in Tibetan religious life. We must assess his scholarly contribution in the most positive terms: his oeuvre is massive and complex; his translations demonstrated a sophisticated understanding of the grammar and intent of his Sanskrit and Apabhraṁśa sources; and his classical Tibetan was, at times, as good as it gets.

In other ways, though, Drokmi's career was quite uncharacteristic of the early translators. His background was nomadic rather than aristocratic or even agricultural. Drokmi was in fact an exceptional personality whose avariciousness and requirements for large amounts of gold and other initiatory presents became legendary in his area and in his time. This facet of his persona eventually passed into popular Tibetan literature, which represents Drokmi as the quintessential greedy lama.[2] Suspicious of competition, he begged his Indian cohort not to give out the Lamdré to anyone else in Tibet, thus assuring himself a monopoly on this most esoteric of teachings. Likewise, he did not allow any of his disciples to obtain from him his full range of learning, making sure that those who received meditative instructions did not gain access to the larger literary corpus, and vice versa. Like a good master strategist, he divided his legacy and conquered his disciples. As a result, we have the Lamdré in its current form because of both Drokmi's personal manipulation of the system and his disciples' ultimate capacity to defeat his best efforts.

This chapter considers in fair detail the career of Drokmi Shākya Yéshé and his primary partner in the transmission of Hevajra systems into Tibet, Kāyastha Gayādhara.[3] The central record of the Sakyapa—Drakpa Gyeltsen's *Chronicle of Tibet*—is translated and discussed, examined for both what it says and what it does not. We also look at the content of the most esoteric text Drokmi is reputed to have translated with Gayādhara, a work called *The Root Text of the *Mārgaphala*, which is fully translated in appendix 2 but hardly comprehensible as it is. As a necessary corollary, we examine the later division of the Lamdré system into the lineage surrounding the transmission and practice of the text of the Lamdré, known as the Lamdré "method of the instruction" (**upadeśanaya*: *man ngag lugs*), and the lineage sustaining the "exegetical method" (**vyākhyānaya*: *bshad lugs*), which involved the exegesis of the *Hevajra-tantra* and allied literature. Drokmi's other contributions also are considered, including his other translations, his reception of what was eventually called the Nine Cycles of the Path (*lam skor dgu*), and his work with a wider variety of other Indian scholars.

THE NOMADIC TRANSLATOR

Like his junior contemporaries Ralo Dorjé-drak, Marpa Chökyi Lotrö, and Gö-lotsāwa Khukpa Lhétsé, Drokmi belongs to the eleventh century, with its exciting explosion of information and something of a frontier spirit. Thanks to the efforts of one of his eventual successors, Mangtö Ludrup Gyamtso (1523–96), writing between 1566 and 1587, we have dates for Drokmi as living from 993 to 1077.[4] The earliest date for Drokmi that I have encountered, however, is found in the description of the Mugulung pilgrimage, written in 1479 by a monk from Tsang, Jampa Dorjé Gyeltsen. He indicates that Mugulung was founded in 1043, which might actually be a decade late.[5] Similarly, we find dates given in the later chronological tables, like that of Sumpa Khenpo's, for around 990 to 1074.[6] Unfortunately, no dates are found in any early source of Drokmi's life, all of which are careful to cite dates for other historical figures whenever possible. Even as late as the completion by Gungru Shérap Zangpo (1411–75) of Ngorchen's earlier unfinished Lamdré chronicle, we are not given any dates for Drokmi. All these dates appear to coalesce in the last quarter of the fifteenth century and achieve currency by the end of the sixteenth. Consequently, we do not have any reliable dates for Drokmi, and it is unlikely that we shall ever have them.

Drokmi probably was born sometime in the decade between 990 and 1000, for he was said to have been the teacher of Gö-lotsāwa Khukpa Lhétsé (born around 1015) and of Marpa (born between 1009 and 1021), after Drokmi's return from studying in Nepal and India for perhaps a decade or more. Assuming that each of these men had begun their Indic studies in their early to mid teens, then Drokmi must have returned from India no later than 1030, and possibly earlier, to allow time for him to establish a sufficient reputation to attract students. We would not be far off, therefore, if we placed Drokmi as studying in the first quarter of the eleventh century and teaching from the second quarter onward, although it is not definite that he lived very far into the third quarter of that century. While Drokmi outlived his most important early disciple (Drom Depa Tönchung), his principal Indian informant in Tibet, Gayādhara, learned of the great translator's death during Gayādhara's own third trip to Tibet.

Drokmi's story unfolds at Drompa-gyang Temple just outside Lhatsé, at the confluence of the Brahmaputra River and its tributary, the Trumchu.[7] This temple is one of the four main "taming temples" ascribed by later myths to Songtsen Gampo and, according to the old chronicles, was intended to pin down the left hip of the cliff demoness in the horn of Tibet called Rulak.[8] Drompa-gyang eventually served as the reputed find spot for scriptural treasures (Terma), including one of the most influential prayers in Tibetan, the *Seven Chapter Prayer* (*gSol 'debs le'u bdun ma*), revealed by Zangpo Drakpa in the fourteenth century.[9] Early Sakyapa chronicles portray Pel Khortsen's three grandsons—the three "dé" of the Eastern section: Peldé, Ödé, and Kyidé—lamenting the fact that the temple lacked an inhabitant. As a result, they decided to invite two of the men of Ü-Tsang, Lotön and Tsongtsün, from their residence in Gyengong to come and act as their chaplains. Lotön, having other pressing matters, elected to send two of his senior disciples, Gya Shākya

Zhönu and Sé Yéshé Tsöndrü, to serve in his stead. These two set about monastic business and provided the ritual of going forth (*pravrajyā*), the novice ordination, for many new disciples.

Now it so happens that there was a certain petty lord of nomads along the Drilchenchu River in the Dungdrok area, since nomads—like agrarian or half-nomad / half-agrarian (*sa ma 'brog*) Tibetans—had a stratified society.[10] This nomad lord, in turn, had two distinct entourages: one was composed of laity, and the other consisted of Bendé, the clerics of questionable venue and uncertain virtue. One individual from the lay entourage asked to receive ordination at the hands of the famous Eastern Vinaya teachers and was granted the name Drokmi Shākya Yéshé, reflecting the fact that he was from a nomadic area (Drokmi), whose teachers were named Shākya (Zhönu) and Yéshé (Tsöndrü).

This was certainly not the first time that a nomad had penetrated the ranks of the elect, for occasionally other "nomad-area persons" (*'brog mi*) show up in Buddhist lineage lists, and the designation Drokmi is sometimes taken to be a specific geographical zone, as in Nelpa's list of the thousand divisions (*stong sde*).[11] Drokmi as the first part of a religious name is especially noted among representatives of the interesting ritual group known as the Mothers (*ma mo*), who appear to be a fusion of indigenous demoness lore and the Indian Mother goddesses (*mātṛkā*) group.[12] For example, at the end of the royal dynastic period there was Drokmi Pelgyi Yéshé, and later in the same system we encounter another translator, Lotsāwa Drokmi Trakgi Relpachen, in the lineage.[13]

Drokmi Shākya Yéshé and a fellow novice, Taglo Zhönu Tsültrim, were the two primary ordinands at Drompa-gyang in that first season, although later authorities expanded the list to include one Leng Yéshé Zhönu, who is otherwise obscure.[14] Whoever were their classmates in this ceremony, Drokmi and Taglo were the two chosen to be sent to India by their teachers, with a quantity of gold to fund them on their journey. They were to study Buddhist scriptures and return with their knowledge so that they might spread the true Dharma in Tibet. Here we catch up with the earliest of our sources, the late-twelfth- or early-thirteenth-century account of Drakpa Gyeltsen, written as the companion to his *Chronicle of the Indic Masters*:

Chronicle of Tibet: the Lineage of Teachers

Homage to the feet of the holy teacher with the fontanel of my head![15] Now as to the Chronicle of Tibet, concerning the lineage of teachers:

1. Gya Shākya Zhönu and Sé Yéshé Tsöndrü acted, respectively, as the Upādhyāya and the Ācārya [in the ordination of monks] at the monastery (Dharmacakra) of Drompa-gyang. [From among these] Sé selected

both Lachen Drokmi Shākya Yéshé and Taglo Zhönu Tsültrim to be sent to India. They were admonished [by Sé Yéshé Tsöndrü], "The root of the dispensation is the Vinaya. The heart of the dispensation is the *Prajñāpāramitā*. The semen of the dispensation is the [texts of] mantra. Go and listen to them!" So admonished, they went to India.

2. Now Lachen [Drokmi] first went to Nepal and entered into the door of mantra through [the teacher] Bhāro Haṁ-thung. Then he went to India itself and, realizing that the Ācārya Ratnākaraśānti was both greatly renowned and learned, he heard extensively the Vinaya, *Prajñāpāramitā*, and mantra. Then having gone to the eastern part of India, he encountered Bhikṣu Vīravajra, who was the greatest direct disciple of Durjayacandra, who himself had held the lineage of Ācārya Virūpa's own disciple, Ḍombiheruka. From Bhikṣu Vīravajra he heard extensively the mantra material of the three tantras of Hevajra, complete in all their branches. He also requested the many instruction manuals of *Acintyakrama* and so forth, so that he heard the "Lamdré without the fundamental text" (*rtsa med lam 'bras*) as well. In this way, Drokmi lived in India for twelve years and became a great translator.

3. But as for Taglo, he never understood anything beyond learning to recite the *Heart Sūtra* in the Indian manner. He just stayed at Vajrāsana, circumambulating the shrine [of Mahābodhi]. Because of his charisma and example in monastic virtue, however, eventually many came to consider themselves members of the Tagtso group.

4. Then Lachen Drokmi returned to Tibet. While he was residing in Namtang Karpo close to Pa-dro[16] and expounding much Dharma, the Guru Gayādhara sent word, "Come and receive me!" Drokmi inquired as to what kind of Dharma Gayādhara knew, and realizing that he was learned in the Vajrayāna, he became quite delighted and went on to receive the guru. They resided at Lhatsé-drak, for what became called the "month of Dharma" and satisfied each other with their learning.[17] Gayādhara told Drokmi, "I'll stay five years." Drokmi replied, "I'll offer you five hundred ounces of gold." Accordingly, they went to live in Mugulung.

5. After three years, though, Gayādhara said that he was going to leave. Drokmi realized that he had yet to offer up the entire five hundred ounces of gold. Drokmi performed the gold-accomplishing ceremony but could not produce even a little. So he sent word to Zur Shākya Jungné, "Come with a gift for Dharma!" Zur, though, was in retreat practicing the meditation of Yangdak. His disciples warned him [not to break his retreat],

"This will be an obstacle for the accomplishment of your practice!" Zur replied to their fears, "Drokmi is a great translator—surely he has oral instructions [mitigating the problem.]" He offered Drokmi about a hundred ounces of gold and was given the instructions known as the *Inconceivable [Nondual] Progress* (*Acintyādvayakramopadeśa*). Zurpoché Shākya Jungné became very happy and declared, "Through the kindness of the great Lama, the younger brother's mental condition has transcended wealth."

6. So there, at one time, Drokmi offered to Gayādhara all five hundred ounces of gold. Gayādhara could not believe it and wondered, "Is this some kind of trick?" So he went out to the street where the people of Mangkhar Drilchen had assembled and he asked, "So, is this stuff gold or isn't it?" They replied in the affirmative, and realizing that it really was gold, Gayādhara became very happy. He said to Drokmi, "I'll give you whatever you want that will make you happy." Drokmi said, "There is nothing that I have to request!" Gayādhara, however, asked him again and again, and finally Drokmi relented, "Well, I could offer you the request that you teach this Holy Speech [i.e., Lamdré] to no other person." Gayādhara agreed to the request and departed for India.

7. Again at a later time, Gö [lotsāwa Khukpa Lhétsé] encountered Gayādhara at Dromo and Gayādhara claimed, "I am Maitrīpā." Accordingly, Gö invited him to Tibet, only to find out that Gayādhara was not Maitrīpā. Gö confronted Gayādhara, "The guru has lied!" Gayādhara, however, simply replied, "I am more learned than Maitrīpā. If it's Dharma you want, you should in fact be happy!" Gö was interested in Dharma, so he greatly reverenced Gayādhara until the guru returned to India.

8. Finally, at a still later time, Gyijo Dawé Öser sent from his home in Ngari-tö an invitation to Gayādhara. He also greatly reverenced the teacher. While Gayādhara was on his way home, though, Gyijo's disciple, Kharak Tsangpa [= Nyö-lotsāwa], invited him to Kharak, where he went. Kharakpa revered him on many occasions, but the teacher began to exhibit the signs of death. "Take me to the peak of that mountain," Gayādhara demanded, "my sons are up there!" "But aren't we your sons?" Kharakpa asked. Gayādhara replied, "This is profitless, take me there!" On the mountain peak were two disciples of Drokmi's, the master meditators Sé and Rok.[18] When he arrived, Gayādhara declared, "My effort for my accomplished sons was not slight. And even though I never meditated, this is how a mantrin encounters the time of death." He picked up

his vajra and ghaṇṭa and just then a globule of light was emitted from his fontanel, and he passed away. Even now, that vajra and ghaṇṭa are to be found in Töpu.

9. Now Lachen Drokmi made it his practice never to impart Lamdré meditation instruction to those disciples he had trained in textual exegesis. Conversely, those he guided in the Lamdré meditations were never trained in the texts. There were five disciples he trained in the texts of the Lamdré: Gyijang Ukarwa from Lhatsé, Draktsé Sonakpa from Shang, Khön Könchok Gyelpo from Sakya, Ré Könchok Gyelpo from Trang-ö, and Lama Ngaripa Selwé Nyingpo. The three who completed the instruction in meditation were Drom Dépa Tönchung, Lhatsün Kali, and Lama Sékhar Chungwa. [The reasons for their special selection to receive the Lamdré meditation instruction are that] Drom performed great service to Drokmi; Lhatsün was Drokmi's brother-in-law; and Lama Sé spent all together seventeen years with Drokmi, seven years at first and then ten years again later on. He offered Drokmi about thirty "lower black" yaks.[19] Drokmi responded to this gift with the observation, "This is a small gift, but it seems necessary." Sékhar Chungwa was said to have obtained the instructions in Lamdré meditation based on his meager service to Drokmi and his great length of time spent with him as well as his application to meditative practice, which satisfied Drokmi. Having completed the Lamdré practice according to direction, he asked to be trained in the texts. Drokmi, though, reiterated his position, "I do not explain texts to those who have received the Lamdré meditative instruction. If you believe in books, then go to Sakya!" So Lama Sé went to Sakya, where he studied for four years with Sakyapa Chenpo [Khön Könchok Gyelpo], hearing the complete corpus of materials. Finally, those disciples of Drokmi who obtained accomplishment (siddhi) were the three men and the four women. The three men were Gyergom Sépo, Shengom Rokpo, and Üpa Dröpoché. The four women were Témo Dorjé-tso, Régom-ma Köné, Shepamo Chamchik, and Chémo Namkhamo. The first six of these seven men and women obtained their accomplishment without leaving their bodies. Chémo Namkhamo, however, merely gained the ordinary accomplishments. Moreover, Drokmi had many disciples who had obtained some kind of accomplishment.

10. For his part, Jé Gönpawa resided for eighteen years with Lama Sé and satisfied his teacher through his devoted service and his practice of the meditative and ritual path. In consideration, he was bestowed all the meditative instructions of the Lamdré. It was while he was staying at Gyichu

> that Sakyapa-chenpo [Kunga Nyingpo] first encountered Lama Sé. Lama Sé asked him many times for stories about Sakya [and his father Khön Könchok Gyelpo]. Taking the young Kunga Nyingpo on his lap, he cried and said, "Although this worn-out old man has some Dharma, please come quickly. If you are tardy, I shall be dead." He then bestowed on Sachen some fragmentary sections of the Lamdré. Realizing that Sachen was going to depart [to follow Lama Sé], Géshé Khönchung said, "There is nothing special about him. What he has accomplished is but the scattered crumbs of our Lama Ngaripa's Dharma" and so did not give Sachen permission to depart. The next year, Sachen left anyway but heard that Lama Sé had passed away. So he asked, "Which of his disciples is the best?" Having heard that Lama Gönpawa was the intense one, Sachen went to see him. Lama Gönpawa realized that Sachen's father had been the teacher of his own Lama Sé, and so teaching Sachen was incumbent on him to uphold the vow of reverence to the lineage. Thus, Jé Gönpawa bestowed on Sachen the complete instructions of the Lamdré.

This is the summary of the *Chronicle of Tibet*. It was composed by the brahmacārin Drakpa Gyeltsen.

DROKMI IN INDIA

We actually have little information about Drokmi's experiences in India. He was one of the first new translation personalities to study in India proper for any length of time. Although Rinchen Zangpo certainly preceded Drokmi by several decades, returning to Gugé toward the end of the 980s from his first period of study, and although his hagiography states that he studied in both Kashmir and India, it is apparent that Rinchen Zangpo was educated primarily in the Kashmir valley rather than in the great monasteries in the Gangetic valley.[20] Lumé's disciple Zhang Nanam Dorjé Wangchuk was said to have studied in Bodhgayā, but the dates of his sojourn to India are unsure, and he seems to have had a lengthy career prior to his departure. The royal monk Tsalana Yéshé Gyeltsen had worked with Kamalaguhya in Central Tibet, producing translations in the first quarter of the eleventh century, but we have no indication that he ever went to India or Nepal, and the translations appear somewhat restricted in circulation. For his part, Drokmi probably embarked for Nepal at the age of twenty or so, perhaps as early as 1010 (or even slightly before) and certainly by 1020. The *Blue Annals* maintains that Drokmi and Taglo were sent to India when Rinchen Zangpo was around fifty (i.e., around

1008), possibly earlier than any other figure from Central Tibet, a circumstance recognized by some Tibetan historians.[21]

Their learned Tibetan teachers are depicted as giving Drokmi and Taglo a triple admonition: they were to study the instructions in proper monastic decorum incumbent on monks (Vinaya); they were to investigate the perfection of insight scriptures (*Prajñāpāramitā*), which had been an important ritual focus in Tibet during the period of disarray; and they were to study the esoteric scriptures and their employment. This last might have been a later exegesis, for at least one early source does not include the admonition to pursue the esoteric path.[22] According to the sources, Drokmi first began studying Sanskrit in Nepal with a certain Bhāro Haṁ-tung (perhaps originally Haṁ-tung Bhāro, for "Bhāro" is used as a last name in Newar documents). This individual was one of the early-eleventh-century Newars who had earned the designation Bhāro, which appears as an aristocratic appellation in the first half of that century. As we have seen, "Haṁ-tung" is a variant of the clerical title Had-du/Haṁ-du sometimes employed by eleventh-century Newars in Pāṭan and Pharping. Later authors identified this Haṁ-tung Bhāro as a Buddhist, with the formal Sanskrit name Śāntabhadra, and it may be concluded that he was a Newar far less concerned with orthodoxy than with ritual—similar to *Kuṇḍa Bhāro, who instructed Ralo Dorjé-drak from around 1030 to 1040.[23] Drokmi was to have received some form of ritual training (he received an initiation) and a smattering of grammar from his Bhāro, but no early source mentions his center of study. Probably it was in Pāṭan, the traditional Buddhist metropolis in the Kathmandu valley and the same city where Ralo trained a decade or two later.

After a year in Nepal, Drokmi and Taglo continued on to India, and the sources agree that Drokmi entered the great convent of Vikramaśīla to study with Ratnākaraśānti. This was an extraordinary figure whose oeuvre includes texts on syllogistic logic, epistemology, perfection of insight, and the voluminous esoteric literature of Buddhist practice in that era. Unfortunately, Ratnākaraśānti's impressive contributions to Buddhist technical literature have been somewhat overlooked by both Tibetan authorities and modern specialists, the former due to the Tibetan assessment that Maḍhyamaka skepticism was the pinnacle of Buddhist thought in India and the latter because of Ratnākaraśānti's daunting scholarship.[24] As difficult as it may seem in the period's zeitgeist, Ratnākaraśānti tried to reassert traditional Buddhist categories, and he formulated a series of sophisticated statements that indicated the priority of meditative experience and gnostic realities in a specifically Buddhist framework. Unfortunately, Ratnākaraśānti's distressing reward for his efforts on behalf of Buddhist identity has been occasional vilification, institutional marginalization, and the classification of his works as lacking an authoritative voice.[25] Nonetheless. it was this eminent figure whose lectures Drokmi elected to attend for his first several years in India.

At the time Drokmi arrived, Indians would have been relatively unfamiliar with Tibetans, even if they were accustomed to Newars from the Kathmandu valley or Kashmiris studying in their centers. It had been almost two centuries since anyone had seen a dedicated personality like Drokmi, and the last Tibetans of the royal dynasty had been less interested in new materials than in reaffirming the precedents already established. Earlier, Rinchen Zangpo may have visited Vikramaśīla before Drokmi, but it is not clear that he spent much time there.[26] At a later date, Tibetans became something of an institution at Vikramaśīla, and we know that several monks came at various times to invite Atiśa to Tibet, until Nagtso finally succeeded around 1037 to 1039.[27] If they followed the same policies that the Tibetan monasteries later used, Drokmi would have been housed in a separate enclave with other "border country folk" from the hills, meaning Newars, Assamese, and probably those from the western Himalayas, excluding Kashmir. We know nothing about Drokmi's personal relationships with either his preceptors or his fellow students, only that his period at Vikramaśīla was consumed with the daunting task of learning both the vernacular and the classical languages of medieval India. The curriculum, though, focused on scholasticism, with its emphasis on debate, syllogism, and rituals appropriate to India rather than to Tibet.

While the early records, like Drakpa Gyeltsen's, are rather general regarding the nature of Drokmi's studies—Drokmi studied Vinaya, *Prajñāpāramitā*, and Vajrayāna (§2, above)—by the mid-thirteenth century, Sakyapa chronicles offered an extensive list of subjects and texts. Martön affirms that Ratnākaraśānti, whom he identified as the Vikramaśīla Eastern Gatekeeper, taught Drokmi grammar, epistemology, the Vinaya, extensive materials on the Perfection of Insight (both scripture and commentary), the three principal tantras of the Hevajra cycle, and the Saṁvara materials.[28] Sources agree that Drokmi went on to study with other Vikramaśīla scholars as well. According to these legends, the Southern Gatekeeper was Vāgīśvarakīrti, whom we may presume was the authority noted for his four short works on practices associated with the *Guhyasamāja-tantra*, as well as other short subjects.[29] Drokmi is said to have studied with him more grammar and epistemology, as well as poetry (*kāvya*) and scripture (*āgama*).[30] The Western Gatekeeper, Prajñākaragupta, taught Drokmi non-Buddhist subjects, a designation probably meant to indicate the Nyāya-Vaiśeṣika system. The Northern Gatekeeper, Lord Nāroṭapa, instructed Drokmi in the literature of the Mahāyāna.

It is a bit difficult to assess this ostensible curriculum, and it is apparent that

Drokmi's student transcripts were creatively elaborated. The list of topics from the thirteenth-century author Martön, in particular, builds on statements by Drakpa Gyeltsen, but the curriculum is not reflected in non-Sakyapa works, which emphasize the role of Indians beyond the walls of Vikramaśīla.[31] The much later *Short Red Book* (*Pusti dmar chung*) specifies concise instructions that are traced from the several personages, along with some brief historical statements. They affirm that when Drokmi had completed his study with Ratnākaraśānti and just before he was to return to Tibet, he had a little gold left over and offered it to the great scholar. In return he received the *Practice Combining Sūtra and Tantra* (*mDo rgyud bsre ba'i nyam len*).[32] Moreover, Nāropā taught Drokmi the *Clarification of the Three Sufferings* (*sDug bsngal gsum sel*); Vāgīśvarakīrti instructed him in the *Clear Recollection of the Natural* (*gNyug ma dran gsal*); Prajñākaragupta transmitted the *Instructions on Protection from Obstacles from the External Demons* (*Phyi rol gdon gyi bar chad bsrung ba'i man ngag*); Jñānaśrīmitra contributed the *Instructions on Protection from Obstacles That Disturb the Body* (*Lus 'khrugs kyi bar chad bsrung ba'i man ngag*); and finally, Ratnavajra taught him the *Instructions on Protection from Obstacles to the Mind in Contemplation* (*Ting nge 'dzin sems kyi bar chad bsrung ba'i man ngag*).[33]

The Indian pedigree of these works might legitimately be questioned, for rather than early-eleventh-century texts from Indic authors, they all appear to be closely associated with the kinds of instructions found in twelfth- and thirteenth-century Central Tibet. Indeed, in a later chapter we look at a longer list of this genre in regard to Sachen Kunga Nyingpo's writings, and these six must be differentiated from the better authenticated eight subsidiary practices (*lam skor phyi ma brgyad*) considered next. The supporting stories for these six instructions are equally at odds with the other evidence and appear to be the result of twelfth- and thirteenth-century appeals for support, perhaps modeled on Kadampa writings about Atiśa or other hagiographical narratives of that time. For example, Atiśa's hagiography verifies that Nāropā visited Vikramaśīla, but it is unlikely that he was a scholar in official residence during Drokmi's period of study.[34] Nagtso-lotsāwa certainly met Nāropā around 1038/39, when Nāropā was an aged siddha in his last few years of life, and even the standard hagiographies do not place him in Vikramaśīla but in Nālandā. There seems to have been much confusion in later Tibetans' minds between these two entirely different establishments, which is reflected in a note (*mchan bu*) to the *Short Red Book* locating all these scholars in Nālandā rather than Vikramaśīla.[35] Likewise, we might wonder why the renowned epistemologist Prajñākaragupta was teaching advanced demonology. Finally, we are most often told that Drokmi did not return from Vikramaśīla to Tibet after completing his studies with Ratnākaraśānti but continued on to Bengal for a more significant meeting.

Eventually becoming dissatisfied with the Vikramaśīla scholastic program after several years, Drokmi is said to have gone on pilgrimage to Khasarpaṇa, a site in southern Bengal dedicated to Avalokiteśvara where Virūpa and other esoteric figures were often said to have worshiped. On the way, he encountered a monk with a begging bowl, who beat his monk's staff on the trunk of a tree in the deep forest in order to receive alms. A spirit living in the tree appeared as two bodiless hands bejeweled with ornaments and placed food in the monk's begging bowl.[36] Drokmi conceived a miraculous faith in this monk, whom he learned was named Prajñendraruci. Prajñendraruci initiated Drokmi into the esoteric system ostensibly derived from the siddha culture of Ḍombiheruka and Virūpa, including scriptures, commentaries, and practical manuals. Indeed, some sources overwhelmingly emphasize this Bengali scholar's importance, ignoring Drokmi's Vikramaśīla career altogether.[37]

Prajñendraruci's system eventually was to become known as the "rootless Lamdré," as opposed to the Lamdré system that was passed down in the root text from Virūpa. The textless Lamdré is paradoxically involved, however, with all sorts of texts, specifically the tantras of Hevajra, their commentaries, and their exegesis. For this reason, it is also called the "exegetical method of Lamdré" (**vyākhyānaya* : *bshad lugs*), and the tradition insists that this system was transmitted uniquely to Drokmi through Prajñendraruci.[38] The Sakyapas have consistently maintained that Prajñendraruci's secret name (*gsang ba'i mtshan*) was Vīravajra, so that the many works ascribed to these two names should be attributed to the same person. It is also said that Prajñendraruci was one of the Indian paṇḍitas with whom Drokmi later worked in Tibet.

We do not know exactly how many years Drokmi stayed in India—some sources say nine, others twelve or even eighteen.[39] All would be easy figures to justify given the quantity of material taught at high-level institutions like Vikramaśīla, but he likely studied in Nepal and India for approximately a decade. In reality, Drokmi became extraordinarily accomplished in his work, although just how much time he actually spent on scholastic topics is uncertain, given that he seemed neither to translate nor to teach them during his career in Tibet. Drakpa Gyeltsen took great pleasure—as scholars are sometimes wont to do—in describing the dismal intellectual accomplishment of Drokmi's initial compatriot, Taglo Zhönu Tsültrim, who stayed for about the same length of time but accomplished little more than learning to recite the *Heart Sūtra* while circumambulating the Mahābodhi Temple at Vajrāsana. Taglo, however, maintained that he was overcome with faith at the tree of awakening (*mahābodhivṛkṣa*) and so could not engage anything else. In this, he received much disapproval, for he had received a grant to become educated and thus had a responsibility to his community and countrymen to return with intellectual skills. But many Tibetan historians offer a degree of redemption to Taglo, as he established himself in monastic leadership and eventually received much acclaim for his virtue, if not for his scholarship.

AN EVENTUAL RETURN TO TIBET

Drokmi returned to Central Tibet and set himself up in the Lhatsé area, eventually founding his center of learning at Mugulung in the Mangkhar valley, south of Lhatsé. He established a monastic presence and began to attract both patronage and Indian paṇḍitas, including one of the more interesting characters of the eleventh century—Kāyastha Gayādhara, whose career we describe later. Why did Drokmi settle in Mangkhar and especially at Mugulung? A glance at map 6 shows that the valley faces northward, with its river, the Mangkhar-chu, intersecting the Tsangpo, the great Brahmaputra River, that runs roughly west to east all along the north side of the Himalayas. In fact, the Brahmaputra and its tributaries define most of traditional Central Tibet, and the majority of the important commercial and religious sites are in its valley or in the valleys stretching from it to the north and south. A few kilometers downstream from the Mangkhar-chu, another river, the Trumchu, flows into the Tsangpo from the area of Sakya. Downstream of these two confluences is the area of Lhatsé, and just east of Lhatsé is the location of Drokmi's home temple, Drompa-gyang, probably a late imperial site.[40]

Beyond the ritual and mythic location, the entire area was important enough to be included in the early lists of organized administrative units under the royal dynasty. Each of the four horns of Tibet was divided into ten "thousand-divisions" (*stong sde*), and three of these in Tsang were Mangkhar, Lhatsé, and the Drompa valley, indicating their value to the imperial military and bureaucratic officials.[41] Since there were only forty "thousand-divisions" in the four horns of Central Tibet, an area containing roughly 8 percent of the empire's human and economic resources can be expected to be of imperial importance, and the Drompa-Mangkhar-Lhatsé region of Rulak was so prized. Much of the area was placed under the control of the powerful Dro and Khyungpo clans—who continued even later to have an overwhelming interest in Tsang Province—and the governors-general (*ru dpon*) were the formidable Dro Gyeltsen Sengé and Khyungpo Yuï-surpü.[42] Drompa was given to another important family, the Ché, whose later advocacy of both Shalu Monastery and the Nying-thik treasure materials is well established.[43] Drompa's centrality to the empire extended even into the period of fragmentation, for Pel Khortsen

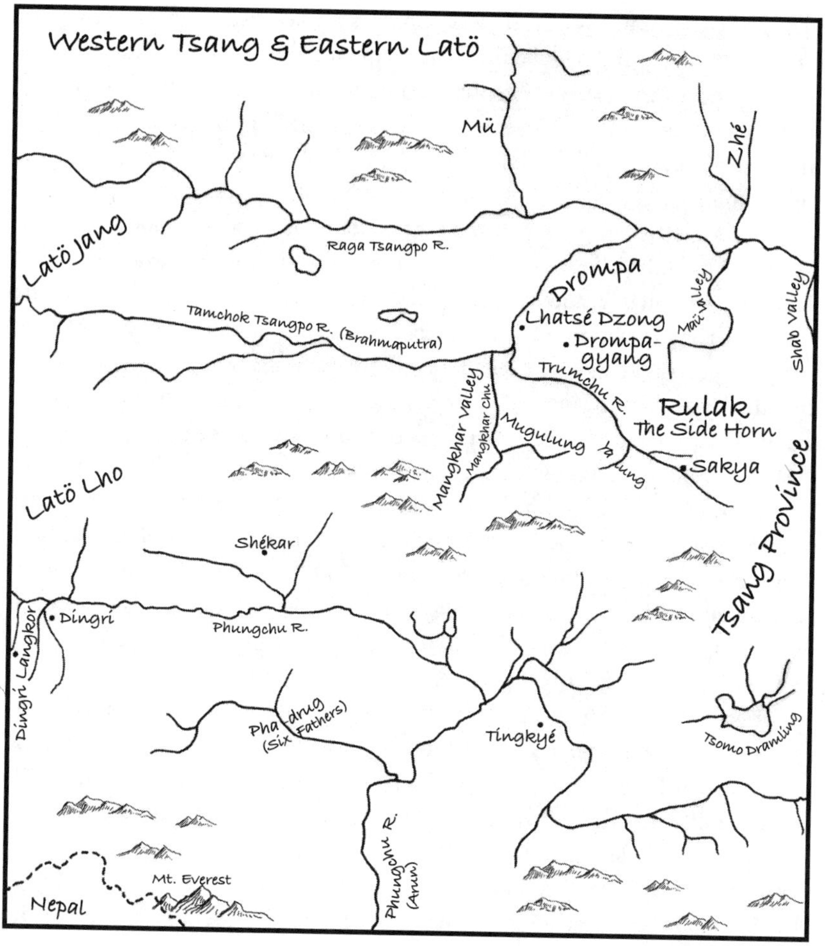

MAP 6 Western Tsang and Eastern Latö.

stayed at a royal residence in Drompa-Lhatsé while making the funerary rites to his father Ösung during the troubles of the divided empire.[44]

The imperial emphasis on this area was for at least one basic reason. The trade route from Lhasa to West Tibet and from there to Kashmir and western Turkestan, and the routes from Lhasa to Nepal, and from there to India all follow the Brahmaputra until Lhatsé, where they divide. It was the strategic point for the trade in salt, precious metals, and other items, as well as being the inner line of Central Tibet. If Lhatsé were lost to an army from Kashmir, Ngari, or

Nepal, then Ü-Tsang would be lost. Conversely, because of its fertile valleys, trade associations, and relative ease in movement to Nepal and to India, the area was inviting to the eleventh-century translators, much more than Lho-drak, where Marpa settled. Yet Drokmi would have wanted to be removed from the intensity of Drompa-gyang, for such ancient temples were both prestigious and highly political, as seen in the Eastern Vinaya monks' relationship to Samyé. So Drokmi evidently adopted an important strategy that Indian Buddhists previously had used: he chose to be close to the regional capital but not in it. The land was less valuable, and religious personnel could still receive feudal largesse without having to choose sides in the daily squabbles that inevitably arose, with potentially drastic consequences in a feudal system, including the loss of lands and life. Even though the imperial machinery was long gone, the area retained many of the ancient clan associations and its importance for Tibet as a whole.

What did this Mugulung look like, where Drokmi settled? I have not found any record left by the early Sakyapa or other Tibetan authorities describing the locale in the eleventh or twelfth century. Mugulung, used as a designation for both Drokmi's residence and the name of the branch valley is actually rather close to Sakya in geographical distance. Indeed, it is possible to walk between them in just a few days, and so description was apparently superfluous.[45] After the rise of alternative institutions like Sakya, lineal representatives clearly wanted the new structures to become the centers of pilgrimage, which is one primary reason that they were the subjects of panegyric depictions. Still, in due course, guidebooks included Mugulung in their itineraries, even if they were distressed at the paucity of physical remains for such an important locale. Certainly, the area must have been conducive to contemplative practice, for we are told that the great Sakyapa teacher Drakpa Gyeltsen had had a meditation cave close by.[46] Mangkhar eventually became the home of Tsarchen Losel Gyamtso (1502–66), who was the founder of the Tsarpa method of Lamdré and who is attributed the development of the fundamental pattern for its teaching. The fifth Dalai Lama's hagiography of Tsarchen emphasizes that there were four cliffs in the Mangkhar valley and that Tsarchen first went into retreat about 1532 in Drakpa Gyeltsen's cave in the west cliff, a cliff known as Chalung Dorjé-drak.[47] Tsarchen established his monastery rather close to Drokmi's old area, and Tsarchen's residence at Tupten Gépel or his tomb at Dar Drongmoché somewhat overshadowed Drokmi's site from that point on. Later pilgrims from elsewhere in Tibet, like Jamyang Khyentsé Wangpo or Situ Chökyi Gyamtso, were rather disappointed in the religious remains in the valley concerning Drokmi and his translation efforts, for Drokmi never seems to have moved beyond a residence housed in rather simple cave structures.[48]

Fortunately, a short pilgrimage manual from 1479 has survived. It was composed by Jampa Dorjé Gyeltsen before Tsarchen's legacy began to dominate the valley.[49] Like most of this class of literature, it provides fanciful etymologies of the names, emphasizes the specific locales where miracles are claimed, and provides a rudimentary description of the area. Mangkhar Mugulung, we are informed, derived its name from the valley's geographical attributes. The name of the larger valley, Mangkhar, means "many fortresses" in modern Tibetan, although it may have initially meant "many encampments" (*mang gar*).[50] From Lhatsé, the Mangkhar valley leads south, and after some distance from the old Lhatsé center, the valley divides, with the major branch continuing south and the smaller valley—Mugulung itself—turning left, east toward Sakya. At a fork in the valley lies a mountain that might have been the source of the valley's name, Mount Muk-chung. Although the guidebook provides two other etymologies for the valley, this is the most convincing one, as Tibetan place-names are often based on a physical characteristic of the area.

Otherwise, our good monk informs us that Mugulung has the meaning of liberation, since liberation is *mukti* in Sanskrit. In this vein, Mount Muk-chung is the small sign of liberation marking the valley where liberation is obtained. Jampa Dorjé Gyeltsen is less moved by the other popular etymology of currency, in which the Tibetan word *mu* means "end" or "conclusion" and indicates the goal of the Dharma or the conclusion of liberation. He is clearly enthralled with the legendary associations of the valley, which has 108 sites of practice where 108 siddhas came to achieve their goals. Likewise, there are 108 monasteries, 108 villages, 108 small markets, 108 willow groves, and 108 whirlpools in the river, indicating the sacred nature of the place. In addition, there is a high verdant mountain (*spang ri*) to the south of the valley and a blue slate mountain (*g.ya' ri*) close by, coiled around like a dragon, indicating the presence of dragon-like yogins, as well as many other religious signs.

The heart of the valley, though, is its thirteen caves, many of which are associated with Drokmi, Gayādhara, and their activities. The guidebook's author says that the great translator first was active there in 1043, although this seems a bit late. Preeminent among the caves is the "white residential cave" (*gzims khang dkar ma phug*), which is actually two caves, upper and lower. Gayādhara resided in the upper level, while Drokmi was in the lower. We are told that in the lower, there was a life-size statue of Drokmi, made of clay, that had embedded in its heart a small stone statue of Gayādhara, the size of a fist with the thumb placed on top. Both the statues were known to have spoken in times of troubles, and the valley was subject to military incursions, from both Central Tibet and an unnamed southern army before 1479. There was also a "translators' cave" (*sgra sgyur lo tsā phug*), in which many of the translations were made, a "consecration cave" (*dbang bskur byin brlabs phug*) associated with the esoteric consecrations, and caves connected with *ḍākinīs* and the Mahāmudrā teachings. Caves connected with other saints are described as well, the most important being the cave of the Indian Vīravajra, the other name of Prajñendraruci, from whom Drokmi received the exegetical method of the Lamdré. Vīravajra is reputed to have composed there a very important Hevajra *sādhana* called the *Blaze of the Jewel* (*Ratnajvalasādhana*), which became a central item in the Sakyapa repertoire.[51] Our monk assures us that Vīravajra lived there for three years, having ridden in on a sunbeam from India, which is, after all, the only way to travel.

THE INDIAN CONTINGENT: GAYĀDHARA AND THE OTHER PAṆḌITAS

Certainly the most significant of all the Indians to have worked with Drokmi in Mugulung was Gayādhara, possibly a native of Bengal and a complex personality whose legacy included collaboration on some of the most significant tantric translations of the eleventh century. Gayādhara's behavior was as problematic as his learning was excellent, and even the most pious sources mention Gayādhara's foibles. In all, Gayādhara is declared to have made three trips to Tibet, and he worked with Drokmi on the first of these, which is said to have lasted between three and five years and certainly culminated in a wealth of translations. Gayādhara is also depicted by all the sources as having significant difficulties in telling the truth, for on his second trip we find him masquerading as Maitrīpā, deceiving the translator of the Guhyasamāja system, Gö-lotsāwa Khukpa Lhétsé, until Gayādhara was recognized by one of his own disciples from the previous sojourn and identified as having deceived his patron. From the beginning, Gayādhara was clearly depicted as a dubious figure who retained his lay status and apparently influenced Drokmi in this direction. As with all our hagiographical subjects, Gayādhara's story becomes more elaborate over time, and the later sources give him an extensive background of questionable veracity.

We do know that Gayādhara was a Kāyastha, a member of a caste that formed in North India at the beginning of the early medieval period around the trade of being a scribe (*kāraṇa*), although Kāyastha is mentioned as an office (not a caste) in a Mathurā inscription as early as the first century C.E.[52] Despite the various lineal mythologies for the Kāyasthas, the epigraphic and literary sources agree that Kāyasthas came from one of three areas: North India, Bengal, or West India (Maharashtra or Gujarat).[53] Of the three, the western branch is unlikely as Gayādhara's kith and kin because of the nature of the literature he transmitted, for it is not clear that Hevajra materials were ever circulated in the west. Moreover, the colloquial pronunciations of various Apabhraṁśa words and verses that Gayādhara purportedly brought with him do not appear phonetically similar to the ostensible old Bengali of the *Caryāgītikoṣa*, calling into question his occasional identification as a Bengali.[54] It is true that the Bengali branch of the Kāyasthas were important outside Bengal, especially in Orissa, but that area also was not well authenticated in either the myth or the literature attributed to Gayādhara.

Even if his original homeland could be conclusively shown as some part of Bengal, we might wonder whether Gayādhara did not belong to the North Indian branch or was at least primarily trained in Bihari traditions. The North Indian was the most important of the Kāyastha branches and had twelve subcastes.[55] Indeed, one of the subcastes was called Gauḍa, probably indicating its involvement with or primary residence in that intermittent capital city of Pāla Bengal, even though Kāyastha sources differentiate the Gauḍa and Bāṅgala Kāyasthas.[56] This North Indian branch regards itself as really a fifth *varṇa*, different from the other four. Whereas the four main castes were created from the creator Brahmā's mouth (Brahmans), his arms (Kṣatriyas), his thighs (Vaiśyas), or his feet (Śūdras), North Indian Kāyasthas maintain that they were formed from the body of the creator and therefore are grounded (*stha*) in Brahmā's body (*kāya*). Their primal progenitor and grand ancestor, Citragupta, who emerged from Brahmā's body, came with a pen and ink bottle, fully endowed with the capacity to be the creator's scribe. The cultic importance of this grand ancestor and his implements are noted in the anthropological literature on Kāyasthas.[57]

Buddhist clerics had been involved with scribal duties for several centuries before this, and the activity of Buddhist monks as scribes (*divira*) is cited in the Kharoṣṭhī documents from Niya in Central Asia.[58] Scribes did not simply take dictation but acted in the range of capacities better indicated by the term "secretary," which may apply equally to a menial clerk, the Secretary-General of the United Nations, and the many levels in between. Scribes used their training in law, literature, court language, accounting, contracts, wills, litigation, evidence adjudication, and many other areas in the range of abilities. Kāyasthas fulfilled all these venues as well, and we frequently read of their acting in the capacity of a medieval office combining the duties of both a secretary of war and a secretary of state (Mahāsandhivigrahin).[59]

It was specifically their office as the village recorders of taxes and deeds, though, that gained Kāyasthas such a notorious reputation for deceit, corruption, and larceny.[60] Gupta noted that Kāyasthas represented a medieval conundrum: they were "highly educated and patronized art and culture," while the "tax-paying common people were much suspicious of the Kāyasthas because deceit lurked both in their tongues as well as in their documents."[61] Even though similar remarks may be found from the time of the dramatist Śudraka onward—Śudraka calls Kāyasthas "snakes" and declares that even criminals will not live in their proximity—it was Gayādhara's approximate contemporaries, Kṣemendra and Kalhaṇa, who most bitterly condemned Kāyasthas.[62] Kṣemendra, for example, maintains that the Kāyasthas' invention of a separate script was a method to defraud people, so that good kings, even knowing their Kāyasthas to be "eager to kill, robbers of others' property, rogues and demons," had to befriend them in order to balance the treasury.[63]

Some of these disparate qualities are seen in Gayādhara as well, from his evident scholarly accomplishments to his moral lapses and avariciousness. According to the 1344 Lamdré annals of Lama Dampa, Gayādhara was a member of a family of scribes assigned to a Bengali king.[64] In the sixteenth century, Khyentsé Wangchuk identified the king as Candrarūpa, a name that cannot be assigned any reliable significance.[65] Gayādhara is said to have met his master, Avadhūti, at the banks of the Lohita River—which branches off the Brahmaputra in Assam toward Arunachal Pradesh—where Avadhūti had been practicing his activity as a naked ascetic (*avadhūtacaryā*), an example of a siddha residing in a tribal area.[66] After he had received the Lamdré from his master, Gayādhara is said to have gone to Tibet to search for the disciple who would continue his teaching, as had been prophesied by the bodhisattva Avalokiteśvara.[67] In Tibet he encountered the translator Purang-lotsāwa Zhönu Shérap, who received teachings and was extremely interested in more, but Gayādhara continued on to Tsang Province in search of his destined disciple. While staying in a meditation cave, we are told, he heard a stream make the sound of liberation (*mu gu*), and the stream ended in Mugulung, so he decided to teach the Lamdré there.[68] He had a dream about Drokmi and sent him a letter requesting that they meet, which they did at Lhatsé-drak, where Gayādhara had a meditation cave, still renowned to the present.[69] At the time they met, we are assured by Mangtö Ludrup Gyamtso, Gayādhara was already 288 years of age.[70]

Realizing that this was a golden opportunity, Drokmi cultivated Gayādhara for three or more years, and they jointly translated an extraordinary quantity of material. All during this time, Drokmi promised Gayādhara five hundred ounces (*srang*) of gold for his teachings, especially the Lamdré, which was destined to become the central meditative system of Drokmi and his most intimate disciples. What Drokmi ultimately asked in return was exclusive rights to use the text and teach the system in Tibet. Gayādhara agreed to this, that he would initiate no one but Drokmi into the Lamdré. The problem was that by the time Gayādhara wanted to go, Drokmi could not come up with the promised money, so he asked his Nyingma colleague Zur Shākya Jungné to come from his hermitage at Tagyapa for teachings and to bring a lot of gold. Zurpoché did exactly that, but not without a certain amount of controversy.[71] When his disciples protested that obstacles would arise by leaving his retreat, Zurpoché replied that Drokmi was a great translator and therefore he certainly must have special meditative instructions (*man ngag*). Zurpoché was given the instructions of the *Acintyādvayakramopadeśa*, examined later, and directions for the meditation on Hevajra.

While this story of gold and transactions survives in the sources, not all the details are uniform. Non-Sakyapa sources, for example, maintain that the person invited by Drokmi was not Zurpoché but his adopted son, Zurchung Shérap Drakpa, although this is not likely.[72] The Sakyapa authors invariably provide a humorous conclusion to the story, at Gayādhara's expense. Not believing that the money given was really gold, Gayādhara sets out for the bazaar in Mangkhar with his pouch full of Drokmi's offering, going from person to person asking whether the material received was really gold. Each person assures him that it really is gold, and he consequently returns to Drokmi and promises to teach the Lamdré to no one else but him. Gayādhara's promise became moot, however, on his third trip to Tibet, for he found that Drokmi had passed away. Consequently, Gayādhara evidently retranslated—or recreated—the Lamdré text with Gyijo Dawé Öser.[73] This second translation seems to have been lost, or at least was exceedingly rare, by the time Khyentsé Wangchuk wrote his history of the tradition in the sixteenth century.[74]

Kagyüpa writers provided an entirely different spin on Gayādhara, for among them he is principally noted as the father of the siddha Tipupa, Rechungpa's Indian master.[75] According to some, Tipupa was the reembodiment of Marpa's son, Darma Dodé, who was the object of Ralo's animosity and who Ralo's hagiographer claimed as having been killed by Ralo's black magic.[76] Since Darma Dodé was skilled in the art of corpse reanimation (*grongs 'jug*), he eventually entered the corpse of Gayādhara's son and became the Brahman Tipupa. One difficulty with this story is exactly the question of Nāropā's dates, since Tipupa was said to have been the disciple of the great siddha, who died around 1040–42, when Marpa perhaps was twenty, yet Darma Dodé was supposed to have been an adult man at the time of his death.

For their part, Indians in Tsang certainly had a profound influence on Drokmi, for Drokmi reputedly worked with several of them: Amoghavajra, Ratnavajra, Prajñāgupta, Prajñendraruci, and the intriguing but obscure yoginī Candramālā from Śrī Laṅka.[77] Through most of their alliances, Drokmi remained a monk, but by the end of his period with Gayādhara, we see in the colophons to the translations that he no longer claimed monastic status. Of the fifty-nine canonical texts and one noncanonical text for which we have colophons, Drokmi identifies himself as a monk fifty-five times, an overwhelming majority. In the other five, it is evident that he had some other status, for he has given up his robes in favor of lay life. Three of these later translations were done with Gayādhara (To. 381, 385, 1220), including his magnum opus, the translation of the *Sampuṭa*, by far the longest of all of Drokmi's translation efforts. Besides this, Drokmi is not represented as a monk in the colophon to one short tantra commentary by Ḍombi (To. 1416), translated with Ratnavajra, and in a short Tārā ritual text (To. 1705) that was translated by Drokmi himself.

Drokmi must have eventually become proud of his status as a person of authority, for by the time he completed the *Sampuṭa* translation he was calling himself an "exalted personality" (*bdag nyid chen po*).[78] He is said to have invited Atiśa and Dromtön to Mugulung, evidently sometime around 1046/47 while the Bengali scholar was on his way to Central Tibet.[79] Drokmi finally married an aristocratic woman while he was staying at Gampé-dzong.[80] Her name was Dzéden Öchak, and she was the sister of one of his foremost disciples, Lhatsün Kali. By her he seems to have had at least two sons, Indra and Dorjé, and there may have been other children as well.[81] Having had so successful a career, Drokmi died before Gayādhara returned for the third time to Tibet, this time to work with Gyijo Dawé Öser.[82] Drokmi apparently requested that his body not be moved for seven days after his death, and during this time we are told that he achieved the highest perfection of the Great Seal.[83] While there are no firm dates for Drokmi's death, he probably did not live beyond the third quarter of the eleventh century, for there is no indication that he was even alive at the time of the great translators' convocation in 1076, under the patronage of Ngadak Tsédé.[84] The *Blue Annals* may provide the most accurate statement, observing that Drokmi passed away at about the same time as Dromtön Gyelwé Jungné, who died in 1064.[85]

Gayādhara himself did not live much longer than his most famous disciple. He had gone to Tibet a second time, in this instance pretending to be the great siddha Maitrīpā, and deceived Gö-lotsāwa Khukpa Lhétsé until his ruse was discovered. On the final trip, he stayed most of the time in West Tibet and by then was famous if not notorious, so that the founder of Shangpa Kagyüpa, Khyungpo Neljor, claimed to have traveled with him to Toling, although we do not know whether Gayādhara ever actually visited that great temple of Gugé.[86] After working for some time with Gyijo Dawé Öser and his disciple Nyö-lotsāwa, Gayādhara understood that his end was near, but he wanted to be near Drokmi's disciples.[87] So he moved to Kharak Töpu, where two of Drokmi's disciples, Sé and Shengom Rokpo, lived.[88] Realizing that his death was close, he crossed his legs in a formal meditative posture, grasped his vajra and bell before him, and announced, "This is how a mantrin dies!" He entered into the contemplation of consciousness transference, passing into the intermediate state as a globule of light emerging from his fontanel.[89] Later historians assure us that Gayādhara's own vajra and bell, along with his reliquary, books, and a painting, came to reside at Sakya by means of diverse paths.[90]

DROKMI'S WORK AND THE ORIGIN OF THE *ROOT TEXT OF THE *MĀRGAPHALA*

Drokmi and the various Indian masters with whom he worked were responsible for a significant number of the translations done in the eleventh century, and the extent of their production is considered toward the end of this chapter. Among those attributed to Drokmi, the translation of the *Root Text of the *Mārgaphala* is held by the followers of the Sakyapa tradition to be the most important, the most secret, and the most closely guarded. This work was sometimes given alternative titles, like the **Vajrapada*, and the question of the title is discussed later. It was understood that Drokmi asked Gayādhara that the text be transmitted to no one else. But some authorities have noted that an alternative version of the *Root Text of the *Mārgaphala* (*Lam 'bras rtsa ba*) seemed to have been available, and in the fifteenth century, Ngorchen Künga Zangpo concluded that another translation had indeed been made of the text by Gyijo Dawé Öser, during Gayādhara's third trip to Tibet.[91] Ngorchen evidently had access to this alternative text, for he mentions a compendium (*yig cha*) of material belonging to this tradition, which he declares to have been complete and once widely spread but no longer available by his day.[92]

The received *Root Text of the *Mārgaphala* is one of the most peculiar works I have encountered in the Tibetan language. There is no indication that an Indic version ever actually existed, for no surviving Indian work cites the text. In the heated world of fifteenth-century Tibetan polemics, Ngorchen could provide no instance of this work having been authoritative in India, and he was forced to rely on Virūpa's identity to validate the tradition. Even then, he had to reinterpret various verses so that Virūpa's name would be found in definitive sources.[93] In reality, both the identity of Virūpa as the author, and Drokmi and Gayādhara as the translation team, are in question, for no example of the received text has a colophon that identifies it as Virūpa's or as translated by this team, an astonishing fact if we are to judge from the exacting credit that Drokmi took for all his other translations. Moreover, there is a problem with the textual transmission, for the Sakyapas maintain that no physical document concerning the Lamdré—neither a copy of the text nor any notes—was either given by Zhang Gönpawa or received by Sachen Kunga Nyingpo in the twelfth century. One tradition declares that the *Root Text of the *Mārgaphala* was not even written down until the time of Zhang Gönpawa, Sachen's teacher.[94] Thus the received *Root Text of the *Mārgaphala* may have been entirely constituted from Zhang Gönpawa's or Sachen's memorization of the work and not from a continuous manuscript tradition. While it is more likely that manuscripts from Drokmi's various disciples were floating around, the peculiarity of the received text combined with the paucity of accompanying documentation leaves much uncertainty about the transmission of this work.

The text itself is a collection of disparate approaches to the esoteric Buddhist path, and it has very little in common with any other work attributed to a/the Virūpa (figure 10). Beyond the short autobiographical verses contained in the canon and in the received hagiographies, there are about an even dozen texts to which the name Virūpa, Śrīvirūpa, Birwapa, or some similar form is attached in the Tibetan *Tengyur*. These works fall into four basic categories: (1) practical manuals for the contemplation of one or another divinity, (2) gritty ritual texts concerned with the concoction of pills or the various tantric karmas, (3) works describing the manipulation of the vital airs and psychophysical yoga, and (4) mystical texts expressing the realization of absolute reality. The first category is dominated by a concern for the divinity and maṇḍalas of Raktayamāri-Raktayamāntaka, although the goddess Chinnamuṇḍā also is represented there.[95] If there is a *sādhana* background to the historical Virūpa, this is probably it, since the hagiographical miracle of Virūpa's holding the sun was considered elsewhere an accomplishment extolled in an anonymous work focusing on Raktayamāri.[96] Moreover, the ritual texts of the second category act in concert with these, as they include instructions for making "nectar" pills from substances running the gamut from disgusting to lethal, and such practices were often associated with the Raktayamāri-Raktayamāntaka system.[97] The Virūpa *Raktayamāntakasādhana* specifically calls for the use of these methods, which is not surprising, as they were frequently enjoined elsewhere in esoteric literature.[98] Moreover, a Yamāntaka yantra work, concerned with manipulating reality through the tantric activities, is attributed to a Virūpa.[99] It might seem that the yogic works of the third category could provide a more fertile field to find similarities with the content of the *Root Text of the *Mārgaphala*, but this does not prove to be the case. Of the two yogic works available, the first is extremely rudimentary, and the second considers the yoga of "self-consecration" (*svādhiṣṭhāna-krama*) in a manner that employs virtually none of the technical terminology found in the Lamdré.[100]

FIGURE 10 Mahāsiddha Virūpa. Chinese, Ming dynasty, Yung-lo mark and period, 1403–1424. Gilt bronze, 43.6 cm. high.
© The Cleveland Museum of Art, 2004, Gift of Mary B. Lee, C. Bingham Blossom, Dudley S. Blossom III, Laurel B. Kovacik, and Elizabeth B. Blossom in memory of Elizabeth B. Blossom, 1972.96

Finally are the three large collections of songs of realization: the *Dohakoṣa*, the *Virūapādacaurāsi*, and the *Sunisprapañcatattvopadeśa*.[101] These are exciting and, indeed, magnificent examples of the song systems used by the later siddha figures in ninth- to twelfth-century India. They provide a philosophical or intellectual counterpoint to the fussy ritualism and village magic exploited in so many of the Yamāri-Yamāntaka works. It is little wonder that Ngorchen turned to the last of these texts to try to vindicate the position of Virūpa and the Lamdré in Indian spiritual geography.[102] Yet these texts do not lead any closer to establishing a Virūpa who might have written both the *Root Text of the *Mārgaphala* and any of the verse collections. In short, it is an astonishing fact that no text is ascribed to a Virūpa that shares the technical lists, the specific terminology, or even the general outline of the *Root Text of the *Mārgaphala*. Perhaps the best gauge of this discontinuity is that, for the most part, the preceding four groups of texts are relatively clear, even sometimes easy to read, with little commentary or elucidation necessary.

This is decidedly not the case for the *Root Text of the *Mārgaphala*. Indeed, the secret nature of this work extends as much from its terse and obscure prose as from its having been sequestered in the hallowed halls of Tibetan institutions. The terminology in the work is sometimes seemingly unique to the text, and the occasional efforts by exegetes to match the content of the work with themes found in various scriptures (especially the *Hevajra-tantra*), simply serve to highlight the differences among them and to illuminate the lack of a true analogue to the *Root Text of the *Mārgaphala*.[103] The text is filled with lists identified by rubric but not specified—for example, the four epistemes (*tshad ma bzhi*) in I.C.—and their articulation in Sachen's commentaries are sometimes just as puzzling, for some of the lists correspond to few known categories of Buddhist thought. Many of the text's categories are sufficiently outside the norms of esoteric Buddhism that they appear to constitute an aborted movement toward an entirely different arrangement of the Buddhist path. Many sections of the *Root Text of the *Mārgaphala* cannot be interpreted without the aid of Sachen's twelfth-century commentaries, and even Sachen sometimes reads the text in defiance of normative Tibetan grammar. Just as curious, Sachen's interpretation of the odd categories is itself idiosyncratic, and some of the examples are identified in the notes to the translation. The current head of the Sakyapa order more than once observed to me that he found the meaning of the *Root Text of the *Mārgaphala* quite difficult to comprehend, and this is no reflection on his own deep scholarly ability.

We may surmise one or more disquieting things from these difficulties. First, Drokmi may have purposely translated the text in a manner that required oral instruction for its correct interpretation. The possible rationale for this practice would have been his desire to maintain total control over the work. Based on his other translations—which are among the best and most polished in the eleventh century—this decision would require an extraordinary departure from the standard that Drokmi himself helped establish. Second, Sachen may not have received the correct interpretation of the text because it was not transmitted correctly by the lineage down to Sachen. This alternative is just as improbable as the first, however. These men were thoroughly invested in the interpretation of this specific work, and I find it unimaginable that they would not have remembered the teaching, for the text is not long, after all. In Sachen's case, the same commentarial structure and phraseology occur verbatim throughout much of the ten lengthy commentaries attributed to him, and, although the tradition denies it, Sachen probably had some written texts from previous masters before him at some time in his career.[104] Thus, it is likely that both Sachen and his predecessors were careful scholars of the work that they considered the actual composition of the celestial goddess Nairātmyā.

A third possibility, however, begs our attention. Gayādhara seems to be exactly the kind of Indian paṇḍita that Rongzom noted in his contemporary criticism of the Sarma system: Rongzom claimed that Indian paṇḍitas find out whatever Tibetans wanted and composed new works en route to Tibet. Certainly, Gayādhara played rather freely with the truth in masquerading as Maitrīpā on his second trip to Tibet. Accordingly, Gayādhara was certainly not above creating an artificial persona for himself, a persona that would provide him with esteem, income, and access to the great clans of Ü-Tsang. Moreover, like many Kāyasthas, Gayādhara was an individual of outstanding learning and dubious ethics, given to opportunism in service of his own position. There can be little doubt, given the extraordinary range of materials he translated, that he was both intelligent and skilled in the special discipline of the esoteric scriptures. Finally, Gayādhara promised Drokmi that he would transmit the *Root Text of the *Mārgaphala* to no one else, but Gyijo Dawé Öser seems also to have received it at a later time, further casting a pall over Gayādhara's veracity.

One possible scenario, therefore, is that Gayādhara appeared in Tibet with much learning and opportunistic ethics, to find Drokmi asking for a text that no one else knew. Because of the great siddhas' popularity, all the other "secret instructions" were relatively well distributed. Drokmi already possessed many of them, but they did not provide him with the monopoly he desired. In the face of such a need, Gayādhara may have produced a text. If this was the case, I do not believe that he would have composed it all himself, for the text of the

Lamdré is so heterogeneous that it is improbably by a single author. Most likely, Gayādhara would already have had in his possession a very short, rather nondescript work embodying much or all of the first section (I), which is a loose grouping of ways to understand the Buddhist path. This very small body of organizing material might then have been augmented by specific instructions that were received by Gayādhara, abstracted by him from esoteric materials that he knew, or simply constructed on the spot. Such a scenario seems more plausible when considering the peculiar title of the work as it occurs in all recensions: *The Instructions on the Path, Together with Its Fruit, Along with Technical Directions*. The "Sanskrit title," *Pratrimatidha-upadeśa*, given in one of the early commentaries, was composed by someone with no knowledge of Sanskrit and is apparently an artifact of the twelfth-century predisposition to fabricate Indic-sounding titles in order to claim Indian authenticity.[105] Thus, whatever its source, the text must have incorporated the technical directions (*man ngag* : *upadeśa*) in addition to the instructions (*gdams ngag*) on the fundamental path structure itself.

In contrast to this model, we should consider the sole surviving text directly attributed to Gayādhara: the *Jñānodayopadeśa* (To. 1514).[106] This work is divided into three sections, the first treating the central mantras of the Saṁvara system, the second describing indirect language, and the third devoted to disparate topics, concluding with a discussion of the relationship between the stages of the bodhisattva/buddha and the twenty-four pilgrimage sites of the Saṁvara system. In all these various topics, there is nary an echo of the Lamdré, and if Gayādhara were the author of the *Root Text of the *Mārgaphala*, then some continuity between its technical language and the terminology of his other work should be expected, as in the case of Virūpa. Yet I cannot move from a sense of Gayādhara's or his immediate predecessor's (Avadhūti's) agency, for the *Root Text* builds on the very latest esoteric directions. For example, the Lamdré's harmony with some late tantras can occasionally be detected, such as the *Yoginīsañcāra*'s pronouncement on the importance of the thirty-seven branches of awakening that also operate as a metanarrative in sections II and III of the *Root Text of the *Mārgaphala*.[107]

Alternatively, perhaps Drokmi was the author of this work. He could have secured this gold simply to pay Gayādhara to support a fallacious Indic source for the material. According to this model, Drokmi would have been sufficiently concerned about his future revenue to fabricate a work requiring exceptional compensation to Gayādhara. I find such a possibility remote at best. While Drokmi cannot be said to have been a perfect monk, I can affirm—having reviewed his oeuvre in some detail—that he was a scholar of extraordinary ability and intellectual integrity, more so in fact than Gayādhara. There is no record of others impugning Drokmi's intellectual credentials, even though some writers satirized his insistent need for funds. So, while the eleventh century produced many willing to question works produced by either Tibetans or Indians, Drokmi does not stand in the ranks of those so accused.

Whoever may have been the author of this most curious work, it is not evident that any part of the *Root Text of the *Mārgaphala* can be definitely attributed to any known Virūpa, and the association of this work with the famous poet/drunkard/yogin of the late tenth century is in strong terminological dissonance with the material included in all other documents containing his name. If Gayādhara was at the center of the text's composition, then Sachen's grammatically problematic readings would be understandable in the context of a continuously evolving work, for the original "translation" would be subject to reinterpretation over the course of the years that Drokmi and Gayādhara worked together. The alternative title **Vajrapada* or **Mūlavajrapada* (*rtsa ba rdo rje'i tshig rkang*) given to the work is unattested in any received edition and appears first specified in Sachen's commentaries.[108] This alternative title is probably a sign of the movement toward legitimacy, for siddhas were understood to have crafted or received such pithy adamantine words (*vajrapada*) as a product of their perfection or as a revelation by a celestial goddess.[109] Indeed, the problems with the *Root Text of the *Mārgaphala* stand as a microcosm of so many of the difficulties seen in other works attributed to late Indian siddhas. I use the slightly more neutral title *Root Text of the *Mārgaphala* simply for convenience, even though this is also one of its later designations.

THE CONTENTS OF THE *ROOT TEXT OF THE *MĀRGAPHALA*

Although the entire *Root Text of the *Mārgaphala* is translated and edited in appendix 2, I will outline the composition here in order to make the various parts and themes a bit more approachable, although this is clearly neither the purpose of this obscure work nor the desire of its lineage. The *Root Text of the *Mārgaphala* is divided into three longer and one shorter sections, each a different length. The commentaries are the sources for these divisions, but there is much merit to their strategy, if only because of the different content exhibited in each of these parts. The three longer sections delineate the "extensive path" and are termed (I) the teaching common to both existence and liberation, (II) the (mundane) path in which the *cakras* are coaxed toward harmony, and (III) the supermundane path that revolves the wheels (*cakra*). Beyond these three is a short section, IV, which is really a catchall conclusion about the Vajrayāna and the specification of the deep, middling, and abbreviated paths, which have little in common with one another except their cursory treatment.

The first section was to be historically the most important for a variety of reasons. It includes seven groupings, two defining the full successive stages of the path and the other five describing standards or specific directions on the path. Presented first is the idea of the triple appearance. This is a restatement of a very old Buddhist conception. Briefly, it means that the nature of existence is analyzed; the nature of the path is expounded; and the circumstances of awakening are articulated. The terminology recognizes that reality appears differently to one in the position of bondage, to one engaged in the practice of the path, and to one who has achieved the full awakening of the Buddha. To the first, existence appears defiled, filled with grief and stained with emotional turbulence. While on the path, however, there is a high degree of variation in the appearance of reality, sometimes seeming pristine and other times seeming polluted. At the point of awakening, though, all reality appears as the non-arisen and in a condition of absolute purity, for it has never been otherwise, merely seeming so from a viewpoint of inadequate understanding.

The antiquity of this schematization is evident when we consider that it was described in such mainstays of Mahāyāna as the *Ratnagotravibhāga*, in which the embryo of the Tathāgata (*tathāgatagarbha*) is described in similar terms: defiled, defiled-undefiled, and stainless, all depending on one's advancement along the Buddhist path.[110] In reality, the Mahāyānist roots of this schema was determinant for its institutionalization, as the triple appearance system became the standard for introducing Lamdré beginners into the context of Buddhist practice, and its content was quite similar to the "stages on the path" (*lam rim*) material so well known from studies of the works of Atiśa, Gampopa, and Tsongkhapa.[111] It must be emphasized that there is nothing in the text's statements on the triple appearance that would necessarily make it an exclusively exoteric explanation, but the semantic associations of this formulation apparently made it both desirable and unavoidable.

Conversely, the next part (I.B) of the first section discusses the triple continuity (*rgyud gsum*), which is potentially similar to the triple appearance as an overview of the path. Briefly, the triple continuity is a similar process applied to the ideology of esoteric Buddhism, as opposed to the normative practices of the Mahāyāna, in the manner of the triple appearance. Thus, the basis of the path is established in a ground that may lead to either defilement or liberation; the physical body is the method; the consecrations are the means for planting the seeds to be ripened in the practice, protections, and confessions of transgressions; and the fruition in the Great Seal (*mahāmudrā*) is described. The language employed in I.B stands in stark contrast with that in I.A, so that the esoteric nature of the triple continuity is apparent in the text. Consequently, this formulation became the mainstay for esoteric exegesis, much as the triple appearance strategy became normative for the exoteric teaching of the Lamdré.

We will return to I.B when discussing Sachen's contributions, but some observations about the actual disposition of the Lamdré path are in order. First, the path in the Lamdré is entirely configured through the ritual authorization of the four consecrations (*abhiṣeka*), so that each consecration allows the yogin to practice a meditation: deity yoga, internal heat, and two different forms of sexual yoga. Even the fruits of each meditation are configured according to the consecrations, so that each section of the stages of the path (*bhūmis* 1–6, 7–10, 11–12 1/2, and 13) and each of the four bodies of the Buddha is realized by one practicing the material authorized in each of the four consecrations. This overwhelming emphasis on consecration as a defining structure for all aspects of the path is without close parallel in any other esoteric Buddhist tradition known to me. In the *Root Text of the *Mārgaphala*, all aspects of the esoteric path are organized into one or another of these consecrations, with the ritual format providing the fundamental grid for all further practice.

Second, there is absolutely no specificity found in the text regarding any individual deity or maṇḍala. The text indicates only that the generation process (*utpattikrama*) should be performed, not which one. The *Root Text of the *Mārgaphala*, therefore, is similar to some other theoretical works that were written from the eighth century onward, like the *Jñānasiddhi*. But because the text is quite specific regarding the internal yoga system, it really needed to be associated with a specific *yoginī-tantra* tradition, and allowances are made for the Lamdré to be practiced with either the Hevajra or the Cakrasaṁvara systems.[112] This allowance recognized that the text had no stated external maṇḍala, but in most instances the interpretation has been on the Hevajra system. At the same time the tradition acknowledges that the internal maṇḍala visualized inside the body conforms more closely to the internal maṇḍala found in the Cakrasaṁvara practices.[113] Thus the text is ambiguous in some areas and not in others; somewhat a Hevajra text and somehow a Cakrasaṁvara work. This ambivalence may reflect both Gayādhara's disposition and his esoteric zeitgeist, for his translation efforts included works from both systems.

Like other *yoginī-tantra* traditions, the Lamdré specifies that the generation process must be followed by the completion process. Normatively, the completion process is embedded in two fundamental practices: a visualized inner yogic heat (the "self-consecration": *svādhiṣṭhāna-krama*) and sexual yoga (*maṇḍalacakra*). The latter may be entirely visualized (*jñānamudrā*) or practiced with a physical partner (*karmamudrā*). The differences between the two fundamental practices are important, if relatively subtle, and both require an internal system of visualization in which the body is seen as inhabited by several—from one to five—internal centers or wheels (*cakra*) in which different arrangements of divinities or letters operate. This internal structure represents the adamantine body (*vajrakāya*), which for many *yoginī-tantras* is not the consequence of practice. Instead, the adamantine body is the natural condition of the human psychophysical continuum, operating in most persons as a ground of human experience that is poorly controlled.

For the Lamdré, the aspects of the *vajrakāya* are principally constituted by three maṇḍalas: the physical body with its channels (*rtsa lus dkyil 'khor*), the "qualities" or genital part of the body with its letters (*yi ge bha ga'i dkyil 'khor*), and the fluid "nectar" processes of the body (*khams bdud rtsi'i dkyil 'khor*).[114] The first two have both a gross and a subtle form. If the sensory organs and limbs are the gross aspects of the physical body, its many different internal channels are its subtle system, transporting around the various elements. The gross form of the "quality" maṇḍala is the individual genital organs, penis and vagina, and the subtle form is composed of letters (especially fourteen) in specific positions inside the channels. Finally, the fluid maṇḍala is composed of semen, blood, and other serous substances. Mobilizing all these three maṇḍalas is the vital wind, which acts as the force for motion and is intimately connected with the mind. The concentration of the mind mixing with the wind can move the wind into the central channel and is capable of transforming the wind from the active wind (*karmavāyu*) into the gnostic wind (*jñānavāyu*). The simplicity of that statement is belied by the overwhelming complexity of the various opinions and differing models of the subtle body proposed in the Lamdré's intersection of medical theories, yogic practice, and textual affiliation.

Although the Kagyüpa also feature several disparate yogic systems, most of the Indian Buddhist yogic schools generally agreed that the completion process is constituted in large part by the two fundamental practices just mentioned, the "self-consecration" psychic heat and *maṇḍalacakra* sexual yoga. This is not true of the Lamdré, which proposes a third major completion process practice. The third practice is called the "adamantine wave" (*rdo rje rba rlabs*), although this term is somewhat misleading. This program is a modification of the sexual practice of the *maṇḍalacakra* but with the visualizations and manipulation of the details done in a different manner. Its purpose is to bring to arrest (*rengs ba*) the vibrations (waves: *rba rlabs*) that constitute the object, the subject, and the conception of duality. Accordingly, the seminal fluid is manipulated through the right channel, the left channel and then brought to rest in the central channel, so that all three come to rest in the adamantine wave that is not separate from bliss and emptiness, since it no longer creates the dualistic distinctions of subject and object, and so forth. While the meditator and his partner also experience the four joys and the four moments as they had done in the *maṇḍalacakra* practice—both practices culminating in the experience of innate bliss (*sahajānanda*)—this practice produces these in the central channel, from the navel to the fontanel, whereas the *maṇḍalacakra* produced them from the fontanel to the navel.[115] Consequently, this third form may have been an attempt to bring together the two different styles of sexual practice, for in India there was a controversy about whether the four joys were in ascent or descent: here both are employed in succession.[116] Lamdré authorities, however, claim that that the adamantine wave experiences are of a different, more intense order than those of the ordinary *maṇḍalacakra*, since they yield the ultimate experience. In the successful meditator, the various vital airs, the serous substances, the letters, and the forms of consciousness all are transformed into the various bodies of the Buddha, with their attendant forms of gnosis.

Returning to the *Root Text of the *Mārgaphala*, items I.C to I.F are discussed as if they were self-evident, even though they are mostly unattested elsewhere. Sachen's commentaries reveal the lists of the four epistemes (I.C), the four aural streams (I.E), and the five forms of interdependent origination (I.F). Only the six instructions (I.D) are fully articulated in the text, and even then their clarity leaves almost everything to be desired. It is not just my English translation that is opaque, and I have tried to rely on annotation to bring out the sense, where such may be found. Moreover, the protective material at the end of the section (I.G) seems not to fit in with the other content and appears to refer to some of the practices discussed in later parts of the text. Whereas I.A through I.F unfolded grand narratives of a path or standards against which that path is measured, I.G provides technical details about certain obstacles and is anomalous in section I.

Section I is explained as pertaining equally to the states of bondage (*saṁsāra*) and liberation (*nirvāṇa*), whereas section II, again according to the commentaries, is occupied with the mundane path (*laukikamārga*), for the various yogic meditations specified can be performed without accomplishing the stages of the bodhisattva. It is section III that concerns the supermundane path (*lokottaramārga*) as the individual stages of the bodhisattva are integrated into the practice and levels of realization are encountered. Like I.G, almost all of section II discusses practices and their impediments, antidotes, and experiences, much of which is refreshingly clear. It is roughly structured around three forms of "seminal coalescence" (*khams 'dus pa*), which differ from one another simply by the level of intensity of the meditative experience. Later writers aligned these three with the three practices of the completion stage—self-consecration and the two forms of sexual yoga—but this subsequent interpretation is presented only as an option in the earliest commentaries, which sometimes specifically resist the easy sequencing.[117] Similarly, section III is independently explained using the categories of the ten stages of the bodhisattva, which here are expanded to thirteen stages, since the esoteric path ostensibly leads to the superior level of the citadel of Vajradhara, the metaphor for ultimate awakening. This structure is invoked for section III in the way that the three forms of coalescence were for section II; since the bodhisattva levels are supermundane and the three coalescences are mundane, there is no overlap. What is both confusing and remarkable, however, is that sections II and III together are given a further Buddhist narrative structure, that of the thirty-seven branches of awakening (*saptatriṁśad-bodhipākṣika-dharmāḥ*). The process is made even more confusing by the addition of various groups, like the six recollections (II.F) and the supercognitions (III.C), which are not included in standard lists of the thirty-seven. Section III is furthermore organized according to the four consecrations, identifying which consecrations leads to which fruit among the stages of the bodhisattva and to which body of the Buddha.

Thus the text reveals a ideological puzzle: doctrinal grid overlaying doctrinal grid overlaying doctrinal grid, none of which precisely coincides. The relationships among the individual members of the different categories become a problematic to be solved by both the teaching master and the individual meditator. As a synthetic series of schematisms, it revels in the complexity of late Indian Buddhist esoteric thought in much the same manner as the *Abhisamayālaṁkāra* does for the Mahāyānist tradition. The received *Root Text of the *Mārgaphala* is clearly the product of a synthetic author (or authors), who is undaunted by the challenge of bringing together the great categories of esoteric and exoteric Mahāyāna but who could not forsake terseness in favor of transparency. The astonishing creativity of the enterprise becomes apparent only when the different systems are sorted out and the text is clarified in the exegetical endeavor. If there is a thread of purpose between this text and Virūpa's hagiography, it is just the playfulness of its layout, the carnival of inadequately expressed topsy-turvy categories.

THE EIGHT SUBSIDIARY CYCLES OF PRACTICE

Beyond the *Root Text of the *Mārgaphala*, the tradition holds that Drokmi was the receptor of eight subsidiary practices, these being subordinate only in the importance placed on them by Drokmi and his followers. Collectively, these and the Lamdré are identified as the "Nine Cycles of Practice," and Sakyapa writers maintain that Drokmi was the only one to unite them as a group, although others transmitted one or another independently. The textual and historical problems of the entire group are excellent examples of two factors previously noted. First is the privileging of short works of yogic instructions (*upadeśa*) over esoteric scriptures, and such pithy texts have human authors and short lineal transmissions. Second, some of these eight subsidiary yogic works are distinguished by alternative versions and were not included in the canon (*bsTan 'gyur*) because there were preferred translations or for some other reason. Most are as "gray" as they can be, for while these instructions claim to be from an Indian author, they often were composed by later Tibetans around very short teachings attributed to Indians. Perhaps most important, the eight subsidiary cycles demonstrate the response of one literate lineage to the wealth of meditative systems and differing traditions coming out of India, Kashmir, and Nepal between the tenth and twelfth century, for most translators at that time received an equally chaotic mass of teaching. In the current emphasis on tracing the formation of the Tibetan Buddhist canon, we might reflect on variant traditions that, for reasons of historical accident as much as for any other cause, were not included in the fourteenth- to eighteenth-century redactions but continued to circulate in limited environments outside the great printing establishments of Central and East Tibet.[118] The following represents these eight systems' order in the modern printing of Drakpa Gyeltsen's *Yellow Book* (*Pod ser*):[119]

1. *ACINTYĀDVAYAKRAMOPADEŚA*. MAHĀMUDRĀSIDDHA-ŚRĪ-KUDDĀLAPĀDA

The *Acintyādvayakramopadeśa*,[120] like many of the works translated during the eleventh century, is a text focused on the completion stage. The received Sanskrit text is relatively short, with 124 verses, and even then is longer than some works of this genre. There are two surviving translations of this text, one included in *Yellow Book* compendium of the Lamdré material used by the Sakyapa and one found in the Tibetan canon.[121] The former translation is attributed to the team of Ratnavajra and Drokmi, whereas the canonical version (To. 2228) is attributed to *Sukhāṅkura and Gö (probably Khukpa Lhétsé). The two translations are different enough to be from different recensions of the *Acintyādvayakramopadeśa*, although they are close enough to be identified with the same basic work. The Sakyapas rounded out the text by providing a commentary and a short discussion of selected sections of the work, as well as a traditional chronicle of its principals.[122] The chronicle, in fact, is derived from a direct statement in the body of the text itself and is amplified in both the two translations, which have somewhat disparate readings of the lineage.[123]

Ngorchen, writing in 1405, maintained that the text was composed based on the *Sampuṭa-tilaka-tantra*, but at most the connection seems to be only indirect. The work itself begins by presenting instructions regarding the correct view, using a vocabulary generally familiar in the Mahāmudrā discussions, and continues on to details of the completion stage path. The text has no obvious structure, but an anonymous commentary included in the modern printing of the *Yellow Book* divides it according to a triple continuity strategy. The "causal" material is devoted to perspective, in which twelve instructions are included: instructions on the psychophysical continuum, on concentration, on the indivisibility of appearance and emptiness, and on the three epistemes that define the path. The path material covers seven goals: grasping the mind, establishing it in reality, cultivating the practices, overcoming obstacles, identifying eight specific activities of benefit, comprehending experiences, and relying on a consort. The result of the path are the forms of gnosis and the bodies of the Buddha. This breakdown, we should emphasize, is not at all evident in the received text and should be considered the product of an emerging exegesis.

2. *SAHAJASIDDHI*. ḌOMBIHERUKA

The *Sahajasiddhi*[124] represented as received by Drokmi appears quite different from the better-known *Sahajasiddhi* work of Ḍombi that survives in Sanskrit and was edited and translated by Shendge.[125] The surviving Sanskrit text is ordered in three sections, the first having to do with the two standard completion process practices, the second discussing issues of the Buddha families (*kula*) and sacraments (*samaya*), and the third presenting standards of nonconceptualization. Conversely, what is found in the Lamdré case is not an Indic text at all, for the work presented is clearly a Tibetan composition based on a teaching concerning the Innate (Sahaja) attributed to Ḍombiheruka. It specifically mentions him in the third person as having composed the *Sahajasiddhi* based on a verse from the *Hevajra-tantra*.[126] The anonymous text found in the *Yellow Book* compendium is, like many Sakyapa works, organized around the triple continuity: the Innate is defined as the ground, the path, and the fruit of meditation. Much of this work overlaps both the *Acintyādvayakramopadeśa* and the *Root Text of the *Mārgaphala*, not to mention other works. But it certainly is not the same as the other texts found in the Tibetan canon under the *Sahajasiddhi* title, although some of its content obviously is shared with all of them.[127] The tension between the Lamdré instructions regarding *Sahajasiddhi* and other works with this title is evident in the *Yellow Book*, in which this text (like many other Tibetan compositions there) is introduced with an Indic title, as if we were about to encounter a translation. Then the text merely claims its status as meditative instruction (*gdams ngag*) based on the *Sahajasiddhi*, and in the conclusion a piece of marginalia of unknown source indicates that this instruction constitutes the precious textless Lamdré received by Ḍombiheruka from Virūpa and passed on to Drokmi by Vīravajra.[128] Its description as the textless Lamdré weakly agrees with Drakpa Gyeltsen's rendition in *Chronicle of Tibet* (§2), translated earlier, but is absent from the Lamdré history presented by Ngorchen.[129]

3. *OBTAINED BEFORE A CAITYA* (*MCHOD RTEN DRUNG THOB*). ASCRIBED TO NĀGĀRJUNA

This work[130] presents many of the difficulties of the previous text. It is described and represented as an Indic work, but at the same time it is presented as an oral instruction based on two Indic works, and the text was written specifically by Drakpa Gyeltsen. Four different titles for this one text are listed in the *Yellow Book*: *Obtained Before a Caitya* (*mChod rten gyi drung tu thob pa*), *The Instruction on Determining the Mind* (*Sems thag gcod pa'i gdams ngag*), *Meditating on the Absolute Thought of Awakening* (*Don dam pa byang chub kyi sems bsgoms pa*), and *Instruction in Mahāmudrā as Natural Reality* (*Phyag rgya chen po rnal du ston pa*). The work is divided into five topics: determining the nature of mind by means of the proper perspective, accumulating merit, concentrating the mind, recognizing the mind as reality, and activity and development based on realization. The text included in the *Yellow Book* maintains that, based on a verse containing the thought of awakening (*bodhicitta*) pronounced by Akṣobhyavajra in the second chapter of the *Guhyasamāja-tantra*, Saraha composed his songs of his *Dohā Treasury*. Likewise, based on a verse containing the thought of awakening (*bodhicitta*) pronounced by Vairocanavajra in the second chapter of the *Guhyasamāja-tantra*, Nāgārjuna composed his *Bodhicittavivaraṇa*. This *Obtained Before a Caitya* is the oral instruction based on both these works and was said to have been obtained by Nāgārjuna from Saraha in front of the Dhānyakaṭaka stūpa built by the demigods, a stūpa close to Śrīparvata.[131]

Assessing one aspect of the source claim is relatively easy, for the Tibetan translation of the *Bodhicittavivaraṇa* begins with the Vairocanavajra verse, and it probably was obtained from the *Guhyasamāja-tantra*, for this work has stimulated the formation of literature on the thought of awakening, especially as the second chapter of the tantra is dedicated to the topic.[132] The *Dohā Treasury* is more difficult, for the text identified in the *Yellow Book* is the one surviving in Apabhraṁśa, and there is no Apabhraṁśa rendering of the verse from the *Guhyasamāja-tantra* found in that text.[133] Although both these two ostensible sources emphasize the relationship of the mind to reality—and are therefore on a continuum with the *Obtained Before a Caitya*, as are all esoteric texts describing meditations on the thought of awakening—there is little in the way of a necessary relationship. It appears, therefore, that the lineage of this work is proposed more for the purpose of establishing its authenticity than for an accurate assessment of its derivation. This impression is reinforced by the later tradition's emphasis on Nāgārjuna's text as the source, with no mention of Saraha thereby reflecting the increased authority of the composite philosopher/siddha Nāgārjuna in the fourteenth and fifteenth centuries.[134] This work was clearly written by Drakpa Gyeltsen, based on the explanation of Sachen Kunga Nyingpo, and it should be understood that there was no previous text, only oral instructions received by Drokmi from Vīravajra.[135]

4. *LETTERLESS MAHĀMUDRĀ* (*PHYAG RGYA CHEN PO YI GE MED PA*). ATTRIBUTED TO VĀGĪŚVARAKĪRTI

The *Yellow Book* again portrays this work in a similar manner.[136] Vāgīśvarakīrti composed his *Saptāṅga* and his *Tattvaratnāvaloka* based on both the *Guhyasamāja* and *Hevajra-tantras* and on the speech of the goddess Tārā. Then, working also with Ḍombiheruka's *Nairātmyayoginīsādhana*, Vāgīśvarakīrti constructed this instruction called the *Letterless Mahāmudrā*.[137] The text is organized into a beginning blessing and instruction of the disciple by the master, who visualizes himself as the goddess Nairātmyā, and includes an instruction on the nature of mind and reality. The second part involves the disciple's visualizations and meditations on the path. The third section is a short discussion of the attributes of the three bodies of the Buddha.

Vāgīśvarakīrti's canonical work indicates that his principal contribution was his emphasis on a rigorous approach to the fourth initiation, the consecration admitting the most variation in representation or in exegesis. Vāgīśvarakīrti's two works cited—his *Saptāṅga* and his *Tattvaratnāvaloka*—along with his autocommentary on the second, are among his most important texts and include interesting developments in the use of painting in the various esoteric initiations.[138] There is no clear connection, however, between the work attributed to him in the *Yellow Book* by the Sakyapas and his canonical texts, and we might wonder whether the same questions of authenticity seen before are not the main issues here as well. Ḍombiheruka's *Nairātmyayoginīsādhana* was apparently mentioned as a source for the *Letterless Mahāmudrā* in recognition of the importance of Ḍombiheruka's work to Drokmi's transmission of visualizations associated with the goddess Nairātmyā. Again, the text of the *Letterless Mahāmudrā* was written by Drakpa Gyeltsen, possibly based on the teaching of Vāgīśvarakīrti, which Drokmi is said to have received from Amoghavajra.[139]

5. *GENERATION PROCESS ORNAMENTED WITH NINE PROFOUND METHODS* (*BSKYED RIM ZAB PA'I TSHUL DGUS BRGYAN PA*). ATTRIBUTED TO PADMAVAJRA (OR SARORUHAVAJRA)

The text,[140] also written by Drakpa Gyeltsen, indicates that it was composed by Saroruhavajra, based on the *Śrī-Hevajrasādhana*.[141] The work is in four sections. First, the perspective is that all of existence and awakening is realized to be indivisible; next are given the nine methods to stabilize the mind through esoteric pacific practices, along with the stages of the path, followed by the generation of certainty through the nine deep means to cut off all the conceptualizations having to do with exteriority; and finally the fruit is explained as the three bodies with the seven branches.[142] Thus the title is slightly misleading in that the full spectrum of ground, path, and fruit is encountered with the basic strategy of a ninefold division of methods of various varieties (including the completion process) on the path.

The *Generation Process Ornamented with Nine Profound Methods* clearly emphasizes the indivisibility of existence and awakening, which is a doctrine not well represented in the *Śrī-Hevajrasādhana* (To. 1218) attributed to Padmavajra. Indeed, the current text of the *Yellow Book* also includes a canonical work attributed to Saroruhavajra, the *Śrī-Hevajrapradīpaśūlopamāvavādaka*, and it looks different in inspiration from the *Generation Process Ornamented with Nine Profound Methods*, in both the discussion of the completion process and its doctrinal positioning.[143] Padmavajra is certainly one of the best known of the ninth-century esoteric authors, having written extensive commentaries on such works as the *Ḍākārṇava* (*Śrī-Ḍākārṇava-mahāyoginītantrarāja-vāhikaṭīkā*, To. 1419), the *Buddhakapāla* (*Buddhakapālatantrapañjikā Tattvacandrikā*, To. 1653), Buddhaguhya's *Tantrārthāvatāra* (*Tantrārthāvatāra-vyākhyāna*, To. 2502), his own *Guhyasiddhi*, and a number of short meditative works, like the *Śrī-Hevajrasādhana*. The identification of the author of the *Generation Process Ornamented with Nine Profound Methods* with Padmavajra is problematic, however, as "padma" is a standard loanword in Tibetan and the Tibetan name Tsokyé Dorjé suggests the Sanskrit Saroruhavajra or a similar equivalent. In the Tibetan translations of the other works attributed to Padmavajra, his name was simply written as is (Padmavajra) or as Péma Dorjé. Thus, the relationship between this instruction written by Drakpa Gyeltsen and the other works ascribed to Padmavajra is not clear. Drakpa Gyeltsen does not provide a lineage for this instruction, but the *Śrī-Hevajrapradīpaśūlopamāvavādaka* was translated by Drokmi in consultation with Gayādhara.[144]

6. *COMPLETION OF THE PATH THROUGH PSYCHIC HEAT* (*GTUM MOS LAM YONGS SU RDZOGS PA*). ASCRIBED TO *MAHĀCĀRYA-CĪRṆAVRATA-KĀṆHA

Drakpa Gyeltsen's introduction to the work[145] declares that Kāṇha, grounded in the understanding of his teacher Śrī-Mahā-Jālandara, composed his works based on his comprehension of a hierarchy in the canon. The entire Buddhadharma was subsumed into the Vajrayāna; all three sections of the tantras were subsumed into the Mahāyoga; both the tantras of skillful means and insight were subsumed into the nondual tantras of *Hevajra* and *Saṁvara*; and these were subsumed into the commentarial tantras of the *Vajraḍāka* and the *Sampuṭa*.[146] Their understanding, if combined, may express the completion process, and so Kāṇha wrote six works on that stage: the *Vasantatilaka*, the *Guhyatattvaprakāśa*, the *Olapati*, the **Garbhasaṁgraha*, the *Saṁvaravyākhyā*, and the **Mahāmudrātilaka*.[147] Drakpa Gyeltsen affirms that all these six may be subsumed into the four topics of the *Olapati*, and its oral instruction is expressed here, adding a fifth section.

I was able to identify four of the six works ascribed to Kāṇha, based on either a surviving Sanskrit text or a translation in the Tibetan canon.[148] Of these four, the *Olapati* certainly has the most anomalous name, for the term *ola* survives in a canonical title as indicating a stage or gradation (*rim pa*, normally equal to *krama*), but this appears unattested elsewhere and may indicate a Prakrit or local expression known to Kāṇha. Descriptions of the content of the *Olapati* by later writers exactly match the content of the *Four Stages* (*Rim pa bzhi pa*: To. 1451), as the canonical title is known, and the *ola* is attested in the autocommentary ascribed to Kāṇha. The work is divided into discussions of the stages of tantra, mantra, gnosis (*jñāna*), and the secret stage.[149] Both this and the other texts ascribed to Kāṇha were popular with the Sakyapa masters, and several of them were commented on or discussed in various ways by Sachen and Drakpa Gyeltsen.[150] This text builds on the *Olapati* in some aspects of its organization, although it is divided into beginning perspective (*lta ba*), meditation (*bsgom pa*), and then the bodies of the Buddha as the fruit of the path. Within the first two, the content is organized in the same way as the

Four Stages—tantra, mantra, gnosis, and secret—but with the addition of a new stage, the nondual. Again we notice the Sakyapas' propensity to take a foundation, path, and goal approach to the material. Both this meditative direction and the following instruction came to Drokmi through Gayādhara.

7. *INSTRUCTION TO STRAIGHTEN THE CROOKED (YON PO BSRANG BA'I GDAMS NGAG)*. ASCRIBED TO ACYUTA-KĀṆHA

The short text presented[151] also was apparently written by either Sachen Kunga Nyingpo or Drakpa Gyeltsen, for even though the authorship is not explicit, it was written at Sakya.[152] In conformity with the other works, this one concerns the completion process, and Ngorchen indicates that it was based on all the Mother tantras (i.e., *yoginī-tantras*), although the *Yellow Book* does not specify the foundation for the work.[153] The text begins with a short, hagiographical scenario in which Acyuta-Kāṇha is depicted encountering a supernormal yogin called Acyuta on the way from Jālandara. His Buddhist/Śaiva split personality is evident here, as it is in three of the songs attributed to Kāṇha in the *Caryāgītikośa*.[154] Here, Kāṇha receives a verse containing the practice from this Acyuta:

> If you seize the vital air by means of the wrathful form [of yoga],
> Then you will eliminate white hair and wrinkles.
> Having been liberated from old age and death,
> One becomes deathless, like the sky.[155]

In its commentary on the verse, the text briefly describes the physical yogic practices (*'khrul 'khor* : *yantra*), as well as the transition between extreme yogic activities patterned on Pāśupata or other Śaiva conduct (*avadhūtacaryā*) and the normative Buddhist behavior (*samantabhadracaryā*). As a consequence of these "wrathful" practices, the text takes great pains to point out that it will relieve the yogin of white hair, wrinkles, and other signs of aging (i.e., crookedness), owing to which Kāṇha is termed "deathless" (*acyuta*). Like many other works in this group, this text concludes with a discussion of the bodies of the Buddha. Ngorchen specifically identifies Acyuta-Kāṇha with the Kāṇha of the previous text, indicating that their identity has been verified through the lineage list and that both are represented as being received by Drokmi from Gayādhara.[156]

8. *CYCLE ON THE PATH WITH A CONSORT* (*PHYAG RGYA'I LAM SKOR*). ATTRIBUTED TO INDRABHŪTI

As its title indicates, this text[157] is exclusively occupied with practices surrounding the use of a sexual partner in the advanced levels of the completion process. The length of the work, one of the longer of the eight subsidiary practices, suggests its importance to the tradition, and in fact its directions are sometimes replicated in discussions in the longest of the eleven commentaries attributed to Sachen, the *Sédönma*.[158] The *Cycle on the Path with a Consort* is concerned with the exegesis of a verse attributed to Indrabhūti:[159]

> On the horse made [i.e., rode] by Devadatta,
> The four doors are to be opened by the nāga.
> Seize desire with the extended bow.
> Increase it with the tortoise gait.
> Since it is blocked and with a sigh,
> The [bodhicitta] is carried in place by the HIK girdle.

The interpretation of this cryptic verse occupies most of the text, a literal interpretation in the first half of the work and an exegesis of specific difficult points in the second half. Devadatta, which is a curious use of the Buddha's heretical disciple's name, indicates the well-prepared tantric yogin, who rides the horse of the Vajrayāna. The "nāga" (a snake) denotes the practice of preparing an implement (the snake) that is to be inserted into the rectum of the female (who is strapped to a saddle), so that the four ends of the psychophysical channels are opened and accessible to the yogin. He controls his desire with mantras (the bow), or, if necessary, increases his sexual ability by means of slow intercourse (the tortoise gait). He blocks the ejaculate by the arrest of the breath (the sigh) or by using the mantra HIK. The work ends with an interesting comment about the nature of Indrabhūti, for the Sakyapas hold that there were three Indrabhūtis: the great, the middle, and the lesser, all organized by their period so that greatness was a function of antiquity, even if all three were emanations of the esoteric bodhisattva Vajrapāṇi. This esoteric instruction came to Drokmi via Prajñāgupta, a name attached to one of the notorious figures of the eleventh century, the Red Master (Ācārya dmar-po). This master was said to have come from Oḍiyāna and have been a disciple of the Kashmiri Ratnavajra; the Red Master's authority was a matter of dispute at least from the time of Podrang Shiwa-Ö.[160]

Any assessment of these eight subsidiary practices must indicate, as I have tried to do, that with one exception (*Acintyādvayakramopadeśa*), they have no attested Indic text. The authors of the works—principally Drakpa Gyeltsen—take great pains to identify these works with well-known Indic materials. Yet their attempts are called into question by the observable discontinuity between these specific works and their putative antecedents. Their textual bases, therefore, are fundamentally Tibetan, a reality obscured by the consistent attempt to posit them as Indic texts with Indic titles in the printed version of the *Yellow Book.* These works represent a disparate variety of content, running the gamut from the fundamentals of esoteric Buddhism to the most advanced instruction in sexual practice and ultimate reality. Their sources are quite varied as well. They came to Drokmi from a range of informants: two (2 and 3) from Vīravajra, perhaps three (5?, 6, 7) from Gayādhara, and one each from Ratnavajra (1), Amoghavajra (4), and Prajñāgupta (8). Their content reveals a clear movement toward homogenization in the vortex of the Sakya institution, for they are consistently capped with instruction in the bodies of the Buddha, and many of them are filled out with a ground (*gzhi*) / path (*lam*) / result (*'bras bu*) structure. Indeed, the movement toward homogenization is often explicit in consideration of the "eight subsidiary practices," and as Gungru Shérap Zangpo pointed out, the Lamdré authors consistently stated that these eight clarify that which is not otherwise clear in the Lamdré and supplement that which is in need of augmentation.[161]

Thus these instructions should provide us with insight into textual formation among the Sarma authorities of the eleventh to twelfth century in terms of both its fluidity and its fragility. Many such disparate meditative directions with no particular textual basis found their way into texts during this time, as we shall see in the compendium of "precious" texts compiled by Sachen Kunga Nyingpo. Doubtless these eight are only the most obvious examples of attempts at resolving the tension among creative developments in meditative techniques, personal positioning, a movement toward institutionalization, and the desire to frame these works in manner amenable to the Tibetan religious public. If this public maintained that the only works acceptable were those authentically Indian, then the only form in which they could be presented must be preceded by an Indic title, a lineage list, and a colophon indicating their origins. Yet the colophons (again with the exception of the *Acintyādvayakramopadeśa*) demonstrate their Tibetan roots and therefore express the personal integrity of their authors. And if they can point to a verse around which the text is constructed (as with the *Yon po bsrang ba'i gdams ngag* and the *Phyag rgya'i lam skor*), so much the better, although the interpretations of these verses are as open to question as are the verses themselves. So, like much of the work of Zhama-lotsāwa briefly reviewed in the previous chapter, most works from the eight subsidiary practices were collectively drawn from the category of "gray" texts, whose inspiration was Indian, even though their actual form is Tibetan.

DROKMI'S OTHER TRANSLATIONS

It would be false to Drokmi and his paṇḍitas to represent the preceding materials as their most significant work, even though these texts represented the basis for Drokmi's ability to establish himself as a spiritual authority in the Mangkhar valley. If these translations and traditions provided authority, the many other translations verified his authenticity as an intellectual leader and scholar of merit. Because of the intensity of Drokmi's effort, there is little point to reciting a relatively meaningless list of names, as many attempts to discuss Tibetan translators have done in the past. Instead, I will divide this collection of translations into significant parts and try to understand Drokmi's total oeuvre. In doing so we must keep in mind certain limitations: the current canonical catalogs really represent later attempts at identifying Tibetan translations and are neither exhaustive nor entirely correct. The *Root Text of the *Mārgaphala* is an excellent example of a work not ascribed to Drokmi in the canon, yet we have no indication that the received work was from the pen of another translator, even if Gyijo Dawé Öser produced another one himself. Likewise, the *Acintyādvayakramopadeśa* version included in the Sakyapa corpus, as shown earlier (1), certainly represents an alternative translation not included in the *Tengyur* canon, although its authenticity is above reproach and was certainly translated by Drokmi. Thus, the core of his production is certain, but around the edges we must presume lost or missing pieces. Drokmi himself was quite aware of the problem of translations becoming dislocated from their translator, and he complained bitterly of plagiarism in the colophon to his final translation of the *Sampuṭa-tilaka*:

> Afterward (after his and Gayādhara's initial translation), some Tibetan "translators" have taken the names of other translators off these scholars' own translations and attached their own names in place of original translators' names while changing the text in a few insignificant places. In order to refute these and other ignorant ones (who accepted these as independent works), I have encountered and collated four (versions) of the Indic tantra text, and have definitively established the translation.[162]

In a series of marginalia to this translation attributed to Sakya Paṇḍita in 1198, the plagiarists were identified as Gö-lotsāwa Khukpa Lhétsé and unnamed others.[163] Gö-lotsāwa was the next Tibetan to work with Gayādhara on the translation of esoteric works, and the marginalia suggest that Gayādhara may have been using his previous work with Drokmi to promote his later patron.

Beyond the texts for the nine cycles of practice just noted, Drokmi's translations consist of thirty-seven tantras and twenty-two esoteric works of other varieties, such as tantra commentaries, instructions in consecration, and meditations.[164] It says something about Drokmi's interest and genre authority in the period that all but one of these fifty-nine works concern either *yoginī-tantras* or material derived from them, the exception being an *Ārya-Tārāmaṇḍalavidhi-sādhana* by *Sahajavilāsa that is concerned with practice more properly Mahāyoga in its content and aesthetics.[165] The standard categories of esoteric writings are not much help in sorting through his selections, for Drokmi's work was overwhelmingly of a single variety. If we make two observations beyond the genre concerns, though, the body of work becomes more accessible. First, all the texts translated by Drokmi either were with Gayādhara (thirty-nine) or not (twenty), and among the latter, Drokmi worked with a variety of Indians or, once (To. 1705), alone. Second, the works can be otherwise divided into short subjects—ten or fewer folia—and longer works. This very convenient heuristic may be questioned in few cases, but the majority of short works actually have fewer than seven folia, and the majority of long works, more than twenty folia. This disparity is striking when we consider the very many short tantras that Drokmi translated, most of them with Gayādhara.

Doubtless, Drokmi's pièce de résistance was his collective translation of the central scriptures associated with Hevajra: the *Hevajra-tantra* itself, the *Sampuṭa*, the *Sampuṭa-tilaka*, and the *Vajrapañjara.*[166] These works in aggregate provided the majority of the maṇḍalas associated with the Sakyapa school and assumed positions of importance in the Kagyüpa and other schools as well. Beyond the Saṁvara-related works, they represent the most important collection of *yoginī-tantra* materials available in eleventh-century India. These scriptures were supplemented with Cakrasaṁvara, Guhyasamāja, and Vajrakumāra (Vajrakīla) practices to provide the mainstay of Sakyapa esoteric ritual and meditation until the present. Drokmi apparently translated no other lengthy tantras except these, so that all the long scriptures were translated in association with Gayādhara.

Just as interesting are all the short tantras translated with either Gayādhara (twenty-five) or with other Indians (eight). These shorter works are extraordinary in both their focus and the information they provide about late-tenth- and early-eleventh-century Indian Buddhism. Most of these works are focused on one or another topics, although a few treat issues applicable to the broader spectrum of Indic esoterism. Thus, the *Śrī-Mahākhatantrarāja* (To. 387) discusses the four Māras, in this case further divided by four, so sixteen Māras are listed. Similarly, the *Śrī-Mahāsamayatantra* (To. 390) extensively redefines the esoteric precepts (*samaya*), invoking the ideology of internal and secret forms as well as external observances. Likewise, the *Śrī-Jvalāgniguhyatantrarāja* (To. 400) is an interesting discussion of postmortem experiences to be encountered by the meditator and postmortem rites performed for these individuals. The *Śrī-Jñānāśayatantrarāja* (To. 404) provides an exegesis of the standard five forms of gnosis as expressed in the esoteric context.

The relationship of title to content is so important to some of the works that they become little more than a discussion of the terms of the title. So the *Śrī-Vajrabhairavavidāraṇatantrarāja* (To. 409) is simply a discussion of the significance of the terms of its title: *vajra*, *bhairava*, *vidāraṇa*, *tantra*, and *rāja*. Similarly, the *Śrī-Ḍākinīsaṁvaratantra* (To. 406) is concerned with questions about the nature of *ḍākinīs* and issues of both the tantric vows (*saṁvara*) and their transgressions. Others seem to start this way but digress into other topics. So the *Śrī-Śmaśānālaṁkāratantrarāja* (To. 402) begins with questions about the terms of the title—what cemeteries, their ornaments, the tantras, and the king are—but is almost exclusively concerned with the eight great cemeteries of the external maṇḍala invoked during the generation process. Other titles are entirely misleading. For example, the *Śrī-Agnimālātantrarāja* (To. 407) looks as if it should be a discussion of a rosary of fire or something like that, whereas actually it is an extensive exegesis on the nature of Heruka (outer, inner, secret), with a concluding addendum on Vajravārāhī.

Perhaps most interesting in this group of short scriptures are the works on wider issues. The *Śrī-Cakrasaṁvaraguhyācintyatantrarāja* (To. 385) is dedicated to the inconceivable (*acintya*) nature of all entities of phenomenal reality, especially mind, mental events, gnosis, and the bodies of the Buddha. The *Śrī-Sūryacakratantrarāja* (To. 397) discusses the importance of acceptance or, more properly, nonrejection, of esoteric practices, especially those of the completion process. Similarly, the *Śrī-Jñānarājatantra* (To. 398) specifies the relationship of defilement, particularly error (*bhrānti*), to the practice of nonrejection in the esoteric path. Even more broadly, the *Anāvilatantrarāja* (To. 414) is very much a *dohā*-like deconstruction of traditional Buddhist categories, with an emphasis on the fundamentals of meditation combined with a caustic criticism of certain unspecified yogins' misuse of esoteric terminology. From a literary perspective, the most interesting of these short works is the *Śrī-Ratnajvalatantrarāja* (To. 396). It is entirely dedicated to a theoretical discussion of three varieties of the highest yoga tantra: identified as means (*upāyatantra*), identified as insight (*prajñātantra*), and identified as nondual (*advayatantra*). In conjunction with other indications, we gain the impression that the category of "nondual" was just beginning to develop in the eleventh century but did not reach its final form before the esoteric momentum turned toward defense rather than creativity. Most later authorities who accepted this category placed the *Hevajra* and *Kālacakra-tantras* in this class, but Drakpa Gyeltsen's work on the *Olapati*, sixth in the Eight Subsidiary Cycles of Practice, states that the *Saṁvara* also was classified by some as a nondual tantra.

In contrast to the esoteric works that were ostensibly the word of the Buddha, the twenty-two other texts that Drokmi translated were more evenly divided between those done with Gayādhara (ten) and those done with others (twelve). Indeed, the most important of these were translated with Prajñendraruci, who reputedly traveled to Tibet, perhaps after he and Drokmi had already worked together in India. Most influential was the translation of Durjayacandra's commentary on the *Hevajra-tantra* (*Kaumudīpañjikā*, To. 1185), a text that configured much of the subsequent Sakyapa scholarship on this scripture. Similarly, Prajñendraruci's *Ratnajvalasādhana*, which the later tradition claims was composed in Mugulung, was translated with the author and was also quite influential in its explanation of the relationship among the topics of consecration, meditative practice, and subsidiary rituals of the cake (*bali* : *gtor ma*) offering, and the like. Two other meditative (*sādhana*) texts were eventually translated with Prajñendraruci, but another meditative work, the *Ṣaḍaṅgasādhana* (To. 1239) of Durjayacandra proved to be especially important later under the influence of Drakpa Gyeltsen. This was translated by Drokmi with Ratnaśrījñāna, one of many obscure Indians seen in Tibet in the mid-eleventh century.[167] The balance of the non-Gayādhara translations were done with Ratnavajra, although once Drokmi worked with Ratnaśrīmitra.

Gayādhara's contribution to nonscriptural translation rested predominantly on short treatises about topics in the Hevajra practice. Two (To. 1305/06) concerned Hevajra's consort, Nairātmyā, but the rest were specifics of the normative Hevajra meditation and featured the work of Saroruhavajra. As stated earlier, Saroruhavajra's exposition of the completion stage according to the Hevajra system, the *Śrī-Hevajrapradīpaśūlopamāvavādaka* (To. 1220), was central to the Sakyapa understanding of normative Hevajra-based yogic practice. It is likely, however, that some of Gayādhara's and Drokmi's work was represented as anonymously translated. Especially inviting are three works (To. 1221–23), said to be by Saroruhavajra, that are embedded in the same section of the canon as other works by this team; they seem to be closely associated with texts in which Drokmi's name is retained.

CONCLUSION: FALLIBLE CHARACTERS WITH LITERARY GENIUS

The esoteric Buddhist transformation of Ü-Tsang, begun by Tsalana Yéshé Gyeltsen and continued by Gayādhara and Drokmi, conforms to the principle that individuals stepping outside the approved social contract may still establish new intellectual or spiritual norms for themselves and others. The eleventh-century personalities were complex, and few achieved either the fame or the notoriety of Drokmi and Gayādhara. They appeared at times to specialize in assaulting the received wisdom of their respective cultures, whether in intellectual excellence, ethical ambiguity, or social ambition. Neither appears especially concerned with his violations of the social structures of Buddhist India or emerging Central Tibet, and the combination of an avaricious Tibetan with a self-absorbed Indian seems, on the face of it, a recipe for disaster. Yet Drokmi's and Gayādhara's achievements belie that estimation, for the larger purpose of literary translation cannot be wholly subsumed into a neat paradigm of self-promotion. Neither promoted himself as an author, even if both were acknowledged authorities. The care and attention to detail evident from the more than sixty translations by Drokmi do not speak of an individual concerned solely with himself, and if his need for wealth was egregious, so was his expenditure of effort on behalf of his tradition. While his insistence on teaching only a few excellent students flies in the face of modern Tibetan practice, it reflected the norm for both Indian esoteric intimacy and good pedagogical method, since the texts they studied were—and continue to be—difficult, complex, and laden with poorly attested nomenclature. Perhaps the best estimation of Drokmi's effectiveness is that many individuals he worked with, Indian or Tibetan, came to be known as experts in their respective fields and as scholars and saints whose contributions to the revival of Tibetan classical culture remain secure to this day.

Even so, we must acknowledge that seldom does a renaissance have such a shaky start. Drokmi, Gayādhara, Gö-lotsāwa Khukpa Lhétsé, Marpa, Ratnavajra, Ācārya Marpo, and others passing through or associated with Drokmi's enclave were assailed from time to time in Tibetan critical literature as having everything from sexual lapses to homicidal tendencies. But even though their portraits collectively might achieve pride of place in a rogues' gallery of eleventh-century Central Tibet, they would equally be called to a command performance in the medieval Central Asian hall of heroes. They all ventured their lives and reputations to cross over the highest mountain range in the world, living in caves while their compatriots died around them, to render the extraordinary thought of one fragile and dying Buddhist subculture into the peculiar language of another in the midst of an uncertain revival. If their behavior occasionally challenges our moral suasion, their linguistic and literary accomplishments should challenge our own dedication to the value of intellectual and spiritual enterprise. It is little wonder that the next generation of Tibetans should find the intellectual task so daunting, even as they discovered the ethical standard of these men to be relatively simple to surpass.

The works that they translated into their literary language provided a stable reference, a secure intellectual compass for later Tibetans to use as a model of the ulterior secret. The emergence of the Tibetan civilization was dependent on such references, which paradoxically remained unstudied by most, for they became textual icons of the culture. Curiously, the great translators, eager for a monopoly on their productions, did not institutionalize their instruction in the language of these icons, so that the contrived titles of putative Indian works could pass without comment. Moreover, the lack of a rigorous course of Sanskrit studies in Tibet meant that the religion could be appropriated creatively without the adjudication skills necessarily promoted by cross-cultural linguistic and scriptural evaluation. Perhaps the greatest irony of the period is that "gray" and apocryphal literature could be written and accepted precisely because there were no continuing standards of linguistic analysis, sustained by printing and institutionalized in schools of learning. Without lexical and literate resources, the production of texts by clans in the service of new visions of religion spoke with the same authority that the translations did. Moreover, they spoke far more intelligibly, in a language familiar, comprehensible, and embodying a symbol system of profound meaning to the civilization.

6

Treasure Texts, the Imperial Legacy, and the Great Perfection

> Now many holy Dharmas teaching the path to Buddhahood in this very life
> Have been translated for His Highness' benefit.
> But because of the great distractions of the king,
> Even though you could not practice them, you have set up the proper karma.
> Therefore bury them as treasure texts,
> So that at the conclusion of seventeen lifetimes, the king will encounter them.
>
> —*Padmasambhava's Copper Island Hagiography* by Nyang-rel[1]

With the activity of the Eastern Vinaya monks and through the aggressive translators of the new dispensation, the Tibetan religious universe began to change in unexpected and disturbing ways. Through their temple constructions, community organizations, land cultivation, linguistic prowess, foreign representatives, social mobility, and new religious expressions, the translators showed that the religious horizon of the eternal Tibetan sky was shrinking year by year. No longer were the mountain and field gods the principal arbiters of power and authority. No longer were their descendants, the members of the royal line, and the landed lords of the old aristocracy the exclusive regents of the Tibetan domain. No longer were the old temples, palace altars, imperial tombs, and mountain shrines the main sources of sacramental potency. No longer were their inhabitants—the lamas, temple guardians, Bendé, mantrins (*sngags pa*), and oracles (*lha pa*)—the primary mediums between gods and men. The sonorous gravitas inherited from the ancient emperors had become lost in a cacophony of new voices, speaking languages of different gods, borne by individuals like Drokmi, who may have come from outside the noble clans.

To make matters worse, the merchants' and translators' new familiarity with India, Nepal, and Kashmir, coupled with their new virtuosity in the languages of South Asian Buddhism, called into question the pedigree of many of the texts and practices sustained by the traditional lamas. As time progressed, it became clear to the literate public that many of the most cherished tantras could not be traced to surviving Indian sources, leaving those newly designated as the Nyingmapa (old school) adrift on a sea of textual and ritual uncertainty. They were not slow to respond, and the complexity of the nativist Tibetan reply is only beginning to become evident as our understanding of the tenth through the twelfth century becomes clearer. For our purposes, the most important parts of the indigenous reaction are the literary trope of the treasure texts as part of the legacy of the emperors, the rejoinders to questions about their own textual authenticity, and the defense of the Tibetan doctrines of the Great Perfection. These entailed reasserting clan and aristocratic functions, defending the new texts and their ideologies that were matured by Tibetans during and after the period of cultural dislocation, and revalorizing imperial (or ostensibly imperial) sites as the sources of true spirituality.

This chapter surveys some of what may be understood about the rise and early development of the treasure texts, the Terma (*gter ma*), derived from the Tibetan word for treasure (*gter*).[2] We look at Buddhist and, to a very limited degree, Bonpo Terma, the early descriptions of their burial and recovery, the legends surrounding their sites and gods, and the imperial mythos that informed almost all aspects of the treasure systems through the renaissance. The chapter also examines an eleventh-century defense of Nyingma works, as well as the Nyingma articulation of a gnoseological correlate to the Great Perfection—the ideology of awareness (*rig-pa*)—which was a remarkable fusion of Indian doctrines and Tibetan spirituality. For all these issues, the chapter can only touch on some of the highlights of an extraordinarily interesting movement. But because to date the scholarship on Terma has tended to avoid its period of origin, some aspects of particular importance to this time will be discussed.

BURIED TREASURES AMID THE RUBBLE OF EMPIRE

Writers on the phenomenon of the treasure texts have tended to emphasize that it arose exclusively as a result of the amazing translation effort, which we have just reviewed.[3] According to this idea, the influx of texts was the principal difficulty, which called for a literary response by those representing the older systems. Other writers have followed Tibetan apologists in highlighting the Indian antecedents of revealed literature, for this is given great weight in the apologetics of treasure by Tibetan writers.[4] In this somewhat different vein, the influx of new texts was less a problem than the actual nature of Indian Buddhism itself, for the Tibetans were putting into practice the same procedure of literary development that lay behind the myth of Nāgārjuna's retrieval of the *Perfection of Insight* (*Prajñāpāramitā*) scriptures from the realm of the Nāgas, or Maitreya's revelation of Yogācāra literature to Asaṅga in the heaven realm of Tuṣita.

Both these positions have much merit but perhaps have overlooked some other considerations, for they emphasized one indisputable factor over all others. If the occlusion of the Tibetan indigenous tradition by the new Buddhist translations had been the exclusive consideration, then Tibetans might have developed treasure texts during the early translation period, when several religious systems were competing. In fact, the Bonpo claimed to have done something similar, for they maintained that their first suppression came under the reign of Drigum Tsenpo, when they buried texts for later revelation, a procedure they insisted again to have adopted at the time of Trihsong Détsen's second suppression of Bon.[5] But there is much reason to doubt the Drigum scenario, for which there is no verification, and it would contradict much of what we know about the formulation of the Tibetan alphabet and the earliest writing. Moreover, Terma is not simply about the burial of texts but about their revelation and subsequent practice, and Bonpo finders were approximately contemporary with their Buddhist colleagues.

Equally, if the Treasure phenomenon were merely a Tibetan development of a ubiquitous Indian form, then its presence would have been detected elsewhere and at other times, so that it would have been expected both during the royal dynastic period and in other Buddhist cultures as well. Neither the metaphor nor the social structure of treasure, however, seems to have appeared in Southeast Asia and also is missing from the phenomenon of reveled scripture in most other Buddhist communities. Even if Indians occasionally used the image of texts discovered as treasure, there was actually nothing like the treasure text movement per se in India. Indeed, India lacked many of the essential ingredients for this development, especially the social and religious values that privileged imperial books and religious artifacts extracted from the ground by members of great clans. While Buddhism in its several cultural milieus tends to replicate its Indian expectation of continued scriptural composition, the social nature and linguistic metaphors of scriptural authorship in the different cultural zones appear to be defined mostly by the cultures and languages in question.

Moreover, the nexus of factors that generated this literature was dependent on the social organization of specific periods, so that the Treasure revelation changed to the degree that Tibetan society itself changed. Consequently—and in contrast to both traditional Tibetans and some modern writers on the Treasure ideology—the models of treasure informing the system adapted to different circumstances between the eleventh and the fourteenth century despite much observable continuity. Those familiar with modern Treasure analysis, for example, may be surprised to find that the triune typology of "earth treasures" (*sa gter*), "knowledge treasures" (*dgongs gter*), and "pure vision" (*dag snang*) is nowhere to be seen, for this is a relatively modern formulation, and this chapter concentrates instead on the earlier descriptions.[6] Second, the Indian saint Padmasambhava had only a very small part in the early Treasure discussions, at least until the late twelfth century, and even then only in selected circles. In his place, the early works focus on the emperors, the unity of their religious and political laws, their legacy in the temples and texts surviving from that time, and the wealth of the saints that they supported. Indeed, later treasure descriptions eventually lost their emphasis on the imperial legacy that was so much the focus of the earlier works.

There can be little doubt that the phenomenon of treasure texts (Terma) is closely connected with the material remains of the Tibetan imperium, the artifacts and hoards of precious materials that flowed into the imperial sites as tribute and booty during the two centuries of Tibetan adventurism and that remained after its fall. "Treasure" (*gter*), after all, may mean exactly that—items buried because of unrest or suppression—and the early treasure texts were often said to be found with specific items associated with the saints or political figures of the empire: statues, jewels, bones, ritual implements, and the like.

Accordingly, the earliest surviving text dedicated to the discussion of treasure, the thirteenth-century Guru Chö-wang's *Magnum Opus on the Origin of Treasure* (*gTer byung chen mo*), simply maintains that there are two main kinds of treasure: Dharma treasure and wealth treasure, a typology found in the twelfth century as well.[7] Elsewhere, Guru Chö-wang specifies "material treasure" (*rdzas gter*) as one of the four kinds.[8] According to this idea, the material wealth supported both the mythology and the search for the treasure texts at a time of poverty or hardship. Along with such treasure items as statues, medicines, and ritual implements, the Terma scriptures declare that the saints or great men of the empire had hidden hoards of wealth because they knew in advance that the Tibetan people would need them in the future. Generally, such ideas are found in the prophecy section of a treasure text, the section describing the circumstances of the ensuing period in the most extreme terms, some of which were surely true. The prophecy goes on to say that at this dark time, such-and-such a person would appear to reveal a specific teaching needed by the few good people living in those times. As Nyang-rel depicts Padmasambhava relating the terms of his hagiography's discovery,

> At the time when these treasures will appear, people will eat cattle dung for their wretched food and clothe themselves in goat hair garments. They will loot every monastery and burn the retreat huts. For their sacred pronouncements they will sell fish and estimate the dead by the thousand. For ethical action they will spread moral pollution and strife, wearing iron coats on their bodies. Teachers will be the generals and monks will be the slaughtering swordsmen. They will make monasteries into redoubts and make their retreats inside the village. Mantrins will increase their families and put poison in the bad food. Chieftains will renege on their oaths and kill heroes with their knives. Tibetans will fall into separate sections like lamellar armor broken into its component plates. Fathers and sons will quarrel; fathers and children will kill their relatives. War gods and demons will call out while thieves guard precipitous cliff trails. Gong-po demons will reside in the hearts of husbands; Sen-mo demons reside in the hearts of women; Teü-rang spirits reside in the hearts of children; all will have come under the influence of devils. Since the eight classes of gods and spirits have been disturbed, the misfortune of disease and famine will arise.
>
> At that time, three inabilities will occur: The earth will not be able to maintain the treasures. All the Dharma treasures and treasures of wealth will be opened. Gold, silver, and jewels will be uncovered. The wealth entrusted to the protectors of religion (*dharmapāla*) will be unable to be protected, so that the wealth dedicated to the Triple Gem will be looted. Finally, Dharma will not be able to be practiced by Bendé. Because they cannot practice religion, they will sell it to others for money. Without their own practice, in pursuit of fame they will teach the Dharma to others.[9]

Thus the time is so bad that both the Dharma treasures and the wealth treasures will be exposed, as if the body of the earth is decrepit and is not being renewed by the virtue of saints. The text goes on to prophesy the coming of Nyang-rel, who will be the treasure revealer of the age and who is represented as the reincarnation of emperor Trihsong Détsen, to whom Padmasambhava is seen granting the prophecy.

Statements like these do not necessarily mean that all these events were literally true, and a few early Dunhuang documents demonstrate a marked Tibetan proclivity to perceive the world as chaotic and humanity as out of control.[10] Indeed, this becomes a literary device in treasure literature, for if we were to believe every statement, then the history of Tibet would be little more than a lengthy catalog of incessant warfare. Moreover, because these works have been continually revealed since at least the eleventh century, if such representations of continual chaos were true, it would mean that no treasure text ever actually did what it claimed to do: restore virtue. But this late-twelfth-century statement—coupled with similar texts from the earlier part of the century, such as the *Pillar Testament* (*bKa' 'chems ka khol ma*)—depicts a pattern of the looting of imperial sites and temple treasuries, the uncovering of hoards left long before, a system of weak religious and civil institutions, and the disclosure of imperial-period texts. These certainly must refer to intermittent real events that contributed to the perception of chaos.

Part of the compelling idea of treasure texts is that during the later tenth century and throughout the eleventh, Buddhist monks, translators, and mantrins were uncovering texts and relics in temples, items that in fact had obscure origins or had been entirely lost to memory. The kings through Relpachen either restricted or outright forbade the translation of the tantras, so the esoteric scriptures were often translated in secret and hidden from imperial agents. Moreover, some of the temples and areas associated with early treasure are located in southern Tibet, relatively close to the Nepalese, Sikkimese, or Bhutanese borders. Such sites are exactly where clandestine translations would have been made or kept, for the translator would have returned from India with the new text or translation in hand and deposited it there. Alternatively, translators might have sent a copy to the periphery of the empire, an area safe from the armies of potential aggressor states. Treasure texts are often represented as written on yellow scrolls (*shog ser*), which might denote their religious status (yellow color) or just the fact that aged paper and silk media turn yellow as they decay.

This is only part of the story, however, for the bulk of the Nyingma tantras—whether classified as continuously transmitted Kahma or revealed Terma—were composed in Tibet. As others have already observed, one part of the treasure texts is surely the consequence of a Buddhist understanding of Indian Buddhism's literary dynamic. Elsewhere I have described Indian Buddhism as a culture of scriptural composition, so that inherent in the institutional culture of Buddhist centers in India is the dynamic that scriptures were supposed to be developed continually as new insights into the world emerged.[11] During the dark period of cultural dislocation, Tibetans put that dynamic into place with the composition of new scriptures, both sūtra and tantra.[12] We know almost nothing about the Tibetan circumstances of the early compositions, but the same is true for Indian scriptures: all the scriptural authors are anonymous. Moreover, Indian tantric literature itself evolved during the hiatus of Tibetan involvement with India, so that the tantras popular or available during the Sarma period emphasized yogic practices that did not exist earlier. It was this material that authorities like Drokmi and Marpa transmitted to Central Tibet. What Indians did not experience, however, was the sudden appearance of authority from a Buddhist source other than their own. Conversely, in the late tenth century the ancient Tibetan traditions were suddenly faced with alternative Sarma voices, ones whose authenticity could not be denied.

In response, the older aristocratic lineage holders began to build on a practice that had already been initiated by Central Asian and Chinese monks, that texts could be produced or revealed in the target civilization, as they had in India. Characteristically, however, an occasional practice in other countries became a cottage industry in Tibet, much as the irregular Indian recognition of incarnate teachers and the employment of debate became mainstays of Tibetan religious institutions. For the Nyingma, the treasure discoveries became a vehicle for self-authentication, both a method for the appropriation of new Indic material and a means for the development of a vision of Tibetan indigenous religiosity. Of these, the latter was by far the more interesting. Rather than a simple restatement of fundamentally Indic materials, the Terma phenomenon allowed Tibetans to cloak their own paradigms in the guise of emerging Indic authority. As the *Pillar Testament* affirms in its formula for Terma composition,

> Having constructed [the Jokhang] in that way, [we know that] the beings of this Tibetan land of snows were not worthy of being converted by the Tathāgata and could not drink the nectar of the holy Dharma because they had no confidence in the holy word. Their minds did not accept the Dharma of awareness, and they were not able to train in the three trainings. However, they have been converted by my [Songtsen Gampo's] laws of Dharma and of the kingdom. So then paint a series of paintings [on the Jokhang] in that way [demonstrating Dharma]. Then impel the ignorance of these beings of the land of snows into learning [through the paintings]. Write what is to be done into a story, so that they will have confidence in the texts. Thus you will dampen their distress at learning and, swelling their interest, will set them to Buddhist training. Having first written Bon doctrines, you then place them in the three trainings of the Dharma.[13]

This formula is interesting and reasonably early and shows both the movement to preserve Tibetan understanding through painting and narratives, which was classified as human religion (*mi chos*), and the sense that Tibet was benighted by Indian standards. The text also recognizes that this dedication to the superiority of Indian ideals was generated at some cost. If all authenticity is derived from Indian Buddhism, then Tibet was fated to labor under the cloud of extraterritorial images of the ideal, denying a simple confidence in indigenous Tibetan spirituality.

GUARDED BY SPIRITS: THE HIDDEN IMPERIAL PERSON

The mythology of Terma has the treasure texts buried or deposited in or around sites dedicated to the dynasty, whether in the ground itself or in pillars or statuary. But this strategy did not implicate, for Tibetans of the renaissance period (as now), the neutral value of a simple repository in the inert earth or elsewhere, as it might for those from a Euro-American society. In Tibet, such places are the habitations of spirits and powers, which are alive with their own traits and desires, their own societies and hierarchies.[14] The simple act of disturbing the earth—whether for the purposes of burying an object, recovering it, digging a foundation, or even plowing a field—was not a simple act, for the denizens of that world must be placated or subdued, or the consequences might be tragic. Below the surface of pillars and fields lurk the spirits of those areas: the Lu (*klu*), who live underground and control springs; the Sadak (*sa bdag*), who possess open ground and fields; and the Nyen (*gnyan*), who live in trees, pillars, and stones.[15] Each of them belongs to large and shifting communities of spirits inhabiting every part of what we might normally consider inanimate nature, whether the weather, clouds, lightning, wind, or almost any other aspect of physical reality. Each of their communities has a hierarchy, so the emperor of Tibet may have paintings of the eight chief Lu as a basis for friendship with the king of the Lu.[16]

There were many kinds of treasure guardians in the eleventh century, and the importance accorded to the feminine *ḍākinīs* in later works is less often mentioned in the earliest texts. The escalating value of Indian models eventually elevated *ḍākinīs* to become the Terma guardians par excellence, and we see the phenomenon of Indianization elsewhere as well. The Lu, especially, became identified with the Indian Nāga snake spirits, for both could appear as snakes and control water.[17] But not all their properties were the same.[18] For example, the Lu preside over the distribution of disease; conversely, the Nāgas shed poison, for disease in India is predominantly under the purview of village goddesses.[19] Nāgas can also appear as elephants and have fertility functions. Indeed, at almost every Indian village shrine is an image of snakes dancing in courtship, for they act as icons of sexuality and fecundity. Conversely, it is sometimes said that in early Terma, all of Tibet was under the authority of the

Lu, placing the human world under the strong influence of the subterranean realm.[20] Perhaps most important to the myths, both Nāgas and Lu controlled treasure, which the Indian snake spirits signaled by keeping a gem in their head, to shed light in the dark when needed.

Supplication of the Lu was particularly associated with the temples during and after the dynasty. Many of the imperial temples, like the Jokhang and Samyé, had important chapels (*klu khang*) dedicated to these creatures, and the king of the Lu was considered one of the most important protectors of these sites (figure 11).[21] In Samyé, for example, part of the treasury we saw exposed when Lumé visited the intermediate circumambulatory pathway (*'khor sa bar ma*) was in one report entrusted to the Lu or named for them, for the treasury was under the purview of such spirits.[22] The Ramoché temple, just to the north of the Jokhang, had a special "palace" dedicated to both the Lu and the Sadak, where the Jowo statue was reportedly installed.[23] The stories of the Jokhang construction indicate that a special *vajra* mud was collected from the realm of the Lu; it was immutable like diamond and acted as a fire retardant or preservative when smeared on the wood.[24] The disturbance of such creatures was troubling in all construction, and builders and carpenters included a class of supervisors (*phywa mkhan*) whose responsibility it was to determine the ritual and esoteric placement of the foundations.[25] It is little wonder that even in the modern period, elite builders were assigned positions in the Tibetan traditional government, for theirs was part of the responsibility over the underground spirit world.[26]

Likewise, the diverse guardian spirits of the Terma, the *yakṣas* and *rākṣasas*, the indigenous gods like Nyenchen Tanglha—the "great big Nyen, god of the plateau," as his name means—are sometimes identified as "place deities" (*yul lha*), sometimes identified with other spirits. Most originated on the Tibetan plateau, however, and convey the idea of a continuity of community between the stratified society of Tibet and the stratified societies of the gods. The mountain gods, like Yarlha Shampo, were considered the ancestors of Tibetans in their areas, so that when Terma was classified as the ancestral treasure, the texts, statues, relics, and so forth came under their dominion as well. Accordingly, their henchmen and lesser sprites were engaged in its defense and protection.[27] The hidden domain with its hierarchy intact was part of a system of interaction and exchange between authorities in the human realm and those in the secret world.

Perhaps the oldest body of lore revealing attempts to conceal sacred items is contained in versions of the *Testament of the Ba/Wa Clan*. One recension indicates that an early Tibetan king, Lha Totori Nyentsen, had a treasure called the Secret Ferocity (gNyan po gsang ba). He would open its container every so often and make offerings, decreeing that all his descendants should do like-

FIGURE 11 Small water shrine to the Lu at Samyé. After a photograph by Richardson

wise; later it was said to be an Indian sūtra written in gold letters.[28] Similarly, the first emperor, Songtsen Gampo, was said to have Buddhist texts translated and then placed under seal in the treasury (*phyag mdzod*) of the Ching-nga fortress, to be taken out in five generations.[29] During Trihsong Détsen's adolescent suppression of Buddhism, before he was converted to the Indic cult, he tried to rid Tibet of the icons of the new religion and wanted the Jowo statue of Śākyamuni returned to China.[30] When that did not work, the statue was buried, but by the next morning it had begun to emerge from the earth. As in the affirmation by Nyang-rel translated at the start of this chapter, the earth could not withstand the treasure, so it was temporarily removed to the Nepalese border. After becoming a Buddhist, Trihsong Détsen decided to suppress Bon instead. He had his agents throw most of the Bon texts into the river, and the rest of them were stuffed inside the Black Stūpa at Samyé.[31] Perhaps the most intriguing story in this regard relates to the aftermath of the controversy between the Chinese and Indian Buddhists. The Chinese texts, considered inappropriate for their time, were hidden in some sort of clay vessel (*rdzas*) so that those with the proper karmic maturation in the future could benefit from them.[32] Not only is this an articulation of the fundamental ideology of the treasure texts, but it resonates with both the early Tibetan practice of pot burial and the Central Asian Buddhist tradition of storing texts in clay jars, which this is how Kharoṣṭhī manuscripts in Afghanistan were preserved.[33]

Most of these narrations date from the early renaissance period and dem-

FIGURE 12 Trandruk imperial temple. After a photograph by Richardson

onstrate that Tibetans assumed that the statues, jewels, and texts of the earlier period were the sacred relics of their ancestors (*yab mes kyi thugs dam*).[34] That ideology was enhanced by the assertion of some early treasure texts, like the *Great Chronicle* of the *Maṇi Kambum*, that they constituted in some sense an extension of the king's soul or person (*rgyal po'i bla*).

> Because the king [Songtsen Gampo] possessed prescient awareness (*abhijñā*), he entrusted this *Testament* [i.e., the *Maṇi Kambum*] to the translators, saying,
>
>> Make two copies of this my teaching. Inscribe one in letters of gold and silver on a blue "river silk," and deposit it as the King's Person in the treasury at Trandruk [figure 12]. Inscribe the second on a scroll of Chinese paper and hide it under the foot of Hayagrīva in the Mahākāruṇika temple [at Samyé].[35]

The notion of the soul/life or person (*bla*) was an indigenous Tibetan idea, for Tibetan theological anthropology maintained that humans were inhabited by a number of elements, including various (sometime five) gods, as well as a vital force (*srog*) and a life identity.[36] There is little early information about such ideas, for they contradict much of Buddhist doctrine, but at best they seem somewhat vague, as many religious ideas of self actually appear. Indeed, the majority of the Tibetan descriptions were written down much later, long after Buddhist institutions were victorious, and these native Tibetan ideas were expressed primarily in epic and medical literature. The treasure descriptions, in fact, are something of an anomaly, for they are among the earliest surviving references to such ideas, which are certainly older than the Terma phenomenon.

Although it is used in different senses, as a noun the term La (*bla*) is usually understood as the "soul/self," and as an adjective it means "exalted" or "appro-

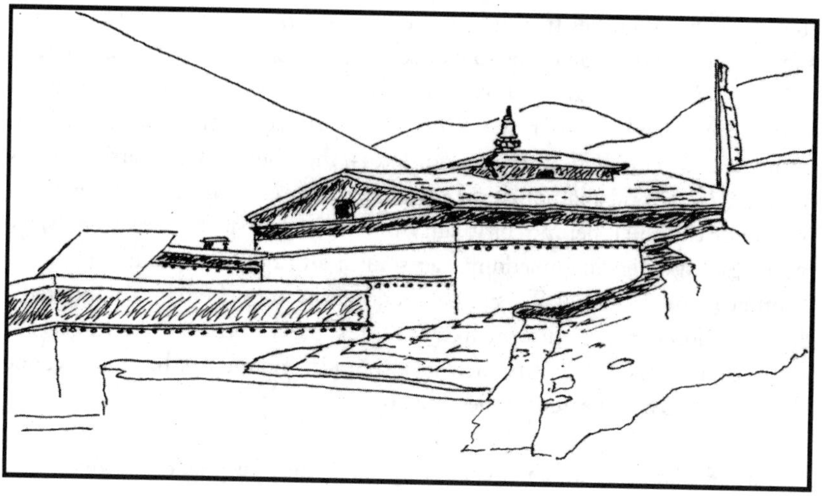

FIGURE 13 Khon-ting temple. After a photograph by Richardson

priate," but in the older texts these meanings are difficult to disentangle. I believe that this word was often used in the sense of the king's (or other) exalted person, much as the term for "person" (*puruṣa*) indicates a self in India, as well as denoting the divinity and authority embedded in the world (*prakṛiti*). Mutatis mutandis, much of this also applies to the Tibetan word La, for it may describe essential or exalted items, without which the individual ceases to be. When Songtsen Gampo unified Tibet, he situated his personal palace (*bla'i pho brang*) at Ching-nga Tak-tse (*phying nga stag rtse*), while the queen and princes settled elsewhere.[37] As Trihsong Détsen began to organize the monks in his empire, the important monk Ba Selnang was installed as the person of the Dharma (*chos kyi bla*), with the military title of commander of the right guard.[38] A little later, when Samyé was to begin construction, Ba Selnang asked to be excused from building the temple of the imperial person (*bla'i gtsug lag khang*) at Samyé but to be allowed to build a temple in his home area of Balam-lak, east of Lhasa.[39] Elsewhere, it is mentioned that physicians were appointed as Songtsen Gampo's personal physicians (*rgyal po'i bla sman*), with their practice evidently on the king's exalted person (*rgyal po'i bla spyad*).[40] These uses harmonize with the Terma category, for the King's Personal Treasure (*rgyal po'i bla gter*) is often placed at the head of a list of other analogous compounds, like incantation Terma (*mthu gter*), mind Terma (*thugs gter*), and medicine Terma (*sman gter*).[41] We are even told that the personal text of the royal ancestor (*yab mes kyi bla dpe*) was buried in Khon-ting in Lho-drak (figure 13).[42]

All these would indicate that the Terma was tied intimately to the king and that the texts and other treasures of the King's Personal Treasure would be in some sense an extension of his soul or self. In this regard, Tibetans understood that the individual or community "person" could be located in a specific object. While they may have been written by the great saints or the celestial bodhisattvas and translated by divine translators, their burials were carried out by imperial decree on behalf of later Tibetans and represented the continued embodiment of the emperors' spirituality in the form of texts. Accordingly, we often read of a person embedding her soul in a turquoise, a mountain, a tree, or other natural material. This phenomenon is even celebrated in some traditional wedding songs, in which the bride's party formally challenges the groom's entourage to identify their locale and its mountains. In response, one of the groom's beer bearers replies,

> The aft mountain like an arrogant elephant is the soul-peak of the great father!
> The fore mountain like a heaped up maṇḍala is the soul-peak of the great mother!
> The right mountain like a coiled white scarf is the soul-peak of the lusty son!
> The left mountain like a coiled purple scarf is the soul-peak of the innocent daughter!
> This place like an eight-petal lotus is the common ground of delight in all happiness![43]

Each of these "soul-peaks" is the translation of *bla ri*, a mountain representing the person or life of an individual. In the modern period, the lake between Dakpo and Ölkha, Lhamo lamtso, was considered both the "soul-lake" (*bla mtsho*) of the goddess Makzorma and also the soul-power residence (*bla gnas*) of the Dalai Lamas.[44] Otherwise, clans were represented by totemic animals, so that sheep, yaks, horses, deer, cattle, oxen, goats, and so on become emblems of the clan's soul (*bla rtags*).[45] Communities could also have such an aggregate soul, and some documents indicate that the suppression of Buddhism by Darma caused the soul-mountain of Tibet to crumble.[46]

As the person/soul treasure (*bla gter*) of the emperor, buried texts were inherently valuable, for they represented his final statement or testament (*bka' 'chems*) as his inheritance left to subsequent generations. So important was this idea that even in the late twelfth century when the *bla gter* was included in an expanded list of various kinds of treasure, it was given pride of place as first on the list, and its initial place of burial was shifted from the Jokhang to Samyé—and the king changed from Songtsen Gampo to Trihsong Détsen—with much of the narrative otherwise left intact.[47] Guru Chö-Wang declared that the King's Personal Treasure liberates its essential meaning in 1,100 ways, for it includes both the Dharma and jewel treasures.[48] Moreover, when the fourteenth-century author Urgyen Lingpa discussed this list, virtually all the Buddhist canon, including the Nyingma tantras, were identified as part of the King's Personal Treasure, far exceeding the textual content included in any of the other seventeen kinds of Terma.[49]

When encountered in texts, the soul/person (*bla*) and the individual, family, or community gods (*lha*) are mutually reinforcing and even fluid categories. Some of the terms interchange the spellings (*bla/lha*), as in the case of the gods of aggression (*dgra lha/bla*) or in the Yumbu Palace, designated as either a personal/chief fortress (*bla mkhar*) or filled with divinity (*lha sgang*), which amounted to much the same thing.[50] For example, epic literature indicates that the first king to be buried in the tombs, Drigum Tsenpo, caused his own demise through the loss of his gods.[51] While preparing for battle against his enemy, Lo-ngam Tadzi, Drigum Tsenpo bound on his person a number of items, including a black silk turban on his head, a fox corpse (pelt?) on his right shoulder, and a dog corpse on his left. These caused, respectively, his hunting god (*mgur lha*), his god of aggression (*dgra lha*), and his god of masculinity (*pho lha*) to fade away. Consequently, when Drigum swung around his sword, he sliced off the magical rope and ladder (*rmu thag rmu skas*) leading to the celestial realms, requiring him to have a tomb in the earth.[52] This tomb was constructed in the earliest royal cemetery area around Mount Gyang-to, where the tomb was regarded as the mound or tent of the royal souls (*gyang to bla 'bubs*).[53] Eventually, the entombment of the kings and emperors of Tibet was understood as establishing a place for the residence of their collective spirits and was identified with many of the properties of the Buddha's relics in stūpas, so that the king's residual presence in the tomb protects all of Tibet.[54]

Some of his courtiers attended the entombed king. By the time our records were compiled, the previous system of human sacrifice had been set aside and had been replaced by a dedication of living humans to be bound to the tomb as its guardians (*dur srung*).[55] The "dead" (*gshin po*), as they were then called, were selected from among the ministers (*nang slon*) of the king or emperor and, once assigned to the service of the king, were not permitted to wander outside the boundary stones of the tomb. In return, they had use of all the food and treasure placed at the tomb, especially during the annual rite of offering. The day before the rite, representatives of the royal family came to the tomb and informed the "dead" of the ritual schedule. The dead ministers then left the tomb, the only time they were permitted to do so. The next day, the royal family approached the tomb and announced, "All the dead have gone to another country!" When no answer was received, they made offerings to the statues and remains of the deceased king. The "dead" tomb guardians then returned to seize these grave goods that had been left for the king.

When we turn from such descriptions to those of the early Terma, the similarities are palpable. In fact, the ideology of royal sites appears to be the primary source for the early Terma descriptions. These sites, temples and tombs, were the repositories and subsequent sources for treasure, whether precious stones and metals or written texts. Their treasuries had dreadful guardians—spirits of the ground and deities of the mountains for the temples, and the human "dead" for the tombs. Each was a place of power and authority, of danger and mystery, where a building intruded into the lethal subterranean world yet also extended into the living world of men. The early descriptions of Terma involved the perception of hidden or buried materials, so that the later sanctified sense of texts embedded in reincarnating consciousnesses (*dgongs gter*) was absent in the early documents and begins to be suggested only in the thirteenth century.[56] Categories like "mind treasure" certainly were present, along with their hiding places, and were understood as material items conveying the spiritual legacy of the king or some great saint.[57]

TERMA IN THE ELEVENTH AND TWELFTH CENTURIES

The historical beginning of the Terma phenomenon is difficult to determine, since the Terma mythology really develops three related and mutually reinforcing constructs. First, texts compiled or revealed at one time are assigned earlier attribution with respect to both their composition and their discovery. This process begins quite early but is cumulative over time, so that by the nineteenth century, Kongtrül's *Precious Treasury* and *Hagiographies of the 108 Treasure Revealers* are filled with late texts and dubious hagiographies posing as early figures. Second, a pattern of texts prophesying subsequent revelations, their sites, and revealers emerges early. By the fourteenth century, Urgyen Lingpa proposed many revealers' names in his works, and the names became formulaic by the end of his list.[58] This trend becomes a classic self-fulfilling prophecy, for later individuals socialized into the treasure system will have appropriated these identities—as in the case of Urgyen Terdak Lingpa (1646–1714)—and seek Terma where they were supposed to be found according to earlier texts. Such directions eventually mature into a formal secret guidebook or statement (*byang bu*), instructing the prospective Terma revealer about the signs and location of other treasure texts, so that one needs Terma to find Terma.[59] Finally, the early impetus for this elaborate mythology is the unbelievable wealth of tantric material being composed by Tibetans, almost all of it anonymously. By the twelfth century the *Old Tantric Canon* (*rNying ma rgyud 'bum*) began to take form, with some of it coming from the Terma literature. We consider each of these three directions in greater detail.

According to the standard stories, the phenomenon of discovering Terma texts began in the tenth century. Treasure revealers (*gter ston*) of both Bonpo and Buddhist persuasion revealed works of royal dynastic origin, and the Bonpo legends state that many of these were discovered serendipitously by traders or itinerant treasure hunters, such as three famous Nepalese scholars strolling through Tibet in search of available gold.[60] Both the chronology published by Kværne and the modern *Treasury of Good Sayings* translated by Karmay indicate that Bon Terma were supposed to have been recovered in the tenth century.[61] However, the earliest Bonpo revealer for whom texts are said to survive is Shenchen Lugah, whose 1017 discovery became an important date for the Bonpos.[62]

The Buddhists identify the earliest revealer as Sangyé Lama, said to be active during the first half of Rinchen Zangpo's life (958–1055), but no surviving works can be traced to him.[63] In the nineteenth century, Kongtrül maintained that his close colleague Jamyang Khyentsé Wangpo mysteriously obtained a work said to have been revealed by Sangyé Lama, then lost, and re-revealed (*yang gter*) by Khyentsé. Kongtrül reproduced this work in his great *Precious Treasury* (*Rin chen gter mdzod*), but its value for early Terma history is dubious.[64] Both *Guru Trashi's History of the Dharma* (*Gur bkra chos 'byung*) and Kongtrül's own *Hagiographies of the 108 Treasure Revealers* (*gTer ston rgya rtsa rnam thar*) include many hagiographical narratives about ostensibly eleventh-century revealers, but almost no texts from these individuals survive or even, in some cases, any early verification of the individual's actual existence. Without other evidence, it is likely that many of these stories were part of a larger strategy of authentication of the documents and their later lineage holders rather than accurate historical representations.

The late eleventh and early twelfth century apparently was when the early treasure texts came into greatest currency. We will look more closely at some of the earliest surviving works, each attributed to eleventh-century figures but probably the result of twelfth-century authors/compilers. It is important to understand that this implicates a double system of apocryphal attribution in these early Terma: not only are the texts identified as the production of royal dynastic personalities, but their discoveries also are attributed to individuals living much earlier than their actual revealers.[65] The most important factor is the profile of the attributed personality, for some of the ostensible tenth- and eleventh-century revealers were otherwise well known or were given important political connections. We find, for example, Lhatsün Ngönmo—a son of Bodhirātsa, the royal patron of Atiśa—listed by Kongtrül as a revealer, but then he shows that the received Terma attributed to him was discovered in the nineteenth century.[66]

There are many such examples, but a few instances are of greatest importance. Drapa Ngönshé (1012–90), we have seen, was an important Eastern Vinaya monk, as he integrated the Nyingma form of tantric praxis into the curriculum of the Eastern Vinaya temples. He eventually gave up his robes, another eleventh-century phenomenon seen in the case of Drokmi, and became a lay guru of the esoteric system. None of our documents discussing his Eastern Vinaya lineage mentions text revelation, and even Nyingma apologists have acknowledged that his received hagiography is silent on treasure revelation.[67] By the twelfth century, though, Nyang-rel singled out Drapa as a treasure revealer in a surprisingly short list, unlike the greatly inflated lists in found in the nineteenth century. "So, Atiśa from the Āyrapalo temple, and that revealed by Drapa Ngönshé, while Lotön, Nyaktön, Druptob Ngödrup extracted Terma from under the statue of Hayagīva in the temple of Mahākāruṇika (i.e., Āyrapalo). I, Nyang-relpachen, revealed Terma from Samyé, Trandruk and Khon-ting temple."[68] No text is attributed to Drapa Ngönshé here, and no text was attributed to him in Urgyen Lingpa's fourteenth-century list either, merely that he would fill up 108 places (with texts?) and would be the head of an imperial-period temple.[69] Medical texts were an important category of Terma, and the treasure status of multiple medical works was affirmed by Guru Chö-wang, but he did not mention Drapa Ngönshé's being associated with them.[70] It appears that only around this time were the classic four medical tantras attributed to Drapa Ngönshé's revelation, and so they appear in Sangyé Gyamtso's *Blue Beryl* (*Baiḍūrya sngon po*), although he was doubtless relying on prior attributions.[71] It is interesting that some traditional Tibetans examining the treasure claims to the medical tantras concluded that Drapa Ngönshé had little to do with medical Terma.[72]

Likewise, there is little reason to believe that either Atiśa or his immediate entourage had anything to do with the remarkable *Pillar Testament* (*bKa' 'chems ka khol ma*), and even the story pushes credulity, for the text itself discusses how Atiśa reveals the *Testament*. Subsequent Kadampa teachers with strong Nyingma leanings—like the twelfth-century Zhangtön Darma Gyeltsen—represent much better candidates, as do a host of Kagyüpas following the renovation of the Jokhang by Dakpo Gomtsül (1116–69), who is mentioned in the *Pillar Testament*.[73] We even find instances of texts clearly claiming revelation by a new translation figure where no such revelation is otherwise recorded, and the claim appears to have been a transparent attempt to gain legitimacy by association. In the Pukdrak *Kanjur*, for example, is a tantra entitled the *Royal Tantra of Remati's Life Mantra* (*Re ma ti srog sngags kyi rgyud kyis rgyal po*).[74] This work claims to be buried by Padmasambhava and eventually revealed by Drokmi. But having reviewed his oeuvre, I find it difficult to believe that Drokmi would have participated in such Terma revelations. Indeed, several eleventh-century translators became the object of Terma hagiographical enterprises, including Ralo, Gya-lotsāwa. and Nyö-lotsāwa.[75] We can only conclude that we have here more examples in which authors use the strategy of placing their works posthumously in the hands of renowned personalities.

Looking in the opposite direction, the *Pillar Testament* also projects where future treasures are to be discovered, in a section that has proved to be one of the most influential in Terma literature. The section, which follows immediately after the directions on how to write Terma and paint pictures, tells where they were to be buried and, by extension, where they were to be revealed. In the middle of his instructions on construction of the Jokhang, Songtsen Gampo is depicted telling his Nepalese queen to bury treasures all around the temple and in other temples of the empire:

> In order to spread the holy Dharma in this snowy land of Tibet, hide the Dharma treasure at a spot close to the "leafy" pillar [of the Jokhang]. By virtue of its qualities, the Dharma will spread through all the beings of this snowy land, my ministers, and royal descendants. Therefore, in order to protect them from ones who would do them harm, hide the treasure of the ferocious incantational magic at a spot close to the "snake-headed" pillar. By virtue of its blessing, no kind of harm will be inflicted on any person or being having faith in Lhasa. In order to ensure no harm is inflicted by evil mantras and to turn back armies from border states, hide the reversing treasure at a spot close to the "lion-milking"[?] pillar. By virtue of its blessing, no kind of harm will be inflicted on any person or being having faith in Lhasa. Hide the medical practice treasures at a spot close to the "leafy" pillar. . . . [many more Jokhang instructions follow] Moreover, hide the treasure appropriate to the Lu at Trandruk Temple in Yoru. Hide the Eternal Bon treasure at Khon-ting Temple in Lho-drak. With that, great benefit will occur for subsequent ordinary people. Hide the astrological treasure at the Long-tang Drölma Temple in Kham. Hide the essential mantra treasure at the Bur-chu Temple in Kongpo. Hide the meditation instruction treasure in the Drompa-gyang Temple in Tsang. By its virtue, many siddhas will arise in Tsang. Hide the treasure of the many divisions of the royal lineage in the Pel-chen Temple of Chang. By virtue of that, the imperial lineage will not be cut off.[76]

Not only were these important eleventh-century temples, but in the imperial period they also had acted as repositories for copies of imperial pronouncements, so that in the early renaissance, real and imagined imperial documents became intermixed.[77] This section of the *Pillar Testament* also became the model for many future Terma prophecies and was augmented from the late twelfth century onward.[78] Such statements validated past apocryphal scriptures, for they were the consequence of an imperial intention and vindicated future compositions, for the future unwritten texts became revealed as the hidden scriptures from the past.

One of Terma's most important purposes was to authenticate the great proliferation of Nyingma tantras (Kahma) from the tenth to the twelfth century, apocryphal works said to have come from the early translation period. This aspect of the logic of treasure texts was relatively straightforward: Terma made questionable Kahma texts into true tantric scriptures, for the authentication of one secured the authenticity of its related works. The question was central to the Tibetan scriptures' survival and their lineage holders' authority, for the early Nyingma tantras were unconventional by the standards of the new tantric scriptures coming from India in the eleventh and twelfth centuries. As pointed out before, the majority of early Nyingma tantras are much more philosophical and abstract than their Indian prototypes, which tend to emphasize rituals. In distinction, both the Kahma and Terma tantras were often concerned with the doctrines and meditative practices of the Great Perfection (*rdzogs chen*), its vocabulary, and its models of reality.

Because the doctrines and meanings associated with the Great Perfection were so distant from normative Indian ideas, the term became one of the lightning rods of anti-Nyingma polemics. The eleventh-century translators knew very well that no cluster of ideas in Indian scriptures could possibly fit the range of conceptions and variations in meditations that were loosely classified as the Great Perfection. The reason was that the Great Perfection was an indigenous Tibetan formulation, and its literature contained some of the most original conceptions in Buddhist history, on a par with the creative work of such East Asian figures as Dogen. In any case, the majority of Great Perfection texts were not initially considered treasure but were part of the continually transmitted legacy of Kahma (*bka' ma*) from the imperial period. Indeed, defenses of treasure texts consistently indicate that the Kahma and the Terma are mutually supporting, that one does not function without the other.[79]

At least one group of texts somehow came to represent both categories. One of the most important of the Great Perfection systems to rise out of the eleventh and twelfth centuries was inscribed in the Seminal Essence (sNying tig) scriptures, the seventeen tantras of the *Collection of Instructions* (*man ngag sde*), as it is frequently categorized.[80] This body of scripture appears to me a product of the eleventh and twelfth centuries and may be traced to the fortunes of an aristocratic clan, the Ché (lCe), later aided by the Zhang. In their involvement with the royal dynastic period, in their survival during the time of dislocation, and in their reemergence in the period of the new diffusion of the Dharma, the Ché represented a clan that developed survival strategies often relying on religion. Its members operated as great authorities in Tsang, specifically in the Nyang River valley, building at least two castles and controlling, as did many of the great clans, the spiritual and temporal affairs of the period.[81] Members of the Ché family founded and oversaw the maintenance of Shalu Monastery, which ultimately played an extremely important role in the formulation of the Tibetan Buddhist canon by becoming the home to Butön Rinchendrup. Ché clan members traveled to India in search of ordination, were lineal holders of the Nyingma systems, and were thoroughly involved in the emergence of Treasure in both Ü and Tsang. Like the Khön, who are examined in the next chapter, and the other great clans, the Ché represented the vitality of the eleventh- and twelfth-century Tibetan religious landscape.

There can be little question that the seventeen tantras were a body of Treasure, even though they were not associated with the great Guru Padmasambhava and were later included in the compendia of the traditionally transmitted Kahma rather than the treasure texts. The reason is that the history of treasure in Tibet during the eleventh and twelfth centuries was a series of competing visions from the early period, featuring figures as diverse as Bairotsana, Songtsen Gampo, Vimalamitra, and Padmasambhava. The seventeen, then, represented themselves as the legacy of Vimalamitra, an eighth-century monk who would have been astonished to find himself the focus of such a tradition. An accepted testimony to the discovery of the seventeen scriptures can found in the colophon of the longest of these works, the *Great Tantra of the Self-Manifestation of Pure Awareness* (*Rig pa rang shar chen po'i rgyud*). This colophon contains the hagiographical revelation of this material by Dangma Lhüngyel, a member of the old Dang(ma) clan and a caretaker of the ancient temple of Zhé-lhakang, one of the old imperial temples of Uru, to the east of Lhasa (figure 14).[82]

> May the Protectors, [Mahākāla] Brother and Sister, watch over the Word! May they cut the life-vein of those defiling their vows, sucking their heart's blood! May the dark crimson Angry Queen, Ekajātī, watch over the Word! May the Lord of Glorious Zhé-lhakang, the owner of the vow, liberate this Word by binding those who have not taken the proper vows! If it is given to those who have defiled their vows, may they be sentenced by the eighteen classes of Ḍākas! Now this secret Explanatory Tantra was translated [by Vimalamitra] from three dissimilar languages and transmitted to the two, the

FIGURE 14 Zhé-lhakhang. After a photograph by Richardson

Lord [Trihsong Détsen] and the Minister [?Ba Selnang, ?Dranka Pelyön], but this great tantra was not further transmitted to Nyang-ben. Having put it between two bejeweled crystal book covers and having placed it in a silver reliquary, the lord [Trihsong Détsen] fastened it with four great nails. The lord then said to Nyang-ben, "Since this is an evil mantra (text) which could fragment Tibet, if it happens that it fragments Tibet, then move it to the outlying areas." Having instructed in this way, he wrapped it in black yak felt cloth and entrusted it alone to Nyang-ben. Then the great Nyang-ben secreted it in Zhé-lhakang, entrusting it to the Lord Dré-tag-chen. This is the unmistaken secret intention of the lord [Trihsong Détsen]. Then the Sthavira Dangma bestowed it on Ché-tsün Sengé Wangchuk and the Lhajé [Dangma] explained in great depth the practical instructions concerning the text. He taught Ché-tsün to practice in a manner utterly dissimilar from any other practice. This holy instruction of the secret array was then hidden separately.

Have confidence that this king of scriptures does not occur elsewhere in Jambudvīpa! It is not necessary to hear [the explanation of the scripture]; merely to possess the text is enough [to realize it]! If one gives this king of instructions to one who is not a fit vessel, then both will be destroyed. May it be found by one of learning, endowed with correct activity! Then may the Doctrine of Secret Mantras endure for a long time! Clarify the fog of ignorance of living beings! The Madman Ché-tsün, who is the same as me, has sent this oral lineage of the learned of India—embedded in this deep instruction on the perfect meaning—down to me. This deep instruction—rare everywhere and unappreciated by all—was hidden as a earthly treasure.[83] "May it be found by one of correct activity!" So the Lord Ché-tsün, having expressed his wish, hid the scripture as an earthly treasure. It was correct.

Although a somewhat different version of the burial and discovery of the Nying-tik materials is found in the *Great Annals of the Seminal Essence Lineage* (*sNying thig lo rgyus chen mo*), there can be little doubt that both narratives represented the affirmation of a number of Tibetan values.[84] First, the standards of spirituality were those attributed to the period of the Tibetan empire, not the period of Tibet's fragmentation, and these standards were understood as unique in the world, no matter how many new scriptures or instructions might be brought in by later translators. Second, the reason the older scriptures were unknown to current Indians is that this later degenerate generation of Indian Paṇḍitas was incapable of contacting the spiritual forces that had sustained and continued to sustain Tibet. Third, the burial and recovery of the scripture was entirely a consequence of the intention of Trihsong Détsen, the emperor. Fourth, the indigenous protectors and minor gods of Tibet played an integral part in this continually emergent spirituality, and their removal from their positions as mediating influences in Tibet (as the new translation traditions proposed) would not only constitute an insult to the great progenitors of the empire but would threaten the survival of Tibet itself. Finally, the representatives of Tibetan religion from the imperial period were still available to Tibetans, so that the continual presences of Vimalamitra, Padmasambhava, Trihsong Détsen, Avalokiteśvara, and so forth, sustained Tibet through the dark days after the fall of the empire, and it is to Tibetans' peril that they ignore the physical scriptures these august beings buried for the benefit of the roof of the world.

This was the genius of Terma: with the treasure texts, Tibet became an active partner in the Buddhist cosmos. Instead of being the disheveled stepchild of the great Indian civilization, by means of Terma the snowy land of Tibet became the authentic ground of the Buddha's enlightened activity. Terma introduced Tibetans to the literary evocation of their royal ancestors as descended ultimately from the Śākya clan, just as Śākyamuni Buddha had been. Through Terma literature, the first emperor of Tibet, Songtsen Gampo, became the emanation of the bodhisattva Avalokiteśvara. With the formalization of Terma around the person of Padmasambhava, the obscure Indian sorcerer became the icon for the interface of the two cultures. He married a Tibetan princess, was both king and Buddha, continually revealed himself to his Tibetan followers, and worked his magic through the entire hierarchy, taming spirits and emperors at a single stroke.

There can be little question that such affirmations were both reassuring and stimulating to audiences high and low, court and village. Treasure scriptures validated the familiar cultural landscape: the tombs of the ancient kings, the families that held Central Tibet together in the midst of civil war, the heritage of the old empire, the royal temples that simultaneously subdued the demoness and operated as points of reference for pilgrimage, the authority of the Tibetan language, and a host of other features. These new materials allowed Tibetans to formulate a nativistic response at a time of insecurity, a response that appropriated the main body of the new learning and re-presented it in a comforting format, with the assurance of Tibetan supremacy in all things sacred.

GIVE ME THAT OLD-TIME RELIGION

The second Nyingma response to Sarma polemics was to embody these attitudes in a direct challenge to the questionable activities of the new translators of esoteric scriptures and their Indian brethren, for sometimes they were accorded license through general public esteem. Indeed. we might consider the charges against the new translation movement attributed to Rongzom Chözang and amplified by Rok-ben Shérap-Ö (1166–1233) in his *Great Final Statement of the History of the Dharma* (*Chos byung grub mtha' chen po*). Not only was Rongzom one of the most learned Tibetans of the latter half of the eleventh century, but he also translated new tantric materials with Indian Paṇḍitas himself.[85] This did not stop him from codifying the ancient Vajrakīla tradition which still sustains his identity, "Rong's system of Vajrakīla" (Rong lugs rdo rje phur pa), or the Nyingma lineage known as Rong's system of the Mental Position of the Great Perfection.[86] He therefore had a dual perspective, for he knew the value of both the new learning and the old spirituality and could understand something of the strengths and weaknesses of either. For example, Rongzom integrated the exegetical movements of both Nyingma and Sarma into his commentarial discussion of the *Mañjuśrīnāmasamgīti*.[87] Yet no one who has read Rongzom's works would regard him as unpartisan, for he was firmly a Nyingma spokesman. Rok-ben amplified Rongzom's scathing observations into one of the most important responses to the polemics of new translators like Gö-lotsāwa Khugpa Lhétsé:[88]

> Now if you wonder why there are dissimilar chronicles of how the various tantras came into being, then we need to observe that in these latter days of the Dharma, the teacher's dispensation had declined in India. The great tantras have gradually begun to disappear, and their manuscripts have become spoiled. With the practice of texts just newly retrieved [as replacements] from the hands of the *ḍākinīs* by the various siddhas, then the chronicles of how the tantras had previously arisen were not internalized [but understood only imperfectly]. Moreover, the Paṇḍitas of today, impelled by their desire for gold, inquire as to what form of Dharma is prized in Tibet, and they then fabricate many of these teachings in response. The translators, impelled by their need for learning, stay the summer in Mangyül

and then go down to Nepal in the winter. Based on the dharmas translated by the bodhisattvas who were the early period translators and their Paṇḍitas, these new translators simply change things according to their own ideas. They base themselves on teachings common with the Tīrthika doctrines of the channels, the winds, and the essences, etc., which they have seen in some extraordinary holy places (*pīṭha*). Yet with this "golden dharma" (*gser chos*), the dispensation of the Tathāgata is crippled and wounded.[89]

Now perhaps you wonder how it is that only the texts of the Nyingma mantra system are no longer seen in India. It is said that generally during the early period, all the Dharma resident in India had been translated. From among them, those texts which were again translated at the later period were designated "New" (Sarma), whereas those which had not been retranslated were called Nyingma. And it is true that there were works, especially among the Mother tantras, which were not translated earlier and later were retrieved from the hands of the *ḍākinīs* and then translated. You might question why these Nyingma tantras were not retranslated. The earlier tantras came into the human sphere in the land of Zahor, which is to the southeast of Vajrāsana (Bodhgayā), and it was thus in that realm [Zahor] that they were popular. Now at that time, Paṇḍitas were educated in Zahor, and thus the Paṇḍitas invited to Tibet during the early period were from Zahor. Even those who were from the east Indian district of *Dhanadāla and elsewhere were generally trained in Zahor. Since the letters in the manuscripts at that time were generally in the script of Zahor, later Paṇḍitas from Magadha did not return to them (i.e., could not read them and therefore did not retranslate the texts). Moreover, the Dharma was eclipsed in Zahor, because a king of a land bordering on Zahor made war on that country. Thus, at the later spread in Tibet, [the Dharma and Paṇḍitas from Zahor] could not be invited. The instruction of the Great Perfection, because it is so very profound, cannot be held in everyone's mind. Its texts were hidden below Vajrāsana and Śrī Siṁha brought out only a bit and taught it to Bairotsana. The rest exists where he buried it. . . . These chronicles are based on the material expressed in the *History of the Dharma in Eastern Tibet* (*mDo Khams smad kyi chos 'byung*) of Khampa Sengé and the *Great Annals, Asked of Smṛti Jñānakīrti, That Cut off Doubt* (*Smṛti Jñānakīrti la dri ba'i the tshom bcad pa'i lo rgyus chen mo*).[90]

The consequences of Tibetans showing up in Indian monasteries loaded with bags of gold have seldom been considered, for this is what Rongzom intends to say. The record is that they did arrive so equipped, and occasionally we become privy to their conversations on the means and difficulties of transporting gold to and from India.[91] Rongzom indicates that a market-driven textual production may have occurred, in which Indians arrived in the highlands of Ü-Tsang with armloads of esoteric works whose ink was barely dry, composed ("revealed") in light of those matters holding the Tibetans' interest. I believe, too, that these forces have been overlooked in the case of the earlier translated royal dynastic materials as well, and even in the case of the Mahāyāna works translated into Chinese, for they all were subject to many of the same tensions. Contrary to the widely accepted elaborate ideology of visionary revelation, at its very worst the production of Buddhist sacred texts was exactly a commodities business. Certain Indians appear to have shown up with whatever text the market wanted, as long as payment was made with the precious yellow metal that Indians continue to adore.

Some of Rongzom's observations ring true: there was a dramatic shift of scripts between the ninth and eleventh century, the Nāgarī shift. In the instance of Kashmiri productions, like the *Nīlamata-purāṇa*, Witzel showed that the Gupta-based *siddha-mātṛkā* scripts occasionally were incomprehensible to the later Paṇḍitas, who would simply free-associate when necessary, although this was, by his account, less a problem in Kashmir than in Magadha and Bengal.[92] It is equally true that the modern history of the Hindu scriptures like the Purāṇas and the tantras is that of a consistent reinvention, frequently in response to what the scribe or Paṇḍita thinks the patron wants to hear. Rocher's review of the Purāṇas presented multiple instances of this process, whether the patron was British or Indian, which simply extends from the social understanding that these texts are performative and emergent rather than inscribed and static.[93]

For many of the Sarma translators, Buddhist scriptures and Indic commentaries became the currency with which they established their personal credentials. It is equally clear from Gö-lotsāwa's accusation that the *Guhyagarbha*'s author was Ma Rinchen-chok, that even learned Tibetans had difficulty determining which work actually came from India and which did not, for we know the *Guhyagarbha* to be authentically Indian in origin. The royal dynastic strategy of cataloging the contents of libraries apparently never occurred to any of the Paṇḍitas and translators ruminating in the libraries left over from the old dynasty, for there is no record of a catalog of Sanskrit manuscripts in the four horns of Tibet. Neither Atiśa, who visited Samyé, nor Ralo, who renovated it in 1106, evidently thought to use their manuscript-reading skills to catalog the Indic holdings. Other libraries holding royal dynastic Indian manuscripts remained uncataloged as well. It is little wonder that the presence or absence of Indic texts could not be the sole determining factor for affirming or condemning a lineage.

Another point of departure for lineal assessment was the deity announced by the scripture or articulated in the *sādhana*. It was the ostensible realization of the individual deity that gave the esoteric translators a sense of authenticity. The attacks on the new translators by Rok-ben and others were calculated to call into question their spirituality and thus their lineage. According to these Nyingma apologists, the new guys in the neighborhood were ordinary people, usurpers cultivating Tīrthika gods, whereas the royal dynastic translators were emanations of Avalokiteśvara. The later apologist Ratna Lingpa (1403–78) was quite vicious in regard to Gö-lotsāwa Khukpa Lhétsé: "I don't know if he's just crazy or actually possessed by a demon, but be sure that he's already in hell."[94]

It is a bit surprising to realize, however, that Rongzom's and Rok-ben's polemics were just as inspired by neoconservative values as were the challenges of Gö-lotsāwa and Lha-lama Yéshé-Ö. All these gentlemen actually had the same two arguments: the opposing party's documents or teachings were not authentically Indian Buddhist in origin, and their conduct was detrimental to the true Dharma. Such responses to the Sarma challenges sharpened the polemical field, so that the last half of the eleventh century became a period of further questioning. For the Nyingma authors, their responses made perfect sense, and later apologists took pains to note that the phenomenon of Terma scriptures was selectively accepted by certain Sarma authorities, an acceptance especially extended to treasure texts like the *Pillar Testament* or the *Maṇi Kambum*, neither of which involved traditions that could be exclusively occupied by a single lineage or other institution.[95] Indeed, part of the attraction of these works—still present today in Tibetans' continued fascination with the Dalai Lama—is the idea that they conveyed a national narrative of divine embodiment for the welfare of all Tibetans. Consequently, those questioning the legitimacy of Terma have seldom extended that critique to those works accepted in their own lineage.

THE ALTERNATIVE CULT OF KNOWLEDGE: RIG-PA

Like other Tibetans, the Nyingma masters were intrigued by the new rush to knowledge that brought prestige and a sense of participation in the international Buddhist movement. In Rongzom's case, as with some Nyingma scholars, he closely followed and amplified the Indian emphasis on gnosis. Ever creative, though, other writers built on their own tradition of revelation to develop an indigenous gnoseology. In this, they matured and articulated some of their own doctrinal materials featuring terms they themselves promoted, preeminently awareness (*rig-pa*) but also including gnosis (*ye shes*: *jñāna*). As it had with Tibetan rituals and local deities, the treasure enterprise provided the legitimacy for the Tibetan self-presentation on issues of realization.[96] Certainly, the Nyingma authors dipped into the archive of seminal works translated from both Indic and Sinic sources, some of which—like the *Avataṁsaka-sūtra* or the *Laṅkāvatāra-sūtra*—proved remarkably fecund in the generation of later literature in both Tibet and China. Attempts by both Sarma Tibetan and modern scholars to categorize the Nyingma developments as the simple consequence of Heshang Moheyan's northern Chan seem to be based on the presumption that Indians and Chinese can have indigenous spirituality but that Tibetans cannot, in contradiction to the remarkable evidence of their history.[97] The centrality of the gnoseology of awareness for the Nyingma, in fact, constitutes one of the distinguishing marks of the Great Perfection doctrines and underscores their differences from the phrases and ideas characteristic of the Chinese dossier in Tibet.[98]

If Indic works featuring knowledge (*jñāna*) seemed privileged in the eleventh century, awareness commanded much of the field in many Nyingma centers. With such titles as the *Great Tantra of the Self-Manifestation of Pure Awareness* (*Rig pa rang shar chen po'i rgyud*) in the Seminal Essence system of the Great Perfection, the eventual development of a specific consecration focusing on the activity of awareness (*rig pa'i rtsal dbang*) seemed to typify the Nyingma spiritual culture. Like many other eleventh- to twelfth-century Nyingma tantras, the *Self-Manifestation of Pure Awareness* text that we now possess focuses primarily on the problem of awareness: *rig-pa*. In the following discussion, I use this work as an important moment in the development of Tibetan gnoseology, although the complexity of Nyingma thought at this time suggests caution with any generalization.[99]

In some ways the indigenous paradigm of awareness was actually a more flexible formulation than the models of gnosis (*jñāna*) surveyed in chapter 4, and this flexibility was used to good effect in the emerging scriptures. Part of the problem in Indian Buddhism is the relationship between directed cognition, or consciousness (*vijñāna*), and gnosis. Early Yogācāra masters like Asaṅga discussed the option of formulating a pure level of consciousness, but this seemed unsatisfactory by Indian standards. This was in part because of the semantic history of *vijñāna*, which required some discursive variety (*vi-jñāna* = *vividhā-jñāna*) in its cognitional field. The difference between consciousness and gnosis required that a system of transition, a process of transformation (*āśrayaparivṛtti*), to be formulated to accomplish the dramatic movement between ignorance and awakening.[100]

Conversely, *rig-pa* required no alternative term and had no such inherent drift toward complexity, so the term could apply to both ordinary awareness and the cognition of the liberated saint. As a technical term, *rig-pa* sometimes appears in translations as a shortened form of the more familiar compound "self-awareness" (*rang gi rig-pa*) and represents the Sanskrit terms *svasaṁvedanā* or *svasaṁvitti* when translating from Indic texts. These terms, meaning "self-referential perception," appeared initially to have been developed by the great Indian epistemologist Dignāga, first in his *Nyāyamukha* and then in his *Pramāṇasamuccaya*. In these, he attempted to describe in precise epistemological terminology both the perceptual and the inferential events as already understood by the Vijñānavāda authors: the identity of the object, means, and result of cognition, distinctions resulting from a mere twist of language applied to the unity of instantaneous perception.[101] Dignāga's initial assessment was superseded by Dharmakīrti, who formulated a more sophisticated definition, particularly in reference to the perceptual event.[102] Consequently, *svasaṁvedanā* retained its perceptual overtones throughout its term of utilization.

The esoteric authors appropriated material from epistemologists, as they did from almost everyone else, and apparently the term *svasaṁvedanā* passed into the esoteric scriptures from their philosophical brethren, for I have not been able to trace the term to the early Ābhidharmika or Yogācāra materials.[103] Vajrayāna traditions used the term extensively, but with a difference. Whereas the epistemologists posited self-referential perception in all cases of the perceptual event, Vajrayāna authors focused on the perception of the awakened individual. The shift in emphasis was significant: instead of concentrating on the means of knowledge of the ordinary individual as a given, the Vajrācāryas concentrated on the gnostic perception of the yogin—thus, "pure awareness"—in terms of the ground of being, the soteriological path, and the goal to be realized.

Particularly significant for the Nyingmas was the *Rosary of Instructional Views* (*Man ngag lta ba'i phreng ba*) attributed to Padmasambhava, for it became an important source for the systematization of some strands of the Great Perfection teaching during the early renaissance.[104] The text identifies self-referential awareness in the "method of the Great Perfection" in the context of the fourth and final postulated realization:

> Now in reference to palpable realization, the state of all phenomena as being awakened from the very beginning is not in contradiction with the scriptures and the explanatory instructions, but neither is it based on merely the letter of the scriptures and the instructions. Rather, one's self-referential awareness (*rang gi rig pa*) comes to palpable realization [of this state] through the certainty [of this fact] in the depth of one's intellect.[105]

The importance of this passage should not be overemphasized, however. It is the only systematic mention of self-referential awareness in the two most influential Vajrayāna *śāstras* written or translated during the early period: the *Rosary of Instructional Views* and the *Bodhicitta-bhāvanā*, the latter a work by Mañju-śrīmitra.[106] The principal gnoseological component in both of these texts is that of gnosis (*jñāna*), the term preferred by the renaissance translators. Even more conservatively, Rongzom appears to have relegated self-referential awareness to its original position as a Vijñānavāda term describing the perceptual event.[107]

Earlier than Rongzom, however, is the work of Nubchen Sangyé Yéshé, a late-ninth- to early-tenth-century author.[108] There are two classes of statements concerning self-referential awareness in Nubchen's *Lamp for the Eye of Contemplation* (*bSam gtan mig sgron*): those relating it to the Mahāyoga *tantras* and those relating it to the system of Atiyoga. The first of these two classes of statements is quite similar to the material discussed in the *Rosary of Instructional Views* and must represent the standard transmission deriving from Indian sources. The most important statement on self-awareness in Nubchen's Mahāyoga chapter, however, dissociates it from the perceptual context and concentrates on its gnoseological function:

> And thus the [unqualified] self-referential awareness is not that dual operator and operation of awareness that turns the field of awareness into an object of perception but is instead the totality of the sphere of phenomena itself (*dharmadhātu*), because it does not grasp at any proper nature in phenomena and does not imagine that any of the extreme views inhere therein. As is said in the tantra, "The sphere of awareness and the gnosis of that sphere are identified as nothing more than self-referential awareness."[109]

Nubchen's Atiyoga chapter is the locus for the other class of qualifications of awareness and apparently represents a transition to the identification of the full-fledged omnipresence of *rig-pa*, which is found throughout the Seminal Essence scriptures:

> It is called the Great Perfection as it signifies that all inconceivable phenomena are without effort and, in their totality, complete. In order to understand the naked liberation [of phenomena], I will explain it in detail. The essential reality of this grand ancestor, this ultimate source of all the various vehicles, is the absolute sphere of simultaneously emerging reality. Having internalized the perception of self-referential awareness, the great actuality of there being no purposeful focusing of the intellect will be clarified in self-referential awareness.[110]

It is necessary to comment that even in this rather rarefied atmosphere of the early trend of the Great Perfection, the terminology maintains, to some degree, continuity with the original usage of awareness and is still tied to some perceptual language. Just how much, though, of this extended interpretation can be ascribed to Indian sources remains problematic, since Nubchen comes from a period in which Tibetans had already begun to radically reinterpret the Indic materials.

So, how does the *Tantra of the Self-Manifestation of Pure Awareness* (*Rig pa rang shar*) relate to this background? The sheer size and diversity of the text make it difficult to identify its phrasing of the central themes of pure awareness. However, the idea—still present in the *Lamp for the Eye of Contemplation*—of self-referential awareness and its underlying perceptual model appears at best vestigial by the time of the text's composition. There are, to be sure, phrases that still can be found, such as the three-line expression "In the lamp of self-manifest pure awareness, the concepts and characteristics of 'mind' and 'intellect,' etc., naturally do not exist."[111] These statements are, however, generally subordinated to two considerations: first, the exposition of the embodiment (*kāya*) doctrine and its extension to include other kinds of awakened forms of the Buddha and, second, to indicate through the use of symbols, the manner of the existence of pure awareness and its functioning.

One of the more telling sections of the *Rig pa rang shar* that illuminates the exposition of the bodies of the Buddha is found in its chapter 21, entitled "The Explanation of the Intention of the Buddhas of the Three Times." The chapter is dedicated to the relation between *rig-pa* and the standard three bodies of the Buddha. Following the statement that the lamp of pure awareness is the most excellent subject of the intentional cognition of the Buddhas of the three times, all of whom are subsumed under the embodiment of reality (*dharmakāya*), the text identifies pure awareness and this reality in the following way:

> Moreover, that *dharmakāya* is complete in the sphere of pure awareness. Because pure awareness does not hold on to anything, it is the proper nature of the *dharmakāya*. Because the appearance of pure awareness is unhindered, it is the proper nature of the *sambhogakāya*. Because pure awareness dawns as all forms of diversity, it is the proper nature of the *nirmāṇakāya*. In this way all phenomena are complete in the sphere of pure awareness.[112]

This basic format is repeated may times and constitutes one of the dominant themes of the scripture.

The text, however, does not stop with the basic three bodies of the Buddha as recognized in Indian Buddhism. Nor does it end its examination with the other three—the *svābhāvikakāya*, the *jñānakāya*, and the *vajrakāya*—which are widely attested in Indic Buddhist works. Rather it seeks to enlarge the entire concept of awakened embodiment, finally to subsume it under the purview of a "fundamental awakened form" (**mūlakāya*) of pure awareness. After defining pure awareness through a number of images, the sixty-second chapter of the *Rig pa rang shar* again addresses the subject of the awakened form:

> Moreover, correctly speaking, pure awareness exists in a continuum like a chain of vajras. While it possesses no substantial existence, it arises in creative appearance, and the awakened embodiment (*kāya*) arises as the ornament of this awareness. From the play of awakened embodiment, gnosis arises; from the ornament of gnosis, light arises; and from the tip of light, rays emerge. Now what is awakened embodiment? There are the basic embodiment of self-awareness (**maulasvasaṁvedanā-kāya*), the expansive embodiment of reality (**vipuladharma-kāya*), the pervasive embodiment of the sphere of reality (**spharaṇadhātu-kāya*), the unchanging adamantine embodiment (**avikaravajra-kāya*), the unchanging natural embodiment (**nirvikara-svābhāvika-kāya*), the correct embodiment of bliss (**samyaksukha-kāya*), the perverse mental embodiment (**mithyācitta-kāya*), the visible embodiment of liberation (**dṛṣṭavimukti-kāya*), the embodiment of the unique point of pure self-awareness (**svasaṁvedanā-tilaka-kāya*), the uninterruptedly expansive spatial embodiment (**avicchinna-vistarākāśa-kāya*), the nonpositional embodiment of the sun and moon (**nairpākṣika-sūryacandra-kāya*), the embodiment cognizant of nondiverse unity (**abhinnaikajña-kāya*), and the nonfixated embodiment of liberation (**nairābhiniveśika-vimukti-kāya*).[113]

The chapter goes on to define each of these in more detail. I have, quite artificially, Sanskritized the Tibetan terms found in this list of thirteen embodiments to demonstrate just how odd they would look in the Indic linguistic context. For the most part, these terms have no Indic counterparts and even, in the case of the "perverse mental embodiment," identify the awakened form—extending from pure awareness—with the state of obvious defilement. This identification reverses the long-standing Indic trajectory to envision awakened embodiment as a result of the path. Moreover, the variety of embodiments, both found in the *Rig pa rang shar* and developed in the later tradition, does not stop here.

Now I shall turn briefly to one of these further developments, called in Tibetan the "ever-youthful jar-like embodiment" (*gzhon nu bum pa'i sku*), an example of how the Indian conceptual field was elaborated by Tibetans in ways that were creative and involved an extensive hermeneutic of category reinterpretation. The Sanskrit for this might be rendered as **Kumārakalaśa-kāya*, but I have found no indication that such a term ever existed in Indian Buddhism. What appears to be an early form of the construct occurs in chapter 41 of the

Rig pa rang shar, in a section praising the lord preaching the scripture: "The grand ancestor of all Buddhas, who are endowed with the purposeful three bodies, is the lord endowed with the power of compassion, the ever youthful embodiment."[114] The context of this quotation echoes the classical formulation found in later works, the image of a lamp hidden in a ceramic or metal jar. The lamp shines and remains forever glowing, but the jar keeps it from being seen outside itself. The image is used to explain the simultaneous inherence of awakened awareness in the individual and his inability to perceive that fact in his obscuration. As it is broached in later works, the question revolves around *the* fundamental Mahāyāna problem: if pure awareness is all-pervasive and endowed with the qualities of light, freedom, and so forth, why does this cognition remain unmanifest in normal perceptual or intuitive states? The *Rig pa rang shar* itself addressed the question by resonating off its own image as a buried treasure:

> Within the expansive *maṇḍala* of the great elements, self-arisen gnosis is hidden as a treasure. Within the citadel of emptiness, the appearance of purity is hidden as a treasure. Within the expansive *maṇḍala* of the sphere of gnosis, the unchanging entities of the five Jinas are hidden as treasures. Within the appearance of the intermediate state of reality, the gnosis of pure awareness is hidden as a treasure. Within the dank dark depths of the bottom of the five defilements (*kleśa*), the unhindered pure awareness is hidden as a treasure. Within the expansive *maṇḍala* of the error of emotive tendencies, clarity of insight (*prajñā*) is hidden as a treasure. Thus, hidden in the *maṇḍala* of one's own heart, in the tomb of the Buddha, these magnificent treasures should be realized.[115]

Likewise, the "ever-youthful jarlike embodiment" represents the hidden lamp, the actuality of awakening, which is revealed when the jar itself (obscuration) is broken. The fact that the lamp is not visible is not the fault of the lamp but is a simple fact of the obstruction of the jar.

Certainly, the narrative materials and the images developed in these and other similar descriptions should alert us to a shift in metaphor in the Seminal Essence scriptures. If jars, lamps, and youths are standard images in the Mahāyānist scriptural metaphors, often denoting the embryo of the Tathāgata, the tradition's spinning a web of images employing treasures, ancestors, jars, lamps, and tombs evokes specifically royal Tibetan associations.[116] In this regard, even the titles of the principal explanatory texts of the Seminal Essence ascribed to Vimalamitra (*gsang ba snying thig zab pa po ti bzhi*)—said to be buried by him and retrieved by Ché-tsün Sengé Wangchuk—elicit images of the imperial letters of commission to ranks during the royal dynastic period. In the same manner that these rescripts were coded "golden" (*gser yig*), "turquoise" (*g.yu yig*), "copper" (*zangs yig*), and so forth, based on the color of the calligraphed letters, the explanatory works contain references to the *Golden Letters* (*gSer yig can*), the *Copper Letters* (*Zangs yig can*), the *Ornamented Discussion* (*Phra khrid*), the *Turquoise Letters* (*g.Yu yig can*), and the *Conch Letters* (*Dung yig can*).[117]

Perhaps more illustrative of the Central Tibetan symbol systems are the explicit appeals to the tomb and ancestral cults of the royal house. In the preceding quotation from the *Rig pa rang shar*, the ever-youthful jar-like embodiment is expressly identified as the grand ancestor residing in the tomb of the Buddha. The burial program of the royal house included the interment of the newly deceased king in a large jar filled with precious metals and gems.[118] The ideology was that his mind was still alive in that jar and that his living presence was indicated by the annual ceremonies conducted down the spirit road marked by the monolithic tablets and the guardian lions.[119] The formulation of this idea of a ever-youthful jar-like embodiment unified specific representations, well known from the Chongyé tumuli, with the Indic doctrines of the eternal embryo of the Buddha—new wine in old jars, as it were. All the associations of continued embodiment, longevity, burial, tomb, revelation, and flight to the celestial realm have an important part in both the doctrinal metaphors and the narrative of translation, entombment, discovery, and rediscovery of the texts of the tradition. Whether we are discussing Ché-tsün or the Seminal Essence texts or the translators, they all were endowed with the paraphernalia and the ritual systems of the ancestral cult and imperial fascination of the Tibetan peoples.

CONCLUSION: THE ABSENT IMPERIUM AS AN ETERNAL TREASURE

With the influx of so many new ideas, texts, lineages, temples, and systems of Buddhist meditation and philosophy, the ancient imperium seemed to fade before the very eyes of its latter-day inheritors. But there was no denying its power and hold on the collective Tibetan conscience, for every temple, every tomb, every monolith, and every ancient text or rusty artifact individually and collectively spoke to the beginning and apogee of Central Tibetan political life. Those maintaining the sites and their rituals never forgot that they alone possessed the legacy, controlling its gods and demons, its divinities and texts, its cosmology that placed Tibet at the center of the universe.

When they therefore "uncovered" texts, works that their various communities had composed and vetted, the Terma revealers actually revealed more than mere words, for the books became signa pointing the direction in which they thought Buddhist community life should go. In this imagined once-and-future history, Terma revealers brought Tibet itself into the realm of the activity of Buddhas and bodhisattvas, so that they did not belong to a border country but to the center of Buddhist mythos. Their new rituals, doctrines, and narratives were not composed of whole cloth, but parts worked into new clothes, clothing that simultaneously revealed and concealed reality. Employing the Tibetan origin myth, the imperial mythologies, the fascination with Avalokiteśvara, and the sense of loss for the empire, the treasure finders brought into written form the oral lore of the tenth to twelfth century.

Especially with the category and content of the emperor's personal treasure, we find the textualization of the emperors' persons, so that the intentions of the imperial will were effected by the continuing process of scriptural revelation. The emperors' mythic decrees were inscribed in these works, which include stories and operate in conjunction with the received paintings in the surviving imperial temples. Eventually, the imperial person was extended from the pillars of temples into the interiors of caves, mountains, rocks, and the very fabric of Tibet, where new treasures are located. Indeed, the process that begins with the textualization of Songtsen Gampo's self ends with the landscape of Tibet inscribed as the self of the emperors. The gods of individual valleys (*yul lha*), heretofore of only localized power and authority, eventually became shared by the Tibetan people, so that pilgrimage to the sites of the Buddhist divinities now inhabiting those areas has been authenticated as religiously efficacious.

The power of the texts was so effective that these works became popularly accepted as indistinguishable from translated Indian works, so that the Indian religion of Buddhism really became Tibetan in scope, nature, and domain. The Tibetans' compelling use of language and their easy claim on all Tibetans' identity made the Terma materials some of the best of all literature and the focus of Tibetan continued self-doubt. Like gravity, however, no Tibetan tradition could ignore the issue of revelation, the question of imperial affiliation, or the consistent claim of clans on public religious life.

7

The Late Eleventh Century: From Esoteric Lineages to Clan Temples

> I built this Sakya Monastery on top of the fortress of the Lu spirits, so that at a later time its fortune would increase. But there is a risk that the Lu will inflict injury on the people if the practice of this place becomes coarsely Tibetan. So take my pure body, embed it in pellets, and put it inside a stūpa planted over the Lance-stand ravine. I will reside there.
>
> —Last testament of Khön Könchok Gyelpo, 1102 C.E.[1]

By the second half of the eleventh century, Tibetans had demonstrated a remarkable achievement. Central Tibet had attained a degree of economic viability and social stability that would have been but a dream in the tenth century, and stories begin to speak of Ü-Tsang clans rich in goods and financial resources, some newly come into their wealth. Tibetans now possessed in their evolving literary language the translations of an extraordinary amount of ritual and philosophical material, executed by translators of increasing learning and sophistication. Tibetans were enjoying a revitalized sense of identity and importance, derived in part from the reformulation of Tibetan ideas under the trope of treasure texts, in which the emperors of the past continued to exercise their care on the land of their descendants. The Eastern Vinaya monks had organized aggressive temple networks enabling a monk to travel from the Nepalese border to Kongpo, and for the most part have access to Buddhist temples and monasteries on his way.

Many challenges remained, however, for the Central Tibetan renaissance was still new and somewhat raw in emotion. Most important, the new tantric lineages were experiencing a degree of institutional instability. Religious traditions become stable when their institutions demonstrate centrality and longevity, but this was a problem for the translators, their immediate followers, and their progeny. Two reasons for this became apparent in the late eleventh century. First, the institutions had been founded with divided purposes, so that religious avocation was not separated from tangible worldly success. Second, the tantric paradigm did not simply inhibit political unification but diminished the stature of the followers and successors of the various paradigmatic leaders, so that tantric teachers—Nyingma or Sarma—continued to occupy the position of quasi-feudal chieftains. Characteristically, the eleventh-century translators left behind both a familial lineage in their sons, who inherited their buildings and wealth, and one or more religious lineages in their disciples, who transmitted their teachings to others, but the two lines seldom coincided. In the next century many of these problems were resolved through a variety of means, some of which began in the late eleventh century.

This chapter reviews those developments in the last part of the eleventh century that have not been previously discussed. The influx of new materials under the aegis of one of the more notorious figures of the eleventh century, Padampa Sangyé, is briefly explored, especially because it exemplifies the continued negotiation between the Indian and Tibetan cultures. We examine the new popular religious expressions of Kadampa and Kagyüpa representatives, showing their creative articulation of Tibetan images. The eleventh century also saw the reemergence of the importance of virtue, with the Kadampa authorities emphasizing Mahāyānist ideologies of purity of mind and karma. The last quarter of the century, in particular, witnessed the development of a new orthodoxy in which emerged a Tibetan sense of the proper handling of the wealth of doctrinal materials from India, stratifying Indian texts and ideas on a scale of values and valorizing Tibetan compositions as necessary. This chapter also looks at the problems in tantric transmission following the death of a famous figure, in this case Drokmi, and concludes with a consideration of the rise of the Khön clan, its mythology, and the foundation of its central institution, Sakya Monastery, in 1073. In all of these, the new systems were in continual renegotiation with the Nyingma and other indigenous traditions of religion and literature, and all successful Sarma lineages eventually reached some variety of rapprochement with the older forms.

THE LITTLE BLACK ĀCĀRYA: PADAMPA AND HIS ZHICHÉ

Padampa was certainly the most influential Indian yogin in late-eleventh- and early-twelfth-century Tibet, challenged in this role by perhaps only another notorious character, Prajñāgupta, who lived somewhat earlier and was mentioned in conjunction with the last of the eight "subsidiary" practices cultivated by Drokmi. More than any other Indian in the late eleventh century, Padampa demonstrates the willingness of Indians to bring the process of creative scripture to Tibet, and he contributed an accelerating sense of openness to the religious zeitgeist. He was quite possibly from South India originally, and the *Blue Annals* declares his father to have been from a caste of jewel merchants, although later hagiographers elevate his stature to a brahman.[2] Padampa was accorded fifty-four siddhas as his gurus, with all the big names represented—Saraha, Virūpa, Nāgārjuna, etc.—and was thought to have traveled to the mysterious land of Oḍiyāna, where he is said to have been involved with more than thirty *ḍākinīs*. Whatever the veracity of this description, there can be little doubt that he was well educated in North Indian tantric literature and practice.

Padampa's hagiography is a wonderland of improbabilities, for he is said to have made as many as seven trips to Tibet over the course of several centuries. According to some claims, he made the first of these visits when the land was still covered by water, as it certainly was by the Neo-Tethys Sea, but it disappeared from Tibet some 40 million years ago. Equally dubious was the more common claim that Padampa had been in Tibet during the royal dynastic period, then known by the Sanskrit name he often used, Kamalaśīla, yet another conflation of two important Indians having the same name. It is probable that he made more than one trip to Tibet and that he had a strong Kashmir connection, as one of his lineages shows. The *Blue Annals* mentions that his fourth trip was to the Nyel valley, along the Arunachal Pradesh border, and he then traveled to Pen-yül in 1073, when he met Magom Chökyi Shérap. He stayed for a while in Pen-yül and Kongpo, then went to China, and returned on his fifth trip to Tibet in the 1090s, settling in Dingri, at Dingri Langkor, between 1097 and his death in 1117. The twenty years he spent in Dingri were the most significant, and most of the documents and traditions attributed to him stem from this time.

Although Padampa worked extensively with Zhama-lotsāwa, whose gray texts were discussed earlier, Padampa's tradition scarcely remembers the work of the translator who rendered Padampa's ideas into intelligible Tibetan. There are a few, seemingly verbatim, transcripts of Padampa's conversations that reveal a person not entirely fluent in Tibetan sentence structure but with a reasonably large vocabulary, given to dramatic statements and in love with symbols, images, and illustrations.[3] Padampa's expansive propensity evidently led beyond verbal interaction to composition, for Chaglo Chöjé-pel accused him of passing off his own work as legitimate tantras:

> Now there is this Indian called Little Black Dampa teaching the *Widespread Position of Simultaneous Awareness (gCig char rig pa rgyang 'dod)*, which is a

> mixture of some perverted teachings and some Great Perfection ideas. Based on these, he composed unlimited perverse Dharmas under the title of *Zhiché of Three Red Cycles*, and the *Tīrtika White Zhiché*, which is placed in a single textual tradition with dissimilar materials that are Buddhist.[4]

This summary suggests that the "pacification" (Zhiché) system was entirely fabricated by Padampa—here called by his nickname, the Little Black Ācārya or Little Black Dampa—with its "white instruction" in mental purification and its "red instruction" in certain forms of tantric practice. Later in the same text, Chaglo Chöjé-pel accuses Padampa of writing a tantra, which can be recognized as the surviving *Tantra of Instruction on the Secret of All Ḍākinīs*, a short, three-chapter work said to have been translated by Padampa himself and apparently not included in any canon.[5] Even the Nyingma Terma authorities understood Padampa's textual revelation, for in an attempted defense of Terma, Ratna Lingpa named another tantra, the *Tantra of the Great River, the Inconceivable Secret of Vowels and Consonants*, as having been revealed by Padampa.[6]

There is little reason to doubt that Padampa could have composed these, for his literate legacy is a summary of how the tantras were written in India, with personal instruction leading to notes and short works, and finally compiled into a scriptural text with a number of short chapters, as exemplified by both the tantras he is accused of authoring. What is different in these two scriptures is the thoroughgoing sense of Tibetan participation, by either Zhama-lotsāwa or others. The work left behind by Padampa was original enough that it stands out as somewhat anomalous by Indian standards, for some of it was influenced by Tibetan social realities and images. The *Tantra of Instruction on the Secret of All Ḍākinīs*, for example, includes a mantra that seems to cite the place-name Dingri: ĀṀ MA DING RI DING RI VAJRA RATNA PADMA VIŚ VASIDDHI SANIRIHA HŪṀ HŪṀ PHAṬ PHAṬ.[7]

Two basic religious directions emerged from Padampa and his coterie—the Zhiché (pacification) lineages and the Chö (cutting off) tradition. The latter is discussed in the next chapter, as it principally entails his female disciple, Machik Labdrön.

The Zhiché is a curious rubric with five lineages appropriating that name, and these transmissions are divided into the early, intermediate, and later Zhiché.[8] According to the available texts, the "early" Zhiché was transmitted to Jñānaguhya of Kashmir during Padampa's third trip to Tibet, and from Jñānaguhya to Önpo Pelden Shérap and on to other Tibetans. The three "intermediate" lineages were those of Magom Chökyi Shérap (rMa lugs), of So Rigpa Cherthong (So lugs), and of Kamtön Wangchuk lama (sKam lugs) and were transmitted during Padampa's fourth and fifth trips. The "later" Zhiché

FIGURE 15 Padampa and Jangsem Kunga. After a thirteenth-century manuscript illustration

was transmitted to Jangsem Kunga, Padampa's greatest Zhiché disciple, who stayed with Padampa until the Indian's death (figure 15).

The curiosity of Zhiché is not its multiple lineages but the fact that there seems to be no core teaching associated with the term Zhiché, which means pacification (of suffering). Padampa was evidently so fluid that whatever was appropriate for him to teach a disciple became subsumed under the aegis of "pacification." For example, the early Zhiché transmitted to Jñānaguhya had five levels of instruction: a tantric version of the Madhyamaka, teaching according to the Father tantras, teaching according to the Mother tantras, Mahāmudrā instruction, and teaching by the *ḍākinī*'s examples, which constitute a fairly straightforward late tantric menu. But the Zhiché (same name) transmitted to Kamtön was a series of meditations on the *Heart Sūtra* of the Perfection of Insight class of Mahāyānist scriptures. Finally, the later Zhiché transmitted to Jangsem Kunga included much from both these earlier systems but featured a "five-path" instruction, breaking up the Vajrayāna path according to the Mahāyānist gradations of the paths of accumulation, application, vision, cultivation, and the final path.

Having spent several decades reading tantric texts, I am used to a degree of inconsistency and discontinuity, but the highly differentiated ideology and practice included with Zhiché pushes the envelope further than I can recall having previously seen. This sense of insubstantiality extended to Padampa's Tibetan disciples as well, for the holders of the several Zhiché traditions imitated Padampa himself and tended to wander hither, thither and yon all over Tibet, collecting odd scraps of teachings and practicing in disparate environments. This was recognized in the literature, and the *Blue Annals* quotes Padampa as saying that because everyone left in their several directions, there was no single famous lineage holder.[9] Although Zhiché became a featured item in many teachers' repertoires, it did not maintain a strong stable environment, a common occurrence among yogic traditions in late-eleventh-century Tibet. This was in great part because those attracted to such eccentric personalities tended to emulate their behavior and were not motivated to construct long-lived centers.

POPULAR EXPRESSIONS AND A ZEAL TO SPREAD THE MESSAGE

Strong institutions require a broad popular base of support, from which the next generation may be drawn, and indications are that the clerical support of a popular Buddhism really came of age in the latter half of the eleventh century, in the interaction of Tibetans with other Tibetans. Most of the systems discussed so far focused on a relatively elite level of religious society—monks, master meditators, and tantric translators—who acted as a privileged aristocratic class with political and economic prerogatives. Conversely, the spread of Buddhism among the ordinary Tibetans (*dmangs*) required the development of ritual systems and accompanying narratives that could be transmitted throughout a large body of people with little financial burden placed on individuals. The strategies that evolved to integrate the laity into Buddhist activities included the promotion of popular teaching methods, the development of the cults featuring loving Buddhist divinities (especially Avalokiteśvara and Tārā), the spread of artistic representations teaching these ideals at sites available to all, and the generation of easily memorized verses set to song.

Many of these strategies were pioneered by Kadampa masters after Atiśa's passing in 1054. Although the monasteries founded by his immediate disciples were modestly successful, they did not command the authority that Samyé and the ancient temples did for the Nyingma lineages or that the new centers of translation—Mugulung, Drowo-lung, and Tanak-pu, to name a few—did among Sarma lineages. We know little about the development of Sangpu Néütok under its founder, Ngok Lekpé Shérap, but Dromtön, Atiśa's lay disciple and founder of Retreng Monastery in 1056/57, had a relatively small number of disciples at this time. The *Blue Annals* states that Dromtön had a regular core of sixty meditators, but other documents assign eighty disciples to him.[10] As we have seen, the few other centers were in tension with the Eastern Vinaya monks, so they were insecure in their positions as dedicated Kadampa convents. This circumstance changed through the agency of the "three brothers" (*mched gsum*), a designation for three Kadampa monks who forged the new identity of meditating Mahāyānist monks spreading the pure Dharma among ordinary Tibetans.

These three brothers were Puchungwa Zhönu Gyeltsen (1031–1109), Chen-nga Tsültrim-bar (1038–1103), and Potoba Rinchen-sel (1027–1105), and all three were primarily disciples of Dromtön at Retreng. It was at this time that the Kadampa denomination really became an entity, and Tibetan writers are uniform in asserting that the name Kadampa or Jowo Kadampa was first used to describe Dromtön's disciples.[11] Born into the Zur clan, Puchungwa Zhönu Gyeltsen was ordained at Gyel Lhakhang as a member of the Eastern Vinaya lineage, the Vinaya tradition of most Kadampa monks.[12] He is reputed to have studied briefly with Atiśa at Nyétang and also to have spent seven fruitful years with Dromtön at Retreng. Even though Puchungwa was very well versed in the *Perfection of Insight* scriptures and ancillary literature, he elected to specialize in Mahāyānist meditative practice.

As in the case of Drokmi and Marpa, Atiśa's lineage became theoretically divided into those specializing in meditation (*sgrub brgyud*) and those who focused on exegetical systems (*bshad brgyud*). Of these, Puchungwa, although trained in both, really represented the former and spent his days in contemplation, with relatively few disciples. His mystical abilities and mysterious persona, however, turned him into the mythic protagonist of Kadampa secret literature—the *Kadampa Book* (*bKa' gdams glegs bam*)—in the twelfth and thirteenth centuries.[13]

The same mystery cannot be applied to Potoba Rinchen-sel, who became something of a celebrity in Central Tibet.[14] He was another member of the Nyö clan to enter religion, being ordained by Lumé's successor Ngok Jangchub Jungné at Yerpa, where he met Atiśa and initially studied with Nagtso. He decided to continue his education with Khutön Tsöndrü (1011–75) and began to specialize in intellectual topics (*mtshan nyid*). After Atiśa's death, he went to Retreng, where he met the other two brothers and continued to work on texts for seven years.

Closely allied to Potoba's life is that of the third brother, Chen-nga, who was the scion of another of the great religious clans, the Wa/Ba, whose members had been central to royal dynastic Buddhism.[15] At the age of seventeen,

Chen-nga took precepts at an Eastern Vinaya temple in Tölung and met Atiśa when he was staying nearby. As a consequence of this encounter, Chen-nga conceived a desire to visit Bodhgayā and began studying Sanskrit in order to become a translator. His plans changed, though, when he met Dromtön at the age of twenty-five, and the Retreng founder told Chen-nga to abandon his aspirations as a translator and to become his disciple instead. Like Potoba, Chen-nga also spent seven years with Dromtön, serving him as his monastic aide-de-camp (whence his name: sPyan-snga = aide) and studying primarily the "stages of the path" literature. Because of their involvement with protecting the Kadampa teachings, the three brothers regarded themselves as reincarnations of three of the sixteen great Arhats who persisted in protecting Śākyamuni's Dharma, but popular acclaim eventually recast the three brothers as the three great bodhisattvas: Avalokiteśvara, Mañjuśrī, and Vajrapāṇi.

Following Dromtön's death in 1064, the Retreng community was gradually expanded by the next abbot, Neljorpa Chenpo (d. 1076), but the three brothers traveled to other areas and started their peripatetic life of missionary activity. In response to the elite bias of most forms of Buddhism spread throughout Tibet at the time, the Kadampas began to promote a more egalitarian ideal. In their literature, they retain a teaching attributed to Atiśa, that monks "from this day forward, pay no attention to names, pay no attention to clans, but with compassion and loving kindness always meditate on the thought of awakening (*bodhicitta*)."[16] This ideal was widespread throughout Indian Buddhism and given lip service in eleventh-century Tibet, but its implementation meant a fundamental change of pedagogical method, for monks would have to deliver Buddhist ideas to the populace. Eventually the change was effected by Chen-nga and Potoba, who devised a style of teaching that included popular images and anecdotes in their presentations.[17] The Kadampa explanation is that Potoba, in particular, had listened carefully to Atiśa's disciple Khutön, had read the scriptures, and had been attentive to popular expressions, always seeking out better ways to communicate the Buddhist message.[18]

Culling his illustrations from the various sources, Potoba brought into his lectures examples that made Buddhist ideas stand out with remarkable clarity.[19] So, when a mother loses her son, she thinks about him all the time, waking and sleeping, and always talks about her deceased boy; in that same way, one should constantly reflect on the triple gem. One should follow a path to awakening like a trader, for whatever happens, the merchant regards it positively: if it snows, then it is good for the horses' hoofs; if it rains, then there will be no bandits.

Several hundred examples, explanations, and stories were collected and organized under twenty-five topic headings, yielding his text *Teaching by Examples: A Profusion of Gems* (*dPe chos rin chen spungs pa*).[20] These examples begin with the refuge idea, through the issues of karma and the Mahāyānist ideal, the six perfections, and conclude with the transference of merit and a summary. Most of the standard topics of introductory Mahāyānist Buddhism are included, so that preachers would have had a handy manual to use for teaching in assemblies. Indeed, the popularity of this approach is evinced even today, for while researching this book, I found that I had heard many of these examples used in modern lectures. Because of the colloquial nature of the teaching, moreover, the commentaries are filled with early Central Tibetan idioms and local words, so that they and the related Kadampa literature are mines of linguistic and cultural information about the late eleventh to twelfth century. As a result of these initiatives, the popular following of the three brothers flourished, with Potoba attracting more than two thousand disciples and Chen-nga several hundred of his own.[21]

Potoba and Chen-nga were definitely not the first to employ indigenous Tibetan images and ideas, as these had already been seen in the Terma literature. But the differences between the Terma presentations—emphasizing the imperial legacy and the power of esoteric spells—and the Kadampa preaching were crystallized in the Kadampa development of the cults of Avalokiteśvara and Tārā. These figures are often said have been promoted by Atiśa, but this is only partly true, for they were important elements in a vast pantheon of deities that the Bengali master brought to Tibet. Tibetans had already shown a predisposition to Avalokiteśvara, for the Āryapalo (a contraction of Āryāvalo[-kiteśvara]) temple at Samyé, the first temple built there, was dedicated to the bodhisattva of compassion.

With the Kadampa emphasis on popular religion, Kadampa preachers like the three brothers turned Avalokiteśvara and Tārā into the religious ancestor/ancestress of the Tibetan people, so that the eventual ideology of Songtsen Gampo and his queens as the emanations of these divinities was made possible by Kadampa missionary activity after Atiśa's demise. The eleven-headed Avalokiteśvara practices, Atiśa's legendary conversations with the goddess Tārā, the difficult law-and-order situation in Tibet, and the emphasis on these two bodhisattvas brought by other Indian masters during the late eleventh century all assisted the focus on the two deities who save devotees from the eight great dangers.[22] This movement eventually spawned such Kadampa mythic and meditative practices as the "doctrine of the sixteen spheres" (*thig le bcu drug gi bstan pa*) and made popular a lay-oriented, Avalokiteśvara-focused fasting program (*smyung gnas*), whose propagation was closely associated with the Kadampa monks.[23]

In this surge of popular religiosity, the position of the Jokhang in Lhasa became central (figure 16). Unlike such big monasteries as Samyé, the Jokhang

FIGURE 16 Entrance to the Jokhang in Lhasa. Photograph by the author

did not have a dual mission, for its main purpose was the intersection between the Tibetan people and the Buddhist divinities. It is instructive to realize that the Jokhang was *not* included in the sites renovated by the Eastern Vinaya monks, and Butön says that they avoided Lhasa in general, for it was the site of punishment, which is rather an enigmatic explanation.[24] According to Atiśa's hagiography, during his tour of Central Tibet, perhaps around 1047/48, the Bengali master both viewed and made elaborate offerings to the famous Jowo statues in the temple when he was invited there by Ngok Legpé Shérap.[25] This may have happened, but it is difficult to separate Atiśa's real activities from his legendary relationship to the building, for he was supposed to have discovered the treasure text the *Pillar Testament* at the Jokhang. A "Lhasa temple" was said to be the site of the translation of four works by Atiśa working with Nagtso, but the extent of the work suggests that it must have been translated at his Lhasa residence, the "Happy suffusion of light" (*dga' ba 'od 'phro*), which was apparently not at the Jokhang.[26]

An elaborate visit by Atiśa would be questionable in part because the Jokhang was evidently first renovated during the renaissance by a Kadampa scholar, Zangskar-lotsāwa, probably in the 1070s. The *Scholar's Feast* (*mKhas pa'i dga' ston*) mentions its dilapidated state: "After the popular revolts, offerings were made at neither of the two temples of Lhasa (Ramoché and Jokhang), but they became inhabited by beggars. In every chapel, stoves belched smoke, soot darkening the walls over a very long period."[27] All the statues were in disarray as well, and Zangskar-lotsāwa, together with the local functionary Dölchung Korpön, moved the beggars out, so that the statues could be replaced, new walls built, and the building turned back into a functioning temple.[28] The *Pillar Testament*, in fact, alludes to presence of a new community supporting the refurbished temple after a period of religious degradation.[29] The *Pillar Testament* is emphatic that the paintings of the west wall, along with those of other imperial-period temples like Trandruk in the Yarlung valley, inform the people how the first emperor Songtsen Gampo became the incarnation of Avalokiteśvara.[30]

Kadampa documents of a later century otherwise offer testimony about Atiśa's seeing miraculous scroll paintings (*thang ka*) of the Buddha and Tārā in Samyé, and we know that such scrolls were essential to the devotional systems surrounding Green Tārā. Indeed, a scroll copy of a form of Tārā popular at Retreng has miraculously survived from the twelfth century, simultaneously demonstrating the devotional image of the green goddess and the means for its cultic propagation.[31] Tantric Buddhist art emphasizes painting far more than sculpture, which is fundamentally neglected in the tantras, and this predisposition in India matured in Tibet in the various directions in regard to making a series of paintings (*rgyud ris*) to spread the message. However, one of the most important images in Retreng was a white bell-metal image of Tārā. Entitled *Tārā Victorious over the Army* (*g.yul rgyal sgrol ma*), it was described as one of Atiśa's two personal statues, the other being the more famous Mañjuvajra image.[32] This particular Tārā statue was said to have protected India from a Turkish army, to have spoken to Dromtön at one time, and to have survived a fire, all elements in the hagiography of the illustrious statue. Together with the relics and reliquaries of great saints like Atiśa, such paintings and statues provided an opportunity for lay participation that did not require the elite.

Beyond the Kadampa effort, the other means for the spread of popular Buddhism was generated and nurtured by the Kagyüpa followers of Marpa, and that was the singing of songs. Oral literature of this nature had been an important part of Buddhism in India, and narrative literature (*sgrung*) had been an essential facet of human religion (*mi chos*) since the early period. Although the Nyingma, certainly, were not slow to assist construction of religious narratives featuring the great saints of the empire, the entire area of poetry and vocal song was not well represented in Tibetan Buddhism until Kagyüpa masters like Mila Repa successfully incorporated the vocal and narrative process into the teaching. Even though the literature depicts these individuals as hermits, they were as much eremitic as cenobitic and tended to mix with people in the marketplaces, at pilgrimage sites, or in local temples, for they often begged for their food and lived by lay largesse. Their poetry was based on the Indian siddhas' *dohā* songs of realization combined with Tibetan poetic forms and folk tunes, and the verses became as accessible to the broader populace in Tibet as their predecessors' stanzas had been in India.

Mila Repa, regarded as one of Marpa's four great disciples, belonged to a branch of the powerful Khyung clan, and his parents were both wealthy and important in the area of Gungtang-tsa, where he was born, perhaps in 1040.[33] As a boy he had a natural gift for song, and his parents named him Happy to Hear (Thos-pa-dga'). But his family was marked by tragedy, first by the death of his father, probably from an epidemic, and second by their impoverishment when their wealth was stolen by family and friends. Consequently, his mother, who belonged to the Nyang clan, became embittered and sent her son to study with one Yungtön Tro-gyel, a master of sorcery (*mthu*), who had Mila Repa study magic under another master, Dr. Nupchung.[34] After more than a year of practice, Mila used his newly acquired skill in magic to kill his opponents and ruin their crops with hail. Then Mila Repa repented his transgressions and went to study the Great Perfection with one Rongtön Lhagah. But because he received no benefit from the practice, he was sent by the Great Perfection teacher to undertake the tribulations inflicted by Master Marpa.

The various trials of Mila Repa are now well known from the early English translations of Tsang-nyön's hagiography, much as their popularity in Tibet became an important aspect of the Mila Repa narrative. Indeed, Kagyüpa literature has tended to feature the trope of a quest for teaching, which played such an important place in Nāropā's hagiography in Tibet, and even Marpa's journey to Phullahari was recast at a later date to conform to the Nāropā plot device of encountering various enigmatic guides, only to be sent out again on a quest until the authentic master was found.[35] Nonetheless, there can be little doubt that Marpa was a difficult teacher, and Mila Repa certainly was required to win instruction under great duress. After some years of training in Kagyüpa yogic practices, when he was in his forties, he finally left to look for his family, and finding all in ruins, he practiced the internal heat yoga in high caves. With his students, Mila Repa traveled to various pilgrimage sites, especially the great mountains—Kailāsa, Bonri, Tsari, etc.—and, by his example, virtually invented the archetype of the white-cotton clad yogin.

Mila Repa's literary legacy is just as noteworthy, for he must have opened the door for Buddhist poetic composition that uses folk-related forms, making the process not only acceptable but also revered. Because we have nothing actually written by him, we cannot be certain that the enormous collections of songs attributed to Mila Repa are actually by the cotton-clad saint. Accordingly, his literary persona became something of a vehicle through which various authors could express their own feelings and intuitions, ones they may not have wanted under their own names. After Mila Repa's time, the collections of "hundred thousand songs" (*mgur 'bum*) became a standard genre in the Kagyüpa literary pantheon, and many of these collections contain some of the best literature in the language, evoking pathos and a recognition of shared frailties, which are notably absent in many saints' repertoires.[36]

For example, the greatest moment of pathos in the Mila Repa story comes when the forty-something yogin returns to his home, which lies in ruins. Half the house is caved in; the fields are but beds of weeds; and he discovers his mother's bones scattered and bleached at the threshold of the home, which is now haunted by spirits. He learns that his sister is wandering as a beggar far away, and the villagers are terrified of the evil spells that Mila Repa had sent in response to his mother's desire for vengeance. The third Karmapa's compilation contains his version of Mila Repa's feeling of renunciation:

This house, Four Pillars and Six Beams,
These days is [worthless] like the upper jaw of a snow lion.
The tower, four corners, eight sides, with its pinnacle as ninth,
These days is [flat and droopy] like a donkey's ear.
The three sided piece of bottom land called Wor-mo,

These days is the fatherland of weeds.
The close kinsmen from whom one hopes for help,
These days make an army of enemies.
This is also an example of impermanence and illusion;
With this image, I will fashion the yogic Dharma.[37]

This is only part of the longer song, and the nature of the preserved verse, coupled with allusions to other earlier collections, shows that these episodes became grist for the wandering bards and petty religious who had been the village storytellers long before Buddhism appeared. The success of the high literary and elite yogic systems represented by both the Kadampa and Kagyüpa was strongly supported by the folk-story purveyors once their own appropriation of Buddhist narratives became not only legitimate but also desirable. With their peripatetic lives and ready-made audiences, the illiterate and quasi-shamanistic poets of the high plains thus added Buddhist yogins and littérateurs to their possessive pantheon of spirits, kings, and magical beings that could be channeled for a good story to the crowd.

The popular religious renaissance in Ü-Tsang in the late eleventh century was the consequence of decisions made at the expense of elitist religious systems, either those supporting the esoteric ideology or those in the hands of clans, and much of Tibetan religion at this time was both. The success of the Kadampa preachers and Kagyüpa poets subverted the imperial narrative and clan origin stories by making religion directly accessible to the ordinary Tibetan nomads, land-bound peasants, and wealthy town traders. Egalitarian in impulse, it allowed believers to have an immediate conversation with Avalokiteśvara and Tārā or with the saints and divinities of emerging Tibetan religion. It would be an error, however, to assume that this was done entirely in opposition to either elite Sarma or Nyingma forms, and nearly all these popular expressions created a very easy alliance with the bardic poets purveying epic royal narratives and articulating other facets of Tibetan spirituality. Eventually, popular religiosity matured into another variety of Terma, like the *Pillar Testament*, where Tibet is seen as the field of the Buddha's activity in which the spiritual agency previously exhibited toward Indians in India was redirected to Tibetans in Tibet.

THE LATE-ELEVENTH-CENTURY INTELLECTUAL EFFLORESCENCE

Besides introducing popular religion, the late eleventh century ushered in an intellectual efflorescence as well. Part of it was stimulated by the translators at that time, who began to question the provenance of the Nyingma scriptures. The nine-vehicle ideology of the Nyingma also was suspect, and the vocabulary of the older tradition was considered questionable. Such criticisms in turn precipitated a reflexive evaluation. As we have seen, the Sarma authorities sometimes had difficulty in determining which texts were authentic, and by the 1092 proclamation of Podrang Shiwa-Ö, even authentically Indian texts and masters were sometimes condemned for their lack of virtue. Increasingly the sense grew, particularly in West Tibet, that Indian Buddhism was alarmingly protean and that Tibetans should obtain from its best representatives the appropriate methods to deal with its complexity. The activity of some of the later paṇḍitas, like Padampa or Prajñāgupta, contributed to this discomfort, for both of them appeared to create new teachings as they encountered new situations. Over time, the strategies began to revolve around doctrinal categories, correct Buddhist vocabulary, and the stratification of texts and teachings, so that exoteric and esoteric (nontantric and tantric) teachings were not conflated with each other.

The Eastern Vinaya monks had dominated exoteric study, and beyond the Vinaya itself they emphasized the *Perfection of Insight* scriptures, the Abhidharma, the *Yogācārabhūmi*, other Mahāyāna scriptures, and related works. We do not know exactly how they used them, but their study was doubtless based on the systems of instruction available during the imperial period. Epistemology was explored as well, and probably in the third quarter of the century, two monks, Dakpo Wang-gyel and Khyungpo Draksé, represented the old study of logic (*tshad ma rnying ma*). These two are said to have challenged each other—perhaps to debate, possibly in a more general sense—on the red hill in Lhasa, where the Potala is located.[38]

Consequently, Central Tibet was ripe for an infusion of nontantric teaching from Indian centers of instruction, and this happened first through the agency of Ngok-lotsāwa Loden Shérap, the nephew of the Sangpu founder, Ngok Lekpé Shérap. Ngok-lotsāwa had not been a disciple of Atiśa, having been born five years after the Bengali scholar's demise, but Ngok was heavily influenced by the legacy of Kadampa learning. In contrast to the Eastern Vinaya monks, who especially studied the scriptures that were ostensibly the word of the Buddha, Ngok Loden Shérap worked with the technical treatises (*śāstra*), which were written by seminal scholars and constituted the texts actually preferred by the intellectuals in the great monasteries of India. These included the more technical works of the Yogācāras—specifically the five works attributed to Maitreya—and particularly the epistemological writings of Dharmakīrti and his followers.

Ngok Loden Shérap was probably motivated to great degree by his participation in an important gathering (*chos 'khor*) of translators in 1076, hosted by Trih Trashi Tsédé in Toling.[39] Other religious gatherings had occurred before and since, but this was a watershed moment, with six or seven translators among the scholars present, including Zangskar-lotsāwa, who had renovated the Jokhang. The tantric translator Ralo Dorjé-drak also was there, but he was something of a peculiarity, as the scholarly emphasis was on nontantric scholasticism. For Ngok, at the age of seventeen, the intellectual stimulation and sense of purpose must have been profound, for he decided to pursue his studies in Sanskrit.[40] His instruction was not in India per se, however, for Ngok worked for seventeen years in Kashmir with Parahitabhadra, Bhavyarāja, Sajjana, and other scholars.

When Ngok Loden Shérap returned, he brought with him some completed translations and many more Indic texts, so that he worked at producing not just more translations but also a wealth of commentarial literature and selected studies, both long and short.[41] This practice was not without some risk, for Tibetans had voiced a degree of disquiet about other Tibetans writing their own materials. Such grumbling from the ranks ensured both that the Tibetan treatises were well written and that potential objections were met. But this extreme conservative position was ultimately doomed, for it was based on a faulty understanding of how Buddhist intellectual culture replicates itself. Independent treatises—coupled with their sources, scholarly lectures, and personal instruction—were both the consequence of good teaching and the further motivation for renewed investigation into problematic ideas. The simple fact is that despite its sophistication and depth, the vast profusion of Buddhist doctrinal structures had, and continues to have, many intractable theoretical and doctrinal problems and paradoxes that resist adequate resolution.

Tibetans were still far from this point, though. Ngok's two treatises published in India (on the *Ratnagotravibhāga* and the *Abhisamayālaṁkāra*) do not represent solutions for areas of controversy but instead outline the basics, examine the structure and content of their root texts, and frame the discussion in a manner comprehensible to those not initiated into the minutia of Mahāyānist thought.[42] They unfold the meaning of the root verses in a straightforward manner, albeit sometimes with a paucity of explanation.[43] In general, Ngok's two treatises are excellent pedagogical manuals for the period, which is perhaps the reason they survived when most of his other works seem lost, leaving only his tomb as a site of pilgrimage (figure 17).

Beyond Ngok Loden Shérap, Kadampa monks began at this time the laborious process of trying to erect a theoretical architecture for the Buddhist path that could include much of what they were learning. The standard technique, as seen in the instance of the tantras, was to establish a path stratigra-

FIGURE 17 Tomb of Ngok Loden Shérap. After a photograph by Richardson

phy that worked in two ways. First, there was to be a description of the relationship among the various Buddhist paths and, second, a description of the method for following these paths. The question was important, for one of the great topics of discussion in Tibet for the next nine hundred years would be whether the Mahāyānist method of the perfections (*pāramitānaya*) following the teaching of the exoteric scriptures yielded a result equal to the method of mantras (*mantranaya*) that employed the tantric practices and was said to lead to complete awakening in this very life. For the Kadampa monks, straddling the divide and using both the paths, the question was much less than purely academic. If their heritage, as represented by the three brothers, did not lead to awakening in the manner of the tantric path, then they would be perceived as spending much effort over a long time for a mediocre goal—hardly a useful perception when seeking financial assistance to establish new and expensive monasteries. Some Kadampa monks had tried to unify the several Buddhist paths under a grand ideology, and some used the highly contested term "Mahāmadhyamaka" in an effort to do just that.[44]

The need to delineate (and to justify) a normative Mahāyānist ideal led Ngok Loden Shérap's followers to develop teachings, and eventually texts, that articulated a graded path (*lam rim*) and graded instruction (*bstan rim*) architecture.[45] The topical structures of these texts were similar to those of the *Teaching by Examples* work of Potoba but were oriented to a more literate audience. They engaged topics similar to those in the popular works but explained them through learned discussions and quotations rather than through folk homilies. Learned Mahāyānist treatises of this variety had a long history before Buddhism came to Tibet, and much of the Yogācāra and Madhyamaka literature is dedicated to similar strategies. But with the new developments in Mahāyānist doctrine and the new missionary field of the expanding number of Central Tibetan temples and monasteries, the need for new synthetic statements became compelling, especially in the polemicized atmosphere of the late eleventh century. This textual trajectory eventually yielded the immensely popular classics of Tibetan Buddhism: the *Jewel Ornament of Liberation* of Gampopa and the *Great Work on the Stages of the Path* of Tsongkhapa.

Another Kadampa contribution was closely related: the meditation manual genre known as the mental purification (*blo sbyong*) texts. Such works were dedicated to the fundamental practices of Mahāyānist meditation and were built on the Kadampa fascination with the *Bodhicaryāvatāra* of Śāntideva, who had included material from Yogācāra meditative practices in his chapter on contemplation. The *Method for Entering Mahāyānist Yoga* by the tenth-century Aro Yéshé Jungné had served somewhat the same purpose and was so influential that it was claimed that Atiśa himself preferred it to any other work by Tibetans.[46] The stages of the path and mental purification books were better developed and worked closely in accord, for the latter demonstrated the practical application of the theoretical structure discussed in the former. Together, they established the authenticity and viability of the Mahāyānist graded path and represented a formidable challenge to the eleventh-century tantric hegemony in Ü-Tsang.

Tantric scholarship, which we might expect to be more widely developed given the resources and interest, was still concerned primarily with translation and ritual. Translators like Marpa and Drokmi certainly wrote independent works, but the few surviving ones and the received titles suggest that their own compositions were mostly short in length and dedicated to discrete clarifications of obscure tantric instructions.[47] Both these eminent translators had disciples, however, who carried on their exegetical lineages (*bshad/gzhung brgyud*) and authored more extensive works. Ngok Chökyi Dorjé (1023–90?), another member of the Ngok clan whose members occupied so many important positions in eleventh-century Tibetan Buddhism, was Marpa's textual disciple and attributed the systematization of seven major maṇḍala systems as well as the founding of Riwo Khyungding temple in Zhung, just south of the modern Gongkar Airport.[48] Drokmi's disciple, Selwé Nyingpo, wrote an indigenous commentary on the *Hevajra-tantra*, one that much later hagiographers said caused tension with Drokmi because of its clarity.[49]

The two most important works of Tibetan tantric scholarship that survive from the period were not commentaries but treatises describing specific tantric paths. The *General Summary of the Guhyasamāja* (*gSang 'dus stong thun*) of Gö-lotsāwa Khukpa Lhétsé is an extensive and excellent introduction to the practice of the Guhyasamāja tradition according to the Ārya school of the siddhas Nāgārjuna, Āryadeva, and their followers. Its six chapters discuss basic personalities, the nature of phenomena, obscurations of the path, introduction to tantra via consecration, the tantric methods of practice, and the final fruit.[50] Most of the chapters are short, and the outline is actually somewhat misleading, for more than 80 percent of the text is in chapter 5, on tantric methods. Clearly, the emphasis is on ritual, so that philosophical topics are introduced as a subset of the "reality of mantras" (*mantratattva*, pp. 369 ff.). Because he scarcely mentions the organization of the tantric literature, it is unfortunate that the *General Introduction to the Tantra Piṭaka* (*rGyud sde spyi'i rnam bzhag*) attributed to this learned yet notorious eleventh-century scholar has yet to be unearthed.

The work of Gö-lotsāwa may be profitably compared with the magnum opus of the best represented of all the eleventh-century tantric scholars: Rongzom Chözang, whose defense of the Nyingma we have already examined. Rongzom worked in the second half of the eleventh century and built on the prior scholarship of the Great Perfection masters of the Mental Position (*sems phyogs*), of whom the most important was Aro Yéshé Jungné. Rongzom was certainly the influential Nyingma intellectual of his day, with a deep and extensive menu of texts attributed to him. Among them, his *Entering the Mahāyāna Practice* (*Theg chen tshul 'jug pa*) is an important marker in Tibetan scholarship.[51] In six almost equal chapters, the text predominantly employs categories from the Abhidharma, Yogācāra, Madhyamaka, and *Prajñāpāramitā* literature in a very sophisticated manner to build up to the affirmation of the Mental Position.[52] Those versed in this literature—which was the continually transmitted inheritance of Tibetans from the dynasty (Kahma)—will appreciate his facility and subtlety, particularly his use of the "three natures" (*trisvabhāva*) ideology of the Yogācāras as an exegetical tool.

When we look at the difference between the work of these two masters, Gö-lotsāwa and Rongzom, their suppositions become apparent. Rongzom scarcely mentions ritual; for him, the Great Perfection is primarily a method of understanding reality, and he consistently revisits questions of perception and the phenomenology of the event horizon. This does not mean that Rongzom was not interested in ritual per se. His involvement with the Vajrakīla system was such that one tradition was named for him (Rong lugs phur ba), and his surviving translations of Sanskrit texts were entirely ritual in nature. Rather, he seems to affirm that ritual belongs to vehicles other than the Great Perfection.[53] Conversely, Gö-lotsāwa comes to philosophical discussions somewhat grudgingly, despite his actual mention of Great Perfection once (p. 73.2) in an examination of the fourth consecration. In his interest and organization, though, he closely reflects the orientation of tenth- to eleventh-century Indian authorities, and his work is a monument to traditional scholarship in its quotations and citations of various texts and authors. In this regard, Rongzom seems lackadaisical and disinterested in other texts; even chapter 5, specifically dedicated to Great Perfection texts, is mostly filled with unattributed quotations, with only a few identified by title.

Rongzom's work is in other ways something of a time warp, a doctrinal curiosity carried over into the late eleventh century. Its emphasis on philosophical ideas and mentalistic doctrine mirrors his own tradition, for like the early Nyingma tantras Rongzom seems inattentive to the new ritualism coming over the Himalayas, and his work is as different from Gö-lotsāwa's as the Nyingma tantras like the *Tantra of the Self-Manifestation of Pure Awareness* (*Rig pa rang shar chen po'i rgyud*) are from Sarma tantras like the *Hevajra-tantra.* Rongzom's text in fact assiduously avoids most of the vocabulary, method of argumentation, and category construction derived from Indian scholarship of the period, even though these were brought to Central Tibet by Ngok Loden Shérap and his successors and became de rigueur for nearly all Tibetans after the twelfth century writing on such topics as perception. In historical hindsight and when considered in the context of his tantric commentaries on Nying-ma works, Rongzom appears to have made a final attempt to reaffirm the traditional scholarship of the imperial legacy, with its unified vision of the Great Perfection as the culmination of all Buddhist soteriology but grounded in Mahāyānist vocabulary.

DROKMI'S LEGACY AND THE NEXT GENERATION

Rongzom and Marpa shared a strategic position in Tibetan religious life as lay tantric scholars. This attribute simplified many aspects of institutional life, for inheritance and succession was not a problem, but it also brought with it the implication that somehow these lamas were not as completely Buddhist as the monks like Gö-lotsāwa. Ralo circumvented the process by enjoying sexual congress at will and still pretending to be a monk. Drokmi, though, maintained his vows until late in life and then married into an aristocratic family. In all these aspects, the teachers were wrestling with issues of clan and family, aristocratic position, and land possession.

Drokmi's religious successors illustrate many of these difficult issues, for the question of succession was perceived in some sense as part of a legacy. Perhaps analogous to Marpa, for both their progeny were religiously unexceptional, Drokmi used the classic technique of divide and conquer among his disciples.

He handled his legacy by determining that if he taught a disciple one of these two traditions, the method of the instruction (**upadeśanaya*) or the exegetical method (**vyākhyānaya*), he would not teach the other. Drokmi also specialized in an exclusive teaching situation, so he declared that he would not teach the Lamdré to four ears (i.e., two people) and would not explain the tantras to six ears (i.e., three people) at one time. Consequently, Tibetan sources tend to identify Drokmi's disciples in a specific pattern: five that completed study of the textual instruction found in the exegetical method, three that received the Lamdré system of the method of instruction, and seven that obtained a degree of accomplishment. The lists, however, are lineage-specific and have led to much disagreement.[54]

Of the disciples studying texts, both Ngaripa Selwé Nyingpo and Khön Könchok Gyelpo, the founder of Sakya, have hagiographical notices.[55] Ngaripa wrote a commentary on the *Hevajra-tantra*, which appears to be the earliest surviving indigenous commentary on that scripture.[56] Ngaripa's father was a cleric from either Mangyül or Purang, the older center of the Gugé kingdom. Like so many figures from this period, he learned to read from his father, who probably specialized in Nyingma rituals, perhaps the Vajrakīla.[57] Ngaripa studied the three texts of the eastern Madhyamaka according to the Nyingma tradition of learning and became widely respected as a teacher.[58] He approached Drokmi for initiation, probably when the translator had advanced in years, and eventually specialized in the tradition of the Padmavajra/Saroruhavajra practice manuals. Ngaripa is reputed to have taught in Kongpo for a while, gaining reputation and wealth, which he offered to Drokmi.

Analogous to the Kagyüpa, however, the Lamdré tradition celebrates those followers who obtained instruction on the Lamdré par excellence: Lhatsün Kali (Drokmi's brother-in-law), Drom Dépa Tönchung, and Sétön Kunrik. Of these, Lhatsün Kali appears as a marital and political connection, but Drom Dépa Tönchung was an important religious figure. He belonged to the Drom lineage, a clan of some political power and authority since the period of the royal dynasty.[59] The Drom, which had been a relatively minor clan, apparently prospered in the period of fragmentation. Two men from the Drom clan stood out in the eleventh century: the Lamdré disciple and Dromtön Gyelwé Jungné, Atiśa's close disciple and the founder of Retreng Monastery.[60] Both were relatively wealthy and well trained in Buddhist practice before they met their principal teachers.[61]

Drom Dépa Tönchung was a skilled ritualist in a Nyingma tradition called the Mothers' Life-Drop (Ma-mo srog tig). Like other eleventh-century Nyingma figures, he is said to have recovered a new cycle of Ma-mo in Samyé as a Terma—entitled the *Goddess's Four-Inch Magical Arrowhead (Lha mo'i mde'u thun sor bzhi)*—and accumulated much wealth on the road to Mugulung by performing associated rituals along the way.[62] Arriving at Drokmi's residence, Drom Dépa Tönchung requested initiation into the Lamdré and was quite liberal in his offerings to the translator. During the consecration ritual, each period of the day he offered a maṇḍala of gold to Drokmi and asked that he be allowed to perform service and to offer a fine silk lower garment (which was then quite rare in Tsang and worth more than a sheep), but the garment was not accepted.[63] He had offering cakes made so large that two men were required to carry each one, and he gave the turquoise named "heap of curds" (*zho spungs*) to the Mugulung translator.

After having received extensive teachings, Drom Dépa Tönchung stayed some time in the area and at one point asked Drokmi to lend him a horse. The translator curtly refused this innocuous request, saying, "Teachers do not make offerings to students!" Drokmi's response understandably dismayed Drom, and so he removed to Latö Dingri-shé. On the way, he contracted an illness and at the point of death regretted his falling out with Drokmi, ascribing it to a blinding lack of faith preventing him from seeing Drokmi as the very Buddha himself. Drom Dépa accordingly requested that all his books and goods, which filled the packs of seventeen horses, be taken and offered to the great translator. Drokmi is reported as having been moved to tears when learning the fate of his devoted disciple, saying that he felt as if his heart would be expelled from his body out of grief, and he offered to instruct any of Drom's disciples in the Lamdré, an offer that startlingly few accepted. Drom Dépa did, though, found one of the two forms of the Lamdré that did not go through the Sakyapa: "Drom's method." Ngorchen's unfinished fifteenth-century study of the Lamdré affirms the existence of a large tome of literature (*po ti shin tu che ba gcig*) from this tradition, including a commentary on the *Root Text of the *Mārgaphala* and more focused works, like that on the "ten secrets."[64]

Drokmi's other great Lamdré disciple, Sétön Kunrik, had a greater influence, for the two most important traditions of Drokmi's teaching were maintained by those whom Sétön trained: the Khön and the Zhama lineages. A little like Drokmi, Sétön started life as a yak-herding nomad, but in Dogmé on the north side of the Brahmaputra from Lhatsé, perhaps in the lower Raga-Tsangpo valley.[65] Unlike Drokmi, Sétön came from the Sé clan, an ancient lineage and mythically one of the first six clans to arise in Tibet.[66] A later author stated that the Sé clan had two branches, the Kya group and the Ché group, and that Sétön belonged to the latter, which apparently was somehow connected to the great Ché clan. The *Blue Annals* says that when Sétön and Sachen Kunga Nyingpo (1092–1158) met, Sétön was eighty-six and Sachen was "about twenty" and Sétön died shortly thereafter.[67] This would mean that Sétön was born around 1026 or so and lived to about 1112 or so.[68] Whatever his dates, Sétön lived a long time, and we have little reason to doubt his meeting with Sachen Kunga Nyingpo sometime after 1110. The fact that he and Drokmi had similar backgrounds may have contributed to both his motivation to study at Mugulung and Drokmi's impetus to accede to his requests.

An amusing legend that has been passed down is that as a young boy, Sétön found a herd of thirty-three wild black yak and, tempting them with sweet grasses, managed to capture some. Crossing south over the Brahmaputra with his herd of yaks, he brought them to Drokmi as an offering for his consecration into the Lamdré. Sétön evidently came at the right time, for he is listed as one of the specific recipients who received the Lamdré after Drom Dépa Tönchung's demise. Still, his meager offering of a few moldy yak must have struck the avaricious Drokmi as both inadequate and somewhat pathetic. He is said to have remarked on how little this was compared with the gifts he was used to receiving, but Sétön's demonstration of both faith and desperation turned the tide. Over the next years Sétön lived near Drokmi and practiced the teaching, although the sources disagree on how long he lived with Drokmi. Drokmi evidently poked fun at him one day, saying, "Sé hopes for a tongue [wants to be a preacher], but he has run off with all my teachings like a thief."[69] This is actually a pretty good pun, for the word Ché in Tibetan may mean a tongue or the Ché noble clan (Sétön was from the Ché branch of the Sé). Thus Drokmi accused Sétön of wanting to be noble but acting like a thief in the night, or wanting to be a preacher but acting like a coward. Sétön was devastated when he heard this criticism, but Drokmi assured him he had been joking.

Sétön eventually founded Kharchung Temple, from which he received his name of Sé-Kharchungwa. It is generally placed in the middle Mangkhar valley, close to where the great reliquary of Tsarchen eventually was located, but there are references to a Kharchung of Sé in other locales as well, and we may wonder whether he used Kharchungwa as a designation for his residence, wherever it was.[70] In order to round out his education, Sétön is said to have studied for some time with Khön Könchok Gyelpo, the founder of Sakya. Although the sources on Sétön are few, they do reveal a person who was not disposed to making grand offerings, in the manner of Drom Dépa Tönchung, for they often note that he gave little "service" (i.e., gifts) to Drokmi but practiced assiduously. If we can read between the lines in his interaction with Zhang Gönpawa, the Zhama family, Sachen, and others, it appears that Sétön was actually a rather reclusive figure who tended to hide his understanding of Drokmi's new teaching but relied on basic rituals to make a living.

THE KHÖN CLAN MYTHOLOGY AND SAKYA BEGINNINGS AS A CLAN TEMPLE

Drokmi's legacy was most concretely nurtured by the Khön clan in Central Tibet. The Khön must be acknowledged as one of the great religious clans of the world, similar in respects to the imperial family of Japan. Indeed, the Khön created a stable institution out of the area of Sakya in southern Central Tibet, building on a meager resource base and surviving cataclysmic social changes from the period of the royal dynasty to the present. They were the most successful clan to maintain, as a single agenda, both the Nyingma Kahma rituals that extended back into the royal dynasty and the Sarma practices based on the later translation materials. The Khön became the rulers of the country under the Mongols for almost a century (ca. 1261 to 1358) and survived both the acquisition and loss of dominant political power, each potentially lethal to a family. Out of their efforts came the Sakya denomination, which maintained a reputation for spirituality even while the family, the order, and the Lamdré were riven with divisions from the fifteenth century forward. While the Khön and the Sakya denomination have not received the attention they merit, it is to some degree precisely because of their conservatism and unwillingness to compromise their principles in the modern world.

Like the Tibetan imperial house, many of the old aristocratic families developed clan mythologies of descent from sky divinities who came to earth at a specific locus and who ruled by means of natural charisma. These myths often combine the Buddhist story of kingship by election (Mahāsammata) with the Tibetan models of the descent by some spiritual avenue between the sky and the mountain peaks. The pedigrees of these legends, however, are uncertain, and we have indications that these mythologies continued to grow over time, particularly after the twelfth century. Given the observable instabilities of Tibetan power after the dynasty's collapse in the mid-ninth century, it is not surprising that aristocratic houses in potential positions of authority would try to augment their perceived stature by presenting themselves as being divine, according to either Tibetan or Buddhist standards of divinity. Evidently unwilling to accept anything less than a supreme appointment, the Khön skillfully articulated a myth that was at once both Tibetan and Buddhist. However, its clan origin myth is relatively recent, for it seems to have been unknown as late as a 1352 clan history, while an early version is apparent in the *Red Annals* of 1363.[71]

The sources relate a story that brings together three themes: the grace of the bodhisattva Mañjuśrī, along with the descent of beings of clear light (*'od gsal lha*), and the descent of divinities of the sky (*gnam lha*). The last two classes of beings are identified in the text with some discomfort, since they derive from different mythologies. The beings of clear light derive from the Indic materials found in the *Mūlasarvāstivāda-vinaya* or related sources and given wide currency in Tibet, while the descent of sky divinities is the ancient Tibetan origin myth.[72] In any case, the purpose is to demonstrate that the Khön clan was the actual vehicle for the incarnations of Mañjuśrī, the bodhisattva of divine intelligence, a story that presents some conceptual difficulties given the behavior attributed to the gods as they descended. The legend begins with three celestial divinities (*gnam lha*): Chiring (longest one), Yuring (long turquoise), and Usé (grizzled hair), who happened to come to the realm of men and were invited to become the lords, an invitation that Usé alone accepted. To him were born the four Séjili brothers, who struggled with the eighteen clans of the Dong tribe, one of the six tribes of standard early Tibetan mythology.[73] In their struggle, their uncle Yuring joined them, and together they subdued the eighteen clans of the Dong, making them their subjects. The *Great Genealogy* is careful to point out that even though the Khön came about through marital alliances with some of these groups, that does not mean that they are of the same genealogical line as the tribes.

Yuring was attracted to a daughter of the Mu (another of the six tribes) named Muza Dembu (unstable Mu queen) and "received her in his fortress," to use the wonderfully allusive vocabulary of Tibetan honorifics.[74] The seven Masang brothers were born to them, and six of these elected to return to the divine realm with their father via the sacred Mu rope. The seventh, Masang Chijé, lived in the world of men, which was somehow located in the intermediate realm (*bar-snang*) between the sky and the earth. His grandson was the boy Lutsa Takpo Öchen, who married Mönza Tsomo-gyel. Their son was born (*skyes*) at the border between a mossy meadow (*spang*) and slate hillside (*g.ya'*) and accordingly was named Yapang-kyé.[75] He took up residence on a beautiful, high mountain northwest of the Shang area of Tibet, a mountain that came to be known as "Yapang's mountain" (g.Ya' spang ri). We are told that Yapang-kyé was one heroic divinity, and he became attracted to the beautiful wife of a demon named Kyareng Tragmé. He fought the demon, killing him, and took the demon widow as his bride. To them a son was born, who was named in honor of his being conceived through the belligerence between divinity and fiend (*lha dang sring po 'khon pa*) and accordingly given the epithet Yapang Khön-bar-kyé. Thus, we are assured, the Khön family name came from the struggle (*'khon*) between a celestial divinity and a demon lord in Central Tibet over a bewitching demoness—which is about as good as clan legends get.

Only at this point, according to the myth, did the divinities actually come to the realm of men, on the peak of a beautiful, high mountain named Shel-tsa Gyelmo, where Yapang Khön-bar-kyé descended.[76] A later Khön descendant, Könpa Jégungtak, seeking a homeland, appealed to the king at Samyé and was told to go hold a place of his own. Looking for a place with the requisite good qualities—excellent earth, water, lumber, grassland, and fieldstone—Könpa Jégungtak came to Latö and established his fiefdom at Nyentsé-tar.[77] Because the king, Trihsong Détsen, esteemed him so greatly, he was entrusted with the high office of minister of the interior (*nang rje kha*) and, as a result, became known as Khön Pelpoché (the Great Glorious Mr. Khön).[78] He married the wife of Lang Khampa-lotsāwa, and to them were born several sons, the elder (or youngest) of whom was Khön Luï-wangpo, one of the seven good men (*sad mi mi bdun*) who were in the first group of Tibetans ordained by Śāntarakṣita at the newly constructed monastery of Samyé. The Khön clan records propose that he was the smartest of the three younger translators (*lo tsā ba gzhon gsum*) among these seven men.

With Khön Luï-wangpo we are on very solid historical ground, so it is appropriate here to assess the lineage mythology. The discontinuities apparently demonstrate that several stories follow in succession: the subjugation of the Dong tribe by divinities who married into the Mu tribe and ruled men, the mythology of the Masang gods as a stage in the development of Tibet, the mythological affirmation of ancestral mountain divinities (Yapang-ri, Shel-tsa Gyelmo) in the area of Shang, the identity of the Khön name as an allusion to the old pan-Eurasian tale of the battle between the gods and the demons, and the strong associations to an imperially granted fiefdom in Latö accorded to the Khön.[79] The narrative discontinuity is evident, for the stories continually place the gods in the realms of men and then remove them again, only to bring them back once more. Actually, the earliest surviving Khön records simply begin with the good translator monk, Khön Luï-wangpo, although Drakpa Gyeltsen does indicate that by virtue of the bodhisattva *Dānaśrī (i.e., Sachen Kunga Nyingpo), the family became one of a stream of religious preceptors.[80] Here the rather self-effacing family description of the twelfth century stands in contrast to the claims of divine incarnation found in later Khön writers from the late fourteenth century onward.[81]

The exact position of this clan during the royal dynastic period remains uncertain. I have not been able to verify the imperial appointment of Khön Pelpoché in the available records, even though many individuals are said to have received these appointments.[82] Neither his name nor the name of the Khön appears in the early surviving documents available to me.[83] Even the association of Khön Luï-wangpo with the "seven good men" is debatable, since some of the earliest materials list "six men," and Luï-wangpo is not among them.[84] What is evident, though, is that the Khön were largely kept at the periphery of the dynasty, irrespective of their court presence. The list of clan dominions under the first emperor, Songtsen Gampo, does not mention the Khön at all, although certainly not all clans are represented, including the important Lang and Gar families.[85] Nonetheless, the aggregate evidence is that the Khön were minor aristocracy, probably in the area of Latö, where they had a well-selected but politically insignificant holding.

It was their favorite son, Luï-wangpo, who held religious esteem as one of the "junior translators" (*lo kyi chung*) of the empire, a very important ecclesiastical position.[86] His training was apparently in Tibet, and it is unclear whether he followed the lead of some of the other well-known luminaries of the eighth century to study in India. There may have been official inhibitions against foreign travel at various times, but sufficient numbers of Tibetans did study in India at that time to warrant questions as to why others did not. In fact, the information about Luï-wangpo is sparse; both Sakya and Nyingma writers include him among the disciples of Padmasambhava, apparently a later perception about the imperial period.[87] We do know that the Khön maintained the ancient practice of the Vajrakīla and the Yangdak Heruka, and it may well be that their involvement with this tradition extended into the dynastic period.[88]

In some ways the Khön clan's penetration into the rarefied world of Tibetan aristocracy is visible in the reputed marital alliance of Luï-wangpo's younger brother (or nephew), Dorjé Rinpoché, with a daughter of the Dro family.[89] This union could not have happened without Khön official recognition in some capacity, because the Dro, along with the Khyungpo, were the powerful clans in Tsang during and immediately following the imperial period.[90] But it was just this involvement with the Dro that brought the Khön to grief after the fall of the dynasty. In the town of Dro Nyentsé, inhabited by both the Dro and Khön clans, a peculiar series of "signs" were seen during three days. On the first day, a white horse with a white woolen cloak was seen; on the second, a red horse with a red cloak was spotted; and on the third day, a black horse with a black cloak was observed in the town. Tibetans being ever suspicious, the rumor went out that someone was challenging the Dro chieftain to a horse race, a metaphor with political significance. Dorjé Rinpoché's seven sons were suspected of trying to challenge the dominion of their Dro relatives; the general opinion was that the Dro chieftain would bring down a group of his armed men to deal with them. The Khöns' position was that this was all the doing of the Dro chieftain, for they had lived peacefully as neighbors for some time. But the die was cast, and the senior six of the seven sons left the area to relocate widely throughout western and southern Tibet—in Mangyül, Gungtang, Sé, Nyaloro, and Nyangshab—and in each of these areas the Khön clan established itself. The youngest son apparently remained in the town and contended with the Dro, eventually succeeding.[91]

After several generations and many vicissitudes, one of the clan's branches found itself in Yalung (not Yarlung), a basin branching to the south in the middle drainage of the Trumchu, just to the west of the eventual site of Sakya and northeast of Mugulung (map 6). Therefore, the later involvement of the Khön with Drokmi was to some degree based on the clan's strength in the immediate area, for slightly later there were members of the Khön family in Mugulung as well.[92] Their many young sons eventually became known as the "eight groups" of the Khön (*'khon tsho brgyad*) in that area. One of their descendants, named Shākya Lotrö, solidified his holdings in the western Shab valley, as well as back in the ancestral lands of Yalung.[93] It is tempting to identify this figure with a lama named Khön Shākya Lotrö, with whom Ralo Dorjé-drak had had a particularly nasty fight and who had estates in Mugulung, apparently complete with serfs. Indeed, almost a small war erupted as a result of Ralo's claimed complicity in the death of his Khön adversary, and the dates are certainly close enough.[94]

Two sons were born in Yalung to Shākya Lotrö, the elder son being Khön Shérap Tsültrim and the younger being Khön Könchok Gyelpo (b. 1034). At an early age Khön Shérap Tsültrim became the disciple of one of the Eastern Vinaya monks, Zhutön Tsöndru, who belonged to a community associated with Lotön. While Khön Shérap Tsültrim did not become a monk during his service to Zhutön Tsöndru, he did remain celibate throughout his life. He apparently took the path of lay celibacy (*brahmacari-upāsaka*) maintained by several notable individuals of this period, with its emphasis on the importance of virtue as a discipline, even while continuing to practice the Vajrakīla and Yangdak Heruka rites.

Conversely, his younger brother, Khön Könchok Gyelpo, became strongly attracted to the newly emerging direction of Buddhist practice and literature.[95] His initial interest was stimulated when he witnessed an event that horrified him.[96] When invited to a ceremony for the benefit of both the living and the ancestral dead (*gson gshin*) of the Dro, he found that twenty-eight yogins in a open marketplace were dancing the masked procession (*'chams*) of the deities of the twenty-eight lunar mansions (*īśvarī*) and were beating drums in the manner appropriate to the propitiation of Ma-mo Relpachen, divinities of the Nyingma pantheon.[97] While this ostensibly secret ritual was being conducted, the market was humming with commercial activity and horse races were being held, so that both the letter and spirit of the esoteric system were being grossly violated. When he asked his elder brother about this event, Shérap Tsültrim acknowledged that this was disgraceful and observed that accomplishment under the older tradition would be henceforth rare. This event was, in reality, to have several serious repercussions for the Khön, repercussions that have lasted into the present. Most interestingly, no Tibetan order has been so assiduously concerned with the edifice of secrecy as the Sakyapa, who have used esoteric occlusion as part of their rhetoric of superiority over other traditions that were not so secretive.[98] This concern even inhibited their printing of the Lamdré textual corpus until around 1905 and has colored their interactions with members of our modern, information-based society.

To be fair to the twenty-eight dancing yogins, it must be said that religious events—including ostensibly secret ones—were sometimes held in market areas during the religious revival of eleventh-century Central Tibet, by the new translation traditions as well as the old.[99] We sometimes read, for example, about Ralo Dorjé-drak presenting his Vajrabhairava consecrations in gatherings assembled in market areas.[100] This was precisely because there were few places at this time where large numbers of people could gather. Even the largest temples being constructed or left over from the old dynastic building program simply could not hold the hundreds of people that would sometimes gather for these "religious circles" (*chos skor*), which might involve anything from instruction in basic Buddhism to the highest teachings, depending on the circumstances. Doubtless, events in which esoteric secrecy was supposed to be observed were more carefully controlled by those in charge, but nonetheless, each of the major Tibetan Buddhist traditions has held large quasi-public gatherings from time to time in which the "ear-whispered" teachings are conveyed to people en masse. This evidently was true in the eleventh century and is certainly true today, so that even selective groups like the Sakyapa, concerned with restricting this material, eventually found themselves making concessions along the way.

Seeking ritual closure, the two Khön brothers took all the dynastic religious materials that they possessed—books, statuary, and paraphernalia of the esoteric system—and entombed them in a stūpa as a formal acknowledgment of the ritual death of the tradition.[101] No sooner had they done so than they were informed by the divine protectors of religion, specifically Karmo Nyida Chamsing, that two of the central meditative rites should not be treated in this way.[102] So the brothers retained the Vajrakumāra system of Vajrakīla and some of Yangdak Heruka materials, which remained part of the Khön clan's rituals. Consequently, the Khön maintain to this day a relatively strong basis in the practice of these traditions that they share with the Nyingma denomination. We can best understand this position by pointing out that most Tibetan orders eventually created a rapprochement with the Nyingmapa by adopting a few of the hidden treasure cycles. Outside the Nyingmapa clans, though, only the Khön can demonstrate that their family have maintained a persistent practice of the Kahma, the continually transmitted royal dynastic systems of religiosity.

With this ritual closure in hand, Khön Könchok Gyelpo set off to study the newly translated scriptures and began with an obscure translator named Khyin-lotsāwa of Belpuk, studying the Hevajra work until the teacher's untimely death.[103] Undaunted, Könchok Gyelpo went to Drokmi himself, who characteristically required a large fee to be accepted. Accordingly, Könchok Gyelpo sold some of the land he owned in Yalung and, with the proceeds, presented seventeen horses to Drokmi, along with funds for their fodder and a rosary entitled "rosary of the lady's gems."[104] He was bestowed instruction on some of Drokmi's teachings, such as the *Acintyādvayakramopadeśa*, but was particularly favored with instruction in the fundamental scriptures of the Hevajra cycle: the *Hevajra-tantra*, the *Sampuṭodbhava*, and the *Vajrapañjara*. As has been seen, this is the material sometimes identified by later writers as the text-less Lamdré (*rtsa ba med pa'i lam 'bras*), because it does not involve the *Root Text of the *Mārgaphala*, and it also has been dubbed the exegetical Lamdré (*lam 'bras bshad brgyud*), because it contains the scriptural material on which the Lamdré is ostensibly based.[105] While this exegetical lineage is somewhat dismissed in Lamdré literature, it actually represents the important intellectual side of the esoteric system, and Sakyapa esoteric scholarship in the ensuing centuries came to depend on this body of literature for its stature in the Tibetan community.

By the time he was finished with Drokmi, Könchok Gyelpo had achieved distinction in his learning and his realization of the exegetical tradition, and he continued his studies with many of the eminent translators and saints of the period.[106] From Gö-lotsāwa Khukpa Lhétsé he studied the *Guhyasamāja*; from Mel-lotsāwa he studied the *Cakrasamvara*; from Paṇḍita Prajñāgupta (the Red Master) he studied the five *Tilaka-tantras*; and he continued his studies with Ma-lotsāwa, Bari-lotsāwa, Purap-lotsāwa, and others, including his own kinsman, Khön Gyichuwa.[107] With all this learning, Könchok Gyelpo set out to perform the correct funerary rites for his father and brother, whose relics were placed in a Buddhist reliquary in Zhangyül Jakshong. Thereafter, he constructed a small center in Drawolung close to Yalung, but it evidently proved to be undesirable after a few years, and the site later came to be called "Sakya ruins" (*sa skya gog po*). While traveling with his some of his disciples, Könchok Gyelpo oversaw the area that would become Sakya and was struck by its excellent characteristics. He accordingly sought out the lord of the region, Jowo Dong-nakpa, who granted him permission to build. But there still were the district chieftains to be reckoned with, for they had the actual control of the immediate land. He approached Zhangzhung Gurawa, as well as the villagers of Four Bendé and Seven Lhami—two towns named for their respective celebrities—and asked what they would like in return for the land. They demurred but finally settled on his paying them a white mare, a rosary of gems, a fine woman's dress, and an armored cuirass for the land. Having completed the transaction, in 1073, the thirty-nine-year-old Khön Könchok Gyelpo formally founded Sakya Monastery, the institutional home of the Sakya denomination for the next nine centuries.

CONCLUSION: NEW BEGINNINGS IN THE WAKE OF THE TRANSLATORS

By the last half of the eleventh century, the translators' ritual and meditative enterprises had yielded vast treasures, but their force seemed to require an overarching intellectual direction. Consequently, the period is marked by the exploration of new ideas, philosophical translations, and the exciting development of indigenous Tibetan composition, on both esoteric and exoteric topics. The lineages extending from the translators had to build on the interest generated by their exploration of the new Indian scriptures, the network of sites developed by the Eastern Vinaya monks, and the background of Nyingma spirituality. With the second generation, figures like Sétön Kunrik for the Lamdré, Ngok Chökyi Dorjé and Mila Repa for the Kagyüpa, the three brothers among the Kadampa, and their peers had to find a new path, one that ultimately led to the complete evangelization of Tibet. They commented on the translated scriptures, organized new institutions, developed a clientele, and assembled disciples, entirely without the benefit of having gone to India or Kashmir to study and attain their authorization.

Buddhism thereby made the great transition required to succeed: it became indigenized and began the long and sometime tortuous process of assimilation. To accomplish this, various traditions found that they needed the strength of the most powerful single institution in Tibet: the sense of cohesiveness of the great clans and aristocratic lords. The clan structure provided the model for inheritance, for the transmission of authority, and for the development of family-based spirituality. The Khön clan was an especially good example of these strengths, for it could legitimately claim descent from royal dynastic personalities, maintained rich traditions of ritual programs, and was excited by the new scriptures and lineages coming into Central Tibet. Khön Könchok Gyelpo's involvement with Drokmi and other translators, including his own clansmen, is a paradigmatic expression of the process unfolding elsewhere among the Zhang, the Ngok, the Zhama, the Ra, the Chim, the Nyiwa, the Zur, the

Ché, and so many other lines of descent. They usually founded temples; passed their teachings onto their relatives; provided instruction in a large body of ritual and literature; obtained lands; and cultivated the minor arts of medicine, prognostication, and astrology, all while accruing wealth and investing their efforts in the internationalization of their countrymen. Their efforts yielded the great efflorescence of indigenous ideas and expressions found in the twelfth century.

8

The Early Twelfth Century: A Confident Tibetan Buddhism

Generally there are two kinds of gurus: those with the eye of insight and those with the eye of the Dharma.

One with the eye of insight, because he knows the universal and individual characteristics of phenomena, will teach the meaning of the Dharma without mistakes and without mixing things up.

One with the eye of the Dharma, however, has supremely realized without error the meaning of the Dharma and has personally experienced that meaning in its own sphere, so that understanding has naturally arisen from within. But arising in that way, by itself [the understanding] pervades and connects, so that he is able to induce the experience in others.

—Gampopa's *Reply to Düsum Khyenpa*[1]

The spiritual and intellectual legacy of the eleventh century set the stage for the developments in the twelfth, when Tibetans truly made Buddhism their own. Even as new esoteric and exoteric systems were being imported and new translations were being made, twelfth-century Tibetans began to feel themselves authentically Buddhist enough to support the process of innovation. Consequently, this century was to see the maturation of Tibetan Sarma scholarship, with new formulations of Tibetan ideas in both epistemology and the new yogic path of later esoteric Buddhism. As the Kadampa and Eastern Vinaya nontantric traditions and the Nyingma tantric systems had done in the eleventh century, in the twelfth century the tantric Kagyüpa and Sakyapa lineages evolved from small sectarian centers to regional denominations, with multiple institutions and an articulated sense of identity. By the end of the century, the Eastern Vinaya monastic institutions had become sufficiently aggressive that their own successes appeared to promote instability, and the ancient Buddhist model of monastic succession based solely on merit proved to be insecure in the Tibetan culture. Consequently, both lay and monastic lineages eventually developed and promoted a new model of monastic succession, in which monks passed on monasteries to members of their own families, so that the very stable aristocratic clans became the foci for Buddhist institutions.

In Ü and Tsang, different Sarma lineages were acquiring the status of denominations. Even prior to this, the Nyingma lineages had been distributed throughout much of Central Tibet, and the Nyingma denominational process both set the stage and was markedly different from that of the Sarma traditions. Among the Sarma, the Kadampa and Kagyüpa became the driving force in Ü, while the Sakyapa and more fragile lineages found a home in Tsang. Through much of the twelfth century, the religious traditions of Ü provided the lead for Tibetan religiosity, with some Tsang figures being a bit more conservative. It is little wonder that Sakya Paṇḍita, the great figurehead of the neoconservatives in the thirteenth century, would represent Tsang neoconservatism, with the Sakyapas promoting a sense of orthodoxy that lasted into the twentieth century.

The twelfth century also saw a greater influx of bright young talent from eastern Tibet (Kham), so that for the first time, Khampa monks and lay scholars became some of the most important leaders in Central Tibet. Even those who, like the first Karmapa, preferred to return to and remain in eastern Tibet, eventually would find themselves pulled back into the dynamism of Ü. By the middle of the century, the aura of Central Tibetan monasteries was so great that scholars from outside Tibet, especially the linguistically and ethnically related Tanguts, came to Tibet to study Buddhism, both from Tibetans and from the increasing number of Indians finding Tibet to be a safe haven. These scholars made their way from the insecure North Indian monasteries, and refugees from Islamic incursions began to speak of an imminent doom that eventually visited all of South Asia.

This chapter focuses on the first half of the twelfth century, to see how the Sarma systems began to follow the path of innovation that in some sense the Nyingma scholars had anticipated in the previous decades. The Nyingma developments—whether the Great Perfection doctrines, indigenous scholarship, or the Terma revelations—were always in the background and remained tantalizing reminders of a possible affirmation of indigenous spirituality. We also review the developments in Kadampa scholarship, especially the new materials brought in by Pa-tsap-lotsāwa and the epistemological innovations of Chapa Chökyi Sengé. I also argue that during the twelfth century, the complex Kālacakra practices achieved widespread acceptance. Following that, we examine the promotion of the Kagyüpa to a monastery-based institution by

Gampopa, along with Gampopa's interpretation of the Great Seal doctrines. Most of the chapter, though, discusses the life and training of Sachen Kunga Nyingpo, considered the first of the great Sakyapa teachers and the inheritor of Sakya Monastery. Sachen bought together the two streams of tantric practice and exegesis that Drokmi had separated. The chapter contends that successful monastic institutions in twelfth-century Ü-Tsang required a strong intellectual component, a strong spiritual practice, a charisma of exalted personalities, and relics from the past, all contained in a clan-based association.

Before this review, a word of caution is in order. Because the twelfth century was so dynamic, many of the same activities taking place in the eleventh century were still being carried out but were less visible in comparison to the charismatic personalities and contemporary developments. Certainly new translations continued to be made, albeit at a decreasing rate and with less overall consequence. New spiritual lineages found their way in, featuring secret instructions that had not yet been revealed by the sacred *ḍākinīs* to previous masters. This was particularly true of the Shangpa Kagyüpa practices of Khyungpo Neljor, the new yogic teachings of Tipupa brought in by Mila Repa's disciple Rechungpa, and the many other new contemplative traditions coming from Indian centers.[2] Terma masters continued to uncover new texts, and the end of the century eventually saw the victory of the Padmasambhava cult. We touch on some of these events, but many more regretfully must be left to other historians.

What was different about this period was that by the early twelfth century, Tibetans had gained a greater sense of themselves in the midst of this wealth of ideas and rituals, of meditations and texts. They began to see accurately that the newer materials were variations on a theme rather than the wholly new themes incorporated since the late tenth century. Thus, they began to take stock of their assets, make catalogs (as they had not done since the collapse of the dynasty), promote individuals as reincarnations of famous Indian masters, and see Tibet as the field for the enlightened activity of the Buddhas and bodhisattvas. Tibet began to look in their eyes—and, increasingly, in the eyes of other Asians—as a new spiritual zone almost on a par with India itself and, after the catastrophes of the turn of the thirteenth century, actually supplanting the homeland of Buddhism as the site of choice for foreign monks eager to learn the authentic Dharma.

THE KADAMPA INTELLECTUAL COMMUNITY

The three brothers Potoba, Chen-nga, and Puchungwa had traveled all through Central Tibet, had evangelized thousands of monks, had promoted the Kadampa to the position of a true monastic order and evolving denomination, but they had not watched over the fortunes of Retreng. Potoba was reputed to have spent three years as the abbot of Retreng before his grand series of lecture tours, but the leadership after him began to falter. All told, three consequences of this weakness were visited on the eleventh- to twelfth-century Kadampa lineage. First, Sangpu Néütok assumed center stage among the Kadampa centers, and Retreng came to be seen and administered as a second satellite of the Sangpu enclave.[3] Second, all these newly evangelized monks had to have some place to stay, so the number of Kadampa centers dramatically increased in the last quarter of the eleventh century and on throughout the twelfth (most famously Nartang in 1153), with a concomitant increase in the number of eminent preceptors and teachers. Many of them, like Atiśa himself, acted as both tantric and nontantric preceptors, so the Kadampa centers offered candidates the opportunity to seriously study the Sarma tantras as well as the proprietary Kadampa curriculum in the sūtras and śāstras. Finally, the strong intellectual tradition brought to Sangpu by Ngok-lotsāwa served as a center of gravity for monks intent on Buddhist intellectual life. Consequently, those concerned mainly with the Kadampa contemplative system of purifying the intellect (*blo sbyong*) and the related *Stages of the Path* literature tended to study at Retreng and its associated retreat centers. Conversely, those focusing on the cutting-edge philosophical works were more often at Sangpu or competing institutions in Lhasa or Pen-yül, for these were the sites where the newly translated material, particularly from Kashmir, was disseminated.

In this regard, the most important translation development for the Kadampas was the return of Pa-tsap Nyima-drak (1055–1142?) from Kashmir around 1100.[4] Actually a contemporary of Ngok Loden Shérap, Pa-tsap's career had the greatest influence in the twelfth century. Until he arrived, Madhyamaka had been predominantly taught through the lens of the Svātantrika school, which owes its origins to Bhāvaviveka (ca. 700 C.E.) and was the school of choice for Ngok. The Tibetan curriculum for this school consisted of the "three eastern Svātantrika works" (*rang rgyud shar gsum*) that had been composed by eighth-century authors: the *Discrimination of the Two Truths* (*Satyadvayavibhaṅga*) of Jñānagarbha, the *Ornament of the Middle Way* (*Madhyamakālaṁkāra*) of Śāntarakṣita, and the *Light on the Middle Way* (*Madhyamakāloka*) of Kamalaśīla.[5] The school generally presumed that logical argumentation and propositions could have a degree of utility in explaining both the relative and the absolute truths, although there was much disagreement within the school on certain key points. Nyingma teaching temples also apparently studied the three eastern Svātantrika works, and Atiśa appears to have favored this school, for the Madhyamaka translations he did with Nagtso predominantly represented this point of view.

Even so, Atiśa's longer hagiography states that the more radical reductionist

Prāsaṅgika school of Candrakīrti was favored in most places in eastern India.[6] An approximate contemporary of Bhāvaviveka, Candrakīrti had proposed in a series of texts and commentaries on the works of Nāgārjuna that Madhyamakas should accept no position whatsoever concerning absolute truth, whereas for ordinary truth the generally accepted ideas of the world were sufficient.[7] Pa-tsap had studied extensively with Sūkṣmajana (the son of Ngok's paṇḍita Sajjana), had stayed in Kashmir between 1076/77 and 1100, and was increasingly concerned with the work of Candrakīrti. When he returned with two of his Kashmiri paṇḍitas to the Pen-yül area, where he had been born, he initially had trouble obtaining disciples, but rumor of his accomplishments brought the attention of Sharwapa (1070–1141), the abbot of Sangpu, who sent some of his own disciples to obtain the new learning. Pa-tsap moved for a while to the Lhasa temple of Ramoché, one of the old dynastic temples, and there he completed several of his translations with different paṇḍitas. He probably moved back and forth between teaching engagements and taught in Pen-yül until about 1130, when Düsum Khyenpa, the first Karmapa, studied Nāgārjuna's works with Pa-tsap.[8]

Pa-tsap's immediate competitor at Sangpu was one of the more original minds of the period, the great master of epistemology and Madhyamaka, Chapa Chökyi Sengé (1109–69).[9] Chapa had himself been the disciple of the master Gyamarpa in matters of Madhyamaka and epistemology, and Gyamarpa was reputedly both highly learned and a strict keeper of the Buddhist rules for monks.[10] He apparently had recognized Chapa's ability when he was still quite young, and at the young age of twenty Chapa was already teaching bright students like Karmapa Düsum Khyenpa and Pagmo Drupa.[11] Unfortunately, his behavior had precipitated some problems, for it was said that by then he had committed some sort of transgression that would take eight years to expiate.[12] As may be expected from such a beginning, Chapa became noted for challenging received opinions, whether those of Indians or even of other Tibetans. Although Chapa espoused a somewhat unorthodox affirmation of the perceptual process according to the old Abhidharma of the Vaibhāṣikas, his great theoretical contribution was in the area of philosophical definition, which had not been treated sufficiently in Indian thought. Chapa tried to make sense of the competing ideas and amplified the tenuous suggestions put forward by earlier Indian thinkers. His Madhyamaka studies were dedicated to promoting Bhāvaviveka's Svātantrika ideology, and he was particularly dismissive of the new Prāsaṅgika literature brought in by Pa-tsab from Kashmir. Because of his contrarious disposition, Chapa's ideas were cited later by Sakya Paṇḍita as the preeminent expression of Tibetan doctrinal innovation, which was the kiss of death for Chapa's proposals.[13] Even worse, Chapa's own disciples apparently abandoned their master's Svātantrika Madhyamaka position, and to a man changed his allegiance to the more radical Prāsaṅgika side.[14] Eventually, any doctrinal innovation—which Tibetans did do—was surreptitiously proposed as the intention of an Indian master, for the neoconservatives had succeeded in condemning as unorthodox any ideas perceived as new or Tibetan.

THE KĀLACAKRA COMES OF AGE

In some way this condemnation of indigenous trajectories was understandable, for Tibetans were continually inundated with innovations from India, which represented for them the same kind of challenge that they had for Chinese and others in the previous centuries. Certainly the last of the great esoteric traditions to arise in India, the Kālacakra was an intellectual challenge on the order of the Prāsaṅgika and other late-eleventh- to early-twelfth-century systems.[15] The Kālacakra had actually come into Tibet sometime earlier. Gyijo Dawé Öser reputedly had fixed the Tibetan calendar's beginning to 1027 C.E. with his computations and the first translations of Kālacakra-related texts, although he probably made most of these calculations in the second half of the eleventh century. Gyijo's disciple Nyö-lotsāwa, the same translator said to have accompanied Marpa to India, is credited with translating the entire standard commentary, the *Vimalaprabhā*, a monumental achievement if true. The same source indicates that the work was again translated by Dro-lotsāwa Shérapdrak, perhaps using the earlier translation as a basis or as a partial guide.[16] In any event, it was Dro-lotsāwa's work with the paṇḍita Somanātha that constitutes the received translation of both the basic tantra and commentary, and it appears to have been completed in the late eleventh or early twelfth century.

This was also the period for the efflorescence of Indian and Tibetan Kālacakra scholarship, with the Indian effort led by scholars like Abhayākaragupta (ca. 1100), Somanātha, Vāgīśvara, and others in Nepal and Kashmir. At the same time, other great Tibetan scholars of the system did their work as well. Ralo Dorjé-drak's nephew, Ra-lo Chörap, had worked with the Nepalese Samantaśrī and others on such works as the *Sekaprakriyā*, the canonical Kālacakra consecration text. Ra-lo Chörap was also an influential and popular Kālacakra preacher. Nyen-chung Dharma-drak, Galo Zhönu-pel (1110–98), and several others in the late eleventh to early twelfth century also helped bring the Kālacakra to Tibet. Moreover, Tibetans were not the only ones interested in the Kālacakra, as Tsami-lotsāwa, the early Tangut scholar (active in the early twelfth century), played an important part in the Kālacakra's transmission to both Tibet and the Tangut kingdom.

Why was this tantric system of such great interest at the turn of the twelfth century, making Indians, Tibetans, Tanguts, and others obsessed with its arcane ideology? For Tibetans the answer was easy but multifaceted. The Kālacakra provided a cosmology that for the first time confirmed the locus of the true Dharma as being outside India, in the northern hidden country of Shambhala. It is not well understood that one possible interpretation of the cryptic directions in the *Kālacakra-tantra* itself—which does not directly agree with the cosmology of the highly influential *Vimalaprabhā* commentary—is that Shambhala might be situated in the neighborhood of the Purang kingdom.[17] Not only did this paradigm work with the indigenous ideology of "hidden mystic valleys" (*sbas yul*) and the Terma tradition, but the mythology also reinforced an emerging Tibetan idea that the Dharma could take refuge and hide in Tibet itself. According to the *Kālacakra-tantra* and related documents, the heretical terrors of Islam and Hinduism would be defeated by a new Dharma king from the north, thus feeding the imperial associations that Tibetans desired in the twelfth century, hoping to cast out the evil enemies of religion, and to erect a strong Buddhist theocracy in its place.

Beyond the cosmology of the Dharma, the *Kālacakra-tantra* is a highly complex document that introduces entire new realms of knowledge. The period's thirst for new information became a motivation for the penetration of the elaborate medical, astrological, embryological, gnoseological, and other lore provided by this most intricate scripture and its supporting literature. Finally, and I believe just as important as all of the preceding reasons, this tantra is a vision of reality in which all these elements are integrated into one another. Unlike the piecemeal notes, ad hoc rituals, and idiosyncratic meditations filling the many short chapters of the other tantras, the *Kālacakra-tantra* is elegantly written by one hand, from a very scholarly position, and by a person of global vision. Each of the five chapters is fully interconnected with the others, and the text requires assiduous study before its secrets are revealed. There is no partial work, no artificial separation of this knowledge here and that practice there. The text speaks of the real union of the transworldly vision and the actual exercise of power, without having to worry so much about minutia of philosophical syntax and religious diction. It represents an all-embracing vision, and once they matured to its message in the late eleventh to early twelfth century, Tibetans seized it with gusto.

GAMPOPA AND THE KAGYÜPA EFFLORESCENCE

It was exactly this idea of an integrated Buddhist vision that others found attractive as well, with the Kagyüpa developing their own synthetic perspective.

While the Kadampa were wrestling with new philosophical ideas, their basic Mahāyānist legacy was assisting other traditions, and there can be few better examples than Gampopa. Gampopa Sönam Rinchen (1079–1153) was an intriguing figure, certainly more complex than either his supporters or detractors have indicated. Since the majority of Kagyüpa lines stem from his disciples, the Kagyüpa transition from a series of fragile lineages into an organized monastic denomination with multiple institutions possessing a common identity really began with Gampopa. He was born in the lower Nyel valley, perhaps close to Lhüntsé, in a fertile area close to the Indian border where the Nyel River flows down to meet the Subansiri as it enters Assam (map 7).[18] His clan was the Nyiwa (*snyi-ba*), which had as modest royal dynastic roots as the Khön did but before then had not specialized in religion.[19] Yet Gampopa's father was able to make an enviable marital alliance for Gampopa, his second son, and the boy was married to a daughter of the powerful and high-status Chim clan, which was something of a coup for the scion of a family of physicians and sorcerers. For this to have happened, the Nyiwa must have been politically powerful in the Nyel valley, which they in fact dominated, and they seemed to have become very wealthy, perhaps as Marpa's family had in Lho-drak, just two valleys to the west. The Nyiwa's status in the Nyel valley may have had something to do with Gampopa's eventually relocating north to Dakpo, along the Tsangpo River, so that his Kadampa-based monastic avocation could thrive outside the clan's shadow.

In any event, Gampopa was first raised in the family business: medicine. Because medicine was part of the dynastic legacy, some hagiographers also state that he was taught the *Guhyagarbha* and other Nyingma tantras, which may have been true.[20] In an autobiographical notice, Gampopa says that he studied other tantras, particularly an unnamed *yoga-tantra* and the *Cakrasaṁvara*, at the age of fifteen with one Géshé Zangskarwa (apparently not Zangskar-lotsāwa), but probably for only a short time until he began his medical studies. Gampopa's happy home, however, was devastated by an epidemic (possibly plague) that caused the death of his wife and children. Consequently, at the somewhat advanced age of twenty-five, he took monastic vows with Géshé Mar-yül Loden shérap at Rongkar in Dakpo. After receiving tantric consecrations and practicing some exoteric meditation, he went to study with Kadampa monks in Pen-yül, in Ü. He appears to have worked with several Kadampa scholars, although his principal teachers were Géshé Gya-yöndak, with whom he studied for three years, and Géshé Jangchup sempa, Géshé Nyuk-rumpa, and Géshé Chak-ri-wa, all of whom are mentioned in Gampopa's works.[21] All told, Gampopa spent about five years studying the Kadampa exoteric and esoteric materials, becoming well versed in the *Stages of the Path* genre but specializing in the Kadampa version of the Mahāyānist contempla-

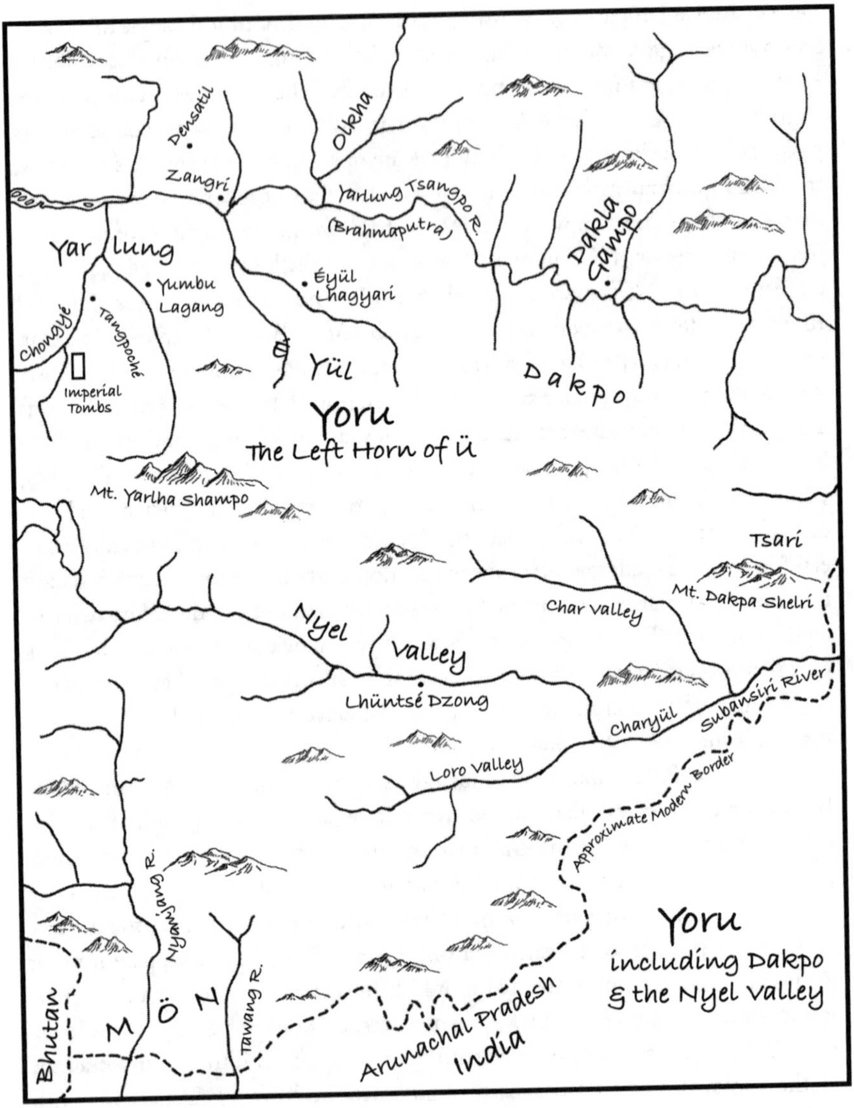

MAP 7 Yoru, Including Dakpo and the Nyel Valley.

tive system. In this, Gampopa was something of a wunderkind, and the sources affirm that he was spiritually gifted all out of proportion to the amount of instruction received or time spent in meditation.

In the spring of 1109, Gampopa heard of Mila Repa and asked his preceptors for permission to find and to study with the famous poet-yogin (figure 18). His Kadampa masters initially were not pleased with the prospect of their prize pupil running off after an itinerant yogin, but eventually he cajoled a tepid acquiescence allowing him to go in pursuit of Mila. After forty days and a certain amount of trouble, Gampopa finally located the peripatetic meditator. Similar to the hagiographies of its other saints, though, Kagyüpa chronicles make Gampopa's search a great trial of his motivation: searching, receiving tantalizing clues, encountering divine guides, and finally discovering the guru revealed before him. Yet there is no denying that he was very well received, and Mila Repa became strongly engaged in the instruction of the gifted monk, who stayed with the colony of yogins for thirteen months. Gampopa was then affirmed in his realization by Mila and in 1100 was sent off to practice meditation on his own.[22] Gampopa returned to Ü, but it became clear that the esoteric teaching he had received did not entirely accord well with the Kadampa Mahāyānist perspective, and Gampopa would struggle with the tension between tantric perspectives and Mahāyānist insight for some time. At this juncture, Gampopa seemed to have returned home, and his father evidently constructed a temple for him in the Nyel valley, where Gampopa practiced meditation and studied the scriptures for six years before going off on his own.[23] Eventually, he and Mila Repa met again just before the great yogin's death around 1123, when Gampopa received some last advanced instruction.

Gampopa's relative lack of direct training—six years total of both scholastic/monastic and meditative training by Buddhist standards is far too brief—became something of an issue with the tradition, and the hagiographers emphasize that he was the rebirth of the bodhisattva Candraprabha-kumārabhūta, the bodhisattva to whom the Mahāyānist classic, the *Samādhirāja-sūtra*, was taught.[24] The problem of sufficient background is especially noticeable in Gampopa's esoteric writings, and their description by Jackson as "anti-intellectual" or "anticonceptual" is a bit wide of the mark, for in regard to conceptualization Gampopa does not generally make statements more extreme than those already present in siddha-based literature of Indian esoteric Buddhism or, for that matter, even in much of normative Mahāyāna texts. He does construct these with his physician's metaphor of a simple panacea (*dkar po chig thub*) for all difficulties, but his relationship to verbal formulas is not as radical as has been portrayed by later neoconservatives like Sakya Paṇḍita, who were completely invested in the scholastic system.[25]

FIGURE 18 Kagyüpa lineage including Marpa, Mila Repa, and Gampopa. After a detail of an early-thirteenth-century painting

What Gampopa does do is violate some unwritten rules that were drawn up in later Indian Buddhist doctrinal systems, by employing esoteric literature to describe conceptual fields appropriate to exoteric study. Thus, in explaining the perfection of insight, a good bodhisattva topic, he crosses the line by quoting from the siddhas and the tantras, even bringing in Chinese apocryphal sūtras in the process. Gampopa also suggests that there is a third path in the Mahāyāna, the "innate yoga" (*sahajayoga*) of the Great Seal (*mahāmudrā*) that goes beyond sūtra and tantra.[26] This innate yoga is of two varieties, one that pertains to the mind itself (*sems nyid lhan cig skyes pa*) and one that pertains to the perceptible world (*snang ba lhan cig skyes pa*). The former is the absolute body of the Buddha (*dharmakāya*), and the latter is the clear light of the absolute body. There are two kinds of "armor" to be used in the practice of the path: the armor of an external view, consisting of virtue, and the armor of internal insight, which consists of internal yogic practices.[27] The Great Seal goes beyond other descriptions in affirming that this ordinary mind is the Buddha, but it is ultimately in conformity with both the sūtras and the tantras.

It is easy to understand that the use of terminology willy-nilly is undesirable, but it is not immediately clear why there is necessarily a line between explanations using sūtras and those using tantras. In actuality the disconnection between these two is a consequence of Indian doctrinal strategies. Once Indian Buddhists began to articulate different systems of thought, proponents of the diverse systems struggled with one another for dominance. In fact, the exoteric and esoteric traditions represent incommensurate ideas, and the simultaneous affirmation of sūtra and tantra worked at the institutional and doctrinal level only if everyone acted as though they applied to separate universes, so that a direct comparison or synthesis of the Madhyamaka and the Vajrayāna descriptions of, say, the value of ethical systems, could be avoided.

Since social stratification is the default position of Indian life, Indians affirmed doctrinal stratification as a means for separating the various trends. This worked because one of the purposes of caste in India is to delimit competition or marriage between groups, for competition in India tends to breed violence and caste requires discrete lines of descent. With the affirmation of the tantras as the word of the Buddha, the stratification of the soteriological system became de rigueur in India, as Mahāyānists of the period wanted to have both the traditional Buddhist path be true and the radical tantras be included in the canon, with little sharing of vocabulary. Thus the model of caste became employed to affirm separate religious applications and separate lines of descent for sūtra and tantra. The way this was actually effected, though, is that the tradition affirmed that sūtras and philosophical śāstras could be used to explain esoteric topics, but not vice versa. In the Indian system, a tantric author like Vilāsavajra could legitimately quote Mahāyānist texts in his commentary on the *Mañjuśrīnāmasaṁgīti*, but Mahāyānist writers were expected to refrain from referencing tantric literature for philosophical validation. Even then, we do occasionally find Indians not adhering to these unwritten rules, particularly in the early phases of tantric composition, and Haribhadra does cite the *Vajrapāṇyabhiṣeka-tantra* in his long commentary on the *Abhisamayālaṁkāra*.[28]

Certainly, much of the study of Buddhist tantric texts is devoted to reaffirming this stratification idiom, but Gampopa was insufficiently trained in that discipline. Ngok Chödor, not Mila Repa, was Marpa's inheritor of tantric textual exegesis, and even in the case of Mila Repa, Gampopa spent only a little more than a year in his teacher's presence. His other study of esoteric literature emphasized its meditative practices rather than its exegetical system, and as he said in the quotation at the beginning of the chapter, Gampopa assumed that a great meditator would intuitively know everything necessary, which actually was an ancient Buddhist idea.[29]

It may be strange to some readers to stress the difference between tantric study and tantric practice, but Marpa himself was said to have obtained Buddhahood without meditating, and Drokmi's paṇḍita Gayādhara was noted for seldom practicing contemplation. In fact, by the late eleventh and early twelfth century, tantric exegesis had become an important area of study and exercise, and Gampopa's received writings seldom quoted the tantras and almost never made reference to the normative points of controversy in the tantric commentaries.[30] In this respect Gampopa was quite different from the well-educated

Gö-lotsāwa Khukpa Lhétsé, whose facile command of the spectrum of tantric literature is evident in his works. Consequently, there are many inconsistencies throughout Gampopa's received writings, and the reader may sometimes sense that Gampopa was trying to find his way through the dense labyrinth of Buddhist texts and ideas.

In defense of Gampopa, it is equally obvious that—if one does not subscribe to the view that there are different universes but that the realms of sūtra and tantra are lines in the Mahāyānist doctrinal sand—then Buddhist doctrines and vocabulary can and perhaps should be considered in conjunction with one another. There are few reasons based on *experience* that there cannot be competition and adjudication as well as cooperation and synthesis between the exoteric and esoteric vocabularies. Indeed, the nonfoundational predisposition of Buddhist social assessment suggests a correspondingly nonfoundational analysis of doctrinal differentiations. This is in fact what various eleventh-century Great Perfection authors, like Rongzom, were suggesting, and in many places in his lectures Gampopa shows himself familiar with and even attracted to the Great Perfection ideas.[31] His work is laced with vocabulary and paradigms closely related to the mental position of the Great Perfection, especially in his expression of awareness (*rig-pa*), which is a central term in Gampopa's corpus, albeit not as highly valued as innateness (*sahaja*).[32] One of his more important works, *Revealing the Hidden Characteristics of Mind* (*Sems kyi mtshan nyid gab pa mngon du phyung ba*), in fact appears to be a Kagyüpa version of one of the teaching traditions of the Rong system of the Mental Position.[33] Most important, though, Gampopa was working toward breaking down the barriers to vocabulary synthesis, so that terminology from one area could be used freely to explain others, and he developed the idea of the "conformity" of the different vehicles with one another.[34] This is probably one basis for his amalgamation of the Kagyüpa traditions and the language of the Kadampa Mahāyānist ideas, which appears in his classic the *Jewel Ornament of Liberation* (*Dwags po thar rgyan*), a fusion that sent his critics into orbit. Yet this is exactly what we should expect of a meditator who was not well socialized into the ideology of vocabulary separation and personally synthetic in his approach to contemplative reality. For Gampopa, it seems that the lines in the doctrinal sand were ephemeral way stations in his personal experience of the ultimate.

That does not mean that stratification was entirely disregarded, and one area in which Gampopa stands accused may be one of the more orthodox of his ideas: the difference between those taking the gradual path (*rim gyis 'jug pa*) and those taking the simultaneous path (*cig char 'jug pa*). By the early twelfth century these terms were carrying much baggage and had been used in

Tibet to discuss Buddhist differences since the dynastic controversy between the Northern Chan of Heshang Moheyan and the Indian Mahāyāna of Kamalaśīla.[35] In the Vajrayāna context, though, it was a legitimate topic of tantric discussion throughout this period, represented in the previous generation by Gö-lotsāwa Khukpa Lhétsé and in the subsequent generation by the Sakyapa hierarch, Drakpa Gyeltsen.[36] Those writers could discuss these ideas, since the Sanskrit terms "by degrees" (*kramavṛtyā*) and "simultaneously" (*yugapad*) had been translated with the Tibetan terms for gradual and simultaneous path in the Tibetan rendering of the tantric Āryadeva's *Caryāmelāpakapradīpa*, a text with a sterling pedigree.[37] Āryadeva in turn based his discussion on their occurrence in the *Laṅkāvatāra Sūtra*, which is the probable source for this distinction in both Chan and Vajrayāna in the first place, since authors from both systems have taken the *Laṅkāvatāra Sūtra* as central to their ideas.[38] There is no question that Gampopa used this categorical distinction more freely and with greater force than some other writers did, but that is a difference of degree rather than of kind, and Gampopa was aware that he had Indian precedent on his side, for he specifically quoted the *Laṅkāvatāra Sūtra* as his source for the two soteriological styles.[39] Conversely, the thirteenth-century neoconservative attempt to align Gampopa's position with that of Heshang Moheyan was based in part on collapsing the distinctions between the Mahāmudrā and Chan while ignoring the topic's orthodox roots.[40]

Around 1120 Gampopa founded his monastery of Dakla Gampo (named for the patron providing the funding) in the Dakpo area of Tibet just east of Yarlung, and he began to gather disciples, who were attracted by the charisma of this highly spiritual personality.[41] His hagiographies emphasize the idea—once again seen in the quotation at the beginning of the chapter—that a contemplative master can transmit his experience to others, and Gampopa was said to have had this quality.[42] Consequently, he attracted some of the best young monks and meditators around, four of whom were considered to have been his greatest disciples: Düsum Khyenpa (Karmapa I), Pagmo Drupa, Barompa, and Dakpo Gomtsül. From these four emerged the "four greater Kagyüpa" lineages. What is not generally realized, though, is that the three really successful lineages extended from the three lamas with excellent Kadampa training: Düsum Khyenpa, Pagmo Drupa, and Dakpo Gomtsül. The Kadampa legacy continued to inform the Kagyüpa practice and ideology for some generations to come, even though the Kagyüpa was a tradition fundamentally yogic in orientation.

In bringing monasticism to the yogic tradition, Gampopa also was nurturing a strong familial association within his monastery. Dakpo Gomtsül was both his successor and his nephew, and in fact Gomtsül's successor was Dakpo

Gomchung, who was his own younger brother. As a result, the Nyiwa clan built and secured the monastery for themselves, much as the Ngok had done elsewhere (initially at Sangpu), as Marpa had done with his sons in Lho-drak, and as Ralo did with his own nephew, Ra Chöbar. By the middle of the twelfth century, there eventually evolved the understanding that a clan may own and occupy important denomination centers, where members of other clans could train but were unlikely to become its successors. The legal basis was clear in these cases, for succession was based on blood. Conversely, the idea of unrelated land inheritance was a murky area in Tibetan life, and the occasional presence of nonaristocratic Tibetans (such as Düsum Khyenpa) at the head of monasteries must have made such a possibility rather jarring for traditionalists, who were already feeling assaulted by the rapid shift of institutional life. While the *Mūlasarvāstivāda-vinaya* made various provisions for the corporate holding and inheritance of land, its authority in India was supported by an ideology of the separation between ecclesiastical and civil precedent.[43] In Central Tibet, though, this had not been established. The legal situation of monastic inheritance had been sufficiently problematic that the Eastern Vinaya monastic groups often challenged one another over valid ownership, as seen in the instance of the early Kadampa monasteries. Conversely, with this strategy of father to son, or uncle to nephew, the legal and religious authority could be successfully transferred to the next generation without question, so that religious domains—whether lay or monastic—could be confidently secured in uncertain times.

THE LADIES MACHIK EXPAND THE REPERTOIRE: CHÖ AND THE ZHAMA LAMDRÉ

While these necessary monastic developments were taking place, Padampa's female followers were promoting their own interesting directions. Padampa's most important female disciple generally has not been included in the Zhiché tradition, apparently because her individual lineage and system were so important. This was Machik Labdrön, about whom much has been written, so I will simply summarize the available scholarship.[44] She was born possibly somewhere in the region of Éyül, east of Yarlung, probably in the third quarter of the eleventh century.[45] Although she was granted the great honorific "Machik" (One Mother) generally accorded mature aristocratic or religious women, there is little indication that she was born into the aristocracy. Her first lama was Drapa Ngönshé, the well-known Eastern Vinaya preceptor who later abandoned his vows and established monasteries associated with Nyingma practices. Machik Labdrön learned to read very well during her training and became a professional reader of religious texts, supported by others for the merit of the ritual performance. She continued her studies with various masters and eventually had several children by one of her teachers, not that uncommon then as now. Most sources indicate that she began studying with Padampa rather late, probably after he returned from China and settled in Dingri in 1097. She ultimately removed to Zangri in Lho-kha, close to her place of birth and just upriver from Gampopa's monastery of Dakla Gampo.

The tradition is content to claim that there were two lineages of Chö, meaning "cutting off the realm of demons," but the practice seems to have been developed primarily by Machik. Its Indian roots are somewhat dubious, and the ritual of mentally offering one's body to demons in a remote or possessed locale was said to have been based on a short *Grand Poem of the Perfection of Insight*, attributed to Āryadeva, which had two translations. Shamanic connections have been sometimes associated with the practice, but it appears that its fundamental visualization was influenced by the Tibetan postmortem rite of offering the body to vultures and other scavengers, sometimes called a "sky burial" in Western literature.[46] The practice was combined with a mentalistic demonology in which the four Māras were described as entirely conceptual in nature, thus amalgamating a postmortem ritual with a Buddhist assessment of its meaning. If this was the case, then the textual source must have been affected by Tibetan or Tibetan-like (Zoroastrian?) rituals. It is certain that the Chö practice was criticized by the neoconservatives, and Chaglo Chöjé-pel (1197–1264) is noted for having accused Padampa of fabricating works that incorporate the un-Buddhist doctrines of Chö into a Buddhist framework.[47] It is more likely, though, that the actual practice came from the ritual conversation of Padampa and Machik Labdrön.

Machik Labdrön was not the only woman to be favored by Padampa. Zhama-lotsāwa's sister, Zhama Machik, was also one of his disciples, but with a less positive outcome. She, like her brother, was born in the region of Six Fathers (Pha drug) in Latö-lho, close to the Nepalese border, and were among the 104 Zhama clan members from that area.[48] The *Blue Annals* states that Zhama-lotsāwa's dates were 1069 to 1144 and that Zhama Machik's dates were 1062 to 1149.[49] When the girl who would come to be known as Zhama Machik was sixteen, she was married to Drom Ramcha Yuné, evidently a Himalayan aristocrat claiming Drom clan connections.[50] The marriage failed, and she left to serve as the ritual assistant and sexual consort of a well-known but relatively minor translator, Ma Chöbar. Shortly thereafter, though, he passed away, and she encountered various psychological difficulties. In addition, she began to experience severe gynecological problems, apparently hemorrhaging frequently and at one point passed a blood clot the size of a bird's egg. These experiences were interpreted by her and her relations as the vital air encountering problems, especially leaking *bodhicitta*—a term that may mean either semen (i.e., blood for a woman) or the thought of awakening. Leaky *bodhicitta* represents a significant impediment for meditators, according to the norms of the completion process yoga, not to mention the excruciating impediments experienced by a woman whose uterine lining is disintegrating at an uncontrolled rate.

Hearing of his great reputation, Zhama Machik traveled to Dingri to ask the opinion of Padampa Sangyé, who informed her that her difficulties were the result of not giving an offering to Ma Chöbar at the time of her initiatory consecration. He counseled her to repair Ma Chöbar's temple, to obtain a pinnacle from Nepal for his reliquary, and to make offerings to his daughter, which she did and gained relief for a year. But then the problem returned, and Padampa again had her on restricted movement for seven years, reading the scriptures. One day Zhama Machik heard a cleric from Nubyül sing a song, and a cognition of great certainty came to her, making her feel much better. In response, Padampa gave her a drum and told her to beat out a rhythm. She did but got only a lot of noise and nothing else. The account of her frustrations with Padampa may or may not be accurate, since we have a profound discontinuity between Padampa's representations in the fifteenth-century *Blue Annals* and the thirteenth-century Lamdré records. The Lamdré chronicles generally depict Padampa as an incompetent, self-promoting, Indian faith healer, whereas dedicated Chö sources show him to be an infallible second Buddha.[51]

Be that as it may, Zhama Machik finally heard of Sétön Kunrik, the Lamdré guru, and hurried off to Kharchung. According to the Lamdré chronicles, Sétön listened to her story and asked her whether she was having this or that experience, which she was, and he confirmed that her problem was meditation without sufficient instruction. He joked that she had had much meditative experience but little direction, whereas he had had much instruction but little experience. He conferred on her new consecrations and instructed her in some of the many techniques the Lamdré has for physical defects in meditation, which seemed to give her relief.

Afterward, with her brother, Zhama Machik developed the "Zhama method" of Lamdré. It is unfortunate that we actually know so little about her and her brother, for the pair continue to show up at the center of both the phenomenon of Padampa—although almost entirely ignored by adherents to the Chö and Zhiché systems after the fifteenth century—and as the most viable alternative to the Khön family's form of Lamdré. In reality, the Zhama tradition was often the preferred method, and some Kagyüpa teachers studied it.[52]

Even Gölo Zhönu-pel emphasized the Zhama as the Lamdré system of choice in the late fifteenth century. The connection between the Lamdré and the Zhama siblings eventually became a feeble footnote with the eclipse of the Zhama system, and more recently, Zhama Machik has assumed a position in the pantheon of individual Tibetan saints associated with sacred geography.[53]

It is appropriate to reflect here on the important positions of Zhama Machik, Machik Labdrön, Padampa's four "*ḍākinī*" disciples, his twenty-four nun followers, and Drokmi's four female disciples who attained realization. Although the evidence indicates that esoteric Buddhism in India was strongly detrimental to women's religious aspirations, this was curiously not the case in the eleventh to the early twelfth century in Central Tibet, especially in Tsang Province where all these women either studied or lived. Indeed, women were important for a limited time but became increasingly silenced by the end of the twelfth century with the emergence of a strong neoconservative stance. It appears that while Tibetans during this period explored their own options in the freer religious climate of the late eleventh to the early twelfth century, women gained greater expressive power. But when Central Tibet became increasingly the focus of international interest and was held up as a paragon of Buddhist practice—eclipsing even India—then Tibetans began to assume some of the unfortunate standards of behavior that called for the suppression of women in India.

That is, as Tibetans became more orthodox, in the process they also became more Indian. We even get a taste of this in the story of Zhama Machik. When three Indian monks arrived to receive instruction in the Dharma, she merely replied that she was a barbarian from a border country, and a woman at that, so what could she teach them? She accepted their gifts but did not teach them any Dharma and sent them home.

SACHEN KUNGA NYINGPO: SAKYA CRISIS AND CONTINUITY

In the face of such extraordinary intellectual and meditative activity, Sakya Monastery appeared to be something of a backwater, a perception that was discarded in the first half of the twelfth century. Having founded his new monastery of Sakya, Könchok Gyelpo, unlike his elder brother, abandoned his celibacy and took a wife. His only son, Kunga Nyingpo, changed the path of the Sakya for the future, and the narrative of his birth is one of those tales that makes the study of Tibetan hagiographical literature so interesting.[54] Kunga Nyingpo's son and hagiographer, Drakpa Gyeltsen, simply recorded that his father was born in the area of upper Drompa, in Tsang.[55] This was generally the region around Sakya, so this information offers no surprise. However, the amazing story of the circumstances of his birth, true or not, as related in the seventeenth century is worthy of our attention simply because of its value as an artifact of Tibetan self-representation and for its literary appeal. It is a story of visionary revelation and drunken seduction, a traveling lama and a feudal lord's daughter.[56]

According to the most reliable accounts, Könchok Gyelpo's first wife, Dorjé Chukmo, did not bear any children, and the Sakya founder seemed content to remain childless.[57] But an eminent visionary in the area, the great Jétsün Chökyi Gyeltsen of Khaü-kyélhé Monastery (his name is conveniently shortened to Nam-khaüpa), had a vision of the Khasarpaṇa form of Avalokiteśvara.[58] He saw the bodhisattva in a rainbow-color tent of clear light, traveling toward the nearby district of Kargong-lung. The holy saint knew in an instant that the bodhisattva of compassion was seeking an appropriate birth and that the proper circumstances were required. In order to establish the correct situation so that Könchok Gyelpo would become the father, the saint issued many invitations to the great lama. Because, however, their residences were near enough to each other to make the round trip in a single day, there was no opportunity to grant the bodhisattva access to an opportune vehicle (a woman) for the bodhisattva's birth. Finally, Nam-khaüpa devised a scheme to introduce the aging Könchok Gyelpo to the young Machik Zhangmo, the daughter of the district lord, the chieftain who had facilitated the sale of Sakya to Könchok Gyelpo. When the lama accepted his invitation one day, the saint Nam-khaüpa delayed him and led him to Kargong-lung, where the lord's manor house was situated. After introducing the young lady to the older lama, they plied the lama with strong, newly made beer. Könchok Gyelpo knew he could not get back to Sakya that night and asked whether there was an inn in the neighborhood, but the young lady invited him to her bed instead. As a result of their night of romance, Kunga Nyingpo was born nine months later, in 1092.

Later Sakyapa sources revel in the prophecy of Kunga Nyingpo's birth.[59] According to legend, when Atiśa arrived at Sakya on his way to Samyé, he predicted that in the future there would be a monastery guarded by two forms of Mahākāla. Furthermore, seven incarnations of Mañjuśrī would reside there, as well as one of Avalokiteśvara and one of Vajrapāṇi. Kunga Nyingpo's birth was the result not only of a saint's scheme but of the divine plan of a number of bodhisattvas as well. However, since Nam-khaüpa was the principal conspirator, he made sure that Könchok Gyelpo knew about the birth and invited him to see his new son.

We can imagine Könchok Gyelpo's consternation to find that he was a father at the age of fifty-eight. He tried to keep the boy's existence a secret, but his wife found out and confronted him. No matter what the lama's charisma, this could not have been an easy conversation. Pointedly, his wife told him that without this child, his family line would be cut off, since his brother had died a celibate layman. She asserted that she was independently well off but that both the child and his mother needed funds for support and education, so she insisted that Könchok Gyelpo bring the boy and his mother to Sakya and make all the proper arrangements for his heir. This he did, and he dedicated the greater part of the Sakya cultivated land for the maintenance of the future Sakya lama and his mother. Unfortunately, Könchok Gyelpo could only begin the child's education, for he passed away in the Gorum building at Sakya in 1102, when the boy was ten.[60]

In a more prosaic manner, Sachen's education established a new standard, for his record of received instruction reads like a catalog of available early-twelfth-century Tibetan Buddhist literature. His own literary contributions extend from this narrowly religious interest, and it would be a mistake to identify him as encyclopedic for precisely this reason. While Sachen's hagiographers assign to him all the knowledge of worldly science, we have little verification of that in fact. His education really began following the last rites of his father. His mother informed him that even though he was the Sakya heir, he had no right to dominion over the monastery, for it would be a joke for a poorly prepared boy to run the establishment that Sakya had become.[61] Machik Zhangmo had another telling observation: Sachen's father had obtained a greater part of his prestige by studying with Indian-trained translators, and so Sachen must emulate that practice. She thus made arrangements to invite Bari-lotsāwa Chökyi Drakpa (1040–1112), a well-respected scholar and translator of ritual manuals, to assume the abbot's seat in Sakya so that her son could become well educated.[62] Bari agreed and instituted the basic presumption of medieval Buddhist education: if intelligence is needed, then the bodhisattva of divine intelligence should be propitiated. Accordingly, Kunga Nyingpo was sent to practice the great mantra of the bodhisattva: ARAPACANADHĪḤ, which is a mantric employment of an esoteric syllabary developed from a language based in the early centuries of the common era in Gandhāra and associated with insight (*prajñā*).[63] Initially, the boy experienced the usual meditative obstacles—visions of big white men, lions, and whatnot—but through the application of the proper meditative antidotes, they were dismissed.

Finally, we are told that after six months Kunga Nyingpo had a grand vision of the bodhisattva Mañjuśrī, who gave him a four-line instruction, called the *Separation from the Four Attachments* (*Zhen pa bzhi bral*), and informed him that his heirs would host the incarnation of this bodhisattva from that point forward.[64] The instruction is actually a standard statement of Buddhist fundamentals:

> If one is attached to this life, he is not a religious.
> If one is attached to existence, there is no dissociation [from it].
> If one is attached to one's own benefit, there is no *bodhicitta.*
> If there is taking (a position), there is not the correct vision.[65]

This episode—at least the vision and the formula—is clearly old, although it is not certain that the prophecy of his lineage was also transmitted to the boy, for it is likely that it was a later addition to the story of this revelation. Both his sons specifically stated that Kunga Nyingpo had a Mañjuśrī vision, and there is nothing in the content of the *Separation from the Four Attachments* that would be inappropriate for one beginning the practice of the Dharma. In reality, it is an elegant statement of exactly the concerns of the beginner and has been taken as such by the Sakyapa.[66]

At that time Kunga Nyingpo was eleven, and after consultation he was sent to study basic metaphysics (Abhidharma) in Rong Ngurmik, which was relatively nearby, with an old member of the Drangti clan named Géshé Drangti Darma Nyingpo.[67] Evidently, metaphysics was a popular topic then—probably featuring the study of the *Abhidharmasamuccaya*—and all residential areas in the lama's center were already filled by his earlier students. Consequently, Kunga Nyingpo had to make do with a nearby ramshackle cave covered up with a black yak-fur felt curtain.[68] A more serious problem arose when his neighbor became ill, apparently with smallpox (*'brum bu'i nad*), and had no one to help him, since he was from a nomadic area. Kunga Nyingpo assisted the unfortunate monk and caught the disease himself, having to return home under distressing circumstances.

Later, after Kunga Nyingpo had completed a rudimentary study of Abhidharma, Géshé Drangti died. Clearly interested in Buddhist doctrinal studies, Kunga Nyingpo went to the temple of Nyangtö Jangché, where he studied with Drangti Zurchöpa Géshé Khyung Rinchen Drakpa, working through Asaṅga's *Bodhisattvabhūmi*, along with the sets of vows it contains.[69] Then, with that teacher and Zurchöpa Pel-midikpa, he started down the epistemological yellow brick road, working on Dharmakīrti's *Pramāṇaviniścaya* and the *Nyāyabindu.* At that point, a very human letter arrived from the Sakya estate stewards (*gzhis-pa*), requesting that the aspiring scholar return to his home institution.[70] "Lama Bari is elderly, and you may not have the opportunity to learn from him later." In reality, the appeal was both for continuity in administration and for the young Kunga Nyingpo to pursue an education in the adhesive that held such communities together: ritual. Ritual not only weds the community of religious into a unified whole but also establishes the basic relationship between the institution and the surrounding valley, over which Sakya and similar monasteries exercised authority and decisions. If Sakya were to have a continuum in its ritual life, the young master would need to learn the esoteric ritual systems that had been the specialty of his father and Bari-lotsāwa. Epistemological texts could not possibly hold together the social fabric of Sakya, and those in positions of authority knew it.

BARI-LOTSĀWA AND THE RITUAL IMPERATIVE

Bari-lotsāwa was one of the preeminent ritualists of his day, specializing in the translation of esoteric meditative manuals (*sādhana*). Born in the Lingkha area of Kham, his parents were unknown, but evidently his father was of the Bari clan, a relatively obscure lineage.[71] Bari was disposed to religious behavior and dreamed that he should study in Central Tibet. He collected funds for his travel and at the age of eighteen (1058)—the common age for Khampas of that time to go to Central Tibet—he journeyed west. In western Uru, he took the novice ordination from Kusulupa Zhang Yönten Rinchen and Lobpön Tencikpa Tsöndrü-drak, and from these masters he obtained the name Rinchen-drak. Like Sachen, Bari began studying the basics with these teachers, and like so many other Khampas of this period, he learned the manuals of graded Buddhist instruction coming through the Kadampa tradition. There is even a strong but apocryphal story that Bari studied with Atiśa himself, which is impossible given the chronology.[72] With Géshé Nya-rawa Döndrup, Bari completed his study of Kadampa literature and went through the basic Yogācāra works of the *Abhidharmasamuccaya* and some of the texts ascribed to Maitreya.

At this point, Bari went to pay his respects to the Jowo statue in the great temple at Lhasa and had a vivid dream that the eleven-headed Avalokiteśvara appeared and foretold great things for him. Bari's response to the dream was to decide to go to the land of the Buddha for study. Bari had been in Central Tibet for fifteen years. and at the age of thirty-three he joined a band of devout Buddhist figures, including a Kadampa Géshé Darma (who was heading to Vajrāsana), an Assamese yogin named Śrī Phalamati, their followers, and other stray individuals: thirteen pilgrims in all. Probably in the fall of 1073 they headed down from Kyirong and would have passed through Navakoṭ and Kathmandu, eventually to the Buddhist centers of Lalitapaṭṭana. Bari, so well trained in Buddhist doctrine and basic moral works, was about to find that the emphasis on ritual was overwhelming the Buddhist centers of South Asia.

Bari's first teacher was a Nepalese, Paṇḍita Ānanda, although we do not know the latter's residence. From him, Bari received a strong dose of the current ritual syllabus: the consecrations, meditations, ritual manuals, tantric authorizations, and study of the commentaries for works associated with Cakrasaṁvara, Vajrayoginī, and the *Catuḥpīṭha* materials. In the standard manner, he also studied Sanskrit grammar in Nepal and was noted as having become accomplished in the language. He then moved on to India and first encountered a Guru Mahāyogin; from this obscure individual, Bari continued his ritual study, especially in Vajravārāhī-related rites. Bari spent the most important period of his study in India with the noted tantric master Vajrāsana, the second in a line to hold that name.[73]

From Vajrāsana, Bari studied extensively in the esoteric texts and also pursued the Mahāyānist scriptures—the *Avataṁsaka*, the *Ratnakūṭa*, and the *Samādhirāja sūtras*. Vajrāsana also taught Bari special rituals for the destruction of enemies and turning back harm by non-Buddhists, one of the many acknowledgments of religious tensions rising in South Asia that we begin to see at this time.[74] Together with Amoghavajra, Vajrāsana went through the texts of a collection of 1,008 sādhanas. He and Amoghavajra eventually selected 108 to be translated into Tibetan, yielding Bari's great ritual compendium, the *One Hundred Esoteric Rites* (*sGrub thabs brgya rtsa*). With this ritual training in hand, Bari returned home in 1082 at the age of forty-two, after nine years in Nepal and India. In Tibet, he pursued the rather pleasant career of the eminent peripatetic translator, newly arrived from India with the very latest in esoteric teachings, and was invited to various places to give consecrations and directions in the new materials. One of these was at Sakya, where he was hosted by Könchok Gyelpo, a connection that later led to his invitation by the Sakya authorities to assume the abbacy after the Sakya founder's death.

The list of Sachen's textual and ritual studies with Bari is a snapshot of important twelfth-century Buddhist works.[75] In an apparent effort to provide Sachen with the background esteemed in India, Bari tossed the young scholar into the same chaotic sea of Mahāyāna and Vajrayāna scriptures in which he himself had swum, including the ritually important *kriyā-tantra* and *caryā-tantra* corpus, and then into the highest yoga class, especially the *yoginī-tantra* materials. This ritual feast was rounded out with Bari's own translation of the *One Hundred Esoteric Rites.*[76]

Fully prepared for his life as a master of ritual, Sachen held a grand stūpa consecration ceremony, in which the great relics of saints past—assiduously collected by Bari—were being interred in the new All Victorious Stūpa (rNam-rgyal mchod-rten).[77] Its name stems from its contents—a mass of sealings containing the *Vijayadhāraṇī* (*Spell of the Victorious One*). In addition, soil from Indian sacred grounds, a piece of the bodhi tree, relics of the Buddha and saints (including body parts), and the greatest relic of them all, the waistcoat (*samghāṭī*) from the robe of the Buddha Kāśyapa, one of the mythic previous Buddhas, were to be interred inside the stūpa.[78] At the end of the ceremony, the stūpa was reportedly encircled with a light like boiling gold, with the sound of bells tinkling in the sky, and a loud disembodied "Well done!" was heard repeated four times. With portents as auspicious as these, there only remained for Bari-lotsāwa to surrender the administration of Sakya and its estates to Kunga Nyingpo, after eight years of his capable stewardship. The translator is also said to have given Kunga Nyingpo a talking stone statue of Mahākāla for protection. Bari returned to his temple of Yu-kharmo and passed away two years thereafter while in retreat in his cave.[79] If the chronology is correct, Bari would have completed his stewardship in 1110 and died in 1112.[80]

His philosophical investigations interrupted, Kunga Nyingpo returned to the study of Dharmakīrti's work with Géshé Mé-lhang-tser nearby and followed this with the introduction to the Madhyamaka, via the three works of the Eastern Svātantrika masters.[81] Then, back with the saint Nam-khaüpa, Kunga Nyingpo worked more systematically through the esoteric canon, including works from virtually every section. Finally, he surveyed more philosophical materials: the five works attributed to Maitreya, the works of Śāntideva, and the study of the versions of the *Prajñāpāramitā* along with its commentaries.

Finding him a glutton for punishment, Kunga Nyingpo's elders sent him to Gyichu Temple where Gyichuwa Draplha-bar resided, a Khön clansman and an eminent translator. With Gyichuwa, Kunga Nyingpo studied the three Hevajra-related tantras, including *Hevajra-tantra* commentaries, the *Kaumudī-pañjikā* of Durjayacandra and the *Yogaratnamālā* of Kāṇhapāda. He also learned both Mahāyānist philosophical and tantric works, including two series of texts that Gyichuwa had received from Maitrīpā's disciple Vajrapāṇi.[82] On the preparatory night just before receiving one consecration from Gyichuwa, Kunga Nyingpo dreamed of three bridges crossing over an enormous river stained all red, as if with blood, and he knew the river was denoted the ocean of existence.[83] In the river were many beings, all calling, "Please save me, won't you please save me!" He rescued them and then saw that many people were on the near bridge, only seven were on the middle bridge, and only three were on the last bridge. He dreamed he would save them but awoke and forgot the dream, only to remember it again later. When he asked Gyichuwa about it, his teacher teased him, "With your current ability, how could you save more than three?"

While he was studying with Gyichuwa, Kunga Nyingpo learned that Sétön Kunrik would be teaching a session at Dogtö, which was Sétön's ancestral area.[84] Although the signs were not particularly auspicious, some of Gyichuwa's younger disciples were going, so Sachen decided to go as well. Lama Sé's disciples began to inquire about his background, and when they found out he was from Sakya, Lama Sétön remarked that one of his teachers, Khön Könchok Gyelpo, had been there but had died. When Kunga Nyingpo indicated that he was Könchok Gyelpo's son, Sétön accused him of lying. Kunga Nyingpo's friends, though, immediately informed the teacher about Könchok Gyelpo's second wife, and then he was duly considerate of his teacher's son. "There is Dharma in this decrepit old man, and I will give it to you, but you must come quickly. If you think you might come slowly, please understand that I will die next year." Sétön then spent the day teaching Kunga Nyingpo a short version of the Lamdré.

Gyichuwa was not impressed with Sétön and did not allow Kunga Nyingpo to return to Sétön. "Your estimation of this man is not correct. That is 'Se-lce-pa-re' (Se who wants to be a preacher) who is entirely lacking in any kind of meditative instruction. He merely teaches fragments broken from my teacher Ngaripa's Dharma." Kunga Nyingpo could do little, according to the standards of the relationship between teacher and disciple and the family ties he had with Gyichuwa. Still, Sétön's prophecy turned out to be correct, and he died the next year. Gyichuwa was also not long to survive, and his dying wish to Kunga Nyingpo was that he should become a monk and take over the Gyichu monastery, thereby entrusting it to a fellow clansman. Kunga Nyingpo went first to Sakya, to gather together the materials for his ordination. Nevertheless, Nam-khaüpa would have none of it, stating that Kunga Nyingpo would benefit beings more by remaining in the lay estate.[85] Again, Kunga Nyingpo found himself in a struggle between teachers with competing agendas, and such disagreements are all too common in Tibetan life.

Having little recourse, Kunga Nyingpo decided to continue his studies in the lay estate and, taking Gyichuwa's texts and notes, went to learn from one of Gyichuwa's teachers, the renowned Melgyo-lotsāwa Lotrö Drakpa at Né-sar in Gungtang. Melgyo had been a disciple of the Nepalese Pamthingpa brothers—two (or four, variously enumerated) of Nāropā's greatest disciples—and the learned translator concentrated on the Cakrasaṁvara cycles of divinity, which became an abiding interest of Kunga Nyingpo's.[86] Beyond the basic scriptures, Kunga Nyingpo also studied the systems of meditation associated with the Indian saints of the Cakrasaṁvara transmission: Luhipa, Ghaṇṭapa, Kāṇhapa, and so on. In addition, he worked on the "adamantine" songs of Nāropā, as well as many of the other esoteric works he had already mastered through other lineages. Some of the translator's disciples, though, became jealous and suspicious of Sachen's ability, and some unfortunate incidents marred his stay in Gungtang.[87] But Gungtang's proximity to Nepal also allowed Sachen to meet three non-Tibetans. Two Nepalese scholars, Padmaśrī and Jñānavajra, had come to southern Tibet and had brought with them the newly developed Kālacakra exegesis of the *Mañjuśrīnāmasaṃgīti* as well as other esoteric teachings. The Indian scholar, Bhadrarāhula, also contributed some instruction.

Yet Sachen had not received the entire Lamdré, and he asked about Sétön's disciples. Opinion was unanimous: the Zhang brothers were the best of Sétön's disciples. The elder was Zhang Gönpawa, also called Zhang Chöbar (figure 19).[88] He and his younger brother, Zhang Ziji, had worked for Sétön during the construction of his monastery.[89] While the younger brother elected to return to their village of Saktang-ding in eastern Tsang, Zhang Chöbar would not accept payment for his efforts and instead asked about receiving instruction. He was told that more gifts would be required, and so he returned later with three hundred loads of barley and many goods, including a coat of mail. Evidently his brother also obtained some instruction, for they were both declared by Sétön in the lineage texts as understanding his Dharma. By Sachen's time, the younger brother had died, but Gönpawa was still living. Namkhaüpa was reportedly scathing in his criticism of Zhang Gönpawa but finally allowed Sachen to go study with the master.

Zhang Gönpawa most interestingly represents himself as a follower of the Brahman (*bram ze lugs*) and Tsa-mundri methods of the Great Perfection system. Although the latter method is obscure, we encountered a variant of the former system earlier, for it involves a Treasure tradition claiming to be from Vimalamitra and represents a transmission close to that depicted in the Seminal Essence colophon translated in chapter 6. Perhaps alternatively, Nyang-rel related a story that ties the Brahman-method texts to the mental manifestation of Avalokiteśvara.[90] Colophons to two of the received Great Perfection tantras mention the Brahman system, and one of them indicates that it was discovered as a member of a group of six tantras.[91] A description of Buddhism in the Nyang valley also mentions a group of six tantras but further elaborates an assembly of twelve items that the text claims constituted one of six cycles of Great Perfection.[92] The related Great Perfection lineages found in the addendum to Nyang-rel's *History*—one of which features Padampa, the Zhama brother/sister team, and Zhang Gönpawa—approximate the other lineages and associates all these figures.[93] Whatever the exact significance of such lists, in aggregate the reports suggest that Zhang did not, unlike Drokmi, represent himself as the purveyor of esoteric secrets newly arrived from India but chose instead to rely on a broader mix of traditions. An analogous accord between old and new is apparent in the activity of others from the period and can be seen in Khön Könchok Gyelpo's maintenance of the Vajrakīla and Yangdak Heruka systems of the old dynastic lineages, even while specializing in the newer dispensation.

FIGURE 19 The Lamdré lineage after Drokmi. Clockwise from upper left: Sékhar Chungwa, Zhang Gönpawa, Sönam Tsémo, and Sachen Kunga Nyingpo. *Sakyapa Monks*, circa 1500. Central Tibet, Sakyapa monastery. *Los Angeles County Museum of Art, Gift of the Ahmanson Foundation. Photograph ©2004 Museum Associates/LACMA*

The hagiographers loved describing Sachen's finding Lama Zhang in a rustic setting, clothed in rude dress and talking in a confused manner: a perfect Tibetan siddha. But Zhang Gönpawa was not impressed with Sachen, claiming that he himself knew only the Great Perfection. After initially sending him away, he discovered that he was Könchok Gyelpo's son; the hagiographers maintain that Zhang Gönpawa felt he had committed a fault by slighting a member of the Lamdré lineage. He consequently called Sachen back and, after ritually expiating his error, granted him the entire Lamdré, along with all the ancillary teachings and the eight subsidiary practices. It is noteworthy that this episode demonstrates the importance of clan identity, so that a slight on the son was regarded as a violation of vows to the father, an idea certainly not part of the Indian tantric vow structure.

Most sources agree that in all, the teaching from Zhang took four years, and it is likely that Sachen received from Zhang Gönpawa the name that sometimes appears in Lamdré lineage lists: Mikyö Dorjé (Skt.: Akṣobhyavajra).[94] The weighty restriction that Zhangtön imposed was that Sachen was not to take any notes during his studies or to explain the text to anyone for eighteen years. Like Zhang's initial statement to Sachen, Sachen was not even to admit that he knew the name "Lamdré" for that length of time. He also was told that if he should only practice, he would receive the accomplishment of the Great Seal. But if Sachen were to teach, then he would have an unlimited number of students, including three who would attain the highest accomplishment of the Great Seal, seven who would achieve the "patience" of a bodhisattva on the mundane path, and eighty who would achieve realization. In the spirit of his teacher's advice, Sachen vowed to recite the entire *Root Text of the *Mārgaphala* six or seven times, every day.

SACHEN AND THE ELEVEN COMMENTARIES

Since we primarily understand the obscure *Root Text of the *Mārgaphala* attributed to Virūpa and ostensibly translated by Gayādhara and Drokmi through the commentaries ascribed to Sachen, we must address the problem of its textual transmission. Despite extensive affirmations of earlier textual transmissions to others (Drom, Zhama), the hagiographical record maintains that the received text came through the agency of Sachen alone, a situation that presents some problems.[95] Because of the seal of eighteen years that Zhang Gönpawa imposed on Sachen, the lama from Sakya supposedly possessed no physical copies of this short work. Many Sakya sources state that when Zhang died, Sachen refused to accept his teacher's books and notes, insisting that they be

TABLE 5 Citations in Sachen's Commentaries

TIBETANS CITED	TEXT AND PAGE
Mugulung-pa / Drokmi	*Sédönma*, 175–76; *Gatengma*, 469
Jé Kharchungwa (= Sétön Kunrik)	*Gatengma*, 175, 267
Jé Gönpawa (= Zhang Gönpawa)	*Gatengma*, 175, 192–93, 267, 320, 331–32; *Sédönma*, 200 (Jé? 110); *Bendéma*, 86
Jomo Lhajéma	*Gatengma*, 195, 267
Gö Khukpa Lhétsé	*Gatengma*, 280
Géshé Gyatsa Jangyé	*Gatengma*, 374
INDIANS CITED	
Ḍombi	*Gatengma*, 186; *Sédönma*, 114
Saraha	*Gatengma*, 243; *Sédönma*, 140
Narotapa	*Gatengma*, 187, 203
Padmapa/Padmavajra	*Gatengma*, 267, 274; *Yumdönma* 74; *Zhuchéma*, 82
Maitrīpā	*Gatengma*, 267
Kuddālapāda	*Gatengma*, 285; *Sédönma*, 179
Indrabhūti	*Gatengma*, 296; *Sédönma*, 29
Nāgārjuna	*Sédönma*, 270
Vasubandhu (pejoratively)	*Gatengma*, 282; *Sédönma*, 179; *Lok-kyama*, 281
Dharmakīrti (pejoratively)	*Lok-kyama*, 281

interred in the stūpa with the other relics of the saint.[96] His son, Drakpa Gyeltsen, acknowledges that prior to his father Sachen, there seem to have been no surviving texts.[97]

Both the hagiographical episode and subsequent testimony, however, are called into question by the occasional quotations from previous authorities in Sachen's commentaries, including statements about the *Root Text of the *Mārga-phala*. While some citations may have eluded me, I have noted in table 5 the following authorities mentioned or quoted in the printed commentaries, omitting only references to Virūpa and Kāṇha:

Most of these persons were either the principal lineage holders of the Lamdré or the "authors" of the eight subsidiary practices that passed through Drokmi and that Sachen was said to have obtained from Zhang Gönpawa. A few are quite curious, since I am uncertain about the identity of Jomo Lhajéma (= Madam Physician) or Géshé Gyatsa Jangyé. The citation of Gö-lotsāwa Kukpa Lhétsé is not extraordinary, as he was the translator of materials in the Guhyasamāja tradition obtained by Sachen.

Most intriguing, however, are a series of quotations from obscure texts, especially *Zhang's Outline* (*rJe sa bcad pa*) and *Little Text* (*gZhung chung*) in the *Sédönma*.[98] Elsewhere, in a short panegyric to the master, Sachen alludes to Lamdré compositions possessed or composed by Zhang Gönpawa.[99] The exact significance of all this information is uncertain, but it appears that at one point Sachen had access to a body of earlier Lamdré materials, probably several short pieces and perhaps a long work, which included some instructions regarding the method of its textual interpretation. These works seemed to have been important to Sachen's understanding of the text. Whether or not he continued to have some material at his disposal—from the materials left behind after Zhang Gönpawa died, obtained from representatives of the Drom or Zhama lineages, or notes bequeathed by his father—it is clear that he used instructions obtained elsewhere to interpret the text as well. In particular, the *Gatengma*'s citations of the "authors" of the eight subsidiary practices indicate that these materials influenced Sachen's understanding the *Root Text of the *Mārgaphala.*

In any event, since the received *Root Text of the *Mārgaphala* is nearly incomprehensible without Sachen's commentaries, we should discuss their composition, identity, and order to the degree that we can. It was said that the reason for their individual composition was that after eighteen years, Sachen began to teach the text and the system. Amé-shep stated that this happened when Sachen was forty-nine, in 1141, although this is another instance in which he provides more precision than the early documents can support.[100] Sachen's first pupil was a lama from Kham, one Jangchub Sempah Aseng, another important Khampa lama in the early twelfth century.[101]

Not surprisingly, Aseng had difficulty understanding the *Root Text of the *Mārgaphala* and requested a summary of its contents, which Sachen produced in the form of an outline, now called the *Asengma.* Beyond that first work, Sachen was said to have produced ten more commentaries, eleven in all. Yet the exact identity of the commentaries is by no means secure, doubtless reflecting the somewhat haphazard nature of pre-Mongol Sakyapa record keeping. In his introduction and table of contents to the later compendium of Lamdré teachings, the *Yellow Book* (*Pod ser*), Drakpa Gyeltsen simply states that his father produced eleven commentaries but neglects to provide their titles, even though two commentaries are included in his work.[102] This omission, coupled with the swift elaboration of other commentaries on this obscure text throughout the twelfth and thirteenth centuries, presented later historians with something of a puzzle. To some degree the question was resolved through the consensual approval of the eighteenth-century printing of one version of the "eleven commentaries," but not because these reflect the only list of the eleven. Printed versions therefore include the following: *Nyagma*, *Asengma*, *Sédönma*, *Zhuchéma*, *Lok-kyama*, *Dagyelma*, *Bendéma*, *Gatengma*, *Yumdönma*, *A-uma*, and *Denbuma*, named after the individuals receiving them. Others have offered different identifications of both the receptors and the commentaries themselves, although the earliest commentators simply affirm that there were eleven commentaries and emphasize the importance of the *Nyagma*.[103]

The authorities consistently maintain that their order of composition is problematic—as we might expect for such an uncertain body of work—but that they have some sense of the beginning and the end. They declare that the *Asengma* was the earliest composed and that the *Nyagma* was the final commentary. Some authorities believe the *Gatengma* to have been composed immediately after the *Asengma*, but the order for the rest remains uncertain.[104] Unfortunately, the similarity of style of all the commentaries inhibits our understanding of possible ways of their development. Nevertheless, there is at least one place where some modification of the message has occurred over time: the definitions of the meaning of "Lamdré" itself. According to later scholars, eleven such definitions are offered in the introductory sections of each text, in which the title is explained. The following list shows how these definitions were understood:[105]

1. Instruction in which the path simultaneously includes the fruit (*lam 'bras bu dang bcas pa'i gdam ngag*).

2. Instruction in which the fruit simultaneously includes the path (*'bras bu lam dang bcas pa'i gdams ngag*).

3. Instruction in which knowing a single element will bring about knowing every element (*gcig shes pas mang po shes par 'gyur ba'i gdams ngag*).

4. Instruction in which difficult experiences are taken as qualities of contemplation (*skyon yon tan du bslang ba'i gdams ngag*).

5. Instruction in which obstacles are taken as siddhi (*bar chad dngos grub tu len pa'i gdams ngag*).

6. Instruction in which hindrances to contemplation are clarified through recognizing [them as arising from] concentration (*ting nge 'dzin ngo shes pas bsam gtan gyi gegs sel ba'i gdams ngag*).

7. Instruction in which demonic hindrances are clarified by recognizing obstacles [as the path itself] (*bar chad ngo shes pas bdud kyi gegs sel ba'i gdams ngag*).

8. Instruction that discloses taking obstacles as siddhi as well as admonishes

TABLE 6 Lamdré Definitions in Sachen's Commentaries

COMMENTARY	ORDER	MISSING
Nyagma (p. 22)	1, 2, 3, 6, 7, 4, 5, 10	8, 9, 11
Sédönma (pp. 21–24)	1, 2, 3, 4, 5, 10, 6, 7, 9	8, 11
Zhuchéma (pp. 5–6)	1, 2, 3, 8, 6, 7, 9, 11, 10	4, 5
Lok-kyama (pp. 195–97)	1, 2, 3, 10, 9, 11, 7, 6, 4, 5	8
Dagyelma (pp. 400–401)	1, 2, 3, 4, 5, 10, 6, 7, 9, 11	8
Bendéma (pp. 4–5)	1, 2, 3, 9, 4, 5, 6, 7, 10, 11	8
Gatengma (pp. 156–57)	1, 3, 4, 5, 10, 11	2, 6, 7, 8, 9
Yumdönma (pp. 5–6)	1, 2, 3, 4, 5, 10	6, 7, 8, 9, 11
A-uma (pp. 165–66)	1, 2, 3, 10, 4, 5	6, 7, 8, 9, 11
Denbuma (p. 298)	1, 2, 3, 4, 10 (?9)	5, 6, 7, 8, 11

taking faults as qualities (*skyon yon tan tu bslang shes shing bar chad dngos grub tu len shes pa'i gdams ngag*).

9. Instruction that unerringly informs the reality of the *Tripiṭaka* (*sde snod gsum gyi de kho na nyid phyin ci ma log par shes pa'i gdams ngag*).

10. Instruction like a nectar that transforms things into gold (*rasāyana*) (*gser 'gyur gyi rtsi lta bu'i gdams ngag*).

11. Instruction in which the short text is like the wish-granting gem (*cintāmaṇi*) (*gzhung chung yid bzhin gyi nor bu lta bu'i gdams ngag*).

Interestingly, not one of the commentaries ascribed to Sachen in the modern printing takes into account all eleven definitions. In a sense, this should not be surprising, since there is a degree of redundancy built into the list. Numbers 1 and 2 imply each other, with the subject and predicate simply reversed. Numbers 4 and 5 are combined into number 8, with little addition, which is one of the reasons that number 8 is the item least frequently encountered in any commentary. Finally, numbers 6 and 7 are almost identical. The order and distribution of these eleven explanations of the title Lamdré is of interest in trying to understand commentarial development, since there is some variation. The results—except for the *Asengma*, which is too short to include other than the title—are summarized in table 6.

It must be emphasized that there is no numbering in the texts, even though these eleven definitions seem to constitute a received list. In addition, a twelfth member found its way into three commentaries: Instruction in which the root

[text] is like a *vajra* word (*vajrapada*) (*rtsa ba rdo rje'i tshig lta bu'i gdams ngag*). This item is clearly an attempt to include the idea that the text is an "adamantine phrase" text—a designation not found in the work itself—and this last interpretation is found in variations in the *Zhuchéma*, the *Lok-kyama*, and the *Dagyelma*. Overall, the shorter commentaries tend to exclude items, although this is not the case for the *Nyagma*, which is one of the shortest.

In both this list and its text, the *Gatengma* is probably the most curious, for some of its properties suggest that its traditional placement as the first of the long commentaries is correct. The *Gatengma* references previous authorities far more often than any other commentary, including the *Sédönma*, although the *Sédönma* is longer than the *Gatengma*. The *Gatengma* has many definitions absent and arranges them in a curious way compared with the other long commentaries. It is the least classical and the most colloquial in style, perhaps because Sachen at this point had not yet mastered the felicitous classical presentation of the later commentaries or because of the colloquial way in which the Lamdré text was presented to him by Zhang Gönpawa, or because of the social circumstances surrounding the *Gatengma*'s composition. I suspect all three were factors at work. Finally, the *Gatengma* indicates that the author is still trying to find his way through the material, whereas other commentaries—notably the *Sédönma*, the *Bendéma*, and the *Nyagma*—seem to pursue their agendas more confidently.

In this regard, Stearns proposed that because of the close identity of the *Gatengma* with the Lamdré text passed down by Pagmo Drupa, the *Gatengma* must be the work of Pagmo Drupa.[106] This is a very curious conclusion and presumes that there were two different texts at one time, one of which (Sachen's) must have been lost, and have been replaced by the Kagyüpa work. A more economical conclusion is simple: as an early disciple of Sachen's, Pagmo Drupa simply copied out the *Gatengma* and included it in his teaching materials, which were naturally assumed by Pagmo Drupa's disciples to be their master's own works. The thirteenth-century hagiography of Pagmo Drupa suggests exactly this idea, that Pagmo Drupa's *Textual Treasury of Lamdré* (*Lam 'bras dpe mdzod ma*) was actually given to him by Sachen.[107] Analogous misidentifications of authorship have occurred before, especially with highly esoteric texts.

Although the authenticity of the *Bendéma* has been questioned, it should be kept in mind that there also are problems with the *Sédönma*. It was certainly pieced together from at least four large sections, and the tradition maintains that the many pieces were unified and edited by a close disciple of Sachen, Géshé Nyen Pül-jungwa, who looked after Sakya after Sachen passed away.[108] In a different direction, the overall confidence in the *Nyagma* is further augmented by its completeness, and over the years I have frequently noticed that the most important points found in the other commentaries are clearly and succinctly stated in the *Nyagma*. The net result is that the traditional affirmations concerning the nature of the texts appear reasonable, for the *Gatengma* demonstrates the uncertainty we would expect of an initial work, whereas the *Nyagma* shows an unmistakable sureness, and the *Sédönma* reveals the greatest detail of all the works. It is little wonder that the *Nyagma* and the *Sédönma* have remained popular to the present, even though I find the *Gatengma* the most intriguing as a document of emerging understanding.

Sachen's strategy in the commentaries is to unpack the practices either explicit or implied in the Lamdré text. The best example of this is the astounding attention his commentaries pay to an apparently innocuous sentence but one that became overwhelmingly important to the Lamdré tradition. In the *Root Text of the *Mārgaphala*, I.B.2.b. simply states, "The teaching by means of the four quinaries on the path, the developing stage, etc." (*lam du bskyed rim stsogs lnga pa bzhis bstan*). This sentence is extraordinarily represented in all the commentaries, in that the entire esoteric path is broken down into the four consecrations, the meditative path authorized by the consecrations, the perspective (understanding) of reality revealed during each consecration, the viewpoint that is to be accomplished during this meditative path, the specific experience or meditation at the time of death for one doing each of the practices, and the final fruit expected from each consecration. Table 7 shows the breakdown.

This table should communicate the emphasis that the Lamdré masters placed on the entire consecration (*abhiṣeka*) ceremonial system, since they ordered all other practices and procedures in reference to one or another of the consecrations. While most esoteric systems place importance on the correct consecration, it is simply the ripening entrance (*smin*) preceding the actual business of the esoteric path that is the process of liberation (*sgrol*). The Lamdré writers certainly recognize this ordering, but they push its employment beyond that found elsewhere, and I know of no other esoteric system that has so thoroughly organized all its practices according to the structures of the consecrations. The consecrations not only are taken at the advent of entrance into the esoteric path but also are visualized daily in the course of its practice, and the fruits of the path are conceived as the fruitional consecrations, so that consecration becomes the central metaphor for the system.

This grand arrangement of twenty different categories, sometimes expanded to twenty-four with the addition of experiences in the intermediate state (*antarābhava*), illustrates important aspects of the tradition.[109] Indeed, one of the more distinctive traits of Lamdré is its continued movement toward both complexity and secrecy, so that the meditations just summarized become the topic of entire treatises in the later history of the Sakyapa order. This trajecto-

TABLE 7 The Four Quinaries of the Lamdré Path

CONSECRATION: *DBANG*	VASE	SECRET	INSIGHT-GNOSIS	FOURTH
Path: *lam*	Formal system of the generation process	Self-consecration practice of the completion process	*Maṇḍala-cakra* practice of the completion process	*Vajra*-wave practice of the completion process
Perspective: *lta-ba*	Three realities: appearance, emptiness, and identity	Four self-born knowledges	Four ascending natural joys	Four descending joys of the reality of the purity of all phenomena
Accomplishment: *grub-mtha'*	Indivisibility of *saṁsāra* and *nirvāṇa*	Completion without contamination	Lesser spread of bliss and emptiness	Greater spread of bliss and emptiness
Experience at death: *'da'-ka-ma*	Transference to a superior state	Clear light	Arrival of Vajrasattva at the moment of death	Transference by means of the *Mahāmudrā*
Fruit: *'bras-bu*	*Nirmāṇakāya*	*Sambhogakāya*	*Dharmakāya*	*Svābhāvikakāya*

ry toward both complexity and the requisite clarity needed to comprehend such complexity—after all, the system must be comprehended by mere mortals who have yet to achieve supernormal powers—collided with the intractable obscurity of the *Root Text of the *Mārgaphala.*

As a consequence, the material in this section (I.B.2.b), which had already achieved the position of constituting a major part of every commentary on the basic text (it takes up most of the I.B space represented in the commentaries outlined in appendix 3), from the fifteenth century onward became the subject of a new series of manuals for the teaching and study of the esoteric tradition. These new manuals were organized around the idea of the triple continuity found in I.B—ground, path, and fruit, an idea that had already stimulated the composition of such extraordinary treatises as Drakpa Gyeltsen's *Jeweled Tree for the Practice of Tantra* (*rGyud kyi mngon par rtogs pa rin po che'i ljon shing*)—and contained in its path section the schema for the twenty items, as shown in table 7. The consequences of this new literary direction were two: First, the Lamdré masters appear to have abandoned the practice of using commentaries on the chaotic text of the *Root Text of the *Mārgaphala* as the vehicle for basic teaching and instruction on esoteric practice, preferring the new, more straightforward manuals on the twenty elements organized into the four consecrations. Second, scholars emphasized the composition of works on either the triple continuity or the specific problems of the path and generally neglected to produce new commentaries on the *Root Text of the *Mārgaphala.* Eventually the text and earlier commentaries on the *Root Text of the *Mārgaphala* began to assume the position of terra incognita, and Khyentsé Wangchuk noted that by the sixteenth century the ritual authorizations of only the *Nyagma*, the *Asengma*, and the *Sédönma* were still available.[110] Amé-shep made a similar statement in 1621, adding that the *Nyagma* was the only text really studied.[111]

SACHEN'S OTHER LITERARY LEGACY

Although Sachen Kunga Nyingpo wrote many interesting works, it is no exaggeration to say that his main emphasis was on his commentaries for the *Root Text of the *Mārgaphala.* This fact is obscured by the printing of Sachen's works in several separate venues—the volumes of Lamdré commentaries, the texts by him collected in the *Collected Works of Sakya Masters* (*Sa skya bka' 'bum*), its recently published supplement, and the specific texts attributed to Sachen in the two Lamdré compendia, the *Yellow Book* (*Pod ser*) and the *Little Red Book* (*Pusti dmar chung*). Even taking into account the disputed nature of some of the materials, the total of Sachen's Lamdré related texts is roughly 60 to 65 percent of his received oeuvre, or about four and a half good-size Tibetan volumes. In a sense, though, this dramatic emphasis is somewhat illusory, for as already indicated, Sachen's multiple commentaries on the same text show a marked redundancy, so that some works appear mostly repetitions of well-established themes.

Sachen's several short texts expanding on or explaining sections of the *Root Text of the *Mārgaphala* were doubtless bundled together sometime during his life and inherited by Drakpa Gyeltsen as an initial compendium of materials. Chapter 9 discusses Drakpa Gyeltsen's reformulation of this material into a full-blown Lamdré corpus, but it depends on Sachen's having composed the twenty-four works listed in Drakpa Gyeltsen's *Contents* (*gLegs bam kyi dkar chags*).[112] Two have already been mentioned: the *Asengma* and the *Nyagma*. Drakpa Gyeltsen specifically names only the former, but he also states that another unnamed commentary by Sachen was used, apparently the *Nyagma*.

Beyond the commentaries, we have three groupings of texts. The first consists of a series of thirteen short (sometimes very short) notes explaining obscure points in the *Root Text of the *Mārgaphala* or practical points in its application.[113] This first group begins with a discussion of visualizing the body as a maṇḍala, in the somewhat unusual manner employed by the Lamdré: The physical attributes of the body were envisioned as the physical attributes of the maṇḍala palace, with the skin becoming both the protective globe and part of the palace itself.[114] Although this description is rare in the later scriptures of esoteric Buddhism, it is by no means unique to the Lamdré, yet this kind of maṇḍala structure became a point of contention between the Sakyapa and the fifteenth-century Géluk author Khedrupjé.[115] Six works are dedicated to aspects of the four consecrations. In these Sachen articulates the "point of death instructions" given during the vase consecration, the details of contemplation on the four internal centers conferred with the secret consecration, the characteristics of an appropriate consort employed during the insight-gnosis consecration, and the point of death instructions for the fourth consecration, connecting many of these together in his exegesis.[116]

Other works in this first group discuss aspects of the advanced consecrations. One is on a difficult phrase in *Root Text of the *Mārgaphala* III.B, "sealed within the four cakras," and another is on the eight forms of dominion accomplished with success in the fourth consecration.[117] Since the teaching on the intermediate state did not completely fit the "four quinaries" schematism, as we have seen, Sachen devoted a text to its elaboration.[118] Likewise, the "five forms of interdependent origination" are the topic of *Root Text of the *Mārgaphala* I.F but remain obscure. Accordingly, Sachen devoted a note to an exegesis of the material.[119] This first group also contains two texts concerned with purification, a fire sacrifice rite and an instruction on the correct means for reciting the hundred-syllable mantra of Vajrasattva/Vajraheruka, done differently than in most other traditions.[120] Finally, the short notes have two more theoretical works, one explaining the all-important fourteen letters in the "bhaga maṇḍala" in the genital region and the other discussing the esoteric moments in the final path during the transition between the twelve-and-a half and the thirteenth stages of the path.[121] The thirteenth stage, the Sakyapa ideal of the final stage of Vajradhara, also was criticized by fifteenth-century opponents of the Sakyapa.[122]

The second group of texts supports Sachen's emphasis on purification and is made up of three slightly longer works on practices for the alleviation of certain psychophysical obstacles.[123] These are followed by two short works on the "deep path, middling path, and abbreviated path" (IV.B) according to standard categories.[124] Finally, there are a group of more disparate works and somewhat uncertain authorship from the colophons. Nonetheless, most of the works show Sachen's ability, and Drakpa Gyeltsen divides them into categories: the four great explanatory texts (*gzhung shing chen po bzhi*, at least one by Drakpa Gyeltsen himself) and the five teachings that precipitate realization (*rtogs pa bskyed pa'i chos lnga*).[125] There is also a peculiar attempt at yogic hermeneutics, trying to align the twelve acts of the Buddha with moments of yogic experience so that Sachen espouses a hagiography of internal yogic components.[126]

Sachen's synthesis of Buddhist narrative and yogic experience reveals another of the tensions evident in the institutional and doctrinal development of the early Khön teachers. If the Lamdré is increasingly esoteric and complex, how can the value systems of nonduality and a holistic integration of all elements of reality into the system be explained? Three texts included in this section of the *Yellow Book* address this issue along broad lines and actually may be considered with another of Sachen's compositions that were not specifically included in the Lamdré. One work, the *Intersection of the Path* (*Lam bsre ba*), considers the issue of the second of the Lamdré definitions: instruction in which the fruit simultaneously includes the path.[127] Here Sachen shows how the Lamdré tries to integrate different benefits experienced into the instructions associated with the path and the complex series of items formally associated with each of the path schematisms: the worldly/transworldly paths, the five paths of the Mahāyāna, the thirteen levels of the bodhisattva, the different consecrations, the bodies of the Buddha, and so forth. In this, Sachen tried to bring clarity to the bewildering mass of simultaneously operating structures, which are found throughout the *Root Text of the *Mārgaphala*, but the text really constitutes notes about their relations rather than an exhaustive analysis.

Apparently, teaching the practical structure of this complex system became difficult, and so Sachen produced his work on Lamdré pedagogical method, the *Text Providing the Arrangement Exactly According to the* [*Lamdré*] *Book and the Disciple's Personality* (*Gang zag gzhung ji lta ba bzhin du dkri ba'i gzhung shing*).[128] This work proved to be extraordinarily influential and gives us a hazy window into how Sachen taught the *Root Text of the *Mārgaphala*. The *Text Providing Arrangement* was evidently a desideratum, for its composition was requested by one of Sachen's disciples, Kartön José Chakyi Dorjé from Lhodrak. It suggests that Lamdré masters had two strategies, according to whether an individual needed the most basic Buddhist perspective or was capable of handling the more advanced Vajrayāna consecrations, instructions, and meditations, an arrangement analogous to that covered in Gampopa's employment of the "simultaneous" or "gradual" paths. This seems to have been Sachen's standard method of teaching the Lamdré: the triple appearance for teaching fundamental Buddhism and the triple continuity for teaching the esoteric path. For a student capable of the esoteric path, the text unfolds the triple continuity: the ground, path, and goal according to the Vajrayāna. The ground provides a philosophical and psychological analysis of the individual, the world, and the inherent nature of awakening. The path briefly formulates the "four quinaries" material of I.B.2.b section of the *Root Text of the *Mārgaphala*, and the goal articulates the final nature of awakening in the thirteenth level of Vajradhara, the primal Buddha.

If the *Text Providing the Arrangement Exactly According to the* [*Lamdré*] *Book and the Disciple's Personality* covered the practical relationship between the exoteric and esoteric forms of Buddhist practice, two of Sachen's other works explored the theory behind the differences between them. His *Entry into and Departure Along the Path* (*Lam 'jug dang ldog pa*) is part of a broader conversation between advocates of the fundamental Mahāyānist method of perfections and proponents of the Vajrayāna.[129] Not everyone in eleventh- and twelfth-century Central Tibet was thrilled at the seeming victory of esoteric Buddhism, and some strong voices were raised in opposition to the system. In this very short work, Sachen broaches the questions of the exact position of the esoteric system on the stages of the path and describes a rough relationship between the two approaches to Buddhism by pointing out that the esoteric system requires the empty perspective of the exoteric perfections, especially during the early stages of practice.

I believe that this work—and the discussions throughout Ü-Tsang that precipitated it—was actually a prelude to the composition of another important contribution: Sachen's *Short General Principles of the Tantric Canon* (*rGyud sde spyi'i rnam bzhag chung ngu*).[130] This may be the earliest surviving work of its kind, although authors from the eighth-century Buddhaguhya onward discussed such questions in the lengthy introductions to their commentaries on specific tantras.[131] Gö-lotsāwa Kukpa Lhétsé had reputedly written a work on this same topic, and Sachen probably followed his organization. In his work, Sachen pursues the same problem addressed in his *Entry into and Departure Along the Path*, but in a much more formal manner: What are the fundamental differences between the two vehicles (Mahāyāna and Vajrayāna) in terms of their starting positions, their paths, and their goals? In the background, we can see the intellectual problem being pursued throughout Tibet at this time: If these two vehicles are fundamentally different in all these areas, by what right do they both claim the designation of Buddhist? Or if they both are Buddhist, what does this say about the Buddha himself?

Sachen's answer to these questions in the *Short General Principles of the Tantric Canon* affirms the unity of their respective goals—absolute awakening—while identifying the psychological and practical differences between these systems' respective adherents. The Mahāyānist adherent rejects the basic stuff of life, so that desire for the objects of the senses is restricted and they are considered poisonous, like the leaves of poisonous plants. By accumulating resources of merit and knowledge, the Mahāyānist practices the six or ten perfections and is most fundamentally concerned with correctly applying himself to restraint of the senses in ordinary existence, so that the method of Perfections is designated the "causal" vehicle, in view of the long time it takes someone to pass through the foundational stages before obtaining awakening. Conversely, the mantrin employs desire for the objects of the senses, not rejecting the ground of the human condition, but cultivating it correctly. Consequently, he uses the secret spells to advance quickly to the citadel of awakening, the thirteenth stage of the path, that of Vajradhara. Because the fruit is inherent in the path, it is called the "resultant" vehicle. Sachen used this opportunity to pursue the arrangement of the esoteric scriptures and discuss the fourfold category system that became the favorite of some Indian exegetes and virtually all Tibetans.[132]

THE VIRŪPA VISIONS AND THE KHÖN SHORT TRANSMISSION

In the fifteenth-century Ngorpa history of the Lamdré, the author takes great pride in the visionary revelations of the siddha Virūpa to Sachen, maintaining that these revelations constituted the defining element demonstrating the superiority of the Khön clan system of Lamdré over the other lineages, especially over the Drom, the Zhama, and later related systems.[133] The final Virūpa revelation was the culmination, we are told, of a series of visions that Sachen received after a very difficult sequence of events and resulted in his obtaining certain instructions that other Lamdré teachers did not. The visions thus constituted the Short Transmission (*nye brgyud*), in which Sachen had direct access to the great siddha, who in turn had received the *Root Text of the *Mārgaphala* from Nairātmyā, so Sachen was only one degree removed from the feminine reflex of the Primal Buddha Vajradhara. Nonetheless, the documents and ideas that support and inform this episode are themselves quite unusual and are probably apocryphal. They speak of the influence of the treasure literature on the Sakyapa tradition during the mid-thirteenth to fifteenth century and of the determination to demonstrate the superiority of the Khön system over other lineages of Lamdré. Although the mid-thirteenth-century frame falls outside the chronological parameters of this study, its claims are about the visionary and textual legacy of Sachen.

The first historically identifiable reference is found in Martön's annals, probably produced in the second quarter of the thirteenth century.[134] Martön summarizes the episode, stating that after Lama Mel died and before Zhang Gönpawa's prohibition had expired, Sachen went to Barpuk-rong and was stricken with a very serious disease (*snyung nad drag po*), which caused him to forget all his teachings. Returning to Sakya he prayed to Jé Gönpawa and had visions of him and subsequently of Virūpa, who transmitted to Sachen the entire seventy-two *tantra piṭakas*, a secret explanation of the cakras in the fourth consecration (*lam sbas bshad*), a teaching about the ten accomplishments, and Virūpa's exegesis and rituals of the *Vajravidaraṇa-dhāraṇī*. Martön declares that the incident was hidden and that the full story was to be found elsewhere, and he also maintains that everything included in his annals had been approved by Sakya Paṇḍita.[135]

We do not know exactly to what Martön was referring by "elsewhere," but the fifteenth-century *Little Red Book* (*Pusti dmar chung*) of the fourth abbot of Ngor Monastery in Tsang, Kunga Wangchuk (1424–78), included the text purported to be a letter by Drakpa Gyeltsen to Kyokpo Gateng (of the *Gatengma*), an epithet descriptive of Gateng's lameness.[136] The letter says that at the age of seventeen, Drakpa Gyeltsen had gone to Gungtang, where he met Lobpön Joden Rong-gom, who remarked, "There seems to be a story of your father encountering Virūpa—haven't you heard of it?" Drakpa Gyeltsen begged him for more, but Joden Rong-gom simply said that he had heard about this when he met a person whose mind was disturbed (*yid yengs pa*) and knew no details. Instead, he referred Drakpa Gyeltsen to Géshé Nyen Pül-jungwa, who had looked after Sakya following Sachen's death, because Pül-jungwa had said he would not tell Joden Rong-gom the story but only would reveal it directly to Drakpa Gyeltsen. Drakpa Gyeltsen returned to Sakya, and Pül-jungwa revealed that Sachen once had gone to Gungtang, where he was stricken with a poisonous illness (*dug nad*) that caused him to lose his memory. He was ill for a month, but the effects lasted for three years. Even when others heard something and remembered it, Sachen could not. He could neither recall letters nor have any knowledge of his friends. Having thought that even if he went to India there would be no help, he prayed to Jé Gönpawa, who came to him in a dream and bestowed on him instructions. Praying with greater vigor, Virūpa came to him in a dream and again taught to him all the teachings.

Over time, the contents of the teaching increase, and the dates become more precise. By the time of Lama Dampa's 1344 annals contained in his *Black Book* (*Pod nag*), the list had become rather long.[137] Moreover, gathered in the collected works of Sakya Paṇḍita are several texts that purport to be many of these teachings, along with a further elaboration of the story by an anonymous author. Collectively, these several texts seem to be designated as the *Special Teaching of Sakya Paṇḍita* (*Sa skya paṇḍi ta'i khyad par gyi gdams pa*) or the *Extraordinary Instruction of Sakya Paṇḍita* (*Sa skya paṇḍi ta'i thun mong ma yin pa'i gdams ngag*).[138] Besides the hagiographical episode, two miraculous events are related, once when Sachen was seen in two places at the same time, and at the moment of his death, when he was seen in four places at once; still later writers maintain that Sachen was seen in six places at once.[139] As an addendum, the anonymous conclusion to Sachen's homage to Virūpa—the homage translated in chapter 1—proposes that the panegyric was composed by Sachen when Virūpa appeared before him.[140] Amé-shep concluded that by 1629 there were two differing traditions on dates for the event: Some writers claim it happened in 1135 when Sachen was forty-three, while others specify 1138, when he was forty-six.[141]

We might assess these records first in regard to style, second in regard to their conformity to what we know elsewhere from the available documents, and finally in regard to the environment of the period. The "letter" is a good place to start, since Drakpa Gyeltsen's materials are available and include several of his letters. Even allowing for the idea that Drakpa Gyeltsen was supposedly young when the letter was written, almost everything about this letter appears difficult to accept as veridical. The style is quite different from Drakpa Gyeltsen's known style, with the uncharacteristic use of the first person (*nga*, which sounds socially illiterate here), whereas his other works almost invariably use the literary humble forms (e.g., *kho bo*) or the more informal I (*bdag*).[142] The letter is also signed "the Great Lord" (Jétsün chenpo), a most unusual way of signing, especially as Drakpa Gyeltsen characteristically employed phrases like "the lay practitioner of the Shākya religion, a yogin of the highest vehicle, Drakpa Gyeltsen" (*Shākya'i dge bsnyen theg pa mchog gi rnal 'byor pa Grags pa rgyal mtshan*).

Moreover, there seems to be no other indication in the works of either Drakpa Gyeltsen or his older brother, Sönam Tsémo, that such an event happened, even though Sönam Tsémo would have been twenty-two when Drakpa Gyeltsen was seventeen, and they certainly would have shared the news of such a momentous event. Both the brothers had their entire literary careers ahead of them, and the vision narrative would surely have appeared in their other works as well. Finally, the episode reflects exactly the kind of circumstances that Drakpa Gyeltsen warns his readers against in his *Contents* to the *Yellow Book.* There he states that one reason for his putting together a list of Sachen's Lamdré materials is that he had seen works attributed to his father that the great lama never wrote.[143] When we go through the record before us, it is hard not to conclude that these later attributions of teachings and their associated story of visionary revelations were the kinds of expansions of the fundamental Sachen corpus that Drakpa Gyeltsen mentioned. The attempt to include these materials in the collections of Sakya Paṇḍita appears similar: the appropriation of Sachen's, Drakpa Gyeltsen's, and Sakya Paṇḍita's identities in service of Sakyapa apocryphal literature.

This is not to say that no visionary events or miracles are recorded in Sachen's life, and the vision of Mañjuśrī played an important part in his young career. Furthermore, after acknowledging the Mañjuśrī vision, Drakpa Gyeltsen also indicates that there were two other miraculous and convincing stories but that the time was not ripe for their expression.[144] While there is no record in Drakpa Gyeltsen's authentic works of a Virūpa vision leading to the Short Transmission, Drakpa Gyeltsen does record other visions, including one with Virūpa:

> Once, when you were teaching the Lamdré,
> In the center of the Offering Assembly, poised in the sky,
> Mañjuśrī, Virūpa and Avalokiteśvara, the three, revealed themselves.
> Homage to you who have become the pure appearance of nineteen [divinities].[145]

It is precisely this sense of a ritual visualization that the episode of the Short Transmission ultimately assumes. According to later texts, Sachen received the manifestation of the great lord of yogins (Virūpa) himself, who appeared as if with a white curtain behind him, his vast form obscuring all of southern Tibet between Nepal and Mön.[146] His hands were in the posture of preaching the Dharma. To his right was Kāṇha, holding a horn trumpet and a skull of nectar; to his left was Gayādhara, dressed in floating white cloth, holding his vajra and bell to his heart; behind him was Kuddālapāda, holding an umbrella; in front was Binasa, who was being offered nectar by a Śabara before him. Their minds were all in deep contemplation and, from their collective trance, were issuing words of praise like "A-la-la!"

The normative collection and codification process probably had something to do with the eventual coalescence of the literature on this apocryphal vision. Generally floating around meditation masters are several teachings that are not precisely formulated. Their lectures or instructions pass from word of mouth to word of mouth and are eventually compiled into collections. Such compilations are sometimes granted authority through a mythology of revelation, while at other times they do not enlist such hagiographical apparatus. Two such collections were evidently important to the evolving mythology of the Short Transmission. The first was a collection of forty-nine short instructions ascribed to Sachen himself, an ascription that is doubtless correct in most aspects. Entitled the *Rosary of Gems, the Precious Collection of Directions of Sakya* (*dPal sa skya pa'i man ngag gces btus pa rin po che'i phreng ba*), the work puts together many of the same kinds of materials attributed to the vision: visualizations of Virūpa as the preeminent teacher, an emphasis on protective rites, confession texts, specific instructions on psychic heat, and so forth. Some are attributed to the Paṇḍita Vajrāsana, who worked with Bari-lotsāwa, while others are from various Nepalese or other individuals who worked in the eleventh and twelfth centuries. Contributing to the overall sense of genuineness is the fact that the style and phraseology of the collection are sometimes very close to that found in the commentaries on the *Root Text of the *Mārgaphala* attributed to Sachen.[147] The authenticity of this collection is further verified by its reformulation by Drakpa Gyeltsen, who put together his own *Precious Collection of Mahāmudrā Instructions* (*Phyag rgya chen po gces pa btus pa'i man ngag*).[148]

Two places in the *Rosary of Gems*, however, contain much later intrusions, since Sakya Paṇḍita's name is found in one lineage list in the compilation, and the learned monk was cited as the author of another work, a short text on alchemy (*bcud len*).[149] Sakya Paṇḍita's appearance in his grandfather's *Rosary of Gems* is illuminating, because some of the works (or instructions) attributed to the Virūpa vision are otherwise known as the "special teaching of Sakya Paṇḍita." The second collection of meditative texts that appears influential in the formation of the mythology of the Short Transmission is the "special teaching of Sakya Paṇḍita," most of which is probably by Sakya Paṇḍita but not identified as associated with a Virūpa revelation. Sakya Paṇḍita's lengthy work on *guruyoga*, one of the topics ostensibly transmitted by Virūpa to Sachen, indicates that this special teaching of the *guruyoga* in the Lamdré was taught in an extremely secret manner, which is similar to language found in the *Root Text of the *Mārgaphala* itself.[150] Elsewhere, in his explanation of the fundamental mantra of Hevajra, the Aṣṭa—another of the Virūpa Short Transmission topics—Sakya Paṇḍita says that this teaching was part of the instructions coming from Sachen (and indeed, Sachen has one such instruction in the *Rosary of Gems*) and that it was ultimately derived from Virūpa.[151] Such mild affirmations of lineal authenticity are historically far from the visionary episode yet are emotionally close for those attempting to formulate a grand narrative that synthesizes traditional visions, floating texts, and the affirmation that the lamas of the tradition are all Vajradhara himself, anyway.

Why would such an apocryphal story occur in this conservative Tibetan Buddhist lineage? The answer is that Buddhist institutional systems have frequently used such artifices for the development and authentication of new practices. Indeed, the eight subsidiary practices used much the same process, so that a later text based on earlier teachings was ascribed to the earlier teacher. Likewise, twelfth-century Central Tibet was a period remarkable for the efflorescence of the Lamdré, with many different traditions—the Zhama, the Drom, the Phagmo Drupa—either spreading through southern Tibet or splitting off from the Sakya. The Drom lineage founder, Drom Depa Tönchung, was said to have revealed Terma in Samyé, and Zhama Machik was associated with Padampa's revelations through her brother. This also was a period of treasure literature efflorescence, through the stimulus provided by Nyang-rel, Guru Chö-wang, and many others. Similarly, most Sarma denominations became involved in revealed literature in several guises. The founder of the Drukpa Kagyüpa, Tsangpa Gyaré (1161–1211), discovered a treasure in 1189 that was said to be written by Nāropā and hidden by Marpa.[152] Apocryphal literature attributed to Dromtön and Atiśa was being developed by the Kadampa in the thirteenth century, and the *Pillar Testament* was being attributed to the Bengali savant.[153] Visions of siddhas became a valuable claim to any lineage, and a later Lamdré scholar, Chagen Wangchuk Gyeltsen, made his Virūpa vision an important addition to his statement of lineal authenticity.[154]

In all likelihood, then, the disciples of Sakya Paṇḍita began to make the very close association between Sakya Paṇḍita and Sachen Kunga Nyingpo, providing a mythology of revelation to the teachings conferred by the great teacher(s) of Sakya Monastery. This connection was further fueled by the series of Virūpa dreams and visions that were apparently much in the psychic life of Drakpa Gyeltsen, Sachen's son and Sakya Paṇḍita's uncle and teacher. These dreams and visions eventually became denoted the Very Short Transmission (*shin tu nye brgyud*), and we examine its content and context in the following chapter. The purpose of such mythologies was simply to collapse the distance between Virūpa, Sachen, and Drakpa Gyeltsen, so that Sakya Paṇḍita would be but a few degrees removed from the Buddha Vajradhara himself. Long before, the Kagyüpa used a similar tactic to collapse the distance between Marpa and Nāropā. The Virūpa narrative also demonstrated the superiority of the Khön clan's Lamdré to other lineages and verified that if other Sarma and Nyingma systems had visionary revelations, certainly the Khön did as well. In these representations they were successful, for all Lamdré annalists from the thirteenth century onward expand and elaborate on the Short Transmission visionary systems.

CONCLUSION: TIBETANS REFORMULATE THEIR RELIGION

The twelfth century stands as the watershed in Tibetan religion, as the time when Central Tibetans confidently established their independent perspective on the architecture of the Buddhist path. The Terma literature of the previous century had advanced the process, but in the twelfth century the Tibetans mythically proposed Tibet as an independent ground for the Buddhas' activities, where the exalted bodhisattvas have incarnated as the great emperors of the royal dynasty. They began to grapple seriously with the consequences of a divided Buddhist path, attempting to integrate the Mahāyāna and the Vajrayāna in a manner unforeseen by Indians, who were much more comfortable with a soteriological stratigraphy based on the analogies offered by caste. Consequently, new ideas about epistemology, philosophy (tantric and nontantric), and doctrine marked the first half of this century. Central Tibetans also began to generate their own literature on meditation and ritual in an accelerating manner, domesticating many of the siddha materials through the time-honored process of exegesis and interpretation.

Finally, the twelfth century was the time when the organization of Tibetan social life offered by the clan structure throughout Central Tibet became a reality for most of the monastic orders and great denominations that prospered during the century. Monasteries were bequeathed to relatives, and the esoteric Dharma became understood as part of the bequest. This was true to such an extent, that an insult to a relative or descendant of a great lama became understood as a insult to the lama himself and therefore a serious breach of the esoteric vows, a formulation not seen in India and fundamentally inspired by Tibetan clan etiquette. The esoteric system, with its paradigms of kingship and filial relations (vajra-brothers and sisters), was extended to generations of the family, to vajra-grandsons, as it were. The implications for Tibetan familial models being extended to the tantric system also meant that women were given a place at the tantric feast as equals, in a manner unseen south of the Himalayas. Women in Tibet enjoyed authority generally unavailable to their sisters in India, and Zhama Machik's dismissal of potential Indian disciples explicitly acknowledged her superior position in the land of her birth. All these developments, however, opened other doors for innovation and creativity, and the deconstruction of behavioral boundaries had unforeseen consequences in the late twelfth century, precipitating a crisis of confidence in Tibetans' practice of Buddhism even while their authenticity was applauded and supported internationally.

9

The Late Twelfth to Early Thirteenth Century: Ethical Crises, International Prestige, and Institutional Maturation

Some go to Vajrāsana (Bodhgayā), but the place is filled with heretics; they have no accomplishment. There are many terrifying bandits on the way—when they cut your throat, you'll repent of having come, dead by a knife.

Others go to the ice field of Kailāsa, but there are many nomads on Kailāsa's glacier. Nomads do all sorts of bad stuff. Having been killed by the glacier of your own perverse views, you'll repent of having come, dead by a knife.

Others go to Tsari Tsagong, filled with the local Lalo Mönpas. But there, even the term "language of Dharma" is not met. Having been killed by your own demons, you'll repent of having come, dead by a knife.

There are so many spots like that, so don't go running to all the "places of accomplishment." But in a secluded retreat of conducive conditions, with the raised [banners of] the two meditative processes engage your discipline.

Then wherever you are is Akaṇiṣṭha, keeping as company your selected divinity. Whatever you eat or drink is nectar. Not to go searching for some external "place of accomplishment" is the vow of the deep secret spells. So don't take up this pilgrimage song, but stay where your are and plow the field!

Yes, this my residence, the glorious Sakya, is just like a site placed in Akaṇiṣṭha heaven.

—*Song of Realization, in Praise of this Place*, by Drakpa Gyeltsen[1]

In the late twelfth and early thirteenth century, Central Tibet achieved a position in Asian religious life that India and, to a certain extent, China had earlier enjoyed. It was at this time that the Tangut emperors began their patronage of Kagyüpa teachers and granted them the titles of "national preceptor" (*guo shi*) and "imperial preceptor" (*di shi*), titles eventually claimed by the Sakyapa teacher Pakpa in the thirteenth century. Tangut monks came independently to Ü-Tsang to study, especially after they saw many Indians fleeing the unrest beginning to engulf areas of West and North India. Occasionally, this resulted in Indians' becoming intrigued with Tibetans, and there are rare instances of Indians or Singhalese attempting to study in Tibet. Individually these events appear isolated, but collectively they marked a profound change in the fortunes of both Tibet and India. To be sure, Tibetans still considered India the holy ground, and many still sought the true Dharma in the land of the Buddha. So, too, learned Indian monks in Tibet were well received and patronized for the latest or most esoteric revelation. But by 1200, Central Tibet had successfully presented itself as a/the place where the Buddha's enlightened activity was fully present, where incarnations of famous Indian monks could be found, and where the rigorous standards of meditation and scholarship of Indian monasteries could be encountered. Rather than a land desperately in need of Buddhist missionaries, Tibet was now sending out its own monks to imperial courts and foreign potentates.

Paradoxically, this was at a time when the Tibetans themselves seemed poorly prepared to become the central distribution point for the Dharma. Their institutions were beginning to achieve longevity and stability, and their scholars were articulating their own understanding of the Dharma, yet whenever it was strained, their society still showed unrest. Whereas the Tanguts and others perceived Tibet as united under religion, Tibetans were experiencing some difficulty simply maintaining the peace, and religious conflict erupted in the last half of the twelfth century in various lineages and denominations. Most important, the Tibetan and Indian feudal systems emulated by religious authorities continued to fuel idiosyncratic behavior and personal aggrandizement under the rubric of enlightened activity, with only occasional checks on outrageous conduct in evidence.

Indeed, Tibetans seemed somewhat oblivious to three things that are striking about the twelfth century: they did not quite appreciate their own accomplishment in the two previous centuries of intensive Buddhist literary and monastic involvement; they did not seek to authenticate independent Tibetan compositions as equivalent to texts from the Indic masters; and they did not understand that the process of religious institution building had become a surrogate for political integration, making national unity difficult for those in positions of power. Buddhist monasteries and their coalescence in the highly fractured political landscape of India were now as much a part of the problem of Tibetan segmentation as they had been the result of Indian political fragmentation five centuries earlier. Tibetans then found themselves in an uneasy series of relationships among the lineal remnants of the dynasty, local aristocrats with pan-Tibetan clan connections, and the growing monastic establishments, which spoke to the feudal lords as equals, which in fact was the case.

By the end of the twelfth century, Tibetans had already translated the vast majority of what they eventually included in the canon. Being a translator, or being associated with a translator, was no longer the *sine qua non* of Tibetan religious life, and the translators' public personas were no longer granted the authority they once were. By the middle of the twelfth century Tibetans became aware that Buddhism in India was under grave duress and that the benefits of studying there were no longer so appealing, for India appeared increasingly lethal. By 1200, the great textual rush was over, and quite rightly, Tibetans began to sit down and digest the contents of this overwhelming mass of intellectual, ritual, and spiritual material. The institutionalization of both the fundamental Buddhist systems and their esoteric offshoots was now almost complete, with Tibetans forming their own denominations according to their own models and the great monasteries of the Central Tibetan region expanding and developing almost by the day. Whereas between the middle eleventh and the early twelfth century, Buddhist esoteric leaders were frequently married laymen, not celibate monks, by the middle of the twelfth century Tibetan indigenous orders were increasingly represented by monks, and even lay teachers often remained celibate.[2]

All this activity left Tibetans with a sense of incompletion, for they were no closer in 1175 to political integration than they were in 1075, 975, or even 875 for that matter. Over three centuries after the loss of the empire, the nostalgia for its sense of purpose and totality seemed to underlie the palpable Tibetan self-denigration in the face of Indian culture, Buddhist spirituality, and the political acumen of other nations: the Tangut, the Chinese, and the Khitan.[3] Tibetans had been building their institutions in imitation of the Indian monastic structures, and references to China were common enough in twelfth-century Tibetan literature that Tibetans had some conception of the magnificence of the now declining Song dynasty, or of the political energy demonstrated by the Tanguts now thriving in the Tarim basin. Accordingly, they realized that they had not achieved in any way an integrated national identity, and so in the twelfth century an abundance of texts on the lineage of the royal dynasty appeared. These included the codification of the received versions of the *Testament of the Ba Clan* (*sBa bzhed*) dedicated to the construction of the grand monastery of Samyé, the finalized mythology of the construction of Lhasa's great Jokhang temple (*bKa' 'chems kha khol ma*), many of the treasures dedicated to the hagiographies of the religious kings, and the beginning of the solidification of the cult to Padmasambhava, who unified Buddhist identity and royal lineage.[4]

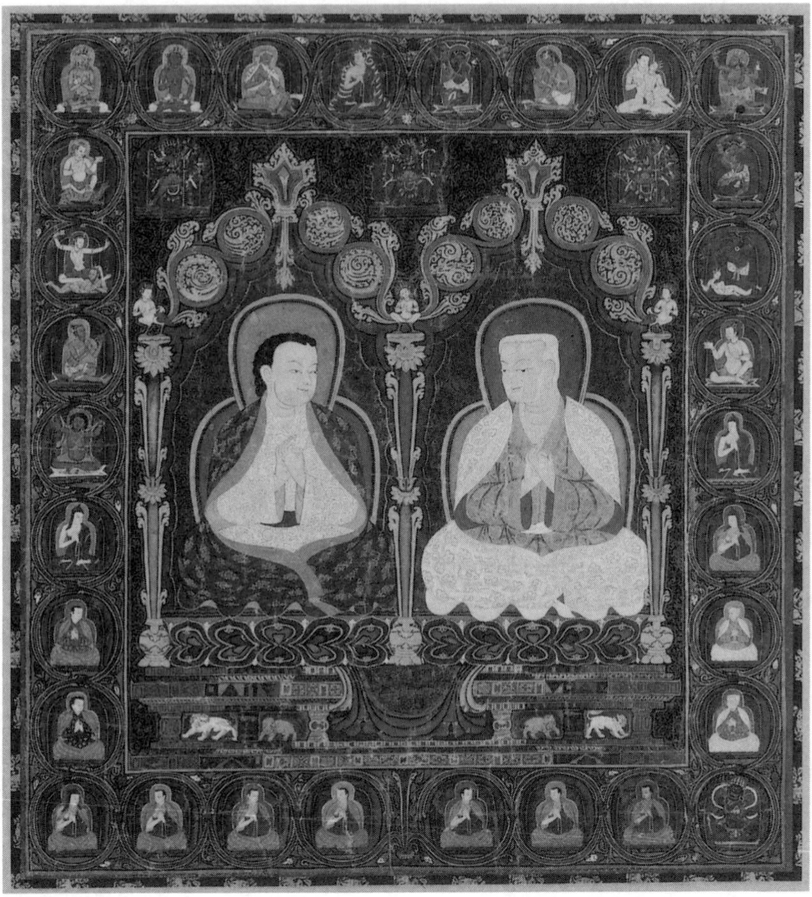

FIGURE 20 Sönam Tsémo and Drakpa Gyeltsen.
Two Sakya-pa Patriarchs. Tibetan, early to mid-fifteenth century.
Museum of Fine Arts, Boston. Gift of John Goelet, 67.831.
Photograph © 2004 Museum of Fine Arts, Boston

This chapter examines the religious instability that threatened the peace, culminating with a subsect of the Kagyüpa establishing a military presence in Central Tibet. We then explore the Kagyüpas' involvement with the Tangut princes and the Kagyüpas' concomitant maturation into an international Buddhist order. The chapter also looks at Sakya, its legacy, and the careers of its two famous lay lamas: Sönam Tsémo and Drakpa Gyeltsen (figure 20). Their literary and scholarly careers take up most of the chapter, especially their maturation of the central tantric system of the Lamdré, for these two authorities provided the spiritual, intellectual, and institutional basis for the eventual flourishing of Sakya under the Mongols. The chapter ends with the death of Drakpa Gyeltsen, as the careers of Sakya Paṇḍita and Chögyel Pakpa are both the fruit of their predecessors' activities and the beginning of an entirely new period of Tibetan religious, social, and political history.

CONFLICT AND CRAZIES IN THE LATE TWELFTH CENTURY

Religious conflict again became a problem in the later twelfth century, harking back to the feuds between the translators or between the Bendé and the Eastern Vinaya monks in the eleventh century. In the mid-eleventh century, the Eastern Vinaya orders of the Dring and the Ba were the most aggressive in their seizure of Kadampa temples and their internecine feuds. Around the turn of the century, perhaps in 1106, the monks of Lumé's faction and of the combined Ba-Rag group started an accelerating conflict at Samyé, with the result that the circumambulatory path (*'khor sa*) was burned, and the destruction of subsidiary temples also was reported.[5] The dispute was apparently resolved by the appearance of the famous (perhaps notorious) Ra-lotsāwa, who insisted, upon pain of black magic, that everyone behave. He used his prestige to restore the monastery and may have realigned Samyé with a less fractious administration.

Aside from this incident, religious figures in the early twelfth century seemed less inclined toward violence until the reemergence of hostilities in Lhasa. The sense of crisis began in the mid-twelfth century, with a great famine engulfing Kham about 1157, an event that motivated more young Khampa monks to seek instruction in Central Tibet.[6] Around 1160, however, the Eastern Vinaya monks again were locked in a struggle for dominance, but this time for control of the Jokhang, and the situation was far more serious than the Samyé incident a half-century before. At this point, four groups were on a collision course: the factions of the Lumé, Ba, Rag, and Dring groups, these four having become the most powerful of the Eastern Vinaya sects. They had come together for some instruction, but the groups swiftly descended into open warfare, and the Jokhang itself and some surrounding buildings were burned, probably including the residence that Atiśa had used while he was in Lhasa in the previous century.[7]

The circumstances of the burning of either Samyé or the Jokhang are not exactly clear, for the record tends to gloss over these events, only to mention that Gampopa's nephew and successor at Dakla Gampo monastery, Dakpo Gomtsül (1116?-69), well served both the cause of peace and the Kagyüpa denomination. He had been completing the construction of a new monastery, Tsur-lhalung, in Tölung, not far away. When he heard news of the battles and conflagration of the great temple, he was reluctant to go to intervene. Nonetheless, he was invited by the secular authority, the Dzong-tsen (Rdzong-btsan), and had visions of multiple divinities like Mahākāla and Remati requesting his efforts. Gomtsül expended much energy at bringing the parties together to achieve concord, initially to no avail. Finally, as he was preparing to leave the city to return to his monastery at the request of his monks, Gomtsül dreamed about the Jowo, who declared that if Gomtsül did not bring resolution to the warfare, no one could. So Gomtsül stayed and finally succeeded in calming the troubled waters.

After peace was established, he entrusted the Jokhang's reconstruction to one of the more colorful figures of the period, Zhang Yu-drak-pa (1123–93).[8] Lama Zhang, as he was known, became a premier disciple of Dakpo Gomtsül and the founder of the last of the "four great" Kagyüpa branches, the Tselpa. He was born into a section of the Nanam clan that obtained the designation of *zhang* (maternal uncle) because of their daughters' marriages to scions of the imperial dynasty, although *zhang* was a title awarded to various branches of several clans.[9] He began his studies quite early and was said to be reciting verses on the Great Perfection by the age of four. Zhang certainly commenced at a young age the study of standard works of Buddhist philosophy (Abhidharma, Madhyamaka, some Yogācāra works, epistemology), but his first love was clearly the tantric systems, and he was said to have pursued for some period the study of black magic involving goat sacrifices. In 1148 he took his final monastic vows and continued his studies in the yogic systems and the Mahāmudrā, including the Zhama Lamdré tradition from a Lama Mel Yerpawa.[10] Zhang was said to have had several dozen teachers, with six most important for his tantric transmissions. He met the great Gampopa before the contemplative master died in 1153 but was said to have obtained decisive realization of awakening from Gampopa's successor, Dakpo Gomtsül, around this time.

Thus well trained in the Kagyüpa religious systems, Lama Zhang began the process of acquiring disciples, building the monastery of Yu-drak in the 1160s, constructing the great center of Tsel in 1175, and following up with Tsel's contiguous edifice of Gung-tang in 1187.[11] Zhang was specifically entrusted with the administration and reconstruction duties of the Jokhang by Dakpo Gomtsül before the latter's death in 1169. It was during this time, and in the development of institutional administration, that Lama Zhang's behavior eventually changed from somewhat eccentric to brutal and bloody. As had Ra-lotsāwa in the previous century, Lama Zhang decided to administer his growing domains by setting up roadblocks to restrict movement on roads, mountains, and rivers, perhaps to collect tariffs but definitely to control access.[12] He also ordered his monks and hired thugs to seize building materials and laborers. Such restrictions and aggressive displays of muscle did not occur without a fight, and the resulting strife with local feudal lords evidently prompted Lama Zhang to form and equip militias or paramilitary forces, some of which were evidently composed of his monastic disciples. Certainly, such irregular paramilitary forces had been assembled before, but Lama Zhang employed them to appropriate domains in Central Tibet from feudal lords in such areas as Lhokha, Drigung, and Ölkha. It took the personal intervention of Karmapa Düsum Khyenpa around 1189 before Lama Zhang ceased belligerent activity with his forces and returned to his monastery.[13] Once the Karmapa intervened, Lama Zhang was said to have grabbed the Karmapa's finger and done a little dance celebrating the moment of resolution before ceasing his criminal behavior.

Perhaps most disturbing in all of this, and revealing in the manner of its employment, was Lama Zhang's attempt at tantric justification for his aggression. Although religious rationalization for personal power, gain, and self-aggrandizement has been common in human history, it has been thankfully rare in Buddhism. Lama Zhang and his disciples, though, determined that they would not be held to the standards of discipline appropriate for the rest of the world, a justification articulated in India for siddhas in general but in Tibet by Ra-lotsāwa and others in particular. This self-serving excuse was based on the idea that the siddha has superior knowledge and is above the mundane standards of the world. Although Indian kings were hardly benign, Indians generally had sense enough not to place siddhas in positions of political and military authority, correctly reasoning that those feeling themselves above social control would have no reason to resist the corrosive influence of power. Tibetans, though, did not observe a theoretical separation of religious and political authority and were at the mercy of any belligerent strongman who could command resources and forces, religious or not.

We can appreciate the challenges Tibetans faced when we see how the siddha theme is played out (sometimes literally) in various venues in Ü-Tsang about this time. Many popular religious movements (*rdol chos*) in the eleventh and twelfth centuries drifted back and forth between inspiration, possession, insanity, and religious praxis. Martin discussed some of these movements, with their populist challenges to Buddhist monastic centers.[14] Other siddha-based developments, as in the case of Lama Zhang's behavior, were found even in Buddhist institutions. Many of these Buddhist institutional movements continued into the twelfth century throughout the southern and central Tibetan areas frequented by Kagyüpa and Nyingma lamas. For example, in the ostensible autobiography of Nyang-rel Nyima-özer (1124–92), the young boy had an extraordinary encounter with a Tibetan "crazy teacher" (*smyon-pa*), a subcategory of religious who put a peculiarly Tibetan valence on the ideal of the siddha persona.[15]

> Then, when I turned twenty (1144 C.E.), I heard of the fame of the precious lama Nyönpa Dönden, and an especial faith in him arose in me. Even just coming into his presence, I found his blessing naturally there, blazing out of him. I requested the Ma Tradition of Zhiché and his instruction in the later transmission [of Zhiché to Jangsem Kunga]. In the midst of the assembly [gathered there for these teachings], the lama declared,
>
>> Now there are before me many learned professors of Dharma and practitioners who are accepted as realized yogins. But your coming is like the rising of the sun in the sky, shining for the welfare of beings.
>
> Then he took off all his clothes, and naked, grabbed my hand, and began to wildly jump and dance about.
>
>> Wake up, all you fortunate ones assembled here! The previous king of this border country is these days the young Nyang, with retreat hair piled on his head (*ral pa can*). The previous translator has nowadays been reborn as my crazy self. This is the deep connection of karma through many lives. Dance away, young Nyang, with retreat hair on your head! You have been reborn for the benefit of beings like the rising of the sun.
>
> So saying, he danced his crazy naked dance. Because of this, those friends of mine previously given to jealously now said their streams of being had been ripened, and all became filled with faith.

Apparently this variety of behavior was an indigenous Tibetan manifestation but was also thematically on a continuum with the wildest of Indian siddha activity. Moreover, the identification of Nyönpa Dönden as associated with Padampa's lineage was in keeping with other records, which list an astonishing number of "crazies" (*smyon pa*) associated with both the Zhiché and Chö systems.

It was common, then as now, for such eccentric personalities to rationalize their behavior, regarding it as a natural expression of the deconstruction of social artifice in the face of the overwhelming experience of the absolute. This was no doubt the case for some, but it is equally true that the defense not only was self-serving but also cultivated a sense of entitlement among the poorly socialized and attracted to the lineage others with severe mental problems. Consequently, by midcentury, Padampa-lineage tantric feasts must have seemed as much a psychiatric outpatient support group as a gathering of awakened masters. Although such individuals may have been entertaining, they were dangerous progenitors of public policy, and the specter of legions of dancing naked clerics wielding weapons seemed to hang like the sword of Damocles over the leaders of most orders at this time. Yet, a simple reading of the Virūpa hagiography would seem to condone behavior that was similar to the crazy yogin of Tibetan life, and some apologists for the meditating warlord pointed out the similarity between Lama Zhang and Virūpa.[16]

Unfortunately, Central Tibet had no institutionalized mechanism to cause such persons to cease their belligerence in the name of the Dharma, and as far as I can tell, Tibetans did not even have a doctrinal system that they would invoke in such a crisis, even though many existed that could have been used. Several sections in the Mahāyāna sūtras, such as the twenty-first chapter of the received *Aṣṭasāhasrikā-prajñāpāramitā*, identify a bodhisattva's failings.[17] Here the Buddha is presented as describing bodhisattvas who stray from the path by being deceived by Māra and becoming seduced by pride (*abhimānapatita*). Many of the same traits cited in that text and elsewhere could be observed in tantric teachers who felt themselves above ordinary morality. The problem was that social inhibitions, combined with an understandable apprehension about their personal safety, appear to have overwhelmed individuals from openly castigating these lineal representatives. Who would wish to oppose a grand lama with an aristocratic clan background, multiple powerful relationships, grand monasteries, belligerent paramilitary forces, and the extensive ritual investment of his teachers? To state the obvious—that Lama Zhang had turned into a pathological tyrant—is to call into question his root lama, the entire lineage, and the form of Buddhism that affirmed his religious position in the first place. It questions the suppositions of the process of spiritual legitimation, subverts approved models of the relationship between spirituality and conduct, and contradicts the ideology of the tantras. As a result, even long afterward, the Kagyüpa annalists tended to gloss over Lama Zhang's conduct by simply alluding to the "Tselpa disruptions."

KAGYÜPA MISSIONARY ACTIVITY AND THE TANGUTS

Of Gampopa's other disciples, Karmapa I Düsum Khyenpa (1110–93) was perhaps the best positioned to subdue Lama Zhang. Curiously, Düsum Khyenpa was one of the most enigmatic of the twelfth-century Kagyüpa masters, even though he had a very high profile and perhaps the greatest stature of his contemporaries.[18] Born in eastern Tibet (Kham) into a nonaristocratic family, he traveled to Ü at the age of eighteen, in the same manner as Bari-lotsāwa had before, as Pagmo Drupa did at the same time, and as Drigung Jikten Gönpo and others approximated later. Düsum Khyenpa and Pagmo Drupa met in Tölung, where they both studied with Gyamarpa and his student prodigy, Chapa Chökyi Sengé. Karmapa went on to Pen-yül to work with Pa-tsap-lotsāwa, the proponent of Prāsaṅgika in the twelfth century, and ended up working on Kadampa texts and meditations for five years and then proceeded to the study of esoteric lineages. Düsum Khyenpa certainly was introduced to the major items in the esoteric syllabus at this time: the Aro system of the Great Perfection, the maṇḍalas of Hevajra, Saṁvara, Mahāmāyā, and the Lamdré. In 1139 he decided to search for Gampopa but first encountered his nephew and successor, the young Dakpo Gomtsül, from whom Düsum Khyenpa received teachings.

When he finally met Gampopa, he received some instruction, but the great master wisely decided that his new disciple needed to practice and so until Gampopa died in 1153, Düsum Khyenpa seems to have been sent to meditate all over the southern area of Tibet and even beyond. He spent some time in Zangri, where the mistress of Chö, Machik Labdrön, lived, came back for three years of rigorous practice in Dakpo, then to Ölkha, and then on to Tsang to study with Mila Repa's disciples. Eventually, Düsum Khyenpa was sent down to the southern lowlands of Mön, where the Nyamjang and Tawang rivers demarcate an ancient territory that once included an area now divided among modern Tibet, Arunachal Pradesh, and Bhutan. Düsum Khyenpa obtained the favor of the king of Mön and was allowed to pass unhindered back and forth along the border between Tibet and Mön. He practiced meditation in areas visited by tigers, which scared the daylights out of the good monk. After Gampopa's death and for the rest of his life, Düsum Khyenpa observed the annual celebration of the master's nirvāṇa, binding his monasteries to related Dakpo Kagyüpa centers where Gampopa's other disciples were similarly engaged. Düsum Khyenpa founded monasteries in Central Tibet, at Tsurpu, as well as in Kham, where he stayed for more than ten years, finally returning to Central Tibet to maintain his vast network of disciples and assist the pacification of various threats to civil order, like that represented by Lama Zhang.

Düsum Khyenpa's comrade in both Kadampa study and Kagyüpa meditation was Pagmo Drupa (1110–70). Pagmo Drupa was born to members of the aristocratic Wa We-na (variant of the Ba) clan in the eastern Tibetan area of Drilung Méshö.[19] He lost his parents when young and began a career of traveling with lamas and receiving teachings. At age eighteen he journeyed to Ü-Tsang, where he was to spend most of the rest of his life. His early career was principally consumed with studying the Kadampa and related systems, and he met Düsum Khyenpa while they both were students of Gyamarpa and Chapa in Tölung. Pagmo Drupa took final monastic ordination at the age of twenty-eight (1138) and decided to stay in Central Tibet, even counseling Düsum Khyenpa not to return to Kham at one point, for fear of his friend's life.[20] Pagmo Drupa studied selected esoteric traditions and met Khampa Aseng, who had been one of Sachen's early disciples.[21] At some time in his thirties, Pagmo Drupa stayed at Sakya for a period, receiving the Lamdré and related transmissions from Sachen. This was probably in the 1140s, although we do not know exactly how much time he spent at Sakya, and it is clear that he visited and studied with other teachers throughout his thirties.[22] He traveled to visit Gampopa in 1151 at the age of forty-one and obtained instruction in Mahāmudrā from the aged master; through his practice of this path, he obtained deep meditative experiences.[23] After the master's death in 1153, Pagmo Drupa meditated throughout wilderness areas, at last constructing his famous grass meditation hut at the place that came to be known as Densatil. There he stayed from 1158 until his death in 1170, and the "lesser eight" Kagyüpa traditions all represent branches from the foundation provided by Pagmo Drupa.

This pattern of sending the best monks out again and again for meditation in various rural environments and non-Buddhist areas actually turned them into de facto missionaries and was one of the most important means for the Kagyüpa to build its patronage and spread its lineage. When such charismatic figures as Düsum Khyenpa or Pagmo Drupa appeared in an area unused to Sarma monks, villagers would hear of the strange saint with an arresting gaze, and everyone would flock to see whether the saint would use his psychic powers to help them find their cattle or cure their children of disease. Over time, religious supremacy was achieved by a thousand appearances, and the fame of Kagyüpa meditators, especially of the three disciples of Gampopa—Düsum Khyenpa, Barompa, and Pagmo Drupa—spread to the Tangut kingdom. The Tanguts had been heavily invested in Buddhism since the mid-eleventh century, and they were capable of producing a great scholar, Tsami-lotsāwa Sangyé-drak, who was instrumental in spreading the Kālacakra system to Tibet in the early twelfth century and was a proponent of Mahākāla activities.[24] Tsami's disciple, Ga-lotsāwa, was a strong influence among Gampopa's disciples as well, so that by the first half of the century the Kagyüpa had already established an important relationship with the Tanguts.[25]

Like other scholars designated Tsami, his name is probably a Tibetan rendition of the Tangut ethnonym Xia with the Bhotic personalizing affix, *mi* (i.e., a man of Xia), and the Tanguts were to be deeply invested in Tibetan Buddhism through the twelfth century until their demise in 1227 by the Mongols.[26] After his experience in Central Tibet, where he debated Chapa Chökyi Sengé, the Indian paṇḍita Jayānanda was hosted by the Tanguts sometime between the 1160s and the 1180s, and Xia Renzong (1139–93) made him a "national preceptor" (*guo shi*).[27] About this time Düsum Khyenpa was invited too, also probably by Xia Renzong, but the Karmapa sent a disciple instead, Tsangpopa Könchok Sengé (d. 1218). Tsangpopa was apparently the first person to earn the designation of "imperial preceptor" (*di shi*), a title given later to Pakpa, under Khubilai Khan.[28]

Following Tsangpopa, another Kagyüpa teacher, Ti-shri Sangyé Réchen (1164/65–1236), served as imperial preceptor. Ti-shri had been trained in both the Barompa and Tselpa lineages and apparently traveled from time to time between the Tangut capital and Tsel Gungtang. In his case, the difference was that, like Tsami-lotsāwa, Ti-shri was a Tangut by nationality, albeit a Kagyüpa by training. All this meant that the Kagyüpa denomination in Ü was well organized for international exchange, one of the reasons that the Karmapa, the Pagmo Drupa, and the Drigungpa subsects all vied with the Sakya as objects of Mongol attention in the next century. This also meant that the Kagyüpa became very wealthy and extraordinarily powerful, far beyond the meager military dreams of Lama Zhang. Eventually the Kagyüpa order extended its involvement with East Asia into China's Ming and Qing dynasties.

When all these factors are considered, it is not surprising that tension between the Kagyüpa and the neoconservatives flared in the late twelfth and early thirteenth century. By the neoconservatives' estimation, Gampopa's idiosyncratic doctrines seemed aligned with the old eighth-century Chinese position, and the new interest in East Asia seemed to them to be a poisonous combination of heresy, personal ambition, political power, and stark greed. The Kagyüpa erosion of the orthodox view (*lta ba*) and correct meditation (*sgom pa*) of Buddhism appeared to be harbingers of an erosion in actual behavior (*spyod pa*). That this rather pessimistic evaluation of the lamas from Ü and Kham was made largely by teachers from (or with strong connections to) West Tibet and Tsang Province tended to add a geographical layer to the denominational tensions.

Some Kagyüpa teachers eventually took a page from the neoconservatives' playbook. The Drigungpa founder, Drigung Jikten Gönpo, and his successor and nephew, Ön Shérap Jungné (1187–1217), both from the O-trön branch of the Kyura clan, formulated the "single intention" (*dgongs gcig*) teachings sometime in the early thirteenth century as a combination of synthetic philosophical vision and neoconservative comments.[29] Not only did this work criticize some of the same practices that later came under Sakya Paṇḍita's disapproval, it attempted to paper over some of the differences between the Sakyapa, on one hand, and the Mahāmudrā, on the other. In some ways this was understandable, for both subscribed to the idea of the triple disciple (*trisaṁvara*), and both considered the Sarma yogic systems to be the pinnacle of the Buddha's dispensation. Like the Karmapa, the Drigungpa became the focus of some Tangut attention as well.[30] Unfortunately, precisely because of their similarities, these Sarma systems came to occupy the same religious niche, making the various Kagyüpa and Sakyapa lineages competitors rather than partners. In the thirteenth century there can be little doubt that similar factors were at work with the success of the Sakyapas of Tsang and even contributed to the resurgence of Central Tibetan Kagyüpas with the victory of Pagmo Drupa Jangchub Gyeltsen in 1358 and the dethronement of the Sakyapa hegemony.

SACHEN'S DISCIPLES, SONS, AND THE CONTINUITY OF TRADITION

In the midst of this effervescent activity, Sakya Monastery appeared remarkably steady, even a bit staid. Sachen Kunga Nyingpo passed away at Sakya in 1158 at the age of sixty-six, after serving as leader of the institution for forty-eight years.[31] Sachen's relics (figure 21) were eventually interred in the stūpa Victorious Pantheon (sKu 'bum rnam rgyal) as objects of wonder and veneration to all who made the pilgrimage to Sakya.[32] Sachen's funerary rite—employing a grand ceremony entitled Closing the Three Times (*dus gsum khegs so*)—was a great religious gathering attended by many renowned religious figures from Sakya and elsewhere. The offerings then made to the assembled religious were stupendous by the standards of the day. Sakya Paṇḍita assures us that about fifty copies of the entire *Perfection of Insight Scripture* in 100,000 verses, more than thirty copies of the 25,000 verse *Perfection of Insight*, and more than eighty copies of the *Ratnakūṭa-sūtra* were distributed to those clerics who attended the funeral.[33] The offerings were so magnificent that it established a standard for postmortem rites in years to come.

This had been a time of Sakya's expansion, enabled by the dynamism of both Bari-lotsāwa and Sachen. Besides the two temples built by Bari and the stūpa of his father, Sachen constructed the Utsé Nyingma temple and a reli-

FIGURE 21 Outer Reliquary of Sachen.
After a photograph by Cyrus Stearns

quary for his mother.[34] Through these activities, Sakya had become a legitimate pilgrimage goal, and the popular practices associated with the Buddhist relic cult found an assured place in Sakya, where pilgrims could receive the blessings of the Buddha Kāśyapa's waistcoat, Rinchen Zangpo's flying mask, the miraculous statuary housed in its temples, the relics of the saints of the Khön clan, and the living lamas of the esoteric dispensation.[35] As a result of his learning, ability, energy, and spirituality, Sachen also cast a very long shadow over the activities of his disciples and his young sons.

Sachen's disciples were important and well known to their contemporaries, and the sources emphasize the groups of disciples and their relationship to two experiences already mentioned. One was Sachen's dream of the three bridges during the preparatory period for a consecration by Gyichuwa. Sachen dreamed of three bridges crossing over an enormous river stained murky red: on the near bridge were many people, but on the middle bridge were merely seven, and on the last bridge were only three. This indicated that he would have three great disciples.[36] Similarly, Zhang Gönpawa said that if Sachen were to teach, he would have unlimited students, including three who would attain the highest accomplishment of the Great Seal, seven mundane bodhisattvas, and so on. Following this lead, the Lamdré records graded his students based on the ubiquitous Tibetan penchant for the rumors of miracles.[37] Such stories are central to Tibetans' perceptions of religious life and cannot easily be separated into a popular versus elite worldview. The miracle tales were understood to be proof (*rtags*) of siddhi, and so the hagiographers assiduously pursued them to prove Sachen's ability to instill miraculous attainment into his disciples.

Accordingly, three of Sachen's disciples were said to have obtained the highest accomplishment: a yogin from Śrī Laṅka, Gompa Kyibarwa from Mangkhar, and Jangchub Sempah-Tak from Latö. Among the other disciples, Gatön Dorjé-drak from Kham stood apart, and Khyentsé Wangchuk (1524–68) considered Drakpa Gyeltsen's letter to that disciple to be among the most important instructions of the Lamdré.[38] In this architecture of accomplishment, however, later authors misplaced several of Sachen's most important disciples. Géshé Nyen Pül-jungwa was one of Sachen's most important followers, for he took over several tasks when his master died and helped educate Sachen's sons. He apparently ran Sakya Monastery for three years while Sönam Tsémo and Drakpa Gyeltsen were continuing their education. He also brought together into a single text the several sections of Sachen's longest commentary on the *Root Text of the *Mārgaphala*. Chapter 8 describes Géshé Nyen Pül-jungwa as the figure who ostensibly informed Drakpa Gyeltsen of the Virūpa visions that constituted the Short Transmission, an admission of Nyen Pül-jungwa's authority even if the story appears apocryphal. However, the good Géshé is only circuitously included in any list of Sachen's disciples.

Also lost was Pagmo Drupa, who was to begin a separate tradition of Lamdré and teach it as a corollary to his own Pagmo Drupa Kagyüpa tradition.[39] Sometime when he was in his thirties, Pagmo Drupa received the Lamdré and related transmissions from Sachen.[40] Later Pagmo Drupa returned to Sakya, probably in 1154 or 1155, and met with Sachen to present him with a gold-lettered copy of the extensive *Perfection of Insight* scripture, as well as other books and items that had been produced during the memorial rites for Gampopa.[41] An early source indicates that Sachen and Pagmo Drupa exchanged presents, and Sachen acknowledged the dramatic change in his disciple's understanding, so that he was to become a "king of the Dharma."[42] In fact, Pagmo Drupa continued to teach the Lamdré at various times in his life, probably using the *Gatengma* commentary and other texts that Sachen gave to him.[43]

Sachen's greatest followers, however, were his two middle sons: Sönam Tsémo and Drakpa Gyeltsen, traditionally counted as the second and third of the five great Sakyapa teachers, beginning with Sachen and ending with Pakpa. In the rankings, however, these two sons are given short shrift. The deficit eventually struck later scholars like Peṇchen Minyak Drakdor as very odd, that Sachen's second son Sönam Tsémo did not figure in the early lists of miraculous disciples, and later scholars chose to place him in a new category: above all the rest.[44] Likewise, Khyentsé Wangchuk felt obliged to rationalize

Drakpa Gyeltsen's rather low position in the traditional list—as a bodhisattva still on the mundane path—given the great scholar's reputation as the emanation of the bodhisattva Mañjuśrī, mythically known as "the teacher of five Buddhas" and a tenth-level bodhisattva.[45]

PERPETUATING THE KHÖN LINE: SÖNAM TSÉMO

Like his father Khön Könchok Gyelpo, Sachen was destined to have two wives, but we do not know when he was first married. Probably it was rather late in his life, after he completed his studies with Mel-lotsāwa, perhaps around the age of forty or so (ca. 1130–35). The meager accounts simply mention that he married two sisters from a clan in Tsamo-rong, from a noble house (*rje btsad*).[46] Sachen's first wife, Jocham Purmo, was the younger of the two sisters, and she gave birth to the first of four sons who were to continue the Khön line at Sakya. Called Kunga-bar, the eldest boy eventually found his way to India, where he achieved success in his studies, becoming a scholar of the "five areas of knowledge."[47] But just as he was preparing to return to Tibet, he caught a fever of some variety and died in Magadha at the age of twenty-one.

Unfortunately, the sources say nothing else about Kunga-bar's motivation to go to India, although we can tentatively suppose a few things from his and his younger brothers' behavior. All these young men were raised in an environment in which their father was embedded in the esoteric paradigm. Despite the thoroughness of his education, Sachen was a specialist in the Vajrayāna, and we have no example of any text written by him on a topic that would be included in a philosophical monastic syllabus of the kind Kunga-bar must have studied. We might then expect that Kunga-bar was studying material that would have rounded out Sakyapa scholarship. Indeed, immediately after Sachen's death, the second son, Sönam Tsémo pursued precisely the philosophical and aesthetic erudition popular in the great Indian monasteries.

Sönam Tsémo was the eldest son of Sachen's second wife, Machik Ödrön, who was apparently the older of the two sisters. She was to bear Sachen the three sons who made all the difference for the Khön line, for even beyond Sönam Tsémo and Drakpa Gyeltsen, the youngest son, Pelchen Öpo, was the father of the great monastic scholar, Sakya Paṇḍita. Sönam Tsémo was born with an exalted list of portents in 1142 at Sakya, when his father was fifty years old.[48] Very soon, the boy's intelligence was clear to all, and his ability doubtless stimulated his eventual assessment as the incarnation of a person who had been born as eleven Indian paṇḍitas, culminating with the great Hevajra exegete Durjayacandra.[49] The sources tell us nothing about the relationship between

Sönam Tsémo and his older brother, Kunga-bar. But if Sachen had had his first child at the age of forty to forty-five (ca. 1132 to 1137), and his second son was born in 1142, the two boys must have known each other. It even is possible that Kunga-bar, in his early twenties, was preparing to return to Sakya because he had learned of his father's illness or death, and Drakpa Gyeltsen's hagiography mentions that Kunga-bar's postmortem ritual was celebrated after the rite for Sachen, suggesting that the eldest son died soon after his father did.[50] If this was the case, Kunga-bar's decision to study in India and pursue a scholarly career probably influenced Sönam Tsémo. Whatever their relationship, the primary influence in Sönam Tsémo's early life was his father, for at a young age he already was reciting some of the esoteric scriptures by heart, such as the *Hevajra* and *Saṁvara-tantras*. By the time he was sixteen, it was said that he knew fourteen such scriptures by heart and was deemed by some (probably half as a jest) to be "*the* scholar of the esoteric system as far as the river Ganges."

Suddenly, however, with the death of Sachen, Sönam Tsémo's life went off in a new direction, for immediately afterward, he decided to study with the great master of epistemology and Madhyamaka, Chapa Chökyi Sengé.[51] As the previous chapter stated, Chapa was a great scholar at Sangpu Néütok, the Kadampa philosophical monastery to the south of Lhasa in Ü. Unfortunately, we know very little about Chapa and his group in the 1160s, when Sönam Tsémo probably spent most of his time at Sangpu Néütok. But it is clear that the institution took the monastic regimen seriously and considered the study of Mahāyānist doctrine to be the centerpiece of the Buddhist path. The environment must have been conducive and influential, for Sönam Tsémo studied with Chapa off and on for eleven years (1158 to 1169), and he certainly became accomplished in the investigation of such works as the *Pramāṇaviniscaya* and the *Bodhicaryāvatāra* in the way that his father had not.

Sönam Tsémo's experience at Sangpu was central to his intellectual development, and his paean to the great master, written at Sakya as a memorial for Chapa in 1173, indicates both his debt and his devotion.[52] It is apparent that Chapa's practice of challenge and defense (*thal-'gyur*) became a facet of Sönam Tsémo's literary persona as well, even though some maintained that Sachen already liked to question his disciples on points of doctrine from time to time as part of their training.[53] Yet the articulation of defensive positions for Vajrayāna doctrines first appears fully developed in Sönam Tsémo's writings, and it is probable that he found himself engaged in this pattern at Sangpu. There the philosophical monks would have taken to task this young esoteric lay representative for some of the perceptions and ideas espoused in the tantras. Indeed, Sangpu was one of the sites in Central Tibet embodying the Kadampa reformist zeal that resulted in their castigation of the tantric lapses attributed to many Indians and Tibetans. This background discourse becomes perceptible in various places in the works of Sönam Tsémo, when he rose to the defense of his tradition against unnamed "persons practicing the perfections," whoever they may have been. Doubtless, too, the extraordinary emphasis on the hermeneutics of esoterism (*bshad thabs*) found throughout Sönam Tsémo's esoteric works, particularly in the chapter in his *General Principles of the Tantric Canon* devoted to the topic, was derived in part from his need to explain esoterism to monks devoted to Buddhist philosophical exegesis and scandalized by the tantric vocabulary.

Sönam Tsémo's work reflects his continuing concern with his father's legacy, especially as noted in the two surviving examples of his correspondence that I have been able to locate. The first is in a short note appended to the mnemonic outline for the consecration of Nairātmyā written to Nétso Beltön sometime before 1165 and possibly before Sachen's death in 1158.[54] There Sönam Tsémo exhorts Nétso Beltön that saintly persons like him are exactly the right ones to perform such consecrations and bring benefit to the doctrine of the Vajrayāna, which is better than that of the Śrāvaka system, since the Vajrayāna is not a simple reflection of the true Dharma in the manner of the lesser vehicle but constitutes the true Dharma itself. Although this early letter does not make clear whether Sachen was still alive, his demise is of particular concern in many of Sönam Tsémo's other documents, which emphasize the ritual of completing Sachen's intention (*dgongs rdzogs*) during the great periods of remembrance (*dus dran*) held each year at Sakya. These periods probably culminated in the anniversary of Sachen's passing on the fourteenth of the ninth month of the lunar calendar. The rite must have been an extraordinary event each year, and it is clear that Sönam Tsémo had a central place in its ritual performance, even if Géshé Nyen Pül-jungwa and Sachen's other disciples were the primary forces behind its continuing celebration. At the end of his panegyric to lineage teachers, for example, Sönam Tsémo notes that in the monkey year (doubtless 1164), Sönam Tsémo made offerings to nine hundred monks during the ritual.[55]

In a longer letter to Gyagom Tsültrim-drak the following year (1165), Sönam Tsémo tries to balance his devotion to his father, his gratitude to his teachers and patrons (as Gyagom Tsültrim-drak seems to have been both), and his interest in his studies.[56] The ritual of the annual celebration of Sachen's nirvana weighed so heavily that Sönam Tsémo mentions it twice in the letter. In his second reference he reveals the intensity of the feeling surrounding this celebration—which continues in Sakyapa monasteries to this day—by his affirmation that the blessing and faith generated were so intense that he had little time to revise either of the two works he was sending to Gyagom Tsültrim-drak. His elder correspondent had previously sent some gifts, especially material for clothing, and in return Sönam Tsémo was sending some items of importance to them both. With the letter, he sent a leather box containing the sash that Sachen had worn, some red-powder pills said to have been from Nāropā, along with an outline of the consecration of Nairātmyā (*bDag med ma'i dbang gi tho yig*) and his recently composed poem in praise of his father (*rJe sa chen la bstod pa*). In the letter, Sönam Tsémo apologizes profusely for the poem's faults and lack of sophistication, and we see in his protestations of insufficiency the emergence of his attention to the requirements of poetic images and prosody that Tibetans had received from India. Since poetic considerations were prominent in Sönam Tsémo's paean to Chapa, poetic criticism was probably part of the curriculum at Sangpu and may have been studied in some detail.[57] While the current scholarship has emphasized the role of Sakya Paṇḍita in the introduction of the Indian critic Daṇḍin's work on poetic standards, it is evident that the principles of poetic composition were of concern to Sönam Tsémo some sixteen years before Sakya Paṇḍita's birth.[58]

Equally clear in this letter was Sönam Tsémo's continued relations with Sachen's elder disciples and their help in keeping the brothers motivated to follow in their father's footsteps. Sönam Tsémo affirmed that both Géshé Nyak and Géshé Nyen Pül-jungwa had been his counselors the previous summer and had assisted him in the composition of the homage to his father. Gyagom Tsültrim-drak also had had a hand in this, for he seems to have been both a corrector of the young man's poetry and a teacher of tantra. Sönam Tsémo indicated that he intended to return to Ü early in the following year (1166), probably to continue his studies at Sangpu with Chapa. If he and Gyagom happened to meet on the way, Sönam Tsémo said that he would feel satisfied if the teacher—whom he addressed with the honorific endearment Old Father (A-po)—would resolve his misunderstandings concerning instructions in meditation and the tantras.

All told, this revealing letter—for we have no other of such depth from Sönam Tsémo—portrays a student who is aware of his own deficiencies and is seeking assistance from trusted teachers and community elders. He clearly is pious and does not pursue his studies simply out of a sense of duty but from a deeply ingrained commitment to the traditions. Sönam Tsémo is torn between his duties at Sakya and his studies in Ü. Yet his pursuit of the scholarly career kept him from Sakya for much of his adult life, and he apparently only served the community as its head for a total of three years. His quest for learning, the later scholar Amé-shep informs us, was such that by the age of twenty-six he had already earned the sobriquet of the "Doctrine's Great Tree of Life in this

TABLE 8 Sönam Tsémo's Dated Works

TEXT	DATE OF COMPLETION
rJe sa chen la bstod pa	1164
rGya sgom tshul khrims grags la spring pa	1165
Chos la 'jug pa'i sgo	1167/8
Yig ge'i bklag thabs byis pa bde blag tu 'jug pa	1167 (or 1179)
sLob dpon Phya pa la bstod pa	1173
dPal kye rdo rje'i rnam par bshad pa nyi ma'i 'od zer	1174
Saṁ pu ṭa'i ṭī ka gnad kyi gsal byed	1175

World System."[59] We also are told that on one of his periods in Sakya, in 1169, he taught the Lamdré in the Old Residence (gZims-khang rnying-ma) at Sakya, but we have little other knowledge of his teaching and may wonder whether instruction to personal disciples—his younger brother's concern—ever occupied much of his time.[60] Unfortunately, few of Sönam Tsémo's works give the date of their composition (table 8).

If it is not possible to trace in detail Sönam Tsémo's intellectual development, we can see that his experience with Chapa was instrumental in influencing him to compose a series of pedagogical manuals, and it is likely that his commentary on the *Bodhicaryāvatāra* and his *Beginners' Guide to Ritual Practice and Advancement on the Path* were composed in the 1160s or early 1170s. It also is likely that the unfinished *General Principles of the Tantric Canon* was conceived and partly written during the late 1160s or very early 1170s, for the 1175 commentary on the *Sampuṭa* indicates that the topics of hermeneutics and practice had been treated elsewhere, doubtless a reference to the treatments of these topics outlined for the third and fourth chapters of his *General Principles*.[61] All told, the few available hints in the compositions of Sönam Tsémo point to his increasing involvement with the esoteric corpus, identifying its central themes, surrounding it with the appropriate ritual expressions that had been missing in his father's work, and bringing it into the mainstream of Sakyapa monastic practice.

In this, Sönam Tsémo was probably influenced by his association with a latter-day wandering Paṇḍita, Ācārya Śrī Ānandagarbha, who was either Indian or Nepalese. Certainly Ānandagarbha's oral explanations of the Hevajra practice ascribed to Saroruhavajra were the source for Sönam Tsémo's own commentary on the *sādhana*, and the two scholars may have had some language difficulties, for Sönam Tsémo acknowledged that there may be some unclear points in the exegesis.[62] If indeed he worked with an Indian or Nepalese for a while, it might explain why he once signed the Sanskrit translation of his regular name, Puṇyāgra, and used the Sanskrit of his initiatory name (Dveṣavajra: Zhe-sdang rdo-rje) in another instance. But Sönam Tsémo had certainly been interested in Sanskrit early on and included a section on mantra pronunciation in his 1167 *Easy Guide to the Pronunciation of Letters.*[63]

Sönam Tsémo's death in 1182 at the age of forty must have come as a shock to the Sakya community, although we cannot even be certain where he died. Amé-shep relates a revealing hagiographical story, said to have been taken from some notes on Drakpa Gyeltsen's panegyric to his brother, that Drakpa Gyeltsen came home one day and simply found a pile of empty clothing, an indication that his brother had risen to the celestial realm without abandoning his body. Some say that the clothing hummed with a peculiar noise.[64] Others declared that "an old woman from Sakya" had a vision that Sönam Tsémo flew up in the air, riding a bitch, over the cliff in western Chumik Dzinkha. Both the saint and his dog left their hand (and paw) prints on the face of the cliff. Some claim that Sönam Tsémo actually died at Chumik Dzinkha, and others maintain that he died in the old Gorum Library, the first building erected by his grandfather at Sakya, a place where Sanskrit manuscripts were kept. So, like the empty robes of the story or the hollow paw prints on the cliff of Chumik, the final narrative of Sönam Tsémo left something of a hollow absence, for he was not to be included in the initial lists of his father's disciples, and no one even thought to record the exact place of his passing. Despite his dedication and talent, it took later teachers to recover his legacy and move him out of the shadows cast by his father and younger brother.

DRAKPA GYELTSEN AND THE SAKYA INSTITUTION

Uncertainties about the life and activity of Sönam Tsémo are to some degree mirrored in the circumstances of his younger brother, Drakpa Gyeltsen. It is not clear that this should have been the case. Unlike his older brother, for whom no hagiography was written, Drakpa Gyeltsen was the object of a standard-length hagiography by Sakya Paṇḍita.[65] Unhappily, though, Sakya Paṇḍita's work is less than complete, and all too frequently he retreats from giving us information with the exclamation that "there is too much to relate about it, so I will not write it here!"[66] Sakya Paṇḍita's reasons for these multiple lapses are obscure, but it appears that he thought that a complete description of physical events was unnecessary to satisfy the requirements of the hagiographical genre as known in his day, for he did provide extensive coverage of dreams, visions, and miracle stories. This may in fact be a direct reflection of the values espoused by Drakpa Gyeltsen himself, for the only autobiographical document he left was his dictated record of especially important dreams that he experienced from the age seventeen until just before his demise.[67]

In any event, Drakpa Gyeltsen was the second son of Sachen's second wife, Machik Ödrön, and was born in Sakya in 1147. He was apparently to become the longest lived of all four of Sachen's sons, as he was at the center of the funerary celebrations for his father and all his brothers.[68] Sakya Paṇḍita assiduously tied every event he reported about his uncle's life into either the mythology of previous generations or the qualities described in Mahāyānist scriptures for the life of a bodhisattva. So like the circumstances of the Buddha, Drakpa Gyeltsen's mother is said to have dreamed that the king of elephants entered her womb, and his birth and childhood are described with the formulaic statements required for aspiring Buddhist saints.[69]

More interesting, Drakpa Gyeltsen evidently followed his brother in becoming a celibate layman (*brahmacari-upāsaka*), taking the vow for this status at age seven from Jangchub Sempah Dawa Gyeltsen. This intriguing figure was probably the teacher who was noted for spreading the message of Buddhist fundamental ethics and had close associations with a wide variety of lineages. He had been a preceptor of Taglungpa, was a holder of the Drom Depa Tönchung's lineage of Lamdré, and had been the disciple for whom Sachen's *Dagyelma* commentary on the Lamdré was written.[70] Amé-shep went so far as to claim that Drakpa Gyeltsen's practice of celibacy was superior to that of a monk, since he benefited from karmic traces of having been a monk in previous lives and was unmoved by sexual desire.[71] Apparently about this age, Drakpa Gyeltsen also decided to forswear the drinking of alcohol or the eating of meat, except as intermittently required in the tantric practice. His other endeavors in his youth were the study of the *Twenty Verses on the Bodhisattva Vow* and, the most basic of Hevajra practices, the visualization of Hevajra according to Saroruhavajra's *sādhana* text. He is said to have received the Lamdré from his father at the age of eight and was forbidden to teach it until the age of twelve, a very peculiar directive given the extreme youth of the boy and the difficulties of the system. Nonetheless, it is clear that this early exposure to the Lamdré via his father established both Drakpa Gyeltsen's authority and his intimate familiarity with the tradition's overall organization.

By all accounts, the pivotal event in the Drakpa Gyeltsen's life was the death of his father, when Drakpa Gyeltsen was only eleven and his brothers were sixteen and eight years of age. He and his elder brother were the foci for many of the great scholars assembled at the funerary ceremony, and we are told that at that time Drakpa Gyeltsen recited the *Hevajra-tantra* from memory. The scholars were dutifully amazed, and some maintained that just as his father was the emanation of Mañjuśrī, he also must be blessed by the bodhisattva of intelligence. Others declared that because Sachen had the vision of Mañjuśrī when he was young, he received the blessing that all his descendants would be granted a similar revelation. It was apparently this event that motivated others to inaugurate the story that all members of the Khön clan would be considered emanations of Mañjuśrī, although we may look in vain for any such claim by Drakpa Gyeltsen himself. Whatever the circumstances of his mythic association with the bodhisattva of insight, it is evident that the recitation of the *Mañjuśrīnāmasaṃgīti*, the *Litany of Names of Mañjuśrī*, would be a primary concern for Drakpa Gyeltsen, and its recitation appeared in his dreams as well as occupying some of his ritual time.[72]

When Sönam Tsémo left Sakya after Sachen's death to study with Chapa at Sangpu, Drakpa Gyeltsen remained behind to continue his esoteric education with Géshé Nyen Pül-jungwa, who assumed the reins of Sakya for three years until 1161. Indeed, Géshé Pül-jungwa and Géshé Nyak Wang-gyel remained important teachers at Sakya at least until 1165. Sakya Paṇḍita also wrote that Drakpa Gyeltsen studied with one "Zhang" (probably Zhang Tsültrim-drak) as well as "other masters," a phrase he used to discount alternative authoritative sources and to occlude, very effectively, most of Drakpa Gyeltsen's teachers beyond Sachen.[73] Amé-shep states that—besides Géshé Nyen, Zhang, and Géshé Nyak—Drakpa Gyeltsen also studied with the Nepalese Jayasena, Lotsāwa Darma Yönten, Sumpa-lotsāwa Pelchok-dangpö Dorjé, and others, but Amé-shep could not provide curricula for their individual instructions.[74] Whoever his preceptors were, we are assured that Drakpa Gyeltsen had a rigorous education in the esoteric tradition, a fact quite evident to anyone perusing his writings. He certainly studied all the four levels of the esoteric canon recognized by the Sakyapa—*kriyā*, *caryā*, *yoga*, and *yogottara*—and in Drakpa Gyeltsen we see for the first time the intrusion of the *Kālacakra-tantra* into Sakya ideas, although Sachen had purportedly studied the text as well. Once Drakpa Gyeltsen became of age (alternatively identified as between twelve and twenty-five) he took responsibility for Sakya, although the few indications we have of his efforts are that he continued to live in the gravity of his elder brother when Sönam Tsémo was in residence.[75] In the elder brother's 1165 letter to Gyagom Tsültrim-drak, Sönam Tsémo was quite grateful for his younger brother's encouragement to express his own understanding of the Vajrayāna. At this time—and probably other times as well—Sönam Tsémo was living at Sakya, for perhaps several months before returning to his studies with Chapa.[76]

Tragedy struck again, however, and Drakpa Gyeltsen hosted another grand funerary ceremony, but this time for Sönam Tsémo, who died in 1182 when Drakpa Gyeltsen was about thirty-five. As a meritorious practice, he had thirty-seven copies produced of the *Perfection of Insight in 100,000 Verses*; approximately eighty copies of the 25,000–verse version; fifty *Ratnakūṭas*; a gold-lettered, 8,000–verse *Perfection of Insight*; and many other offerings. Drakpa Gyeltsen also outlived his younger brother, Pelchen Öpo (1150–1203), who married and produced two sons, and for his younger brother's funerary rites, he again sponsored the copying of texts on a par with those of his elder brother. Indeed, funerary ceremonies became so important to Drakpa Gyeltsen's life that Sakya Paṇḍita made them an important facet of his uncle's religious activity. Sakya Paṇḍita tells us that, in aggregate, more than 250 copies of the *Perfection of Insight in 100,000 Verses*, written in ink mixed with gems, were offered by his uncle. Many of these scriptures were the result of the Khön postmortem rituals, and a hundred copies still remained in the main temple of Sakya around 1216.[77] Jétsün Rinpoché (as Drakpa Gyeltsen came to be known) also sponsored the copying of an early canon, both sūtras and tantras, in golden letters. When we see this scriptural patronage in relationship to the many images, silk banners, canopies, and various other items he offered at Sakya and to many other monasteries, it is little wonder that Drakpa Gyeltsen became famous for his largesse in service of the Buddhist cause. Sakya Paṇḍita noted that when his uncle passed away, he had almost no assets left, besides the clothes on his back and a few personal items.

As the quotation at the beginning of this chapter shows, Drakpa Gyeltsen did not like to travel, and Sakya Paṇḍita mentions no other place where his uncle lived other than his beloved monastery. But according to other sources, Drakpa Gyeltsen established at least one retreat in a cave in the Mangkhar valley, which is listed in both the pilgrims' guides and Tsarchen's hagiography.[78] In all likelihood, this period or periods of retreat came at a mature age, and Drakpa Gyeltsen mentioned a series of dreams at age forty-eight in which he climbed up cliffs, as well as another dream that he had while staying on a "shelf" in Mangkhar.[79] This is certainly different from another hermitage described as the "eastern remote site" of Gyangdrak Nyipak, where his commentary on the *Yoginīsañcāratantra* was composed in 1206.[80] Between his long life and restricted movements, it is not surprising that Drakpa Gyeltsen was able to become a wide-ranging author, writing on topics throughout the esoteric canon and completing the directions taken by his father and brother. Table 9 lists those of his works, all too few, that contain dates (or approximate dates) in the colophons.

As with the works of his brother, we cannot begin to ascertain Drakpa

TABLE 9 Drakpa Gyeltsen's Dated Works

TEXT	DATE OF COMPLETION
Khams bde dri ba'i nyams dbyangs	1171
Lam 'bras brgyud pa'i gsol 'debs	1174
dGa' ston la spring yig	mouse year (1192?/1204/1216)
rGyud kyi mngon par rtogs pa rin po che'i ljon shing	by 1196[81]
brTag gnyis rnam 'grel dag ldan	1204
bDe mchog kun tu spyod pa'i rgyud kyi gsal byed	1206
Ga ring rgyal po la rtsis bsdur du btang ba'i gsung yig	1206
'Khor 'das dbyer med tshig byas rin chen snang ba	1206
'Phags pa rdo rje gur gyi rgyan	1210
Rin chen snang ba shlo ka nyi shu pa'i rnam par 'grel pa	1212
rJe btsun pa'i mnal lam	1213/14

Gyeltsen's own intellectual development, for these titles represent just a smattering of the approximately 150 works attributed to him, as contained in the *Collected Works of the Sakya Masters*, its supplement, and the *Yellow Book* (*Pod ser*). The *Yellow Book* was Drakpa Gyeltsen's greatest contribution to the Lamdré system, in the narrowest sense. However, by the twelfth century such a narrow application was increasingly restricted to consecration lineages, and "Lamdré" began to assume the position of a general rubric for esoteric studies related to the *Hevajra-tantra* as taught at Sakya.

For all his writing, Drakpa Gyeltsen's activity on behalf of others and his interaction with them remain somewhat obscure. The colophons for two works show that he was occupied with instructing his young nephew, Kunga Gyeltsen—destined to become Sakya Paṇḍita—from 1196 until the young man's association with Paṇ-chen Śākyaśrī in the early years of the thirteenth century, especially teaching the texts of the tantras.[82] Kunga Gyeltsen eventually studied a wide variety of works with his aging uncle, and the relationship between the two became a hagiographer's delight, with a plethora of titles being taught to the young scholar by the elderly sage. No doubt the list has been inflated to some degree, and there is little evidence that Drakpa Gyeltsen, for example, could have taught Sanskrit or the Nyingma tantras to his nephew.[83] In the same way that Sakya Paṇḍita's narrative of his uncle obscures

Drakpa Gyeltsen's teachers after Sachen, Sakya Paṇḍita's own hagiographies do likewise, emphasizing the young scholar's studies with his uncle above all else, so that the Khön clan connection became the defining reality of these individuals' educations.[84]

If Drakpa Gyeltsen did not travel extensively, the world came to him, and Sakya became caught up in a the larger geopolitics of the period, just as Tsurpu and the other Kagyüpa monasteries did at the same time. On a holy war of conquest, the Turks and Afghans had conquered much of North India and had ridden east to destroy the great monasteries of Bihar and Bengal. The Western Tarim was taken by the Karakhitai in the early twelfth century, with the Eastern Tarim under the expanding power of the Tangut state, which had conquered the Uigurs in Turfan in 1028. The Tangut Renzong emperor was a powerful supporter of Buddhism at home and seemed to embody the model of a Dharmarāja.

These and related factors had several consequences. Most important, Tsang Province was overrun with Indian monks in the last quarter of the twelfth and the first quarter of the thirteenth century. This was when Śākyaśrī, Vibhūticandra, Sumatikīrti, and others traveled in the western and southern areas of Tibet, and Drakpa Gyeltsen had the opportunity to host many of them in Sakya. He used the presence of Indian monks for his own studies as well and received transmissions on aspects of esoteric literature rather late in his life from Indian monks fleeing to Tibet. Drakpa Gyeltsen thus received a Vajravārāhī meditation attributed to Advayavajra from Jayaśrīsena, and his collected works contain other stray Indian ritual texts probably received from Indians or their immediate translators.[85] It may have been at this time that Drakpa Gyeltsen was influenced by the presence of Indians—as his brother may have been, by the presence of Nepalese—signing his name in Sanskrit translation, Kīrtidvaja. The foreigners, though, occasionally clashed with Tibetan manners on the nature of important teachers and their position in Tibetan society. For example, there was the well-authenticated episode that some monks, especially Vibhūticandra, did not wish to prostrate themselves to a layman, in this case Drakpa Gyeltsen himself.[86] According to the Vinaya code, they were forbidden to do so, and this had been part of the conflict almost two centuries earlier, between the lay Bendé and the monks of Lumé and Lotön, when the Vinaya was reintroduced into Central Tibet from Tsongkha.

At the same time, many monks entered Central Tibet from the Tangut empire, eastern Tibet, Ladakh, Kashmir, and elsewhere. The presence of the Tanguts, especially, was notable, and it may be inferred that there was a drive for continued Tangut religious education under the auspices of Renzong, whose strong Buddhist support has already been noted in the case of the Kagyüpa.[87]

About this time, according to Kychanov, "knowledge of the Tibetan language and Tibetan Buddhist texts was a compulsory requirement for educated Buddhists in Hsi Hsia (i.e., the Tangut country), in any case an indispensable condition for occupying a post in the management of a Buddhist community."[88] Because Tibet had become a safe haven for Indian monks, Tangut monks could both study esoteric literature under Tibetans and receive the final Vinaya transmission to come into Tibet, the "middle" Vinaya (*bar 'dul*), brought by Śākyaśrī with his fellow Paṇḍitas and established in 1204. Writing in 1745, the Tibetan historian Tséwang Norbu stated that this latest Vinaya was the most influential of the monastic systems of the later spread, much more than the Western transmission (*stod 'dul*) through Gugé and actually rivaling the Eastern Vinaya transmission (*smad 'dul*) of Lumé and the others.[89]

This influx of foreigners directly affected Sakya in other ways. One work by Drakpa Gyeltsen, on ten kinds of esoteric activities using rituals associated with Vajravārāhī, was dictated to Tsingé-tönpa Gélong Shérap-drak, a Tangut.[90] Another text, an outline of consecration rituals involving maṇḍalas of the *kriyā* and *caryā* class, was written for Tsingé-tönpa Dülwa-dzinpa, probably another Tangut.[91] Apparently "Tsingé-tönpa," like "Tsami," was used for something like "Tangut teacher," and twelfth-century Tibetan works might contribute to our understanding of Tangut phonology. Other names of those requesting works—like a certain Tsāmi or Malu-lotön Gélong Könchok-drak—indicate their foreign origin, not to mention those monks from Lle'u (probably sLe'u, or Leh, Ladakh) and those from Tsongkha or Amdo.[92] The Amdo monks were so prominent that a monastery seems to have been built by one of them in Tsang, for Drakpa Gyeltsen, perhaps rather early in his career, wrote a text on fundamental rituals for Wangchuk-özer at Tsongkha Gönpa.[93] The earliest dated text by Drakpa Gyeltsen is actually a song of realization written for Yéshé Dorjé from Kham in 1171 and was an early example of a series of these texts that Drakpa Gyeltsen eventually produced.[94]

Closer to home, one of Drakpa Gyeltsen's most interesting correspondents was Gah-ring Gyelpo, to whom Drakpa Gyeltsen directed his genealogical letter of 1206 and who figures in Sönam Tsémo's letter of 1165 to Gyagom Tsültrim-drak.[95] The 1165 letter says that Gah-ring Gyelpo offered an extraordinary piece of Chinese silk to Drakpa Gyeltsen. Such offerings were marks of distinction and tended to elevate the importance of the receiver in the eyes of his immediate peers, which was especially important in this case, as Drakpa Gyeltsen then was only about eighteen. Evidently, Gah-ring Gyelpo and Drakpa Gyeltsen exchanged letters throughout the great teacher's maturity, for theirs is the longest correspondence by Drakpa Gyeltsen on record. Other figures in the great Sakya lama's life were doubtless his other disciples, but except for a few names, we know little about their personal lives, and they were omitted from the lineage lists and writings of the tradition in favor of Sakya Paṇḍita, whose scholarly reputation and sanctity overwhelmed all others in the first half of the thirteenth century.

DREAMS, REVELATION, AND DEATH

The most revealing work about Drakpa Gyeltsen was his record of his religious dreams, *The Lord's Dreams* (*rJe btsun pa'i mnal lam*). Here he recounts dreams he had at ages seventeen (1164/65), eighteen (1165/66), nineteen (1166/67), thirty-six (1183/84, after Sönam Tsémo's death), forty-eight (1195/96), sixty (1207/08), and sixty-six (1213/14).[96] Some were allegorical, like the dream at age forty-eight, which he believed to be a prophecy about himself and his disciples. Others were more mythical or even contained doctrinal observations. The following is the first part of the dream he had at sixty-six years of age:

> [Beltön Sengé Gyeltsen writes,] Generally, when Jétsün [Drakpa Gyeltsen] had a dream, he encountered his teachers, and it was to clarify various doubts that he had:
>
>> Again, at the age of sixty-six, I had a dream at dawn following the sixth of the ninth month, which is the final month in autumn. I met with the Great Lama (Sachen) and asked a question, and his answer clarified many doubts I had about the path. Then he said, "So, what do you think? Is the Enjoyment Body (*sambhogakāya*) of the Buddha better, or is the Manifestation Body (*nirmāṇakāya*) better?"
>>
>> I answered that principally the Victorious Bull (i.e., Buddha) exudes a Manifestation Body for the welfare of others, so that in reality good and bad have no place in the emanations of a Buddha. If this manifestation appears good or bad, it would simply be the magical display, so isn't the Enjoyment Body better?"
>>
>> He responded, "Son, that is exactly it! You have understood!"[97]

In the continuation of the dream, Sachen appeared surrounded by the eight great bodhisattvas, displaying his essential identity with Śākyamuni and the eight Arhats on one side and the maṇḍala of Hevajra and the eight goddesses on the other, finally resolving all into himself. The moral of the dream—lost on neither Drakpa Gyeltsen nor the Sakyapa lineage as a whole—was that

Sachen Kunga Nyingpo was the paradigmatic teacher who embodied the entire authentic Buddhist tradition, whether the vows of the śrāvaka, the bodhisattva, or the vidyādhara, for these collectively constituted the triple vow (*trisaṁvara*) so significant for Tibetan Buddhism.

One dream, in particular, became overwhelmingly important to later Sakyapa writers and was termed the Very Short Transmission (Shin tu nye brgyud) in the seventeenth century.[98] As stated in chapter 8, the formulation of the Short Transmission (Lam 'bras nye brgyud) had first appeared in the mid-thirteenth century and represented the probably apocryphal projection of an extraordinary wealth of textual and meditative material onto a vision of Virūpa by Sachen. Drakpa Gyeltsen's vision of his father, though, is more tangible, for the verse said to have been transmitted is contained in Sakya Paṇḍita's hagiography of his uncle, written just after Drakpa Gyeltsen's death in 1216.[99] It is not clear when the vision occurred, for the fifteenth-century Ngorpa chronicle declares that it happened thirty-six years after Sachen's death, which would place it about 1194/95, whereas later authors insist that it happened in Drakpa Gyeltsen's fifty-fifth year (1202/3).[100] Sakya Paṇḍita's hagiography places the vision directly following the prophetic dream in Drakpa Gyeltsen's thirty-sixth year (1183/84).[101] Sakya Paṇḍita records that Drakpa Gyeltsen appeared before his father in the divine realm and that the old master dismissed his other disciples there assembled. He then said,

> Son, listen up, for I am going to summarize all explanations
> of the Dharma, just as it is!
> The real master of *bodhicitta*
> Will first make his seat on absolute reality,
> And then grab a handful of the element wind.
> He generates well the fiery experience of psychic heat,
> So that the viscous *bodhi*[*citta*] will flow in the central channel,
> And tame the element earth and other elements.
> Having come face-to-face with the five forms of gnosis,
> He will obtain the position of deathlessness![102]

This summary of the teachings proved to be part of the larger claim that the Khön were superior to all other Lamdré lineages, for theirs was a transmission that continued to have short circuits of spirituality, crossing over intermediate generations so that the lineage began to assume the proportions of Virūpa > Sachen Kunga Nyingpo > Drakpa Gyeltsen > Sakya Paṇḍita > Phakpa > Khubilai Khan. It is not surprising that by the end of the thirteenth century, when the Sakyapa had achieved supremacy over the political and spiritual fortunes of Tibet, the Khön version of the Lamdré achieved the paramount position in Central and East Asia.

Before Drakpa Gyeltsen died at the age of sixty-nine, he had another series of dreams and visions that prophesied his future and his time of demise. He had dreamed at the age of thirty-six that he eventually would be reborn in *Suvarṇa, a realm inconceivably far to the north of this world; there he would be born as the universal conqueror *Guṇāparyanta. Sakya Paṇḍita relates that toward the end of his life, Drakpa Gyeltsen was visited by *ḍākinīs* and heroes, who acknowledged that he had developed the spirituality of the accord between the inner and outer qualities of interdependent origination, as understood in the Lamdré. Many times he had such visions, and many times Drakpa Gyeltsen sent back the celestial heroes and maidens, insisting each time that he was not yet ready to enter the pure realms. Finally, he could not hold off death any longer and passed on into the lands of bliss. Sakya Paṇḍita noted that although his passing was announced by spiritual beings, the aftermath of his demise was a time of misfortune. It is said that

> when that Great Being passed into nirvana, all the accumulated merit shared among beings became exhausted. All the areas that had not experienced evil years during the lives of previous men suddenly found themselves encumbered by frost, hail, strong winds, and unnatural rains. The various species of beings will be grievously harmed by all kinds of disease. The world will become unlivable with social chaos and infectious diseases.[103]

By the time he died in 1216, Drakpa Gyeltsen was considered by some Tibetans to be the emanation of the bodhisattva Mañjuśrī, the teacher of five Buddhas. With the death of Sachen's fourth and last surviving son, the age of lay teachers at the head of prestigious monasteries filled with monks had mostly passed. From that time forward, the fully ordained monk became the standard against which other forms of spirituality were measured.

THE BROTHERS AS COMPLEMENTARY LITTÉRATEURS AND THE DOMESTICATION OF THE LAMDRÉ

Not only were Sönam Tsémo and Drakpa Gyeltsen close in age and in agenda, but they operated in a tandem fraternal manner that was unprecedented in Tibetan literary life and perhaps was not seen again until the seventeenth-century Nyingma team of Urgyen Terdak Lingpa and Lo-chen Dharma-śrī. There was no question as to the leader in this relationship, for Sönam Tsémo risked much to propel himself into the unknown world of Sangpu Néütok, leaving his brother behind to work with the members of Sachen's entourage. Drakpa Gyeltsen seemed to regard himself as the follower in the footsteps of his brother, and he made known his debt to his brother and teacher over and over again. Yet it would be misleading to see the younger brother as less than the elder, for Drakpa Gyeltsen lived a life almost thirty years longer than that of his older sibling, and he continued to compose a legacy that survived in Sakyapa monasteries to the middle of the twentieth century. Their collective influence was overwhelming in the Sakyapa literary persona. I have been told by Ngorpa teachers, for example, that the abbot of that elite monastery in Tsang was expected to memorize four basic works, one by Sönam Tsémo, one by Sakya Paṇḍita, and two by Drakpa Gyeltsen.[104]

This is not to say that the work of the two brothers was so similar as to be indistinguishable, for each proved the complement and, sometimes, the supplement of the other, in both style and content. For example, if Sönam Tsémo's works were known for their concern with Indic standards of style and attention to prosody, and if Sakya Paṇḍita's works were famous for their neoconservative insistence on Indic orthodoxy, then Drakpa Gyeltsen's writings were renowned for their ease of understanding and accessibility.[105] Indeed, of the twelfth- and thirteenth-century Sakyapa legacy, the only works that appear to be sustained in popular Tibetan memory are the songs of realization composed by Drakpa Gyeltsen and Sakya Paṇḍita's *Treasury of Good Sayings* (*Sa skya legs bshad gter*), the Tibetan *Poor Richard's Almanac*. I have seen recent modern printings of and have heard Tibetans recite verses from both these works.

The brothers' greatest challenge was the complete domestication of the Lamdré system. The *Root Text of the *Mārgaphala* is, as we have seen, a technical, cryptic, and detailed articulation of internal yogic systems that were the primary focus and purpose of the siddha culture of early medieval India. Furthermore, all of the nine cycles of practice (*lam skor dgu*) maintained by Drokmi and transmitted by the Khön reflected this kind of yogic technique. Such systems were generated in and supported by a culture of itinerancy and personal empowerment and could easily have led to the conduct of the "crazies" of Padampa's lineage and the radical behavior of Lama Zhang Yu-drak-pa. Seldom did this siddha culture validate the development of strong Buddhist institutions, for such was the prerogative of institutional esoterism. The later movement built and supported its institutions through its sacralization of hierarchical relationships and sāmanta feudalism in the ritual system of the Buddhist maṇḍala and the consecratory rites to enter such maṇḍalas. While siddha systems used maṇḍalas, they did so with the intention that these representations were eventually to be destroyed, abandoned, deconstructed, and decoded, for they expressed all the institutional ideology that siddhas considered inferior to their own internal yogic processes and resultant psychic powers.

Conversely, Tibetan aristocratic values were protective of institutional longevity, for the chaos at the beginning of the period of fragmentation was still fresh in Tibetans' minds. Nonetheless, the benefits of yogic systems for the clans were enormous, in prestige, charismatic complexity, and the image of power and authority that accrued to religious clansmen. Moreover, Tibetans have consistently been fascinated with wild behavior and miracle tales, so that the magical component of religious life stood as a insistent beggar at the door of Sakya. Accordingly, the process of domestication required that behaviors promoting institutional instability be tamed, thwarted, subverted, interpreted, or just plain denied. This domestication was effected by several very potent means, which we consider in order of importance.

Masters of the Lamdré deemed the teaching's first consideration to be hagiography, the lives of its saints, which integrated the yogic practice into a narrative framework. Sachen's hagiography of Saroruhavajra is among the earliest surviving hagiographies of an Indian saint. Sönam Tsémo contextualized the study of the Dharma in light of the received hagiography of the Buddha and wrote about the Indian Amoghapāśa lineage.[106] He also authored a short but essential hagiography of Bari-lotsāwa, whom he never met. Together with Drakpa Gyeltsen, the brothers recorded the earliest surviving genealogies of the old dynasty and the early genealogy of the Khön.[107] Drakpa Gyeltsen also excelled at the hagiographer's art: his Virūpa story became the seminal version against which all others were measured, and he wrote relatively extensive materials on Kāṇha, the Cakrasaṁvara lineages, as well as notes on siddhas and their practices. Indeed, Drakpa Gyeltsen's work is a veritable cornucopia of curious lore about India.[108] He also provided the most complete early list on the spread of Eastern Vinaya communities (*sde-pa/tsho*) from the tenth century into Tsang Province and on the relationship of these groups to monastic communities in India.[109] For the Lamdré lineage in Tibet, Drakpa Gyeltsen offered rudimentary sketches of Drokmi, Sétön, and Zhang Gönpawa—in *Chronicle of Tibet: The Lineage of Teachers*, translated in chapter 5 of this book—and wrote the first piece on the lives of his grandfather and father.

The hagiographies accompanying the siddha technical literature, like Virūpa's story accompanying the Lamdré, depict these yogins as adversarial to non-Buddhists and amused by monks, even as the orthodox Buddhist clerics expelled them from their monasteries. Consequently, in the Sakyapa hagiographies, civic virtues eventually had to triumph. Virūpa, notoriously destructive of Hindu sites, was reined in by Avalokiteśvara and made to cease his destructive activity. Gayādhara, lying to Gö-lotsāwa about his identity, was unmasked in the end. Drokmi, unable to pay his debt to Gayādhara, gained the assistance of Zur Shākya Jungné, exchanging good teaching for solid gold.

Coupled with these social and narrative factors was the fact that the Lamdré had no necessary relationship to any specific maṇḍala. Sachen's commentaries acknowledged that the text could be used with either the Cakrasaṁvara or the Hevajra maṇḍalas, even though it did not agree exactly with the yogic systems enjoined in either of their tantras. Indeed, the popularity of the short pithy meditation manuals in the last half of the eleventh century was partly a result of these texts' posturing as being more direct and, in some sense, superior in validity to the tantras themselves. Thus, the tantric maṇḍalas simply served as instructional aids, tools on the path of meditation, and the practices associated with the lowest consecration. Conversely, the yogic treatises were the liberating trajectory, the shooting star that took the yogin right to the center of the cosmos. The grand schematisms of the visualized external maṇḍalas might bring the yogin to the bodhisattva path, but the forms of higher yoga could conduct him to the citadel of Vajradhara himself.

But for the Lamdré to be thoroughly at home in Sakya, it would need to become part of a larger ceremonial domain, one that articulated the ritual requirements and behavioral restrictions incumbent on its practitioners. According to a fifteenth-century chronicle, an initial collection of Lamdré materials occurred when Sachen placed his final commentary on the *Root Text of the *Mārgaphala*, the *Nyagma*, together with several short meditative works, in a special goatskin book case kept under lock and key. This initial collection was identified as the *Sag-shubma*, the *Goatskin Box*.[110] Sachen probably was familiar with a similar collection in the possession of his master, Zhang Gönpawa, but the tradition denies that Sachen received this work, even though a group of texts may actually have been offered to him by Zhang Gönpawa's widow.

Whatever the precedent, we now have little evidence to assess the tradition concerning the *Goatskin Box*. One other compilation of meditative works by Sachen is preserved in the collected works of the Sakyapa masters, however, and it serves to verify Sachen's practice of bundling texts. This is the *Rosary of Gems, the Precious Collection of Directions of Sakya* (*dPal sa skya pa'i man ngag gces pa btus pa rin po che'i phreng ba*), a collection of forty-nine abbreviated practices that was briefly examined in chapter 8.[111] The importance of this particular collection has not been acknowledged by the tradition much after Drakpa Gyeltsen, but an investigation of the eleven commentaries ascribed to Sachen Kunga Nyingpo demonstrates that some of the abbreviated practices appear to have been incorporated into the exegesis of the *Root Text of the *Mārgaphala*.[112] It is clear that the collection of forty-nine texts was sufficiently important for Drakpa Gyeltsen to compile his own compendium of thirty-two short texts, based on his father's precedent.[113]

Compendia of this variety had a lengthy history in Buddhist meditative traditions and operated as a de facto quintessence of canonical materials. Such compendia were particularly emphasized in meditative systems, where their ritual, meditative, and exegetical materials would often be found bundled together into a text of extraordinary importance. Moreover, other lineages were becoming invested in the same process, and at this time, the Kadampa began to put together their own *Kadampa Book* (*bKa' gdams glegs 'bam*), for many of the same mythic and ritual reasons.[114]

Whatever earlier bundling of Lamdré materials may have existed, the earliest surviving Lamdré compilation is Drakpa Gyeltsen's *Yellow Book.* Fortunately, the *Yellow Book* has preserved for us Drakpa Gyeltsen's criteria, for it was ordered according to the short *Contents of the Compendium* (*gLegs bam gyi dkar chags*) placed at its head. Drakpa Gyeltsen expressed his purpose for the *Contents*: "In order to eliminate the increase or decrease of the [number of] works placed in this volume, I have written this table of contents."[115] Drakpa Gyeltsen drew together material from several sources for his compilation; the term *Yellow Book* became its nickname because the autograph was wrapped in yellow-gold cloth.[116] Drakpa Gyeltsen himself humorously admitted how lazy he had been in completing the *Yellow Book*: when half of the first version of the *Yellow Book* had been accidentally lost, he finally was motivated to finish the *Contents* through the continual requests of a big-headed, short, fat, smart disciple of his, Shākya-drak.[117] Since his autocommentary on his versified discussion of the indivisibility of existence and nirvana (*Rin chen snang ba shlo ka nyi shu pa'i rnam par 'grel pa*) is dated 1212 and is mentioned in the *Contents*, the *Contents* must have been composed sometime between 1212 and Drakpa Gyeltsen's death in 1216. Thus the *Yellow Book* as described in the *Contents* was the result of a lifetime of teaching the Lamdré.

Drakpa Gyeltsen's *Contents* is actually the earliest document of this variety known to me: a self-contained, separately produced list of short works bundled together according to a sacred plan and accorded authenticity by its carrying out the intention of that quasi-scriptural dictum. Later in Tibet, very well developed examples of compendia catalogs were found, as in the works of Khampa writers of the late nineteenth and early twentieth century, Jamyang Loter Wangpo and Kongtrül Lotrö Tayé, whose statements of ritual compendia and their organizing principles are illuminating.[118] But for around the turn of the thirteenth century, Drakpa Gyeltsen's work appears to have been groundbreaking.

In reality, his *Contents* did not entirely close the work to minor adjustment, despite his affirmation that such was his purpose. It includes a statement that texts in sections IV and VIII could be set aside, which they seem to have been in practice. Such regulating principles, however, were not in the minds of later editors. Far from following Drakpa Gyeltsen's dicta in the *Contents*, all modern editions of the *Yellow Book* actually include many more materials than he enjoined, and the precise enumeration of the texts in the compendium has been a matter of contention since at least the seventeenth century.[119] Whatever the eventual disposition of the materials in manuscript and printed versions, the *Contents* calls for the following sections:

CATEGORY	NUMBER OF TEXTS	PAGES IN *LL* II
I. *Yellow Book Contents*	1 by Drakpa Gyeltsen	1–8
II. *Root Text* and *Nyags ma*	2—1 asc. Virūpa; 1 by Sachen	11–19, 21–128
III. gsal ba'i yi ge nyi shu rtsa gsum	24: 13 by Sachen (plus *A seng ma* becomes 14) 10 by Drakpa Gyeltsen	128–91
IV. gsung ba'i yi ge dum bu bcu bdun (not all present)	17: 3 by Sachen; 2 by Sönam Tsémo, 12 by Drakpa Gyeltsen	191–292
V. lam 'bring bsdus	2 by Sachen	292–99
VI. gzhung shing chen po bzhi	4: 2 or 3 by Sachen; 1 or 2 by Drakpa Gyeltsen	300–32
VII. rtogs pa bskyed pa'i chos lnga	5: 4 or 5 by Sachen, 1 or none by Drakpa Gyeltsen	323–44
VIII. dpe chung (not all present)	9: 6 by Sachen; 3 by Drakpa Gyeltsen	481–581
IX. bla ma brgyud pa'i lo rgyus	2 by Drakpa Gyeltsen	581–99

Thanks to the *Contents*, we can see the compilation as essentially nine larger units, ignoring for the moment the inclusion of later materials.[120] The first is the *Contents* itself (I). Next is the *Root Text of the *Mārgaphala* and its commentary, the *Nyagma* (II), and its presence here was perhaps one of the motivating factors in the continuing popularity of the *Nyagma*.[121] The next major section (III) consists of twenty-three short works that clarify parts of the *Root Text of the *Mārgaphala* and conclude with the *Asengma*, the summary of the *Root Text of the *Mārgaphala*. Many of these short works reflect the discussions in Sachen's commentaries and explain how the commentaries were composed, especially since the thirteen attributed to Sachen can be identified relatively easily and can be distinguished from his son's compositions.[122]

The next section (IV) contains seventeen titles, seven of which are not represented in the current printing. These seven covered the extensive consecration, the generation process practices, the tantric vows, tantric feast, homa sacrifice, and other issues; Drakpa Gyeltsen maintained that they could be either included or kept apart, since they were suitable for beginners as well as advanced students.[123] At the start of these seventeen works are two of the most influential treatises among the Sakyapa: Drakpa Gyeltsen's verse text and commentary on the viewpoint of the indivisibility of existence and nirvana (*'khor 'das dbyer med*), worked out along lines quite different from those of the Nyingma, for example, or of the exegetes of the *Guhyasamāja-tantra.*[124] The correspondence is structured through the completion process (*sampannakrama*) system of the Lamdré, in which the internal maṇḍalas of the adamantine body are given the dominant role in identifying bondage and liberation. The ramifications of this system are finally analyzed in the works of the Tsar-pa subsect of the Sakyapa from the sixteenth century onward and are acknowledged as one of the Sakyapa's contributions to esoteric doctrine.[125] Following these are works dedicated to specific questions of practice, and four short discussions of clarifying psychophysical obstacles, three of which were written by Sachen.[126]

Section V contains works elaborating the medium and abbreviated paths, which were broached at the end of the *Root Text of the *Mārgaphala* but not explained there. The sixth section (VI) consists of the "four great central pillars," delineating the more important theoretical considerations not included in the materials on the indivisibility of existence and nirvana. Because most are attributed to Sachen (the exact number by him is unclear), we looked at them in chapter 8. The seventh and eighth (VII and VIII) sections return to the specific practices incompletely described in the *Root Text of the *Mārgaphala*, such as the sexual practices and psychic heat, and many of the texts listed in the *Contents* also are excluded from the current printing. Three by Drakpa Gyeltsen that are included, though, show something of his exegetical direction.[127] They represent attempts to locate the scriptural sources for the practices found in the *Root Text of the *Mārgaphala* and, contrary to his intention, simply demonstrate that some practices can be anchored in the canon only through extraordinary interpretive gymnastics. Finally, section IX contains the hagiographical materials concerning the story of Virūpa and the record of Drokmi's career in India and Tibet, which was translated in chapter 5.

As mentioned earlier, section IV acknowledges that some materials were suitable for beginners, that is, the works on the Hevajra maṇḍala, its consecration, and related rites, which were required for the Lamdré to stabilize its institutional base according to the esoteric principles. Sachen had been concerned about meditative manuals (*sādhana*), especially those relating to either the Cakrasaṁvara lineage of Kāṇha or the Hevajra maṇḍala of Saroruhavajra.

Sachen apparently identified this latter figure as the exemplar for Hevajra meditative materials, an estimation that was doubtless held by his predecessors in the Lamdré lineage, and presumably Saroruhavajra's was the maṇḍala most closely associated with the Lamdré from the time of Drokmi. Sachen appears to have written consecration texts for Hevajra that were directly tied to the special characteristics of the Lamdré, and short texts are both found in the *Yellow Book* and scattered throughout Sachen's other materials.[128] Most of them address the issue of the body as the maṇḍala, as observed in the completion process, rather than the external formal maṇḍala, as used in the generation process. Although some of these works consider the integration of the Lamdré into the greater institutional dynamic, Sachen did not appear to have produced a single unified consecration text or a specific ritual manual for this purpose.

By the second half of the twelfth century, however, Sakya was seemingly a much different institution, and the need for such a text was clearly felt by the brothers. As mentioned before, the earliest identifiable text by Sönam Tsémo was an outline of Nairātmyā's consecration (*bDag med ma'i dbang gi tho yig*), which is closely associated with Hevajra's consecration, as Nairātmyā was considered Hevajra's mythic consort and the hierophant of Virūpa. When he was older, Sönam Tsémo contributed the first dedicated systematic texts for both the consecration and meditation on Hevajra according to the Lamdré. Whereas his father's consecration texts concerned the internal bodily maṇḍalas and were sparsely written, these works were specifically on the external formal maṇḍala (*phyi dbyibs dkyil 'khor*) and proposed an extensive ritual system for the Lamdré. Most of Sönam Tsémo's works that tied the Lamdré to a larger ritual pattern appear to have been based on the precedents of Saroruhavajra. For example, the fundamental meditative text uses the "four-limbed" arrangement, in which the generation process occurs in four stages, the quadruple adamant (*vajracatuṣka*): service (*sevā*), proximate accomplishment (*upasādhana*), accomplishment (*sādhana*), and great accomplishment (*mahāsādhana*). This was the strategy for meditation Saroruhavajra used but had been a commonly accepted pattern since the time of the *Guhyasamāja-tantra*.[129]

Drakpa Gyeltsen's contribution in this regard was somewhat different, for he apparently saw that despite its abbreviated outline, the four-limbed ritual was quite long in practice. His motive and method of developing an abbreviated version say much about the domestication of the Lamdré, for if he had been as dedicated to maintaining small groups of disciples as Drokmi had been, then it is unlikely that Drakpa Gyeltsen would have offered the shorter text. In his composition, Drakpa Gyeltsen also abandoned the four-limbed form of ritual and moved to a six-limbed form. He further decided to use a relatively obscure work whose author was instrumental in defining the exegetical method of the Lamdré: Durjayacandra's *Ṣaḍaṅgasādhana* (To. 1239), which had been translated by Ratnaśrījñāna and Drokmi. Durjayacandra based his meditative text on the six stages specified in fourth chapter of the *Vajrapañjara-tantra*, and so his own work could claim canonical precedent.[130] The six stages identify the normative generation process visualizations: the palace, the passion of being divine, the consecration by the "gnostic entities" collected before oneself, the tasting of the nectar of the five serous substances, offerings to Hevajra and retinue, and the praise by the attendant goddesses. In selecting Durjayacandra's work, Drakpa Gyeltsen evidently wished to emphasize the relationship between the two lineages of Lamdré and to promote the work of Durjayacandra, whose other compositions were so influential in Drakpa Gyeltsen's own development.[131] Based on Drakpa Gyeltsen's emphasis, the six-limbed form of the Hevajra maṇḍala became the norm for the Sakyapa from that time on and led to many more developments and some contentious issues.[132]

These works were the best expressions of a much larger effort by Sachen's sons to produce an authoritative textual basis for the rituals necessary to integrate the Lamdré into its institutional home. Accordingly, independent works on cake offerings, a wide variety of fire sacrifice manuals, and texts on other related rites were composed, based on the precedents of ritual works translated by Drokmi or others associated with the lineages collected and transmitted by Sachen himself. Even the metanarrative of the sorcerer's discipline (*vidyādhara-saṁvara*) received treatment, and Drakpa Gyeltsen composed a very long and influential exposition of the fourteen root tantric vows and the eight subsidiary commitments.[133]

ESOTERIC CLARIFICATION AND THE INTEGRATION OF THE EXEGETICAL SYSTEM

If the purpose of the previous works was to integrate the instructional method of the Lamdré into the larger institutional ritual world, then the task was only half done. The twelfth-century Sakyapa authors believed that the exegetical system was also an equally legitimate lineage stemming from Virūpa, although it proved much more protean in its form and boundaries. Accordingly, the "textless" Lamdré, as it was sometimes called, was just as important for the Khön overall, since it included commentaries on the *Hevajra* and related esoteric scriptures. As part of the process, the brothers were generally concerned with overarching questions about the tantric canon, as shown in Drakpa Gyeltsen's early catalog of the tantras.[134] Two specific domains, however, stand out as areas of complementary exegesis by the brothers: the commentaries on specific tantras, especially the *Hevajra*, and the development of the *General Principles of the Tantric Canon* genre. It is interesting that in both areas, Drakpa Gyeltsen conceived his contributions to be only addenda to the works of his father and elder brother, but his works in fact became paradigmatic to the tradition and, as in the case of the ritual texts, essentially superseded those of his predecessors.

Tantric commentaries are difficult to assess, for they usually draw from a number of sources. Yet we see Tibetan lineages like the Khön investing an inordinate amount of energy in exegetical composition, and we must believe that the institution continued to support the interpretive process as a mark of its vitality. Most of these factors hold true for the Sakyapa commentaries, and the lineage of its *Hevajra* exegetical texts is relatively clear. The fundamental basis for the *Hevajra* exegesis in the Sakyapa was the *Kaumudīpañjikā* of Durjayacandra, which had been translated by Drokmi and Prajñendraruci. Based on Drokmi's instruction, his most important pupil in esoteric exegesis was Ngaripa Selwé Nyingpo, whose commentary on the *Hevajra-tantra* remained influential.[135] Sachen wrote his own explanation of difficulties in the *Hevajra-tantra*, but it is not a work for the faint of heart, as it is difficult and requires a fairly good knowledge of the *Hevajra* before it becomes clear.[136] Sönam Tsémo's 1174 commentary on the *Hevajra-tantra* was an extensive elaboration of the ideas he espoused regarding the hermeneutic method for tantric exegesis, much of which he gathered from Ngaripa's earlier work.[137] Drakpa Gyeltsen wrote his own commentary in 1204, thirty years after his brother's version, which he relied on for his general outline and its chapter-by-chapter method.[138] Drakpa Gyeltsen, however, was less attentive to Indic models of composition and prosody, so that his writings tend to be clearer Tibetan.

Tantric commentaries alone, though, did not facilitate the understanding of the entire path, and one of the brothers' great contributions was their work on a grand map of the esoteric system. Sachen had already begun such an effort, with his *Short General Principles of the Tantric Canon* (*rGyud sde spyi'i rnam bzhag chung ngu*), perhaps modeled on the previous work of Gö-lotsāwa Khukpa Lhétsé. But the intellectual climate in Ü-Tsang had changed markedly since the composition of Sachen's work, and Sönam Tsémo's exposure to the questions and intellectual challenges at Sangpu evidently convinced him of the necessity for an expansion and restatement of some central issues, particularly concerning how the highly charged esoteric language of the tantric canon was to be properly understood.

Sönam Tsémo's unfinished *General Principles of the Tantric Canon* (*rGyud sde sphyi'i rnam par gzhag pa*) is in many ways a development of the ideas in his father's shorter work and is in some ways an independent treatise. The work has four parts, only three of which Sönam Tsémo addressed before his death. The initial section of the *General Principles of the Tantric Canon* begins with a discussion of the ultimate goal, which Sönam Tsémo also accepts as the unique condition of absolute awakening. He then proceeds to acknowledge that the Mahāyāna has two paths, the first being the method of the perfections and the second being the vehicle of the secret mantras. Sönam Tsémo next sets out to demonstrate the superiority of the Mantrayāna, but in a manner different from his father's, for he states that not only is it quicker than the normative path of perfections but also yields a superior result: Buddhahood on the thirteenth level of Vajradhara. There is nothing peculiar about this claim, for Mahāyānists had made similar statements about their superiority to the earlier schools on matters of ultimate awakening. But it does mean that Sönam Tsémo's doctrine of a single Buddhahood requires some manipulation of goal-related terminology, for how could there be only one goal for both Mahāyānist paths when the esoteric system yields a superior result? Sönam Tsémo also classifies the major titles in the tantric canon and expands on the "nondual" classification that the Sakyapas use for their most important works. In general, the balance of the first chapter of Sönam Tsémo's work is an elaboration on Sachen's earlier composition.

The very short second chapter analyzes the idea of "tantra," first by examining the name based on the well-known statements found in the final chapter of the *Guhyasamāja-tantra*: tantra is the threefold continuity of the ground, of nature, and of inalienableness.[139] Sönam Tsémo then discusses the triple continuity (*rgyud gsum*), noting that the triple continuity will be described in more detail in the (missing) fourth chapter.[140] Finally, the third chapter treats the difficult category of hermeneutics (*bshad thabs*). Buddhists have resorted to all sorts of hermeneutical techniques, and Sönam Tsémo collected six major systems for tantric exegesis and explained their employment according to his understanding.[141] The systems include the well-known methods already introduced in the *Sandhivyākaraṇa-tantra* and employed by the tantric Candrakīrti, as well as systems embedded in such tantras as the *Jñānavajrasamuccaya*, the *Khasama-tantrarāja*, the *Hevajra-tantra*, and the *Sampuṭatilaka*.[142]

Besides its importance to the emergence of a genre of works dedicated to the systematic taxonomy of tantra, the *General Principles of the Tantric Canon* is interesting for two reasons, one pertaining to the intellectual history of the twelfth century and the other at a more human level. Intellectually, the work offers a series of arguments that various members of the Buddhist monastic community used against the esoteric system as they saw it. Doubtless many of these arguments were actually encountered while Sönam Tsémo was studying under Chapa, for they are almost invariably phrased as coming from an unidentified "person practicing the perfections" (*pha rol tu phyin pa po*). Collectively, they show that the Tibetans then did not necessarily walk lockstep into the mystical future but reflected (as they have done before and since) on both the content and consequences of accepting the potentially destabilizing tantric material in their midst. One argument is particularly trenchant in its deconstruction of the esoteric paradigm:[143]

> Now for the contention that because we claim that the esoteric path has many methods and is without difficulties, therefore this path must be in error: [Opponent] You (tantrikas) maintain as a means for the realization of reality the many methods in the accomplishment of the highest siddhi—such as the "generation process" and the [completion process] use of channels, wind, and semen—your claims about these are incorrect. The "generation process" is the coming into being of the formal body of the Buddha (*rūpakāya*), and its reality is entirely in accord with the path of the perfections. The "many means"—the semen, wind and channels—also exist in the path of the Tīrthikas, and so how could they become the "means" [to Buddhahood]? Even more, the "many means" for ordinary siddhi, such as the means for killing beings and attracting consorts, these just represent animosity towards sentient beings. How could you see supreme awakening in them when even passage to the heaven realms is very far from one behaving in that manner? With respect to your "path without difficulties," you are claiming that the accomplishment of awakening is by means of bliss. Now if awakening is achieved by a lack of hesitation toward desires, then every ordinary being in the universe has achieved it. But if you claim that you will achieve awakening because one remains unstained if one examines the sense object with an understanding of reality [and not being involved with the field of desire]—this is straight Sāṁkhya, not the Buddhist path!

Sönam Tsémo's reply to these objections is indicative of the presuppositions of the esoteric system: he reasserts hierarchy, establishes their performance on different planes of reality, and dismisses the objection, since the standards of comparison are so obviously inferior to his own system. Thus despite their clear similarity, the Mahāyānist visualization of the formal body of the Buddha cannot be the same as the generation process, because the esoteric system produces awakening in a single lifetime and is therefore superior. The obvious dependence of the completion process on Śaiva practices and the dependence of both Śaiva and Bauddha esoteric systems on Sāṁkhya theoretical structures cannot be entirely true because the Buddhists frame their rites with the practices of going for refuge, generating the thought of awakening, and so forth. Concerning the use of drastic means to kill and control beings, Sönam Tsémo points out (correctly) that even Mahāyānists have admitted that these may be used by superior beings for the welfare of all, as seen in the instance of Asaṅga's *Bodhisattvabhūmi* and enacted by Lhalung Pelgyi Dorjé in his assassination of Darma in 842. Mahāyānists can therefore hardly be aghast at the esoteric elaboration of a doctrine they themselves inaugurated. Overall, Sönam Tsémo demonstrates that the strategy of hermeneutical stratification continued to be the apologetic method of choice for those defending systems developed in the early medieval environment.

The human side of the *General Principles of the Tantric Canon* is apparent from the final section of the last chapter that Sönam Tsémo completed, on exegetical method. The entire chapter is somewhat rough and would doubtless have been polished later, even though its current state is the result of Sakya Paṇḍita's editorial attention, and we do not know how extensive this was. The final section of the chapter is not announced at the beginning, however, showing that Sönam Tsémo added it without going back and changing the chapter outline. It begins with a refutation of objections by unnamed opponents, who protested the use of these elaborate exegetical techniques. One of the opposition, at least, pointed out that the importance of these methods was called into question by their lack of unanimity, for seldom do two esoteric exegetes explain a single section from a tantra in a similar manner. Sönam Tsémo, however, concludes the hard-nosed rebuttal of his opponents with a touching affirmation of his own tradition and the way in which it was handed to him. He offers a short summary of the two lineages from Virūpa: that through Ḍombi down to Prajñendraruci and that through Kāṇha down to Gayādhara. For a moment, we are allowed a glimpse into the core values of a twelfth-century author and his need to validate his father's legacy.

The final section, on the practice of the esoteric system according to the Sakya authorities, was announced by Sönam Tsémo but completed by Drakpa Gyeltsen in the latter's the *Jeweled Tree for the Realization of Tantra* (*rGyud kyi mngon par rtogs pa rin po che'i ljon shing*). We do not know exactly what sort of communication occurred between the two brothers on the nature of Sönam Tsémo's intention for the last section of his text, although a line in Drakpa Gyeltsen's introduction indicates that his brother had ordered him to write on this topic.[144] It is also somewhat misleading to describe the *Jeweled Tree* as the fourth section of Sönam Tsémo's *General Principles*, since the final work is almost twice as long as its parent text. We do know from references in the *General Principles* that Sönam Tsémo intended the text to discuss the triple continuity, and thus the *Jeweled Tree* is organized according to this strategy: the universal fundament of the causal continuity (*kun gzhi rgyu'i rgyud*), the path as the continuity of method (*lam thabs kyi rgyud*), and the conclusive fruitional continuity (*mthar thug gi 'bras bu rgyud*).

This overarching structure is somewhat misleading, however, for the first section is quite short, and the final section also of modest length, whereas the path material occupies more than 80 percent of the received text, analogous to the dissimilar sizes of the chapters seen in *General Summary of the Guhyasamāja* (*gSang 'dus stong thun*) of Gö-lotsāwa Khukpa Lhétsé. The causal continuity summarizes the idea of different categories of humans and the principle that certain individuals require specific methods. This had been a favorite topic of Buddhist authors since the inauguration of scholastic analysis, and Drakpa Gyeltsen modestly builds on the results of his predecessors, in part because he intended to examine the issue in greater detail in the path section. The fruitional continuity also covers familiar ground and is devoted to the layout of the levels of the bodhisattva, the level of the Buddha, the difference among general Mahāyānist ideas, and the esoteric system of thirteen levels. This final section concludes with a discussion of the different enumerations of the bodies of the Buddha, the idea of fundamental transformation (*āśraya-parivṛtti*), the five forms of gnosis, the concept of nonlocalized nirvana (*apratiṣṭhita-nirvāṇa*), nonduality, and the continuous activity of the Buddha on behalf of beings.

The path section, however, is different. Drakpa Gyeltsen could have simply followed the exegetical technique of his father embedded in the various Lamdré commentaries, with the "four quinaries," which were noted in the previous chapter. But perhaps following the lead established by Gö-lotsāwa, Drakpa Gyeltsen chose to start with an entirely different tactic and organized this lengthy section according to the nature of the candidate to be taught. Thus, prospective yogins were either those less fortunate that enter into the path by stages (*rim gyis pa*) or those of acute understanding who enter the path by encountering all its aspects at the same time (*cig char 'jug pa*). These are provocative terms, used by such disparate authorities as the Chinese Chan masters, Gö-lotsāwa, and Gampopa. Unlike the Chan authors, though, Drakpa Gyeltsen uses this terminology to discuss entrance into the esoteric path, not for the stage of final awakening, and in this he follows the precedent established by Āryadeva. Accordingly, the less fortunate novice might study in succession the path of the śrāvaka, the bodhisattva, and the vidyādhara, going through each in turn.[145] Conversely, the fortunate disciple would enter directly into practice of the higher yoga espoused in such nondual tantras as the *Hevajra*.[146]

In actuality, most of the text is taken up with the various materials presented under the rubric of simultaneous entrance, which is divided in a traditional manner according to the ritual of consecration, which ripens the disciple, or the actual practice of the esoteric system, which brings the disciple to liberation. Under the category of ripening, Drakpa Gyeltsen presents a very useful summary of the essential components of the *abhiṣeka* ritual as practiced in his day, and it is clear that at this time, Tibetans had already accepted the replacement of a real feminine partner (*shes rab dngos*) by a visualized partner. Similarly, in the practical section, he articulates the process of the visualization of maṇḍalas as a result of the vase consecration, the process of realization according to psychic heat as a consequence of the secret consecration, and the process of realization employing a real or imagined sexual union as a consequence of the insight-gnosis consecration.

This short summary cannot begin to convey the interesting and, in many ways, extraordinary nature of this text. Perhaps the most remarkable part of the *Jeweled Tree* is the long section on philosophical view or perspective, a section situated between the presentations of consecration and practice. Under this seemingly innocuous rubric, Drakpa Gyeltsen provides a fairly close analysis of the major Buddhist philosophical schools, concluding with the Madhyamaka. In accordance with the spirit of Chapa and the preference of some at his time, he concludes that extreme skepticism exhibited by the Prāsaṅgika school of Buddhapālita and Candrakīrti and promoted by Pa-tsap-lotsāwa is incapable of supporting the major ideas central to the Buddhist perspective. Instead, he shows that the Svātantrika Madhyamaka school of Bhavya is superior to its more extreme brethren in providing a nuanced assessment of issues of truth.[147]

Why is this important? Drakpa Gyeltsen was committed to the system that considered the ultimate nature of reality to be gnosis (*jñāna*), an interesting and exciting development in the later esoteric system, especially evident in the *yoginī-tantras*, but one that has received almost no attention in scholarly secondary literature. There are, however, different varieties of gnosis, specifically the kind of gnosis generated by example at the time of the insight-gnosis consecration (*mtshon byed dpe ye shes*) and the absolute gnosis achieved by the yogin at the time of achieving the thirteenth level of Vajradhara (*mtshon bya don gyi ye shes*). Likewise, there are different kinds of candidates, those with an ordinary perspective and those who have accumulated both merit and knowledge in previous lives. These categories must be maintained at the technical level and must be expressed in a manner that does not try to deconstruct their systematic relationship, for the root of the relationship between the disciple and master is trust, not suspicion. It is difficult to see how the Prāsaṅgika system—with its very heavy-handed dismissal of the validity of all Buddhist technical vocabulary—could act in concert with any meditative praxis while the greater subtlety of the Svātantrika could serve Drakpa Gyeltsen's need to provide an intellectual substructure to the esoteric system.

Having set up this substructure, Drakpa Gyeltsen moves to the establishment of the perspective of the indivisibility of existence and nirvana (*'khor 'das dbyer med*), which is the most basic of the Lamdré doctrinal statements. Here he takes the reader through the idea that the perceptible world is nothing but mentality, that mentality is finally illusory, and that the illusory nature is itself empty. The emptiness, though, is not an absence of any predication, for Drakpa Gyeltsen points out the commonsensical reality that the much touted "no position" of the Madhyamaka is itself a position. Instead, he goes on to affirm some basic Buddhist values in the process of delineating the position of his esoteric system. One value is that there is a relationship between the psychophysical continuum and the act of awakening. Similar to many *yoginī-tantra* systems, the Lamdré refers to the ordinary mind-body system as the "adamantine body" (*vajrakāya*) in which all the requirements for final awakening already are present but not functioning correctly. Thus the winds, the channels, the serous substances, the resonant structures, the mental systems, and the movement of gnosis already exist inside each human but are poorly developed. In this way, Drakpa Gyeltsen integrated the esoteric ideology of an infinite series of internal processes into the doctrinal structure of the greater Buddhist world and affirmed the system most appropriate to support the practices of the Lamdré. In both this and other works, Drakpa Gyeltsen does not shy away from encountering critics, much as his brother had done in the *General Principles of the Tantric Canon*.[148] In the process, Drakpa Gyeltsen gives us interesting insights into the tension between monasteries, like Sakya, that represented the superiority of the Vajrayāna and those that called its rhetoric into question.

THE BUDDHIST CONTEXT AND EARLY SAKYA PEDAGOGICAL WORKS

We also begin to sense the importance of education as a value for Sönam Tsémo, who always sought improvement in his own work. That sense of pedagogical method reached a degree of fruition in 1167 with the composition of one of his most famous works, the *Door to Enter the Dharma* (*Chos la 'jug pa'i sgo*).[149] The work is divided into several loosely organized sections and is dedicated to explaining the fundamental axioms of the Buddhist path, with a special emphasis on ideas of hagiography and historical narrative. The text begins with an examination of issues associated with the definition and understanding of Dharma, its primary term. The next section explores questions of motivation, purification, and encountering a good spiritual friend, who assists in the path. Then the text discusses the Buddhist path, inasmuch as the path is the means for entering the Dharma. This direction takes Sönam Tsémo into the major part of the text, which is a retelling of the previous embodiments of the Buddha, his incarnation into this world, and his twelve acts. Sönam Tsémo considers objections, based on dissimilar sources, but presents his own view about the nature of the Buddha and relates his cremation, distribution of relics, and the three collections (or councils) of the Dharma. The author then summarizes the lineage of Indian scholars before turning to the introduction of Buddhism in Tibet, which includes a genealogy of the Tibetan kings. Sönam Tsémo finishes with a chronology containing some dates very important to the reconstruction of the prerenaissance period, from the mid-ninth to the late-tenth century. At the conclusion, Sönam Tsémo reveals his concern for the future of the Buddhist religion, for there are few who speak the words of the Buddha, and most people seem angry at them. In Magadha, the adversaries of the Dharma increase; in Tibet, false doctrines spread; and evil border kings destroy the great monasteries of India. Sönam Tsémo accordingly wrote this work on the essentials of the Buddhadharma, so that the threats on both sides of the Himalayas would be answered by renewed effort by those few who esteemed the religion.

Besides this, Sönam Tsémo also wrote a short work on the manner for Tibetans to pronounce the letters of their language and the words of mantras and makes a plea for Tibetans to learn a uniform pronunciation.[150] His list of pronunciations by territory is apparently a very early description of Tibetan dialects and serves as a resource for the historical phonology of the language.[151] Likewise, the description of Indian pronunciation as known to him in the mid-twelfth century is an underused resource for Indic phonology. In a similar vein, it is certain that Drakpa Gyeltsen used Smṛti's grammar of the Tibetan language to teach the correct principles of pronunciation, orthography, and composition, for a work purporting to be his teaching notes has been published.[152] Based on his exposure to the work of Chapa, Sönam Tsémo also wrote a commentary on the *Bodhicaryāvatāra*. This exercise started out as a commentary on its important ninth chapter but was eventually expanded to include the entire text and is still used as the commentary of choice when Sakyapa teachers instruct their charges in this elegant Mahāyānist work.[153] Finally, we should note that both the brothers composed introductory ritual texts for beginners in the monastic environment, so that the archive of normative prayers and correct ritual conduct in the halls of Sakya could be observed.[154]

The efforts of these two accomplished scholars on behalf of neophytes to the Buddhist path did not go unnoticed, even though this is most often the case for those writing introductory materials. Amé-shep maintained that Sönam Tsémo was so concerned with pedagogy that these and other works were unprecedented (*sngon med*) in their assistance to aspiring scholars.[155] To comprehend this praise, we must understand that in normative Tibetan jargon, "unprecedented" is a pejorative term. Nonetheless, Amé-shep declared that in Sönam

Tsémo's case, progress was possible and even admirable, rather than his innovation's being simply a semantic equivalent of ineptitude or willful perversion of the tradition. Amé-shep made similar statements about Drakpa Gyeltsen, that however difficult the text, he always wrote it so his disciples could easily understand it, even when it was being read aloud for the first time.[156]

CONCLUSION: A SECURE SOURCE OF BUDDHIST SPIRITUALITY

By the early thirteenth century, Tibetan Buddhism had assumed its place on the stage of Asian religion. Overcoming some measure of social instability, the neoconservative agenda of Sakya Paṇḍita, Drigung Jikten Gönpo, and Chaglo Chöjé-pel afforded a strong social and ritual locale for the important Sarma institutions and provided the rationale for their self-promotion. With Indian literary principles assuming the central position, Tibetans found their institutions being judged on the same standards. Consequently, the "monasteries" that had sometimes been founded and controlled by nonmonastics—Dromtön for the Kadampa, Marpa for the Kagyüpa, and Könchok Gyelpo for the Sakya—became increasingly brought under the aegis of the Vinaya and the authority of Indian models of decorum. When the system failed, as in the case of the crazy masters like Lama Zhang or though the machinations of the Eastern Vinaya monks, Tibetans patched together ad hoc solutions, but the structural faults remained.

Between the time Sakya was built in 1073 and Drakpa Gyeltsen died in 1216, not quite a century and a half had passed. Yet the Tibetan model of institutional security succeeded, in large part by each generation's performing its appointed tasks with an acute sense of timing and a large measure of good luck. Sakya Monastery was lucky enough to enjoy both excellent leadership and extraordinarily good fortune, and the two litterateurs among the sons of Sachen were instrumental in both these directions. It is unfortunate that they sometimes did this at the cost of scholarly accuracy, for it is known that Butön Rinchendrup, writing more than a century after the great work of Sönam Tsémo and Drakpa Gyeltsen, found many errors in their quotations and attributions to sources in the Buddhist archive.[157] To his credit, Butön dealt with these errors with relative tact and delicacy, which were probably required in the case of writings by such icons of the systems. Drakpa Gyeltsen's discussion of the esoteric vows also created quite a stir, for he affirmed that the three vows of the śrāvaka, bodhisattva, and vidyādhara have a single essence, much as early Buddhism affirmed that all Dharma has the single taste, that of liberation.[158]

The famous Kālacakra scholar Vibhūticandra felt called on to refute Drakpa Gyeltsen's position, even though this did not diminish regard for the text, which is still maintained as the standard today. Yet minor questions like these simply demonstrate that these brothers' works were extraordinarily successful in moving forward the agenda of domestication. They managed to set the stage for one of the most important developments in Central Asian history, the fact that the Mongols left Tibet largely alone and delegated its administration to a Sakya monk.

Amé-shep relates an amusing tale, that the deities of Tibet and Mongolia appeared to Drakpa Gyeltsen in a dream one night while he was staying in a meditation cave. They all drank from the wine offering placed in a skull on Drakpa Gyeltsen's esoteric altar, got roaring drunk, and danced and sang the night away, babbling in a variety of languages. Amé-shep affirms that this was how the Sakyapa established a special relationship with the state of Mongolia, for the connection had been smoothed ahead on the spiritual plane through an uproarious evening of imbibing esoteric nectar.[159] Such stories are delightful literary episodes, but the reality is that the Khön invested more than a century of hard work to domesticate the antinomian systems of Indian esoteric Buddhism and bring them into line with the aristocratic values espoused by houses of merit in eleventh- and twelfth-century Ü-Tsang. They required the complicity of an entire maṇḍala of remarkable personalities who were willing to subordinate themselves and occlude their contributions so that the Khön star might shine that much brighter. The dozens of figures who served the Khön—Bari-lotsāwa, Géshé Nyen Pül-jungwa, and Géshé Nyak Wang-gyel, to mention a few—did so to contribute to an institution larger than themselves, and they must have understood the consequences of institutional instability in Central Tibet. Like this maṇḍala of human agents for the Khön, the domestication of the Lamdré text embedded it in a much larger field of literary and spiritual endeavors even while it always was reserved pride of place in the religious life of Sakya and its various affiliate institutions. The achievement of all these individuals is an outstanding example of the protean nature of the medieval Indian Buddhist institutional culture, its adaptability, and its ability to service both religious and political needs.

10

Conclusion and Epilogue: The Victory of the Clan Structure, Late Tantric Buddhism, and the Neoconservative Vision

Esoteric Buddhism arose from the regionalization of Indian polity and religion during India's early medieval period, especially from the seventh century onward. In India, it represented a partially successful reorganization of the various religious communities to encounter and overcome the challenges of economic destabilization, population relocation, loss of patronage, the new fluid politics of sāmanta feudalism, and the increasing importance of caste, gods, and regional valorization. These same communities were also facing a dramatic change in Buddhist identity, through the decline in women's participation, the shift in intellectual values toward Brahmanical models, and the loss of both ethical and intellectual centers of gravity. In the face of such challenges, Indian Buddhists responded by appropriating and sanctifying selected aspects of the sociopolitical sphere, although this response embodied a tension new to the Buddhist tradition. On one side were those affirming and sacralizing the real politik of the day, the Buddhist monks of the great institutions of the Gangetic valley and, to a limited degree, elsewhere as well. Using the model of becoming the "supreme overlord" (*rājādhirāja*), they developed and propagated a meditative system and attendant rituals that displayed a thorough grasp of the ideals and methods of sāmanta feudalism. Constructing sacred Buddhist paradigms of the power relations grounded in the political maṇḍalas surrounding them, they articulated an idea of core zones of authority and buffer client states in the relations between the Buddhas and bodhisattvas in the visualized sacred circles.

At the other end of the spectrum was the newly emergent siddha form, whose goal was individual dominion over the sorcerers (*vidyādharas*), and the gods themselves, by whose authority an overlord rules. The siddha traditions also imported a politics of dominion and control, but for the benefit of the single siddha and not for the betterment of the surrounding community. Appropriating and altering methods derived from Śaiva and other sources, Buddhist siddhas both developed radical meditative techniques not seen before in the Buddhist world and wrapped them in language that was simultaneously playful and ferocious, erotic and destructive. Siddhas from the Buddhist persuasion—of whom Virūpa was a paradigmatic example—became the proponents of regional languages and cultures, of tribal affirmation, and of the segmentation of power in medieval India. They forced the monasteries to grapple with the new rituals and yogic systems, to develop new forms of hermeneutics, to comprehend a rapidly evolving iconography, to use song and dance in offerings to the new forms of the Buddhas, and to become invested in an entirely new canon, in which the *mahāyoga* and *yoginī-tantras* sometimes took second place to the new yogic instructions (*upadeśa*) handed to a specific siddha by an often feminine manifestation of the absolute.

Tibetans, Newars, and other Himalayan peoples became the receptors of these seventh-eleventh century developments, and they used the new forms to regenerate their own fragmented cultures. Whereas the institutional and siddha esoteric systems of India were the result of a society reeling from a series of difficulties, in Central Tibet these forms of religion became the mortar that the eleventh-century translators used to resurrect Tibetan identity and indelibly associate it with esoteric Buddhist practice. Tibetans had just passed through a dark period of their history, following the fragmentation of the empire, and sought a reinvigorated form of Buddhism able to provide a common discourse of transmuting the poison of chaos into the nectar of civilization. The rough language of the new scriptures, the magical fascination of its practitioners, the slippery ethics of its representatives, and the emphasis on charismatic personalities all appealed to a section of the emerging Tibetan intelligentsia and to the many representatives of the great clans on the plateau. They based themselves in the foundational temples and small monasteries resurrected by Eastern Vinaya monks, who had been ordained at surviving temples in Tsongkha and brought its monastic curriculum to Central Tibet. With ability and dedication, the next generation arose as translators of great merit, reconnecting Tibetan spirituality with Indian Buddhism, in order to bathe the stains of the broken imperial vision in the healing waters of Indian religion.

Aspiring translators sought out the new scriptures in the great monasteries and small retreats of India, Kashmir, and Nepal. Once accomplished in their avocation, the translators of the esoteric rites put together a feudal formulation of personal charisma, clan affiliation, subtle learning, occasional sanctity, ritual virtuosity, and undeniable dedication. Drokmi Shākya Yéshé and his contemporaries used the medieval Indian world to recreate and reform Tibetan culture, all the while cementing that same culture in a public ethos that affirmed fragmentation and political disunity. Neither Drokmi's personal avariciousness nor the ethical lapses of Gayādhara did much to persuade Tibetans that such systems of religiosity came at a cost to themselves and to their society. In recompense, the esoteric translators of the eleventh century accomplished one of the great intellectual feats of history, rendering into the classical Tibetan language a vast corpus of ritual, medical, and philosophical doctrine. While the translators' temples seldom achieved durable distinction, the monasteries constructed by their immediate followers found a new social form by aligning the religious lineage with the stable system of the inheritance of clan domains, a problem that had not been successfully solved for the Eastern Vinaya monks.

Throughout the renaissance, Tibetans tested the limits of their religious heritage and began the process of indigenization. Grounded in the forms of religion surviving from the fragmentation of the dynasty, the Nyingma traditions developed new varieties of ritual and literature. They were motivated partly as a response to the new translations, partly to validate the sanctity of clan chieftains so often the leaders of the old lineages, partly to verify the authenticity of indigenous Tibetan composition, and partly to express the simultaneous loss of and faith in the great dynastic accomplishments. They revealed treasure, both literature and material remains, at the old dynastic sites throughout Central Tibet, declaring these to be the personal treasures of the emperors, sent to sustain the Tibetan people in the royal absence. The Terma employed indigenous aesthetics, affirmed autochthonous spirits and gods, and moved Tibet from the periphery of the Buddhist world to the center of the Buddhas' and bodhisattvas' activity. In a similar vein, Sarma authorities also developed new ideas through the eleventh and, particularly, the twelfth century. Whether the topic was the new formulation of Mahāmudrā under Gampopa, the epistemological developments of Chapa, or the rise of Chö rites with Machik Labdrön, Sarma representatives in Ü-Tsang began to understand that the eventual disposition of Buddhism in Tibet required that the religion of India be open to a specifically Tibetan articulation. All were caught up in the possibilities of knowledge, awareness, and the many new gnoseological formulations of the renaissance.

Consequently, the esoteric texts—both Nyingma and Sarma, both Terma and translations—provided an iconic formation, yielding multiple points of reference for the individual communities in the society. The highly esoteric and jealously guarded meditative instructions became both the vehicle for their practitioners' liberation and the emblems of their status and superiority. In the process, many different kinds of textual communities emerged, each focused on its individual works, each claiming ultimate sanctity for its lineages and traditions. Underpinning all such claims, though, was the remarkable fact of the textualization of Tibet, so that even while their religious were haggling over the definition of textual authority, Tibet was seen and evaluated as the land of texts, and the landscape itself was the source of religious works of the great saints and the all-knowing emperors.

As part of Tibetan indigenization, clans like the Ché, the Ngok, the Nyö, the Nyiwa, and the Kyura began to specialize in religion, and the Khön were a preeminent example of this process. Creating a mythology that ultimately combined bodhisattvas' incarnations with divine descent from the Tibetan gods, the Khön were among the most successful of the eleventh- to twelfth-century religious clans. Khön Könchok Gyelpo constructed Sakya in 1073, and the institution was maintained thereafter by Khön clan members, who used their extraordinary intelligence and skills to create a fortress of learning in the feudalized spiritual culture of Tsang Province. Through the assistance of a large number of learned associates, they developed the translations of Drokmi and Bari-lotsāwa, particularly the esoteric system of the Lamdré, into a vision of a ritual ground, in which Tibetan practice rivaled anything to be found in India, with the relic cult similarly advanced. Like other successful clans in Central Tibet, the Khön moved from a father-son lineage to an uncle-nephew form, with celibacy and monastic vocation eventually displacing the married sage as the ideal.

The collapse of Indian centers in the twelfth and thirteenth centuries cemented the reputation of Sakya and other monasteries, forcing Indian monks to pay homage to Tibetan laymen, who were both more fortunate and more skillful at maintaining the Buddhadharma than their Indian patrons had been. Sachen Kunga Nyingpo and his two highly accomplished sons developed the institution and domesticated the wild image of Virūpa, making the Lamdré, one of the most esoteric systems of siddha practice, the mainstay for perhaps the most conservative Buddhist center. This simultaneous domestication of the *yoginī-tantras* and the explanatory yogic manuals required internal meditations to be tied to a maṇḍala ritual form, emphasizing a single series of scriptures and impressing a community structure on the siddha's image of quintessential individuality. The emergent form was that of the mystic hierophant, a successor to Indian monks and siddhas, skillful in the world, spiritually mature, with magical and administrative ability, possessed of internal divinities and external alliances—powerful in every sense of the word. The Khön success at this endeavor became a great part of the ground from which the seeds for the association of the Sakya patriarchs with Khubilai Khan would eventually be grown.

At the same time, the troubles in twelfth-century Tibet—the burning of

Samyé and the Jokhang, the infighting among the Shangpa disciples of Khyungpo Neljor, and the religious warfare of Lama Zhang, among others—created a sense of a potential for the collapse of social forms, as had happened before in the ninth and tenth centuries. Combined with the Islamic invasion of North India, the loss of Central Asia to Islamic armies, the rise of the Mongol powers, and the conflagration at its borders, Tibetans developed a perception of orthodox Buddhism under duress, a perception that was fundamentally correct. Internally, Tibetans understood that they preserved much of the great monastic system of North India, even as it was lost to Indians in real time. The sense of international Buddhist crisis, combined with the Indian and Tangut fascination with Tibet, assisted the development of the neoconservative movement, including Drigung Jikten Gönpo, Sakya Paṇḍita, Chaglo Chöjé-pel, and others. They saw what they understood as the Buddha's pure message being eroded within as well as without, and the natural creativity of the Tibetan people embodied in the work of Chapa, Gampopa, the Terma masters, and others was perceived as heresy and doctrinal betrayal. Consequently, they worked to suppress any deviation from the norm, criticizing the Buddhist activity that they understood to be un-Indian, and in doing so, they adopted a standard that was a theoretical position rather than a real Indian construct. Unknown to or unacknowledged by the neoconservatives, many of the same behaviors and ideas that they criticized in early-thirteenth-century Tibet had been found in India for many centuries.

Three factors aided their position. First, the Mongols realized that the neoconservative vision would be good for Mongolia, so Khubilai Khan institutionalized the identity of Sakya Paṇḍita as the paragon of Tibetan religion. The Mongols simply were fascinated with the sage that could do it all—yogic systems, magical rites, monastic decorum, clan connections, intellectual acumen, administrative ability, medicine, logic, language, and so forth—for most of the teachers selected by the Mongols throughout their centuries of involvement with Tibetan religion had the maximum number of skills. Sakya Paṇḍita was, after all, in many ways the culmination of seventeen hundred years of Buddhist history. Second, Tibetans began to see that their social health rested in greater part with the institutional health of the large, well-run monasteries, which had by then completely embodied the symbiosis between aristocratic clan and late Indian Buddhism. In this, the Mongols followed their lead; historically unfamiliar with such stable institutions, they were intuitively suspicious of the many Chinese versions, which embodied aesthetic and intellectual directions unattractive by Mongol standards. Finally, the neoconservatives, good Buddhists that they were, did not elect to mandate their vision through the force of law, even when given the opportunity by their Mongol lords. They would be magnanimous rulers: having achieved victory, they could afford to grant religious freedom to those at the margins. In this, they were similar to other Buddhists who were satisfied that eventually all the world would see the truth.

The neoconservative movement in the early thirteenth century, aided by Indian monastic refugees and the Mongol warlords, would formulate much of the institutional structure for Tibet from that point on. After the fall of the Sakya from power and the rise of the Pagmo Drupa hierarch Jangchub Gyeltsen in 1348, the same vision of an orthodox Buddhist monk representing a strong yogic and canonical tradition remained viable. Intermittently successful, the person of the monk hierarch would stand in tension with the ideology of a lay political leader until the rise of the Dalai Lama's government in the seventeenth century. The roots of all of these, however, lay with the bold efforts of a few obsessed men in the tenth to twelfth century, men who overcame unimaginable challenges, gambling on their intellectual and spiritual abilities at a time when Tibet so desperately needed their efforts. Throughout all their activities, the Buddhist religion provided the correct materials for reconstructing Tibetan society, and the doctrine of awakening in its various guises became the social, intellectual, and spiritual catalyst for the renaissance of Tibetan culture.

This is not to say that all Tibetan innovations or the crazies of the Tibetan siddha expression were content to leave the field, for these were indelible patterns of human behavior. The Nyön-pa craziness continued on among the Kagyüpa and Nyingma figures, and peripatetic Tibetan siddhas continued to flavor meetings of religious institutions for some time to come. They were offset in some measure not just by the neoconservative ideology but also by the development of the reincarnate lama paradigm, which in most cases institutionalized clan structures, for the clans accepted the smaller Labrang units of Buddhist monasteries as their own property to be administered as such while the reincarnations were predominantly recognized among the aristocracy. Tibetan innovations continued, with the great heresy yet to come: the "other emptiness" of the Jonangpa. But the pattern of struggle for and against stratified intellectual systems and stratified social systems has remained a dominant theme of Tibetan religious life to the present.

Notes

NOTES TO INTRODUCTION

1. Pakpa's letter to Khubilai, ca. 1255–59, *rGyal bu byang chub sems dpa' la gnang ba'i bka' yig*, *SKB* VII.238.3.2–4. This letter was noticed by Szerb 1985, p. 165, n. 2. He is undoubtedly right in identifying this letter as addressed to Khubilai, and it was written to Khubilai before he achieved his election as Khan on May 5, 1260; Rossabi 1988, pp. 51–52; Ruegg 1995, pp. 38–40. In his new years' greetings of 1255–58 to Khubilai, 'Phags-pa generally uses the phrase "Prince-Bodhisattva" when addressing Khubilai, once adding Khubilai's name (Tib: go pe la); see *rGyal po go pe la sras dang btsun mor bcas la shing mo yos sogs la gnang ba'i bkra shis kyi tshigs bcad rnams*, *SKB* VII.300.3.7 (1255), 301.1.4 (1256), 301.4.7 (1258); the undated text between 1256 and 1258 has bsod rnams dbang phyug rgyal ba'i sras po go pe la instead (301.2.1). One of 'Phags-pa's other compositions addressed to Khubilai Khan, his *bsNgags par 'os pa'i rab tu byed pa*, written in response to Khubilai's successes against the Song dynasty in 1275, is almost as obsequious.

2. The consequence of Sa-skya Paṇḍita's effective imprisonment was that he produced virtually nothing while in Mongol internment; Jackson 1987, vol. 1, pp. 28–29, 68. Tucci 1949, vol. 1, pp. 10–12, translated a letter to Tibetans attributed to Sa-skya Paṇḍita on their dire position; its authenticity was challenged in Jackson 1986.

3. Petech 1990, pp. 16–22. On the office of national preceptor, see Ruegg 1995, pp. 18–19, 46–52. On the antecedents of the imperial preceptor, see Dunnell 1992; Sperling 1987.

4. Franke 1981, pp. 58–69; Heissig 1980, p. 24. It is difficult to follow Ruegg 1997, p. 865, that neither Sa-skya Paṇḍita nor 'Phags-pa was "in a position to compose a full theoretical treatise on the 'constitutional' relation between the two orders represented by the Officiant/Spiritual Preceptor and the Donor-Ruler" because of excessive responsibilities. I would instead argue that such an idea was without Indic precedent and would have proved extraordinarily problematic in both theory and practice. Compare *rGyal po la gdams pa'i rab tu byed pa'i rnam par bshad pa gsung rab gsal ba'i rgyan*, esp. *SKB* VII.95.1.6–4.1, on the esoteric vows between master/disciple.

Szerb 1985, p. 168, indicates that the work was by Shes-rab gzhon-nu but supervised by 'Phags-pa.

5. Franke 1978, pp. 58–61; Szerb 1980, p. 290; Rossabi 1988, p. 143; Grupper 1980, pp. 47–63, app. 1; and Sperling 1991 and 1994, most of whom emphasized the role of Mahākāla rituals in the Mongol and Tangut worlds; Sperling 1994, p. 804, observed that "one pivotal element in the relationship was a shared belief in the efficacy of rituals linked to Mahākāla as a means for manifesting powers that could be harnessed to the Mongol imperium." While the statement is doubtlessly the case, the texts cited are from the sixteenth and seventeenth centuries, a time when Mahākāla became especially important. Heissig 1980, pp. 26–27, 56, shows that Mahākāla became for later Mongols a ritual system devoted to mediating relationships with animals, which was perhaps also true for the early Mongols.

6. Rossabi 1988, pp. 145–47.

7. For a summary, see Petech 1990, pp. 39–140.

8. Petech 1990, p. 9. Like most modern historians, Petech glosses over the availability of descendants of the royal family to be taken by the Mongols as Tibetan representatives and their hostages.

9. Rossabi 1988, pp. 143–44.

10. Jagchid 1970, pp. 121–24.

11. Wylie 1977, pp. 113–14.

12. Rossabi 1988, pp. 16, 41. Grupper 1980, pp. 53–54, app. 1, cites the 1739 *Altan Kürdün Mingyan Gegesütü Bic' 'ig*.

13. Szerb 1980, p. 290, sums up the difficulty of this fuctionalist-reductionist supposition: "The primary reasons for the growing influence of the Sa-skya sect were no doubt political. But as Mongol rulers were generally enthusiastic about magic . . ."

14. Ratchnevsky 1991, pp. 96–101; Cleaves 1967.

15. Meyvaert 1980, pp. 252–53.

16. Boyle 1968, pp. 538–42; Petech 1990, pp. 11–12.

17. Heissig 1980, pp. 26–28; Jagchid and Hyer 1979, pp. 180–82.

18. Szerb 1985; Sperling 1994; and Ruegg 1995 have made contributions in this direction.

19. For example, Petech 1990, p. 2; Wylie 1977, p. 103. We may note that even as late as Ruegg 1995, who is certainly not a functionalist, the early (1283) 'Phags-pa hagiography in the *Lam 'bras slob bshad* collection, *bLa ma dam pa chos kyi rgyal po rin po che'i rnam par thar pa rin po che'i phreng ba*, by Ye-shes rgyal-mtshan, was overlooked.

20. On the Mongol patronage of the Kashmiri master Na-mo, see Jagchid 1970, pp. 117–20; 1980, pp. 80–84.

21. For a translation of the biography of Kumārajīva's captor, Lüguang, see Mather 1959, esp. pp. 4–6, 35, 86–87; on Kumārajīva's life and position, see Robinson 1967, pp. 71–95.

22. Wright 1990, pp. 34–67 (originally published in *HJAS* 11 [1948]: 321–71). Wright's analysis of Fotudeng's relationship to Shile and the Shi clan is somewhat more sophisticated than most later proposals of 'Phags-pa's interaction with Khu-

bilai. Wright maintained that the Kuchean monk demonstrated the "fetish power of Buddhism in four fields": rain making, military advice, medicine, and politics.

23. For a list of the Mongols and their Tibetan teachers, see Wylie 1977, p. 108, n. 16.

24. Heissig 1980, p. 25: "Not only Chinese sources but also Mongolian sources describe the orgies celebrated at the Mongol court as the result of the profane misunderstanding of this doctrine, and the degeneration of the Mongolian ruling class which went along with this, as one of the most important causes of the collapse of Mongol rule over China (1368)."

25. For a recent assessment of the process, see Ehrhard 1997.

26. The problem of Bon sources is discussed by Martin 2001b, pp. 40–55. I have perused most of the literature he mentions, but with such meager results that I feel the topic would be better pursued by Bon specialists.

27. This date has been consistently represented as 1253 or 1258; see Szerb 1985, p. 166; Ruegg 1995, pp. 33, n. 42 (1258, relying on the *mKhas pa'i dga' ston*, pp. 1414–15), pp. 48–49, nn. 88, 54. Most scholars apparently follow the 1736 *Sa skya gsung rab dkar chag*, p. 316.4.2, which gives 1253. The early hagiography in the *Lam 'bras slob bshad* collection, *bLa ma dam pa chos kyi rgyal po rin po che'i rnam par thar pa rin po che'i phreng ba* by Yes-shes rgyal-mtshan is entirely silent about the ostensible three consecrations ('Phags-pa's relationship to Khubilai is specified on pp. 304–6, 327–29), but 'Phags-pa's own *bsTod pa rnam dag gi phreng ba SKB* VII.143.3.2 gives the date of Khubilai's initiation as 1263 (chu mo phag). The *rGya bod yig tshang chen mo* of 1434 gives the date of the consecration sometime after the fifth month of 1255 (p. 326.8) and before 'Phags-pa's return to Tibet in 1256 (p. 328.4). The tradition that Tibet was a consecration gift (dbang yon) from Khubilai to 'Phags-pa seems first to appear in the *rGya bod yig tshang chen mo*, p. 327, and is possibly a post Yuan Sa-skya attempt to claim continued authority in Tibet, long after actual political dominion had been lost to Phag-ma gru-pa Byang-chub rgyal-mtshan. My suspicion is that the consecration was given only once, in 1263, but that it kept getting conflated with other events, eventually to be combined with the myth of Tibet as a gift for consecration.

28. Stearns 2001 is referenced throughout, and our differences in reading the material will be apparent.

29. Davidson 2002c, pp. 1–24, is devoted to this issue. Intellectuals in traditional societies perceive their agenda as the reaffirmation of the religious culture, by glossing over difficult issues of discontinuity, innovation, and unethical conduct and by restricting the questions asked to those already affirmed by the tradition. For traditionalists, the preferred method of treating modern, critical history is to launch an ad hominem attack discounting the historian and his or her motives, behavior, or psychology.

30. Davidson, *Indian Esoteric Buddhism—A Social History of the Tantric Movement.*

31. Spitz 1987, vol. 1, p. 2; Cochrane 1981, pp. 14–20.

32. See Green 1988, pp. 120–21; See Maristella Lorch, "Petrarch, Cicero, and the Classical Pagan Tradition," in Rabil 1988, vol. 1, pp. 71–114.

33. The social position of medieval artisans is treated in *Mayamata*, chap. 5; compare Dubois 1897, pp. 34–35, 63, who believes the problems of bad government are at fault. A good modern study is that by Kumar 1988, pp. 12–62, which looks at the social status of artisans in Banaras. For the rise in artists' status in sixteenth-century Europe, see Martines 1988, pp. 244–59; Burke 1986, pp. 74–87. The relationship of medicine to religion took some time to emerge; the *Deb ther sngon po*, for example, does not mention the *rGyud bzhi* or the other medical or artisan works. There is material on medicine and other arts in the 1434 *rGya bod yig tshang chen mo*, yet the author seems to indicate that, as in the case of his discussion of swords (p. 232), precious little had been written earlier. Earlier works on medical history seem to stem from the twelfth century; see Martin 1997, nos. 17, 35–37, 105, etc. The twelfth century is the time we also see medicine in the Sa-skya, and Grags-pa rgyal-mtshan devoted a work to the science, which is conspicuously placed as the last item in his collected works; *gSo dpyad rgyal po'i dkor mdzod*, *SKB* IV.354.3.1–396.1.6.

34. An example of the application of these categories to the visual arts in Tibet is Klimburg-Salter 1987.

35. Stark and Bainbridge 1985. More recent interesting studies on emerging religions phenomena include Barrett 2001; Dawson 2001; and Fink and Stark 2001, among many others.

36. Gould 2002, pp. 745–1022, is an extended treatise on this model and its application to culture.

NOTES TO CHAPTER 1

1. Edited and translated into German in Dietz 1984, pp. 360–65. I differ from her translation on small points. I am well aware that the text as it stands cannot be entirely authentic; see Karmay 1998, p. 25.

2. Chattopadhyaya 1994, pp. 183–222; Burton Stein 1991 is an update of the segmentary state model.

3. On this phenomenon, see Nath 2001; compare Sharma 1965 and 2001, pp. 235–65.

4. *Dravyasamgraha*, pp. 42–44, 115–16.

5. On these classifications as inherited by Tibetans, see Orofino 2001.

6. See Davidson 1991, for Ngor-chen's two works examining the ritual systems of texts classified as *kriyā* and *caryā-tantras*: the *Bya rgyud spyi'i rnam par bshad pa legs par bshad pa'i rgya mtsho* (written in 1420) and the *sPyod pa'i rgyud spyi'i rnam par gzhags pa legs par bshad pa'i sgron me* (written in 1405).

7. These experiences are nicely outlined in Gyatso 1982.

8. *Guhyasamāja-tantra* XII.58–65, XVIII.135–39, XVIII.171–77.

9. For a good traditional Tibetan discussion of these schools and controversies about their literature, see A-mes zhabs, *dPal gsang ba 'dus pa'i dam pa'i chos byung*

ba'i tshul legs par bshad pa gsang 'dus chos kun gsal pa'i nyin byed, esp, pp. 24.5–48.3, covering India and Indian literature.

10. Mañjuvajra is mentioned in *Guhyasamāja-tantra* XII.3, XIV.37, XVI.68, XVI.86; and Akṣobhyavajra is mentioned in *Guhyasamāja-tantra* VI.prose intro., XI.26 and XVII.1; neither of these figures are necessarily primary in the tantra, however.

11. I discuss the Buddhajñānapāda legend in some detail in *Indian Esoteric Buddhism*, pp. 311–16; the lore of the tantric Nāgārjuna has hardly been examined beyond Tucci 1930a.

12. From *Pañcakrama* II.4–23. I have translated the forms of śūnya as if śūnyatā, for that is effectively the way it is glossed, for example, *Pañcakrama* II.23ef: mahāśūnyapadasyaite paryāyāḥ kathitā jinaiḥ ||. For the importance of this material, see Wayman 1977, pp. 322–24, unfortunately obscured by Wayman's impenetrable style; more approachable is Kværne 1977, "The Religious Background," pp. 30–34, in the introduction to his *Caryāgītikośa* edition.

13. Introductory Remarks to *Pañcakrama*, p. x, n. 12.

14. See Davidson 1991; Stein 1995; Mayer 1998.

15. For a discussion of the source of this list of sites, see Davidson 2002c, pp. 206–11.

16. *bKa' 'chems ka khol ma*, pp. 131, 138, 156; the same text identifies Tibet as being like Śrī Laṅka in that it is Rākṣasapuri; pp. 46, 145, 202.

17. For a short examination of these lineages, see Davidson 1992.

18. For a discussion of these maṇḍalas, see Davidson 2002c, pp. 294–303.

19. This table is actually an amalgamation of two tables formulated by Snellgrove in his introduction to the *Hevajra-tantra*, pp. 34, 38. For a more detailed discussion of these issue of the origin of such ideas, see Davidson 2002d.

20. Reported in *Deb ther sngon po*, vol. 1, p. 127.18–19; *Blue Annals*, vol. 1, p. 97. The *gDams ngag mdzod* vol. 10, pp. 2–6, preserves a text on *sādhana* translated by Gyi-jo that may be part of chapter 4 of the *Kālacakra-tantra.*

21. *dKar brgyud gser 'phreng*, pp. 59–135; compare with the Ras chung bsnyan brgyud tradition of Lha-btsun-pa Rin-chen rnam-rgyal, 1473–1557, represented in Guenther 1963, pp. 7–109, which has some convergence with my text. Other Nāropā hagiographies that I have looked through to understand the difficult sections of the preceding text include the early hagiography attributed to sGam-popa in the *sGam po pa gsung 'bum*, vol. 1, pp. 4.6–16.3; *Lho rong chos 'byung*, pp. 18–29; *sTag lung chos 'byung*, pp. 77–91; *mKhas pa'i dga' ston*, vol. 1, pp. 760–771; *'Brug pa'i chos 'byung*, pp. 186–204; *dPal Nā ro pa'i rnam par thar pa*. The odd hagiography of Abhayadattaśrī is found in Robinson 1979, pp. 93–95 (translation), pp. 338–39 (ms. text, ff. 108–11) = **Caturaśītisiddhapravṛtti*, fols. 25b4–26b1. A comparative study of the Nāropā hagiographies would be instructive.

22. *dKar brgyud gser 'phreng*, vv. 20–32 of the Nāropā chapter; the verses are given on pp. 62.7–64.4 and commented on pp. 85.2–132.4.

23. The Lha-btsun-pa Rin-chen rnam-rgyal hagiography translated in Guen-

ther 1963 is different from earlier works precisely because it emphasizes content in the hagiography. This strategy was also followed in the *dPal Nā ro pa'i rnam par thar pa* of dBang-phyug rgyal-mtshan.

24. This is from *sTag lung chos 'byung*, pp. 56–77; compare *mKhas pa'i dga' ston*, vol. 1, pp. 739–54, which organizes these lineages by direction; *Lho rong chos 'byung*, p. 16.

25. There are several versions of the "six yogas," but the bKa'-brgyud-pa tend to follow this one; it is from the *Ṣaḍdharmopadeśa*, To. 2330, and *gDams ngag mdzod*, vol. 5, pp. 106–7.

26. This was proposed by Ngor-chen Kun-dga' bzang-po in his section of the *Lam 'bras byung tshul*, p. 110.2.3, by associating the Dharmapāla of the legend with the Dharmapāla of the *Buddhabhūmisūtra* transmission. For the dates 530 to 561 of the scholastic Dharmapāla, see Kajiyama 1968/69, pp. 194–95.

27. *Lam 'bras byung tshul*, p. 110.2.4.

28. *Lam 'bras byung tshul*, p. 111.3.5–6. The old royal chronology is defended by Sa-skya Paṇḍita in his hagiography of Grags-pa rgyal-mtshan, *bLa ma rje btsun chen po'i rnam thar*, pp. 147.1.1 ff., based on apocryphal Khotanese sources, and he rejects the Indian chronology of Paṇḍita Śākyaśrī, which the Indian master computed in 1210, identifying the Buddha's nirvāṇa in 543 B.C.E., a much more accurate date. See Yamaguchi 1984 and Davidson 2002a.

29. This is a translation of the *dPal ldan Bi ru pa la bstod pa*, *SKB* I.1.1.1–2.2.4.

30. An intentional contradiction is inserted to indicate that Virūpa is beyond duality, part of standard Mahāyāna hermeneutics. The identification of contrapositives is seen elsewhere, for example, v. 3, where Virūpa is considered the play of the immovable.

31. kun tu rgyu ba—possibly an indication of Virūpa's Avadhūta status, although Avadhūta is normatively rendered kun tu 'dar ba; compare *Hevajra-tantra*, Snellgrove 1959, vol. 2, p. 161.

32. Ripening is done through the four consecrations, and liberation is performed through the practice of the generation and completion paths; see Grags-pa rgyal-mtshan's *rGyud kyi mngon par rtogs pa rin po che'i ljon shing*, p. 17.1.3.

33. 'Gros bzhi thims; Lam-'bras masters consistently define the final fruit by means of the dissolution of these four gradations or functions of the body; *Sras don ma* 437.3–440.3; *sGa theng ma* 481.3–485.3.

34. The text continues with an articulation of a vision and teachings said to have been received by Sa-chen. Thus the great lord of yogins appeared with four other siddhas. Sa-chen visibly saw his face, and Virūpa preached to him. Sa-chen's panegyric was said to arise out of the force of this experience. For an evaluation of the report on this ostensible vision, see chapter 8.

35. *bLa ma rgya gar ba'i lo rgyus*, *SKB* III.170.3.2–5.

36. The "four aural streams" (*snyan brgyud bzhi* : **catuḥkarṇatantra*, see To. 2337 and 2338; *snyan-brguyd* is perhaps a rendering of either *karṇaparamparā* or *karṇatantra*) are one of the important defining systems erected by the Lam-'bras authors, the other major one being the "four epistemes" (*tshad-ma bzhi*). Together

they verify the unbroken and undiminished authenticity of the lineage from the Buddha to the lama of initiation; compare *Sras don ma* 197.5–201.3; *sGa theng ma* 296.2–299.2; Davidson 1999. For the appropriation of the tshad ma bzhi by bKa'-brgyud-pa masters, see Martin 2001b, pp. 158–76.

37. The use of "heat" as an image of meditative success is of long duration in India, whether in the Brahmanical sense of *tapas* or the specifically Buddhist usage of *uṣman*, which is the term used here in its Tibetan rendering, *drod.* Within the Lam-'bras, this use of heat is preeminently indicative of the experience generated on the worldly path, not the experience of the path of vision and above. Its presence is a prerequisite for further experience on the path. See Grags-pa rgyal-mtshan's *rGyud kyi mngon par rtogs pa rin po che'i ljon shing*, pp. 47.2.5–50.2.1; *Sras don ma*, pp. 252.6–58.2. The capacity to turn the poisons of the personality (latent demons) into the qualities of liberation (forms of gnosis) is at the base of the Vajrayāna theoretical structure and was definitively elaborated in the environment of the Sa-skya, especially Grags-pa rgyal-mtshan; see *rGyud kyi mngon par rtogs pa rin po che'i ljon shing*, pp. 63.2.2–69.1.4; compare *Jñānasiddhi* I.37–64.

38. Thapar 2004 has reexamined the history of Somanātha. I am preparing a monograph on Virūpa and his Apabhraṁśa materials.

39. *bLa ma brgyud pa'i rnam par thar pa ngo mtshar snang ba*, p. 116.6; *mKhas grub khyung po rnal 'byor gyi rnam thar*, pp. 27–29.

40. *gDams ngag byung tshul gyi zin bris gsang chen bstan pa rgyas byed*, p. 7.1–2; see Nihom 1992 for an edition and discussion of the *Chinnamastā sādhana* attributed to Virūpa.

41. In the *gLegs bam gyi dkar chags*, p. 5.3–4, Grags-pa rgyal-mtshan identifies the lam 'bring po of *Lam 'bras rtsa ba* IV.B as the rtsa ba med pa'i lam, meaning that the "textless path" would be one holding merely to the precepts; compare *sGa theng ma*, p. 487.4; *Sras don ma*, pp. 443.6–444.4. Conversely, in *Sahajasiddhi*, *Pod ser*, p. 395.5, a note indicates that it is the *rtsa ba med pa'i lam 'bras* and that the inclusion of the eight other practices was justified by a line in the *gLegs bam gyi dkar chags*, p. 6.4, that he could not mention all the little teachings associated with the Lam-'bras. This was used to include various teachings like the eight subsidiary practices; see *Lam 'bras byung tshul*, p. 125.1.2. The *Lam 'bras lam skor sogs kyi gsan yig*, p. 32.4.3–5, said to have been received from 'Phags-pa, appears to collapse the *Sahajasiddhi* and the exegetical lineages from Ḍombi into a single line.

42. As far as I am aware, the earliest recognition of this division is in the lineages found in bSod-nams rtse-mo's *rGyud sde spyi'i rnam par gzhag pa*, pp. 36.4.2–37.1.3. bSod-nams rtse-mo, though, does not employ the nomenclature of "man ngag lugs" and "bshad lugs," and it is not clear when this terminology came into use. Grags-pa rgyal-mtshan simply numbers them: first lineage and second lineage; *rGyud kyi mngon par rtogs pa rin po che'i ljon shing*, p. 69.1.5–6. I noted "birwa pa'i man ngag brgyud," but not distinguished from a "bshad brgyud," in Grags-pa rgyal-mtshan's *rTsa ba'i ltung ba bcu bzhi pa'i 'grel pa gsal byed 'khrul spong*, p. 235.3.2. The earliest use of terms close to "man ngag lugs" and "bshad lugs" that I have noted is in Ngor-chen's *Thos yig rgya mtsho*, pp. 48.4.1–49.3.6, where we find mang

ngag lugs kyi dkyil 'khor du rgyu dus kyi dbang gi chu bo ma nub par bskur ba'i brgyud pa, but its contrast is with the bshad bka' legs par thos pa'i brgyud pa, 49.1.6. This specific terminology is missing in 'Phags-pa's *Lam 'bras lam skor sogs kyi gsan yig*, p. 32.4.2–5, where we find lam 'bras kyi brgyud pa and gzhung gi rgyud pa. The distinction between the two lineages was important enough that Ngor-chen dedicated separate works to their lines of transmission: his *Lam 'bras byung tshul* for the "method of instruction" and his *Kye rdo rje'i byung tshul* as a partial discussion of the "explanatory method." See the bibliography for these works. For a more general discussion, see Davidson 1992, pp. 109–10.

43. A version of this verse is used at the completion of the ceremony for bodhisattva precepts, *Bodhicaryāvatāra* III.25; the form here is from the *Vajrāvalī*, Sakurai 1996, p. 475; another version is found in the *Saṁvarodaya-tantra* XVIII.34c-35b.

44. For example, *Sarvadurgatipariśodhana-tantra*, p. 238.32; this use of vajra is specified in *Sarvatathāga-tatattvasaṁgraha*, Chandra, pp. 59–60, there done as part of the consecration.

45. *Vajrayānamūlāpattiṭikā-mārgapradīpa*, To. 2488, fols. 208b7–210a4; for a review of tantric rules, see Davidson 2002c, pp. 322–27.

46. *Sarvabuddhasamāyoga-gaṇavidhi*, To. 1672, fol. 196b4; see Davidson 2002c, pp. 318–22; and Snellgrove 1987, vol. 1, pp. 160–70.

47. van der Veer 1988, pp. 85–130; this situation may be contrasted with the Nāth yogis studied by Bouillier 1997, pp. 142–57, 206–9.

NOTES TO CHAPTER 2

1. *bKa' 'chems ka khol ma*, translating pp. 277.19–78.2, 278.13–79.1.

2. The standard history is Beckwith 1987.

3. A survey of the court involvement with Buddhism is found in Dargyay 1991.

4. This is a point that Kapstein 2000, pp. 11–12, makes convincingly. The term *feudalism* has been contested in its application to Tibet's modern period, but the primary criteria—decentralization, dissolution of a central state apparatus, and insecurity—inhibiting the application of feudalism to Tibet as proposed in such protests as Thargyal 1988 are in fact found in our period. Because of these and other traits, it was similar to Indian feudalism, for which see Davidson 2002c, chap. 2.

5. Tucci 1947, p. 463. This same observation has been made many times.

6. Hackin 1924, p. 18; *Chos la 'jug pa'i sgo*, p. 343.3. Tucci 1947, table between pp. 462–63; Tucci 1956a, pp. 51–63, considers the later lineage. The perhaps late-twelfth-century *Bod kyi rgyal rabs* of Grags-pa rgyal-mtshan, p. 296.1.5–4.2, and the *Chos 'byung me tog snying po sbrang rtsi'i bcud* of Nyang-ral nyi-ma 'od-zer, pp. 446 ff., appear to be the earliest of our surviving sources to provide a somewhat more extensive discussion of the period. By the thirteenth century, the 1283 Ne'u chronicle *sNgon gyi gtam me tog phreng ba*, Uebach 1987, pp. 118 ff.; the *lDe'u chos 'byung*,

pp. 137–63; and the *mKhas pa lde'u chos 'byung*, pp. 364 ff., seem to present well-developed stories of the period; their similarity to the *sBa bzhed zhabs btags ma*, Stein 1961, pp. 78–92, would seem to argue for a late date to the completion of this latter work; see Martin 1997, pp. 23–24, for a bibliography on *sBa bzhed* scholarship.

7. Sørensen 1994, p. 410, n. 1420, provides the references to Tibetan literature. The *Xin Tangshu* gives 838.; see Pelliot 1961, p. 183; compare Vitali 1996, p. 541, n. 923.

8. *Chos 'byung me tog snying po sbrang rtsi'i bcud* pp. 417.20–18.4; *sBa bzhed zhabs btags ma*, Stein 1961, pp. 70.14–71.

9. Sørensen 1994, p. 412, n. 1431, notes the Sad-na-legs 812 chronology but misunderstands the significance of the bkas bcad rnam pa gsum and does not consider that reforms took time to implement; that is why the Ral-pa-can materials emphasize his position in the revision. Compare the recent work of Scherrer-Schaub 2002 on this process.

10. See Herrmann-Pfandt 2002 for a recent discussion of these catalogs.

11. For these and their sources, see Uebach 1990; I thank Janet Gyatso for drawing my attention to this article.

12. *Bu ston chos 'byung*, p. 191.5–7; *mKhas pa'i dga' ston*, vol. 1, p. 417.12–16; the final part of this is in *Chos 'byung me tog snying po sbrang rtsi'i bcud* p. 423.6–7.

13. This is the reading of *Bu ston chos 'byung*, p. 191.6; *mKhas pa'i dga' ston*, vol. 1, p. 417.14, makes the restriction apply solely to the mātṛ-tantras, the later scriptures not translated in the early period. rNying-ma authors like Nyang-ral do not accept this restriction on translation and engage in lengthy descriptions of the material translated, most of which, however, is actually apocryphal and assigned to Ral-pa-can as a matter of chronological defense. See, for example, *Chos 'byung me tog snying po sbrang rtsi'i bcud* pp. 420–23, which introduces aberrations like the translation of the Byams-chos-lde-lnga (p. 422.8), mostly done later by rNgog bLo-ldan shes-rab.

14. *dBa' bzhed*, p. 88 (fol. 24b5–6).

15. Richardson 1998, pp. 176–81.

16. As found in the *dKar chag ldan dkar ma*; Lalou 1953, Herrmann-Pfandt 2002.

17. *Bod sil bu'i byung ba brjod pa shel dkar phreng ba*, pp. 78–88, shows how much the sources disagree over the birth, death, and regnal dates of this figure.

18. Weinstein 1987, pp. 114–37.

19. Kapstein 2000, p. 52, rightly rejects the explanation that Buddhism was the sole cause of collapse, and he also looks to the issues of empire maintenance to explain the question. But he does not fully consider Relpachen's excessive expenditure on behalf of the clergy as a primary factor or the catastrophic assassination as important. For an estimate of dissatisfaction with the Buddhist faction, see Sørensen 1994, p. 423, n. 1488.

20. Woghihara, ed., *Bodhisattvabhūmi*, pp. 165–66; Demiéville, "Le Bouddhism de la guerre," reprinted in Demiéville 1973, pp. 261–99, esp. p. 293; Tatz 1986, 70–71.

21. This is according to the Ne'u Paṇḍita's *sNgon gyi gtam me tog phreng ba*, Uebach 1987, p. 120; it is also accepted by the *sBa bzhed zhabs btags ma*, pp. 81–82.

22. Her name is given as sNa-nam bza' in the *mKhas pa'i dga' ston*, vol. 1, p. 430, but the Nyang-ral's twelfth-century *Chos 'byung me tog snying po sbrang rtsi'i bcud*, p. 446, provides 'Bal-'phan bza'-ma; the *lDe'u chos 'byung*, p. 141, and the *mKhas pa lde'u chos 'byung*, p. 369, give 'Phan-bza' 'phan-rgyal.

23. Petech 1994, pp. 652–56; Vitali 1996, pp. 196–97.

24. *mKhas pa'i dga' ston*, vol. 1, p. 430; *lDe'u chos 'byung*, p. 141; *Deb ther dmar po*, p. 40; Nor-brang O-rgyan presents several reasons why he believes the story should be dismissed, *Bod sil bu'i byung ba brjod pa shel dkar phreng ba*, pp. 103–11.

25. Petech 1994, p. 649.

26. Petech 1994, pp. 651–52.

27. Nor-brang O-rgyan is particularly interested in the popular revolts; *Bod sil bu'i byung ba brjod pa shel dkar phreng ba*, pp. 128–56.

28. Petech 1994, p. 651; Beckwith 1987, pp. 169–72; *lDe'u chos 'byung*, p. 144; *mKhas pa'i dga' ston*, vol. 1, p. 431; *mKhas pa lde'u chos byung*, p. 372. We have a wealth of variation on the orthography of this man's name; Kho-byer lde stong sbas (*mKhas pa lde'u chos 'byung*), Kho-bzhir stong sde sbas (*lDe'u chos 'byung*), dBa's kho bzher legs steng (*mKhas pa'i dga' ston*), and the Chinese Shang Kong-zhe (Petech 1994, p. 651); I have followed Beckwith's reproduction of the Dun Huang annals' orthography. It is quite possible that he was only distantly related to the sBa, and Petech notes that the Chinese transcription of his name was as if it were 'Bal, another important clan.

29. Petech 1994, p. 651, discusses this man's career; see also Richardson, "The Succession to Glang-dar-ma," in Richardson 1998, p. 110.

30. Vitali 1996, p. 546; *Chos 'byung me tog snying po sbrang rtsi'i bcud*, p. 447; *mKhas pa lde'u chos 'byung*, pp. 321, 327.

31. *mKhas pa lde'u chos 'byung*, p. 376.

32. Vitali 1996, p. 542, n. 923.

33. Vitali 1996, pp. 190, n. 545; *lDe'u chos 'byung*, pp. 142–43; *mKhas pa lde'u chos byung*, p. 371. I believe Vitali misinterpreted this passage, for it is clear that the two figures of 'Bro Tsug-sgra lha-ldong and Cang-rgyan A-bo (with their variant spellings) did not try to "protect dPal-'khor-btsan's throne in gTsang" but acted in the capacity of officers of an institution, a common use of the verb bskyangs.

34. *lDe'u chos 'byung*, p. 142.

35. *lDe'u chos 'byung*, p. 143.

36. Vitali 1996, p. 548; *mKhas pa lde'u chos 'byung*, p. 376; Petech 1997, p. 231, puts this date at 923.

37. For a general discussion, see Vitali 1996 and Everding 2000, vol. 2, pp. 260–69.

38. This passage is taken from the *mKhas pa lde'u chos byung*, pp. 372–73, supplemented by the *lDe'u chos 'byung*, pp. 144–46. Similar language is included in the *mKhas pa'i dga' ston*, vol. 1, p. 431. This section continues in all three sources, but the language of omens and conversations with divinities is very obscure and is apparently related to the ancient Tibetan of the dynastic religion.

39. A curious narrative about him is related in *mKhas pa lde'u chos 'byung*, pp. 373–74. The traditional scenario for the story of his death is discussed in Richardson 1998, pp. 144–48; *mKhas pa'i dga' ston*, vol. 1, pp. 420–22; compare *Chos 'byung me tog snying po sbrang rtsi'i bcud*, p. 446; *lDe'u chos 'byung*, p. 138.

40. For Bran-kha dpal-yon as a later divinity, see Nebesky-Wojkowitz 1956, pp. 232–33. Karmay 1998, pp. 437–38, relates that as a demon he challenged the authority of the nine mountain deities of Central Tibet. Richardson 1998, p. 147, saw what was said to be Bran-kha dpal-yon's stuffed body set up in Yer-pa.

41. *mKhas pa lde'u chos 'byung*, p. 371. A different form of this phrase is cited in *lDe'u chos 'byung*, p. 143; here, I understand res mos as being from the cognate ris mo, a diagram or image.

42. *lDe'u chos 'byung*, p. 143.3–6.

43. *Chos 'byung me tog snying po sbrang rtsi'i bcud*, p. 446.17–19.

44. *Chos 'byung me tog snying po sbrang rtsi'i bcud*, p. 446.15–16; the "dar gyi mdud pa" indicates a protective silk string with a knot in the center guaranteeing life; some Tibetans apparently believed that this dissolution of political and religious order was impossible; see *mKhas pa'i dga' ston*, vol. 1, pp. 420–21.

45. *mKhas pa'i dga' ston*, vol. 1, p. 433.4–8; compare *sNgon gyi gtam me tog phreng ba*, Uebach 1987, p. 85, n. 321, which dates the tomb desecration as 877. However, the date of the breaching of the tombs was more plausibly during or after the long insurrection of 905 to 910. Tucci 1950, p. 42, and Petech 1994 and 1997 discussed the difficult chronology involved. Tucci's conclusion that it happened in 877 conflicts with more recent studies; see Hazod 2000b, p. 185; Hazod 2000a, p. 197, n. 6; and Vitali 1996, pp. 544–47. For the titles of the tombs, see Haarh 1969, pp. 391–92; and *mKhas pa lde'u chos 'byung*, pp. 377–79.

46. *mKhas pa'i dga' ston*, vol. 1, p. 455.10–11; on the palace at Khra-'brug, see the *bKa' 'chems ka khol ma*, p. 104.7–8.

47. Kaḥ-thog Tshe-dbang nor-bu's *Bod rje lha btsan po'i gdung rabs tshig nyung don gsal*, pp. 78–81, presents a good summary of the differing opinions about the time elapsed between the collapse of the royal dynasty and the reintroduction of the Dharma into Central Tibet; compare *mKhas pa'i dga' ston*, vol. 1, p. 481.19–21.

48. Petech 1994, p. 653; both he and Vitali follow the long chronology, which is best represented in the Sa-skya records. See Vitali 1996, pp. 541–51, but the results of their calculations are slightly different.

49. Exceptions are Beckwith 1977; Dunnel 1994; and Petech 1983 and 1994.

50. Wang 1963, p. 16; Somers 1979, pp. 727–54.

51. *bKa' thang sde lnga*, p. 152; for the phrase "thousand district," see Uray 1982; Richardson 1998, pp. 167–76.

52. The monolith at sPu was described by Francke 1914–26, p. 19, reedited in Thakur 1994, whose interpretation was challenged by Richardson 1995. The inscription is discussed by Vitali 1996, pp. 207–8. Richardson 1998, pp. 286–91, discusses a monolith, probably of the eleventh or twelfth century, carved in imitation of those erected during the royal dynasty.

53. On this distinction, see *kLong chen chos 'byung* pp. 413–14; *rGya bod yig tshang chen mo*, pp. 447–448.

54. David Germano proposed applying the term *post-tantra* to the rNying-ma compositions because of their radical difference from the Indic models of tantra.

55. Hackin 1924, pp. 30, 21; the perceptive reader will see that there the term *paripūrṇa* might be seen in compound with the eighty characteristics and thirty-two marks but has been separated for pedagogical purposes; *paripūrṇa* generally denotes fulfillment, as when all the perfections have been completed. On the early use of rdzogs chen, see van Schaik 2004.

56. See *Kṛṣṇayamāri-tantra* 17.9–11, and Kumāracandra's informative discussion of this material in his commentary to *Kṛṣṇayamāri*, pp. 123–29. Wayman 1977, pp. 156–59, noted its use in the Ārya exegesis of the *Guhyasamāja-tantra*.

57. Hackin 1924, pp. 2, 5.

58. The following discussion is based on the *Chos 'byung me tog snying po sbrang rtsi'i bcud*, pp. 435–36; for more detail, see the excellent discussion in Germano 2002.

59. Works dedicated to these systems are found in the *rNying ma bka' ma rgyas pa*, vol. 17, pp. 371–411, 426–517, and are included in the *gDams ngag mdzod*, vol. 1, pp. 213–371; this list of the important traditions is found in *kLong chen chos 'byung* pp. 393–94.

60. The problem of A-ro is recognized in Karmay 1988, p. 133. *kLong chen chos 'byung* p. 393, makes A-ro Ye-shes 'byung-gnas a disciple of gNyags Jñānakumāra, which is highly unlikely. A-ro does not seem to be quoted in the works by sNubs-chen, like the *bSam gtan mig sgron*, so he would appear to have been active after the early tenth century. The *Deb ther sngon po*, vol. 2, p. 1163, *Blue Annals*, vol. 2, pp. 999–1000, provides a short hagiography of dubious value. *Chos 'byung me tog snying po sbrang rtsi'i bcud*, p. 491, features A-ro in two rdzogs chen lineages.

61. *Deb ther sngon po*, vol. 1, p. 211; *Blue Annals*, vol. 1, p. 167.

62. *sNyan brgyud rin po che'i khrid kyi man ngag mkha' dbyings snying po'i bde khrid* by dPal mKha'-spyod-pa; this author is mentioned in *Deb ther sngon po*, vol. 2, p. 1151, *Blue Annals*, vol. 2, p. 991, as the disciple of Karma-pa Rang-byung rdo-rje (1284–1339); it is possible that he should be identified with Zhwa-dmar-pa II mKha'-spyod dbang-po, as does *gDams ngag mdzod*, table of contents, vol. 1, although the dates provided (1350–1405) are problematic.

63. *kLong chen chos 'byung*, p. 393–94.

64. I thank David Germano for making this very rare work available to me. The chapters are 'khor bar sdug bsngal nyes dmigs mang po'i gzhi (pp. 7.2–12.1), rnam rtog bdag tu 'dzin pa 'khor ba'i rgyu (pp. 12.2–19.4), mya ngag 'das pa zhi ba bde ba'i mchog (pp. 19.4–25.3), and bdag med rtogs pa mya ngan 'das pa'i rgyu (pp. 25.3–47.4).

65. See the long list of bKa'-gdams-pa figures listed in the lineage lists in the *sLob dpon dga' rab rdo rje nas brgyud pa'i rdzogs pa chen po sems sde'i phra khrid kyi man ngag.* pp. 436–37, 516–17, some of whom were disciples of Paṇ-chen Śākyaśrī. The work was written by rGya-sman-pa Nam-mkha' rdo-rje, probably in 1273 (cho mo bya lo). rGya-sman-pa was a teacher of the famous Ku-mā-ra-rā-dza (1266–1343); see *Deb ther sngon po*, vol. 1, p. 246; *Blue Annals*, vol. 1, p. 199.

66. On the early lineages in general, see *Chos 'byung me tog snying po sbrang rtsi'i bcud*, pp. 482–92.

67. *Chos 'byung me tog snying po sbrang rtsi'i bcud*, p. 485.13.

68. Nagano 2000 is an excellent recent study of such practices.

69. Karmay 1998, pp. 382; for an excellent discussion of the issue of purity, see pp. 380–412; compare Tucci 1980, pp. 163–212, which emphasizes the auspicious-inauspicious continuum.

70. On the somewhat neglected marriage ritual, see Karmay 1998, pp. 147–53; Shastri 1994. The *gNa' rabs bod kyi chang pa'i lam srol* of Bar-shi Phun-tshogs Dbang-rgyal is an interesting modern Tibetan work on marriage. On travel to the realms of the dead, see Lalou 1949; Macdonald 1971b, pp. 373–76; Kapstein 2000, pp. 7–8; and Cuevas 2003, pp. 33–38.

71. On the sources for this idea, see Stein 1986, pp. 185–88.

72. Lalou 1952; Snellgrove 1967, p. 16; Martin 2001b, pp. 12–15.

73. These have been well studied by Lhagyal 2000.

74. *mKhas pa'i dga' ston*, vol. 1, p. 192.12–23; on mi chos as the ritual of the tombs, see vol. 1, p. 170.12.

75. An early catalog of the items included in mi chos is found in *sBa bzhed*, p. 62.8–11; *sBa bzhed zhabs btags ma*, p. 53.6–8.

76. Their names are given as Chen-po rGyal-ba and his disciple Zhang-lcang-grum in the *sBa bzhad zhabs btags ma*, p. 86, and *Chos 'byung me tog snying po sbrang rtsi'i bcud*, p. 448.16, which identifies their residence as 'Chims-smad and the entire issue of reading a text and commentary for postmortem or prophylactic purposes is given in much greater detail.

77. *mKhas pa'i dga' ston*, vol. 1, pp. 430–31; analogous material found *sBa bzhed zhabs btags ma*, pp. 86.5–87.2, 90.11–91.1; *Chos 'byung me tog snying po sbrang rtsi'i bcud*, pp. 448.10–449.3. I thank Dan Martin for suggestions and corrections to this passage.

78. The 'ban 'dzi ba of *sBa bzhed zhabs btags ma*, p. 86.9, are evidently the same group spelled 'ba' 'ji ba in the received version of the proclamation of Lha bla-ma Ye-shes-'od; see Karmay 1998, pp. 3–16. Martin 2001b, p. 109, n., believes the name to be un-Tibetan. However, I am inclined to interpret 'ban/'ba' 'dzi ba as an orthographic oddity to render Bande 'dzi ba, for the 'a in 'ba' may be pronounced with a nasal, as 'ban, and 'dzi and 'ji are easily confused in *dbu med* manuscripts. As noted by Karmay 1998, p. 7, n. 30, other editions have 'ban 'ji ba, such as the modern printed version of the bka' shog in the *dGag lan nges don 'brug sgra*, pp. 182.21, 186.11; Karmay 1998, p. 16, n., suggests other foreign etymologies.

79. Karmay 1998, pp. 3–16.

80. Vitali 1996, pp. 215–18.

81. *bKa' 'chems ka khol ma*, pp. 282–85.

82. See Childs 1997 for an indication of this problem. The problem of animal sacrifice in Buddhist ceremonies—whether Tibetan, Newar, or other Himalayan group—is much more widespread than Childs's essay indicates. For some indication of its severity, see Owens 1993; Locke 1985, p. 14; Cüppers 1997; Diemberger and Hazod 1997.

83. I thank David Germano and Matthew Kapstein for their sharing their perspective on this issue.

84. *Bod kyi gdung rus zhib 'jug* makes a start on identifying clans in the various periods, but the work must be handled carefully, sometimes conflating place names with clan names; on the ancient clans, see Stein 1961.

85. *Bod kyi gdung rus zhib 'jug*, pp. 58–83, identifies the clans of the royal dynastic period. Tucci 1956a, p. 80, n. 7, believes that some of the names in table 2 are geographical designations rather than clans and proposes that the clan names are missing from this one entry; the syntax, though, would seem to argue for these as clans.

86. This is from *lDe'u chos 'byung*, pp. 145–46; there are several variations of this list, indicating the god of the domain and other details, which are studied in Dotson, forthcoming.

87. For modern class mobility, see Carrasco 1959, pp. 128–31.

88. For modern clan names, see *Bod kyi gdung rus zhib 'jug*, pp. 160–208.

89. On these grades in the dynastic period, see Richardson 1998, pp. 12–24, 149–66.

90. *Deb ther sngon po*, vol. 1, p. 125.1–2; *Blue Annals*, vol. 1, p. 95.

91. *Deb ther sngon po*, vol. 1, p. 147.11–14; *Blue Annals*, vol. 1, 114; in this case, both were from the Zur clan; on this clan, see Tsering 1978.

92. Some of these have been studied; see Tucci 1949, vol. 2, pp. 656–73; Vitali 1990, pp. 94–96; Stein 1962; for the Khön, see chapter 7.

93. The *rNgog gi gdung rabs che dge yig tshang* is mentioned in the *Lho rong chos 'byung*, p. 50.16–17.

94. See Vitali 2002 for an excellent study on the involvement of clans with gNas-rnying temple.

NOTES TO CHAPTER 3

1. Slightly summarized from *mKhas pa lde'u chos 'byung*, p. 390.5–11.

2. *Chos 'byung me tog snying po sbrang rtsi'i bcud*, p. 459; *mKhas pa lde'u chos 'byung*, pp. 390–91; *rNam thar rgyas pa yongs grags*, p. 113.

3. Wang 1963, p. 5.

4. Dunnel 1994, pp. 168–72.

5. Backus 1981, pp. 159–64.

6. *Bod kyi rgyal rabs*, p. 296.3.3; compare *Deb ther dmar po gsar ma*, pp. 132–33. Note that Tucci 1947, p. 458, neglects to translate this section and glosses it with "Follows a short insertion on the spread of Bon and Buddhism," despite the importance of the passage.

7. For a discussion of these, see Uebach 1990.

8. Hagiographical literature is replete with citations of the interaction of Tibetan translators and merchants; see, for example, the hagiography of Rwa-lo, *Rwa*

lo tsā ba'i rnam thar, esp. pp. 20, 36–37. For the modern importance of this phenomenon, see Lewis 1993.

9. See Aris 1979, pp. 3–33; see also Janet Gyatso's 1987 discussion of the implications of this system.

10. *mKhas pa lde'u chos 'byung*, pp. 390–92; *mKhas pa'i dga' ston*, pp. 466–68; *Chos 'byung me tog snying po sbrang rtsi'i bcud*, pp. 449–50; *lDe'u chos 'byung*, pp. 154–55; *sNgon gyi gtam me tog phreng ba*, Uebach 1987, pp. 120–24. The significance of the ethnonym or place-name Hor here is elusive; perhaps it is to render the identity of a Turkic people, for the *Deb ther dmar po*, p. 41, places this area in proximity to the Qarlok kingdom.

11. This material is from *sNgon gyi gtam me tog phreng ba*, Uebach 1987, p. 122.

12. *sBa bzhed zhabs rtags ma*, p. 83.3–5; *sNgon gyi gtam me tog phreng ba*, Uebach 1987, p. 120; *Chos 'byung me tog snying po sbrang rtsi'i bcud*, p. 441.6–8; *Bu ston chos 'byung*, p. 192.11–12.

13. *Chos 'byung me tog snying po sbrang rtsi'i bcud*, p. 446.5–11; compare *mKhas pa lde'u chos 'byung*, pp. 391.18–93.10, for the body of individuals trained under the direction of these monks.

14. *Chos 'byung me tog snying po sbrang rtsi'i bcud*, p. 446.4, mentions a rMe-gral or rMe tradition, beyond the mKhas-gral (one variant for mkhan-brgyud) and bTsun-gral accepted by others, but this lineage is not otherwise identified.

15. The mkhan rgyud (texts' orthography) is sometimes referred to as the mkhas rgyud; for the two lineages, see *sBa bzhed zhabs rtags ma*, p. 85.15; *sNgon gyi gtam me tog phreng ba*, Uebach 1987, p. 128; *mKhas pa lde'u chos 'byung*, p. 392.1–10.

16. *sNgon gyi gtam me tog phreng ba*, Uebach 1987, p. 128; *sBa bzhed zhabs rtags ma*, p. 87.

17. The best discussions are Dunnel 1994; Petech 1983; Stein 1959, pp. 230–40; Iwasaki 1993; compare Schram's 1961 historical study of the complexity of this area.

18. Iwasaki 1993, p. 18.

19. Petech 1983, p. 175.

20. Dunnel 1994, p. 173.

21. Iwasaki 1993, p. 24.

22. These kings seem to show up suddenly in the fourteenth century: *rGyal rabs gsal ba'i me long*, p. 200; *Yar lung jo bo'i chos 'byung*, p. 73; *Deb ther dmar po gsar ma*, Tucci 1971, pp. 166–70.

23. Petech 1983, p. 177.

24. Iwasaki 1993, p. 22.

25. Iwasaki 1993, p. 19.

26. Iwasaki 1993, p. 25.

27. *Bod rje lha btsan po'i gdung rabs tshig nyung don gsal*, pp. 77–81. Nor-brang O-rgyan's chronology is unacceptable, as he places these figures much too early and then explains away the time between the building of the temples and the early translators. See *Bod sil bu'i byung ba brjod pa shel dkar phreng ba*, pp. 291–93.

28. Richardson 1957, pp. 58–63, appears to be the first to identify this correctly.

29. Sources for these names include *sBa bzhed zhabs rtags ma*, p. 87.4–5; *sNgon gyi gtam me tog phreng ba*, Uebach 1987, p. 128; *mKhas pa'i dga' ston*, vol. 1, p. 467.7–8; *Chos la 'jug pa'i sgo*, *SKB* II.343.4.3; *Chos 'byung me tog snying po sbrang rtsi'i bcud*, p. 450.5–7 (which includes dGongs-pa-gsal); *Bu ston chos 'byung*, Szerb 1990, p. 60.15–16. Some include Thul-ba Ye-shes rgyal-mtshan (*Chos la 'jug pa'i sgo*, p. 343.4.3), but I believe this a corruption of 'Dul-ba Ye-shes rgyal-mtshan.

30. *lDe'u chos 'byung*, p. 156: de ltar bskos kyang mkhan po'i gsungs la ma nyan te | rang re ci dga' byas |. This list, similarly but not exactly described, also occurs in the *Chos 'byung me tog snying po sbrang rtsi'i bcud*, p. 450, but has a slightly different import.

31. *sBa bzhed zhabs rtags ma*, p. 87, describes the process, and *mKhas pa'i dga' ston*, vol. 1, p. 473, discusses the hats as a hallmark of their association.

32. *rGya bod yig tshang chen mo*, pp. 458–59; for another version in the *Bu ston chos 'byung*, Szerb 1990, pp. 61.8–62.5.

33. *Chos 'byung me tog snying po sbrang rtsi'i bcud*, p. 449.

34. *mKhas pa lde'u chos 'byung*, p. 394; *Bod rje lha btsan po'i gdung rabs tshig nyung don gsal*, pp. 78–81; *mKhas pa'i dga' ston*, vol. 1, p. 481.19–21; *Deb ther sngon po*, vol. 1, p. 86.13–14 (*Blue Annals*, vol. 1, p. 62); *rGya bod yig tshang chen mo*, p. 459.17; for a discussion of this issue, see Vitali 1990, p. 62, n. 1.

35. *Chos 'byung me tog snying po sbrang rtsi'i bcud*, pp. 451–52, and *sBa bzhed zhabs rtags ma*, pp. 87–88; the Nyang-ral text has consistently misread lo-tshong as lo tsā ba.

36. This area is described in the *sBa bzhed*, pp. 45–46, and this must correspond to the 'khor-sa chen mo of the texts. This section in the *sBa bzhed* seems to be the source for all later descriptions, including that in the eighty-sixth chapter of the *Padma bka' thang*, p. 510.

37. This room has irregular spellings: rnga-khang in *sBa bzhed*, p. 44, and *Chos 'byung me tog snying po sbrang rtsi'i bcud*, p. 451; it is spelled mnga'-khang in *sBa bzhed zhabs rtags ma*, p. 87; and snga-khang in the recent printed edition of the *Padma bka' thang*, p. 510.

38. My surmise on the interpretation of the text. Skam bu indicates something completely dried, which is the appearance of rotten wood. We erroneously call this "dry rot," even though the conditions are the ones described here: exposure to intermittent moisture without protection.

39. I believe that phyir rdzab zhal byas of Nyang-ral and phyir zha la la of the *sBa bzhed zhabs rtags ma* derived from some colloquial usage like phyir zhal rdzongs, "Let's get [these keys] out of here!" but the sources are unclear, so I translate Nyang-ral.

40. From the *sBa bzhed zhabs rtags ma*, p. 88.6: g.yu' ru'i lam rgyag bya 'di gzung gsungs nas bzhes |.

41. Note that the *sBa bzhed zhabs rtags ma*, p. 88.10, indicates that kLu-mes's attempt to repair the dbU-rtse temple was rebuffed by sBa and Rag, achieving success after only the intervention of Khri-lde mgon-btsan.

42. *sBa bzhed zhabs rtags ma*, p. 88.10.

43. Vitali 1990, pp. 37–39 (but compare p. 63, n. 29), and van der Kuijp 1987, p. 109, in contrast to Tucci 1949, vol. 1, p. 84, have understood these as "divisional areas" or "districts," which is close to the recent use of the term; see Diemberger and Hazod 1999, pp. 42–45. Yet at this early stage a strong place identity is misleading. Tsho is cognate with tshogs, 'tshogs pa, tshogs-pa, sogs, and other forms, indicating groups of people, and tsho was and is commonly the pluralizer for some nouns and pronouns. Before the "ten men of dbUs-gTsang" even arrived in central Tibet, they were described as a common group (byin po tsho yar 'ongs) for they all were ordained at the same time; see *mKhas pa'i dga' ston*, vol. 1, p. 473.3. The term sde[-pa] is preferred by some authors, such as Nel-pa (*sNgon gyi gtam me tog phreng ba*, Uebach 1987, pp. 132–36), while others use tsho. It appears that there was some difference in regional usage as well, for gTsang groups appear to be described as tsho more frequently. Grags-pa rgyal-mtshan's record indicates that tsho, sde-pa, and [b]rgyud were terms of varying association; see *rGya bod kyi sde pa'i gyes mdo*, pp. 297.1.3 ff.

44. The sources for the activity of the monks establishing the groups in dbUs-gTsang are principally *mKhas pa lde'u chos 'byung*, pp. 392–96; *Chos 'byung me tog snying po sbrang rtsi'i bcud*, pp. 452–54; *lDe'u chos 'byung*, pp. 155–59; *sNgon gyi gtam me tog phreng ba*, Uebach 1987, pp. 130–36; *rGya bod kyi sde pa'i gyes mdo*; *Bu ston chos 'byung*, Szerb 1990, pp. 59–81; and *rGya bod yig tshang chen mo*, pp. 459–68, which seems to furnish much of the data taken by dPa'-bo in the *mKhas pa'i dga' ston*, pp. 473–81. For schematics of the temples, see Tucci 1949, vol. 1, chart between pp. 84–85; and Uebach 1987, pp. 37–43.

45. This temple is also spelled rGyal-'gong, *lDe'u chos 'byung*, p. 157; *rGya bod yig tshang chen mo*, p. 462.1.

46. *lDe'u chos 'byung*, p. 158.

47. *sNgon gyi gtam me tog phreng ba*, Uebach 1987, p. 132.

48. These eight are emphasized in the *sNgon gyi gtam me tog phreng ba*, Uebach 1987, p. 132, but the others remain obscure.

49. *mKhas pa'i dga' ston*, p. 478: glang tsho stod smad tu gyes.

50. For the founding of Zha-lu and the disparate evidence on the date of its founding, see Vitali 1990, pp. 89–122; Tucci 1949, vol. 2, pp. 656–62.

51. For a discussion of the process at gNas-rnying, see Vitali 2002.

52. *rGya bod yig tshang chen mo*, pp. 464–65; *mKhas pa'i dga' ston*, p. 479.

53. *mKhas pa'i dga' ston*, p. 474, *lDe'u chos 'byung*, p. 157; *rGya bod yig tshang chen mo*, p. 460; *sNgon gyi gtam me tog phreng ba*, Uebach 1987, p. 132; *Chos 'byung me tog snying po sbrang rtsi'i bcud*, pp. 452–53.

54. *Deb ther sngon po*, vol. 1, p. 103.13; *mKhas pa'i dga' ston*, vol. 1, p. 474.

55. *sNgon gyi gtam me tog phreng ba*, Uebach 1987, p. 136, and *Chos 'byung me tog snying po sbrang rtsi'i bcud*, p. 452, refers to these four disciples as his "[four] sons" (bu bzhi), rather than four pillars. Compare *Deb ther sngon po*, vol. 1, p. 86.

56. *Chos 'byung me tog snying po sbrang rtsi'i bcud*, p. 452; *sNgon gyi gtam me tog phreng ba*, Uebach 1987, p. 136, dos not place this activity at Yer-pa but at g.Yu sgro

lha khang dmar and acts as if the temple existed before the activity of kLu-mes or Sum-pa, for they simply came there but did not construct it. There seems to be much difference of opinion on the nature and origin of this temple(s): *mKhas pa'i dga' ston*, vol. 1, p. 474, lists this as one of rNgog Byang-chub 'byung-gnas's temples; the *Deb ther sngon po*, vol. 1, p. 103, acts as if it is two temples built by Sum-pa; *Blue Annals*, vol. 1, p. 75. The attribution to Sum-pa probably follows the line in the *rGya bod yig tshang chen mo*, p. 460, which does so.

57. Tucci 1956b, p. 107.

58. The modern *sGrub pa'i gnas mchog yer pa'i dkar chag dad pa'i sa bon*, written in 1938, is found in the *gNas yig phyogs bsgrig* collection, pp. 3–49; the preceding reference is from p. 10.1. This text contains much material from the ancient *Brag yer pa'i dkar chag*, as may be seen from its continuity with the quotations in *mKhas pa'i dga' ston*, vol. 1, pp. 456–58; for example, the line referred to here is found on p. 457.6.

59. *mKhas pa'i dga' ston*, vol. 1, p. 474.8–14, lists his death date as 1060 (lcags byi) at the age of eighty-five (that is, eighty-four in European reckoning), but the chronology is problematic. *rGya bod yig tshang chen mo*, p. 460, spells the earlier temple as Ra-tshag. rGyal lha-khang is the subject of Richardson 1957.

60. Vitali 2002, pp. 100–102; Richardson 1957.

61. *mKhas pa'i dga' ston*, vol. 1, p. 474; compare *Chos 'byung me tog snying po sbrang rtsi'i bcud*, p. 452.

62. *Chos 'byung me tog snying po sbrang rtsi'i bcud*, p. 453.11.

63. *mKhas pa lde'u chos 'byung*, p. 397.

64. *rNam thar yongs grags*, pp. 157.4, 176.7–10.

65. Tables 3 through 7 in *sNgon gyi gtam me tog phreng ba*, Uebach 1987, pp. 39–43, provide a convenient schematization of the relationships and construction.

66. Vitali 1990, pp. 1–35, has unfortunately done exactly that with the conflation of Ka-chu and Ke-ru temples; see Richardson 1998, pp. 212–13, 317.

67. *rNam thar yongs grags*, pp. 164.3, 169.13–14.

68. The term khral is understood as sham thabs khral in the *rNam thar yongs grags*, pp. 156.15, 187.21–88.5. Vitali 1990, p. 38, interprets the taxation as applying to divisions of area, but taxation in early Tibet by household or commercial transaction rather than on land, which was owned by the gentry; Róna-Tas 1978; Thomas 1935–55, vol. 2, p. 327. Thus, the khral tsho was a dutiable monastic group.

69. *rNam thar yongs grags*, p. 156.15–16.

70. *rGya bod kyi sde pa'i gyes mdo*, *SKB* IV.297.2.3–4; the text seems somewhat garbled.

71. *Bu ston chos 'byung*, Szerb 1990, pp. 72.12, 76.10–77.4; this material reproduced in *rGya bod yig tshang chen mo*, pp. 464.12, 466.6–9.

72. One of Lo-btsun's disciples, Kyi Ye-shes dbang-po, was said to have four revenue communities in his stod tsho; *rGya bod kyi sde pa'i gyes mdo*, *SKB* IV.297.3.2.

73. *sNgon gyi gtam me tog phreng ba*, Uebach 1987, p. 126.

74. *Deb ther sngon po*, vol. 1, p. 104.12–13, *Blue Annals*, vol. 1, p. 76; reproduced in *mKhas pa'i dga' ston*, vol. 1, p. 476.16.

75. *Deb ther sngon po*, vol. 1, pp. 122–124 provides a summary of the figures involved; *Blue Annals*, vol. 1, pp. 93–94; Ferrari 1958, p. 52; *Kaḥ thog si tu'i dbus gtsang gnas yig*, p. 202.

76. Gra-pa mNgon-shes's hagiography is found principally in the *Deb ther sngon po*, vol. 1, pp. 124–32; *Blue Annals*, vol. 1, pp. 94–101; see also *mKhas pa'i dga' ston*, vol. 1, pp. 475.16–76.16. Vitali 1990, p. 39, reproduces much of this material; see also Ferrari 1958, pp. 54–55.

77. For one list of his disciples and their monasteries, see *sNgon gyi gtam me tog phreng ba*, Uebach 1987, pp. 138–41, and table 3.

78. *Deb ther sngon po*, vol. 1, pp. 104.12, 122.3–5, 127.1–2; *Blue Annals*, vol. 1, pp. 76, 93, 96–97. An early-twentieth-century description of Grwa-thang can be found in *Kaḥ thog si tu'i dbus gtsang gnas yig*, pp. 123–25.

79. *Deb ther sngon po*, vol. 1, p. 126.17–18; *Blue Annals*, vol. 1, p. 96.

80. sPyan-g.yas lha-khang; see Ferrari 1958, p. 53.

81. *Chos 'byung me tog snying po sbrang rtsi'i bcud*, p. 478.7, connects him to the new translation work of Zangs-dkar lo-tsā-ba and his nephew; the same work p. 501.9, connects him to revelations from the Āyrapalo temple.

82. *mKhas pa lde'u chos 'byung*, p. 394; *lDe'u chos 'byung*, pp. 157–58.

83. *bKa' 'chems ka khol ma*, p. 280.

84. Martin 2001b, pp. 93–104.

85. The Pe-har cult is taken as indicative of this inclusiveness; see Vitali 1996, pp. 216–18; Karmay 1991; Martin 1996c, pp. 184–91.

86. *Vajraśekhara*; To. 480, fol. 199b4–5, becomes the locus classicus of the trisaṁvara (Tibetan: sdom gsum). The Ordinance of Lha-bla-ma, Karmay 1998, pp. 3–16, appeals to three vows. For a systematic study of the later sdom-gsum literature, see Sobish 2002.

87. A widely distributed example of this favoring of the Gu-ge kingdom is Snellgrove 1987, vol. 2, pp. 470–509.

88. For a broad survey, see Snellgrove and Skorupski 1977–80, both vols. A more specialized discussion of chronology and sources is Vitali 1996, and Klimburg-Salter 1997 provides an excellent investigation of a Tabo temple founded in the late tenth century.

89. The *Rin chen bzang po'i rnam thar shel 'phreng* published and translated in Snellgrove and Skorupski 1977–80, vol. 2, pp. 85–111, places his departure at 975. For the mortality total, see also the *rNam thar yongs grags*, p. 114.

90. For specific temples, see Vitali 1996, pp. 249–87, 303–10.

91. Unless specified, all the material on Atiśa and Nag-tsho is drawn from the *rNam thar yongs grags*; this episode is found on pp. 117–25.

92. For some of these issues, see Ruegg 1981; for Prajñāgupta's influence on 'Brog-mi and 'Khon dKon-mchog rgyal-po, see chapters 5 and 7. The *rNam thar yongs grags*, p. 192.12, anachronistically has rGya-gar nag-chung (= Pha-dam-pa sangs-rgyas) sending a disciple to make offerings to Atiśa.

93. *rNam thar yongs grags*, p. 117.11–12.

94. In the *rNam thar yongs grags*, for on p. 118.4–5, Nag-tsho is depicted as having studied Abhidharma with rGya brTson-seng on his first trip to India.

95. Fragments of Nag-tsho's record of his itinerary are contained in the *rNal 'byor byang chub seng ge'i dris lan*, *SKB* III.277.4.4–78.1.6; I have used some of this material in Davidson 2002c, pp. 316–17, and consider this record in more detail later in this book.

96. See Decleer 1996, Bajracharya 1979, Locke 1985, pp. 404–13, Petech 1984, pp. 42–43, Stearns 1996, pp. 137–38.

97. For a short review of the Vinaya lineages, see Kaḥ-thog Tshe-dbang nor-bu's *Bod rje lha btsan po'i gdung rabs tshig nyung don gsal*, pp. 82–85; compare *mKhas pa'i dga' ston*, vol. 1., pp. 481–83; *Chos 'byung me tog snying po sbrang rtsi'i bcud*, p. 446.

98. *rNam thar yongs grags*, pp. 178–79.

99. *rNam thar yongs grags*, pp. 164.3, 169.13–14; the former was at sNan-mda', whereas the latter temple was in Yar-lung at Bya-sar-chags.

100. Stark and Bainbridge 1985, pp. 27–28.

101. *rNam thar yongs grags*, pp. 159, 163, 174, 186.

102. *rNam thar yongs grags*, pp. 156, 187–88.

103. *rNam thar yongs grags*, pp. 156, 187–88.

104. *rNam thar yongs grags*, p. 169, 15–20.

105. *Chos 'byung me tog snying po sbrang rtsi'i bcud*, pp. 455.18–56.1.

106. *rNam thar yongs grags*, pp. 158, 166, 179.

107. *rNam thar yongs grags*, pp. 169.17–70.3.

108. *Rwa sgreng dgon pa'i dkar chag*, pp. 76–84, discusses the founding of this section of Rwa-sgreng. According to this description, although this main temple and stūpa section was constructed after some smaller, mostly residential, buildings, it was the first large construction that turned it into a real monastery.

109. *rNam thar yongs grags*, p. 221.9–20.

110. *rGya bod kyi sde pa'i gyes mdo*, *SKB* IV.297.2.2; this material is treated differently in van der Kuijp 1987, pp. 108–10.

111. *rNam thar yongs grags*, p. 212.21–13.3, compared with the preceding statement.

112. From *Chos 'byung me tog snying po sbrang rtsi'i bcud*, p. 449, but the list of the royal supporters and their descent from Yum-brtan becomes increasingly less clear; *lDe'u chos 'byung*, p. 154; *mKhas pa'i dga' ston*, vol. 1, pp. 433–34; *Deb ther dmar po gsar ma*, pp. 170–71.

113. *Chos la 'jug pa'i sgo*, *SKB* II.344.2.3, emphasizes the West Tibetan contributions.

114. Colophon to the *Śrī-Guhyasamājasādhana-siddhasambhava-nidhi*, fol. 69b6; Petech 1997, pp. 237, 253, n. 51.

115. Petech 1997, p. 253, n. 51, provides a few incorrect references; the following are attributed to Tsa-la-na Ye-shes rgyal-mtshan: To. 451, 1214, 1320, 1846, 1850, 1853, 1859, 1866, 1870, 1872–78. Of these, it appears that the *brDa nges par gzung ba* may have been composed by the royal monk himself.

116. The chronology is from Hazod 2000b, p. 182.

117. *dPal gsang ba 'dus pa'i dam pa'i chos byung ba'i tshul legs par bshad pa gsang 'dus chos kun gsal pa'i nyin byed*, p. 185; compare *Deb ther sngon po*, vol. 1, p. 451; *Blue Annals*, vol. 1, p. 372; *Chos 'byung me tog snying po sbrang rtsi'i bcud*, p. 477.7–18.

118. *Deb ther sngon po*, vol. 1, pp. 213–14; *Blue Annals*, vol. 1, pp. 168–69; most of the works identified by 'Gos-lo gZhon-nu-dpal as containing the word rdzogs-chen were translated by Tsa-la-na Ye-shes rgyal-mtshan.

119. Hazod 2000b, p. 176.

120. *Chos 'byung me tog snying po sbrang rtsi'i bcud*, pp. 460–72, considers the West Tibetan connection a supplement to the great activity already taking place. *sNgon gyi gtam me tog phreng ba*, Uebach 1987, p. 153, mentions it only in passing; *mKhas pa lde'u chos 'byung*, pp. 397 provides only a bit more; *Bu ston chos 'byung*, Szerb 1990, pp. 86–89, treats Western Tibet and the bKa'-gdams-pa in passing as well; greater respective attention is given in *sBa bzhed zhabs rtags ma*, pp. 89.12–91.9. In *Chos la 'jug pa'i sgo*, *SKB* II.343.4.6–44.2.6, the review of the events does not even mention Atiśa or the bKa'-gdams-pa. The twelfth-century *bKa' 'chems ka khol ma*, pp. 2–5, 276, 319, is the earliest text to be strongly concerned with Atiśa, in this case the apocryphal connection between Atiśa and Srong-btsan sgam-po. From the time of the 1363 *Deb ther dmar po*, pp. 61–81, we see the bKa'-gdams-pa receiving their own chapter and approaching parity with the Eastern Vinaya monks; this direction was followed in the 1434 *rGya bod yig tshang chen mo*, pp. 472–81.

121. We see this in both the 1529 sectarian history of Paṇ-chen bSod-nams grags-pa, *bKa' gdams gsar rnying gi chos 'byung*, pp. 4.4–45.5, and in the more mainstream *Deb gter sngon po*, vol. 1, pp. 297–425; *Blue Annals*, vol. 1, pp. 241–350.

NOTES TO CHAPTER 4

1. *Rwa lo tsā ba'i rnam thar*, p. 10.9–10.

2. **Catuḥkrama*, fol. 358b6–7; Grags-pa shes-rab must be an approximate contemporary of rNgog-lo bLo-ldan shes-rab (1059–1109), for both worked with Sumatikīrti. De Jong 1972, p. 516, maintains that the phrases la gtugs pa or dang gtugs pa indicate "to compare [one text] with [another]." While this is the implied meaning in some circumstances with respect to texts (not here, where the text secured is the only one), gtugs actually means to encounter or to consult, in these cases with the purpose of collation. De Jong's interpretation causes him some problems, pp. 533–34, when colophons indicate that individuals are encountered (or not: paṇḍi ta la ma gtugs shing), which do not indicate that a text was compared with a paṇḍita but that a paṇḍita had not been met who could solve textual difficulties.

3. *Rwa lo tsā ba'i rnam thar*, p. 310.1–7.

4. Snellgrove 1987, vol. 2, p. 470, sums up the received wisdom: "The second diffusion of Indian Buddhism in Tibet, regarded primarily as a necessary scholarly enterprise, was a very important phase in the history of the conversion of Tibet,

but it represented a new beginning only so far as the collation and translating of Indian Buddhist scriptures were concerned."

5. The literature on this phenomenon is vast; a convenient summary is in Rabil 1988, pp. 350–81.

6. For the Shong-ston bLo-gros brtan-pa, see Davidson 1981, p. 14, n. 38; the unacceptable translation system of Bu-ston is evinced in his work on the *Tārāmūla-kalpa*, To. 724.

7. This explanation is based in the discussion in *Chos 'byung me tog snying po sbrang rtsi'i bcud*, p. 459; compare *mKhas pa lde'u chos 'byung*, p. 396; the *rNam thar yongs grags*, p. 113, is especially adamant that doubts about the correct path were the issue.

8. *Chos 'byung me tog snying po sbrang rtsi'i bcud*, p. 462.18–21, mentions the unsuccessful search for sections of esoteric literature in old temple libraries.

9. Indicating the textual history, Sørensen 1994, pp. 14–22, and van der Kuijp 1996, p. 47, pointed to one of the two lineage lists in the conclusion of the text printed in Lanzhou (p. 320: Atiśa, Bang-ston, sTod-lung-pa [1032–16], sNe'u-zur-ba [1042–1118/19], 'Bri-gung-pa [1143–1217], rGya-ma-ba [1138–1210], Rwa-sgreng-ba, dKon-bzang, rDor-je tshul-khrims [1154–1221], and then the redactor), although both suggested that the list might be made more historical than it is by emending 'Bri-gung-pa to Lha-chen 'Bri-gang-pa [ca. 1100/10–1190]. However, I believe the real message here is that some bKa'-brgyud monks appropriated the Atiśa legend to augment their position in the midst of the rise of the Sa-skya in the thirteenth century and were unable to invoke the bKa'-gdams lineage in a logical chronology, resulting in the chronological inconsistency. The text recognizes (p. 321) that it is the longest version of a threefold short, medium, and long version circulating in gTsang and mentions (p. 287.10) one whose name ends in snying-po (snying po'i mtha' can), undoubtedly indicating Dwags-po sGom-tshul (1116–69; full name: Tshul-khrims snying-po, see his short hagiography appended to the *mNyam med sgam po pa'i rnam thar*, p. 166.9), and thus the text is probably the product of his followers who participated in the renovation of the Jo-khang around 1165.

10. See, for example, the **Vajrayānamūlāpattiṭīkā*, To. 2486, fol. 190b4.

11. On this topic, see Davidson 1990.

12. This is important and neglected evidence about a Candrakīrti. If this Indian proves to be the same as the author of the *Pradīpodyotana* commentary on the *Guhyasamāja*, then that would assist our chronology of Indic tantra. See *Chos 'byung me tog snying po sbrang rtsi'i bcud*, p. 459; compare *mKhas pa lde'u chos 'byung*, p. 394, where he gives a delightful narrative of a second translation team, sNubs Ye-ses rgya-mtsho and Dhanadhala (?), and the latter's evil mantras.

13. A helpful review on the opinions of the circumstances of the later diffusion is found in Kaḥ-thog Tshe-dbang nor-bu's *Bod rje lha btsan po'i gdung rabs tshig nyung don gsal*, pp. 77–85.

14. Early versions of the Smṛti story are found in *Chos 'byung me tog snying po sbrang rtsi'i bcud*, pp. 459–60, and *mKhas pa lde'u chos 'byung*, p. 396.

15. For this character, the text reads khyeng rje shag btsan bya ba la btsongs te; I understand khyeng / kheng / rgyen as cognates, the former unattested but the latter well known.

16. It probable that gLan Tshul-khrims snying-po is referring to a disciple of kLu-mes; see *sNgon gyi gtam me tog phreng ba*, Uebach 1987, p. 144.

17. The *sMra sgo mtshon cha* (To. 4295) is examined in some detail in Verhagen 2001, pp. 37–57.

18. *Datang xiyu ji*, T.2087.51.918b16—24; Beal 1869, vol. 2, pp. 135–36.

19. Sachau 1910, vol. 1, p. 19.

20. *Datang xiyu qiufa gaoseng zhuan*, T. 2066 passim; Lahiri 1986, p. xvii.

21. Verhagen 1994, pp. 185–98, 231–57, discusses these grammars and their associated literature.

22. Verhagen 1994, pp. 9–107, reviews this effort.

23. Colophon to the *Ārya-tathāgatoṣṇīṣasitātapatrāparājita-mahāpratyaṅgirā-paramasiddha-nāma-dhāraṇī*, fol. 219a7.

24. Colophon to the *Bhikṣāvṛtti-nāma*. I have not been able to locate a Nye-ba'i 'thung-gcod-pa in Kathmandu. For a translation of Si-tu Paṇ-chen's visits to Kathmandu in 1723 and 1744, see Lewis and Jamspal 1988. None of the sites mentioned by Si-tu Paṇ-chen seems to correspond to this one. Cf. Lo Bue 1997.

25. The colophons to three texts contain virtually the same lines: *Raktayamārisādhana*, To. 2084, rgyud, tsi, fol. 161a4–5; *Kāyavākcittatrayādhiṣṭhānoddeśa*, To. 2085, rgyud, tsi, fol. 162b4–5; *Trisattvasamādhisamāpatti*, To. 2086, rgyud, tsi, fol. 162b3–4. Note that the Tohuku catalog has no translator listed for the first (To. 2084) of these, just one of many places where this catalog is in error. On Tirhut, see Petech 1984, pp. 55, 119, 207–12.

26. Colophon to the *rJe btsun ma 'phags pa sgrol ma'i sgrub thabs nyi shu rtsa gcig pa'i las kyi yan lag dang bcas pa mdo bsdus pa*, To. 1686, *bsTan-'gyur*, rgyud, sha, fol. 24b6. For Stam Bihara as Vikramaśīla, see Stearns 1996, p. 137, n. 37.

27. *Rong zom chos bzang gi gsung 'bum*, vol. 1, p. 238.

28. See the remarks in Hattori 1968, pp. 18–19; *Mañjuśrīnāmasaṃgīti*, Davidson 1981, p. 13.

29. Witzel 1994, pp. 2–3, 18–20.

30. Sachau 1910, vol. 1, p. 18; discussed in Witzel 1994, pp. 2–3.

31. Colophon to *Śrī-Hevajrābhisamayatilaka*, fol. 130a6.

32. The following is taken from the *Rwa lo tsā ba'i rnam thar* 1989; Decleer 1992 considered some of the problems of this document.

33. *Rwa lo tsā ba'i rnam thar*, p. 9.

34. Decleer 1992, pp. 14–16, showed the disagreement among the sources on this betrothal. While the *Rwa lo tsā ba'i rnam thar*, p. 9, indicates that he did not wish marriage, Tāranātha's telling of the same tale indicates that his fiancée could not stand Rwa-lo; both may still be true in some measure.

35. *Rwa lo tsā ba'i rnam thar*, pp. 11–13.

36. The designation Transitional was suggested by Slusser 1982, vol. 1, pp. 41–51;

adopted by Petech 1984, pp. 31–76; and questioned to some degree by Malla 1985, p. 125.

37. The following political description follows Petech 1984, pp. 31–43, except as noted. See Malla 1985, although this is an excessively harsh review of Petech 1984.

38. Compare Petech 1984, pp. 37–39, who provides the regnal dates of 1010 to 1041, while the editors of the *Gopālarājavaṁśāvalī*, p. 236, suggest 1023 to 1038.

39. Petech 1984, pp. 39–41; *Gopālarājavaṁśāvalī*, p. 127; *Nepālavaṁśāvalī*, p. 98.

40. Regmi 1983, vol. 1, pp. 132–33, vol. 2, pp. 82–83, vol. 3, pp. 221–23; the date is Mānadeva era, beginning October 576 C.E., year 199. For this era, see Petech 1984, p. 12.

41. Eimer 1979, §§ 248 to 251.

42. *Rwa lo tsā ba'i rnam thar*, p. 60.

43. *Rwa lo tsā ba'i rnam thar*, pp. 11, 20–21, 38, 68, 81, etc.

44. Regmi 1983, vol. 1, pp. 76–77, vol. 2, pp. 46–47, vol. 3, pp. 139–46; Guṁ Bāhā in Sankhu is the only one clearly identifiable; see Locke 1985, pp. 467–69.

45. Locke 1985, pp. 533–36.

46. Locke 1985, pp. 28–30, considers this grouping.

47. Based on the descriptions of geography, Decleer 1994–95 hypothesized that Ye-rang nyi-ma steng be located in the Chobar Gorge, but the evidence is not compelling and the site unlikely. I prefer to look for the monastery exactly where the text locates it and read the geographical descriptions as Pure-Land inspired.

48. Locke 1985, pp. 70–74, discusses this monastery.

49. *Rwa lo tsā ba'i rnam thar*, p. 72: specifically, Maitrīpā was said to have been the Upādhyāya, but this siddha figure was ejected from Vikramaśīla by Atiśa for sexual impropriety, and it is questionable whether he would have gotten a hearing at Nālandā at about the same time.

50. Two of the scriptural materials are edited and translated in Siklós 1996; the colophons are available on pp. 114, 155. Siklós's analysis of the transmission to Tibet, pp. 10–11, is weak. The representation of Bha-ro phyag-rdum as essential to the Yamāri materials is bolstered by his presence in the lineage received by Sa-chen Kun-dga' snying-po, *bLa ma sa skya pa chen po'i rnam thar*, p. 83.3.1.

51. The *Mayamata* 25.43–56 contains a description of the construction of various kinds of kuṇḍa.

52. For the current usage, see Kölver and Śākya 1985, p. 19; compare Gellner 1992, pp. 162–86.

53. Petech 1984, pp. 190–91; Kölver and Śākya 1985, pp. 72, 91, 107, 128. The earliest Bhāro attested is Kaḍhā Bhāro, in a document dated 1090/91, sixty years after Rwa-lo's arrival. It is difficult to extrapolate from current caste designations as far back into the eleventh century, and we know that the remarkable changes in the twentieth century could just as easily have occurred before. For the changes in Newar sociology in the last two centuries, see Rosser 1978.

54. *rNam thar rgyas pa*, Eimer 1979, §§ 271, 393; Petech 1984, p. 190.

55. *Rwa lo tsā ba'i rnam thar*, p. 66.

56. *Rwa lo tsā ba'i rnam thar*, p. 13; for bhari = wife, see *Gopālarājavaṁśāvalī*, p. 181. Locke 1985, p. 484a, specifically questions the depiction of medieval Pāṭan under the "thesis [that] posits a great (celibate) monastic and scholarly tradition on the model of the Indian Buddhist Universities which then deteriorated to produce a sort of corrupt Buddhism in the Malla period. Did this [model actually] ever exist, or has Nepalese Buddhism from its inception been mainly ritual Buddhism supported mostly by householder monks?" Note, however, that the bāhīs maintained an ideology of conservative Buddhist monasticism, even after becoming entirely lay, which may indicate that at one time they were the centers of celibate Mahāyānist orthodoxy; see Gellner 1992, pp. 167–68; Locke 1985, pp. 185–89.

57. *Rwa lo tsā ba'i rnam thar*, pp. 20–21, 39–40; in this latter place, the merchant's name is given as Zla ba bzang, perhaps *Candrabhadra or some similar name.

58. *Rwa lo tsā ba'i rnam thar*, pp. 15–16: nga rta la babs nas bong bu zhon pa mi 'ong.

59. *Rwa lo tsā ba'i rnam thar*, p. 35.

60. *Rwa lo tsā ba'i rnam thar*, p. 43; Decleer 1992 showed this episode to be reported in a dramatically different manner by Tāranātha.

61. *Rwa lo tsā ba'i rnam thar*, pp. 30–31, for the warning, in strong contrast to Rwa-lo's propagation in public environments, pp. 45, 54, 143, 145, 158, 159, 162, 181, 183, 188, 200, 217, 229, 234, 241, 243, 291, 300, etc.

62. *Rwa lo tsā ba'i rnam thar*, p. 48.

63. *Rwa lo tsā ba'i rnam thar*, p. 49.

64. *Rwa lo tsā ba'i rnam thar*, p. 50.

65. *Rwa lo tsā ba'i rnam thar*, p. 100.

66. *Rwa lo tsā ba'i rnam thar*, p. 63; I have not been able to locate the precise meaning of this designation in medieval Nepalese documents, but Tibetan materials treat Ha-du (or Haṁ-du, Had-du) as a class of Newari religious; compare *Rwa lo tsā ba'i rnam thar*, pp. 64, 66. In the latter section, two hundred of these individuals are assembled. Hang-du dkar-po is also mentioned as Sa-chen's source for some Yoginī, Guhyasamāja, and Kālacakra teachings; see *bLa ma sa skya pa chen po'i rnam thar*, p. 85.4.2–3. Compare Stearns 2001, pp. 206–7, n. 15.

67. We note that none of the rNying-ma annalists of the Vajrakīla agrees with this outcome. For them, Rwa-lo was killed by Lang-lab Byang-chub rdo-rje, and this constitutes a great item of pride; see, for example, Sog-bzlog-pa, *dPal rdo rje phur pa'i lo rgyus chos kyi 'byung gnas ngo mtshar rgya mtsho'i rba rlabs*, in *Sog bzlog pa gsung 'bum*, vol. 1, pp. 168–77, esp. pp. 168.4–70.3.

68. *Rwa lo tsā ba'i rnam thar*, p. 309.

69. *Rwa lo tsā ba'i rnam thar*, p. 310; one of the verses in this sung reply is translated at the head of this chapter; see n. 2. The episode of Kong-po A-rgyal's daughter is related on pp. 293–95; Rwa-lo's survival and escape were, of course, miraculous.

70. *Sog bzlog pa gsung 'bum*, vol. 1, p. 168. We note that Sog-bzlog-pa had his own reasons for propagating this number, for he claimed that Lang-lab Byang-

chub rdo-rje was the only figure to escape Rwa-lo's net of magic, thus articulating the superiority of the Vajrakīla system over that of Vajrabhairava.

71. *Rwa lo tsā ba'i rnam thar*, pp. 102–3.

72. *Rwa lo tsā ba'i rnam thar*, pp. 64, 142; *Chos 'byung bstan pa'i sgron me*, p. 148.1–2.

73. *Rwa lo tsā ba'i rnam thar*, pp. 166–68; Davidson (forthcoming b) further examines this conflict.

74. *Deb ther sngon po*, vol. 1, pp. 438–43; *Blue Annals*, vol. 1, pp. 360–64.

75. *Deb ther sngon po*, vol. 1, p. 159.9–10; *Blue Annals*, vol. 1, p. 123.

76. *Deb ther sngon po*, vol. 1, p. 438.9–10; *Blue Annals*, vol. 1, p. 360.

77. *dPal gsang ba 'dus pa'i dam pa'i chos byung ba'i tshul*, pp. 115–17; Vitali 2002, p. 90, n. 6, relates the *gNas rnying skyes bu rnams kyi rnam thar* version of the story.

78. *bLa ma brgyud pa bod kyi lo rgyus*, p. 173.3.5, translated in chapter 5.

79. *Deb ther sngon po*, vol. 1, pp. 151–52, 156; *Blue Annals*, vol. 1, pp. 117, 121.

80. *Lho rong chos 'byung*, p. 50, mentions the *rNgog gi gdung rabs che dge yig tsang* of the rNgog clan.

81. Snellgrove 1987, vol. 2, pp. 470–526, contains many cogent observations on this point.

82. *Rwa lo tsā ba'i rnam thar*, p. 122.

83. See Jackson 1990, pp. 102–4.

84. *Deb ther dmar po*, p. 74.2, gives a bird year; the thirteenth-century *dKar brgyud gser 'phreng* gives no dates, pp. 137–87, nor does the *mKhas pa'i dga' ston*, vol. 1, pp. 774–75; *Lho rong chos 'byung*, p. 49, is the most informative on the chaos of dates: "This lord was born in the sa-mo-phag year (999 or 1059) and passed away at eighty-six (that is, 85); we can also accept the difference of two years so that he was born in the chu-pho-stag year (1002 or 1062), but there are others accepting a difference of five years (1004?), and which among these is correct should be examined. The *Chos 'byung mig 'byed* (?) says he was born in a shing-pho-byi (1024) and died at eight-four in the me-mo-phag (1107), but that would put Mila at age sixty-eight and rNgog mdo-sde at age thirty-one when he died, and the time doesn't fit." Only the later bKa'-brgyud sources, like the *sTag lung chos 'byung*, pp. 132–44, accepts the date of the *Blue Annals*, pp. 404–5.

85. For the relationship of Mar-yul to the current Ladakh, see Vitali 1996, pp. 153–61.

86. *Kha rag gnyos kyi rgyud pa byon tshul mdor bsdus*, dated 1431?, pp. 5–16. This hagiography clearly has its own problems, and gNyos-lo is accorded an age of more than 140 years at his death, p. 16.3.

87. *Deb ther dmar po*, p. 74.16, has Mar-pa study for six years and six months with Nāropā.

88. Decleer 1992, pp. 20–22, examined this curious episode; Stearns 2001, p. 220, n. 62, discussed charges that gNyos-lo-tsā-ba fabricated tantra rather than translating them.

89. The problems with the exact death date of Nāropā extends to testimony of

the bKa'-gdams-pa. As we will see, the report of Nag-tsho in Grags-pa rgyal-mtshan's letter makes 1041 the most likely date, with the news of his death received by Atiśa and Nag-tsho after they had already arrived in Nepal. Yet the *rNam thar rgyas pa* has Nāropā die twenty-one days after Nag-tsho sees him back in Vikramaśīla; see Eimer 1979, § 232.

90. For example, *sTag lung chos 'byung*, pp. 131–45.

91. *Mar pa lo tsā'i rnam thar*, p. 84; this strategy was followed by gTsang-smyong's follower Brag-dkar Lha-btsun Rin-chen rnam-rgyal (1457–1557) in his hagiography of Nāropā, which is the one translated by Guenther 1963; see pp. 100–102; for gTsang-smyong, see Smith 2001, pp. 59–79.

92. *rNal 'byor byang chub seng ge'i dris lan*, *SKB* III.277.4.4–78.2.7.

93. There have been many who have noticed this problem; Wylie 1982 is representative; compare Guenther 1963, pp. xi-xii.

94. For example, *Ṣaḍdharmopadeśa*, To. 2330, fol. 271a2–3; compare *Guhyaratna*, To. 1525, fol. 83b1–2.

95. *mKhas pa'i dga' ston*, vol. 1, p. 760; rNgog's dates from *Lho rong chos 'byung*, p. 52, but other sources place his birthdate at 1036.

96. *sGam po pa gsung 'bum*, vol. 1, p. 326.8; on this figure, see *Deb ther sngon po*, vol. 1, p. 485.2–67, *Blue Annals*, vol. 1, p. 400; on sGam-po-pa locating Puspahari in Kashmir, see *sGam po pa gsung 'bum*, vol. 2, pp. 8, 392.

97. *dKar brgyud gser 'phreng*, p. 173; this prophecy is often repeated; see *Deb ther dmar po*, p. 74, *mKhas pa'i dga' ston*, vol. 1, p. 775; *'Brug pa'i chos 'byung*, p. 325.

98. *sGra sbyor bam po gnyis pa*, fol. 132b6–33a1.

99. *Rwa lo tsā ba'i rnam thar*, p. 104, identifies three kinds of *ḍākinīs*: flesh-eating (sha za), worldly ('jig rten), and gnostic (ye shes). It is not clear whether these categories are in fact Indian. For the Lam-'bras definitions of five *ḍāka*, see app. 2, §I.B.2.d. note 7.

100. For a fuller elaboration of the concerns in this section, see Davidson 2002a.

101. For example, *Pha dam pa'i rnam thar*, pp. 60–61.

102. *Dam chos snying po zhi byed las rgyud kyi snyan rgyud zab ched ma*, vol. 1; this very interesting collection is in need of much work; Hermann-Pfandt 1992, pp. 407–15, has begun the process; compare Davidson forthcoming a.

103. *Śrī-Vajraḍākinīgītā*, To. 2442, fol. 67a1–2.

104. *rNal 'byor pa thams cad kyi de kho na nyid snang zhes bya ba grub pa rnams kyi rdo rje'i mgur*, To. 2453.

105. Examples of the normative view of gSar-ma traditions being almost universally authentic include Mayer 1997b, pp. 620–22.

106. There are two received versions of the *sNgag log sun 'byin*. One is in *Sog bzlog gsung 'bum*, vol. 1, pp. 475–88, which includes the interlinear annotations and refutations of the translator's position. The second version is found in the *sNgags log sun 'byin gyi skor*, pp. 18–25. The texts diverge in significant ways.

107. *gSang sngags snga 'gyur la bod du rtsod pa snga phyir byung ba rnams kyi lan du brjod pa Nges pa don gyi 'brug sgra*, in *Sog bzlog gsung 'bum*, vol. 1, p. 444.4.

108. On Bai-ro tsa-na, see Karmay 1988, pp. 17–37.

109. On this canon, see Karmay 1988, pp. 23–24. Kaneko 1982 lists five works having *rMad du byung ba* in the title: nos. 10, 20, 38, 40, and 42. Karmay 1988, p. 24, identifies no. 20 as the text in the *sems-sde* canon.

110. *sNgags log sun 'byin gyi skor*, pp. 13, 26.

111. Mayer 1996, p. 142, n. 29, reports that Alexis Sanderson argued that because of its citation in the received manuscript of Vilāsava's *Mantrārthāvalokinī*, the real name of this work is *Guhyakośa*. The Dun-huang manuscript studied in Hackin 1924, p. 7, however, reads *Guhyagarbha*, and the text provides a close approximation of the phonetics we expect from an Indian—Devaputra—in the tenth century.

112. David Germano called my attention to this translation by Thar-pa lo-tsā-ba Nyi-ma rgyal-mthsan being preserved in the Phu-brag, no. 754, Samten 1992, pp. 233–34; compare *Sog bzlog pa gsung 'bum*, p. 479. Sog-bzlog-pa reports that the Maṇika Śrījñāna translation was done in the iron monkey (lcags pho spre'u) year. gZhon-nu-dpal, writing in 1478, mentions that the bSam-yas text was actually found by Kha-che paṇ-chen Śākyaśrī, at the beginning of the thirteenth century, and came eventually to bCom-ldan rig-ral and was translated by Thar-pa lo-tsā-ba, a teacher of Bu-ston, and that gZhon-nu-dpal himself had the surviving Sanskrit folia in his possession. See *Deb ther sngon po*, vol. 1, p. 136; *Blue Annals*, vol. 1, p. 104.

113. Karmay 1998, pp. 29–30.

114. Karmay 1998, p. 30, correctly identified him with the Paṇḍita Prajñāgupta.

115. On this issue, see Davidson 1990.

116. To. 378, 379, 392–94, 398, 404, 410, 421, 422, 447, 450.

117. Davidson 1981, p. 13, for a discussion of this point.

118. Rinpoche and Dwivedi, eds., *Jñānodaya-tantram*.

119. On this point, see the introduction by Tsuda 1974 to his edition of the *Saṁvarodaya-tantra*, p. 30.

120. Jackson 1996, p. 235, first notes this was in the twelfth century but that its roots were in the eleventh; Rong-zom devotes two surviving works to the issue, although it is discussed elsewhere in his oeuvre as well: the *Sangs rgyas sa chen po*, *Rong zom chos bzang gi gsung 'bum*, vol. 2, pp. 69–87; and the *Rang byung ye shes chen po'i 'bras bu rol pa'i dkyil 'khor tu bla ba'i yi ge*, *Rong zom chos bzang gi gsung 'bum*, vol. 2, pp. 111–30. The question is discussed in the hagiography/contents by Mi-pham, *Rong zom gsung 'bum dkar chag me tog phreng* ba, *Rong zom chos bzang gi gsung 'bum*, vol. 1, pp. 15–21; I thank Orna Almogi for drawing my attention to these works.

121. Spitz 1987, vol. 1, p. 148.

122. *Bu ston chos 'byung*, pp. 3–9; Obermiller 1931, vol. 1, pp. 8–17.

123. *Rwa lo tsā ba'i rnam thar*, p. 205; for this event, see Shastri 1997; van der Kuijp 1983, pp. 31–32.

124. On European textual cultures, see Irvine 1994, and on the problems of definition for a textual culture, see Stock 1990, pp. 140–58. The situation appears more complex than reported in Blackburn 2001 for Śrī Laṇka.

NOTES TO CHAPTER 5

1. *Suparigraha-maṇḍalavidhi-sādhana*, fol. 154a6–7.

2. For example, *Deb ther sngon po*, vol. 1, p. 484; *Blue Annals*, vol. 1, p. 399; see also *Chos 'byung me tog snying po sbrang rtsi'i bcud*, pp. 474–75.

3. Given the attention that macrons have received in the spelling of Atiśa's name—precipitated by Eimer's observation that Atiśa is never spelled Atīśa in Tibetan—I must inform the reader that Gayādhara is always spelled Gayadhara/Ghayadhara in Tibetan literature, the latter being very common, albeit the least probable. So why the change? Because I have never seen the name spelled Gayadhara in inscriptions, only Gayādhara. For example, Banerji 1919–20, l. 27; Kielhorn 1886, v. 81. Having worked with medieval Bengali and Newar manuscripts, I must conclude that the concern for vowel length has perhaps received more attention than is warranted.

4. *bsTan rtsis gsal ba'i nyin byed*, pp. 81–83.

5. *gNas chen muk gu lung gi khyad par bshad pa*, in *Bod kyi gnas yig bdams bsgrigs*, p. 299, indicates that Mu-gu-lung was founded 436 years before 1479.

6. *Chos 'byung dpag bsam ljon bzang*, p. 834, with the birthdate inferred from the assumption that 'Brog-mi was to have been 84 when he died; compare *bsTan rtsis gsal ba'i nyin byed*, p. 83.

7. *bLa ma brgyud pa'i rnam par thar pa ngo mtshar snang ba* 13–20; compare Tucci 1947 for the various lineages in Central Tibet, and Richardson 1998, pp. 106–13, for the question of the reliability of these lists.

8. Aris 1979, pp. 3–34; Gyatso 1987.

9. Ferrari 1958, pp. 66, 154.

10. Ekvall 1968 provides a good introduction to traditional nomad life.

11. *sNgon gyi gtam me tog phreng ba*, Uebach 1987, pp. 19–24, and p. 53; *Chos 'byung me tog snying po sbrang rtsi'i bcud* apparently has one place where 'brog mi is used as a collective noun, p. 461.6–7.

12. Nebesky-Wojkowitz 1956, pp. 269–73.

13. 'Brog-mi dPal ye-shes is found in *mKhas pa'i dga' ston*, vol. 1, p. 613; Lo-tsā-ba 'Brog-mi Phrag gi ral-pa-can in *Chos 'byung me tog snying po sbrang rtsi'i bcud*, p. 490. The mTshams-brag manuscript of the *rNying ma rgyud 'bum*, vol. tsha, fols. 26a6–7, represents the shorter text of the *Sarvabuddhasamāyoga* to be the translation of Paṇḍita [?Buddha-] Guhya and 'Brog-mi dPal gyi ye-shes; equally, Kaneko 1982, no. 207, for the gTing-skyes manuscript.

14. *bsTan rtsis gsal ba'i nyin byed*, p. 82, *Lam 'bras khog phub*, p. 121.1.

15. *bLa ma brgyud pa bod kyi lo rgyus*, *SKB* III.173.1.6–74.1.6.

16. The *SKB* edition reads snga dro'i tshur nye ba rnam thang dkar po na, but the place name sPa-gro was evidently overwritten by the editor into sNga-dro (morning), and the correct name and alternative spelling is retained in other editions of the text; see *LL* XI.595.5 : spa gro'i tshur nye ba gnam thang dkar po na; compare *Pod-nag*, *LL* XVI.17.6–18.1.

17. The story as related by Grags-pa rgyal-mtshan is far too elliptical to be translated directly, so I have supplied the sense from the *Pod-nag*, *LL* XVI.18.1–23.3.

18. Again the text makes little sense. The editing of the *LL* XI.597.2, compared with *bLa ma brgyud pa'i rnam par thar pa ngo mtshar snang ba LL* XVI.22.2, has been accepted: der bla chen gyi slob ma sgom chen se rog gnyis can du bzhugs nas |.

19. gNag-smad, evidently a kind of wild black yak. An expanded version of the story of these yak and the position they played in the family of Se-mkhar chung-ba is found in the *bLa ma brgyud pa'i rnam par thar pa ngo mtshar snang ba*, *LL* XVI.32.6–33.1, in which Se, while a boy, is sent to graze them on a mountain, a fairly common experience among 'brog-pa, even those from a quasi-aristocratic lineage.

20. The problems surrounding Rin-chen bzang-po's chronology is examined in Vitali 1996, pp. 186–89 and n. 263. An edition and translation of the earliest Rin-chen bzang-po hagiography are provided in Snellgrove and Skorupski 1977–80, vol. 2, pp. 83–116. Please note that this hagiography sets Nāropā in Kashmir; thus it is subject to all the problems besetting the Nāropā hagiography.

21. *Deb ther sngon po*, vol. 1, p. 257; *Blue Annals*, vol. 1, p. 205; *bsTan rtsis gsal ba'i nyin byed*, p. 81.

22. *Lam 'bras snyan brgyud*, p. 436.

23. Stearns 2001, p. 207, n. 15.

24. For an attempt to demonstrate the need for a reassessment of Ratnākara-śānti's work, see Davidson 1999. Fortunately, other scholars like Isaacson 2001, have begun to edit and reassess his material.

25. For example, for the inferiority of Ratnākaraśānti's view, see *rNam thar yong grags*, pp. 49, 71, 75–76, 86.

26. *rNam thar yong grags*, p. 114.

27. *rNam thar yong grags*, pp. 114–26.

28. *Zhib mo rdo rje*, Stearns 2001, pp. 85–87; compare *bLa ma brgyud pa'i rnam par thar pa ngo mtshar snang ba*, pp. 15–16.

29. In the sDe-dge *bsTan 'gyur* are collected his treatise on cheating death (*Mṛtyu-vañcanopadeśa*, To. 1748), four instructions on the *Guhyasamāja-tantra* (To. 1887–90), a ritual for image consecration (To. 3131), and short sādhanas to Vajrapāṇi (To. 2887) and Tārā (3682)

30. The following is from *Zhib mo rdo rje*, Stearns 2001, pp. 85–89; compare *bLa ma brgyud pa'i rnam par thar pa ngo mtshar snang ba*, p. 16.

31. Compare *Lam 'bras snyan brgyud*, p. 437; *Bhir ba pa'i lo rgyus*, p. 395.

32. This work is also given three other titles, the *Instruction of Śāntipa*, the *Autolocomotion of the Essential Meaning*, and the *Instruction on blessing the Awareness of Appearance*; the work is in the *Pusti dmar chung LL* XIII.394–398.

33. *Pusti dmar chung LL* XIII.398–410 contains these various instructions; the importance of these is emphasized in the *Lam 'bras khog phub*, pp. 124–25.

34. *rNam thar rgyas pa*, Eimer 1979, §§ 231–32.

35. *Pusti dmar chung LL* XIII.398.3: nā lendra'i mkhas pa sgo drug las.

36. *Zhib mo rdo rje*, Stearns 2001, pp. 86–87; *bLa ma brgyud pa'i rnam par thar pa ngo mtshar snang ba*, p. 16.

37. *Lam 'bras snyan brgyud*, p. 437, and *Bhir ba pa'i lo rgyus*, p. 395, give nine years; Grags-pa rgyal-mtshan has twelve; *Zhib mo rdo rje*, Stearns 2001, pp. 88–89, has thirteen for both Nepal and India; *Lam 'bras khog phub*, p. 124, gives eighteen years.

38. For the sources of this nomenclature, see chap. 1, nn. 41 and 42.

39. *Lam 'bras snyan brgyud*, p. 437; *Bhir ba pa'i lo rgyus*, p. 395.

40. Aris 1979, pp. 3–34; Gyatso 1987.

41. *sNgon gyi gtam me tog phreng ba*, Uebach 1987, p. 52; *mKhas pa'i dga' ston*, vol. 1, p. 187.19–20; the importance of Ru-lag was noted by Everding 2000, vol. 2, pp. 279–89.

42. *mKhas pa'i dga' ston*, vol. 1, pp. 187.4–5, 188.15–16.

43. *mKhas pa'i dga' ston*, vol. 1, p. 187.6; *Chos 'byung me tog snying po sbrang rtsi'i bcud*, p. 492; Vitali 1990, pp. 89–96.

44. *Chos la 'jug pa'i sgo*, p. 345.1.5; the date is interpreted following Vitali 1996, p. 547, n. 934.

45. mKhyen-brtse'i dbang-po maintained that the trip could be done in a day; Ferrari 1958, p. 64.

46. *Tshar chen rnam thar*, p. 500; Ferrari 1958, p. 65.

47. *Tshar chen rnam thar*, p. 500; the cave was called Cha-lung rdo-rje-brag rdzong.

48. Ferrari 1958, p. 23; similarly, the visit by Si-tu Chos kyi rgya-mtsho, who visited Mu-gu-lung in 1919, devotes only a couple of lines to 'Brog-mi; *Kaḥ tog si tu'i dbus gtsang gnas yig*, pp. 328–29.

49. The text is not really given a title in the work outside the title provided by the editor—*gNas chen muk gu lung gi khyad par bshad pa*—but it is included in a collection of "sacred site letters" (*gnas yig*) entitled *Bod kyi gnas yig bdams bsgrigs*, pp. 295–99.

50. We see mang-'gar, mang-kar, mang-gar, mang-dkar, etc.; see *Zhib mo rdo rje*, Stearns 2001, pp. 90–107, 117, 180, 226, 229, 235; *sNgon gyi gtam me tog phreng ba*, Uebach 1987, p. 52; *mKhas pa'i dga' ston*, vol. 1, p. 187.19–20.

51. The *Ratnajvalasādhana*, To. 1251, ascribed to Prajñedraruci.

52. The earliest instance with which I am familiar is that of a Kāyastha Bhaṭṭipriya from Mathurā. See the inscription edited and translated in Sharma 1989, p. 312, dated to the first century C.E.; compare Russell 1916, vol. 3, pp. 404–22; Gupta 1996, pp. 8–49. There are many more inscriptions, however, than Gupta notes, and the history of the medieval Kāyasthas has yet to be written.

53. For a succinct account of the caste, see Leonard 1978, pp. 12–15.

54. *bLa ma rgya gar ba'i lo rgyus*, *SKB* III.173.1.1–6, and note the Apabhraṁśa forms found in Gayādhara's own *Jñānodayopadeśa*, fols. 363b7–368a2.

55. Gupta 1996, pp. 50 ff.; Russell 1916, vol. 3, pp. 416–18.

56. This is disputed by Gupta 1996, pp. 61–62, although his reasoning is questionable, given the overwhelming specificity of the term Gauḍa; compare Russell 1916, vol. 3, p. 418.

57. Russell 1916, vol. 3, p. 421.

58. Boyer, Rapson, and Senart 1920–29, nos. 330, 338, are by divira Budharačhi, who in 419 is identified as an important monk. Lin 1990, p. 285, was written by the monk Saṁghamitra; compare the remarks of Salomon 1999, p. 54, in which the monks are scribes (here Kāyastha) who were permitted to retain their equipment and, evidently, exercise their skills on behalf of the Dharma.

59. There are too many inscriptions to note, compare Rajguru 1955–76, vol. 4, pp. 97, 103, 109, 155, etc.; compare Gupta 1996, pp. 94–99, for some others.

60. Gupta 1996, pp. 156–62.

61. Gupta 1996, pp. 156, 158.

62. *Mṛcchakatika*, pp. 182–83, 324–25 (act 5, v. 7, prose, act 9, v. 14); compare *Rājataraṅgiṇī* 5.180–84, 8.131.

63. Kṣemendra's *Kalāvilāsa*, discussed in Gupta 1996, pp. 160–61; for Kṣemendra's criticism of tantrikas in general, see Baldissera 2001.

64. *bLa ma brgyud pa'i rnam par thar pa ngo mtshar snang ba*, p. 117.

65. *Tshar chen rnam thar*, pp. 413–14.

66. *gDams ngag byung tshul gyi zin bris gsang chen bstan pa rgyas byed*, p. 43; *Lam 'bras byung tshul*, p. 111.1.5–6.

67. *gDams ngag byung tshul gyi zin bris gsang chen bstan pa rgyas byed*, p. 43.

68. *Tshar chen rnam thar*, p. 414.

69. *gDams ngag byung tshul gyi zin bris gsang chen bstan pa rgyas byed*, pp. 43–44.

70. *bsTan rtsis gsal ba'i nyin byed*, pp. 92–93.

71. *Deb ther sngon po*, vol. 1, p. 145; *Blue Annals*, vol. 1, p. 112; *Zhib mo rdo rje*, Stearns 2001, pp. 90–93.

72. *Lam 'bras snyan brgyud*, p. 438; *Bhir ba pa'i lo rgyus*, p. 396.

73. *Lam 'bras byung tshul*, p. 114.3; *Zhib mo rdo rje*, Stearns 2001, pp. 96–97.

74. *gDams ngag byung tshul gyi zin bris gsang chen bstan pa rgyas byed*, p. 49.

75. For example, *'Brug pa'i chos 'byung*, p. 221.

76. *Lho rong chos 'byung*, p. 47.

77. The colophon to the *Śrī-Jñānajvala-tantrarāja* identifies her as such; To. 394, fol. 223a6: sing gha la'i gling gi rnal 'byor ma tsandra mā la. 'Brog-mi may have been party to the revision of the *Abhidhānottara-tantra* which is found in the Phug-brag canon, Samten 1992, no. 446, in which case he would have worked with Prabhākara as well; see Samten 1992, p. 163, which lists the revisers as Prabhākara and Shākya Yes-shes, but the chronology is difficult and it is possible this is another Shākya Yes-shes or an error in the name.

78. *Sampuṭa*, fol. 158b6.

79. *rNam thar yong grags*, p. 159; *mKhas pa'i dga' ston*, vol. 1, p. 683; *bsTan rtsis gsal ba'i nyin byed*, p. 103.

80. Stearns 2001, pp. 91, 213, n. 39; *gDams ngag byung tshul gyi zin bris gsang chen bstan pa rgyas byed*, pp. 77–99. mKhyen-brtse portrays Lha-btsun Ka-li as the son of mNga'-bdag dPal-lde, indicating that 'Brog-mi's wife was a princess of the royal house. None of our lists for dPal-sde's progeny support this claim; compare, for ex-

ample, *Bod rje btsan po'i gdung rab tshig nyung don gsal*, p. 71, in which dPal-lde is given two sons: the elder, 'Od-dpal-lde, and the younger, Dharma Tsakra. Stearns 2001, p. 213, n. 39, seems to accept the marriage of a princess and a nomad, even though he acknowledges on p. 232, n. 114, that no non-Lam-'bras documentation supports this position. It would be unlikely indeed if a commoner like 'Brog-mi were capable of marrying a princess. It is possible that the aristocratic house into which he married postured as one of the pretenders that arose during the period of fragmentation.

81. The annotation to the *Zhib mo rdo rje*, Stearns 2001, pp. 90–91, indicates this about his sons, followed by bLa-ma Dam-pa, *bLa ma brgyud pa'i rnam par thar pa ngo mtshar snang ba*, p. 17; compare the names for the sons listed in *bLa ma brgyud pa'i rnam par thar pa ngo mtshar snang ba*, p. 35.6. Nyang-ral's *Chos 'byung me tog snying po sbrang rtsi'i bcud*, however, mentions a 'brog mi sras po lo tsā ba, p. 480.15; Stearns 2001, p. 213, n. 39, discusses legends of the sons. The *Phag mo gru pa'i rnam thar rin po che'i phreng ba*, p. 13.2, mentions a bLa-ma Mang-dkar-ba, who may have been a descendant of 'Brog-mi.

82. *Zhib mo rdo rje*, Stearns 2001, pp. 96–97; *gDams ngag byung tshul gyi zin bris gsang chen bstan pa rgyas byed*, p. 49.

83. *Zhib mo rdo rje*, Stearns 2001, pp. 100–101.

84. For a list of the participants, both Indian and Tibetan, see Shastri 1997, pp. 877–78.

85. *Deb ther sngon po*, vol. 1, p. 100; *Blue Annals*, vol. 1, p. 72.

86. *mKhas grub khyung po rnal 'byor gyi rnam thar*, p. 33; the claim is unclear as to which trip of Gayādhara's is meant, and we are not certain that Khyung-po rnal-'byor's hagiographer knew that the Bengali scholar had made multiple trips.

87. *Lam 'bras snyan brgyud*, pp. 439–40; *Kha rag gnyos kyi rgyud pa byon tshul mdor bsdus*, pp. 12.4–13.2.

88. While it is clear that the Rog here is sGom-pa Rog or gShen-sgom Rog-po, it is not clear that this Se is Se-ston Kun-rig; *bLa ma brgyud pa'i rnam par thar pa ngo mtshar snang ba*, p. 22; compare *gDams ngag byung tshul gyi zin bris gsang chen bstan pa rgyas byed*, p. 49; *Lam 'bras khog phub*, pp. 138–39; Stearns 2001, p. 233, n. 120, discusses the problem.

89. *Bhir ba pa'i lo rgyus*, p. 398; *bLa ma brgyud pa'i rnam par thar pa ngo mtshar snang ba*, pp. 21–22; *gDams ngag byung tshul gyi zin bris gsang chen bstan pa rgyas byed*, p. 49; *Zhib mo rdo rje*, Stearns 2001, p. 97.

90. *Zhib mo rdo rje*, Stearns 2001, p. 99; bLa-ma Dam-pa maintains that they were offered to Sa-chen by Nags-ston lo-tsā-ba at the time of his receiving the Lam-'bras from Sa-chen; *bLa ma brgyud pa'i rnam par thar pa ngo mtshar snang ba*, p. 22.

91. *Lam 'bras byung tshul*, 114.1.2–5.

92. *Lam 'bras byung tshul*, 114.1.3–4; Ngor-chen lists the following texts: a translation of the [*Lam 'bras*] *rTsa ba rdo rje'i tshig rkang*, the annals of the lineage of the Gyi-jo'i slob-brgyud, both a lengthy commentary on and a summary of the *Lam 'bras rtsa ba*, and an unspecified number of texts on topics like the letters in the *bha*

ga dkyil 'khor. The lineage is Gyi-jo zla-ba'i 'od-zer, Zhu 'khor-lo, Zhu dar-ma rgyal-mtshan, Zhu-ston Hor-mo, 'Od-pa don-ne, mChims Tshul-khrims shes-rab.

93. *Lam 'bras byung tshul*, 110.3.5–11.2.5.

94. *Zab don gnad kyi sgron me* of Go-rams bSod-nams seng-ge, p. 2.

95. *Raktayamāntakasādhana*, To. 2017; *Raktayamārisādhana*, To. 2018; *Uḍḍiyānaśrīyogayoginīsvabhūta-sambhoga-śmaśānakalpa*, To. 1744 (fol. 113b1 of this work associates it with the *Mahāmāyā-tantra*, or the *Khasamatantra*), *Chinnamuṇḍasādhana*, To. 1555; a variant version of this last work was edited and examined by Nihom 1992.

96. *gShin rje gshed kyi yid bzhin gyi nor bu'i phreng ba zhe bya ba'i sgrub thabs*, To. 2083, fol. 159a7.

97. Schaeffer 2002 introduces this literature but glosses over (p. 523) the fact that the literature principally describes a substance, ambrosia (*amṛta*), rather than immortality per se.

98. *Raktayamāntakasādhana*, To. 2017, fol. 78a2; there is little surprising about this, but the confirmation is satisfying. The nectar texts are *Amṛtasiddhimūla*, To. 2285, and *Amṛtādhiṣṭhāna*, To. 2044.

99. *Yamāriyantrāvalī*, To. 2022.

100. These are, respectively, the *'Od gsal 'char ba'i rim pa*, To. 2019, and the *Karmacaṇḍālikā-dohakoṣa-gīti*, To. 2344. Despite the dohā form of this latter, it is really an instructional text.

101. *Dohakoṣa*, To. 2280; *Virūapādacaurāsi*, To. 2283; *Suniṣprapañcatattvopadeśa*, To. 2020.

102. *bsKyed rim gnad kyi zla zer*, p. 178.3.

103. There are three specific works like this in the *Pod ser: Lung 'di nyid dang mdor bsdus su sbyar, Lung 'di nyid dang zhib tu sbyar ba, Lam 'bras dang bcas pa'i don rnams lung ci rigs pa dang sbyar.* Collectively, they occupy *Pod ser*, pp. 481–581.

104. Differences of opinion by various teachers, Indian and Tibetan, are especially noted in the *sGa theng ma*, pp. 175, 180, 186–87, 192–93, 195–96, 203, 223, 267, 280, 282, 319–20, and 331–32.

105. *lDan bu ma*, p. 298.1.

106. It is possible that this work is related to the recently published *Jñānodayatantra*.

107. *Yoginīsañcārya* 1.1, and chaps. 2 and 3, are largely dedicated to this idea; *Yoginīsañcārya*, ed. Pandey 2002, pp. 8–13, 19–41.

108. For example, *Sras don ma*, pp. 11.2, 21.1, 22.4, 27. 5, etc.

109. We might note the continuity of use from the *Ratnagotravibhāga* forward, for that Mahāyānist work starts with seven "adamantine words" (*vajrapada*); *Ratnagotravibhāga*, I.1; Takasaki 1966, pp. 141–42. Compare the discussion in the *Pañcakrama*, I.11–12.

110. *Ratnagotravibhāga*, 1.23–26; Takasaki 1966, pp. 186–95.

111. For example, Jackson 1996; Levinson 1996.

112. For example, *Sras don ma*, pp. 51–52, which allows for both Saṁvara and Hevajra visualization systems, even though evidently preferring the former.

113. *Sras don ma* 24.1–2.

114. This material is taken from the *rGyud kyi mngon par rtogs pa rin po che'i ljon shing* 30.3.5–35.1.5, and supplemented by *sGa theng ma* 386.4–400.2, *Sras don ma* 323.6–34.4.

115. One of the curiosities of Sa-chen's descriptions are that the four joys of the *maṇḍalacakra* practice are called in "ascending" order, despite the descent of the fluid from the fontanel to the navel, and the four joys of the adamantine wave are in the "descending order," despite their ascent from the navel to the fontanel. I have not encountered an explanation of this variance in terminology. Both go through the sequence of ānanda-paramānanda-viramānanda-sahajānanda. For a discussion of these and the controversy on their order, see Snellgrove's introduction to *Hevajra-tantra*, p. 38; see also Kværne 1975; Davidson 2002d.

116. On this controversy and the lore of *sahaja*, see Davidson 2002d.

117. For example, all three 'khams 'dus pa are applied to the rdo rje rba labs in *kLog skya ma*, pp. 254–55. However, Sa-chen in the *Gang zag gzhung ji lta ba bzhin du dkri ba'i gzhung shing*, *Pod ser*, pp. 312–13, equates the two lists of three items.

118. I have pointed out that alternative Tibetan translations of the *Mañjuśrī-nāmasaṁgīti*, for example, were the most frequently encountered in monastic liturgical syllabi (*chos spyod*), and these did not conform to its late canonical translation (To. 360) by Shong bLo-gros brtan-pa; Davidson 1981, p. 13; cf. Wedemeyer, forthcoming.

119. *LL* XI.347–479; we note a different order observed by Ngor-chen in his *Lam 'bras byung tshul* 109.3.2–10.1.6.

120. The received Sanskrit is edited by Samdhong Rinpoche and Dvivedi, *Guhyādi-Aṣṭasiddhi-Saṅgraha*, pp. 195–208; 'Brog-mi's translation is found in *Pod ser LL* XI.347–62, and at that time the text apparently had the title *Acintya-kramopadeśa*; these eight subsidiary cycles are presented briefly in Stearns 2001, p. 210, n. 30.

121. See the bibliography; it is worth noting that Grags-pa rgyal-mtshan's *gLegs bam gyi dkar chags* makes no mention of the eight subsidiary texts, so their inclusion is apparently a later addition to the *Pod ser LL* XI.1–8.

122. *LL* XI.362–87.

123. *Acintyādvayakramopadeśa* vv. 87–89; *LL* XI.358.4–5; To. 2228, fol. 103a7–b1.

124. The text is found *Pod ser LL* XI.387–95.

125. Shendge 1967 (*Sahajasiddhi*); Samdhong Rinpoche and Dvivedi, *Guhyādi-Aṣṭasiddhi-Saṅgraha*, pp. 181–91; compare *Pod ser LL* XI.387–95.

126. *Hevajra-tantra* I.x.41; compare *Pod ser LL* XI.387.4.

127. These are reviewed by Shendge 1967, p. 128.

128. *Pod ser LL* XI.395.5: 'di la rtsa ba med pa'i lam 'bras bya ba'ang ming 'dogs te |.

129. *Lam 'bras byung tshul*, p. 109.4.3; compare his discussion of Ḍombiheruka's position in the "exegetical system," (bshad brgyud), *Kye rdo rje'i byung tshul*, p. 282.1.1–2.5; for Ngor-chen's consideration of this lineage, see Davidson 1991 and 1992.

130. The text is found in *Pod ser LL* XI.400–406.

131. *Pod ser LL* XI.405.5–6.

132. *Guhyasamāja-tantra*, p. 10, has both verses, even if the verse attributed to Vairocanavajra is not identified with a number by Matsunaga; the Akṣobhyavajra verse is II.4. The former verse is found right at the beginning of the *Bodhicittavivaraṇa*, To. 1800, fol. 38a7. Namai 1997 has begun to explore the complexity of the bodhicitta texts and their relationship to the *Guhyasamāja*.

133. *Sarahapādasya dohākoṣa*, Bachi 1935, pp. 52–120.

134. *Lam 'bras byung tshul*, p. 109.4.2.

135. *Pod ser LL* XI.401.4, 406.1.

136. The text is found in *Pod ser LL* XI.406–419.

137. *Pod ser LL* XI.406.3–4; note that Ngor Chen, *Lam 'bras byung tshul*, p. 110.1.2–3, indicates that rather than Ḍombiheruka's *Nairātmyayoginīsādhana*, Vāgīśvarakīrti used his own *De kho na nyid rin po che'i phreng ba* as a source text. We seem to have no surviving text by that name attributed to Vāgīśvarakīrti, however, and I wonder whether Ngor-chen was confusing Vāgīśvarakīrti with Advayavajra, who did write a *Tattvaratnāvalī*, found in the *Advayavajrasaṁgraha*, pp. 14–22.

138. *Saptāṅga* (To. 1888), esp. fol. 190a-b; *Tattvaratnāvaloka*, ed. Janardan Pandey (To. 1889).

139. *Pod ser LL* XI.406.5, 418.6.

140. The text is found in *Pod ser LL* XI.419–441.

141. *Pod ser LL* XI.419.4–5; we note that Ngor-chen makes this work based on both the *Śrī-Hevajrasādhana* and the *Śrī-Hevajrapradīpaśūlopamāvavādaka*; *Lam 'bras byung tshul*, p. 109.3.6–4.1.

142. *Pod ser LL* XI.420.2–3.

143. *Pod ser LL* XI.441–445; compare To. 1220, which is the same translation.

144. *Pod ser LL* XI.445.3.

145. The text occurs in *Pod ser LL* XI.445–57.

146. The identity of the *Saṁvara* as a nondual tantra is anomalous; see bSod-nams rtse-mo's *rGyud sde spyi'i rnam par gzhag pa*, p. 18.1.2.

147. *Pod ser LL* XI.445.4–46.1.

148. The *Vasantatilakā* has been edited by Samdhong Rinpoche and Dvivedi; the *Guhyatattvaprakāśa* is found as the *gSang ba'i de kho na nyid rab tu gsal ba* (To. 1450), and the *Saṁvaravyākhyā* is found as the *sDom pa bshad pa* (To. 1460); the *Olapati* is discussed later.

149. The commentary's title is imperfectly Sanskritized to *Olacastustayavibhaṅga* : *Rim pa bzhi'i rnam par 'byed pa*; fol. 358b7.

150. Sa-chen's works on Kāṇha's tradition are found in *SKB* I.216.4.2–256.3.6, which mention the "six texts" (gzhung drug) of Kāṇha and especially attend to the *Olapati* and the *Vasantatilakā*. Grags-pa rgyal-mtshan's materials are primarily on the consecration ritual and lineage, although the "six texts" topics are covered in some detail; *Nag po dkyil chog gi bshad sbyar* and *bDe mchog nag po pa'i dkyil chog lag tu blang ba'i rim pa*.

151. The text gives U-tsi-ta-'chi-ba-med-pa, and it appears that acyuta > ucyata >

ucita in a series of copying errors, as acyuta exactly translates 'chi ba med pa, deathless. The text is in *Pod ser LL* XI.457–61.

152. *Pod ser LL* XI.461.1.

153. *Lam 'bras byung tshul*, p. 110.1.4–5.

154. *Caryāgītikośa*, nos. 10, 11, and 18.

155. *Pod ser LL* XI.458.5.

156. *Lam 'bras byung tshul*, p. 110.1.5.

157. The text occurs in *Pod ser LL* XI.461–79.

158. *Sras don ma*, pp. 364.4–66.1.

159. *Pod ser LL* XI.461.2–3.

160. *Pod ser LL* XI.479.3–4; compare *Blue Annals* (1949), vol. 2, p. 697, Prajñāgupta is attributed the position of the Indian informant in *Mahāmudrātilaka* (To. 420), and other tantras (To. 421–22). Ruegg 1981, pp. 220–21, discusses his career and incorrectly reconstructs his name, while the colophon to the *Jñānatilaka-yoginītantrarāja-paramamahādbhuta*, To. 422, fol. 136b4, provides the correct Prajñāgupta. See also Karmay 1998, pp. 30–35; Stearns 2001, pp. 52–53; Vitali 1996, p. 238, n. 336.

161. *Lam 'bras byung tshul*, pp. 124.4.6–25.1.2; I am presuming this section belongs to the part completed by Gung-ru Shes-rab bzang-po; Gung-ru Shes-rab bzang-po refers to a line in the *Pod ser LL* XI.6.4.

162. *Sampuṭatilaka*, To. 382, fol. 194a6–7; de Jong 1972, pp. 26–27, notes and translates this colophon but does not interpret it satisfactorily. Interestingly, a manuscript of 'Brog-mi's initial translation of the tantra before his final revision exists in the Phug-brag canon no. 461; Samten 1992, p. 168.

163. *rGyud kyi rgyal po chen po saṁ pu ṭa zhes bya ba dpal ldan sa skya paṇḍi ta'i mchan dang bcas pa*, fol. 300a3 (p. 667.3); the date is provided fol. 300b4 (p. 668.4).

164. This enumeration is taken from the Tohoku catalog, ed. Ui et al. 1934. Respectively, this indicates numbers To. 381–411, 413–14, 417–18 (one work, the *Hevajra-tantra*), 418–19, 426–27, 1185, 1195, 1207–8, 1210–13, 1220, 1225–26, 1236, 1241, 1251, 1263, 1305–6 (note the incorrect numbering, 1306 given twice, but 1304 missing so that the numbers once again coincide by 1306), 1310, 1416, 1514, 1705. We may also note that To. 429, listed in the catalog as by Gayādhara and ('Brog-mi) Shakya ye-shes, is an incorrect reading of the colophon, which gives the translators as Gayādhara and 'Gos khug-pa lhas-btsas. Similarly, To. 1209 and To. 1240 are not clearly by 'Brog-mi, according to the printed text, which provides no translator, although the designation of 'Brog-mi to To. 1210 and To. 1241 may indicate that these were considered concluding sections of their immediately preceding works. Phug-brag 446 [Samten 1992, p. 163] is a revision ascribed to Prabhākara and Shākya Ye-shes, but it is possible that this is not 'Brog-mi.

165. This work describes a maṇḍala of ten divinities and features a Gold Tārā with four heads and eight arms. It is not clear why 'Brog-mi should have translated this work, although he did it alone and it may have been done toward the end of his life; *Ārya-Tārāmaṇḍalavidhi-sādhana*, To. 1705.

166. Respectively, To. 381, 382, 417–418, and 419; To. 417 is in fact only the first half (kalpa) of the two parts of the work, so that the translators' colophon indicates their agency in the entire translation, and the Tohoku catalog needs emendation. For observations on the importance of different renditions of the *Hevajra*, see van der Kuijp 1985, whose errors in Sanskrit have been noted by Nihom 1995, p. 325, n. 29. Samten 1992, pp. xiv, 167, notes that the *Vajrapañjara* found in Phug-brag no. 458, while ascribed to this team, is in fact quite different from the edition found in the other canons.

167. In his *bsKyed rim gnad kyi zla zer*, p. 175.2.2, Ngor-chen identifies Ratna-śrījñāna with Gayādhara, although this identification appears to be another of Ngor-chen's idiosyncratic readings of history.

NOTES TO CHAPTER 6

1. *Zangs gling ma*, p. 129.13–17.

2. A good survey of the phenomenon, primarily from a later point of view, is Gyatso 1996; for Bonpo *gter* traditions, see Martin 2001b.

3. This is the emphasis in Snellgrove 1987, vol. 2, pp. 397–99.

4. Especially seen in Mayer 1994, p. 541; Gyatso 1994 discusses the earliest apology, that of Gu-ru Chos dbang, whose ideas will play a part here.

5. Karmay 1972, pp. 65–71.

6. For these categories, see Gyatso 1998, pp. 147–48; for a modern Tibetan representation of *gter-ma*, see Thondup 1986.

7. *gTer byung chen mo*, pp. 101.7, 104.1.

8. *gTer byung chen mo*, pp. 81.5–82.3; these are discussed in Gyatso 1994, p. 276.

9. *Zangs gling ma*, pp. 132–133.

10. Thomas 1957, pp. 45–102.

11. Davidson 1990, 2002a, 2002c, p. 147.

12. For some reason, the sūtra side of this has received little attention, but several sūtras are quoted in the *gter* literature, most notably variations on the title *Chu klung sna tshogs* [*rol pa'i*] *mdo* and the *rNam rol mdo*; see *bKa' 'chems ka khol ma*, pp. 14.17, 15.8–9, 107.13–14; the *Maṇi bka' 'bum*, pp. 173.3–75.4; and Guru Chos-dbang's *gTer 'byung chen mo*, pp. 89.5, 91.6. Martin 2001b, p. 23, seems to presume an Indian text and provides one of these sūtras with the Sanskritized title *Nāḍīlalita Sūtra*, an improbable combination. See Davidson 2003, forthcoming a.

13. *bKa' 'chems ka khol ma*, p. 258.2–12; compare statements in Guru Chos-dbang's *gTer 'byung chen mo*, p. 83.6–84.1; Gyatso 1994, p. 280–83.

14. Denjongpa 2002, p. 5, "One day, my teacher Lopen Dugyal mentioned that there are many more spirits and deities inhabiting the environment in Sikkim than there are human beings."

15. Karmay 1998, p. 254; Tucci 1949, vol. 2, pp. 721–24; Nebesky-Wojkowitz 1956, pp. 287–300.

16. *bKa' thang sde lnga*, p. 137.18.

17. Lalou 1938 translates and studies Atiśa's text on the eight Nāgas.

18. This is also true of their comparison to the Chinese dragon, which has traits accorded to the Tibetan klu, the Tibetan dragon, the 'brug, and the Tibetan wind horse, the lung-rta; for this latter, see Karmay 1998, pp. 414–15.

19. On Nāgas, see Sutherland 1991, pp. 38–43; Vogel 1926.

20. For example, *Zangs gling ma*, p. 111.12–15, has Padmasambhava do many ceremonies focused on the klu because of their dominion; similarly p. 120.12–14.

21. *bKa' 'chems ka khol ma*, pp. 257.12, 247.8; *sBa bzhed*, p. 46.5; *sBa bzhed zhabs btags ma*, p. 38.1; Richardson 1998, pp. 247–50, locates the chapel to the klu and gnod-sbyin nos. 12 and 16.

22. The *sBa bzhed* p. 45.12–14 makes no mention of the klu, and the treasury is called the "treasury of things" (rdzas kyi bang mdzod), but *sBa bzhed zhabs btags ma*, p. 37 leaves it out; compare *bKa' thang sde lnga*, p. 139.12: 'khor sa bar ma klu la gtad pa yin.

23. *bKa' 'chems ka khol ma*, pp. 37.14, 203.8; *mKhas pa'i dga ston* 1: 221.6.

24. *bKa' 'chems ka khol ma*, p. 221.5–7; *mKhas pa'i dga ston* 1: 223.15–17.

25. *sBa bzhed* p. 53; *sBa bzhed zhabs btags ma*, p. 45; *dBa' bzhed*, pp. 53 (11a), 55 (12a), 63 (14b); for a discussion of the issue of phywa, see Karmay 1998, pp. 178–180, n.; 247, n.

26. Tucci 1956b, p. 77.

27. Aspects of this have been studied in the fine collection of essays in Blondeau and Steinkellner 1996.

28. *dBa' bzhed*, pp. 24–25 (text fol. 1b3–6 has been rather freely interpreted by the translators); Sørensen 1994, p. 150; Haarh 1969, pp. 335–38; Stein 1986, pp. 188–93; Richardson 1998, pp. 74–81. On the gnyan po gsang ba, *mKhas pa'i dga ston,* vol. 1, pp. 168–70; *rGya bod yig tshang chen mo*, p. 137.6; *Chos 'byung me tog snying po sbrang rtsi'i bcud*, pp. 164.8–166.7.

29. *dBa' bzhed*, pp. 24–25 (fol. 2a1).

30. *dBa' bzhed*, p. 36.

31. *sBa bzhed*, p. 35.2–3; *sBa bzhed zhabs btags ma*, p. 28.5–6.

32. *sBa bzhed*, p. 32.15–17; *sBa bzhed zhabs btags ma*, p. 26.6–7.

33. Haarh 1969, pp. 348–49; for the Kharoṣṭhī materials, see Salomon 1999, pp. 240–47.

34. This phrase is employed in the *rGyal rabs gsal ba'i me slong*, p. 61.4, for the gnyan po gsang ba.

35. *Maṇi bka' 'bum*, fol. 96.5–6; the Punaka edition cited here reads the temple name incorrectly as phra 'brug, but the Zhol spar khang (fol. 90b6) has khra 'brug; this treasury was probably at the Khra-'brug palace; see *bKa' 'chems ka khol ma*, p. 104.7–8. The temple is the Ārya-palo (i.e. Āryāvalokiteśvara] temple close to the south entrance of the compound, which was built first by Khri-srong lde'u-btsan; its certification here by Srong-btsan sgam-po is an anachronism; *sBa bzhed*, p. 339.5–6; *sBa bzhed zhabs btags ma*, p. 32.1–4. The "river silk" is *chu dar*, a board-like

or felt-like material made from pounding water weeds (*Tshig mdzod chen mo*, p. 802b); the water weed described by *chu bal* (*mo*) remains uncertain, and the attempt by Arya 1998, p. 65b, to identify it with spirogyra varians (a form of algae) may not be correct, since a solid paper would need fibers. The consistent reference to *chu dar* in *gter ma* means that it may have been an early (sacred?) form of paper employed by Tibetans before the importation of Chinese products; see *bKa' thang sde lnga*, pp. 160.19, 195.21. It is placed first on the list of materials on which *gter ma* may legitimately be copied (*bris gzhi*) in Guru Chos-dbang's *gTer 'byung chen mo*, p. 102.4.

36. The best material on the ideas of the *bla* is collected in Karmay 1998, pp. 310–38; see also Tucci 1980, pp. 190–93.

37. *mKhas pa lde'u chos 'byung*, pp. 254.21–55.1.

38. That is, g.yas kyi tshugs dpon; *dBa' bzhed*, p. 60, fol. 14a7; *sBa bzhed*, p. 34.7; the title chos kyi bla is left out of *sBa bzhed zhabs btags ma*, p. 27.10.

39. *sBa bzhed*, p. 35.14; *dBa' bzhed*, fol. 15a2; *mKhas pa'i dga' ston*, vol. 1, p. 333.13; missing *sBa bzhed zhabs btags ma*, p. 26.11. The identity of the bla'i gtsug lag khang with bSam-yas is evident in the *sNgon gyi gtam me tog phreng ba*, Uebach 1987, p. 112 (*Bod kyi lo rgyus deb ther khag lnga*, p. 28.2), in which the same episode mentions bSam-yas. For the Ba-lam-glag temple, see *dBa' bzhed*, Wangdu and Diemberger 2000 (under *dBa' bzhed*), pp. 41 n. 90, 63, n. 203.

40. *rGya bod yig tshang chen mo*, pp. 192.8, 192.15.

41. *Zangs gling ma*, pp. 130–32.

42. *Chos 'byung me tog snying po sbrang rtsi'i bcud*, p. 437.5.

43. *gNa' rabs bod kyi chang pa'i lam srol*, p. 37.

44. Ferrari 1958, pp. 48, 122, n. 207.

45. Karmay 1998, pp. 327–28.

46. Karmay 1998, p. 314.

47. *Zangs gling ma*, pp. 130–32.

48. *gTer 'byung chen mo*, p. 98.5–6.

49. *bKa' thang sde lnga*, pp. 166–77.

50. *rGya bod yig tshang chen mo*, p. 136.13; *Chos 'byung me tog snying po sbrang rtsi'i bcud*, p. 164.8.

51. *Tun hong nas thon pa'i bod kyi lo rgyus yig cha*, pp. 34–35 (= Pelliot Tibetan 1287).

52. Haarh 1969, p. 144; *mKhas pa'i dga' ston*, p. 161.15–21.

53. Haarh 1969, p. 381, and Macdonald 1971b, p. 222, n. 133, pointed out that a tent provided the fundamental metaphor for the tombs, a point that Karmay 1998, p. 225, does not accept. I believe he is incorrect in this, although he is to be commended for discovering the site.

54. This line of thought is particularly noticeable in rNying-ma-pa literature; see chap. 38 of the *gTam gyi tshogs theg pa'i rgya mtsho* by 'Jigs-med gling-pa, pp. 278–303. This chapter was used by Tucci 1950, pp. 1–5, and Haarh 1969, pp. 114–17, 362–64, 381–91; compare the Bon-po text studied in Lalou 1952.

55. *bKa' thang sde lnga*, p. 146; discussed in Tucci 1950, p. 10, and translated

Haarh 1969, pp. 350–52, but his translation is in need of revision, and Haarh has misunderstood the tomb guardians as different from the ministers.

56. Guru Chos-dbang's *gTer 'byung chen mo*, p. 102.3, mentions that *gter* has an inexhaustible location, as it may be hidden in the mind; this may lead to the system of *dgongs gter*, but is not quite there yet, for it is missing the question of Padmasambhava's disciples' reincarnating consciousnesses revealing at a later date the texts buried earlier.

57. *Zangs gling ma*, p. 130.15, has the *thugs gter* buried in mChims phu'i dben gnas, that is, the Chimpu hermitage, a placement followed in *Padma bka' thang*, p. 551.17, but not in the same text, p. 551.5–7; *gTer 'byung chen mo*, p. 98.7, has the *thugs gter* buried at rNam skas brag (unidentified). There is a *dgongs gter*, but it too is placed in the ground, and the *bKa' thang sde lnga*, pp. 74.21–75.1, indicates that the three *dgongs gter* were to be hidden in the three Jo mo gling.

58. *Padma bka' thang*, pp. 558–74.

59. A later example is presented in Gyatso 1998, pp. 57–60, 168, 173–75, 255–56; we see the beginning of this process in the kha-byang statements found in the *Zangs gling ma*, p. 140.2.

60. Karmay 1972, pp. 118–22.

61. Kværne 1971, p. 228; Karmay 1972, pp. 112–26; Karmay 1998, pp. 122–24.

62. Martin 2001a, pp. 49–80, 93–99; Karmay 1972, pp. 126–32.

63. There earliest reference I have seen to Sangs-rgyas bla-ma is in the *Padma bka' thang*, p. 558.9; this section is quoted and expanded in the *Gu bkra'i chos 'byung*, pp. 365–66, which is essentially copied in *gTer ston brgya rtsa'i rnam thar*, fols. 36a3–37a5.

64. This is the *Yang gter rtsa gsum dril sgrub*, found in *Rin chen gter mdzod chen mo*, vol. 97, pp. 521–52. The dubious nature of this work is evident when we take into account the statement of Gu-ru bKra-shis that the fifth Dalai Lama could not locate any texts by Sangs-rgyas bla-ma; *Gu bkra'i chos 'byung*, p. 366.1. It is interesting that Kong-sprul sought out verification of this work from mChog-gyur gling-pa and others before including in the *Rin chen gter mdzod chen mo*; see *gTer ston brgya rtsa'i rnam thar*, fol. 37a4–5.

65. Martin 2001a, p. 53, notes that a number of texts associated with gShen-chen klu-dga' were found by later gter ston.

66. *gTer ston brgya rtsa'i rnam thar*, fol. 60a2–b5; again much of the material is taken from the *Gu bkra'i chos 'byung*, pp. 398–99.

67. *rGyud bzhi'i bka' bsgrub nges don snying po*, pp. 235.4–36.2; first noted by Karmay 1998, pp. 228–37, esp. p. 230, n. 12.

68. *Chos 'byung me tog snying po sbrang rtsi'i bcud*, p. 501.8–12.

69. *Padma bka' thang*, p. 563.1–4.

70. *gTer 'byung chen mo*, pp. 84.7–85.7.

71. *Baiḍūrya sngon po*, pp. 206.6–10.4; compare *Gu bkra'i chos 'byung*, pp. 376–78, and *gTer ston brgya rtsa'i rnam thar*, fols. 45b6–46b5.

72. Karmay 1998, pp. 228–37, has given this his usually meticulous attention.

73. The 1302 *Zhu len nor bu phreng ba*, for example, mentions the *bKa' 'chems ka khol ma* revelation only in association with Zhang-ston Dar-ma rgyal-mtshan (p. 454). He was a disciple of Zhang-ston Dar-ma-grags (1103–74), whose dates are found *Blue Annals*, vol. 1, p. 284. For the bKa'-brgyud-pa evidence, see chap. 4, n. 9. There also were several thirteenth-century bKa'-gdams-pa masters strongly associated with the khams lugs sems sde in Central Tibet: see *sLob dpon dga' rab rdo rje nas brgyud pa'i rdzogs pa chen po sems sde'i phra khrid kyi man ngag*, pp. 436–37, 516–17.

74. Phug-brag no. 772; Samten 1992, pp. 240–41.

75. Compare *Padma bka' thang*, p. 558.9–13, *Gu bkra'i chos 'byung*, pp. 366.10–17, and *gTer ston brgya rtsa'i rnam thar*, fol. 37a5–b4.

76. This passage translates *bKa' 'chems ka khol ma*, pp. 258.14–59.8, 260.17–61.7. For ease of reading, I have altered the ra-sa of 259.1 to lha-sa, which is the reading for the same sentence 259.5–6, and have altered Khrom-pa-rgyan to Grom-pa-rgyang, as it is evidently an unusual spelling of the temple's name. The meaning of seng ge lag zan ma of 259.4 is not clear to me; apparently it has been changed in later recensions to ka ba seng ge can, the lion pillar (*bKa' thang sde lnga*, p. 159.9).

77. *mKhas pa'i dga' ston*, vol. 1, pp. 372–76.

78. *Zangs gling ma*, pp. 130–32; *bKa' thang sde lnga*, pp. 74–75, 155–207, 529–32; *Padma bka' thang*, pp. 548–57; compare the quotation in *mKhas pa'i dga' ston*, vol. 1, pp. 246–47.

79. *gTer byung chen mo*, pp. 105.2, 111.5.

80. I thank David Germano for many conversations on the question of the sNying-tig lineages.

81. A good introduction to the position of the lCe can be found in Vitali 1990, pp. 91–96; much remains to be said on this clan, however, as well as on other clans in the Myang-stod area.

82. *Rig pa rang shar*, A-'dzom chos-gar ed., pp. 852–55; the mTshams-Brag, pp. 696–99; and the gTing-skyes, pp. 332–34. I thank David Germano for suggestions and corrections to the colophon translation.

83. I have read "kun gyis ma tshims sa yi gter du bzhag" where the texts are problematic.

84. Compare *sNying thig ya bzhi*, vol. 9, pp. 162–72; *rNying ma bka' ma rgyas pa*, vol. 45, pp. 643–52. Karmay 1988, p. 209, n. 16, dates this to the twelfth century. While I have erred in my previous dating of the text by attributing it to kLong-chen-pa (Davidson 1981, p. 11) and have no objection to the twelfth-century date, Karmay, though, has far more confidence than I that the single occurrence of the first person *bdag* indicates that the text should be definitely ascribed to Zhang-ston-pa (1097–1167), for such first-person identities are often hagiographically manipulated.

85. I have been able to identify eight translations on which he worked: To. 604: *Khrodhavijayakalpaguhyatantra*, working alone [see Samten 1992, p. xv]; To. 1301: Mañjuśrījñāna's *Hevajrasādhana*, working with the author; To. 1319: anon. *Kuru-*

kullesādhana, working again with Mañjuśrījñāna; To. 1922: Padmapāṇi's *Kṛṣṇayamāritantrapañjikā*, working with Parameśvara; To. 1982: *Amoghavajra's *Vajrabhairavasādhanakarmopacāra-sattvasaṁgraha*, revised translation with Mañjuśrījñāna and Phyug-mtshams dBang-phyug rgyal-po; To. 2014: *Vilāsavajra's *Yamāntakavajraprabheda-nāma-mūlamantrārtha*, with Upāyaśrīmitra; To. 4432: anon. *Tripratyayabhāṣya*, on his own; and *Vilāsavajra's *Vajramaṇḍalavidhipuṣṭi-sādhana*, which noncanonical and is found in *Rong zom chos bzang gi gsung 'bum*, vol. 1, pp. 355–67. For his hagiographical sources, see Almogi 2002.

86. Rong-lugs rdo-rje phur-pa; *Sog bzlog pa gsung 'bum*, vol. 1, pp. 145–56, treats the rong zom lugs kyi dbang lung; for the four lineages of Rong lugs sems sde, *kLong chen chos 'byung*, p. 394.

87. Rong-zom's oeuvre has been mapped out by his great-great grandson, sLobdpon Me-dpung, *Rong zom chos bzang gi gsung 'bum*, vol. 2, pp. 235–39, and it is distressing how little has been preserved; the relationship of this figure to Rong-zom is found in the hagiography, *Rong zom chos bzang gi gsung 'bum*, vol. 1, p. 30. The principal materials ascribed to Rong-zom are collected in his *Rong zom gsung thor bu*, the *rNying ma bka' ma rgyas pa* collections (esp. his *rdo rje phur pa* and *gsang snying* texts in vols. 8–9), the *Theg chen tshul 'jug*, and the *Rong zom chos bzang gi gsung 'bum*. I do not have access to the recently published Khams edition of his collected works; see also Martin 1997, p. 25, n. 6. We may note that he is ascribed a *Chos 'byung* which is missing in action; see Martin 1997, p. 25, n. 5.

88. *Chos 'byung grub mtha' chen po*, pp. 43.3–47.4; the material I have not translated (. . .) includes a discussion of Bai-ro tsa-na's banishment and Vimala's problems with other Paṇḍitas, with the result that there are no more texts in India. Compare also the partial quotation of this passage in Ratna gling pa's *Chos 'byung bstan pa'i sgron me*, pp. 72–73. Compare the Rong-zom chos-bzang quote, Rog Bande Shes rab 'od, *Chos 'byuṅ grub mtha' chen po*, pp. 115–18, on the superiorities of the rNying-ma system over the gSar-ma, discussed as well in Ratna gling-pa, pp. 136–40. Rog-ban has been given the dates 1166–1233 by the *Tshig-mdzod chen-mo*, pp. 3223 and 3228.

89. Either Rong-zom or Rog-ban is making a sarcastic pun; more than one of the gSar-ma traditions entitled their teachings the "Golden Dharma," but the text indicates that these *lo-tsā-ba* and *paṇḍitas* were really interested in the religion (*chos*) of gold (*gser*).

90. These historical works were not included in Martin 1997; Ratna gling-pa, *Chos 'byung bstan pa'i sgron me*, p. 106, cites the same sources, possibly taken from Rog-bande.

91. Eimer 1979, § 239.

92. Witzel 1994, pp. 1–21.

93. Rocher 1986, pp. 49–59.

94. *Chos 'byung bstan pa'i sgron me*, pp. 166–67.

95. For example, the *gTer 'byung chen mo gsal ba'i sgron me* of Ratna gling-pa, pp. 46.1–47.2, 52.5–54.5, takes pains to identify the category of *gsar-ma-gter*. We may

even note that the issue of *gter* per se apparently did not become an area of contention until the time of Chag-lo-tsā-ba, and his *Chag lo tsā bas mdzad pa'i sngags log sun 'byin pa*, in *sNgags log sun 'byin gyi skor*, pp. 13.2–14.2.

96. Karmay 1988, pp. 175–200, views rig-pa from a somewhat different perspective.

97. On the *Rig pa rang shar*, Tucci 1958, vol. 2, pp. 63–64, states, "This tantra preaches the doctrine of the non-existence of a path and the non-existence of cause and effect." This seriously misrepresents this scripture, as will be seen. By means of such misrepresentations, Tucci was trying to prove that the rNying-ma tantras are reformulations of Chan doctrines. Cf. van Schaik 2004.

98. For these phrases, see Broughton 1983; Gómez 1983; Ueyama 1983; and Meinert 2002, 2003, and forthcoming. My own reading of such documents as Pelliot Tibetan 116, 823; Stein Tibetan 468, and others convinces me of little influence visible in the oldest strata of rDzogs chen, that of the sems sde. For example, the limited use of so so'i rang gi rig pa, found in Pelliot Tibetan 116, indicates the translation of pratyātmavedanīya (individually perceived) or some similar Sanskrit word through the Chinese and does not render the gnoseological force of rig-pa; see Mala and Kimura 1988, p. 90 (f. 157, lines 3–4); see a similar use fols. 111.4–12.1, 237.5. The only use I have noted in Pelliot Tibetan 116, similar to the rNying-ma sense is fol. 194.4, followed immediately by a lengthy discussion of myed pa'i sems and myed pa'i gnas, which have no connection to rNying-ma use. Stein Tibetan 468, fol. 1b1, uses rig-pa as a term of beginning understanding, equivalent to shes-pa, and I could not find rig-pa in Pelliot Tibetan 823 at all.

99. In particular, I would like to acknowledge that the contents of some sNying-tig tantras, like the *sGra thal 'gyur chen po'i rgyud* (Kaneko 1982, n. 155) *rNying ma rgyud 'bum*, gTing-skyes manuscript, vol. 10, pp. 386–530, do not consider rig-pa in the definitive sense of the *Rig pa rang shar*. But many others do, and it remains the main gnoseological term for the rNying-ma tradition.

100. For a review of the Yogācāra documents, see Davidson 1985.

101. Tucci 1930b, p. 51; Hattori 1968, pp. 28–31, 101–6; Bandyopadhyay 1979.

102. *Pramāṇavārttika*, pp. 190–210, 223–45.

103. Davidson 1981, p. 8 n. 21; Davidson 1999; Sthiramati uses the word in his *Madhyāntavibhāga-ṭīkā*, pp. 79.12, 122.16. The first of these two references is the more important as it occurs in a quotation of an unnamed sūtra. The sūtra identifies *svasaṁvedyạ* as the description of nonconceptual gnosis (*nirvikalpajñāna*) through which one enters the *dharmadhātu*.

104. It is not generally noted that this work is featured in the two later recensions of the *Testament of the Ba-clan* and played an important in the early renaissance rNying-ma self representation; *sBa bzhed*, p. 32.5–7; *sBa bzhed zhabs btags ma*, pp. 25.16–26.1.

105. My translation; compare Karmay 1988, pp. 159, 167; this passage in a slightly different form is quoted in *bSam gtan mig sgron*, p. 192.4–5. For a discussion of this passage and the antiquity of the *Man ngag lta phreng*, see Karmay 1988, pp. 140–44.

106. Tohoku 2591; Mañjuśrīmitra's text is edited and translated in Norbu and Lipman 1986.

107. Rong-zom Chos kyi bzang-po, *Theg chen tshul 'jug*, pp. 319.4, 333.2–6; we note the sparse discussion of rig-pa in his *Man ngag lta ba'i phreng ba zhes bya ba'i 'grel pa*, p. 104.2. At one place in his commentary to the *Guhyagarbha-tantra*, the *rGyud rgyal gsang ba snying po'i 'grel pa rong zom chos bzang gis mdzad pa*, p. 207.1–2, the tantra quotation seems to cry for an explanation of rig-pa, but he interprets it as a perception of ye-shes. Again, in the same commentary, he emphasizes the perceptual interpretation of rig-pa; for example, pp. 148.5, 151.5.

108. Karmay 1988, pp. 99–103, discusses the problem of gNubs-chen's dates and proposes a tenth-century date; Vitali 1996, pp. 546–47, arrives at the same date based on other sources.

109. gNubs-chen, *bSam gtan mig sgron*, p. 196.1.

110. *bSam gtan mig sgron*, p. 290.6.

111. *Rig pa rang shar*, gTing-skyes, p. 106.7; A-'dzom, p. 539.5.

112. *Rig pa rang shar*, gTing-skyes, p. 62.4–6; A-'dzom, pp. 473.6–74.2.; almost identical language elsewhere, for example, gTing-skyes, p. 42.1–5; A-'dzom, p. 446.1–4.

113. *Rig pa rang shar*, gTing-skyes, pp. 205.5–206.2; A-'dzom ed., p. 683.2–6.

114. *Rig pa rang shar*, gTing-skyes, p. 134.4; A-'dzom ed., p. 583.6; compare gTing-skyes, pp. 99.7–100.6.

115. *Rig pa rang shar*, gTing-skyes, p. 57.2–5; A-'dzom ed., p. 465.6–66.3.

116. See *Nye brgyud gcod kyi khrid yig gsal bar bkod pa legs bshad bdud rtsi'i rol mtsho*, p. 26; Karmay 1988, p. 185, considers some of the early materials; *Ratnagotra-vibhāga* I.42–44; Takasaki 1966, pp. 225–29; Ruegg 1971, p. 464, n. 73; 1973, p. 79, n.3.

117. *mKhas pa'i dga' ston*, vol. 1, pp. 190–91; this list was reviewed by Tucci 1956a, pp. 88–89; compare Chang 1959–60, pp. 133, 153, n. 21. The texts are found in *sNying thig ya bzhi*, vols. 8–9. The term *phra khrid* may be understood in light of the Old Tibetan *phra-men*, which was argued by Tucci 1950, p. 79, n. 45, to correspond to silver-gilt, as is understood by Dunhuang Chinese equivalents. Compare Richardson 1985, p. 105, n. 1, where lapis lazuli may be this item, although he is uncertain; see Stein 1986, p. 193. On these appointments, see Stein 1984; Demiéville 1952, pp. 284–86.

118. Haarh 1969, pp. 380–91.

119. Richardson 1998, pp. 219–33; Tucci 1950, *passim*; compare with the spirit roads illustrated and discussed in Paludan 1991.

NOTES TO CHAPTER 7

1. *gDung rabs chen mo*, pp. 24.22–25.2. For the location of the 'Khon sku 'bum, where the remains of 'Khon dKon-mchog rgyal-po are said to be housed, see Schoening 1990, pp. 14 and 24 (#11 on map 4).

2. *Blue Annals*, vol. 2, p. 868; compare the nineteenth-century hagiography of Khams-smyon Dharma seng-ge, *Pha dam pa'i rnam thar*, p. 12.

3. There are many short works of the *zhu len* and *tshogs chos* format that appear

to be his direct expressions; see *Dam chos snying po zhi byed las rgyud kyi snyan rgyud zab ched ma*, vol. 2, pp. 165–358, vol. 3, pp. 1–83; the works in the earlier sections appear more heavily edited; on the end of the Dharma, especially interesting is the *zhu len* in *gDams ngag mdzod*, vol. 9, pp. 435–40.

4. *sNgags log sun 'byin gyi skor*, p. 14.2–4; reading rgya gar ba for rgya gar na at the beginning.

5. *Dam chos snying po zhi byed las rgyud kyi snyan rgyud zab ched ma*, vol. 1, pp. 411–16; this is identified in *sNgags log sun 'byin gyi skor*, p. 16.2–3, by the goddess Seng-ge gdong ma who is the interlocutor in the work.

6. *Ā li kā li gsang ba bsam gyis myi khyab pa chu klung chen po'i rgyud*, found in *Dam chos snying po zhi byed las rgyud kyi snyan rgyud zab ched ma*, vol. 1, pp. 6–114. Three selected chapters with annotations were published in *gDams ngag mdzod*, vol. 9, pp. 2–16. This work is identified as *Zhi byed chu klung gi rgyud* in Rat-na gling-pa's *gTer 'byung chen mo gsal ba'i sgron me*, p. 47.1.

7. *Dam chos snying po zhi byed las rgyud kyi snyan rgyud zab ched ma*, vol. 1, pp. 413.7–14.1; ding ri is repeated on p. 414.7. I also take the mention of two languages and zangs kyi ri, p. 413.5, as indicative of the translation art and the residence of Ma-gcig lab-sgron later in her life.

8. The only reasonable record of the Zhi byed lo rgyus known to me is the *Deb ther sngon po*, vol. 2, pp. 1015–1135; *Blue Annals*, vol. 2, pp. 867–979. This is either the basis for the Zhi-byed section of the *Zhi byed dang gcog yul gyi chos 'byung rin po che'i phreng ba*, pp. 573–96, or they have a common source. I would not have been able to understand much of the following discussion without the valuable summary of Lo-chen Dharma-Shrī, *Zhi byed snga phyi bar gsum gyi khrid yig rnams phyogs gcig tu bsdebs pa bdud rtsi'i nying khu*, *gDams ngag mdzod*, vol. 9, pp. 308–404.

9. *Deb ther sngon po*, vol. 2, p. 1019.20; *Blue Annals*, vol. 2, p. 871.

10. *Deb ther sngon po*, vol. 1, p. 322; *Blue Annals*, vol. 1, p. 264; compare *bKa' gdams rin po che'i chos 'byung*, p. 304; *bKa' gdams chos 'byung*, p. 102.

11. *bKa' gdams rin po che'i chos 'byung*, p. 301; *bKa' gdams chos 'byung*, p. 99; *Zhu lan nor bu'i phreng ba*, pp. 316, 318.

12. *bKa' gdams rin po che'i chos 'byung*, pp. 310–12; *bKa' gdams chos 'byung*, pp. 109–11; *Zhu lan nor bu'i phreng ba*, pp. 352–96. This latter source is highly hagiographical; see Ehrhard 2002.

13. Ehrhard 2002 discusses this process.

14. Hagiographical material on Po-to-ba is found in *bKa' gdams rin po che'i chos 'byung*, pp. 312–15; *bKa' gdams chos 'byung*, pp. 111–14; Po-to-ba and sPyan-snga appear as characters in *Zhu lan nor bu'i phreng ba*, pp. 368–86. *Blue Annals*, vol. 1, p. 269, *Deb ther sngon po*, vol. 1, p. 329, gives Po-to-ba the birthdate of 1031; this should be questioned in the face of its other unreliable eleventh-century dates and the bKa'-gdam-pa opinion for 1027 as his birthdate.

15. Hagiographical material on sPyan-snga is found in *bKa' gdams rin po che'i chos 'byung*, pp. 315–19; *bKa' gdams chos 'byung*, pp. 114–18; compare *Zhu lan nor bu'i phreng ba*, pp. 368–86.

16. *dPe chos rin chen spungs pa*, p. 364.

17. sPyan-snga's images are mentioned in *bKa' gdams rin po che'i chos 'byung*, p. 318; *bKa' gdams chos 'byung*, p. 117.

18. *dPe chos rin chen spungs pa*, p. 5.

19. These examples are found in *dPe chos rin chen spungs pa*, pp. 25, 167.

20. The twenty-five topics are itemized in *dPe chos rin chen spungs pa*, pp. 18–21.

21. *bKa' gdams rin po che'i chos 'byung*, pp. 314.2, 319.2 (300 monks for sPyan-snga); *bKa' gdams chos 'byung*, pp. 112.21, 118.5 (700 monks for sPyan-snga); *Yar lung jo bo'i chos 'byung*, p. 98; *Deb ther dmar po*, pp. 61–62.

22. On this mythology, see Beyer 1973, pp. 229–36; Willson 1986, pp. 169–206; Lienhard 1993. On the importance attached to Atiśa's translation of Avalokiteśvara practices, see the relatively extensive colophons translated in Chattopadhyaya 1967, pp. 477, 485.

23. *Blue Annals*, pp. 1008; the 'Phags-pa Wa-ti temple and its images are associated with the sku mched gsum in the documents studied in Ehrhard 2002. This temple is also noted in *Sras don ma*, p. 36.6. Atiśa and Rin-chen bzang-po translated dGe-slong-ma dPal-mo's classic text (To. 2737); see Chattopadhyaya 1967, pp. 485–86; Vitali forthcoming.

24. *Bu ston chos 'byung*, Szerb 1990, p. 62.15: chad pas gcod pa'i sa yin pas | 'gro ma nus par. This phrase usually means that there were limbs and heads left over from punishment decrees, but why would the entire city be so described?

25. *rNam thar yong grags*, pp. 176–77.

26. The texts translated are the *Madhyamaka-upadeśa* (To. 3929 and 4468), the *Nikāyabhedavibhaṅga-vyākhyāna* (To. 4139), the *Bhikṣu-varṣāgrapṛcchā* (To. 4133), and the *Tarkajvālā* (To. 3856). These are presented in Chattopadhyaya 1967, pp. 455, 483, 486–87. The *rNam thar yong grags*, p. 177, indicates that the dga' ba 'od 'phro was a separate "island," gling cig, which would usually be the description of a separate establishment different from the 'Phrul snang gtsug glag khang. The same source indicates that it was destroyed during the troubles of the twelfth century and now was called the dkar chung gi skya khang chung chung, which I have not been able to locate.

27. *mKhas pa'i dga' ston*, vol. 1, p. 447.10–12.

28. For this process and the argument that Zangs-dkar lo-tsā-ba did this after the chos skor of 1076, see Vitali 1990, pp. 69–88.

29. *bKa' 'chems ka khol ma*, pp. 286–89.

30. For example, *bKa' 'chems ka khol ma*, p. 104.7–8. These are identified as painting no. 1 in Vitali 1990, p. 76.

31. Catalog no. 3, pp. 54–59, in Kossak and Singer 1998. The inscription on the back of the painting reads: bya rtson 'grus 'od kyi thugs dam | se' spyil phu ba'i rab gnas gzhugs | mchad kha ba'i | spyil phu ba'i chos skyong la gtad do |. While the inscription is a bit enigmatic, it appears to have been misinterpreted by Kossak and Singer. I understand the inscription to indicate that the form of Tārā was used and taught by Bya rTson-'grus-'od (d. 1175), and his disciple Se sPyil-phu-ba (d. 1189)

performed the consecration of this particular painting. The painting was thus probably completed around 1175, not a century earlier, as the authors argue.

32. *Rwa sgreng dgon pa'i dkar chag*, pp. 103–4; the same image was mentioned by Si-tu Chos-kyi rgya-mtsho, *Kaḥ thog si tu'i dbus gtsang gnas yig*, p. 53.

33. The standard dates generally repeated for Mid-la ras-pa are 1040–1123, but as with most eleventh-century dates, these are by no means certain; *dKar brgyud gser 'phreng*, p. 198.7, has him born in a sheep (lug) year rather than the lcags pho 'brug of later texts like the *Lho rong chos 'byung*, p. 72.18. The following discussion is predominantly drawn from *dKar brgyud gser 'phreng*, pp. 189–265, except as noted. For a useful discussion of the principal sources, see Tiso 1997. See Ramble 1997, pp. 492–95 for the Khyung clan.

34. An excellent discussion of these figures is found in Martin 1982.

35. For example, *sTag lung chos 'byung*, pp. 132–137.

36. On the folk song genre, see Roger Jackson 1996.

37. *mDzod nag ma*, vol. 1, p. 117.2–5; I have read dgro as dgra bo, which does not follow the meter, but neither does rnor = rnal 'byor of the next line.

38. *Deb ther sngon po*, vol. 1, p. 123; *The Blue Annals*, vol. 1, p. 93; on Khyung-po Grags-se, see Vitali 1990, pp. 97–98.

39. For a discussion of the sources of and participants at this gathering, see Shastri 1997.

40. On rNgog's life and studies, see van der Kuijp 1983, pp. 29–48; Kramer 1997.

41. It is well known that Bu-ston's list of rNgog bLo-ldan shes-rab's works is the standard list; *Bu ston chos 'byung*, rDo-rje rgyal-po 1988, p. 313. On the works of rNgog in general, see Jackson 1985, 1993a, 1993b, 1994a; Kramer 1997.

42. These texts are, respectively, the *Theg chen rgyud bla'i don bsdus pa* and the *Lo tsā ba chen po'i bsdus don*. The former text, although it represents the type of commentary known in India as a *piṇḍārtha* (as pointed out by the introduction of Jackson 1993b, p. 5), the actual name *don bsdus pa* was evidently in imitation of the *arthasaṁgraha* commentary (*don bsdus pa*) attributed to Asaṅga (To. 4025; the accurate title is contained in the colophon, fol. 129a), which rNgog himself translated. Both texts comment on verses from all five chapters, with the most effort expended on the first and, by far, the longest chapter. I have not located quotations from other texts in the rNgog-lo commentary. Conversely, rNgog's influences in the *Abhisamayālaṁkāra* commentary are revealed by his references to Haribhadra, fols. 13a3, 30b4, 31a3, 44b6, 51b4, 54b6, 61b5, 77a2, 83a6, 85b1, 86b1, 92a2, 92b1, and 98a3; to Ārya Vimuktisena, fols. 20a2, 27b1–4, 31a4, 33a6, 37a1, 51b4, 62a2, 75a3, 84a1, 92a2–5; to the *Ratnagotravibhāga*, fol. 54a1; and to the *Mahāyānasūtrālaṁkāra*, fols. 53b3, 95b3. Interestingly, in many controversies, he sides with Vimuktisena against Haribhadra. The *Lo tsā ba chen po'i bsdus don* is also put into *Abhisamayālaṁkāra* exegetical context by the attached learned discussion by bLo-bzang mkyen-rab rgya-mtsho, pp. 1–252.

43. The works are curiously prescient of the method used in the texts of the rDzong-gsar yig-cha of gZhan-phan chos-kyi snang-ba (1871–1927); see Smith 2001, pp. 26, 232–33, 277, n. 39, 332, n. 835.

44. *Zhu lan nor bu'i phreng ba*, p. 317; for a discussion of this term, see van der Kuijp 1983, pp. 36–42, Stearns 1999, pp. 86–105.

45. For the lam rim literature, see Levinson 1996; for the bstan rim literature, see David Jackson 1996.

46. *rNam thar yong grags*, p. 199.1–4.

47. *Lho rong chos 'byung*, p. 50, lists works by Mar-pa known to the author.

48. *mKhas pa'i dga' ston*, vol. 1, p. 777.10; attributed to a rNgog (probably Chos-rdor) is a *Sre 'pho'i zhal gdams* (*mKhas pa'i dga' ston*, vol. 1, p. 760.9). Otherwise, the contents of rNgog Chos-rdor's *yig cha* are listed in *Lho rong chos 'byung*, p. 52.19–53.3. His dates are from the *Lho rong chos 'byung*, pp. 50.20–52.12. The *Blue Annals*, vol. 1, p. 404, gives the dates 1036–1102. It may be noted, though, that rTa-tshag Tshe-dbang-rgyal had recourse to the *rNgog gi gdung rabs che dge yig tshang*, the rNgog clan records, while we do not; see *Lho rong chos 'byung*, p. 50.16–17.

49. *bLa ma mnga' ris pas mdzad pa'i brtag gnyis kyi tshig 'grel*, *SKB* I.13.4–65.4. Stearns 2001, p. 231, n. 112, offers the story that gSal-ba'i snying-po displeased 'Brog-mi but acknowledges that no earlier source supports this assessment. There are many problems with the annals of Cha-rgan dBang-phyug rgyal-mtshan, on which Stearns often relies.

50. *gSang 'dus stong thun*: rten gyi gang zag (pp. 5–12), sbyang gzhi rang bzhin gyi chos (pp. 12–31), sbyang ba mi mthun pa lam gyi dri ma (pp. 31–36), dmigs bya yul (pp. 36–84), nyams len thabs (pp. 84–523), mthar phyin 'bras bu (pp. 523–38).

51. A summary of the text is in Karmay 1988, pp. 125–33, but it does not consider Rong-zom's investigation of the three natures or the other interesting aspects of his Mahāyānist philosophical architecture. Rong-zom's oeuvre is mapped out by his great-great grandson, sLob-dpon Me-dpung, *Rong zom chos bzang gi gsung 'bum*, vol. 2, pp. 235–39. For biographical references, see Almogi 2002. The only date I have found for him is his being "discovered" as a young scholar by the Yum-brtan scion Pha-ba on or after a 'brug year; *Rong zom chos bzang gi gsung 'bum*, vol. 2, p. 393.1; this is probably either 1040 or 1052.

52. David Jackson's description of Rong-zom as having "stressed the need for faith over reasoning" (Jackson 1994b, p. 29) is not compelling. *Theg chen tshul 'jug*, p. 410.1, makes a place for faith, but it is posed as the technique for those who cannot otherwise enter the rdzogs chen method. The reasoning is explicitly and implicitly affirmed throughout (especially in chaps. 2 and 3, dedicated to objections and analysis), although, as with most Mahāyānists, Rong-zom presents absolute truth as beyond predication. Jackson's predilection for epistemological authors perhaps is behind his focus on this narrow variety of analysis as "reasoning," whereas historically many kinds of reasoning have been used in Buddhism, and the word cannot legitimately be restricted to late Buddhist dialectical or syllogistic forms. The reification of authors' positions into a dialectic of faith versus reason is surely inadequate to do justice to esoteric Buddhist complexity.

53. *rDo rje phur pa'i chos 'byung ngor mtshar rgya mtsho'i rba rlabs*, pp. 145–56; compare the brief descriptions of the nine vehicles in *Theg chen tshul 'jug*, pp.

349–53, and his ritual statements in his *Man ngag lta ba'i phreng ba zhes bya ba'i 'grel pa*, pp. 75–93, and especially his ambivalence, pp. 105–121. For Rong-zom's translations, see chap. 6, n. 85.

54. Stearns 2001, pp. 102–23, reviews this material in depth. See also *bLa ma brgyud pa'i rnam par thar pa ngo mtshar snang ba*, pp. 24–41; *gDams ngag byung tshul gyi zin bris gsang chen bstan pa rgyas byed*, pp. 77–99. 'Brom De-pa ston-chung is depicted by mKhyen-brtse, p. 78, as a gTer ston during his stay at bSam-yas, although the 'Brom lugs documents do not maintain this relationship.

55. *Zhib mo rdo rje*, Stearns 2001, pp. 111–13; *bLa ma brgyud pa'i rnam par thar pa ngo mtshar snang ba*, pp. 28–29; *gDams ngag byung tshul gyi zin bris gsang chen bstan pa rgyas byed*, pp. 75–77.

56. *bLa ma mnga' ris pas mdzad pa'i brtag gnyis kyi tshig 'grel*, *SKB* I.13.4–65.4. The editor, Ngor-thar-rtse mkhan-po, clearly believed that the following work, *dPal Kye rdo rje'i rtsa ba'i rgyud brtag pa gnyis pa'i dka' 'grel man ngag don gsal*, *SKB* I.66.1–78.3, was also an eleventh-century work, by sGyi-chu-ba, but this was the result of his inferring it from various "teachings received" texts, rather than its being clear in the text itself; see his note in the contents, *SKB* I.xvii. Compare Ngor-chen's *Kye rdo rje'i 'grel ba'i dkar chag*, p. 284.4.4, where the "seven superior texts" are listed.

57. *gDams ngag byung tshul gyi zin bris gsang chen bstan pa rgyas byed*, p. 75.

58. For the nature of these texts, see Jackson 1985, p. 21.

59. Stearns 2001, pp. 113–17, 232–35, provides much detail on the 'Brom hagiographies.

60. Nyang-ral's *Chos 'byung me tog snying po sbrang rtsi'i bcud*, mentions a 'Brom-ston rDo-rje rin-chen living in the mid-eleventh century, p. 470.10.

61. *Zhib mo rdo rje*, Stearns 2001, pp. 112–13, and *bLa ma brgyud pa'i rnam par thar pa ngo mtshar snang ba*, p. 30, make 'Brom De-pa ston-chung a native of dbUs, in the area of 'Phan-yul, but this affirmation is not accepted by Ngor-chen in his *Lam 'bras byung tshul*, p. 114.1.6–2.1. Much of this latter text is drawn from a document quite similar to the 'Brom record included in the *Bhir ba pa'i lo rgyus*, p. 399: 'brom de mdo' smad kyi 'khams pa mi chen phyug po byin brlabs shin tu che ba |. Compare *gDams ngag byung tshul gyi zin bris gsang chen bstan pa rgyas byed*, pp. 77–82, which demonstrates mKhyen-brtse's proclivity toward the storyteller's art. The following discussion is drawn from these sources.

62. *gDams ngag byung tshul gyi zin bris gsang chen bstan pa rgyas byed*, p. 78.

63. This is the best interpretation I can provide for a sentence differently explained in all our sources about a silk garment being offered (dar sham) either to 'Brog-mi or to his wife.

64. *Lam 'bras byung tshul*, p. 114.4.4.

65. The best source for Se-ston-pa is the *Zhib mo rdo rje*, Stearns 2001, pp. 116–17, followed by *bLa ma brgyud pa'i rnam par thar pa ngo mtshar snang ba*, pp. 32–36, and *gDams ngag byung tshul gyi zin bris gsang chen bstan pa rgyas byed*, pp. 82–90, although the later texts emphasize hagiographic issues.

66. Stein 1961, pp. 4–19, 24–25. Cf. Ramble 1997.

67. *Deb ther sngon po*, p. 267.7–8; *Blue Annals*, vol. 1, p. 215, seems to have a block print that says twenty-five (i.e., Western twenty-four) and died the next year, but our text is much more qualified.

68. Mang-thos klu-sgrub rgya-mtsho listed 1025 as his birthdate and says that he lived for ninety-seven years, but this is questionable; *bsTan rtsis gsal ba'i nyin byed*, p. 89; many of the dates in this text appear erroneous or without verification.

69. *Zhib mo rdo rje*, Stearns 2001, pp. 120–21; compare *bLa ma brgyud pa'i rnam par thar pa ngo mtshar snang ba*, p. 35.3.

70. The normative placement is found in the guidebook of mKhyen-brtse'i dbang-po, Ferrari 1958, pp. 24, 65. A mKhar-chung in eastern Ding-ri is mentioned by Ngor-chen, *Lam 'bras byung tshul*, p. 115.3.1, and a lDog-mkhar-chung founded in 1064 in the table of years (re'u mig) in the *Chos 'byung dpag bsam ljon bzang*, p. 833. The old Tibetan term phro brang, later meaning palace, early indicated the residence of the king, wherever that was, and mKhar-chung may have been so understood as well.

71. The myth is unknown in early documents, like *Chos la 'jug pa'i sgo*, pp. 343.1.2–344.2.6, *Ga ring rgyal po la rtsis bsdur du btang ba'i gsung yig*, p. 104.2.1; *bLa ma sa skya pa chen po'i rnam thar*, p. 84.1.4, and the 1352 *Sa skya'i gdung rabs*, p. 310, by sGra-tshad-pa Rin-chen rnam-rgyal. Fourteenth-century versions are in the *Deb ther dmar po*, p. 46; *Yar lung jo bo'i chos 'byung*, pp. 136–44, with fully formed versions in the *rGya bod yig tshang chen mo*, pp. 305–20, and the *gDung rabs chen mo*, pp. 6–13. The *rGya bod yig tshang chen mo* material was translated in Smith 2001, pp. 99–109, and summarized from the fifth Dalai Lama's Chronicles, Tucci 1949, vol. 2, p. 625.

72. For the Indian sources and first Tibetan assimilation of this myth, see Davidson 2003.

73. See Stein 1961, pp. 18–70, for the identity of these tribes; the lDong are found on pp. 31–41.

74. See Stein 1961, pp. 50–66, for the dMu.

75. *Deb ther dmar po*, p. 46, refers to g.Ya'-spang-skyes as from the eastern section of Yar-lungs.

76. An alternative place in mNga'-ris, at mThos-zhing-sa, is cited in *gDung rabs chen mo*, p. 10.

77. Please note the difference between the *Yar lung jo bo'i chos 'byung*, p. 137, and *gDung rabs chen mo*, p. 11, on the precise nature of these eight (A-mes-zhabs allows for another two as well) qualities.

78. His position is indicated in different ways in each of our sources; *bLa ma brgyud pa'i rnam par thar pa ngo mtshar snang ba*, p. 25, nang mi (la gtogs pa); *Yar lung jo bo'i chos 'byung*, p. 138, nang rje kha; *rGya bod yig tshang chen mo*, p. 308, nang che ba; and *gDung rabs chen mo*, p. 11, nang blon.

79. On marriage to the rMu divinities, see Stein 1985, p. 107; on the ma-sangs, see *mKhas pa'i dga' ston*, vol. 1, p. 152, and note that gNya' g.Ya'-spang skye is one of them; this list is discussed in Haarh 1969, p. 293.

80. *bLa ma sa skya pa chen po'i rnam thar*, p. 84.1.3: dge ba'i bshes gnyen brgyud pa'i rigs su gyur pa; compare Grags-pa rgyal-mtshan's letter to Ga-ring rgyal-po,

Ga ring rgyal po la rtsis bsdur du btang ba'i gsung yig, p. 104.2.2, which simply begins the lineage rather than characterizing it.

81. *bLa ma sa skya pa chen po'i rnam thar*, p. 84.3–4; compare *gDung rabs chen mo*, p. 7.

82. *mKhas pa'i dga' ston*, vol. 1, pp. 411–13, provides a list of ministers, none of which is a 'Khon. Compare *sBa bzhed*, pp. 58–59; *sBa bzhed zhabs rtags ma*, p. 51, where the young men number six and do not include kLu'i dbang-po.

83. Bacot and Toussaint 1940–46, index; *Tun hong nas thon pa'i bod kyi lo rgyus yig cha*, pp. 202–7; Thomas 1935–55, vol. 3, p. 117–19; compare Chang 1959–60, pp. 171–73; *sBa bzhed zhabs rtags ma*, pp. 95–96.

84. *Chos 'byung me tog snying po sbrang rtsi'i bcud*, pp. 310; legends of their individual troubles in their study in India are related on pp. 310–12. *gDung rabs chen mo*, p. 13, acknowledges the difficulties.

85. *mKhas pa'i dga' ston*, vol. 1, pp. 186–87.

86. Nyang ral mentions this as his title; *Chos 'byung me tog snying po sbrang rtsi'i bcud*, p. 393.4.

87. Emphasized in *rGya bod yig tshang chen mo*, p. 309.

88. Grags-pa rgyal-mtshan's *Phyag rgya chen po gces pa btus pa'i man ngag*, pp. 305.1.6–3.4, includes a transmission purportedly from the royal dynastic period, the "gNubs nam mkha'i snying po'i nag po 'bru bdun."

89. *bLa ma sa skya pa chen po'i rnam thar*, p. 84.1.4–5, indicates that kLu'i dbang-po's younger brother is one Phal-pa, and rDo-rje rin-po-che was his son; compare *rGya bod yig tshang chen mo*, p. 309; *gDung rabs chen mo*, p. 14.6.

90. *mKhas pa'i dga' ston*, vol. 1, pp. 187. 4, 188.15.

91. *rGya bod yig tshang chen mo*, p. 310. The other sources do not make as specific a claim.

92. *Rwa lo tsā ba'i rnam thar*, p. 50.

93. The *Yar lung jo bo'i chos 'byung*, p. 139, does not have them return to g.Ya'-lung.

94. *Rwa lo tsā ba'i rnam thar*, p. 50.

95. The earliest surviving example of a hagiography for 'Khon dKon-mchog rgyal-po is in Grags-pa rgyal-mtshan's *bLa ma sa skya pa chen po'i rnam thar*, p. 84.2.2–6. This is a hagiography of Sa-chen but includes a short one of his father as well. Other sources include *Yar lung jo bo'i chos 'byung*, pp. 140–42; *bLa ma brgyud pa'i rnam par thar pa ngo mtshar snang ba*, pp. 25–30; *gDung rabs chen mo*, pp. 18–22 (again the first part of Sa-chen's section is again his father's hagiography); *rGya bod yig tshang chen mo*, pp. 312–16; *rJe btsun sa skya pa gong ma gsum gyi rnam par thar pa dpag bsam ljon pa*, pp. 67–70; and *gDams ngag byung tshul gyi zin bris gsang chen bstan pa rgyas byed*, pp. 71–77.

96. *gDung rabs chen mo*, p. 18; *Yar lung jo bo'i chos 'byung*, p. 140; this episode is curiously lacking in *bLa ma brgyud pa'i rnam par thar pa ngo mtshar snang ba*, p. 26, where his study with 'Brog-mi is precipitated by his brother's death instead.

97. The *Yar lung jo bo'i chos 'byung*, p. 140, reads de lta bu'i bla ma de la 'bro'i gson gshin byed ba'i gdan 'dren byung bas byon |. I have not located a satisfactory

reference to gson gshin as a ritual. Thomas 1935–55, vol. 2, pp. 412–13, seems inapplicable. *rGya bod yig tshang chen mo*, p. 309.12, also is questionable, but the *rGya bod yig tshang chen mo*, p. 312, designates it a 'Bro'i lung ston chen po gcig byung ba'i tshe, "when there was a great prophetic gathering on behalf of the 'Bro." Compare Tucci 1980, p. 228; Snellgrove 1967, p. 118.8.

98. Previously (Davidson 1991, p. 218) I typified the Sa-skya as "pugnaciously secretive," which caused Stearns 2001, p. 174, n. 36, to say that I seemed "offended" by the tradition, an unfortunate misperception on his part. The Sa-skya used its emphasis on secrecy as a basis for its claim of superiority over other traditions, to the point that some Sa-skya-pa claimed that the rNying-ma meditators would no longer be able to obtain any accomplishment because of their lack of secrecy (e.g., *Ngor chos 'byung*, p. 301.6). This use is certainly pugnacious.

99. Snellgrove 1987, vol. 2, p. 510, highlights the change to large gatherings in the Tibetan context.

100. *Rwa lo tsā ba'i rnam thar*, pp. 53–4, 119–120, etc. There may be a question about whether the term *khrom* refers to a simple gathering anywhere or a market gathering, as I have elected to interpret it.

101. *gDung rabs chen mo*, p. 18; *Yar lung jo bo'i chos 'byung*, p. 140; *rGya bod yig tshang chen mo*, p. 312.

102. *gDung rabs chen mo*, p. 18; *rGya bod yig tshang chen mo*, p. 313; *Yar lung jo bo'i chos 'byung*, p. 140; these figures are briefly discussed in Nebesky-Wajkowitz 1956, pp. 87, 259, 275.

103. *bLa ma brgyud pa'i rnam par thar pa ngo mtshar snang ba*, p. 26, also has dKon-mchog rgyal-po study with another of 'Brog-mi's disciples, dbRad dKon-mchog rgyal-po; *gDams ngag byung tshul gyi zin bris gsang chen bstan pa rgyas byed*, p. 72, identifies 'Khyin lo-tsā-ba with that association, as well as specifying another name, sBal-ti lo-tsā-ba, which would indicate his affiliation with the far western mNga'-ris area or with the actual location of Baltistan, southeast of Gilgit. However, we must use mKhyen-brtse judiciously, for he frequently presents material that is provided in no earlier source.

104. Jo-mo nor phreng-ba; *bLa ma brgyud pa'i rnam par thar pa ngo mtshar snang ba*, p. 26; *rGya bod yig tshang chen mo*, p. 313.

105. We note, for example, that Ngor-chen wrote two different "origin" texts, one for each side of the system: his incomplete *Lam 'bras byung tshul*, and his *Kye rdo rje'i byung tshul*.

106. *bLa ma sa skya pa chen po'i rnam thar*, p. 84.2.2–6.

107. *bLa ma brgyud pa'i rnam par thar pa ngo mtshar snang ba*, p. 26, correctly identifies Prajñāgupta as Ācārya dMar-po, as we saw in the previous chapter. The five *tilaka tantras* would probably be the *Sampuṭa-tilaka* (To.382), the *Mahāmudrā-tilaka* (To. 420), the *Jñānatilaka* (To. 422), the *Candraguhya-tilaka* (To. 477), *and the Guhyamaṇi-tilaka* (To. 493), although I have no confirmation of this list. Both the *Mahāmudrā-tilaka* and the *Jñānatilaka*, however, were translated by Prajñāgupta, and the proclamation of Pho-brang Zhi-ba-'od condemns them as compositions

of this Uḍḍiyāna Paṇḍita; see Karmay 1998, p. 35. gZhon-nu-dpal, *Deb ther sngon po*, vol. 2, p. 1221 (*Blue Annals*, vol. 2, p. 1049; followed by Karmay 1998, p. 30), has made the error of identifying Sa-chen Kun-dga' snying-po as the student of Prajñāgupta, probably because dKon-mchog rgyal-po's hagiography is included in the same document as his son's; *bLa ma sa skya pa chen po'i rnam thar*, p. 84.2.5–6. Apparently this was the cause for gZhon-nu-dpal postulating two trips by Prajñāgupta to Tibet, for there seems to be no other source for this story. *gDung rabs chen mo*, p. 18.8–9, has dKon-mchog rgyal-po study the *Cakrasaṁvara* with rMa-lo, but I have followed Grags-pa rgyal-mtshan's *bLa ma sa skya pa chen po'i rnam thar*. Martin 1996a, p. 36, n. 35, shows that some Tibetan sources confuse Ācārya dMar-po with a Tibetan figure, La-stod dMar-po.

NOTES TO CHAPTER 8

1. *sGam po pa gsung 'bum*, vol. 1, p. 452.3–4; the exact sense of rang gis khyab 'brel is obscure.

2. The Shangs-pa bka'-brgyud-pa are discussed in Snellgrove 1987, vol. 2, pp. 499–504, and in Kapstein 1980, 1992.

3. *bKa' gdams rin po che'i chos 'byung*, pp. 307–9; *bKa' gdams chos 'byung*, pp. 106–8.

4. The following material on sPa-tshab is taken almost exclusively from Lang 1990, and the reader should see her fuller treatment for further details; see also Ruegg 2000, pp. 27–55.

5. The first of these has been translated in Eckel 1987.

6. *rNam thar yong grags*, p. 190.2–4.

7. For an assessment of the consequences of this position in India, see Davidson 2002c, pp. 99–102.

8. The sources disagree on this issue; the *mKhas pa'i dga' ston*, vol. 2, p. 860.10, indicates that Dus-gsum mkhyen-pa learned these at gSang-phu, where he was one of the "three khams-pa," but the first Karma-pa's hagiography places this at 'Phan-yul, which is more likely; see *rJe dus gsum mkhyen pa'i rnam thar* by rGwa-lo rNam-rgyal rdo-rje (1203–82), *Dus gsum mkhyen pa'i bka' 'bum*, vol. 1, p. 59.3.

9. For Phya-pa, see van der Kuijp 1978 and 1983, pp. 59–70.

10. According to gZhon-nu-dpal, rGya-dmar-pa had also been the student of Zha-ma lo-tsā-ba's son, Lha-rje Zla-ba'i 'od-zer; *Deb ther sngon po*, vol. 1, p. 283; *Blue Annals*, vol. 1, p. 231–32. However, since Lha-rje Zla-ba'i 'od-zer was reputed to have been born in 1123, or fourteen years after the birth of Phya-pa, it is unclear how Phya-pa's teacher would be the disciple of a man so junior to himself.

11. van der Kuijp 1983, p. 60.

12. *Phag mo gru pa'i rnam thar rin po che'i phreng ba*, p. 11.1.

13. Jackson 1987, vol. 1, pp. 129–31, 169–77.

14. van der Kuijp 1983, p. 69.

15. For an overview of the history of this system, see Newman 1985, 1998; Orofino 1997.

16. *Kha rag gnyos kyi rgyud pa byon tshul mdor bsdus*, p. 14.

17. *Kālacakra-tantra* 1.150; on this point, see Davidson 2002a.

18. The following sources have been used for his biography: autobiographical accounts are in the *sGam po pa gsung 'bum*, vol. 1, pp. 401–2; *mNyam med sgam po pa'i rnam thar*, *dKar brgyud gser 'phreng*, pp. 267–339; *Lho rong chos 'byung*, pp. 168–77; *mKhas pa'i dga' ston*, vol. 1, pp. 789–800. We may note that there was a dispute on sGam-po-pa's dates as well; *dKar brgyud gser 'phreng*, p. 277.2, says that he was born in a bird year (1069 or 1081); a date refuted in *Lho rong chos 'byung*, p. 175, in its questionable chronology. Si-tu identifies a site said to have been sGam-po-pa's birthplace; *Kaḥ thog si tu'i dbus gtsang gnas yig*, p. 258.

19. *mKhas pa'i dga' ston*, vol. 1, p. 789.9–10, states that there were three branches of sNyi-ba: rGya-snyi, g.Yu-snyi, and Bod-snyi, this last the Tibetan branch. His source for this is unclear to me. A sNyi-ba participated in the tomb looting after the collapse of the dynasty; see *mKhas pa'i dga' ston*, vol. 1, p. 433.4–8.

20. *dKar brgyud gser 'phreng*, p. 280.2, says that he studied this and other rNying-ma works with sLob-dpon Jo-sras rGyal-mtshan grags-pa.

21. *sGam po pa gsung 'bum*, vol. 1, pp. 401–2; *mNyam med sgam po pa'i rnam thar*, pp. 55–56.

22. *sGam po pa gsung 'bum*, vol. 1, p. 402.5; *mNyam med sgam po pa'i rnam thar*, p. 98; this period of thirteen months is expanded to forty months in *dKar brgyud gser 'phreng*, p. 320.

23. *'Brug pa'i chos 'byung* p. 386.

24. *Samādhirāja-sūtra, passim*; *mNyam med sgam po pa'i rnam thar*, pp. 2–51, relates some of the myths accorded that bodhisattva through the later chapters of the work.

25. Jackson 1994b, p. 39. Jackson's analysis of sGam-po-pa is done from the position of the affirmation of Sa-paṇ's perspective and primarily through the lens of later Tibetan scholars; it does not take sufficient account of Indian literature generally and Vajrayāna literature in particular. *sGam po pa gsung 'bum*, vol. 1, pp. 173, 217–30, vol. 2, pp. 328–29, repeatedly makes the point of Saraha's importance to sGam-po-pa, and one does not need to go very far through Saraha's dohā corpus to find a castigation of scholars on a par with those identified by Jackson 1994b, pp. 39–41. Rather than sGam-po-pa's idiosyncratic personal position, it appears to be the heritage of his lineage. More to the point, I know of no normative Indian Mahāyānist that maintains that conceptualization (*vikalpa*) is appropriate to awakening; compare *Mahāyānasūtrālamkāra* 1.11–14, which discusses why it is that *vikalpa* is the only *kleśa* for the bodhisattva and therefore the Mahāyāna is not within the purview of scholasticism, echoed in sGam-po-pa's *rJe phag mo gru pa'i zhus len*, *sGam po pa gsung 'bum*, vol. 1, p. 471.7–72.1, and noted by Jackson 1994b, pp. 150–51. References like this could be multiplied at great length, but it appears that sGam-po-pa's metaphor of the dkar po chig thub builds on well-established models.

26. Jackson 1994b, pp. 14–28, does a good job of introducing this problem; Mathes forthcoming, shows that sGam-po-pa's position has roots in the writings of Advayavajra and Sajahavajra.

27. For his discussions of this material, see *sGam po pa gsung 'bum*, vol. 1, pp. 333–35, vol. 2, pp. 329–378.

28. *Abhisamayālaṁkārāloka*, p. 270.13.

29. One of the sixteen Arhats, Cūḍapanthaka, was said to have realized all the *Tripiṭaka* by contemplation; *Divyāvadāna*, p. 429.

30. *sGam po pa gsung 'bum*, vol. 1, pp. 460–62, contains some quotations, but the one text that is a curious amalgam of odd bits of textual references, with little in the way of continuity or argument, is the *bStan bcos lung gi nyi 'od*, which was missing in the older edition of the *sGam po pa gsung 'bum* but is included in the *sGam po pa gsung 'bum yid bzhin nor bu*, vol. 4, pp. 91–184.

31. *sGam po pa gsung 'bum*, vol. 1, pp. 219, 269, 304, 368; p. 303, shows himself to be familiar with the system of A-ro ye-shes byung-gnas, though it is not clear whether this is from a text or from oral exposure. On similarities between rDzogs-chen and the bKa'-gdam-pa views, see *sGam po pa gsung 'bum*, vol. 2, p. 300.5. In *sGam po pa gsung 'bum*, vol. 1, pp. 438–39, he voices frustration with rDzogs-chen claims, as noted by Jackson 1994b, p. 30, n. 71.

32. See *sGam po pa gsung 'bum*, vol. 1, *passim*, but the section discussing his most important term, sahaja, and its relationship to rig-pa, 267.5–268.6, is particularly interesting. On p. 273, sGam-po-pa even uses the term rig pa rang shar.

33. *sGam po pa gsung 'bum*. For the Rong-lugs fourfold categories, see *kLong chen chos 'byung*, p. 393.

34. *sGam po pa gsung 'bum*, vol. 1, pp. 281.2–83.5, 285.4–88.1.

35. The bibliography for this issue is now enormous; important sources include Ruegg 1989; Karmay 1988, pp. 86–106; Demiéville 1952; Broughton 1983; Gómez 1983; Ueyama 1983; and Meinert 2002, 2003, forthcoming.

36. *gSang 'dus stong thun*, p. 301.1; *rGyud kyi mngon par rtogs pa rin po che'i ljon shing*, pp. 3.1.6, 17.1.3.

37. *Caryāmelāpakapradīpa*, Skt. text, pp. 3–7; Tibetan text, pp. 158–67.

38. *Caryāmelāpakapradīpa*, p. 4, quotes *Laṅkāvatāra-sūtra*, p. 55.2–14. See also *Laṅkāvatāra-sūtra*, pp. 82, 84. Ruegg 1989, p. 120, notes the use of the *Laṅkāvatāra-sūtra* but does not refer to Āryadeva's use. This same *Laṅkāvatāra* material is quoted in Pelliot Tibetan 116, fol. 129, and Pelliot Tibetan 823, fols. 9b-10a, indicating a Chan awareness; see also Demiéville 1952, p. 18. The influence of this scripture on the Northern Chan was contested by McRae 1986, pp. 24–29.

39. *bsTan bcos lung gi nyi 'od*, pp. 173–74; this text was not accessible to Jackson 1994b, p. 24, when he voiced his consternation at sGam-po-pa's sources.

40. Compare Mayer 1997a, a review article of Jackson 1994b.

41. On the patron, see *rGya bod yig tshang chen mo*, p. 530.3.

42. *mNyam med sgam po pa'i rnam thar*, pp. 142–43.

43. This was explored by Schopen 1992, 1994a, 1994b, 1995.

44. Gyatso 1985; Edou 1996; Rossi-Filibeck 1983; Kollmar-Paulenz 1993, 1998.

45. There is some disagreement on her place and date of birth; see Gyatso 1985, p. 329, and Edou 1996, p. 111.

46. Martin 1996b also proposed this connection; I thank Bryan Cuevas for bringing the article to my attention.

47. See *sNgag log sun 'byin kyi skor*, p. 14, about Dam-pa nag-chung, an alternative name for Pha-dam-pa.

48. The following is from *Lam 'bras byung tshul*, pp. 115.1.1–16.2.4 (spelling the name Zhwa-ma), which is very close to the Zha-ma lineage work, the *Lam 'bras snyan brgyud*, pp. 440–47; *Zhib mo rdo rje*, Stearns 2001, pp. 124–31; *bLa ma brgyud pa'i rnam par thar pa ngo mtshar snang ba*, pp. 43–48; *gDams ngag byung tshul gyi zin bris gsang chen bstan pa rgyas byed*, pp. 102–8. The Zha-ma lineage text, or one of the other Lam-'bras works, is evidently the source for *Deb ther sngon po*, vol. 1, pp. 271–80; *Blue Annals*, vol. 1, pp. 218–26. This inference is especially important, since the Lam-'bras is primarily represented in the *Blue Annals* through the Zha-ma system. For a map and discussion of the current Pha-drug area, see Diemberger and Hazod 1999, p. 36.

49. *Deb ther sngon po*, vol. 1, pp. 274, 279–80, 283; *Blue Annals*, vol. 1, p. 221, 226, 229. Even though widely acknowledged, we should still note Roerich's confusion between Zha-ma ma-gcig and Ma-gcig Lab-sgron in *Blue Annals*, 1949, vol. 1, p. 225, vol. 2, p. 919. The correction was made by Gyatso 1985, pp. 328–29, n. 34, and is the subject of LoBue 1994.

50. The husband is called A-ba lha-rgyal, and the marital age is fourteen in *Deb ther sngon po*, vol. 1, p. 274; *Blue Annals*, vol. 1, p. 221.

51. For an especially colorful hagiography, see the *Pha dam pa'i rnam thar.*

52. For example, Phag-mo gru-pa studied with Zha-ma Ma-gcig; *Blue Annals*, pp. 226, 557, and *sTag-lung chos 'byung*, p. 177.

53. Compare Zha-ma Ma-gcig in Diemberger and Hazod 1999, who wrote an entire article on this fascinating woman without mentioning the Lam 'bras connection, a reflection of her later employment in Tibetan sacred geography.

54. The following sources were available to me for Sa-chen's hagiography: *bLa ma sa skya pa chen po'i rnam thar*, pp. 84.2.6–87.3.5; *Zhib mo rdo rje*, Stearns 2001, pp. 132–49; *bLa ma brgyud pa'i rnam par thar pa ngo mtshar snang ba*, pp. 48–66; *Yar lung jo bo'i chos 'byung*, pp. 142–44; *rGya bod yig tshang chen mo*, pp. 316–21; *rJe btsun sa skya pa gong ma gsum gyi rnam par thar pa dpag bsam ljon pa*, pp. 70–85; *gDams ngag byung tshul gyi zin bris gsang chen bstan pa rgyas byed*, pp. 108–28; *gDung rabs chen mo*, pp. 22–62.

55. *bLa ma sa skya pa chen po'i rnam thar*, p. 84.1.2: ru lag gtsang stod grom pa'i yul gyi stod du sku 'khrungs pa'i bla ma chen po sa skya pa zhes gnas las mtshan du grags pa.

56. *gDung rabs chen mo*, pp. 20–23.

57. I have found no confirmation of a later story that 'Khon dKon-mchog rgyal-po was first a monk and then later was asked to renounce his vows. This appears tied into a much later story of Atiśa and the Sa-skya prophecy; see Cassinelli and Ekvall 1969, p. 12.

58. We may recall the importance of the Khasarpaṇa form of Avalokiteśvara

for later esoteric Buddhism in general and the Virūpa myth in particular; see chap. 1.

59. For example, *gDams ngag byung tshul gyi zin bris gsang chen bstan pa rgyas byed*, p. 109; *gDung rabs chen mo*, pp. 23–24.

60. The name for this building as it was known to sNgags-'chang Kun-dga' rin-chen was sGo-rum gZim-spyil dkar-po; Schoening 1990, pp. 13–14. Schoening relies on the description of the building as seen during Kaḥ-thog Si-tu's 1919 visit; see *Kaḥ thog si tu'i dbus gtsang gnas yig*, pp. 315–27, esp. pp. 323–24.

61. The early sources in fact begin Sa-chen's story at this point; *bLa ma sa skya pa chen po'i rnam thar*, p. 84.2.6; *Yar lung jo bo'i chos 'byung*, p. 142; *Zhib mo rdo rje*, Stearns 2001, p. 132.

62. *bLa ma ba ri lo tsā ba rin chen grags kyi rnam thar*, fols. 5a5–5b6; the importance of this hagiography is recognized in *gDung rabs chen mo*, p. 29.11.

63. Solomon 1990 argues that its origin is in Gāndhārī.

64. Several sources, apparently beginning with the *Yar lung jo bo'i chos 'byung*, p. 143, indicate that the vision was received in the building then housing the bLa-brang-shar; compare *rGya bod yig tshang chen mo*, p. 317.

65. From rGya-mtsho 1981, p. 27.

66. *rJe sa chen la bstod pa*, p. 38.2.3; *bLa ma sa skya pa chen po'i rnam thar*, p. 88.2.2–3. See also the discussion of *Zhen pa bzhi bral* literature in rGya-mthso 1981.

67. This extended episode is found in the *Yar lung jo bo'i chos 'byung*, p. 143; *bLa ma brgyud pa'i rnam par thar pa ngo mtshar snang ba*, pp. 50–51; *rGya bod yig tshang chen mo*, pp. 318–19; *gDams ngag byung tshul gyi zin bris gsang chen bstan pa rgyas byed*, pp. 111–12; *gDung rabs chen mo*, pp. 27–28. Grags-pa rgyal-mtshan's *bLa ma sa skya pa chen po'i rnam thar*, p. 85.1.1, has Sa-chen study Abhidharma after he works with Ba-ri, and places it in his twelfth year. The shift in later hagiographers is possibly due to the fact that it would be impossible for anyone to complete the range of studies under Ba-ri outlined in Grags-pa rgyal-mtshan's narrative within a single year, whereas rudimentary Abhidharma can be accomplished in that period.

68. *bLa ma brgyud pa'i rnam par thar pa ngo mtshar snang ba*, p. 50.

69. Note that A-mes-zhabs expands the already impressive list of titles for both dKon-mchog rgyal-po and Sa-chen; *gDung rabs chen mo*, p. 28.4.

70. Intimations of this episode are found in the *Zhib mo rdo rje*, Stearns 2001, pp. 136–37.

71. The following material is based on Ba-ri's hagiography written by bSod-nams rtse-mo, *bLa ma ba ri lo tsā ba rin chen grags kyi rnam thar*, especially fols. 3a-5b.

72. *rNam thar yong grags*, pp. 201–2; *Deb ther sngon po*, vol. 1, p. 101.5; *Blue Annals* vol. 1, p. 73. Chattopadyaya 1967, pp. 493, 498, lists two works (To. 1866, 2704) said to have been translated by Atiśa and Ba-ri in Tho-ling, where Atiśa was between 1042 and 1045; this means that Ba-ri would have had to learn Sanskrit and classical Tibetan between the ages of two and five; the colophons are clearly apocryphal here.

73. *bLa ma ba ri lo tsā ba rin chen grags kyi rnam thar*, fols. 1a-1b, 4a; while the

hagiography calls them rDo-rje gdan-pa che-ba, and rDo-rje gdan-pa chung-ba, it is not clear that these designations would have been reflected in their Indian names: Mahā-Vajrāsana-pāda?, Cūḍa-Vajrāsana-pāda?, or something analogous.

74. Many such texts are included in the core of the *Ba ri be'u bum*, pp. 1 through 23 of which are actually by Ba-ri lo-tsā-ba; the rest accreted over time with much *gter ma* material, and by the end of the text (p. 581.3) there is a reference to rDo-rje gling-pa (1346–1405).

75. *bLa ma sa skya pa chen po'i rnam thar*, p. 84.4.2–6; *gDung rabs chen mo*, pp. 28–29.

76. For a discussion of Ba-ri's work and analogous *sādhana* collections, see Thomas 1903.

77. Also now called the rNam-rgyal sku-'bum, its location is shown by Schoening 1990, pp. 24–25 (no. 10); *bLa ma ba ri lo tsā ba rin chen grags kyi rnam thar*, fols. 5a-b (pp. 263–64); *gDung rabs chen mo*, pp. 28.21–29.12.

78. The *dhāraṇī* was possibly the *Sarvadurgatiparśodhanī-uṣṇīṣavijaya-dhāraṇī* (To. 597 [= 984]). For the use of spells in stūpas, see Schopen 1985. Ba-ri's hagiography, *bLa ma ba ri lo tsā ba rin chen grags kyi rnam thar*, fol. 5a6, claims that 3,140,000 ('bum ther gsum dang khri tsho bdun bzhugs pa'i rnam rgyal gyi sātstsha) clay sealings of the *dhāraṇī* were included in this reliquary, an improbable number.

79. According to Jeffrey Schoening, reported by Stearns 2001, n. 170, this is a temple in Sa-skya itself.

80. *bLa ma ba ri lo tsā ba rin chen grags kyi rnam thar*, fol. 5a5, indicates that Ba-ri came to Sa-skya at the age of sixty-two, maintained the monastery for ten years, and (fol. 5b5) transferred it to Sa-chen when Ba-ri was seventy; this is mathematically impossible, and we must consider that the ten years were from 1102 until his death in 1112. The chronological calendar in the *Tshig mdzod chen mo* lists 1111 as both the year of Kun-dga' snying-po's ascension to the position of Sa-skya Khri-pa and Ba-ri's death. This is probably based on two different chronologies. The *rGya bod yig tshang chen mo*, p. 317, maintains that Sa-chen's father died when he was eleven (i.e., 1103, but incorrect), while most other sources give ten (1102, correct); compare *gDung rabs chen mo*, p. 28.22.

81. For the Sa-skya emphasis on this school, see Jackson 1985.

82. This material is obscure; *bLa ma sa skya pa chen po'i rnam thar*, p. 85.1.6–2.2: yang bla ma de nyid la rje btsun me trī ba'i slob ma rje btsun phyag na rdo rje zhes bya ba la bla ma de nyid kyis nos pa'i grub pa sde bco brgyad grub pa'i khongs su gtogs pa du ma dang bcas pa | snying po skor phra mo dang bcas pa nyis shu rtsa lnga yan lag du ma dang bcas pa shin tu zab pa'i man ngag gis brgyan pa rnams khong du chud par mdzad do |. I had initially suspected much of this was included in Sa-chen's odd collection of bits in instruction, the *dPal sa skya pa'i man ngag gces btus pa rin po che'i phreng ba*, but none of these forty-nine texts is attributed to Vajrapāṇi.

83. *bLa ma brgyud pa'i rnam par thar pa ngo mtshar snang ba*, p. 52; *rGya bod yig tshang chen mo*, p. 318; *gDung rabs chen mo*, p. 31.2–9.

84. This episode is found from the *Zhib mo rdo rje*, Stearns 2001, pp. 136–39; compare *bLa ma brgyud pa'i rnam par thar pa ngo mtshar snang ba*, pp. 53–54; *gDams ngag byung tshul gyi zin bris gsang chen bstan pa rgyas byed*, p. 113, has an alternative version of the dream. This episode from mKhyen-brtse was translated in Stearns 1997, pp. 192–93.

85. *gDung rabs chen mo*, pp. 33.22–34.3.

86. See the short hagiographical notice in the *Deb ther sngon po*, vol. 1, pp. 463–65; *Blue Annals*, vol. 1, pp. 381–83.

87. *gDams ngag byung tshul gyi zin bris gsang chen bstan pa rgyas byed*, p. 117; *gDung rabs chen mo*, p. 35.

88. This individual is not to be confused with the dGe-shes dGon-pa-ba who was a well-known bKa'-gdams-pa disciple of Atiśa; compare *rNam thar yong grags* p. 193, or with another Zhang-ston Chos-'bar, *Deb ther sngon po*, vol. 1, p. 125; *Blue Annals* vol. 1, p. 95.

89. *bLa ma brgyud pa'i rnam par thar pa ngo mtshar snang ba*, p. 42.1, lists their skills as being gsung rab kyi rtsi dras mkhan po, an office that is unknown to me, perhaps involved in enumerating costs (rtsis) for the writing of the canon. See also *gDams ngag byung tshul gyi zin bris gsang chen bstan pa rgyas byed*, pp. 100–101.

90. *Chos 'byung me tog snying po sbrang rtsi'i bcud*, pp. 187–90.

91. The two tantras are the *rDo rje sems dpa' nam mkha' che bram ze rgyas pa'i rgyud*, with sixteen chapters that consistently announce themselves as from the *Extensive Brahman Tantra* [Kaneko (1982), no. 19] and the *rDzogs pa chen po lta ba'i yang snying | sangs rgyas thams cad kyi dgongs pa | nam mkha' klong yangs kyi rgyud* [Kaneko 1982, no. 114] in fifty-three chapters, which represents itself as a member of six tantras buried by Myang Ting-nge-'dzin bzang-po. I thank David Germano for drawing my attention to this latter work.

92. *Myang chos 'byung*, p. 207.

93. *Chos 'byung me tog snying po sbrang rtsi'i bcud*, p. 492. Germano (personal communication) suggested that this may be an incipient canon of eleven tantras based on his readings of the colophons of various tantras.

94. *gDams ngag byung tshul gyi zin bris gsang chen bstan pa rgyas byed*, p. 118, is an exception, for it has Sa-chen study Lam-'bras four years and then another four on the eight ancillary cycles of practice, but this is a measure of the questionable nature of this narrative. A-mes-zhabs indicates that Sachen was twenty-seven when he began his studies and they lasted until he was thirty-one, or from 1119 to 1123, although we must doubt that the early record can support this level of specificity; *Lam 'bras khog phub*, p. 176. The name Mi-bskyod rdo-rje is explicit in the version of the Tibetan hagiographies found in the current printing of the *Pod ser*, p. 593, translated in chap. 5, and is reflected in Grags-pa rgyal-mtshan's *gNas bstod nyams dbyang*, p. 348.2.1.

95. Several of Stearns's (2001) arguments are based on the proposition of there being no text of the Lam-'bras prior to Sa-chen. He points out (p. 173, n. 20) that the colophon to the *A seng ma* verifies this. The colophon indicates that Virūpa's

work was not committed to writing and that to do so would be a sin. I would take this as the circumstances known to him at that time, but the situation had evidently changed later, for he himself commits the work to writing, and I expect that he had encountered manuscripts by others having done the same.

96. *Zhib mo rdo rje*, Stearns 2001, pp. 146–47; bla ma Dam-pa has Zhang-ston-pa's wife offer the texts to Sa-chen, *bLa ma brgyud pa'i rnam par thar pa ngo mtshar snang ba*, p. 62; a version of this episode is translated in Stearns 2001, p. 250, n. 215.

97. *gLegs bam gyi dkar chags*, p. 2: cung zad gsungs pa rnams sngar yi ge med kyang.

98. *Sras don ma*, 127–28, 175–77.

99. *sGa theng ma*, pp. 192, 267, 320, 331–33; *Sras don ma*, p. 200; *Bande ma*, p. 88. In his *Zhang ston la bstod pa*, p. 2.3.1, Sa-chen provides a cryptic allusion to Zhang-ston-pa's literary holdings: rdo rje'i tshig rnams rgya cher 'grel mdzad sdud pa por | nges par mchis kyang mi yi gzugs 'dzin bla ma mchog |. This seems to indicate that Zhang collected extensive commentaries, or (if sdud pa is taken as a variant for sdus pa) perhaps composed a summary. Without some other reference, the verse remains obscure. The colophon indicates that this panegyric was composed when Sa-chen took the Lam-'bras initiation, but since it mentions Lam-'bras vocabulary, we still have the question of its textual transmission.

100. *Lam 'bras khog phub*, p. 184.

101. Note that A-seng evidently appears an occasional teacher of Sa-chen's, for Grags-pa rgyal-mtshan traces at least one of the lineages in his *Phyag rgya chen po gces pa btus pa'i man ngag*, p. 304.1.1, from bla-ma A-seng to bla-ma Sa-skya-pa. We see the same text and lineage in *dPal sa skya pa'i man ngag gces btus pa rin po che'i phreng ba*, p. 273.3.4, but here with the bla-ma A to Sa-skya-pa, apparently indicating that "bla-ma A" found in so many of these short works is A-seng or was understood to be so by Grags-pa rgyal-mtshan.

102. *gLegs bam gyi dkar chags*, speaking about his composition of the dkar chags, p. 3. The formal title of the *A seng ma*, *Don bsdus pa*, is mentioned under the designation *Thams cad kyi don bsdud kyi tshigs su bcad pa*, *gLegs bam gyi dkar chags*, p. 4.2.-3.

103. For example, the *gSung sgros ma*, p. 4.3; bLa-ma Dam-pa's *bLa ma brgyud pa'i rnam par thar pa ngo mtshar snang ba*, pp. 62–63, mentions only the *A seng ma*, the *sGa theng ma*, the *kLog skya ma*, and the *gNyags ma*. Specifics on the acceptance of the commentaries are found in Stearns 2001, pp. 24–25.

104. For example, *Lam 'bras khog phub*, p. 187.

105. This master list is taken from the *Lam 'bras khog phub*, p. 5; the items are interpreted according to *Sras don ma*, pp. 21–24, or according to *Zhu byas ma*, pp. 5–6.

106. Stearns 2001, p. 30. In an e-mail (dated January 14, 2004), Stearns informed me that he no longer holds this position but believes the *sGa theng ma* to be authentic and the original *dPe mdzod ma* of Phag-mo Gru-pa to be lost, replaced by the *sGa theng ma*.

107. *dKar brgyud gser 'phreng* p. 404.4.

108. The breaks are *Sras don ma*, pp. 205, 241, and 381. the colophon, pp. 445–46, seems to indicate that rJe Phul-byung-ba did this when he occupied the abbot's position of Sa-skya for three years training Sa-chen's sons. Compare mKhyen-brtse's *gDams ngag byung tshul gyi zin bris gsang chen bstan pa rgyas byed*, p. 128.

109. The intermediate state (Tib.: bar do) is articulated in most detail as a separate category in the *lDan bu ma*, pp. 361–65.

110. *gDams ngag byung tshul gyi zin bris gsang chen bstan pa rgyas byed*, p. 128.

111. *Lam 'bras khog phub*, p. 187.

112. See p. 357 on the contents of the *Pod ser* in the following chapter.

113. These works are in section II in the *Pod ser*; see chapter 9, p. 357; with the *A seng ma*, fourteen works by Sa-chen are found in that section.

114. I will provide the titles for these works in the notes so as not to burden the reader; here the reference is to Sa-chen's *Lus kyi dkyi 'khor*, *Pod ser*, pp. 135–38.

115. For some of this material and references, see Davidson 1991.

116. *Bum dbang gi snang bsgyur ba'i 'da' ka ma*, *gSang dbang gi skabs su thig le'i rnal 'byor bzhi*, *Shes rab ye shes kyi phyag rgya'i mtshan nyid*, and *dBang bzhi pa'i 'da' ka ma dang bum dbang dang thun mong du yi ges sgo dgag pa dang bcas pa*; these are collectively represented in *Pod ser*, pp. 144–51.

117. *'Das pa'i lam la gsang dbang gi skabs su 'khor bzhi'i rgya*, *dBang bzhi pa'i skabs su dang phyug gi don brgyad*, *Pod ser*, pp. 185–87; the former topic was to be taken up later in a text attributed to Sa-skya Paṇḍita, *Lam sbas bshad*, *SKB* IV.349.1.2–3.6.

118. *Bar do bzhi'i gdams ngag*, *Pod ser*, pp. 151–54.

119. *rTen 'brel lnga*, *Pod ser*, pp. 163–66.

120. *Grib sel gyi sbyin sreg bsdus pa*, *Yi ge brgya pa gdon pa'i gdams ngag*, *Pod ser*, pp. 166–67, 171–73.

121. *Bha ga'i yi ge bcu bzhi*, *Sa bcu gsum pa'i phyed kyi mngon rtogs*, *Pod ser*, pp. 183–85, 187–88.

122. Davidson 1991.

123. *'Phrang bdun gsal ba*, *Byung rgyal du mi gtong ba'i gnad bzhi*, *'Byung ba lus 'khrugs rlung dang spyod lam gyi gsal ba'i brtse chen thub pas legs bar gsungs*, *Pod ser*, pp. 260–88; see section IV in the *Pod ser* table in chap. 9, p. 357.

124. *rTsa ba med pa'i lam 'bring po*, and *Lam 'bras bsdus pa zhes bya ba'i rtsa ba*, *Pod ser*, pp. 292–99 (which also includes two short works not found in the *gLegs bam kyi dkar chags*); these constitute section V in the *Pod ser* table.

125. *gLegs bam gyi dkar chags*, pp. 5.4–6.1; these are in sections VI and VII in the *Pod ser*, table 10.

126. *Phyi nang gi mdzad pa bcu gnyis*, *Pod ser*, pp. 339–44.

127. The *Lam bsre ba* is found in *Pod ser*, pp. 327–36.

128. One of the gzhung shing chen po bzhi, *Pod ser*, pp. 300–14.

129. *Pod ser*, pp. 323–25.

130. *SKB* I.2.3.4–7.4.6.

131. For example, in Buddhaguhya's *Vairocanābhisambodhitantrapiṇḍārtha*, fols. 2a3–4a4.

132. Now well known by the translation of mKhas-grub-rje's manual in Lessing and Wayman 1968.

133. It is unclear at this section of the text whether it is by Ngor-chen himself or completed by Gung-ru Shes-rab bzang-po; *Lam 'bras byung tshul*, p. 118.2.4–5.

134. *Zhib mo rdo rje*, Stearns 2001, pp. 152–53.

135. *Zhib mo rdo rje*, Stearns 2001, pp. 152–53, and compare p. 255, n. 235.

136. *Pusti dmar chung*, pp. 13–15. This text is also called *Pod dmar*, but because there exists another *Pod dmar* by dMar-ston Chos-kyi rgyal-po, the designation *Pusti dmar chung* is sometimes used by the tradition to avoid confusion.

137. *Pod nag*, p. 64. Stearns 2001, p. 255, n. 234, indicates that the exact nature of this list was problematic for the tradition but that it was "clarified" in the work of gLo-ba mkhan-chen bSod-nams lhun-grub (1456–1532). The fact that the tradition required more than three hundred years to identify the materials transmitted supports my evaluation of its apocryphal nature.

138. These start with a *Grub chen bcu* according to the current edition of the *SKB* and conclude with a *Phra mo brgyad kyi man ngag*, *SKB* V.349.3.6–54.3.1, but the compiler's organization is belied by the designations found on pp. 350.1.1 and 354.3.1. In fact the text on pp. 350.2.2 to 353.2.1, actually entitled in the text "Teachings from the mouth of the Yogeśvara Virūpa" (*dPal rnal 'byor gyi dbang phyug chen po birwa pa'i zhal gyi gdams pa*, pp. 350.2.1–53.2.1), appears to be a simple expansion or commentary on the *Grub chen bcu*, with the short hagiographical episode added.

139. *Grub chen bcu*, *SKB* V.350.1.5–2.2; compare *gDung rabs chen mo*, pp. 45, 53.

140. *dPal ldan Bi ru pa la bstod pa*, pp. 2.2.2–2.2.4.

141. *Lam 'bras khog phub*, p. 180.

142. See, for example, his *rNal 'byor byang chub seng ge'i dris lan*, his *gLegs bam kyi dkar chag*, *Ga ring rgyal po la rtsis bsdur du btang ba'i gsung yig*, and the delightful series of "songs of my experience" (nyams dbyangs) collected in *SKB* IV.345.3.2–54.2.6. There are a few places where I have located Grags-pa rgyal-mtshan's use of "nga" for the first person. These include his *gNas bstod kyi nyams dbyangs*, pp. 348.2.6 and 348.3.3, and even there tends to use "bdag." This is not, though, a letter to a disciple of his father, one who is, moreover, an honored member of the eastern Tibetan community, as sGa-theng certainly was. There is also one "nga rang" towards the end of his long letter to Ga-ring rgyal-po, *Ga ring rgyal po la rtsis bsdur du btang ba'i gsung yig*, p. 104.4.1, but again this was written at the age of sixty, not as an adolescent.

143. *gLegs bam gyi dkar chags*, p. 7.1–2.

144. *bLa ma sa skya pa chen po'i rnam thar*, p. 87.2.3.

145. *bLa ma rnam thar bstod pa khyod nyi ma*, p. 83.1.4.

146. *gDung rabs chen mo*, p. 44; for the location of Mon in the early period, see Pommaret 1999.

147. The discussion on the use of one, two, or four cakras in the practice of psychic heat, for example, is found in the *Sras don ma*, pp. 95–99; yet this practice appears to have derived from a text in the collection, the *Pulla ha ri'i paṇḍita'i man*

ngag, found in the *dPal sa skya pa'i man ngag gces btus pa rin po che'i phreng ba*, p. 275.1.5–4.3. The former is one recension of the same text also found in Grags-pa rgyal-mtshan's own compendium of directions, the *Phyag rgya chen po gces pa btus pa'i man ngag*, p. 309.2.1–4.3.

148. *Phyag rgya chen po gces pa btus pa'i man ngag*, *SKB* IV.302.3.1–11.4.5.

149. *dPal sa skya pa'i man ngag gces btus pa rin po che'i phreng ba*, pp. 278.2.4–4.1, 280.3.2–4.4.

150. *Lam zab mo bla ma'i rnal 'byor*, p. 339.4.4–5.

151. *Aṣṭa'i gzhi bshad*, p. 355.3.4.

152. *dKar brgyud gser 'phreng*, pp. 509–11; *Myang chos 'byung*, pp. 23–24; *Lho rong chos 'byung*, p. 650; *Brug pa'i chos 'byung*, pp. 429–35; *mKhas pa'i dga' ston*, p. 847; a text of the *'Brug lugs ro snyoms rtsa gzhung* is contained in *gDams ngag mdzod*, vol. 7, pp. 59–73.

153. On the development of the *bKa' gdams glegs bam*, see Ehrhard 2002.

154. *Lam 'bras byung tshul*, p.117.1.4–5; I presume that we must read the sentence: de la cha gan gyi[s] zhwa ma lugs kyi chos skor to make Cha-gan the subject of the visionary experience.

NOTES TO CHAPTER 9

1. *gNas bstod kyi nyams dbyangs*, p. 348.1.3–6. The very unpolished nature of this "song," may be noted, especially as the syllables vary idiosyncratically between seven and nine. However, the marked tendency for Sa-skyas to question pilgrimage practices began at least with Grags-pa rgyal-mtshan, although it reached its full value later; see Huber 1990 for some of the polemics engaged in by Sa-Paṇ and others.

2. Noted by Martin 1996c, p. 188, n. 65, and 1996a, pp. 23–24. The prevalence of laity throughout the early Buddhist traditions in Tibet dilutes the premise of Martin 1996a, as he seems to acknowledge.

3. Kapstein 2000, pp. 141–62, examined this issue in the *Maṇi bka' 'bum* and other texts.

4. Good observations on the nature of the *sBa bzhed* chronicle are found in Kapstein 2000, pp. 23–50.

5. The basic record is in the *Rwa lo tsā ba'i rnam thar*, pp. 283–84, and is summarized in *Deb ther sngon po*, vol. 1, p. 458, *Blue Annals*, vol. 1, p. 378. dGos-lo places the date of me pho khyi on the event, probably from reading the age of Rwa-lo in the hagiography as eighty (he was born in 1016). This apparently is why Martin 2001a, p. 48, proposed this date. I have less confidence in the *Deb ther sngon po* early chronologies, however. Martin 2001a maintains that the outlying temples and the wall around the compound were damaged by the sMad 'dul monks.

6. *'Bri gung chos rje 'Jig rten mgon po bka' 'bum*, vol. 1, p. 50.1.

7. *mKhas pa'i dga' ston*, vol. 1, pp. 448, 801; *bKa' 'chems ka khol ma*, p. 287; *mNyam med sgam po pa'i rnam thar*, p. 167; *Lho rong chos 'byung*, pp. 178–79. I am inferring

that this is how the 'Bring-tsho destroyed Atiśa's residence; see *rNam thar yong grags*, p. 177.

8. Except as noted, the following is based on Martin 1992 and 2001a, as well as Jackson 1994b, pp. 58–72.

9. On part of the mChims clan becoming Zhang, see *Deb ther sngon po*, vol. 1, p. 125.1; *Blue Annals* vol. 1, p. 95. For an obscure discussion of other Zhang clans, see *rGya bod yig tshang chen mo*, pp. 236–37.

10. *mKhas pa'i dga' ston*, vol. 1, p. 807.9.

11. *Deb ther dmar po*, p. 127.22–23. For these two institutions, see Richardson 1998, p. 306.

12. *mKhas pa'i dga' ston*, vol. 1, p. 808.11.

13. *Dus gsum mkhyen pa'i bka' 'bum*, p. 78.1, indicates that the Karmapa mediated Lama Zhang's dispute with a Dag-ra-ba (?).

14. Martin 1996c, pp. 185–86, and 1996a, *passim*.

15. *Nyang ral rnam thar*, pp. 90–92.

16. *mKhas pa'i dga' ston*, vol. 1, p. 808.18–19.

17. *Aṣṭasāhasrikā-prajñāpāramitā-sūtra*, pp. 191–96.

18. The following is based on his hagiography by rGa-lo in the *Dus gsum mkhyen pa'i bka' 'bum*, vol. 1, pp. 47–128. This work is closely followed by all the standard histories.

19. Phag-mo gru-pa's hagiographies include the *Phag mo gru pa'i rnam thar rin po che'i phreng ba*, *dKar brgyud gser 'phreng*, pp. 387–435; *sTag lung chos 'byung*, pp. 171–87; *Lho rong chos 'byung*, pp. 306–27; *rLangs kyi po ti bse ru rgyas pa*, p. 103; *Deb ther sngon po*, vol. 1, pp. 651–66; *Blue Annals*, vol. 1, pp. 552–65; *mKhas pa'i dga' ston*, vol. 1, pp. 811–19; and *'Brug pa'i chos 'byung*, pp. 401–8. *rGya bod yig tshang chen mo*, pp. 534–35, provides an anomalous chronology of Phag-mo gru-pa, having him born in the fire-tiger year (1086?) rather than the iron-tiger year (1110) and traveling to Central Tibet at the age of 24 (1110?) rather than at the age of eighteen in 1128. Jackson 1990, pp. 39–45, and 1994b, pp. 39–42, 60–61, 77, contributed to our understanding of this important figure.

20. *Deb ther sngon po*, vol. 1, p. 655, and *Blue Annals*, vol. 1, p. 555, has him ordained at 25 (1135), but this is contradicted by the *dKar brgyud gser phreng*, p. 403, and the *Lho rong chos 'byung*, p. 307.

21. *Phag mo gru pa'i rnam thar rin po che'i phreng ba*, p. 12.1.

22. *Lam 'bras byung tshul*, p. 118.1.1, has Phag-mo gru-pa living at Sa-skya for twelve years, an improbable number; this is evidently followed by A-mes-zhabs, *gDung rabs chen mo*, p. 48.

23. *dKar brgyud gser phreng*, pp. 407–11, emphasizes both Phag-mo gru-pa's faith and the experiences he receives. As Jackson 1994b, p. 60, notes, the Zhang writings on this period have a peculiar chronology.

24. Sperling 1994.

25. This is rGwa-lo gZhon-nu-dpal (1110/14–1198/1202). For this figure, see Sperling 1994 and *Blue Annals*, vol. 2, pp. 469, 475, 555. We note that there was a

later rGwa-lo rNam-rgyal rdo-rje (1203–82), who was the hagiographer of Dus-gsum mkhyen-pa and was apparently considered the reincarnation of the earlier disciple of rTsa-mi.

26. On this affix, see Kychanov 1978, p. 210. This article treats the special position of Tibetans among the Tangut.

27. Dunnall 1992, pp. 94–96; van der Kuijp 1993.

28. On this issue, see Sperling 1987 and Dunnel 1992.

29. Martin 2001b, pp. 148–60, provides an excellent introduction to this material. The composition of the verses is discussed in *Dam chos dgongs pa gcig pa'i yig cha*, pp. 156–58.

30. *'Bri gung chos rje 'Jig rten mgon po bka' 'bum*, p. 166; *'Brig gung gdan rabs gser phreng*, p. 83.

31. *bLa ma sa skya pa chen po'i rnam thar*, p. 87.2.5–3.1.

32. *gDung rabs chen mo*, p. 53.

33. *bLa ma rje btsun chen po'i rnam thar*, p. 144.2.5.

34. Schoening 1990, p. 14.

35. On Rin-chen bZang-po's mask, see Vitali 2001.

36. *bLa ma brgyud pa'i rnam par thar pa ngo mtshar snang ba*, p. 52; *rGya bod yig tshang chen mo*, p. 318; *gDung rabs chen mo*, p. 31.2–9.

37. The disciples are mentioned in *Zhib mo rdo rje*, Stearns 2001, pp. 149–51; *bLa ma brgyud pa'i rnam par thar pa ngo mtshar snang ba*, pp. 66–70; *gDams ngag byung tshul gyi zin bris gsang chen bstan pa rgyas byed*, pp. 128–34; *Lam 'bras khog phub*, pp. 188–90.

38. *gDams ngag byung tshul gyi zin bris gsang chen bstan pa rgyas byed*, p. 133; a letter is mentioned in the *bLa ma brgyud pa'i rnam par thar pa ngo mtshar snang ba*, p. 68. This is probably the *dGa' ston la spring yig*, *SKB* III.272.3.6–74.3.2, also contained in the fifteenth-century *Pusti dmar chung*, pp. 41–49: *rJe btsun gyis dga' ston rdo rje grags la gdams pa*.

39. For a different perspective of Phag-mo gru-pa, see Stearns 2001, pp. 26–31.

40. *dKar brgyud gser phreng*, pp. 407–11, emphasizes both Phag-mo gru-pa's faith and the experiences he receives.

41. *dKar brgyud gser phreng*, pp. 414–15; *Lho rong chos 'byung*, p. 314.

42. *dKar brgyud gser phreng*, p. 414–15; compare *Lho rong chos 'byung*, p. 314. Jackson 1990, pp. 39–47, discusses the unfortunate proposition (based on Roerich's interpretation of *Blue Annals*, 1949, vol. 1, p. 559) that Sa-chen and Phag-mo gru-pa had a falling-out, but Jackson rejects this interpretation on good textual grounds.

43. *Lam 'bras byung tshul*, p. 118.2.2. See chap. 8 for questions about the *sGa-theng-ma*.

44. This is in a supplement to the homage to Sa-chen by Zhu-byas, *gDung rabs chen mo*, pp. 49–51, which A-mes-zhabs follows.

45. *gDams ngag byung tshul gyi zin bris gsang chen bstan pa rgyas byed*, p. 130.

46. *gDung rabs chen mo*, p. 62.

47. Jackson 1987, vol. 2, pp. 344–47, presents Sa-skya Paṇḍita's summary of the thirteenth-century Tibetan understanding of the five Buddhist and five non-Bud-

dhist areas of knowledge: Buddhist areas constitute the philosophical systems of the Vaibhāṣika, Sautrāntika, Vijñapti[-mātratā-vāda], and the Niḥsvabhāvavāda (Madhyamaka); non-Buddhist systems are *Vaidaka (Mīmāṁsā), Sāṁkhya, Aulūkya (Vaiśeṣika), Kṣapaṇaka (Jaina), and Cārvāka. The areas of knowledge listed in the *Mahāvyutpatti*, nos. 1554–59, 4953–71, do not include any specifically Buddhist studies and collectively demonstrate the changing nature of these rubrics.

48. *gDung rabs chen mo*, p. 63.

49. *Lam 'bras byung tshul*, p. 120.1.4; *gDung rabs chen mo*, p. 63.

50. *bLa ma rje btsun chen po'i rnam thar*, p. 144.2.6.

51. For Phya-pa, see van der Kuijp 1978 and 1983, pp. 59–70.

52. *sLob dpon Phya pa la bstod pa*, p. 41.1.5. He evidently sent a copy to gSang-phu Ne'u-thog as an offering, p. 41.2.2. Phya-pa's death date, offerings made on his behalf, and the areas of his intellectual emphasis are mentioned in this panegyric as well.

53. This was maintained in the episodes in which Phag-mo gru-pa was favored by Sa-chen, who liked the way he answered questions put to him; for example, *Deb ther sngon po*, vol. 1, p. 656; *Blue Annals*, vol. 2, p. 556.

54. *bDag med ma'i dbang gi tho yig*, p. 404.3.2–6. This short work is mentioned in his *rGya sgom tshul khrims grags la spring ba* of 1165, p. 39.3.2–3.

55. *brGyud pa dang bcas pa la gsol ba 'debs pa*, p. 39.1.5.

56. *rGya sgom tshul khrims grags la spring ba*; p. 39, *passim*, is very difficult, with very obscure twelfth-century words and honorific usages.

57. *sLob dpon Phya pa la bstod pa*, p. 40.2.2–5, is especially significant.

58. This emphasis on Sa-skya Paṇḍita's position is found, for example, in Jackson 1983, p. 7. A-mes-zhabs notes the importance of prosody in bSod-nams rtse-mo's compositions; *gDung rabs chen mo*, p. 66.

59. *gDung rabs chen mo*, p. 64: 'dzam bu gling pa'i bstan pa'i srog shing chen po.

60. *gDung rabs chen mo*, p. 64.

61. *Saṁ pu ṭa'i ṭī ka gnad kyi gsal byed*, p. 189.3.5.

62. *dPal kye rdo rje'i sgrub thabs mtsho skyes kyi ṭī ka*, p. 131.6.

63. The *Yig ge'i bklag thabs byis pa bde blag tu 'jug pa* is discussed later. Puṇyāgra is found in the colophon to his *Dang po'i las can gyi bya ba'i rim pa dang lam rim bgrod tshul*, p. 147.1.6; Dveshavajra is found in *dPal kye rdo rje rtsa ba'i rgyud brtag pa gnyis pa'i bsdus don*, p. 176.1.5.

64. *gDung rabs chen mo*, pp. 66–67.

65. *bLa ma rje btsun chen po'i rnam thar*, *SKB* V.143.1.1–154.4.6. The other essential sources are *gDung rabs chen mo*, pp. 69–85, and his dream record in *rJe btsun pa'i mnal lam*.

66. *bLa ma rje btsun chen po'i rnam thar*, pp. 144.1.2, 144.1.6, 144.2.3, 144.4.4, 145.1.2.

67. *rJe btsun pa'i mnal lam*. The *SKB* editor includes a note (V.x) that Ngor-chen claims the letter was dictated by Grags-pa rgyal-mtshan to mKhas-pa sbal-ston at an uncertain date, and this also is indicated in the colophon to the text as contained in *LL* I.64.1: rje btsun pa'i mnal lam sbal ston seng ge rgyal mtshan gyis bris so |.

68. *bLa ma rje btsun chen po'i rnam thar*, p. 144.2.4–3.2; *Ga ring rgyal po la rtsis*

bsdur du btang ba'i gsung yig, p. 104.2.6, includes the death date of his youngest brother, dPal-chen 'od-po (1150–1203).

69. *bLa ma rje btsun chen po'i rnam thar*, p. 143.2.2. Here nāgarāja (klu'i rgyal po) would be understood as the king of elephants in India (since elephants and snakes are frequently seen as variations of the same entity), and I presume that Sa-skya Paṇḍita would be using the term in this manner.

70. *Deb ther sngon po*, vol. 1, p. 661; *Blue Annals*, vol. 1, p. 561. He is listed as a disciple of Sa-chen and is considered an incarnation of Avalokiteśvara in *gDung rabs chen mo*, p. 50. For his connection to the 'Brom-lugs, see *Lam 'bras byung tshul*, p. 114.4.2.

71. *gDung rabs chen mo*, p. 69.

72. *rJe btsun pa'i mnal lam*, p. 98.3.1–4.2; *bLa ma rje btsun chen po'i rnam thar*, p. 144.4.4–6.

73. For example, *bLa ma rje btsun chen po'i rnam thar*, pp. 143.4.1, 144.1.1–2; *gDung rabs chen mo*, p. 51, gives Paṇ-chen Mi-nyag grags-rdor's supplementary list of Sa-chen's disciples, which includes two Zhang: Zhang-ston gSum-thog-pa and Zhang-ston sPe'i dmar-ba.

74. *gDung rabs chen mo*, p. 70; *gDams ngag byung tshul gyi zin bris gsang chen bstan pa rgyas byed*, p. 140.2, adds rGya-sgom tshul-khrims-grags to the list of Grags-pa rgyal-mtshan's important teachers.

75. *gDung rabs chen mo*, p. 83, mentions some of the different reports.

76. *rGya sgom tshul khrims grags la spring ba*, pp. 39.3.5 and 39.4.1–2.

77. *bLa ma rje btsun chen po'i rnam thar*, p. 144.4.1; compare *gDung rabs chen mo*, p. 75, which numbers more than three hundred and places the hundred in the temple housing the remains of the great Sa-skya teachers (*gong ma*), a designation usually meaning Sa-chen, his two sons, Sa-paṇ and 'Phags-pa, although it is not clear that their remains were housed together at this time.

78. *Tshar chen rnam thar*, p. 500; Ferrari 1958, p. 65.

79. *rJe btsun pa'i mnal lam*, *SKB* IV.99.1.2–3.4.

80. *bDe mchog kun tu spyod pa'i rgyud kyi gsal byed*, p. 55.2.4.

81. This may be inferred by Sa-skya Paṇḍita's observation at the end of the outline, *rGyud sde spyi'i rnam gzhag dang rgyud kyi mngon par rtogs pa'i stong thun sa bcad*, *SKB* III.81.2.4–5, that he was fourteen years old when he edited the summary. These works are also referenced in his *brTag gnyis rnam 'grel dag ldan*, p. 162.3.3.

82. *rGyud sde spyi'i rnam gzhag dang rgyud kyi mngon par rtogs pa'i stong thun sa bcad*, *SKB* III.81.2.4–5; *rGyud kyi rgyal po chen po saṁ pu ṭa zhe bya ba dpal ldan sa skya paṇḍi ta'i mchan dang bcas pa*, p. 668.4 (fol. 300b4), indicates that Sa-paṇ had heard from Grags-pa rgyal-mtshan the *Sampuṭa* five times and the *Sampuṭa-tilaka* two before he wrote the notes at age sixteen (1198).

83. For example, *dPal ldan sa skya paṇḍi ta chen po'i rnam par thar pa*, pp. 434.1.4–436.3.2, provides a long list of topics and titles, most of which are attributed to Grags-pa rgyal-mtshan's teaching; pp. 436.1.3 and 436.3.1 specifically list rNying-ma esoteric works and the study of Sanskrit.

84. Jackson 1985, p. 23, acknowledges that the disparity between Sa-skya Paṇ-

ḍita's list of his uncle's studies and the lists provided in the latter's hagiographies—in this case, concerning Madhyamaka studies—but refrains from concluding that we have the hagiographer's art at its source.

85. *Vidyādharīkelī-śrīvajravārāhī-sādhana*, *SKB* IV.29.2.3, and see *SKB* IV.28.2.5–30.4.4.

86. Stearns 1996, pp. 132–34, provides sources for this issue.

87. Dunnel 1996, p. 158.

88. Kychanov 1978, p. 208.

89. *Bod rje lha btsan po'i gdung rabs tshig nyung don gsal*, p. 84. The discussion of Vinaya is on pp. 82–85. Śākyaśrī becomes an important culture hero celebrated in the *Myang chos 'byung*, pp. 68–73.

90. *Phag mo las bcu'i gsal byed*, *SKB* IV.28.2.3. For Mi-nyag as a national designation, see Stein 1951, 1966, p. 288.

91. *Bya spyod rigs gsum spyi'i rig gtad kyi cho ga*, *SKB* IV.255.1.3–5.

92. *Nges brjod bla ma'i 'khrul 'khor bri thabs*, *SKB* IV.45.4.5, requested by rTsā-mi; *Arga'i cho ga dang rab tu gnas pa don gsal*, *SKB* IV.252.2.6, requested by sNge-ston (? = sDe-ston) dKon-mchog-grags and mDo-smad gling-kha'i yul du skyes pa yi dGe-slong lDe-ston-pa; *Kun rig gi cho ga gzhan phan 'od zer*, *SKB* IV.228.1.4, requested by Lle'u dge-slong Seng-ge-mgon; *gZhan phan nyer mkho*, *SKB* IV.237.2.4, requested by gTsang-kha (= Tsong-kha) snyid-ston dGe-slong Rin-chen-grags; *rTsa ba'i ltung ba bcu bzhi pa'i 'grel pa gsal byed 'khrul spong*, *SKB* III.265.3.4, requested by bTsong-ga'i dGe-slong rDor-rje grags-mched; *rTsa dbu ma'i khrid yig*, *SKB* IV.42.4.2, requested by mDo-smad gyar-mo-thang gi ston-pa gZhon-nu; *Chos spyod rin chen phreng ba*, *SKB* IV.320.2.6, requested by rTsong-kha'i cang-ston (?) dGe-slong brTson-'grus-grags.

93. *Byin rlabs tshar gsum khug pa*, p. 95.3.3–4.

94. *bDud rtsi 'khyil pa sgrub thabs las sbyor dang bcas pa*, *SKB* IV.67.2.6. This is the only time that I have found he used this designation.

95. *rGya sgom tshul khrims grags la spring ba*, p. 39.4.3; *Ga ring rgyal po la rtsis bsdur du btang ba'i gsung yig*, p. 104.4.4–5.

96. The section beginning *rJe btsun pa'i mnal lam*, *SKB* IV.99.4.4, which mentions his looking toward sixty-nine years of age, I take to be a continuation of the dream at sixty-six beginning on p. 99.4.1. This is how it is understood in *gDung rabs chen mo*, p. 81, whereas *bLa ma rje btsun chen po'i rnam thar*, p. 145.3.2, seems to say that it happened two years before his death.

97. *rJe btsun pa'i mnal lam*, p. 99.4.1–4. Compare *LL* I.62.3–5.

98. The term is used in describing the episode in the *Lam 'bras khog phub*, p. 190.5; I know of no instance where it is used before this text.

99. *bLa ma rje btsun chen po'i rnam thar*, p. 145.1.2–2.2.

100. *gDung rab chen mo*, p. 79; *gDams ngag byung tshul gyi zin bris gsang chen bstan pa rgyas byed*, pp. 139–40; *Lam 'bras khog phub*, p. 190.5.

101. *bLa ma rje btsun chen po'i rnam thar*, p. 145.1.2–4, is almost identical with *rJe btsun pa'i mnal lam*, pp. 98.4.6–99.1.2.

102. *bLa ma rje btsun chen po'i rnam thar*, p. 145.1.5–2.1. While all the preceding sources report the verse, none agrees, so Sa-skya Paṇḍita's version appears to be the most authentic.

103. *bLa ma rje btsun chen po'i rnam thar*, p. 146.2.2–3.

104. Personal communications from Ngor Thar-rtse zhabs-drung (1981) and Ngor Thar-rtse mkhan-po (1982). These works were the *rGyud sde spyi'i rnam par gzhag pa*, the *rGyud kyi mngon par rtogs pa rin po che'i ljon shing*, the *brTag gnyis rnam 'grel dag ldan*, and the *sDom gsum rab dbye*.

105. *bLa ma rje btsun chen po'i rnam thar*, p. 144.1.4–5; see a similar expression in *gDung rab chen mo*, p. 74.

106. His *Chos la 'jug pa'i sgo* is examined later; the Amoghapāśa lineage materials are found in his *'Phags pa don yod zhags pa'i lo rgyus*.

107. Genealogical material is included in *Chos la 'jug pa'i sgo*, pp. 343.1.2–46.2.4, of bSod-nams rtse-mo and in the dedicated *Bod kyi rgyal rabs* of Grags-pa rgyal-mtshan. 'Khon lineal matters occupy the *bLa ma sa skya pa chen po'i rnam thar*, p. 84.1.4–2.2, and is the topic of *Ga ring rgyal po la rtsis bsdur du btang ba'i gsung yig*.

108. Besides the hagiography of his father, his major hagiographical contributions are Virūpa's in his *bLa ma rgya gar ba'i lo rgyus*; Kāṇha's in his *Nag po dkyil chog gi bshad sbyar*, pp. 304.3.4–306.2.2; Ghaṇṭapāda's in the *sLob dpon rdo rje dril bu pa'i lo rgyus*; and Luïpa's in the *bDem mchog lu hi pa'i lugs kyi bla ma brgyud pa'i lo rgyus*. Both his *Notes on Vajrayāna Systems* (*rDo rje 'byung ba'i yig sna*) and his *Notes on Individual Sādhanas* (*sGrub thabs so so'i yig sna*) also contain odd bits of curious stories.

109. *rGya bod kyi sde pa'i gyes mdo*.

110. *Lam 'bras 'byung tshul*, p. 120.1. Note that A-myes-zhabs presents the reading gseg shubs ma, indicating a standard book case (gsegs); *Lam 'bras khog phub*, p. 275.

111. *dPal sa skya pa'i man ngag gces btus pa rin po che'i phreng ba*, *SKB* I.268.2.1–81.2.6. The numbering is uncertain, for some texts appear to work in conjunction with works before or after, and there is no *dkar-chag* to enumerate the works as intended.

112. For example, compare *Sras don ma*, pp. 95–99, and *dPal sa skya pa'i man ngag gces btus pa rin po che'i phreng ba*, *SKB* I.275.1.5–75.4.3.

113. *Phyag rgya chen po gces pa btus pa'i man ngag*, *SKB* IV.302.3.1–11.4.5. The uncertainty of numbering for Sa-chen's collection applies to Grags-pa rgyal-mtshan's as well.

114. Ehrhard 2002, p. 40.

115. *gLegs bam gyi dkar chags*, p. 3.1.

116. For the relationship of Tibetan color terminology to English, see Nagano 1979, pp. 11–23.

117. *gLegs bam gyi dkar-chags*, p. 8.1–2.

118. See his *gSung ngag rin po che lam 'bras bu dang bcas pa ngor lugs thun min slob bshad dang | thun mong tshogs bshad tha dad kyi smin grol yan lang dang bcas pa'i brgyud yig gser gyi phreng ba byin zab 'od brgya 'bar ba*, *LL* XX.417–511; compare Smith 2001, pp. 235–58.

119. *Lam bras khog phub*, pp. 301–3.

120. Stearns 2001, pp. 32–35, already summarized the *Pod ser* contents, but his discussion emphasizes elements different from mine, so they are complementary rather than redundant.

121. *Lam-bras khog phub*, p. 187.

122. Grags-pa rgyal-mtshan was apparently responsible for the following works (with their pages in the *Pod ser*): *Kun gzhi rgyu rgyud* (128–31); *gDan stshogs kyi yi ge* (131–35); *Bum dbang gi 'da' ka ma'i skabs su 'chi ltas | 'khrul 'khor | 'chi bslu dang bcas pa* (138–44); *Lam dus kyi dbang rgyas 'bring bsdus gsum* (154–58); *Tshad ma bzhi'i yi ge* (158–61); *gDams ngag drug gi yi ge* (161–63); *Grib ma khrus sel* (167–69); *Grib ma satstshas sel ba* (169–70); *Thig le bsrung ba* (170–71); and the *'Jig rten pa'i lam gyi skabs su rlung gi sbyor ba bdun gyis lam khrid pa* (173–83). The others are by Sa-chen, according to the *gLegs bam kyi dkar chags*.

123. *gLegs bam kyi dkar chags*, p. 5.1–2.

124. Wayman 1977, pp. 137–80, is still the only significant treatment of the Guhyasamāja material.

125. Tachikawa 1975 is devoted to an examination of this issue with respect to the dGe-lugs understanding found in the *sGrub mtha' shel gyi me long* of Thu'u-bkwan bLo-bzang chos kyi nyi-ma.

126. Stearns 2001, pp. 30–32, argues that some short works in the *Pod ser* are based on Lam-'bras writings of Phag-mo gru-pa. This may prove to be true, but his argument as presented is not entirely compelling, as it relies on the idea that Sa-chen used no texts; compare Stearns 2001, pp. 32–35.

127. *Lung 'di nyid dang mdor bsdus su sbyar* (*Pod ser*, pp. 481–93), *Lung 'di nyid dang zhib tu sbyar ba* (*Pod ser*, pp. 493–529), and *Lam 'bras bu dang bcas pa'i don rnams lung ci rigs pa dang sbyar* (*Pod ser*, pp. 529–81).

128. Besides *Pod ser*, sec. IV, pp. 144–51 and 185–87, there is a longer work, *Kye rdor lus dkyil gyi dbang gi bya ba mdor bsdus pa*, ascribed to bLa-ma Sa-chen-pa and close to the language associated with Sa-chen's other works. On fol. 7a4 (p. 19.4), the signature of the Lam 'bras, the rdo rje rba rlabs bsgom pa, is mentioned; compare a supplemental work on the Vajrācāryabhiṣeka, *Gong tu ma bstan pa'i rdo rje slob dpon gyi dbang gi tho, Sa skya'i rje btsun gong ma rnam lnga'i gsung ma phyi gsar rnyed*, vol. 1, pp. 21–25. There is another short text, *sMon lam dbang bzhi'i bshad par sbyar ba*, which is not definitely a Lam-'bras-related work; *Sa skya'i rje btsun gong ma rnam lnga'i gsung ma phyi gsar rnyed*, vol. 1, pp. 81–84.

129. *Guhyasamāja-tantra* XII, vv. 60–76, pp. 42–44.

130. For references, see Davidson 1992, pp. 178–79, n. 20.

131. For a discussion of this ritual and related concerns, see Davidson 1992, pp. 114–20.

132. For a discussion of many of these issues, see Nor-chen's *bsKyed rim gnad kyi zla zer*, pp. 190.1 ff.; and Go-rams-pa's *bsKyed rim gnad kyi zla zer la rtsod pa spong ba gnad kyi gsal byed*, pp. 597 ff.

133. *rTsa ba'i ltung ba bcu bzhi pa'i 'grel pa gsal byed 'khrul spong*.

134. Eimer 1997.

135. *bLa ma mnga' ris pas mdzad pa'i brtag gnyis kyi tshig 'grel.* Compare the acknowledgement of Durjayacandra's and mNga'-ris-pa's commentaries in *dPal kye rdo rje'i rnam par bshad pa nyi ma'i 'od zer*, p. 109.3.1.

136. *Kye rdo rje'i rtsa rgyud brtag gnyis kyi dka' 'grel.*

137. *dPal kye rdo rje'i rnam par bshad pa nyi ma'i 'od zer.*

138. *brTag gnyis rnam 'grel dag ldan.*

139. *Guhyasamāja-tantra* XVIII.34.

140. *rGyud sde spyi'i rnam par gzhag pa*, pp. 22.3.5, 34.3.3, 35.4.5, 36.1.3, 36.3.3.

141. See Steinkellner 1978; Broido 1982, 1983, and 1984; Arènes 1998.

142. His sources are identified in *rGyud sde spyi'i rnam par gzhag pa*, pp. 31.4.5, 32.1.2, 32.1.6, 32.3.1, 32.3.3, 32.3.4, 33.1.5, 33.2.6, 34.2.1, 34.2.4, 34.3.6, 35.1.1, 35.2.4, 35.3.4, 35.4.6.

143. *rGyud sde spyi'i rnam par gzhag pa*, pp. 11.4.4–12.1.2.

144. *rGyud kyi mngon rtogs rin po che'i ljon shing*, p. 2.1.3.

145. Grags-pa rgyal-mtshan's scriptural source for this is *HT* II.ii.14–15, and *HT* II.viii.9–10.

146. *rGyud kyi mngon rtogs rin po che'i ljon shing*, 17.1.6–2.3, citing the *Sarvatathāgatatattvasaṁgraha* and the *Sampuṭa*; compare *HT* II.iv.76.

147. *rGyud kyi mngon rtogs rin po che'i ljon shing*, pp. 22.1.1–4, 26.3.2–4.

148. *rGyud kyi mngon rtogs rin po che'i ljon shing*, pp. 22.3.2, 26.1.3. We also see his interest in this level of encounter and refutation in his *rTsa ba'i ltung ba bcu bzhi pa'i 'grel pa gsal byed 'khrul spong*, pp. 261.2.6–65.2.6, where he refutes four "incorrect opinions" with respect to the Vajrayāna.

149. The identity of this place is not certain. The *Rwa lo rnam thar*, p. 46, mentions a sNye-nam na-mo-che in La-stod, and the *rNam thar rgyas pa yong grags*, p. 157, mentions a sNe-len in La-stod.

150. *Yi ge'i bklag thab byis pa bde blag tu 'jug pa.*

151. Verhagen 1995, 2001, pp. 58–63, studies this work.

152. *sMra sgo'i mtshon cha'i mchan rje btsun grags pa rgyal mtshan gyis mdzad pa*; *gDung rabs chen mo*, p. 74; Jackson 1987, vol. 1, pp. 116–117; Verhagen 2001, p. 52.

153. *Byang chub sems dpa'i spyod pa la 'jug pa'i 'grel pa*; see p. 515.2.5 for his debt to Phya-pa.

154. bSod-nams rtse-mo's *Dang po'i las can gyi bya ba'i rim pa dang lam rim bgrod tshul*, and the *Chos spyod rin chen phreng ba* of Grags-pa rgyal-mtshan.

155. *gDung rabs chen mo*, p. 64.

156. *gDung rabs chen mo*, p. 72.

157. Ruegg 1966, pp. 112–13, discusses this episode.

158. For a discussion of this controversy, see Stearns 1996, pp. 152–55.

159. gDung rabs chen mo, pp. 80–81.

Glossary

For the correct orthography of Tibetan terms, see the Tibetan Orthographic Equivalents.

* = Denotes a hypothetical Sanskrit reconstruction.

Abhiṣeka	Esoteric consecration or initiation, modeled after Indian coronation rites.
Atiyoga	Highest yoga, often equated with Dzogchen.
Bodhicitta	Occurs on several levels: it may indicate the Mahāyānist "thought of awakening" leading to the bodhisattva's vow; it may indicate semen, as the yogic "relative *bodhicitta*"; or it may indicate absolute mind, the very substance of the universe.
Bendé	Clerics, sometimes having a family, sometimes monks.
Cakrasaṁvara	A deity and accompanying *yoginī-tantra* literature emphasizing *sampannakrama*.
Chö	"Cutting off," the practice of liberation through offering the body.
Chongyé	The area of the imperial necropolis in the Yarlung valley.
Ḍākinī	Mythic feminine beings, who may lead to liberation.
Dzogchen	Great Perfection, a Nyingma doctrine and practice.
Guhyasamāja	The *mahāyoga tantra* and its system of the "secret assembly" maṇḍalas.
Hevajra	A late *yoginī-tantra* featuring the deity Hevajra and his eight *ḍākinīs*.
Jokhang	The temple in Lhasa built by Songtsen Gampo or his queens and the center of popular devotion.
Jonangpa	A thirteenth-century tradition emphasizing the *Kālacakra-tantra*.
Kagyüpa	Indicates a tantric lineage but has come to signify preeminently the lineage from Marpa lotsāwa.

Kahma	Nyingma literature and traditions said to have been passed down without interruption from the royal dynasty period.
Kālacakra	A late-tenth- or early-eleventh-century tantric tradition, the *Wheel of Time*.
Lamdré	The esoteric yogic system said to be from Virūpa, embodied in a text; see appendix 2.
Lotsāwa	The Tibetan word for translator.
Lu	Indigenous Tibetan subterranean spirits, later identified with Indian snake spirits (nāga).
Madhyamaka	An Indian philosophical-religious system emphasizing the negation of all properties.
Mahāmudrā	The Great Seal, meaning the concluding practice in the esoteric path for Sarma lineages.
Mahāyoga-tantra	A variety of tantra, also called a father tantra, that emphasizes maṇḍalas. The preeminent *mahāyoga-tantra* is the *Guhyasamāja-tantra*.
Mamo	Tibetan goddesses identified with Indian mother goddesses (mātṛkā)
Maṇḍalacakra	Sexual yoga, real or visualized; one of the two major varieties of *sampannakrama*.
Mantrayāna	One of the orthodox names for tantric Buddhism, the "vehicle of mantras."
*Mārgaphala	The reconstructed Sanskrit for Lamdré, the esoteric yogic system said to be from Virūpa.
Mudrā	Seal, meaning a hand gesture or the final state of visualization or being.
Mūlasarvāstivāda	The monastic Vinaya tradition of all Tibetan monasteries.
Nyingma	"Old Tradition," referring to the early systems developed from the royal dynastic translations and their indigenous literature.
Nyön-pa	"Crazy," a sage considered insane by the standards of the world and acting as such.
Sakyapa	Tibetan tradition based in Sakya Monastery, founded in 1073 C.E.
Sādhana	A meditative rite visualizing a Buddhist divinity, generally as oneself.
Sāmanta feudalism	Indian medieval feudalism, emphasizing the position of the vassal (sāmanta).
Sampannakrama	"Completion process" consisting of internal yogic fire visualization (*svādhiṣṭhānakrama*) and sexual yoga (*maṇḍalacakra*).

Samyé	The first monastery in Tibet; a dynastic foundation.
Sarma	Indicating the traditions and translations introduced into Tibet from the late tenth century onward.
Śāstra	A technical treatise or commentary with a specific human author; different from sūtra.
Śrāvaka	Monk of the early Buddhist tradition, adhering to the more than two hundred vows.
Sūtra	Exoteric text that contains the word of the Buddha.
Svādhiṣṭhāna	Internal heat yoga practice of the completion process (*sampannakrama*).
Tantra	Esoteric text said to be the word of the/a Buddha.
Terma	Treasure or treasure text, mythically buried during the royal dynasty.
Trisaṁvara	The three vows of the śrāvaka, the bodhisattva, and the vidyādhara.
Utpattikrama	The generation process, including the visualization of the maṇḍala, especially the external maṇḍala, in which the meditators visualize themselves as a deity surrounded in a palace by a maṇḍala of other deities, subordinate to themselves.
Ü-Tsang	Central Tibet, defined by the four horns: Uru and Yoru (Ü), and Yéru and Rulak (Tsang).
Vairocana	The Great Sun Buddha of the Mahāyāna, who became a fundamental deity of great maṇḍala systems developed in the tantras and favored by the Tibetan emperors.
Vajrakīla	Deity and maṇḍala of the Nyingma system; Vajrakīla had both Kahma and Terma forms.
Vajrasattva	The Adamantine Being, Original Buddha, and hierophant.
Vajrayāna	A name for tantric Buddhism that emphasizes its immediate speed (thunderbolt-like) and the royal scepter (vajra) as its symbol.
Vidyādhara	An imperial sorcerer having esoteric knowledge, the model for tantric yogins.
Yamāntaka	The destroyer of death, another *mahāyoga-tantra* deity, maṇḍala, and text.
Yangdak	A Nyingma deity and maṇḍala having both Kahma and Terma forms.
Yarlung	The valley of early Tibetan royalty, containing the imperial necropolis at Chongyé.
Yogācāra	An Indian philosophical-religious system emphasizing the description of mind and mental events.

Yoginī-tantra	A tantric text emphasizing *sampannakrama*. Especially important were the *Cakrasaṁvara*, *Hevajra*, and *Buddhakapāla tantras*.
Zhiché	A "pacifying" meditative tradition brought in stages by Padampa Sangyé.

Tibetan Orthographic Equivalents

Amé-shep = A-mes-zhabs
Anchung Namdzong = An-chung gnam-rdzong
An Shākya-kyap = An Shākya-skyabs
Apo Pentön = A-pho pha-ston
Aro Yéshé Jungné = A-ro Ye-shes byung-gnas
Aseng = A-seng
Asengma = *A seng ma*
A-uma = *'A 'u ma*
Ba/Bé = sBa[s]
Ba Gyelpo tagna = sBa rGyal-po stag-sna
Balam-Lak = Ba-lam-glag
Balam-né = Ba-lam-gnas
Barompa = 'Ba'-rom-pa
Bangtön = Bang-ston
Bari-lotsāwa = Ba-ri lo-tsā-ba
Barpuk-rong = Bar-spug-rong
Ba Selnang = sBa gSal-snang
Ba Tsültrim Lotrö = sBa Tshul-khrims blo-gros
Bharo Chagdum = Bha-ro phyag-rdum
Batsün Lotrö Yönten = sBa-btsun bLo-gros yon-tan
Batsün Lotrö Wangchuk = rBa-btsun bLo-gros dbang-phyug
Bé = sBas
Bé Gyelwa Lotrö = sBas rGyal-ba blo-gros
Bel = 'Bal
Belpen Zama = 'Bal-'phan bza'-ma
Belpuk = sBal-phug
Beltön Sengé Gyeltsen = sBal-ston Seng-ge rgyal-mtshan
Bendé = ban-de

Bendéma = *Bande ma*
Ben-dziba = 'ban-dzi-ba / 'ba'-ji-ba
Bepsa Wamo-shung = 'Bebs-za Wa-mo-zhung
Béso Kerwa = Be-so Ker-ba
Bon-nag Rewa Dzugu = Bon-nag Re-ba 'dzu-gu
Büldok-lhak Lhakhang = Bul-rdog-lhag lha-khang
Bumtang = Bum-thang
Butön = Bu-ston
Butön Rinchendrup = Bu-ston Rin-chen-grub
Butsel Serkhang-ling = Bu-tshal gser-khang-gling
Cha = bya
Cha = Phya
Chag = Chag
Chagen Wangchuk Gyeltsen = Cha-gan dBang-phyug rgyal-mtshan
Chag-gong = Chag-gong
Chaglo Chöjé-pel = Chag-lo Chos-rje dpal
Chalung Dorjé-drak = Cha-lung rdo-rje-brag
Changtsa Jerong = Byang-tsha bye-rong gi dgon-pa
Chapa Chökyi Sengé = Cha-pa (or Phya-pa) Chos-kyi seng-ge
Char Ratna = Car-rad-na
Cha-tsang gung-nang = Bya-tshang gung-snang
Cha-uk sa-tsik = Bya-'ug sa-tshigs
Ché = lCe
Chégom Nakpo = lCe-sgom Nag-po
Chémo Namkhamo = 'Phyad-mo Nam-mkha'-mo
Chen-nga Tsültrim-bar = sPyan-snga Tshul-khrim-'bar
Chen-ngok Lotrö Gyelwa = sPyan-rngog bLo-gros rgyal-ba
Chenyé = sPyan-g.yas
Chépong = Che-spong
Chétön Shérap Jungné = lCe-ston Shes-rab 'byung-gnas
Ché-tsün Sengé Wangchuk = lCe-btsun Seng-ge dbang-phyug
Chidar = Phyi-dar
Chim = mChims
Chimpu = mChims-phu
Ching-nga = 'Ching-nga
Ching-yül = 'Ching-yul
Chiri = Phyi-ri
Chiring = sPyi-ring
Chö = gCod
Chog = lCogs

Chog-ro = lCogs-ro
Chog-ro Pelgyi Wangchuk = Cog-ro dPal-gyi dbang-phyug
Chomden Rigrel = bCom-ldan Rig-ral
Chongyé = 'Phyong-rgyas
Chuk-tsam = Phyugs-mtshams
Chumik Dzinkha = Chu-mig rdzing-kha
Chuwori Gomdra = Chu-bo-ri'i bsgom-grwa
Dagyelma = Zla rgyal ma
Dakla Gampo = Dwags-la sgam-po
Dakpo Gomtsül = Dwags-po sGom-tshul
Dakpo Wang-gyel = Dwags-po dbang-rgyal
Dam-shö karmo = 'Dam-shod dkar-mo
Dangma Lhüngyel = lDang-ma lhun-rgyal
Darchen-pel = Dar-chen-dpal
Dar Drongmoché = mDar-grong-mo-che
Darma Dodé = Dar-ma mdo-sde
Darma Trih Udum-tsen = Dar-ma Khri 'U-dum btsan
Dashö-tsel = Zla-shod-tshal
Dé = lDe
Denbuma = lDan bu ma
Denkar = lDan-dkar
Denma = lDan-ma
Densa = gdan-sa
Densatil = gDan-sa-mthil
Dentik = Dan-tig
Détsug-gön = lDe-gtsug-mgon
Déü José = lDe'u jo-sras
Dhartön Shākya Lotrö = Dhar-ston Shākya blo-gros
Dingri = Ding-ri
Dogmé = mDog-smad
Dogtö = mDog-stod
Dölchung Korpön = mDol-chung bskor-dpon
Dong = lDong tribe
Dorjé Chukmo = rDo-rje phyug-mo
Dorjé-drak = rDo-rje-grags
Dorjé Peldzom = rDo-rje dpal-'dzom
Dorjé Purpa = rDo-rje phur-pa
Dorjé Raptenma = rDo-rje rab-gtan-ma
Drag-rum tö-mé = Brag-rum stod-smad
Drakpa Gyeltsen = Grags-pa rgyal-mtshan

Drakpa Shérap = Grags-pa shes-rab
Draktsé Sonakpa = Brag-rtse so nag-pa
Drak Yerpa = Brag yer-pa
Dranang = Grwa-nang
Drang-jé pa-nga = Drang-rje pha-lnga
Drang-khar Ché-chen = sBrang-mkhar sbre-can
Drangti = Brang-ti
Drangti Zurchöpa Géshé Khyung Rinchen Drakpa = Brang-ti Zur-chos-pa dge-bshes Khyung rin-chen grags-pa
Dranka = Bran-ka
Dranka Pelgyi Yönten = Bran-kha dPal-gyi yon-tan
Drapa Ngönshé = Gra-pa mNgon-shes
Dratang = Gra-thang
Drawolung = Bra-bo-lung
Dré = ’Bre
Dré = Brad
Dré Kyiru = Dra’i kyi-ru
Dreng Chökhu = Greng ’phyos-khu
Drengyi Lhading = ’Dren gyi lha-sdings
Dré-tag-chen = Gres-thag-can
Drigum Tsenpo = Gri-gum btsan-po
Drigung Jikten Gönpo = ’Bri-gung ’Jig-rten mgon-po
Drigung Pel-dzin = ’Bri-khungs dPal-’dzin
Drilung Méshö = ’Bris-lung rme-shod
Dring = ’Bring
Dring Yéshé Yönten = ’Bring Ye-shes yon-tan
Drisiru = Gri-zi-ru
Dro = ’Bro
Dro = sGro
Dro Gyeltsen Sengé = ’Bro rGyal-mtshan seng-ge
Drokmi = ’Brog-mi
Drokmi Lotsāwa = ’Brog-mi lo-tsā-ba
Drokmi Pelgyi Yéshé = ’Brog-mi dPal-gyi ye-shes
Drokmi Shākya yéshé = ’Brog-mi Shākya ye-shes
Dro-lotsāwa Shérap-drak = ’Bro-lo-tsā-ba Shes-rab-grags
Dro Mañjuśrī = sGro Mañ-’dzu-shrī
Dromchu = Grom-chu or Khrum-chu
Drom Dépa Tönchung = ’Brom De-pa ston-chung
Dromo = Gro-mo
Drompa = Grom-pa

Drompa-gyang = Grom-pa-rgyang
Drom Ramcha Yuné = 'Brom Ram-cha yu-ne
Dromtön = 'Brom-ston
Dromtön Gyelwé Jungné = 'Brom-ston rGyal-ba'i 'byung-gnas
Drong-chung = Grong-chung
Dro Nyentsé = 'Bro-gnyan-rtse
Drowo-lung = Gro-bo-lung
Dru = Bru
Dru = 'Dru
Drukpa Kagyüpa = 'Brug-pa bKa'-brgyud-pa
Drum Barwa Jangchub = Brum 'Bar-ba byang-chub
Drum Chinglak-chen = Grum Phying-slag-can
Dru-mer = Gru-mer
Dru-mer Tsültrim Jungné = Gru-mer Tshul-khrims 'byung-gnas
Drum Yeshé Gyeltsen = Grum Ye-shes rgyal-mtshan
Druptob Ngödrup = Grub-thob dngos-grub
Dungdrok = gDung-'brog
Dung-tsuk = mdung tshugs
Düsum Khyenpa = Dus-gsum mkhyen-pa
Dütsi = bdud rtsi
Dzéden Öchak = mDzes-ldan 'od-chags
Dzongkha = rDzong-kha
Galo Zhönu-pel = rGwa-lo gZhon-nu-dpal
Gampé-dzong = Gam-pa'i rdzong
Gampopa = sGam-po-pa
Gar = mGar
Gah-ring Gyelpo = Ga-ring rgyal-po
Gatengma = sGa theng ma
Gatön Dorjé-drak = sGa-ston rDo-rje-grags
Gégyé = dGe-rgyas
Gélo = dGe-blo
Géluk = dGe-lugs
Géshé Chak-ri-wa = dGe-bshes lCags-ri-ba
Géshé Drangti Darma Nyingpo = dGe-shes Brang-ti Dar-ma snying-po
Géshé Gyatsa Jangyé = dGe-bshes rGya-tsha byang-ye
Géshé Gya-yöndak = dGe-bshes rGya yon-bdag
Géshé Jangchup sempa = Byang-chub sems-dpa'
Géshé Khönchung = dGe-bshes 'Khon-chung
Géshé Mar-yül Loden shérap = dGe-shes Mar-yul blo-ldan shes-rab
Géshé Mé-lhang-tser = dGe-bshes Me'i-lhang-tsher

Géshé Nyak Wang-gyel = dGe-bshes gNyag dbang-rgyal
Géshé Nya-rawa Döndrup = dGe-bshes gNya' Ra-ba don-grub
Géshé Nyen Pül-jungwa = dGe-bshes gNyan Phul-byung-ba
Géshé Nyuk-rumpa = dGe-bshes sNyug-rum-pa
Géshé Tréü-chok = dGe-shes Kre'o mchog
Géshé Zangskarwa = dGe-shes Zangs-dkar-ba
Géwasel = dGe-ba-gsal
Gö = 'Gos
Gö-lotsāwa Khukpa Lhétsé = 'Gos lo-tsā-ba Khug-pa lhas-brtsas
Gölo Zhönu-pel = 'Gos-lo gZhon-nu-dpal
Gompa Kyibarwa = sGom-pa sKyi-'bar-ba
Gön = mGon
Gönchö = mGon-spyod
Gongpa-sel = dGong-pa-gsal
Gön-né = mGon-ne
Gön-nyön = mGon-smyon
Gorum = sGo-rum
Götön = mGos-ston
Gugé Purang = Gu-ge pu-hrangs
Gungru Shérap Zangpo = Gung-ru Shes-rab bzang-po
Gungtang = Gung-thang
Gurmo Rapkha = 'Gur-mo rab-kha
Guru Chö-wang = Gu-ru Chos-dbang
Guru Trashi = Gu-ru bkra-shis
Gyagom Tsültrim-drak = rGya-sgom Tshul-khrims-grags
Gya-lo Tsöndrü Sengé = rGya-lo brTson-'grus seng-ge
Gyamarpa = rGya-dmar-pa
Gyangdrak Nyipak = rGyang-grags gnyis-'phags
Gyasar-gang = Gya-sar-gang
Gya Shākya Zhönu = rGya Shākya gzhon-nu
Gya Tsülseng = rGya Tshul-seng
Gyelbu Yöndak = rGyal-bu yon-bdag
Gyel-luk Lhékyi Lhakhang = rGyal-lugs lhas kyi lha-khang
Gyel-tangpa Déchen Dorjé = rGyal-thang-pa bDe-chen rdo-rje
Gyengong = rGyan-gong
Gyenkor = rGyan-skor
Gyéré Langra = Gye-re glang-ra
Gyergom Sépo = sGyer-sgom se-po
Gyichu = sGyi-chu
Gyichuwa Draplha-bar = sGyi-chu-ba dGra-lha-'bar

Gyijang Ukarwa = Gyi-ljang dbu-dkar-ba
Gyijo Dawé Öser = Gyi-jo Zla-ba'i 'od-zer
Haḍu Karpo = Haḍu dkar-po
Heshang Genbak = Ha-shang Gan-'bag
Heshang Kawa = Ha-shang Ka-ba
Jampa Dorjé Gyeltsen = Byams-pa rDo-rje rgyal-mtshan
Jamyang Khyentsé Wangpo = 'Jam-dbyangs mKhyen-brtse'i dbang-po
Jamyang Loter Wangpo = `Jam-dbyangs bLo-gter dbang-po
Jangchub-Ö = Byang-chub-'od
Jangchub Sempah Aseng = Byang-chub sems-dpa' A-seng
Jangchub Sempah Dawa Gyeltsen = Byang-chub sems-dpa' Zla-ba rgyal-mtshan
Jangchub Sempah-Tak = Byang-chub sems-dpa' sTag
Jangchub Sengé = Byang-chub seng-ge
Jangsem Kunga = Byang-sems Kun-dga'
Jé Gönpawa = rJe dGon-pa-ba
Jé Kharchungwa = rJe mKhar-chung-ba (= Se mKhar-chung-ba)
Jétsün = rJe-btsun
Jétsün chenpo = rJe-btsun chen-po
Jétsün Chökyi Gyeltsen = rJe-btsun Chos kyi rgyal-mtshan
Jétsün Rinpoché = rJe-btsun rin-po-che
Jocham Purmo = Jo-lcam Phur-mo
Joga = 'Jo-dga'
Jokhang = Jo-khang (= 'Phrul-snang gtsug-lag-khang)
Jomo Lhajéma = Jo-mo Lha-rje-ma
Jowo = Jo-bo
Jowo Dong-nakpa = Jo-bo gDong-nag-pa,
Kadam = bKa'-gdams
Kadampa = bKa'-gdams-pa
Kahma = bka'-ma
Ka-ö Chog-drakpa = Ka-'od mchog-grags-pa
Kargong-lung = dKar-gong-lung
Karmo Nyida Chamsing = dKar-mo nyi-zla lcam-sring
Kartön José Chakyi Dorjé = dKar-ston jo-sras lCags kyi rdo-rje
Kawa Shākya Wangchuk = Ka-ba Shākya dbang-phyug
Kek Né-nying = sKegs gnas-snying
Kelkor = sKal-skor
Kham = Khams
Khampa Dorgyel = Khams-pa rDor-rgyal
Khampa Sengé = Khams-pa Seng-ge

Khamsum Sangkhang = Khams-gsum zangs-khang
Khangsar Yari-puk = Khang-gsar ya-ri-phug
Kharak = Kha-rag
Kharak Töpu = Kha-rag thod-phu
Kharak Tsangpa Kha-rag gtsang-pa
Kharchungwa = mKhar-chung-ba
Khaü-kyélhé = Kha'u-skyed-lhas
Khedrupjé = mKhas-grub-rje
Khépa-déü = mKhas-pa lde'u
Khyin-lotsāwa = 'Khyin lo-tsā-ba
Khölpo Sémong = Khol-po sre-mong
Khön = 'Khon
Khön Gyichuwa = 'Khon sGyi-chu-ba
Khön Könchok Gyelpo = 'Khon dKon-mchog rgyal-po
Khön Luï-wangpo = 'Khon kLu'i dbang-po
Khön Pelpoché = 'Khon dPal-po-che
Khön Shākya Lotrö = 'Khon Shākya bLo-gros
Khön Shérap Tsültrim = 'Khon Shes-rab tshul-khrims
Khon-ting = Kho-mthing
Khor-ré = 'Khor-re
Khu = Khu
Khutön Tsöndrü Yungdrung = Khu-ston brTson-'grus g.yung-drung
Khyentsé Wangchuk = mKhyen-brtse'i dbang-phyug
Khyungpo Draksé = Khyung-po Grags-se
Khyungpo Neljor = Khyung-po rNal-'byor
Khyungpo Sengé Gyeltsen = Khyung-po Seng-ge rgyal-mtshan
Khyungpo Yu'i-surpü = Khyung-po g.Yu'i zur-phud
Kongpo Agyel = Kong-po A-rgyal
Kongpo Yéjung = Kong-po Ye-'byung
Kongtrül = Kong-sprul
Kongtrül Lotrö Tayé = Kong-sprul bLo-gros mtha'-yas
Könpa Jégungtak = dKon-pa rJe-gung-stag
Kunga = Kun-dga'
Kunga-bar = Kun-dga'-'bar
Kunga Gyeltsen = Kun-dga' rgyal-mtshan
Kunga Nyingpo = Kun-dga' snying-po
Kunga Wangchuk = Kun-dga' dbang-phyug
Kuring dé-nga = Ku-rings sde-lnga
Kusulupa Zhang Yönten Rinchen = Ku-su-lu-pa Zhang Yon-tan rin-chen

Kya = sKya
Kyareng Tragmé = sKya-rengs khrag-med
Kyi Atsarya Yéshé Wangpo = Kyi Atsarya Ye-shes dbang-po
Kyichu = sKyid-chu
Kyidé = sKyid-lde
Kyirong = sKyi-grong
Kyobpa Pel-zangpo = sKyob-pa dPal bzang-po
Kyokpo Gateng = Kyog-po sGa-theng
Kyotön Shérap Dorjé = sKyo-ston Shes-rab rdo-rje
Kyura = sKyu-ra
Lachen = bLa-chen
Lama Dampa = bLa-ma dam-pa bSod-nams rgyal-mtshan
Lamdré = lam 'bras
Lamo Chagdéü = La-mo chag-de'u
Lang = rLangs
Langchung Pelgyi Sengé = rLangs-chung dPal-gyi seng-ge
Lang Darma = gLang dar-ma
Lang Khampa lotsāwa = bLang Khams-pa lo-tsā-ba
Langlap Jangchub Dorjé = Lang-lab Byang-chub rdo-rje
Langpa = Lang-pa
Langtön Jampa = gLang-ston Byams-pa
Latö = La-stod
Latö Dingrishé = La-stod Ding-ri-shed
Latö-lho = La-stod-lho
Latö-mar = La-stod-mar
Lé = gle
Leng Yéshé Zhönu = Leng Ye-shes gzhon-nu
Len Tsültrim Nyingpo = gLan Tshul-khrims snying-po
Len Yéshé Shérap = rLan Ye-shes shes-rab
Lha chenpo = Lha chen-po
Lha Dépo = Lha lDe-po
Lha Détsen = Lha lDe-btsan
Lha Kadampa = Lha bKa'-gdams-pa
Lha-lama Yéshé-Ö = Lha-bla ma Ye-shes-'od
Lhalung Pelgyi Dorjé = Lha-lung dPal gyi rdo-rje
Lhalung Rapjor-yang = Lha-lung Rab-'byor-dbyangs
Lhamo lamtso = Lha-mo bla-mtsho
Lha Totori Nyentsen = Lha Tho-tho-ri gnyan-btsan
Lhatsé = Lha-rtse
Lhatsé-drak = Lha-rtse'i brag

Lhatsün Kali = Lha-btsun ka-li
Lhatsün Ngönmo = Lha-btsun sngon-mo
Lhatsün Tönpa = Lha-btsun ston-pa
Lho-drak = Lho-brag
Lhüntsé = Lhun-rtse
Lingkha = gLing-kha
Lobpön Joden Rong-gom = sLob-dpon Jo-gdan rong-sgom
Lobpön Tencikpa Tsöndrü-drak = sLob-dpon sTan-gcig-pa brTson-'grus-grags
Lok-kyama = kLog skya ma
Lonak Tsuksen = Lo-nag gtsug-san
Lo-ngam Tadzi = Lo-ngam rta-rdzi
Longchen Chöjung = kLong chen chos 'byung
Long-tang Drölma = gLong-thang sgrol-ma
Lön Gungzher = bLon Gung-bzher
Lopo Lojung-bé = Lo-pho lo-byung sbas
Lotön = Lo-ston
Lotön Dorjé Wangchuk = Lo-ston rDo-rje dbang-phyug
lotsāwa = lo-tsā-ba
Lotsāwa Darma Yönten = Lo-tsā-ba Dar-ma yon-tan
Lotsāwa Drokmi Trakgi Relpachen = Lo-tsā-ba 'Brog-mi Phrag gi ral-pa-can
Lotsün = Lo-btsun
Lowo-lotsāwa Pelden Jangchub = bLo-bo lo-tsā-ba dPal-ldan byang-chub
Lu = klu
Lu Kargyel = kLu sKar-rgyal
Lumé = kLu-mes
Lumé Shérap Tsültrim = kLu-mes Shes-rab tshul-khrims
Lung-shö nampo = kLungs-shod nam-po
Lutsa Takpo Öchen = kLu-tsha stag-po 'od-chen
Ma = rMa
Machik Labdrön = Ma-gcig Lab-sgron
Machik Ödrön = Ma-gcig 'Od-gron
Machik Zhangmo = Ma-gcig Zhang-mo
Ma Chöbar = rMa Chos-'bar
Magom Chökyi Shérap = rMa-sgom Chos-kyi shes-rab
Makzorma = dMag-zor-ma
Ma-lotsāwa = rMa lo-tsā-ba
Malu-lotön Gélong Könchok-drak = sMa-klu lo-ston dGe-slong dKon-mchog-grags

Mamo Relpachen = Ma-mo ral-pa-can
Mañdzu-lingpa = Mañdzu-gling-pa
Mangkhar = Mang-mkhar
Mangkar Drilchen = Mang-kar dril-chen
Mangtö Ludrup Gyamtso = Mang-thos kLu-grub rgya-mtsho
Maṇi Kambum = *Maṇi bka' 'bum*
Ma Rinchen-chok = rMa Rin-chen mchog
Marpa Chökyi Lotrö = Mar-pa Chos-kyi blo-gros
Marpa Dorjé Yéshé = Mar-pa rDo-rje ye-shes
Mar Shākya Sengé = dMar Shākya seng-ge
Martön = dMar-ston
Mar-tsün Gyelwa = dMar-btsun rGyal-ba
Masang = Ma-sangs
Masang Chijé = Ma-sangs spyi-rje
Melgyo Lotrö Drakpa = Mal-gyo bLo-gros grags-pa
Mel-lotsāwa = Mal lo-tsā-ba
Mel Yerpawa = Mal Yer-pa-ba
Mé-tsönpo Sönam Gyeltsen = Mes-tshon-po bSod-nams rgyal-mtshan
Meü = rMe'u
Mikyö Dorjé = Mi-bskyod rdo-rje
Mila Repa = Mid-la ras-pa
Mogar Drésa = Mo-'gar 'bras-sa
Mora-gyel = Mo-ra-'gyel
Mönza Tsomo-gyel = Mon-bza' mtsho-mo-rgyal
Mu = dMu
Mugulung = Myu-gu-lung
Mushang-kyi Rokam = Mu-shangs kyi ro-skam
Muza Dembu = dMu-za ldem-bu
Nagtso-lotsāwa = Nag-tsho lo-tsā-ba
Nagtso Tsültrim Gyelwa = Nag-tsho Tshul-khrims rgyal-ba
Namdé = gNam-lde
Namdé Ösung = gNam-lde 'Od-srung
Namké Nyingpo = Nam-mkha'i snying-po
Nam-khaüpa = gNam-kha'u-pa
Namo shampo = sNa-mo sham-po
Nam-ra = Nam-ra
Namtang Karpo = rNam-thang dkar-po
Nanam = sNa-nams
Nang = sNang
Nartang = sNar-thang

Neljorpa Chenpo = rNal-'byor-pa chen-po
Neljorpa Shérap Dorjé = rNal-'byor-pa Shes-rab rdo-rje
Né-nying = gNas-rnying
Népo Drakpa Gyeltsen = sNe-po Grags-pa rgyal-mtshan
Né-sar = gNas-gsar
Nétso Beltön = Ne-tso sBal-ston
Néütang = Ne'u-thang
Nézhi = gNas-gzhi
Ngadak Trihchung = mNga'-bdag Khri-chung
Ngadak Trihpa = mNga'-bdag Khri-pa
Ngadak Tsédé = mNga'-bdag rTse-lde
Ngak-chang Ngagwang Kunga Rinchen = sNgags-'chang Ngag-dbang kun-dga' rin-chen
Ngak-nag Taktsa = sNgags-nag sTag-tsha
Ngakpa = sngags-pa
Ngari = mNga'-ris
Ngaripa Selwé Nyingpo = mNga'-ris-pa gSal-ba'i snying-po
Ngari-tö = mNga'-ris stod
Ngendzong Repa = Ngan-rdzong ras-pa
Ngenlam Gyelwé Wangpo = Ngan-lam rGyal-ba'i dbang-po
Ngok = rNgog
Ngok Chökyi Dorjé = rNgog Chos kyi rdo-rje
Ngok Dodé = rNgog mDo-sde
Ngok Jangchub Jungné = rNgog Byang-chub 'byung-gnas
Ngok Lekpé Shérap = rNgog Legs-pa'i shes-rab
Ngok-lotsāwa Loden Shérap = rNgog lo-tsā-ba bLo-ldan shes-rab
Ngoktönpa = rNgog-ston-pa
Ngoling = sNgo-gling
Ngom-shö = Ngom-shod
Ngönmo = sNgon-mo
Ngorchen Künga Zangpo = Ngor-chen Kun-dga' bzang-po
Ngozher nyiwa = sNgo-bzher snyi-ba
Nön = gNon
Nup = sNubs/gNubs
Nubchen Sangyé Yéshé = gNubs-chen Sangs-rgyas ye-shes
Nupchung = sNubs-chung
Nub Pelgyi Jangchub = sNubs dPal-gyi byang-chub
Nub Sangyé Rinchen = gNubs Sangs-rgyas rin-chen
Nubyül = gNubs-yul
Nyagdé = Nyag-lde

Nyagma = gNyags ma
Nyak = gNyags
Nyaktön = gNyag-ston
Nyak Tokpo = sNyags thogs-po
Nyalam = gNya'-lam
Nyaloro = gNya'-lo-ro
Nyang = Myang
Nyang-rel = Nyang-ral
Nyang-rel Nyima-özer = Nyang-ral Nyi-ma 'od-zer
Nyang-ro = Nyang-ro
Nyangtö Jangché = Nyang-stod byang-'chad
Nyel = gNyal
Nyen = gnyan
Nyen-chung Dharma-drak = gNyan-chung Dharma-grags
Nyénam-lang = sNye-nam-glang
Nyenchen Tanglha = gNyan-chen thang-lha
Nyen-lotsāwa Darma-drak = gNyan lo-tsā-ba Darma-grags
Nyentsé-tar = gNyen-rtse-thar
Nyétang = sNye-thang
Nyéwé Tungchöpa = Nye-ba'i-'thung-gcod-pa
Nyima-gön = Nyi-ma mgon
Nyima Gyeltsen = Nyi-ma rgyal-mtshan
Nyima Gyeltsen Pel-zangpo = Nyi-ma rgyal-mtshan dpal-bzang-po
Nyingma = rNying-ma
Nying-tik = sNying-tig
Nyi-ö Pelgön = Nyi-'od dpal-mgon
Nyiwa= sNyi-ba
Nyö = gNyos
Nyö-lotsāwa Yönten-drak = gNyos lo-tsā-ba Yon-tan-grags
Nyönpa Dönden = sMyon-pa don-ldan
Öbar = 'Od-'bar
Ödé = 'Od-lde
Odren Lotrö Wangchuk = 'O-bran bLo-gros dbang-phyug
Ogam Khudöl Sumdruk = 'Og-'am khu-dol gsum-'brug
Ökyi-bar = 'Od-skyid-'bar
Ölkha = 'ol-kha
Ompuk = 'Om-phug
Önpo Pelden Shérap = dbOn-po dPal-ldan shes-rab
Öser Bumé = 'Od-zer 'bum-me
Ösung = 'Od-srung

O-trön = ’O-phron
Pa = sPa
Padampa Sangyé = Pha-dam-pa Sangs-rgyas
Pa-dro = sPa-gro
Pagmo Drupa Dorjé Gyelpo = Phag-mo gru-pa rDo-rje rgyal-po
Pagor Bairotsana = sPa-gor Be-ro-tsa-na
Pakpa = ’Phags-pa bLo-gros rgyal-mtshan
Pakpa Wati = ’Phags-pa Wa-ti
Pangtang = ’Phang-thang
Pa-tsap = sPa-tshab
Pa-tsap lotsāwa Nyima-drak = sPa-tshab lo-tsā-ba Nyi-ma-grags
Pawa-désé = Pha-ba lDe-se
Pelchen Öpo = dPal-chen ’od-po
Peldé = dPal lde
Pelden Lhamo = dPal-ldan Lha-mo
Pelgi Dorjé = dPal-gyi rdo-rje
Pel Khortsen = dPal-’khor-btsan
Pelmo Pelta = dPal-mo dpal-tha
Pelsang Kharchak drilbu = dPal-bzang ’khar-chags dril-bu’i dgon-pa
Péma Dorjé = Pad-ma rdo-rje
Pema Marutsé = Padma ma-ru-rtse
Peṇchen Minyak Drakdor = Paṇ-chen Mi-nyag grags-rdor
Pen-yül = ’Phan-yul
Podrang Shiwa-Ö = Pho-brang Zhi-ba-’od
Po-gyü tsékhar = Pho-rgyud rtse-mkhar
Pön Gyel-lé = dPon-rgyal-le
Potoba Rinchen-sel = Po-to-ba Rin-chen-gsal
Puchungwa Zhönu Gyeltsen = Phu-chung-ba gZhon-nu rgyal-mtshan
Pukdrak *Kanjur* = Phug-brag *bKa’-’gyur*
Pukpoché = Phug-po-che
Purang = Pu-hrangs
Purang lotsāwa Zhönu Shérap = Pu-rangs lo-tsā-ba gZhon-nu shes-rab
Purap-lotsāwa = Pu-hrab lo-tsā-ba
Ra = Rwa
Rachak = Ra-chag
Rakshi Tsültrim Jungné = Rag-shi Tshul-khrims ’byung-gnas
Ralo Dorjé-drak = Rwa lo-tsā-ba rDo-rje-grags
Ra Lotrö Zangpo = Rwa bLo-gros bzang-po
Ra-lotsāwa = Rwa lo-tsā-ba rDo-rje-grags
Ramoché = Ra mo che

Ratna Lingpa = Ratna gling-pa
Ratön Könchok Dorjé = Rwa-ston dKon-mchog rdo-rje
Rechungpa = Ras-chung-pa
Régom-ma Köné = dbRad-sgom-ma dKon-ne
Ré Könchok Gyelpo = dbRad dKon-mchog rgyal-po
Relpachen = Ral-pa-can
Retreng = Rwa-sgreng
Rigpa-gön = Rig-pa-mgon
Rinchen Zangpo = Rin-chen bzang-po
Riwo Khyungding = Ri-bo khyung-lding gi lha-khang
Rok = Rog
Rok-ben Shérap-Ö = Rog-ban Shes-rab-'od
Rongkar = dbRong-kar
Rong Ngurmik = Rong Ngur-smig
Rongtön Lhagah = Rong-ston lha-dga'
Rongtön Sengé-drak = Rong-ston seng-ge-grags
Rongzom Chözang = Rong-zom chos-bzang
Rulak = Ru-lag
Sachen Kunga Nyingpo = Sa-chen Kun-dga' snying-po
Sadak = sa-bdag
Sag-shubma = Sag shubs ma
Saktang-ding = Sag-thang-sdings
Sakya = Sa-skya
Sakya Labrang = Sa-skya bla-brang
Sakyapa = Sa-skya-pa
Samyé = bSam-yas
Sangpu Néütok = gSang-phu ne'u-thog
Sangyé Gyamtso = Sangs-rgyas rgya-mtsho
Sangyé Lama = Sangs-rgyas bla-ma
Sangyé Rinpoché = Sangs-rgyas rin-po-che
Sarma = gsar ma
Sé = Srad
Sédönma = Sras don ma
Sédur = Se-rdu
Séjili = Se-byi-li
Sékhar Chungwa = Se-mkhar chung-ba
Sékhar Gutok = Sras-mkhar dgu-thog
Sénalek = Sad-na-legs Khri-sde srong-btsan
Sera Pukpa = Se-ra phug-pa
Sétön Kunrik = Se-ston Kun-rig

Sétön Sönam Öser = Se-ston bSod-nams 'od-zer
Sétsa Sönam Gyeltsen = Se-tsha bSod-nams rgyal-mtshan
Sé Yéshé Tsöndrü = Se Ye-shes brtson-'grus
Shabkyi Go-nga = Shabs kyi sgo-lnga
Shak-tsen = Shag-btsan
Shākya-drak = Shākya-grags
Shākya Shérap = Shākya shes-rab
Shalu = Zha-lu
Shang = Shangs
Shang Kharlung = Shangs-mkhar-lung
Shangpa Kagyüpa = Shangs-pa bKa'-brgyud-pa
Sharwapa = Shar-ba-pa
Shel-tsa Gyelmo = Shel-tsha rgyal-mo
Shen = gShen
Shenchen Lugah = gShen-chen kLu-dga'
Shengom Rokpo = gShen-sgom rog-po
Shepamo Chamchik = Shab-pa-mo lCam-gcig
Shiwa-Ö = Zhi-ba-'od
Shong Lotrö Tenpa = Shong-ston bLo-gros brtan-pa
Shöbu = Shod-bu
Shüpu = Shud-pu
Situ Chökyi Gyamtso = Si-tu Chos kyi rgya-mtsho
Sogdokpa Lotrö Gyeltsen = Sog-bzlog-pa bLo-gros rgyal-mtshan
Sölnak Tangboché = Sol-nag Thang-bo-che
Songtsen Gampo = Srong-btsan sgam-po
Sönam Gyamtso = bSod-nams rgya-mtsho
Sönam Tsémo = bSod-nams rtse-mo
Song-ngé = Srong-nge
Sumpa Khenpo = Sum-pa mkhan-po
Sumpa-lotsāwa Pelchok-dangpö Dorjé = Sum-pa lo-tsā-ba dPal-mchog dang-po'i rdo-rje
Sumpa Yéshé Lotrö = Sum-pa Ye-shes blo-gros
Sumtön Pakpa Gyeltsen = Sum-ston 'Phags-pa rgyal-mtshan
Sumtrang = gSum-'phrang
Sum-tsek = gSum-brtsegs
Taglo Zhönu Tsültrim = sTag-lo gZhon-nu tshul-khrims
Taglungpa = sTag-lung-pa
Tagtso = sTag-tsho (=sTag-lo)
Tagyapa = Thag rgya-pa
Taktsé = sTag-rtse

Taktsé-nyak = rTag-rtse-snyags
Tanak = rTa-nag
Tangpoché = Thang-po-che
Tangchen = Thang-chen
Tang = Thang
Tarpa lotsāwa = Thar-pa lo-tsā-ba
Témo Dorjé-tso = rTad-mo rDo-rje-'tsho
Tentreü = brTan-spre'u
Terma = gter-ma
Thar-pa lam-tön = Thar-pa lam-ston
Ti-shri Sangyé Réchen = Ti-shri Sangs-rgyas ras-chen
Tokpo = Thog-po
Toling = mTho-ling
Tölung = sTod-lung
Tön-kharda = Don-mkhar-mda'
Töpu = Thod-phu
Trandruk = Khra-'brug
Trang-ö = 'Phrang-'od
Trashi-gön = bKra-shis mgon
Trashi Tsekpel = bKra-shis brtsegs-dpal
Trihchung = Khri-chung
Trihdé = Khri-lde
Trihdé-bar = Khri-lde-'bar
Trihdé Göntsek = Khri-lde mgon-brtsegs
Trihdé Göntsen = Khri-lde mgon-btsan
Trihdépo = Khri-lde-po
Trihdé Songtsen = Khri-lde srong-btsan
Trihdé Yumten = Khri-lde Yum-brtan
Trihgong = Kri-gong
Trih Kyidé Nyimagön = Khri sKyi-sde nyi-ma mgon
Trih Namdé Tsenpo = Khri gNam-lde btsan-po
Trihpa = Khri-pa
Trih Öpo = Khri-'od-po
Trih Trashi Tsédé = Khri bkra-shis rTse-lde
Trihtsuk Détsen = Khri-gtsug lde-btsan
Trihsong Détsen = Khri-srong lde'u-btsan
Trölma = Khrol-ma
Trülgyel = 'Phrul-rgyal
Trumchu = Khrum-chu
Tsalana Yéshé Gyeltsen = Tsa-la-na Ye-shes rgyal-mtshan

Tsāmi = rTsā-mi
Tsami Lotsāwa Sangyé-drak = rTsa-mi lo-tsā-ba Sangs-rgyas-grags
Tsamo-rong = Tsha-mo-rong
Tsang = gTsang
Tsang tö-mé = gTsang stod-smad
Tsangdar Dépa Yéshé = gTsang-dar Dad-pa ye-shes
Tsangdram = gTsang-'gram
Tsang-nyön = gTsang-smyon
Tsangpa Gyaré = gTsang-pa rGya-ras
Tsangpopa Könchok Sengé = gTsang-po-pa dKon-mchog seng-ge
Tsang Rapsel = gTsang rab-gsal
Tsarchen Losel Gyamtso = Tshar-chen bLo-gsal rgya-mtsho
Tsé = Tshe
Tsédé = rTse-lde
Tsel = Tshal
Tselpa Kunga Dorjé = Tshal-pa Kun-dga' rdo-rje
Tsépongza = Tshe-spong-bza'
Tséroduk = rTse-ro-dug
Tséwang Norbu = Kaḥ-tog mkhan-po Tshe-dbang nor-bu
Tsi-lhakhang = rTsis lha-khang
Tsingé-tönpa Dülwa-dzinpa = Tsing-nge ston-pa 'Dul-ba 'dzin-pa
Tsingé-tönpa Gélong Shérap-drak = Tsing-nge ston-pa dGe-slong Shes-rab-grags
Tsokyé Dorjé = mTsho-skyes rdo-rje
Tsongdü = Tshong-'dus
Tsongkha Gönpa = gTsong-kha dgon-pa
Tsongtsün Shérap Sengé = Tshong-btsun Shes-rab seng-ge
Tsuglak Trengwa = gTsug-lag 'phreng-ba
Tsültrim Jangchub = Tshul-khrims byang-chub
Tsur-lhalung = mTshur lha-lung
Tsurpu = mTshur-phu
Tsur-tsün Gyelwa = mTshur-btsun rGyal-ba
Tupten Gépel = Thub-bstan dge-'phel
Tülwa Yéshé Gyeltsen = Thul-ba Ye-shes rgyal-mtshan
Tüsong = Dus-srong
Üpa Dröpoché = dBus-pa Grod-po-che
Urgyen Lingpa = U-rgyan gling-pa
Urgyen Terdak Lingpa = U-rgyan gter-bdag gling-pa
Uru = dBu-ru
Usé = dBu-se

Ü Shatsar = dBus-sha-tshar
Ü-Tsang = dBus-gTsang
U-tsé = dBu-rtse
Utsé Nyingma = dBu-rtse rnying-ma
Wa / Wé = dBa'/dBa's
Wangchuk-özer = dBang-phyug 'od-zer
Wangchuk-trih = dBang-phyug-khri
Wangdé = dBang-lde
Yalung = g.Ya'-lung
Yamdrok nak-khim = Ya-'brog gnags-khyim
Yamshü Gyelwa-ö = Yam-shud rgyal-ba-'od
Yangdak = Yang-dag
Yapang Khön-bar-kyé = g.Ya'-spang 'khon-bar-skyes
Yapang-kyé = g.Ya'-spang-skyes
Yarlha Shampo = Yar-lha Sham-po
Yarlung = Yar-lung
Yarlung sog-kha = Yar-lungs sog-kha
Ya-tsün Könchok Gyelwa = dBya'-btsun dKon-mchog rgyal-ba
Yé = g.Yas
Yerpa = Yer-pa
Yéru = g.Yas-ru
Yéshé Dorjé = Ye-shes rdo-rje
Yéshé Gyeltsen = Ye-shes rgyal-mtshan
Yéshé-Ö = Ye-shes-'od
Yöl-togbep = Yol thog-'bebs
Yo-gejung = g.Yo dge-'byung
Yoru = g.Yo-ru
Yönru = g.Yon-ru
Yuchen = g.Yu-spyan
Yu-drak = g.Yu-brag
Yu-kharmo = g.Yu-mkhar-mo
Yumbu Lagang = Yum-bu gla-sgang
Yumdönma = Yum don ma
Yumten = Yum-brtan
Yuné = g.Yu-[s]ne
Yungtön Tro-gyel = g.Yung-ston Khro-rgyal
Yung-wa ché-chung = Yung-ba che-chung
Yuring = g.Yu-ring
Yuru = g.Yu-ru (= g.Yo-ru)
Yutok = g.Yu-thog

Zangpo Drakpa = bZang-po grags-pa
Zangri = zangs-ri
Zangskar lotsāwa = Zangs-dkar lo-tsā-ba
Zha-gé désum = Zha-gad sde-gsum
Zhama Chökyi Gyelpo = Zha-ma Chos-kyi rgyal-po
Zhama Macik = Zha-ma Ma-gcig
Zhang Chöbar = Zhang Chos-'bar
Zhang Gönpawa = Zhang dGon-pa-ba
Zhangjé Séné = Zhang-rje Sad-ne
Zhangtön Darma Gyeltsen = Zhang-ston Dar-ma rgyal-mtshan
Zhang Nanam Dorjé Wangchuk = Zhang sNa-nam rdo-rje dbang-phyug
Zhang Tsültrim-drak = Zhang Tshul-khrims-grags
Zhang Yu-drak-pa = Zhang g.Yu-brag-pa
Zhangyül Jakshong = Zhang-yul 'Jag-gshong
Zhangzhung Gurawa = Zhang-gzhung Gu-ra-ba
Zhang Ziji = Zhang gZi-brjid
Zhé-lhakang = Zhwa'i lha-khang
Zhi-ché = Zhi-byed
Zhong-pa = Zhong-pa
Zhu = Zhu
Zhuchéma = Zhu byas ma
Zhutön Tsöndru = Zhu-ston brtson-'grus
Zhutön Zhon-nu Tsöndru = Zhu-ston gZhon-nu brtson-'grus
Zugah Dorjé = gZu-dga' rdo-rje
Zurchen = Zur-chen
Zurchöpa Pel-midikpa = Zur-chos-pa dPal mi-dig-pa
Zurchung Shérap Drakpa = Zur-chung Shes-rab grags-pa
Zurpoché = Zur-po-che
Zur Shākya Jungné = Zur Shākya 'byung-gnas

Appendix 1

EASTERN VINAYA TEMPLES, CAVE TEMPLES, AND RESIDENCES IN THE MID-ELEVENTH CENTURY

Ka chu
Ka tshal
Ke ju
Kri gong
dKar sna
sKul gyi khe ldir
Kha rag labs so
Kha rag so gcig
Khams gsum
Kho lha khang
Khyim phu'i dge dgon
Khra sna'i gnyan po gnas
Khra pa'i gnang khang
Khra'i sgom ra
Khra'i dben chen
Khrig gi sgang bu
Khris kyi kha chad dgon pa
Khrol ma
'Khor re skyi sgang
'Khor re ba khor
mKhan gyi zu ra phug
Gangs bar lha khang
Gan pa'i she btsun gnas
Go ro mtshar rna
Go shul lha rtag
Gya ba'i dang gnya'
Gye re glang ra
Gye re'i mda' grong
Grang chung
Gra'i se lung
Gri phug
Gru gu sgang
Gru shul cha khrod
Gro mo che
Grom pa rgyang
gLang mda'
dGe rgyas
dGon ser
mGur mo lha khang
mGos ston
rGya gar
rGya thang
rGyags mda'i lha khang
rGyan gong ri phug
rGyal sar sgang
rGyal lug blangs lha khang
rGyud kyi ber chung
sGa thang skar ma thang
sGa ra sgal po kha
sGyi'i khrig
sGre mkhar
Ngan lam pa'i dbyi mo
Ngur smrig
sNgo gling
bsNgur gyi ste dkyus
lCags mkhar

lCe pa'i la'i gnas
Cha khrod
Cha chung 'gur
Cha tog
Cha rags gong pa kha
Chags ra sgang
Chag sa
Chang sdong
Chu mig ring mo
Chu shul na bo
mChil ka'i rgyal thang
Jo mo
'Jed kyi gnas brgyad
rJem gyi gnas
Nyang ro bud mdo
Nyangs smad khri'u gnas
Nyan po dgon pa
Nyan rdzing skam
Nyi rong khon ba rkyang
Nyug gi 'U lung
gNyal gyi bzang ru
sNyan btsun gnas
sNye thang brag sna
sNye mo sgo mo
bsNyems
Ta mo ra
gTam shul gyi mda'i dgon po
rTa nag phu'i bya tshang
lTu'i rgyan gong
sTag gi gras po che
sTag tshal dkyus thang
sTag tshal gyi bya cho mkhar po che
sTag lo lha khang
sTod lung yab kyi ra tshag
sTod lungs cha thog
sTod lungs thag ma
Thag ma lha khang
Thang skya
Thang chung
Dug chung
De kha rgal
Do la ri mo
Dong mkhar phug
Don mo ri
Drung gi sgo 'dul
gDang gi drug spyid
'Dol chung
'Dres tshe stag nag bye tshang
lDan gyi dre shod
lDing pa'i gnas
bsDag gi gad lnga
bsDag gi gral lnga
Nang khol gyi gral ma thang
Ne'u'i gnas
gNam khang
gNam gyi rtse ldeng
gNas rnying
gNas gzhi
gNas gsar
sNa nam 'dre brdes
sNa bzhi lha khang
sNang gsal lha khang
Pa tshab kyi mjo phug lha khang
sPa ra rte dkyus
sPang dkar lha lung
sPun gsum
sPyil gyi 'dzim pa lung
Pho 'gal
Phyag gi kham khung
Phyi nas thang sgrong dgon pa
Phyi lung
'Phan yul 'jog po'i klu gong
'Phan yul gyi brag rgya
'Phan yul 'Tshar sna
Phrang 'og gi lha khang
'Phrang
Ba shi
Ban gyi bya tsha
Ban pa thib spyi
Ban pa drug ral
Ban pa'i sgro ba
Ba'ang kyi ra gor
Bar thang bye
Bu tshal
Bum thang
Bur gyi 'dzangs pa

Bya rgyus
Byang thang Wal gnas
Byang phyi'i sribs mda' gnas
Brag rgyab
Brag dmar
Brag rum gnas gsar
Brang gi chu bskor gnas
Brang ra mo che
Bran ma sgang
dbUs sde lto gong
dbYe'i lha khang
sBu sde lho gong
sBre lha khang
Mang mkhar mu gu lung
Man lung chu ngu
Mar la thad
Mi chos kyi sa khul du ba gnas lam
Mu shangs kyi ro skam
Mes phreng
Mon mkhar 'gan
Mon gra
Myang ro 'dre brdas
Myu gu sna'i gyang ra dmar po
Mrug gi gnas gsar
dMar sgang
dMe ru at 'Bro sa thang
sMa ris gong ma
sMon gro
gTsang 'gram
gTsang gzhug gnas
bTsan po ldings
rTsis kyi yang dben
rTsis lha khang
rTswa thang
Tsha mig
mTsal chung
mTshur gyi snyan dmar
mTsho smad lha khang
rDzing stag
rDzi'i skyer lung
Zha phu
Zha lu
Zhal gyi bsnams khang
Zhal gyi tshul chen
Zho brang
Zhog pa
Zhwa'i lha khang
gZha'i spang ri
gZhu po
gZhung sgre mkhar
gZhu'i kun dga' ra ba
gZhu'i zangs can
gZho'i 'chad kha
bZang yul spang bzangs
bZad kyi lding ba
bZad kyi sogs pa ri
bZad bu'i rog dom
Yugs kyi zham tshong stengs
Yungs 'gur
Yer pa
Yer pa Bab rang
Yol thang
g.Yag sde'i sog po dgon pa
g.Yu sgro khang dmar
g.Yo ru gra thang
'U yug mda'i ra shag
'O yug gi spen phug
'Om phug
'Ol tshal grags pa de
Ra chag
Ra sog mtshar la
Rab btsun gnas
Ri mer chad thib
Re lha khang
La chung
La stod ma la thang
La mo chag lde'u
La mo ze sna
Lan 'gro ba'i stag tshang
Lan pa spyil bu
Lan pa'i pho brang
Lab so
Las stod seng rtser
Lung kha phu
Shangs kyi bye phug bzung
Shangs mkhar lung

Shab kyi 'dar sgang
Shab kyi lha mo lung
Sa la tshugs
Ser gyi brag shong
So kha
Sol nag Thang po che
Srad kyi gung gsum
Srad kyi ltang ldang
Sri'i rgya phibs

gSas khang
gSer gyi sgong thog
bSam yas dbU rtse
bSam yas dbU tshal
Lha khang rma ru
Lha mdo
Lhan gyi ba so thang
Lhas kyi lku mgon
Lhing pa'i gnası

Appendix 2

THE *ROOT TEXT OF THE *MĀRGAPHALA*: TRANSLATION AND EDITION OF THE *LAM 'BRAS BU DANG BCAS PA'I GDAMS NGAG DANG MAN NGAG TU BCAS PA*

The Instructions on the Path, Together with Its Fruit, Along with Technical Directions

Homage to the lotus feet of the holy teacher! I should now note the succinct expression of the "Path & Fruit."

[The Extensive Path]

I. [Teaching the Path Common to Both Existence and Nirvāṇa.]

A. [The path taught as the triple appearance.][1]

1. Sentient beings perceive impure appearance based on their defilements.

2. Yogins perceive the appearance of meditative experiences based on their concentration.

3. Sugatas perceive pure appearance based on the ornamental circle of their inexhaustible body, speech, and mind.

I. B. [The path taught as the triple continuity.]

1. The causal continuity of the universal field is the root continuity because it contains all of existence and nirvāṇa.[2]

2. But for the physical body, which is the continuity of method, etc.,[3] *there is:*

a. The causal consecration by means of the four trinities of site, etc., etc.[4]

b. The teaching by means of the four quinaries on the path, the generation stage, etc.[5]

c. The protection of the contemplative commitments, etc.[6]

d. Reparations made to Vajraḍāka, etc.,[7] *for faults and transgressions are to be done by satisfaction, etc., through the five objects of the senses, etc.*[8]

e. Through meditation on the four consecrations during the four times of daily practice of the path, based in the body, obscurations to great bliss become the articulate continuity with their clarification in the awakened state.[9]

3. The fruitional continuity of the Great Seal is omniscience through the four fruitional consecrations.[10]

I. C. [The path taught as the four epistemes.]

Having defined the fruit by the four epistemes,[11]

I. D. [The path taught as the six instructions.][12]

1. Meditative poisons are expelled by the three modes without the fault of incongruity, etc.[13]

2. (a) [Avoidance of and] reliance on food, activity, breath, semen, and a consort; (b) bliss of the five essences; and (c) nonseparation from the experience of the five senses: with these one will rely on [i.e., partake of] the nectars.[14]

3. (a) The four channels of existence, the cakras, and the others.[15] *(b) On the first and last plane [one knot is released]; by the ten triples there is release through the untying of knots on the intermediate [ten stages].*[16]

4. The poisons of one's perspective are expelled through meditation on the pure conceptualization on the path of clarifying the occurrence of thoughts.[17]

5. Since the five sense fields are not rejected by the five varieties of sensory consciousness, there is reliance on the nectar [of sensation].[18]

6. There is release through the pure phenomena dawning as primordially empty.[19]

I. E. [The path taught as the four aural streams]

There is the nonseverance of the four, the aural stream of the secret mantras, etc.[20]

I. F. [The path taught as the five forms of interdependent origination][21]

1. Based on a physical body with distinguishing characteristics,

2. There is the interdependent origination of the limit of existence.

3. This is the interdependent origination dependent on another (paratantra).

4. The path here is the path [leading to] great awakening.

5. The interdependent origination of all phenomena is the sequential episteme.[22]

6. The purified great awakening is the underlying consciousness (ālayavijñāna).

7. The path is entirely completed by the five forms of interdependent origination.

I. G. [The special explanation of the protection from obstacles applying to the paths occupied with skillful means, insight, or both.]

1. Obstacles[23] *to the path for a yogin occupied with skillful means will be protected against as follows: by firm faith; or by the circle of protection, by muttering of mantras, and by the knot of protection; or by the appearance of phenomena as mind, being interdependent origination, namely, dependent on another. Since the latter is like the reflection in a mirror, he will be thus protected by the nonseparation from the meaning of the ocean of reality.*

2. Obstacles to the path for a yogin occupied with insight will come in two forms: external demons, which come when one does not comprehend them as the transformation of the two paths and eight perspectives and accomplishments; and the internal obstacles, which will come when one does not comprehend the signs and the ten paths, etc. There will be protection for these yogins when these obstacles are comprehended correctly.[24]

3. There is protection from the veils, the obscurations, and the loss of seminal fluid.[25]

II. [Teaching the Existential Path in which the Cakras Are Coaxed.][26]

A. [Summary of the cause for the arising of concentration.]

1. Having obtained, from the path of accumulation, the four fruits separating one from the ordinary body speech and mind,[27]

2. By means of the three ways of coalescing the essence in the [seven] balanced modes,[28]

3. If one traverses the path according to the thirty-seven elements of awakening,[29] *having self-empowered*[30] *the vital wind and the mind,*

4. Then there are the four bases of psychic power (ṛddhipāda)[31] *relating to undissipated cultivation:*[32] *the wind of activity and the masculine, feminine, and neuter winds.*[33] *Because there is incineration by the gnosis of crossing over,*[34] *at the first coalescence of the essence the channels open up as if by the winter wind with its "implement" [its frigid bite].*[35] *[Thus there is discomfort,] such as mental experience,*[36] *dreaming of horses, etc., and physical discomfort in the channels. There are the knots of the various channels, etc.*

5. The primary [and subsidiary] vital winds make ten. By the seven determinants of their constraint, the [five] subsidiary vital winds are by degrees internally arrested.[37] *Many of the seminal nuclei open up and become blended together with the foundation.*[38] *Based on that [meditation], the mind resides internally; the five consciousnesses are collected internally; the five aggregates are tamed; and there is the intermittent arrival and departure of gnosis.*

6. There are visions, dreams, and [physical] experiences relating to undissipated cultivation, in three sections each [resulting in nine items total]. In the case of that ["heat"] preceded by conceptualization, the experience modifies the appearance of the triple world.[39]

7. (a)[40] *When "earth" merges into "water," there is an illusion. When "water" merges into "fire," there is smoke. When "fire" merges into "air," there is the appearance of fireflies. When "air" merges into consciousness, there is the ignition of a butter lamp. When consciousness merges into clear light, it is like the sky on a cloudless day. When the vital wind of "earth," "water," "fire," or "air" coalesces with the mind, then [in the case of the vital wind of fire,] the entire triple world appears as if on fire. With the vital wind of water, the follicles of the body feel cold. With the vital wind of air, the mind cannot concentrate, and [in sleep, one dreams of] one's own flight and the rising of flocks of birds.*[41] *With the equal operation of all four of the elemental vital winds [earth, water, fire, and air], various goddesses offer their dance [in visions and dreams]. With the various mixtures of the vital winds of the four elements, one experiences smells and tastes. With the preponderance of the vital wind of "space" [coalescing with the mind], there is the physical feeling of bliss in the follicles.*[42]

b. With the five nectars there is [the vision of] the bodies, etc., of the Sugatas.[43] *Through the Sihla [menstrual blood] there is the experience of the sun. Through the Gapura [semen] there is the experience of the moon. By the subtle seminal nuclei in the minor channels, there is the experience of the many stars.*

c. (i) In controlling the channels, etc., there are the experiences of [the body as] a tree trunk and of the five emotions: desire, anger, and the rest [present as letters in the heart].[44] *There are the channels of anxiety, of sorrow, of demons, and the appearance of tears and yawning through the tear channel.*

c. (ii) One might coalesce in equal measure the vital wind and mind into the letters of the six families which first come together in the navel [during gestation].[45] *If so, then the whole triple world appears in light of the experience of being led into [birth among] the six families [of beings, feeling] their dances and [vocalizing] their mantras; the experience is carried over into dreams and physical sensations.*

c. (iii) From OṀ *there is the concentration (samādhi) of meditation (dhyāna), etc.*[46] *If [the mind/vital wind] correctly merges into the* ĀḤ *of the woman's "sky," then the entire triple world appears as space. If they are merged into the citadel of the great mother, the perfection of insight, etc., then one experiences the dharmakāya and the liberation of subject and object. If [merged] into the clarity and lightness developed from the* HŪṂ, *then one experiences the very pure sky of the self-originated gnosis. The channels are opened by the gradually abating "implement" of the wind in the intermediate coalescence of the essence.*[47] *So, even with the discomfort of the seminal nuclei, there is stability of the visions in the world.*[48]

II. B. [Explanation of the path that extensively delineates the cause for the rise of meditation.][49]

Briefly, in [the letters] RAKṢA, *etc., the demons, etc., there is the sound from that which has a bell and vision like the pure eye of the gods.*[50] *These are considered the occurrence of meditative experience from the "zenith of existence" (bhavāgra) on down.*[51] *Showing what is inexpressible, this method is hidden to [those on] the five [paths] and the ten [stages of the method of the Mahāyāna perfections].*[52]

II. C. [The explanation of the path separate from hope and fear.]

The triple ternaries of inverted vital wind, etc., are the external interdependent origination of undissipated cultivation.[53] *The internal [interdependent origination] consists of the five ḍākinīs [= five winds] and the five bodies of the Tathāgatas [= five secretions].*[54] *These [external and internal interdependent originations] are made the interdependent origination of great awakening. By this action, the yogin knows that the perfected powers (siddhi) arise from his own body. With this understanding, the thought of hoping or searching for these (siddhis) is cleansed. Knowing that the demons and obstacles to meditation are one's own path and interdependent origination, then the defects are taken up as qualities. Thus, the intensity (heat: ūṣmagata: drod) of the path, in order or out of order, is accepted for the chaos it is.*[55]

II. D. [The path explained as the four awakenings.][56]

As the Devaputra Māra comes on the path for a yogin occupied with insight, he is protected by the four awakenings.[57]

II. E. [Explanation of the path of the four bases of recollection.][58]

Now the four bases of recollection pertaining to undissipated cultivation: As the sensory fields have been obstructed, the yogin thinks of the necessity of summoning and generating one's chosen divinity, since there must be equal divisions within the meditation.[59]

II. F. [Fruit of the four bases of recollection][60]

At the final coalescence of the essence, the channels are opened as if by [the summer] wind, which is without an "implement" [harsh bite].[61] *With the coalescence of the seminal fluid within the six senses, the yogin correctly cognizes the six recollections (anusmṛti).*[62] *He sees some nirmāṇakāyas. Now as to the four correct renunciations (samyakprahāṇa)*[63] *relating to undissipated cultivation [during the fourth consecration]: The disciple reflects on the cognition arisen following the third consecration by [his guru who is the same as] the nirmāṇakāya. He seeks for the hidden vein in his consort, a twelve-year-old "padminī," who is a "happy one," etc.*[64] *The heart's* A *[goes] to the tip of the "nose" of the avadhūtī [central channel] and the "leisurely" and "mobile," etc., forms of the vital wind are pushed within [the central channel] by the intellect with seasoned intelligence.*[65] *By this means, there occurs the vajra posture of the body, speech, and mind.*[66] *Then the vital wind is pressed by the seminal fluid [into the central channel]. Thus, one does not hear the sound of drums, etc., [and becomes unreceptive to the senses]. By these and indicative of them, one overcomes the Māras [obstacles] of thinking "this is sufficient," etc. At that point, the path of the internal Buddhas has proceeded to the zenith of existence. Although [previously] tolerance toward unarisen phenomena (anutpattikadharmakṣānti) was difficult, now [the yogin experiences] tolerance toward emptiness. In the central channel, his mind returns to the nonconceptual, and even if the mind should migrate, there is tolerance. This is beyond all existential phenomena. Since the phenomena on the path of nirvāṇa is completely perfected, this path constitutes the best of all phenomena (agradharma).*

II. G. [Conclusion.]

*In that manner—whether the experience is defective or not—the mind and vital wind are brought together into the "*A *of external form" and moved upward. Those elements arisen on the path are essence, proper nature, and characteristics.*[67]

III. [Teaching the Supermundane Path That Revolves the Cakras.]

A. 1. On the supermundane path, by means of the path of external and internal interdependent origination,

The yogin obtains the naturally spontaneous nirmāṇakāya. Because of the generation stage path, one completes the vase consecration which purifies the body.

Now as to the seven branches of awakening that constitute the sign of this obtainment's reality: they are the four citadels of the precious veins and the three ladies.[68] *Having thus seen the physical maṇḍala, one engages the coming and going of conceptualization.*[69] *He vibrates*[70] *a hundred pure lands of the nirmāṇakāyas, listens [to the nirmāṇakāyas in these hundred pure lands preach the Dharma], gives a hundred gifts, diffuses a hundred lights, teaches a hundred of those below himself, and becomes able to enter into a hundred different contemplations.*[71] *Having in particular seen the basis for human existence*[72] *in the vein of the six realms of beings, he experiences both happiness and apprehension.*[73] *He is repulsed by [his previous] shameful behavior. At this moment he realizes the doctrines of the indivisibility of saṁsāra and nirvāṇa ('khor 'das dbyer med), which the teacher had previously imparted during the causal consecration.*[74] *Then compassion is born, and tears naturally come. The yogin understands the different mentalities of others and bursts into laughter when he sees the various sensory objects. Because he sees the interior pure lands, [he can demonstrate] all the various miracles in a single moment.*[75] *What is not seen internally is likewise not observed externally. At this moment, his penis becomes erect. In the same way as it is experienced when the seminal fluid is held at the tip of the vajra in the natural level,*[76] *his entire body is intoxicated with bliss, and he feels overcome. He does not recognize the differentiation of self or other. The internal sign is that the breaths of inhalation and exhalation are each arrested by an inch.*[77] *The external sign is that half the genital cakra is firm with the seminal fluid. This is the first stage, that of the path of vision.*

2. Moreover, from the nirmāṇakāya the four fourfold consecrations are received.[78] *From the second stage, which is on the path of cultivation, the yogin is able to vibrate, etc., a thousand purelands of the nirmāṇakāya, etc. His qualities, etc., increase, and the coming and going [of conceptualization] cease. The internal sign is that inhalation and exhalation are each arrested by six inches. The external sign is that genital, navel, and heart cakras are firm with the seminal fluid. He sees some of the sambhogakāyas. This is the sixth stage, on the path of cultivation.*

III. B. Again, from the sambhogakāya the four fourfold consecrations are received. Through the path on which is practiced the self-consecration, the yogin obtains the naturally spontaneous sambhogakāya. This is the conclusion of the secret consecration that purifies speech. The sign of its reality is that the yogin obtains authority over the five faculties and over the five vital winds of the five vital fluids.[79] *He is unhindered in five abilities and unhindered in his use of the gazes.*[80] *He sees the seeds of the six families of beings within the bhagamaṇḍala and gains authority over the six seed syllables.*[81] *He is able to teach the Dharma to beings in their own languages, and [his understanding] is unhindered toward the general and specific characteristics of phenomena.*[82] *Having seen the eight source letters in the navel as [i.e., transform into] the vowels and consonants, he becomes unhindered toward the twelve branches of the Dharma announced by the Buddha and contained in the sūtrapiṭaka.*[83] *He is able to enjoy the five nectars and the six flavors. The "pure sounds" are clarified by the six verse feet of "the syllable A," etc.*[84] *From the seventh stage up, he is able to vibrate, etc., the 108 pure lands of the sambhogakāyas, etc., sealed within the four cakras.*[85] *The internal sign is that inhalation and exhalation are each arrested by fully ten inches. The external sign is that as far as the throat and eyebrow cakras, the cakras are firm with the seminal fluid. This is the tenth stage, on the path of cultivation.*

III. C. Again, from the dharmakāya the four fourfold consecrations are received. The path on which is practiced the method of the maṇḍalacakra, purifies the mind.[86] *By means of that path, the yogin obtains the naturally spontaneous dharmakāya; this is the conclusion of the insight-gnosis consecration. The sign of its reality is that the yogin sees the fundamental bodhicittamaṇḍala, which is the quintessential essence that controls the five powers and the five vital winds of bodhicitta; with the vision the signs become apparent.*[87] *Having obtained the consecration of the three bodies of the Buddha and the five forms of gnosis, etc., if one sees the five nectars coalescing into the appropriate vein, then one views the Buddhas working for the benefit of others.*[88] *If one is sees the seminal fluid coalesced into [central channel from] the nirmāṇacakra [in the navel] to the mahāsukhacakra [in the fontanel], then he sees the Buddhas subtly residing in the locus of Akaniṣṭha. If he sees the five nectars and the five vital winds coalesce into the nirmāṇacakra in the navel, then he sees the five families of the sambhogakāya, who, resident in the mothers' bhaga, disseminate the secret [mantra path] to worthy bodhi-*

sattvas.[89] *If he sees the mudrā's quintessential essence, then he becomes unhindered toward the supercognitions.*[90] *If he leads the essence into the letters inside the veins, then he will be unhindered toward magical powers. If he is subsequently reincarnated, then he will remember his previous existences. The internal sign is that inhalation and exhalation are each arrested by all twelve inches.*[91] *The external sign is that the entire fontanel cakra is firm with the seminal fluid. This is the twelfth stage, on the path of cultivation.*

III. D. 1. Again, there is the four fourfold consecration. Through this path of culmination there is the ultimate purification by means of the ultimate interdependent origination. Through this path of the adamantine wave (rdo rje rba rlabs), there is the highest perfection of the Great Seal (mahāmudrā). It is the knowledge being (vidyāpuruṣa), the path of the purification of ordinary existence. With this, the yogin obtains the naturally spontaneous svabhāvikakāya. This stage is the culmination of the fourth consecration of the body, speech, and mind. The sign of its reality is that the eightfold noble path consists of the obtainment of the two fruits with the purification of the eight consciousnesses.[92] *Then this great earth is happy, delighted, and overjoyed, so that it quakes in six different ways.*[93] *Sound [of defeat] resounds in the residence of Māra.*[94] *The yogin sees the triple world in the place of the mudrā.*[95] *Ḍākas assemble coming from distant areas. The eight varieties of dominion arise: minuteness and the rest.*[96] *The internal sign is that both the vital winds of inhalation and exhalation enter into the central channel. The external sign is that half the uṣṇīṣa is firm with the seminal fluid. This is the twelfth and a half stage.*

2. Proceeding to the culmination of the fourth, or mental, consecration, the yogin obtains the unique fruit, which is the sign of its reality.[97] *By means of bodhicitta, he breaks open the realm of existence which is the city of the Vindhya prince (*vindhyakumāranagaradharmadhātu).*[98] *The yogin is able to vibrate, etc., myriads (prasuta) of the fruitional dharmakāya pure lands, etc.*[99] *As soon as he obtains the thirteenth stage, he attracts consorts of the tenth stage, etc. The coalescence of the savor of the Tathāgatas of the three times becomes the preceptor. By means of the interdependent origination that obtains accomplishment in the vagina through the indivisibility of the chosen divinity and the teacher, there is the path that completely purifies existence. Obtaining the naturally spontaneous exceedingly pure svabhāvikakāya is the culmination of the fruit. The sign of its reality is that he is able to vibrate, etc., the fruitional svabhāvikakāya pure lands without exception, etc. The internal sign is that the vital winds of inspiration and expiration are arrested in the central channel. The external sign is that the entire uṣṇīṣa is firm with seminal fluid. By means of the dissolutions of the four gradations ('gros bzhi thims)—which constitute the interdependent originations of exterior and interior—since there is a transformation and elimination of defects in the experience of cultivation that has previously occurred, the yogin arrives at the thirteenth stage.*[100] *Then he becomes omniscient.*

3. On this thirteenth stage, that of Vajradhara, interdependent origination appears as if in complete conformity. At the point at which he becomes a Buddha, all his retinue also become Buddhas as a unit.

IV. A. Now the adamantine vehicle of secret spells is really constituted by consecra-

tions: those of the cause, the path, and the fruit. Although it is marked by conceptual thought, it realizes nonconceptual reality. Accordingly, there is the appearance of gnosis.

B. [The Deep Path, Middling Path, and Abbreviated Path]

*The deep path of the teacher, the esoteric commitment, and the individual suppression through the physical body (*vāpuḥpratisaṁkhyānirodha).*

[Colophon]

The Instructions on the Path, Together with Its Fruit, Along with Technical Directions is completed. Finished.

Lam 'bras bu dang bcas pa'i gdams ngag dang man ngag du bcas pa[1]

bla ma dam pa'i zhabs pad la[2] *btud de | lam 'bras gsung mdo bri bar bya |*

[Lam rgyas pa][3]

[I. 'Khor 'das thun mong gi lam bstan pa]

A. [sNang ba gsum du bstan pa'i lam]

1. sems can la | nyon mongs pa la | ma dag pa'i snang ba[4] *|*

2. rnal 'byor pa la[5] *| ting nge 'dzin la*[6] *| nyams kyi snang ba |*

3. bde bar gshegs pa la[7] *| sku gsung thugs mi zad pa rgyan gyi*[8] *'khor lo la | dag pa'i snang ba'o ||*

B. [rGyud gsum du bstan pa'i lam]

1. kun gzhi rgyu rgyud la 'khor 'das tshang bas[9] *rtsa rgyud |*

2. lus thabs rgyud stsogs[10] *la a. gdan stsogs stsogs*[11] *gsum pa bzhis*[12] *rgyu'i dbang | b. lam du bskyed rim stsogs*[13] *lnga pa bzhis bstan | c. mnyam gzhag gi dam tshig stsogs bsrung | d. rdo rje mkha' 'gro stsogs kyi*[14] *nyams chag*[15] *bskang | 'dod yon stsogs lngas*[16] *mnyes pa stsogs [11] bya | e. lam gyi thun bzhi la dbang bzhi bsgoms*[17] *pas lus la brten nas bde chen gyi sgrib pa 'gag*[18] *cing 'tshang rgya bar gsal bas bshad rgyud |*

3. phyag rgya chen po 'bras bu'i rgyud ni 'bras bu'i dbang bzhis thams cad mkhyen to |

C. [Tshad ma bzhi ru bstan pa'i lam]

tshad ma bzhis 'bras bu gtan la phab nas |

D. [gDams ngag drug tu bstan pa'i lam]

1. 'gal 'dus[19] *skyon med stsogs gsum gyis bsam gtan gyi dug dbyung |*

2. a. zas | spyod lam | rlung | thig le | phyag rgya ma bsten | b. dwangs ma[20] *lnga'i bde ba dang | c. dbang po lnga nyams dang ma bral bas bdud rtsi*[21] *bsten |*

3. a. 'khor ba'i rtsa bzhi dang | 'khor lo rnams dang[22] *| gzhan rnams dang | b. sa thog mtha' la*[23] *re re | gsum pa bcus*[24] *bar gyi rtsa mdud dral bas la dor |*

4. 'jug pa sel ba'i lam yid 'dag pa'i rnam rtog bsgoms[25] *pas lta ba'i*[26] *dug dbyung |*

5. rnam shes lngas yul lnga ma [12] spangs bas[27] *bdud rtsi bsten |*

6. dag pa'i chos rnams gdod nas stong par shar bas la dor |

E. [sNyan brgyud bzhir bstan pa'i lam]

gsang sngags snyan brgyud[28] *stsogs bzhi ma chad pa*[29] *|*

F. [rTen 'brel lngar bstan pa'i lam]

1. lus khyad par can la brten nas |

2. dngos[30] *po'i mtha' rten cing 'brel bar 'byung ba |*

3. gzhan dbang rten 'brel |

4. byang chub chen po'i lam |

5. chos thams cad rten cing 'brel bar 'byung ba lo rgyus kyi tshad ma[31] *|*

6. kun gzhi'i[32] *rnam shes dag pa'i byang chub chen po |*

7. rten cing 'brel bar 'byung ba lngas lam yongs su rdzogs pa'o |[33]

G. [Thabs shes kyi phyogs su lhung ba'i lam gyi bar chad srung ba'i bye brag bstan pa[34]*]*

1. thabs kyi phyogs su lhung ba'i rnal 'byor pa'i lam gyi bar chad ni | dad pa brtan pos bsrung[35] *| srung ba'i 'khor lo*[36] *| sngags zlos | sngags mdud*[37] *| chos rnams sems nyid snang ba | gzhan dbang rten 'brel | gzugs brnyan yin phyir de kho na nyid rgya mtsho'i don dang ma bral bas bsrung |*

2. shes rab la phyi'i bdud la[38] *lam gnyis | lta grub*[39] *brgyad bsgyur ba 'ong*[40] *| nang lam*[41] *stsogs bcu dang brda ma shes na 'ong | shes pas*[42] *bsrung |*

3. grib dang sgrib pa thig le 'dzag pa bsrung ||

II. ['Khor lo 'cham pa 'jig rten pa'i lam bstan pa]

A. [Ting nge 'dzin skye ba'i rgyu mdor bstan pa]

1. tshogs lam nas tha mal pa'i lus ngag yid dang bral ba'i[43] *'bras bu bzhi*[44] *thob nas*[45] *|*

2. khams 'du lugs gsum gyis[46] *phyogs med rnams dang |*

3. rlung sems bdag byin gyis brlabs[47] *nas | byang chub kyi phyogs dang mthun pa'i chos sum cu rtsa*[48] *bdun ltar lam bgrod na |*

4. bsgom pa[49] *mi 'chor ba'i rdzu 'phrul gyi rkang pa bzhi ni*[50] *| las kyi rlung | pho | mo | ma ning gi rlung | thod rgal ye shes*[51] *kyi me 'bar bas khams 'dus pa dang po dgun gyi rlung po*[52] *lag cha can gyis rtsa dral | sems gnas | rta rmi | rtsa lung gi zug 'byung | rtsa sna [13] tshogs mdud stsogs |*

5. gzhi rtsa ba'i rlung stsogs bcu[53] *| zin pa'i bye brag bdun gyis yan lag gi rlung rim gyis nang du 'gag*[54] *| thig le*[55] *mang du kha 'bu | rten mnyam du 'dre*[56] *| de la brten nas sems nang du gnas | rnam shes lnga nang du*[57] *'dus | phung po lnga dul | ye shes kyi 'gro ldog byed |*

6. bsgom pa mi 'chor ba'i mthong snang | rmi lam | nyams gsum gsum ni rnam rtog sngon du song ba ltar khams gsum kun du snang ngo |

7. a. sa chu la thim na smig rgyu | chu me la thim na du ba | me rlung la thim na srin bu me khyer | rlung rnam par shes pa la thim na mar me 'bar ba | rnam par shes pa 'od gsal la thim na nam mkha' sprin med[58] *lta bu | sa chu me rlung dang rlung sems mnyam par 'dus na khams gsum kun tu me lta bur snang ngo |*[59] *chu rlung dang*[60] *spu lus grang | rlung gi rlung 'du 'phro dang | rang 'phur | bya 'byung | 'byung bzhi'i*[61] *rlung mnyam rgyu dang | lha mo sna tshogs kyis gar mchod | 'byung bzhi'i rlung sna tshogs dang dri ro | nam mkha'*[62] *dang mnyam pa dang spu lu*[63] *bde |*

b. bdud rtsi lnga dang de[64] *bzhin gshegs sku stshogs | sihla dang nyi ma | ga bur dang zla ba | rtsa bran*[65] *rnams su thig phran*[66] *dang skar ma |*

c. i. rtsa 'dzin stsogs su shing sdong stsogs | chags sdang rnam pa lnga dang | nyam nga[67] *| mya ngan | 'dre'i rtsa | mchi ma'i*[68] *rtsar g.yal dang mchi ma | ii. lte bar dang po chags pa'i rigs drug gi yi ger rlung sems mnyam par 'dus na | rigs drug gi gar | sngags | der khrid pa | rmi lam | nyams lta bur khams gsum kun tu snang ngo*[69] *| iii.* OṀ *las bsam gtan stsogs kyi ting nge 'dzin | yum gyi mkha'* ĀḤ *la*[70] *yang dag par thim na* *khams [14] gsum nam mkha' | yum chen mo shes rab kyi pha rol tu phyin ma stsogs kyi pho brang du thim na[71] chos sku nyams su myong zhing gzung 'dzin[72] grol |* HŪṀ *las gsal zhing yang la[73] rang byung[74] gi ye shes nam mkha' shin tu dri ma med | khams 'dus pa bar pa rlung po[75] lag cha bri bas rtsa dral | thig le'i zug[76] dang mthong snang brtan no |*

B. [Ting nge 'dzin skye ba'i rgyu rgyas par bstan pa'i lam bstan pa]

mdor na rakṣa stsogs su srin po stsogs | dril[77] can gyi sgra | lha'i mig rnam par dag pa bzhin | srid pa'i rtse mo man cad ting nge 'dzin gyi nyams su 'byung ba snyam byed pa | bshad kyis mi lang ba[78] mtshon cing | lnga bcu la gsang |

C. [Re dogs dang bral ba'i lam bstan pa]

bsgom pa mi 'chor ba'i phyi'i[79] rten 'brel rlung log[80] stsogs gsum gsum ni | nang gi mkha' 'gro lnga[81] | de bzhin gshegs pa'i sku lnga byang chub chen po'i rten 'brel mdzad pas | dngos grub rnams rang las[82] 'byung bar shes shing | shes pas[83] re zhing rtsol ba'i[84] blo sel to | bdud dang gol sa rnams rang gi lam[85] dang rten 'brel du shes pas skyon yon tan du bslang zhing | rim pa yin min du skye ba'i drod[86] byung rgyal du gtang ngo[87] |

D. [Sad pa bzhir bstan pa'i lam bstan pa]

shes rab kyi phyogs su lhung ba'i lam la lha'i bu'i bdud 'ong bas[88] sad pa bzhis bsrung |

E. [Dran pa nyer gzhag gi lam bstan pa]

bsgom pa mi 'chor ba'i[89] dran pa nye bar gzhag pa bzhi ni | yul 'gags pas[90] rang yi dam gyi lha dang gug skyed kyi dgos pa bsam zhing | ting nge 'dzin cha mnyam pas[91] |

F. [(Dran pa nyer gzhag) de'i 'bras bu bstan pa]

khams 'dus pa tha ma rlung po lag cha bral bas rtsa dral |[92] skye mched drug gi nang du thig le 'dus pas rjes su dran pa drug yang dag par shes | sprul sku 'ga' mthong | bsgom pa mi 'chor ba'i yang dag par spong ba bzhi ni | sprul sku las | dbang gsum gyi rjes la[93] 'byung ba'i[94] shes pa bsam zhing | dgyes[95] stsogs pad can bcu gnyis ma'i rtsa btsal [15] zhing | snying po'i A *kun 'dar[96] gyi sna rtser dal rgyu[97] stsogs rigs pas[98] yid 'jug pas | lus ngag yid rdo rje'i[99] skyil krung bcas[100] | thig les[101] rlung non pas rnga sgra stsogs mi thos pas | chog shes pa stsogs kyi bdud choms bas so[102] | nang gi[103] sangs rgyas rnams kyi lam srid pa'i rtse mor phyin cing | ma skyes pa'i[104] chos la bzod par dka' ba[105] stong pa nyid kyi bzod pa[106] | dbu mar sems rtog med log sems 'phos na[107] bzod pa | 'khor ba'i chos las 'das shing | mya ngan las 'das pa'i lam chos rnams yongs su[108] rdzogs pas chos rnams kyi nang na[109] mchog go |*

G. [mJug bsdud bstan pa]

de ltar nyams skyon can dang[110] | skyon med dang | phyi dbyibs kyi A *na[111] yar rlung sems mnyam par 'dus nas | lam du 'byung ba rnams ngo bo | rang bzhin | mtshan nyid do[112] ||*

III. ['Khor lo bskor ba 'jig rten las 'das pa'i lam bstan pa]

A. 1. 'jig rten las 'das pa'i lam la |

[rgyu] phyi nang rten[113] cing 'brel bar 'byung ba'i lam gyis

['bras bu] sprul sku rang bzhin gyis lhun grub 'thob par byed pa[114] | bskyed pa'i rim pa'i lam nas[115] | lus 'dag par byed pa[116] bum pa'i dbang mthar phyin |

[rtags] de kho na nyid kyi rtags byang chub kyi yan lag bdun ni | rtsa rin po che'i

pho brang bzhi | gtso mo[117] *gsum ste lus kyi dkyil 'khor mthong nas*[118] *| rtog pa'i*[119] *'gro ldog byed | sprul sku'i zhing khams brgya bsgul zhing | nyan*[120] *| sbyin brgya | 'od brgya 'gyed | mar brgya 'ched*[121] *| ting nge 'dzin mi 'dra ba brgya la snyoms par 'jug nus | rigs drug gi rtsar khyad par du mi'i rten mthong na*[122] *| dga' la*[123] *g.yang za | ngo tsha la skyug bro | sngon bla mas rgyu dus na bstan pa'i*[124] *'khor 'das dbyer med de tsam na rtogs*[125] *| snying rje skye | mchi ma ltung*[126] *|[16] gzhan gyi sems sna tshogs shes | 'dod yon sna tshogs mthong bas dgod bro*[127] *| rdzu 'phrul sna tshogs skad cig mas*[128] *'byung ba rnams nang gi zhing khams mthong bas so | nang ma mthong bar phyi mi mthong | de tsam na lingga brtan | rdo rje'i rtser*[129] *lhan cig*[130] *skyes pa'i sar thig le gnas pa ltar*[131] *lus bde bas myos shing brgyal*[132] *| rang gzhan ngo mi shes | nang rtags rlung sor gcig 'gag*[133] *| phyi rtags gsang gnas phyed thig les brtan |*

[mjug bsdud] mthong lam[134] *sa | dang po'o ||*

2. *[rgyu] yang sprul sku las*[135] *dbang bzhi bzhi*[136] *|*

[rtags] sgom lam sa gnyis nas[137] *sprul sku'i*[138] *zhing khams stong la stsogs pa sgul ba*[139] *la stsogs pa nus | yon tan stsogs 'phel | 'gro ldog stsogs 'gag*[140] *| nang rtags rlung sor drug 'gag | phyi rtags gsang gnas lte snying*[141] *thig les brtan | longs sku 'ga' mthong |*

[mjug bsdud] sgom lam sa drug pa'o[142] *|*

B. *[rgyu] yang longs sku las dbang bzhi bzhi |*

['bras bu] bdag byin gyis rlabs[143] *pa'i rim pa'i lam nas longs sku rang bzhin gyis*[144] *lhun grub 'thob par byed pa | ngag 'dag par byed pa gsang ba'i*[145] *dbang mthar phyin |*

[rtags] de kho na nyid kyi rtags dbang po lnga dang | dwangs ma lnga'i rlung lnga la[146] *mnga' brnyes | nus pa lnga dang | lta stangs rnams*[147] *la thogs pa med | bha ga'i dkyil 'khor du*[148] *rigs drug gi*[149] *sa bon mthong | sa bon drug la mnga' brnyes | sems can rnams kyi skad du chos ston cing | chos spyi dang rang gi mtshan nyid la thogs pa med | lte bar yi ge'i phyi mo*[150] *brgyad* Ā LI KĀ LIr *mthong nas*[151] *| mdo sde'i chos gsung rab yang lag bcu gnyis la thogs pa med | bdud rtsi lnga dang ro drug la longs spyod nus | tshangs pa'i dbyangs su gyur pa rnams* A *ni [17] yig 'bru zhes stsogs*[152] *drug gis gsal lo | sa bdun pa yan chad longs sku'i zhing khams 'khor bzhi'i rgya dung phyur*[153] *la stsogs pa sgul ba*[154] *la stsogs pa nus | nang rtags rlung sor bcu 'gag*[155] *| phyi rtags mgrin*[156] *smin thig les brtan |*

[mjug bsdud] sgom lam sa bcu pa'o[157] *||*

C. *[rgyu] yang chos sku las*[158] *dbang bzhi bzhi |*

['bras bu] sems 'dag par byed pa[159] *dkyil 'khor 'khor lo'i thabs*[160] *kyi lam nas chos sku rang bzhin gyis*[161] *lhun grub 'thob par byed pa shes rab ye shes*[162] *kyi dbang mthar phyin |*

[rtags] de kho na nyid kyi rtags stobs lnga dang[163] *byang chub kyi*[164] *sems kyi rlung lnga spyod pa'i*[165] *dwangs ma'i dwangs ma rtsa ba byang chub sems kyi dkyil 'khor mthong nas rtags bstan pa*[166] *| sku gsum ye shes lnga stsogs dbang*[167] *thob nas | bdud rtsi lnga rtsa gar 'du ba mthong na*[168] *| sangs rgyas rnams gzhan don mdzad pa mthong | sprul pa bde chen du*[169] *thig le 'du ba mthong na | sangs rgyas rnams 'og min gyi gnas na zab mo la bzhugs pa mthong | lte ba sprul par bdud rtsi lnga dang rlung lnga 'du ba*[170] *mthong na | longs sku*[171] *rigs lnga yum gyi bha ga na bzhugs nas skal ldan byang chub sems dpa' la*[172] *gsang ba sgrogs pa mthong | phyag rgya ma'i dwangs ma'i dwangs*

ma mthong na mngon shes la thogs pa med | rtsa yig rnams su dwangs ma 'drongs na rdzu 'phrul la[173] *thogs pa med | de nyid slad spos na*[174] *sngon gyi gnas rjes su dran | nang rtags rlung sor bcu gnyis 'gag*[175] *| phyi rtags spyi gtsug hril thig les brtan*[176] *|*

[mjug bsdud] sgom lam[177] *sa bcu gnyis pa'o ||*

D. 1. [rgyu] yang dbang bzhi bzhi[178] *|*

['bras bu] mthar phyin gyi lam nas[179] *| mthar thug rten 'brel gyis mthar thug [18] 'dag par byed pa*[180] *| rdo rje rba rlabs kyi lam nas*[181] *| phyag rgya chen po mchog gi dngos grub | rig ma'i skyes bu srid pa rnam par dag pa'i lam | ngo bo nyid kyi sku rang bzhin gyis*[182] *lhun grub 'thob par byed pa | bzhi pa lus ngag yid kyi*[183] *dbang mthar phyin |*

[rtags] de kho na nyid kyi rtags 'phags pa'i lam yan lag brgyad ni | rnam shes brgyad 'dag kar 'bras bu gnyis thob ste[184] *| sa chen 'di ni*[185] *dga' zhing rangs la mgu | de rnam pa drug tu g.yos*[186] *| bdud gnas su sgra grag | phya rgya ma'i gnas su khams gsum mthong | mkha' 'gro rnams*[187] *ring nas 'du |* HA RI MA *la stsogs pa dbang phyug gi don brgyad 'char | nang rtags srog rtsol* A VA DHŪ TĪr *'jug*[188] *| phyi rtags gtsug tor phyed thig les brtan |*

[mjug bsdud] sa phyed dang bcu gsum pa'o ||

2. bzhi pa yid kyi dbang mthar phyin | de kho na nyid kyi rtags 'bras bu gcig thob ste[189] *| 'bigs byed gzhon nu'i gron khyer chos kyi dbyings byang chub sems kyis ni 'bigs | 'bras bu chos sku'i*[190] *zhing khams rab bkram la stsogs pa sgul ba*[191] *la sogs pa nus | sa bcu gsum thob kar sa bcu ma la stsogs pa yid kyis bkug ste | slob dpon dus gsum bder gshegs bcud 'dus yin*[192] *| yi dam lha dang bla ma dbyer med las*[193] *bha gar*[194] *dngos grub len pa'i rten 'brel gyis | srid pa rnam par dag pa'i lam | ngo bo nyid kyi sku shin tu rnam par dag pa rang bzhin gyis*[195] *lhun grub*[196] *'thob par byed pa*[197] *'bras bu mthar phyin | de kho na nyid kyi rtags 'bras bu ngo bo nyid kyi sku'i zhing khams*[197] *ma lus pa la stsogs pa sgul ba*[198] *la sogs pa nus*[199] *| nang rtags srog rtsol* A VA DHŪ TĪr *'gag*[200] *| phyi rtags gtsug tor hril [19] thig les brtan*[201] *| phyi dang*[202] *nang gi rten 'brel 'gros bzhi*[203] *thim pa rnams kyis sgom nyams*[204] *skyon yod med phyed pas*[205] *| sa bcu gsum pa'o*[206] *| thams cad mkhyen to |*

3. bcu gsum rdo rje 'dzin sar[207] *rten 'brel 'grigs pa ltar snang*[208] *| 'tshang rgya kar 'khor tshom bu gcig dang bcas te 'tshang rgya*[209] *|*

IV. A. gsang sngags rdo rje theg pa ni[210] *| rgyu dang lam dang 'bras bu'i dbang | rtog pas brtags kyang rtog med rtogs*[211] *| ye shes snang ba de bzhin no |*

B. [Lam zab 'bring gsum du bstan pa]

lam zab bla ma | dam tshig | lus so sor brtags pa'i 'gog pa |

[Colophon] lam 'bras bu dang bcas pa'i gdams ngag dang man ngag du[212] *bcas pa rdzogs sho || samāptam ithī ||*

Appendix 3

CONCORDANCE OF AVAILABLE EARLY LAM-'BRAS COMMENTARIES, TWELFTH TO FOURTEENTH CENTURY

LAM-'BRAS SECTION	GNYAGS MA	SRAS DON MA	ZHU BYAS MA	KLOG SKYA MA	ZLA RGYAL MA	BANDE MA	SGA THENG MA	YUM DON MA	'A 'U MA	DAN LBU MA	GSUNG SGROS MA	POD NAG MA	RGYUD-LUGS RNAM 'GREL[a]
Intro	21.3	11.2	2.1	192.1	398.1	2.1	150.1	2.1	162.1	298.1	2.1	124.1	104:2.1
I.A	23.1	30.5	8.1	201.1	404.3	6.1	162.4	10.4	166.4	302.1	21.5	143.4	24.6
B	26.1	44.1	10.5	205.3	408.1	8.4	171.3	13.6	168.2	304.4	33.1	154.5	52.3
C	52.4	170.5	84.1	275.6	455.5	69.5	276.5	75.2	201.4	375.3	139.4	269.4	105:18.4
D	53.1	175.5	88.1	279.5	458.1	72.3	280.2	78.3	202.2	376.4	144.3	275.4	35.2
E	59.5	197.5	96.6	290.2	463.3	79.1	296.2	85.2	208.6	396.2	163.6	289.1	90.2
F	60.6	201.3	98.2	291.6	464.2	80.2	299.2	86.6	210.6	397.6	166.4	290.6	94.4
G	61.2	205.3	100.6	294.2	465.4	81.3	303.1	88.5	212.4	400.2	170.4	296.5	102.1
II.Intro	67.5	241.4	114.2	307.2	475.4	92.3	333.5	99.4	218.5	412.4	192.1	320.2	104.5
II.A	70.3	253.6	116.6	307.5	475.6	94.6	342.1	100.1	220.1	414.2	199.3	327.5	153.6
B	91.4	341.2	140.3	343.4	500.3	115.1	405.2	125.5	243.5	449.3	233.4	369.2	212.5
C	93.2	351.5	142.2	345.5	501.3	116.3	409.5	127.2	246.2	449.4	236.1	372.3	229.4
D	95.3	358.1	143.6	349.2	502.6	117.5	414.2	129.3	248.1	451.5	238.4	376.1	236.3
E	95.5	358.6	144.2	349.4	503.1	117.6	414.4	129.3	248.2	452.1	239.1	376.5	236.4
F	98.1	364.1	146.3	352.2	504.3	119.3	418.5	130.6	249.3	455.2	241.4	379.5	242.5
G	101.2	378.6	150.5	357.6	507.1	123.1	429.1	134.3	255.1	460.6	248.5	387.2	257.2
III.A	101.6	381.1	151.1	358.4	507.3	123.4	429.5	134.5	256.1	461.2	249.1	388.3	365.4
B	109.2	398.3	159.6	367.4	513.2	129.4	445.1	140.4	266.2	474.4	260.6	399.3	386.2
C	112.5	407.3	165.3	373.5	516.3	133.2	454.3	144.5	271.4	478.4	267.5	406.6	391.3
D	117.6	417.4	171.5	379.5	519.3	138.1	467.1	148.4	278.5	483.6	275.5	414.4	395.6
IV.A	126.1	442.6	185.4	392.2	526.4	146.3	486.3	156.3	291.1	496.1	292.1	429.2	408.1
B	126.5	443.6	186.2	393.1	527.1	147.2	487.4	157.2	292.1	496.5	292.6	430.3	409.2
Colophon	127.3	445.1	186.6	393.6	527.4	147.5	488.4	157.5	292.5	497.2	293.5	431.2	410.3

NOTE: [a] The *rGyud lugs rnam 'grel* is was given the fuller name of *rTsa ba rdo rje'i tshig rkang rgyud lungs kyi rnam par 'grel pa bshad pa* by the editors of the *Bo dong gsung 'bum*, although the name by which it was known is uncertain and its authorship is in question. It is found in the *Encyclopedia Tibetica*, vols. 104.2.1 through 105.414.4; section I.B continues from 104.52.3 to 105.18.4, as the table indicates, but may be unclear.

Notes to Appendices

NOTE TO APPENDIX 1

1. Sources for this appendix include *mKhas pa lde'u chos 'byung*, 390–94; *sBa bzhed zhabs btags ma*, Stein 1961, pp. 87–89; *Chos 'byung me tog snying po sbrang rtsi'i bcud* pp. 451–53; *mKhas pa'i dga' ston*, vol. 1, pp. 467–81; *rGya bod kyi sde pa'i gyes mdo*, pp. 297.1.3 ff.; *rGya bod yig tshang*, pp. 458–70; and *Bu ston chos 'byung*, Szerb 1990, pp. 62–80. For the *sNgon gyi gtam me tog phreng ba*, the tables in Uebach 1987, pp. 39–43, are most helpful for that important source.

NOTES TO APPENDIX 2

1. The *sGa theng ma* (162.4) organizes the exegesis of this section as the basis for a certain kind of appearance (*rten*: sentient beings, yogins, and Sugatas), the appearance (*snang ba*: impure, experience, pure), and the cause of the appearance (*rgyu*: defilements, concentration). Other commentaries follow a *rten*, *rgyu*, *snang ba* scheme, which is reflected in the sentence syntax (*Bande ma* 6.1; *Sras don ma* 30.6; *gNyags ma* 23.3). The commentaries emphasize that the cause of pure appearance is *not* specified and is the "dissolution of the four movements" (*'gros bzhi thims pa*; *Sras don ma* 43.1; *gNyags ma* 25.5; *sGa theng ma* 170.5; *Bande ma* 8.2;) which the text later identifies (see sections I.B.3 and III.F) as the means of entering the thirteenth stage of Vajradhara. This explanation is not entirely satisfactory, for it ignores the strong parallelism of the text here, indicating that the means might be considered the *sku gsung thugs mi zad pa rgyan gyi 'khor lo*, although this is doctrinally problematic.

2. This idea is quite old, being at least evident from the time of the *Mahāyānābhidharmasūtra's* statement, quoted, for example, in *Ratnagotravibhāgabhāṣya* to I.152: anādikāliko dhātuḥ sarvadharmasamāśrayaḥ | tasmin sati gatiḥ sarvā nirvāṇādhigamo 'pi ca || There is a beginningless element, the basis of all phenomena. When it occurs, all avenues of being occur, as well as the realization of nirvāṇa. See Johnston (*Ratnagotravibhāga*), p. 72, n.; and Takasaki 1966, p. 290, n., for some references.

3. Here the commentaries indicate that the physical body is also the articulate continuity (*bshad rgyud*) as well as the continuity of method. Sa-chen explains that it is the articulate continuity as well, because it is the means to realize the poten-

tials in the causal continuity of the underlying consciousness (*Sras don ma* 50.5–6; *sGa theng ma* 183.5; *gNyags ma* 27.2–4; these do not entirely agree with one another). The explanation is minimally incomplete and indicates the problems of the early commentaries yet reflects the text in some sense, since the term "articulate continuity" is included in I. B.2.e.

4. The three sites (*gdan* : *pīṭha* according to *Pod nag* 162.2) are those of (a) the Buddhas and bodhisattvas, (b) the *vidyās* and the goddesses, and (c) the masculine and feminine angry guardians (*krodha*). These are recognized in four *maṇḍalas*: the colored dust *maṇḍala* (*rdul mtshon gyi dkyil 'khor*), the gnostic beings' *maṇḍala* (*ye shes kyi dkyil 'khor*), the commitment beings' *maṇḍala* (*dam tshig gi dkyil 'khor*), and the mantric *maṇḍala*. Alternatively, the *sGa theng ma* (177.3) lists five: the colored dust *maṇḍala*, the physical *maṇḍala* (*lus dkyil*), the qualities' *maṇḍala* (*bhaga'i dkyil 'khor*), the *bodhicitta maṇḍala*, and the absolute awakening *maṇḍala* (*don dam pa byang chub*). Each of these *maṇḍala*s is also employed during the causal consecration, that is, the fourfold initiatory events that occur: the vase, secret, insight-gnosis, and fourth initiations. Both the *sGa theng ma* (183.6) and *Sras don ma* (51.2, 55.3) state that the first "etc." indicates the vase consecration, while the second indicates the three higher consecrations. Other explanations are, for example, found in *Bande ma* 14.1–5. *gNyags ma* 28 is unclear on the text at this point.

5. Each of the four consecrations—vase, secret, insight-gnosis, and fourth—is divided into five further topics (a quinary for each), although at least one source adds a sixth topic before the five. See chapter 8, table 7, page 310.

6. For each of the consecrations there are five *samaya*, a term that includes both vows and sacramental behavior: contemplative, performative, consumptive, shielded, and inseparable *samayas*, according to the following chart (*sGa theng ma* 260.3–262.5; *Bande ma* 63.2–64.3):

SAMAYA	VASE CONSECRATION	SECRET CONSECRATION	INSIGHT-GNOSIS	FOURTH CONSECRATION
Contemplative	*Utpattikrama*	*Svādhiṣṭhāna-krama*	*Maṇḍala cakra*	Three vajra waves
Performative	Three realities	Four self-born joys	Four ascending joys	Four descending joys
Consumptive	Five nectars and meats	Emptiness and clarity	Bliss	Bliss and emptiness
Shielded from	Twenty-two breaches of commitments	All problems within the veins or wind	Six forms of semen release	Obscurations from ignorance
Inseparable	Never apart from the vajra and *ghaṇṭa*	Soft and harsh breath as appropriate	Physical or imaginary consort	Padminī consort, physical or imaginary

Notice that the *samaya* are, in part, a restatement of the twenty categories in the "four quinaries of the path" given in the previous section (chapter 8, table 7), especially noticeable in the contemplative and performative rows, which mimic the path and perspective of the previous diagram.

7. Five *ḍāka* are listed to whom reparations are to be made: (a) the Vajraḍāka, who is the guru; (b) the Jñānaḍāka, which is concurrent with the sambhogakāya; (c) the Mātrikāḍāka, who is the nirmāṇakāya; (d) the *Māṁsabhakṣanaḍāka, who is the Śmaśānādhipati; and (e) the Samayaḍāka, who are the adamantine relatives and friends in the sacred community. See *sGa theng ma*, 265.1–3, *Bande ma*, 65.3.

8. Depending on the variety of fault, offerings of external goods and their appropriation, along with the internal experiences of enjoyment, may be offered to a physical consort dressed in ornaments, or she may be offered to the teacher. Alternatively, for the more important transgressions of the five *samaya* noted in the preceding table, the five *ḍāka* may be appeased. These variations are indicated by the "etc." of the line.

9. This idea is an extension of the doctrine that in the Vajrayāna, the defilements of the individual become the nature of his path: *skyon yon tan du slong ba'i gdams ngag* (*Sras don ma*, 22.6–23.2). Compare *Hevajra-tantra* I.ix.19 and see the discussion of the epithets of the Lam-'bras in chapter 8.

10. The four fruitional consecrations are identified as the four ways of dissolution (*'gros bzhi thim*), those pertaining to the channels, the syllables, the nectar, and the vital air (*rtsa yi ge mdud bdud rtsi rlung gi 'gros*) made possible by the four causal consecrations. These four result in the four (or five) bodies of the Buddha. See *Sras don ma*, 168.5–70.4; *sGa theng ma*, 275.2–76.5. There is an alternative discussion in *sGa theng ma*, 267.3–5, which says that an idea of fruitional consecration is known in nonesoteric Buddhism as well, a recognition that the idea of abhiṣeka first arose to show that a bodhisattva was coronated as the successor of the Buddha(s); see *Daśabhūmika*, chapter 10, *passim*.

11. Three extremely important lists are mentioned in passing but are not actually specified in this first part of the *Lam 'bras rtsa ba*: the four epistemes, the four aural streams, and the five forms of interdependent origination. The first list (*sGa theng ma*, 276.5–80.2; *Sras don ma*, 170.5–75.5) indicates the authoritative nature of knowledge gleaned from (a) the scriptures, which are the word of the Sugata (*bde bar gshegs pa'i bka' yang dag lung gi tshad ma*); (b) the instructions of the guru (*rang gi bla ma rdo rje slob dpon gyi nyams kyi man ngag tshad ma*); (c) the experience gained in yoga (*rnal 'byor pa bdag nyid nyams myong rjes su dran pa'i tshad ma*); and (d) the interdependent continuity as sequential (*dngos po'i mtha' rten cing 'brel bar 'byung ba lo rgyus kyi tshad ma'o*). The final one needs some comment. It is interpreted in Sa-chen's commentaries simply as *pratītyasamutpāda* defined in a time-space continuum, that is, not the interrelation of events in the horizon of present experience but through time as well, definitely in keeping with normative Indic descriptions of the doctrine. This definition is explicitly encountered in section I.F.5. In the exegesis for that section, Sa-chen specifies that *lo rgyus tshad ma* indicates

the gradations of realization, from the mundane path through the absolute awakening of the Buddha (*sGa theng ma*, 301.3–5, and see the note to I.F.5). However, the later tradition almost invariably interprets this as the authoritative nature of the lineage and uses this to justify giving the lineal hagiographies (*lo rgyus*) pride of place in the bundled materials comprising the Lam-'bras, and the lineage intersection is broached in a single note in *Sras don ma*, 203.4–5: "And in one sense, this episteme indicates the realization of interdependence, so that from the Ādibuddha Vajradhara until one's own teacher, there has been the lineage of instructions from mouth to ear." I have not seen this application of *pratītyasamutpāda* in Indic materials. While *pratītyasamutpāda* certainly does define the interrelation among elements composing the ostensible continuity of a person through the previous, present, and future lives, I have never seen it represented as the continuum of relations among lineal teachers, meant to include their hagiographical identities. Conversely, *lo rgyus* clearly means the chronology of events and points to a genre of literature: the annals. Perhaps the Sa-skya use indicates a greater semantic field in the tenth and eleventh century, which was excluded as the term became completely identified with the hagiographical genre. For the context of the esoteric appropriation of epistemological language, see Davidson 1999; for the *tshad ma bzhi* as appropriated by bKa'-brgyud-pa masters, see Martin 2001b, pp. 158–76.

12. Generally Sa-chen's commentaries invert the order of the members of this section, dealing with perspective first (I.D.4–6) and then with meditation (I.D.1–3). The *'A 'u ma*, 202–8, is a curious exception to this practice, for it retains the order as given in the *Lam 'bras rtsa ba.* According to *sGa theng ma*, 287.3–4, the three on perspective apply to pacific contemplation (*śamatha*) as the antidote to obscurations on the defiling emotions (*kleśāvaraṇa*), whereas the three concerning meditation (*bsam gtan* : *dhyāna*) apply to superior insight (*vipaśyanā*) as an antidote to obscurations about the knowable (*jñeyāvaraṇa*).

13. The *gNyags-ma*, 56.3–4, lists the three as the mode without the fault of incongruity with the nonduality in thusness (*ngo bo nyid la zung 'jug 'gal 'dus skyon med*), the mode without the fault of incongruity with the emptiness and clear light of self-originated great gnosis (*rang byung ye shes chen po gsal stong 'gal 'dus skyon med*), and the mode without the fault of incongruity with the bliss and emptiness of simultaneous joy found in the natural and the pure (*lhan skyes dang shin tu rnam dag la lhan cig skyes pa'i dga' ba bde stong 'gal 'dus skyon med*). The poisons here are enumerated as eight; *sGa theng ma*, 287.5.

14. *sGa theng ma*, 289.4–5, says that members of each of the categories should be avoided, for example, onions, and specific members should be enjoyed, partaken of, consumed, experienced, and other forms of consumptive significance under the general aegis of "relied on" (*bsten pa* : **ālambayitavya*).

15. The four channels of existence are the two main veins on either side of the body, which separate into four below the navel, a front and a back branch for each of the two. The cakras are rather complex in the Lam-'bras system: within two the bodhicitta is nonmoving (*acala* : *mi g.yo*), but within four it is mobile. Beyond them,

the twelve great joints of the body (*tshigs chen*) have their own cakras. The "others" reference the thirty-two subsidiary veins, and their thirty-two knots; *sGa theng ma*, 293.5–94.4.

16. Section I.D.3.b refers to the central or the "nirvāṇa vein" (*mya ngan las 'das pa'i rtsa*), whereas section I.D.3.a identifies the release of the *saṁsāra* veins. The line indicates that only one knot is untied on both the first and twelfth stages of the bodhisattva. Yet each of the intermediate stages (2–11) is responsible for the release of three knots, at the beginning of each stage, in the middle of each stage, and at the conclusion of each stage. The term *la dor ba* found in sections I.D.3 and I.D.6 is rare. It appears connected to *la zlo ba*, *la zla ba*, and related cognate forms (e.g., *la zlas pa*). The *Tshig mdzod chen mo* defines the former as an old (*rnying*) term, signifying a decision (*thag gcod pa*) or conclusively surpassed an obstacle (*la brgal zin pa*). This latter is probably the metaphorical nexus, crossing over (*rgal ba / zlo ba*) a mountain pass (*la*). Its semantic field indicates the conclusion or accomplishment with finality and, in the Sa-skya usage, has a decisiveness to its cognitive value, indicating that the individual has arrived at this conclusion with intellectual as well as meditative effort, since it is applied to the environments of both contemplation and perspective. Here, for example, it indicates that when a bodhisattva stage is accomplished by untying one or three knots, then the bodhisattva does not reverse down the path; *sGa theng ma* 295.5; compare *Sras don ma*, 183.1, 191.2–197.5, and *sGa theng ma*, 287.2.

17. The poisons here are two: ignorance and the pursuit of conceptualizations; *sGa theng ma*, 281.2. The definition of *'jug sel lam* in *sGa theng ma*, 283.5–6, involves the use and understanding of rudimentary breathing techniques.

18. This statement is the essence of the esoteric technique and is ostensibly meant to attract those entrapped in the enjoyment of the senses; *sGa theng ma*, 285.1–2; and *rGyud sde spyi'i rnam par gzhag pa*, *SKB* II.7.2.6–9.1.2.

19. For the Sa-skya tradition in general and the Lam-'bras in particular, this statement denotes the recognition of three levels of realization: the elements of reality for all beings are constituted by mind; that very mind is illusory; and the illusion is without self-nature. See *sGa theng ma*, 286.5–6.

20. The second of the important unarticulated lists in this section, the *snyan brgyud bzhi*, are regarded by nearly all Sa-skya authorities as one of the great defining strategies for the Vajrayāna in general and the Lam-'bras in particular. Briefly, (a) the nondiminution of the river of consecration (*dbang gi chu bo ma nub pa*) indicates that the consecration has been maintained undiminished during the ritual of consecration, during the visualized consecration practiced daily, and through the receipt of the fruits of consecration at the moment crossing through the twelfth-and-a-half stage of the Buddha to the citadel of Vajradhara. (b) The nonseverance of the stream of benediction (*byin rlabs kyi brgyud pa ma nyams pa*, or *ma chad pa*) indicates that the teachers of the tradition have themselves retained the four conclusions of practice, experience, benediction, and accomplishment. (c) The nonreversal of the thrust of instruction (*gdams ngag gi sarga ma log pa*) would seem to

indicate—and was explained to me by Thar-rtse mkhan-po—as not confusing the order of instruction, but Sa-chen's commentaries unequivocally declare this to be the capacity of the lineage to instruct the individual on how signs of impediment may be turned into ornaments of accomplishment. The problem is with the word *sarga*, an Indic term, normatively meaning a category in a progression, a definition that recognizes multiple hermeneutic strategies. Finally, (d) the ability to satisfy the concerns of the faith (*mos gus kyi bsam pa tshim par nus pa*) denotes the capacity of the teacher to provide correct instruction and motivation, so that the student comes to the conclusion that the teacher is in reality indistinguishable from the very Buddha himself. See *Sras don ma*, 197.5–201.3; *sGa theng ma*, 296.2–99.2; and Grags-pa rgyal-mtshan's short work on (a), his (*dBang dus dang lam dus dang mthar phyin gyi lam 'bras bu'i dus kyi*) *'Gros bzhi thim pa* contained in the *Pod ser*, 336.5–39.6. For its hagiographical background, see chapter 1.

21. This section is even more peculiar than the previous allusions to important categories in that it is quite extensive yet never identifies the five *pratītyasamutpāda*, which it contextualizes without specific identification. According to the commentaries ascribed to Sa-chen, the five are the external, the internal, the secret, the reality, and the final interdependent origination (*phyi, nang, gsang, de kho na nyid, mthar thug gi rten cing 'brel bar 'byung ba*); *Sras don ma*, 204.5–205.2; *sGa theng ma*, 301.3–302.6. The discussion in I.F is about seven circumstances contextualizing these forms of interdependence: (a) their basis for actualization; (b) their conclusion; (c) their self-nature; (d) among the four paths (the incomplete awakening of *śrāvaka*, *pratyekabuddha*, bodhisattva, or the great awakening of the Buddha), to which they apply; (e) among the four epistemes, to which they apply; (f) their object of realization; and (g) the forms of interdependent origination that are referred to here.

22. As is clear from the discussion of I.C, the term *lo rgyus* principally indicates a sequence of years and has come to mean a genre of literature: traditional annals. Here, the text refers to a sequence of phenomena, and in Sa-chen's commentaries, to the sequence of realization, from the mundane path, through the stages of the bodhisattva, concluding with the final realization of Vajradhara. See *sGa theng ma*, 301.3–5; *Sras don ma*, 203.1–5.

23. The *Sras don ma*, 205.4–213.5, seems to read this and the corresponding line in I.G.2 as *rnal 'byor pa'i lam gyi bar chad bzhi ni*, indicating four obstacles for each of the two paths. This is an important interpretation, and Sa-chen states that the yogin involved in skillful means has four obstacles and eight protections (four using skillful means, three using insight, and one using interdependence), as does the yogin in I.G.2. The circumstances common to both, I.G.3, has fourteen protections for this obstacle. This means there are thirty forms of protection in all. See *sGa theng ma*, 303.2–3; *Sras don ma*, 205.4–5. Clearly, this is a topic with multiple consequences proposed for the psychological and spiritual health of the yogin, and separate treatises were written from Sa-chen onward to respond to threats to the yogin's health and practice through the agency of these obstacles. See the materi-

als collected in the *Pod ser*, 166–71, the *Pusti dmar chung*, 104–91, and the *Man ngag gces pa btus pa*, 268–71.

24. The two paths are the generation and completion paths (*utpatti-sampanna-krama*), outlined in chapter 1. For each of the four categories of consecration discussed by the Lam-'bras teachers, there are four views and four accomplishments; see section I.B.2.b and table 7 in chapter 8. The signs are the three varieties of corporeal, dexterous, and vocal, which are called for at the time of consecration or the tantric gathering (*gaṇacakra*) but which are not universally employed. The ten paths, etc., indicates the two paths of *utpatti-sampannakrama*, and the previously mentioned perspectives and final positions. Later, the text discusses the dedication of the "four awakenings" (*sad ma bzhi*, II.D) to the category of the path of insight, but the *Sras don ma* both acknowledges this statement and extends its application to protection applied to both paths; see *Sras don ma*, 213 ff.

25. The commentaries identify fourteen required forms of protection that are common to both kinds of yogins: those pertaining to the six veils, the six forms of seminal fluid loss, and the two obscurations from which protection is needed. These protections apply to both the paths of skillful means and insight; see *sGa theng ma*, 319.1–33.5; *Sras don ma*, 222.5–41.4.

26. The interpretation of *'khor lo 'cham pa* is difficult because it is described as both a process and a result. It seems to be an earlier spelling of 'jam pa, especially as used in 'jam khrid, "to lead by coaxing or cajoling," or perhaps from 'chams pa, "to harmonize." The most developed description is that found in *Sras don ma*, 18.1–3: "coaxing of the cakras' indicates that leading up through the worldly path, the four—the vein/physical maṇḍala, the letters/bhaga maṇḍala, the fluid/bodhicitta maṇḍala, and their pervading winds—intermittently the interdependant origination is sometimes correct and sometimes not. When it is correct and they are in harmony together (*'cham*), then good experiences arise. But when they are not correct, then one needs to coax along (or harmonize, reading 'cham for 'char) the collection of interdependant elements. This is similar to an unfinished water mill or an unfinished wagon wheel (which needs coaxing to move when out of kilter)." A similar description is found in *sGa theng ma*, 333.5–34.1. While Thar-rtse mkhan-po explained 'cham pa to me in the sense of "to dance," it also has a subsidiary sense of bringing disparate elements into harmony or the gentle methods to lead it to that state. The commentaries are unanimous in declaring this second section to be entirely occupied with the mundane path (*'jig rten pa'i lam*), while the third section is supermundane (*'jig rten las 'das pa*), and that is where the cakras turn easily (*'khor lo bskor ba*). Whatever the precise semantic value of *'khor lo 'cham pa*, it is clear that it was understood to apply to the practice of the yogic regimen by those yet to accomplish the first stage of the bodhisattva.

27. The commentaries identify more than one list of "four fruits" here, the first being based on four of the five fruits known to the Sarvāstivāda Abhidharma and subsequently used in Mahāyānist analysis: *visaṁyogaphala*, *vipākaphala*, *niṣyanda/sahajaphala*, *puruṣakāra/vimalaphala* (*gNyags ma*, 71.2–3); these are applied to the

mundane path. Moreover, four fruits of the first of the accomplishments (*grub mtha' dang po*) are listed along with fruits applied separately to each accomplishment of the four *abhiṣeka*. It is unclear which of these many lists of the four fruits were referenced in the text; see *Sras don ma*, 254.1–58.2; *sGa theng ma*, 345.4–49.4.

28. The "three means of coalescing the essence" (*khams 'du lugs gsum*) identifies three ways in which experience is developed by those on the path: those who obtain their experience based on the maturation of practice accrued in a previous lifetime (*las 'phro can rang gis khams 'du ba*), those who experience based on their devotion and interest (*mos gus can byin rlabs kyis khams 'du ba*), and those who experience based on their effort and exertion (*brtson 'grus can 'bad rtsol gyis khams 'du ba*). To each of these are applied the seven categories of the seven balanced modes (*phyogs med pa*). In each, the first of the balanced modes is that of the means of coalescing the essence itself. So *gNyags ma*, 73.1–2: "awakening to the balanced maturation accrued from a previous lifetime, the vital wind is turned back in a balanced mode. Accordingly, the fire of internal heat blazes in a balanced mode, the channels experience discomfort in a balanced mode, the essence is coalesced in a balanced mode, the defiled super consciousness (*sāsravābhijñā*) arises in a balance mode, and the undefiled super consciousness (*anāsravābhijñā*) arises in a balanced mode." The other two categories of "coalescence of the essence," "through devotion and interest," and "through exertion and effort," are practiced in this way as well. The *gNyags ma* continues to explain that if one goes through all twenty-one of these levels, then supreme success will certainly be obtained in this lifetime. Similar explanations found in *Sras don ma*, 258.2–63.1; *sGa theng ma*, 349.4–51.6.

29. The use of normative Mahāyānist categories to explain esoteric practice is a peculiar emphasis of the Sa-skya system and is seldom more curious than in this application. The *gNyags ma*, 69.6–70.1, explains: "If one traverses the path according to the thirty-seven elements of awakening, then at first the four bases of psychic power act as an antidote to taking the phenomenal world as an impediment [literally, an enemy]. Then the four bases of recollection act as an antidote for those taking emptiness as an impediment. Finally, the four correct renunciations operate as an antidote for those overcome by bliss. These twelve eliminate the mundane path. As for the supermundane path, up through the sixth level of the bodhisattva, there are the seven factors of awakening, on the next four levels operate the five faculties, on the next two operate the five powers, and the eight consciousnesses based in the 12–1/2th level are the eight-fold noble path. Thus the root supermundane path is cut off by the twenty-five factors of awakening." Yet we may note that the use of these categories are in practice redefined to describe esoteric practice, fitting the new esoteric wine into the old Mahāyānist bottles.

30. According to the commentaries, this section is the middle of a list of "three ways the mind is stabilized" (*sems gnas lugs gsum*): the mind is stabilized by reversing the vital wind (*rlung log pas sems gnas*), by the self-empowerment of vital wind and mind (*rlung sems bdag byin gyis brlabs pas sems gnas*), and by the complete intermingling of the mind and the physical basis (*rten mnyam du 'dres pas sems gnas*); *Sras don ma*, 263.1–3; *sGa theng ma*, 351.6–352.5.

31. The four *ṛddhipāda* are normative to Buddhism, but here they are clearly forms of internal wind; compare Gethin 1992, pp. 82–85; Dayal 1932, pp. 104–6; *sGa theng ma*, 353.4–5; *Sras don ma*, 266.2–3.

32. "Undissipated cultivation" is the translation of *sgom pa mi 'chor ba* (perhaps **asaṁhārya-bhāvanā*, but with no attestation seen), an important term in the Lam-'bras. The term is used as a qualifier in three other contexts: *bsgom pa mi 'chor ba'i phyi'i rten 'brel* in I.C, *bsgom pa mi 'chor ba'i dran pa nye bar gzhag pa bzhi* in II.E, and *bsgom pa mi 'chor ba'i yang dag par spong ba bzhi* in II.F. The most complete definition is provided by the *Sras don ma*, 266.1–2: "Undissipated cultivation is the harmonization of interdependence within oneself so that it is known as the contemplation itself. Undissipated cultivation is the arising of experience without reference to other methods which have in fact no means for the harmonization of interdependence within one's body. Because of the essential nature of the internal interdependence, and because it is known as that which is the contemplation of the path, it is called undissipated cultivation." This is a clarification and expansion of the definition found in the *sGa theng ma*, 353.3–4.

33. The commentaries do not exactly agree with the evident sense of the text. The masculine, feminine, and neuter winds are treated as the activities (*'jug pa*) of *karmavāyu*, as is *thod rgal ye shes me 'bar ba'i rlung*, making this the fourth. Indeed, the commentaries separate the *rdzu 'phrul gyi rkang pa bzhi* (as a different set of *rlung* based on the four elements of earth, wind, water, and fire) from the subsequent set, even though it appears clear that this is the significance of the text, and attempt an integration of the various lists of vital wind; see *sGa theng ma*, 353.4; *Sras don ma*, 266.2–3; *gNyags ma*, 74.

34. *Thod rgal ye shes kyi me 'bar ba. Thod rgal* became one of the grand operative terms of the sNying-thig movement within the rDzogs-chen path of the rNying-ma. Clearly, those communities wishing to define the hermeneutics of the psychophysical yogic practices employed this term, and they were evidently drawing on its use in the context of the *Prajñāpāramitā* literature. While there is a modern disinclination to see these individual applications of the word *thod rgal* as similar in any manner, such disinclination apparently stems from the institutional desire to harden boundaries.

35. The "implement of the winter wind" is glossed as its frigid bite; see *gNyags ma*, 74.1. With the middling and final "coalescence of the essence," the discomfort will diminish, and eventually only benefit will remain. The significance of the term *rtsa dral* is somewhat difficult, since the normal meaning of *'dral ba* is "to burst or render apart" and is cognate to *ral ba*, "to tear," "to be slashed by a sword." Here, though, the early use of *dral ba*, the perfect participle, is the action of opening channels (*rtsa dral*) or loosening knots (*mdud dral*); compare *sGa theng ma*, 424.5.

36. *Sems gnas* is glossed as *sems nyams. Sras don ma*, 269.2; *sGa theng ma*, 355.1; *gNyags ma*, 75.1.

37. The five primary vital winds are the *prāṇa/srog 'dzin*, the *samāna/mnyam gnas*, the *apāna/thur sel*, the *udāna/gyen rgyu*, and the *vyāna/khyab byed.* See Guenther 1963, p. 271, for these equivalents, although reassessment seems overdue. The

subsidiary vital winds are the *rgyu ba*, the *rab tu rgyu ba*, *shin tu rgyu ba*, the *mngon par rgyu ba*, and the *yang dag par rgyu ba.* Each of these ten is understood according to the seven determinants of its names, locus, function, discomfort encountered when constrained, meditation, fault of its stiffening, and method of preparation; *gNyags ma*, 76.4. This results in the seventy instructions (*man ngag* : *upadeśa*) of the vital wind. The commentaries introduce around this area of the *Lam 'bras rtsa ba* a new discussion, which is not directly reflected in the text, concerning the seven essentials of the practice of vital wind (*rlung gi nyams su blang ba'i gnad bdun bstan pa*); *Sras don ma*, 269.6–93.1; *sGa theng ma*, 355.4–68.6.

38. *gNyags ma*, 80.1–2, indicates that the essences open up like the unfolding of butter in curd being churned and that these nuclear essences become fused to their respective cakras (known as "citadels") by the combination of their presence there and the activity of contemplation, in the way that the *samayaḍākas* and the *jñānaḍākas* become fused and empowered; compare *sGa theng ma*, 369.5–70.1.

39. This differentiation is according to the three categories of "heat": that preceded by conceptualization (*rnam rtog sngon du song ba'i drod*), that relating to the coalescence of essences (*khams dgu 'dus pa'i drod*), and that heat arising from the incineration of the seminal fluid and its coalescence (*thig le 'bar zhing 'dus pa'i drod*); each of these is further divided into the divisions of visions, dreams, and physical experiences; see *Sras don ma*, 36.5–37.6; *gNyags ma*, 81–84; *sGa theng ma*, 371.4–6. Later, II.C, "undissipated cultivation," is equated with the external dependent origination and defined in the context of II.E with the preponderance of mental control (*Sras don ma*, 359.1–2): "Concerning undissipated cultivation, beyond this point the body and speech are accorded less importance and mind becomes the chief component, so we call the cultivation undissipated."

40. According to the *gNyags ma*, 81.3, this section begins the first of the three ways of explaining the path (*lam khrid lugs gsum*): that by means of vital wind (*rlung gis lam khrid*), that by means of the essential nectars (*khams bdud rtsis lam khrid*), and that by means of the channels and letters (*rtsa yi ges lam khrid*). This is one of the two principal hermeneutical techniques in the path, which is begun here with the mundane path and completed later under different conditions with the supermundane path; *gNyags ma*, 67.6–69.2; *sGa theng ma*, 334.6–38.5; *Sras don ma*, 241.6–47.2.

41. Again, we must rely on the commentaries to make sense of the text. The *gNyags ma*, 81.2–83.3, explains that when one or another of the vital airs associated with one of the five elements becomes empowered and supreme, it provides the three: physical experience, dreams, and visionary experience. Not only does the empowerment of the vital air of fire cause the vision of the burning of the triple world, but one also dreams of a city of fire, and one's bodily hair and skin feel hot and sensitive. Not only does the empowerment of the vital air of water make one feel cold, but one also dreams of a boat on the ocean and has visions of the four oceans, etc. Not only does one dream of flying, but also one feels like one is racing like a horse and dreaming that the whole universe is like a whirlwind. The commentaries also rearrange the text, by pulling up from below the phrase *nam mkha'*

dang mnyam pa dang spu lus bde as a form of experience of vital wind to be explained with the other forms of vital wind. So not only does one have the physical sensation of pleasure in the follicles, but one also experiences a vision of predominant emptiness and dreams of unhindered appearance in all directions. All five elemental vital winds accordingly have three experiences, making the fifteen experiences. These are substantially different from another list of fifteen experiences listed in the context of the "triple appearance"; see *Sras don ma*, 34.3–39.5. We may note that the element of earth has been left out of the discussion in the Lam-'bras text and must be inferred; *gNyags ma*, 83; *sGa theng ma*, 375.6.

42. The term *spu lu(s)* is apparently unattested in our lexicons; I take it to indicate the follicles of the bodily hairs (*spu*) taken as a whole, encompassing the entire surface of the skin. We note again that the commentaries reorder the discussion and that this last line is considered in conjunction with similar discussions after the element water and before considering all four great elements together, for example, *sGa theng ma*, 375.1.

43. *gNyags ma*, 84.3, has the second of the three ways of explaining the path, that through the essential nectars (*khams bdud rtsi'i lam khrid*) beginning in this section and completed later in the supermundane path.

44. Finally, *gNyags ma*, 85.2, has the third of the three ways of explaining the path, that through the channels and letters (*rtsa yi ges lam khrid*) beginning in this section and also completed later in the supermundane path.

45. This continues the explanation of the path, but through fourteen letters (*rtsa yi ge bcu bzhi'i lam khrid*). The importance of this section is not immediately evident in either the text or in such a modest title as "fourteen letters." However, both the *Sras don ma* (323.6–34.4) and the *sGa theng ma* (386.4–400.2) use this section as a heuristic to express the fundamental subtle arrangement of the veins, the letters, and the operation of the subtle body, technically known as the "natural condition of the *vajrakāya*" (*rdo rje'i lus kyi gnas lugs*).

46. *gNyags ma*, 89.5, says that this means the experience of all four of the levels of *dhyāna* found in the world of form.

47. *gNyags ma*, 91.1–2, following the same theme of the wind, explains that the intermediate level of mundane practice brings lesser discomfort, like the cold suffered from the spring wind.

48. These visions of the intermediate coalescence of the essence (*khams 'dus pa bar pa*) are real in a way that those of the first coalescence are not but do not have the transcendental valence of the final coalescence. Technically, these are given different nomenclature: *sGa theng ma*, 385.6–86.1: "These [visions] in the case of the first coalescence are uncertain and erroneous appearance; for the intermediate they are certain and visionary appearance; for the final they are very certain and arise as the appearance of clarity."

49. One of the more curious titles, given that this section is so short.

50. While the *Sras don ma* and *sGa theng ma* agree that these letters are the fourteen letters of the *bha ga'i dkyil 'khor*, they do not precisely agree on the arrange-

ment of the letters and even observe that there is no common opinion in the tantras about the location of the *bha ga'i dkyil 'khor.* See *Sras don ma*, 323.6–34.2; *sGa theng ma*, 386.1–400.2; see also the *Bha ga'i yi ge bcu bzhi* in *Pod ser*, 183–85. Generally, however, the section refers to the fourteen letters at the base of the spine where the three major veins come together in a triangle. There the veins form knots or ganglia (*mdud*), which appear in the shape of letters: OṀ, AḤ, HŪṀ, with letters representing the six realms of existence in close proximity, and five other letters (mostly inverted) below these, one of them being KṢA. The letter RA, however, is not noted, and there is no explanation why the text indicates this—although it appears clear that it relates directly to demons (*srin po* : *rākṣasa*). These letters were first mentioned in the commentary to I.7.c.ii, but not directly in the text itself. The demons, etc., means that all demons and demonesses are available and are also seen within these knots, as are images of tigers and snakes, corresponding to these items in the external world; *Sras don ma*, 344.1–5, 346.4–48.6. "That which has a bell" indicates the central channel, since the lower end of the central channel is bell-like, but the sound emitting from it is like the sound of a bee buzzing around a flower, not the sound of a bell; *sGa theng ma*, 406.4.

51. *Bhavāgra* is frequently taken, as it is here, as the limit of mundane existence, to be transcended with the supermundane path; see *Abhidharmakośa* VI.44–45, 73.

52. The five paths are those of accumulation, application, vision, cultivation, and the final path; the ten stages are those of the bodhisattva. A useful demonstration of the relationship of these two arrangements can be found in Conze 1957.

53. The ternaries are the three kinds of experiences occurring to meditators: signs, visions, and dream experiences; each of these is graded by the three levels of intensity (*drod*) on the path, lower, medium, and supreme; see *Sras don ma*, 352.2. Here undissipated cultivation is simply identified with the external dependent origination; for its definition, see note 32.

54. This explanation is consistent with other interior explanations found in esoteric commentaries; see Ratnākaraśānti's *Mahāmāyātantraṭīkā Guṇavatī*, 3–4. The definition of a *ḍākinī* given in the *Sras don ma* is interesting: "Traveling and journeying to the spaces in the citadels of the precious veins, it is called *ḍākinī*."

55. Here and in II.F, the text invokes the well-known four aids to penetration (*nirvedhabhāgīya-dharma*): heat (*ūṣmagata*), zenith (*mūrdhan*), tolerance (*kṣānti*), and highest worldly dharmas (*laukikāgradharma*). For this material, see *Śrāvakabhūmi*, Shukla 494.20–500.15. Our text, however, interprets these in a very idiosyncratic manner, not in a manner familiar to the *Abhidharma* or *Prajñāpāramitā* literature. Zenith, for example, is equivalent here to the zenith of existence (*bhavāgra*), and tolerance is identified with the tolerance toward unarisen phenomena (*anutpattikadharmakṣānti*). These interpretations are highly irregular, and the former specifically calls into question the Indic nature of this section of the text. We note that *Sras don ma* (27.3, 357.4) and *sGa theng ma* (414.2) read *bskyang* for *gtang*, that is, "guarding" for "accepting."

56. Another group of items alluded to in the text but not enumerated. All the

commentaries discuss this item in relation to I.G.2, since the yogin occupied with insight is first mentioned there. The four awakenings (*sad pa bzhi*) are those by experience (*nyams kyis sad pa*), by meditation (*ting nge 'dzin gyis sad pa*), by mantras (*sngags kyis sad pa*), and by the combination of the four perspectives and the four accomplishments, as indicated in table 7, chapter 8, on the twenty aspects of the path (*lta grub gyis sad pa*). See *Sras don ma*, 213.5–18.5; *gNyags ma*, 63.4–5; *sGa theng ma*, 311.2–15.2.

57. Devaputra Māra is the last of the standard grouping of the four Māras, including the Māras of death, the aggregates, and the defilements; see *Śrāvakabhūmi*, 343–45. This last form is the Māra identified with the divinity tempting the bodhisattva immediately before awakening. See *Lalitavistara*, 218–34, 254–56 (esp. 22.9); Dayal 1932, pp. 306–16. The difference between yogins occupied with skillful means and yogins occupied with insight was discussed earlier in I.G.1–3.

58. Another group of four not identified in the text, although this group is far more standard, as the four bases for recollection: body, feelings, mind, and events (*kāyavedanācittadharmasmṛtyupasthānāni*) of normative Buddhism that form part of the thirty-seven branches of awakening. See Dayal 1932, pp. 82–101; Pagel 1995, pp. 381–89; Gethin 1992, pp. 29–68. We may note, though, that the explanation of these in the Lam-'bras commentaries is exclusively esoteric. The four bases for recollection are thought to be the antidote suitable for a yogin experiencing emptiness as a problem; *Sras don ma*, 359.3.

59. During the generation stage, the yogin dissolves himself into emptiness and then must regenerate himself as a divinity out of emptiness in the form of the *samayasattva* while summoning the *jñānasattva*. The text makes a case for the equivalence of both meditation on form and emptiness—the equal divisions—and this section focuses on those for whom emptiness has become an impediment. We also may note that the "chosen divinity" (*iṣṭadevatā*) is unspecified, indicating that the association of the text with the Hevajra system is purely adventitious, although in keeping with the principles of the *yoginī-tantra* practices.

60. This section is somewhat chaotic and multidimensional, causing the commentaries generally to introduce the section as the fruit of the previous section, whereas at the end it is sometimes identified with the four bases of psychic power; compare *Pod nag ma*, 138.5, *Sras don ma*, 378.6, *sGa theng ma*, 341.6.

61. The discomfort of the practices no longer afflict the channels of the yogin, so the winds are without the bite associated with winter.

62. The six recollections are not part of the normative list of the *bodhipakṣika-dharmas* and are not included in the twelve *bodhipakṣika-dharmas* classified in the mundane path in the Lam-'bras. Here they are simply defined as the objects of the six senses; *Sras don ma*, 367.4.

63. Note that the term *prahāṇa* (*spong ba*) is interpreted here according to its literal and evidently erroneous etymology, rather than according to its normative Buddhist reading as equivalent to *pradhāna*, primary effort. Compare Dayal 1932, pp. 101–3; Pagal 1995, pp. 397–99; Gethin 1992, pp. 69–103.

64. I thank Cy Stearns for pointing out to me that the commentaries interpret "12" as if it were "20," apparently in the interests of social propriety, for all versions of the text agree on a twelve-year-old girl. A *padminī* is considered ideal, especially for the practice during the fourth consecration; she has images of a lotus (*padma*) on the palms of her hands and the soles of her feet and naturally exhibits the moods of happiness, joy, and the like. The yogin searches for the vein by a surprising ritual involving strapping the young lady to a saddle, tying cloth around parts of her torso, and working a greased oblong ball of felt and cotton up her rectum. This is supposed to bring the convergence of the three channels in her vaginal passage and cause a pointed "nose" to emerge from the central channel. This "*ḍākinī's* nose" is like a pointed spike and is supposed to penetrate the head of the disciple's penis while engaged in the intercourse required for the fourth consecration in this system; *sGa theng ma*, 423.1–24.5; *Sras don ma*, 364.4–66.1.

65. Here, as elsewhere, there are insufficient grammatical markers to reveal the significance of the text without the commentaries. *Sras don ma*, 370.1–6; *sGa theng ma*, 424.3–25.3 state that the A comes from the heart area and merges with one of the A letters (*phyi dbyibs A*) among the fourteen just noted. The two forms of vital wind simply indicate that all the ten primary and subsidiary winds are also forced into the central channel, and the "seasoned intelligence" means that they disciple has practiced this for some time.

66. *Sras don ma*, 370.6–71.1; *sGa theng ma*, 424.6–25.3: the body (= right channel) and the speech (left channel) merge with the mind (= central channel) in a configuration reminiscent of the fully cross-legged position referred by Haṭhayogins as the "lotus position," but often by esoteric Buddhist representatives as the vajra position.

67. The "A of external form" is one of the fourteen letters in the pelvic region and represents the "nose" at the end of the central channel; *Sras don ma*, 379.3. "Essence" indicates the experience of the emptiness of essence; *Sras don ma*, 379.6–80.1. "Proper nature" signifies the experience of nonduality; *Sras don ma*, 380.1. And "characteristics" indicate the experience of the provisional reality of skillful means, which is summarized as superimposition; *Sras don ma*, 380.1.

68. Each of these sections is predominantly composed of signs: the signs of reality (*de kho na nyid kyi rtags* : **tattvacihna*), the internal signs and the external signs. The commentaries point out that these are the reverse of the natural order, as we have seen elsewhere, for example, I.D.; *Sras don ma*, 385.2–3. Here, the marks of reality are metaphors: the four citadels for the four cakras (navel, heart, throat, head) and the three ladies for the three principal veins; *Sras don ma*, 387.6–88.1. They have been equated with the seven factors of awakening (*saptabodhyaṅgāni*), which are normatively referred to as the penultimate of the seven categories of the thirty-seven limbs of awakening. Compare Dayal 1932, pp. 149–55; Genthin 1992, pp. 146–89.

69. *sGa theng ma*, 436.4–6, indicates that this is the method for eliminating the gross and moderate conceptualization that is to be eliminated.

70. Note that the Lam-'bras follows the model given in the *Daśabhūmika* that increases the realization by powers of ten for each level of the bodhisattva, starting from the hundred of the first level. The verb *sgul ba* normatively indicates agitation or trembling and may render some form of the Sanskrit √*kamp*, "to vibrate." The descriptive apparatus, both here and later in the text, describes the capacity to see or visit these pure lands, in accordance with the standard descriptions found in the *Daśabhūmika*, 30.4, "and he rattles a hundred world systems" *lokadhātuśataṁ ca kampayati*; p. 36, II. 22d, "they shake, illuminate, and cross over a hundred fields" *kaṁpenti kṣetraśatu bhāsi samākramanti* |. It is not exactly clear why the scripture has bodhisattvas engage in rattling all these worlds, except perhaps as an extension of the old Buddhist mythology about the quaking of the earth during specific events in the Buddha's life, like the defeat of Māra.

71. The *Sras don ma*, 389.1–2, says that these are the standard Mahāyāna contemplations, such as the *śūraṁgama-samādhi, the siṁhavijṛmbhita-samādhi*; similarly *sGa theng ma*, 438.1.

72. This is the perception of the letter NṚ among the fourteen letters in the *bha ga'i dkyil 'khor*; *sGa theng ma*, 438.6.

73. He is apprehensive that he might yet return to birth among the other realms of existence; *sGa theng ma*, 439.3–4, *Sras don ma*, 390.2–3.

74. This is the *grub mtha'* to the vase consecration; see table 7, chapter 8.

75. *gNyags ma*, 106.3–4, and *Sras don ma*, 257.3, describe the capacity to perform the miracles, some of which are associated with Virūpa in the hagiographical literature: turning back a river, holding the sun and moon in place, passing effortlessly through walls and mountains, and so forth.

76. This means that during the practice of the completion process, the yogin does not ejaculate, but in the fourth or "natural" moment (*sahajakṣaṇa*) with the "natural" bliss (*sahajānanda*), the yogin's body is filled with bliss and he is overcome.

77. The commentaries indicate that the normal inhalation is twelve inches and exhalation is the same, making a total movement of the breath of twenty-four inches. With this stage, the inhalation/exhalation cycle is reduced by one inch in either direction, making a total cycle of twenty-two inches. With succeeding stages, the breath is reduced by an inch, so that on the twelfth stage, the breath is entirely arrested and the twelve steps in dependent origination are entirely reversed, indicating that ignorance is eliminated; see *Sras don ma*, 393.5–94.4.

78. This indicates the consecrations received during the practice of the path (*lam dus*). Because of the yogin's accomplishment, from the second to sixth stages, he gets them from the *nirmāṇakāya*, whereas we see ascending orders of the bodies of the Buddha granting consecrations further along the path.

79. The five faculties (*pañcendriyāni*) are, in addition to those found in normative articulation of the thirty-seven branches, the specifically esoteric faculties of immunity from being afraid or disturbed by various manifestations of the winds associated with the great elements (earth, air, fire, water, space) because these vital

airs have been subdued. Compare Dayal 1932, pp. 141–49; Gethin 1992, pp. 104–40; Pagel 1995, pp. 399–401; *Sras don ma*, 399.3–5; *sGa theng ma*, 446.5–47.1.

80. The five abilities are forms of *siddhi*, like passing through earth or rendering himself invisible; *Sras don ma*, 399.5–6. The gazes, here classified as either four or eight, are a development of the four gazes recognized in the *Hevajra-tantra* I.xi.1–7. Compare Dayal 1932, pp. 141–49; Gethin 1992, pp. 1 ff.; *sGa theng ma*, 447.3–5.

81. The six seed syllables are A (for gods), NṚ (for humans), SU (for demigods) PRE (for ghosts), DU (for animals), and TRI (for denizens of hell). These are part of the architecture of the *bhagamaṇḍala*; for mutually incommensurate descriptions of this *maṇḍala*, see *Sras don ma*, 324.3–34.2, and *sGa theng ma*, 386.1–400.2.

82. The general characteristics (*sāmāṇyalakṣaṇa*) of the dharmas constitute the "four seals of reality": all compounded elements are impermanent; all defiled elements are distressing; all dharmas are nonself; and only nirvāṇa is peace. The specific characteristics (*svalakṣaṇa*) of the dharmas change with each. Generally, because of the influence of the *Abhidharmakośa*, the later Indian Buddhists and most Tibetan Buddhists accepted the seventy-five dharma schematism of the Sarvāstivāda, and each of these bears its own characteristic. See *Abhidharmakośa*, I.27, VI.14.

83. The eight source letters are A KA CA ṬA TA PA YA ŚA. The term *phyi mo* can denote a root (*rtsa ba*) or foundation (*gzhi*) for something. The *sGa theng ma* (448.4–5) states that from the short A in the navel cakra, the two syllables E WAṂ arise. From the E, the short A (of the eight letters) arises. From the WAṀ, the syllables KA CA ṬA TA PA YA ŚA arise. From the A, the sixteen vowels (*āli*) separate off as the external circle. From the KĀ (*sic*), the thirty-four consonants (*kāli*) separate out. From these vowels and consonants, all letters arise; from letters come names, and from names arise words. Thus, command over the scriptures is through seeing and controlling the letters arising in the navel cakra. Compare *Sras don ma*, 401.1–4.

84. This is a reference to vv. 28c-29d of the *Mañjuśrīnāmasaṁgīti*: "The syllable A, the foremost of all phonemes, of great meaning, the supreme syllable. Aspirated, unoriginated, without uttering a sound, [Mañjuśrī] is the foremost cause of all expression, shining forth within all speech." The context of the six-foot verse clearly indicates the bodhisattva Mañjuśrī, and his capacity for expression is the cause for his sometimes identification as the lord of speech (*vāgīśvara*). For the entire text and translation of the *Mañjuśrīnāmasaṁgīti*, see Davidson 1981. Normatively, "pure sounds" (*brahmasvara*) indicate the quality of the Buddha's speech and constitute one of the thirty-two marks of the Buddha. Here they refer to the three A-s: the "heart A, the navel A, and the external form A"; *Sras don ma*, 402.3, *sGa theng ma*, 449.6–50.4. The first and last are found in the *bhagamaṇḍala* in the genital area, so that the metaphor and terminology of heart may be misleading.

85. This difficult sentence has become a focus for rearrangement and rereading. The *Sras don ma* reads *'khor bzhi rgyal ba* instead of *rgya* and rearranges the syntax

to have this follow *sa bdun yan cad*, whereas the rest of the early commentaries read it as printed but interpret it differently. Perhaps the most persuasive interpretation is found in the *gZhu byas ma*, that the four seals are found in the four cakras: *karmamudrā* in the *nirmāṇacakra* in the navel, the *dharmamudrā* in the *dharmacakra* in the heart, the *mahāmudrā* in the *sambhogacakra* in the throat, and the *samayamudrā* in the *mahāsukhacakra* in the fontanel; *gZhu byas ma*, 162.6. The commentaries use this opportunity to develop a grand arrangement, linking the vision of pure lands with a triple continuity (*rgyud gsum*), triple appearance (*snang gsum*) system, the four *maṇḍalas* of the channels, the letters, the seminal fluid, and the essential gnostic wind, and the physical container/mental contained system; *Sras don ma*, 403.3–406.3; *sGa theng ma* 450.5–53.3.

86. The *sGa theng ma*, 454.6–55.1, says that the ground to be purified, in this case the mind, is in the text here associated with the path, whereas in III.A and B it is associated with the consecration.

87. The *bodhicittamaṇḍala* is understood here as the "quintessential essence" (*dwangs ma'i dwangs ma*) because it has arrived at the fontanel and represents the great essence which has been repeatedly purified by the interdependence of the path of the winds, the mind, and the serus substances; *Sras don ma*, 408.4–5. The five powers (*pañcabalāni*) arise out of the control of each form of wind as it is brought into the central channel, and the five vital winds of the *bodhicitta* mean that each essential wind is mixed inseparably with one of the five nectars as a physical manifestation of the *bodhicitta*; *Sras don ma*, 408.4. For the five powers as functions of the thirty-seven branches of awakening, see Dayal 1932, pp. 1141–49; Gethin 1992, pp. 140–45; Pagel 1995, pp. 401–3.

88. *Sras don ma*, 408.6–412.6, discusses the practice of the internal stages of the *maṇḍalacakra* practice and how one then obtains the consecrations of the three bodies of the Buddha, the consecrations of the five forms of gnosis, the consecrations of the five *mudrā*, the consecrations of the eleven Herukas, the consecrations of the twenty-four realities of the divinities, and the consecrations of the four factors of reality. See similar lists with a somewhat different explanation in *sGa theng ma*, 456.4–463.2.

89. *Yum gyi bha ga* is often glossed as the *dharmodaya* in which the *maṇḍala* is constructed by visualization, or the *dharmodaya* as the vaginal form. The *dharmodaya* is an inverted triangle or tetrahedron, inside the protective walls of vajra and within which the palace is visualized. *Sras don ma*, 414.3–4, however, gives four interpretations of *bhaga*; compare *sGa theng ma*, 464.4.

90. The six supercognitions are not part of the normative list of the thirty-seven *bodhipakṣikadharmas*.

91. This means that the yogin no longer breathes at all, since he does not need external breath to survive and since the vital wind has been entirely drawn into the central channel and all the vowels have been arrested along with all the forms of conceptualization; *Sras don ma*, 416.5–17.1.

92. The last section of the thirty-seven branches of awakening is the eightfold

noble path (*aṣṭa mārgāṅgāni*), which is so well known. Here, though, the eight are reinterpreted esoterically as the purification of the eight forms of consciousness; compare *Sras don ma*, 426.3–5; Dayal 1932, pp. 155–64; Gethin 1992, pp. 190–226; Pagel 1995, pp. 391–95. The two fruits are the path to liberation through signlessness (*ānimittavimokṣamukha*) by means of the stiffening of the right (channel) object wave and the path to liberation through wishlessness (*apraṇihitavimokṣamukha*) by means of stiffening the left (channel) subject wave; *Sras don ma*, 426.5–6.

93. One of the standard signs of the great acts of the Buddha, especially awakening; see the *Lalitavistara*, 254.12: ṣaḍvikāraṁ ca daśasu dikṣu sarvalokadhātavo 'kampat prakampat samprakampat |.

94. *Sras don ma*, 427.4, describes a scenario in which there is a great sound because the four Māras have been defeated, resulting in the noise of a rain of meteorites, the roaring of the ocean, the shocking crash of cymbals, and so forth. The sounds mentioned at this point in the *Lalitavistara* seem to be primarily those of joy and acclaim, 254.17–18: daśasu dikṣu bodhisattvāś ca devaputrāś cānandaśabdaṁ niścārayāmāsuḥ — utpannaḥ sattvapaṇḍitaḥ |, and compare 256.12.

95. *Sras don ma*, 427.6, says that all the phenomena of saṁsāra and nirvāṇa are now seen within the mustard seed-size essential essence of the consort's vagina, without any differentiation of existence or size or quality, and so forth.

96. *Ha ri ma* of the text is a corruption (Prakrit haṇima?) of *aṇiman*, the first of a standard list of the eight forms of dominion (*aiśvārya* or *īśvaratvam* = *dbang phyug*), identified in such references as the *Yogasūtra-vyāsabhāṣya* to *Yogasūtra* 3.44: the capacity to become minute (*aṇiman*), buoyant (*laghiman*), massive (*mahiman*), obtaining everything (*prāpti*), unrestrained (*prākāmya*), controlling (*vaśitvam*), with mastery (*īśitṛtvam*), and concluding things as he likes (*kāmāvasāyitvam*); see Prasâda 1912, pp. 248–50; compare *Sras don ma*, 429.2–30.6. *Bande ma*, 140.5–6, indicates that the verse containing these qualities is from a *Thun mong ma yin pa'i gsang ba*, which I have not been able to identify, although the list is alluded to in various sources. See *Kṛṣṇayamāri-tantra*, 74.20.

97. This is the final of the three realities, that of the entrance to the liberation of emptiness (*śūnyatāvimokṣamukha*), the concluding member of the two fruits listed in III.D.1. It indicates the complete arrest of the wave of conceptualization; *Sras don ma*, 432.1–2.

98. I have not seen this metaphor before. The commentaries explain it away by indicating the fontanel as this city and its opening up as the conclusion of the yogic practice, for example, *Sras don ma*, 432.3.

99. The multiple etc. indicates that the other activities mentioned above in conjunction with vibration, such as teaching (III.A), are also included.

100. Lam-'bras masters consistently define the final fruit by means of the dissolution of the four gradations or functions of the body. By means of the vase consecration, the fruit acquired is the dissolution of the various channels into the central channel, which is ultimately transformed (*gnas gyur* : *parāvṛtti*) into the *nirmāṇakāya*. The secret consecration causes the letter *maṇḍala* to dissolve finally into the

HAṀ in the fontanel, and the transformation of these letters brings the *sambhogakāya*. Likewise, the relationship between the third consecration, the nectar *maṇḍala*, and the *dharmakāya*. Finally, the fourth consecration dissolves the vital wind into the gnostic wind in the central channel, which is transformed into the *svabhāvikakāya*. None of these is the mind itself, and the mind is transformed into a fifth body, in which the *suviśuddhasvabhāvikakāya* is called the **anābhogakāya*; *Sras don ma*, 437.3–40.3; *sGa theng ma*, 481.3–85.3. The problems previously experienced were primarily on the mundane path, although some continued through the supermundane path; *Sras don ma*, 442.1–6.

NOTES TO THE EDITION

1. The following abbreviations are used in the apparatus: (*PS*): *Pod ser*, 11.9.1–19.3; (*PTT*): *Peking Tibetan Tripitaka*, Pe. 3131 *bsTan-'gyur*, rgyud 'grel, tsi, fols. 152a8–55b8; (*DG*): *bDe-dge bsTan-'gyur*, To. 2284, rgyud, zhi, fols. 139a6–42b7; (*Co*): *Co-ne bsTan-'gyur*, rgyud, zhi, fols. 139a-43a; (*rGyud kun*): *rGyud sde kun btus*, vol. 26.92–102; (*DNg*): *gDams-ngag mdzod*, 4.1.1–11.1.1; (*Bo dong*): *Bo dong gsung 'bum* (*Encyclopaedia Tibetica*), vol. 105.415–28. The numbers in brackets, for example, [11], are the *PS* page numbers. Occasional readings from the *Sras don ma* and the *sGa theng ma* also are provided. The title of the text is extracted from the end of the work and is something of an issue. The preceding title is that given at the end of the text (*PS* 19.3). *Co* (143a1), *DG* (142b7), *Po-dong* (428.4), and *PTT* (vol. 69.134.3.8) has *man ngag du bcas pa*. *DNg*, *rGyud kun* have *man ngag dang bcas pa*. The titles given at the beginning of the various editions, however, reflect a much wider variation: To. 2284 in the catalog has perhaps the most commonly used title, *Lam 'bras bu dang bcas pa'i rtsa ba rdo rje'i tshig rkang*, evident in the *sDe-dge bstan 'gyur dkar chag* (699: lam 'bras bu dang bcas pa'i rtsa ba rdo rje'i tshig rkang dang | bdud rtsi grub pa'i rtsa ba zhes bya ba slob dpon chen po bi rū pas mdzad pa). *DNg*, *rGyud kun* have *gSung ngag rin po che lam 'bras bu dang bcas pa'i gzhung rdo rje'i tshig rkang*; the *LL* edition in the *PS* does not offer any beginning title, similar to the canonical editions, while the *gLegs bam kyi dkar-chags* of the *PS* (2.2) uses the common abbreviation *rTsa ba rdo rje'i tshig rkang*, **Mūla-vajrapada*.

2. *DNg* omits la.

3. Most of the titles for the section divisions contained in [brackets] are from the *sGa theng ma*, 159 ff., or the other commentaries, and are provided for convenience; they are not in the original text. See chapter 8 for a discussion of the priority of the *sGa theng ma*.

4. *PTT* nyon mongs pa'i snang ba la ma dag ba'i snang ba la |; *DG*, *Co* nyon mongs pa'i snang ba la ma dag pa'i snang ba|.

5. *DG*, *Co* omit la.

6. *PTT* omits la.

7. *PTT*, *DG*, *Co* pa'i; *PTT*, *DG*, *Co*, *DNg* omit la.

8. *PTT* gyis.

9. *Co* tshad pas.

10. *PTT, Co, DG,* and *DNg* use the new orthography (*la*) *sogs* throughout. *PS* uses the archaic stsogs, which is retained.

11. *PTT, DG, Co, DNg, Bo dong, rGyud kun* sogs.

12. *PTT, DG, Co* bzhi yis and throughout.

13. *PTT* skyed rim la sogs.

14. *DNg, rGyud kun* kyis.

15. *DNg, rGyud kun, Co* chags.

16. *DNg, rGyud kun* omit sogs; *DG* 'dod yon sogs la yis.

17. *DNg* bsgom.

18. *PTT* bgag; *DG, Co* 'dag.

19. *DNg* 'du'i.

20. *PTT, DG, Co, Bo dong* dangs ma for dwangs ma throughout.

21. *DNg* rtsir.

22. *PTT* rnam lnga dang |.

23. *DNg, rGyud kun* omit la.

24. *DNg* bcu'i; *rGyud kun* bcus.

25. *DNg* bsgom; *Bo dong* sgoms.

26. *Bo dong* blta ba'i.

27. *PTT* las.

28. *PTT* rgyud.

29. *PTT, DG, Co* ma chad pas |.

30. *PTT* dbang.

31. *PTT* tshad ma'o |; *DG, Co* lo rgyus kyis tshad ma'o |.

32. *PTT, DNg, DG, Co, rGyud kun* kun gzhi.

33. *DNg, rGyud kun* lam thams chad yongs su rdzogs pa'o |.

34. *sGa theng ma* reads rtan pa, clearly a misprint.

35. *DNg, rGyud kun* dad pa brtan po |; *Bo dong* dad pa rtan po | = omit bsrung.

36. *PTT* dad pa brtan pos bsrung ba'i 'khor lo |; *DG, Co* dad pa brtan pos srung ba'i 'khor lo |.

37. *Bo dong* 'dud.

38. *DNg, PTT, DG, Co, rGyud kun* omit la.

39. *Bo dong* blta grub.

40. *DNg, PTT, rGyud kun* bsgyur ba'o |; *DG, Co* rgyur ba'o |.

41. *PTT* nang gang bdud lam; *DG* nang gi bdud lam; *Co* nang gis dud lam.

42. *PTT, Co* brda shes pas; *DG* brda ma shes na 'od brda shes pas.

43. *PTT, DG, Co* bral bas bral ba'i.

44. *DNg* 'bras bus gzhi.

45. *Co* thobs nas; *DG* thabs nas.

46. *PS* gyi.

47. *DNg* rlabs.

48. *DNg, rGyud kun* so.

49. *DNg, PTT, DG, Co, Bo dong* sgom pa mi 'chor ba throughout.

50. *DNg, rGyud kun* omit ni.

51. *PTT, DG, Co* thod rgal gyi ye shes.

52. *DNg* dang po la rlung po; *rGyud kun* dang po la rlung so; *PTT, Co* dang po rgyun gyi rlung po; *DG* mas 'dus pa dang po | rgyun gyi rlung po; here, as elsewhere, *PTT, DG, Co* give lag ca for lag cha.

53. *PTT, DG* [omit rtsa] sna tshogs 'dud la sogs | gzhi rtsa ba'i rlung la sogs |; *Co* [omit rtsa] sna tshogs 'dud la sogs bzhi rtsa ba'i rlung la sogs zin.

54. *DNg* 'gags.

55. *PTT, DG, Co* de tsa na thig le.

56. *DNg* 'gre |; *DG* 'dro.

57. *DNg, Bo dong, rGyud kun* omit nang du.

58. *DNg, rGyud kun* med pa.

59. *PTT, DG, Co* me 'bar ba lta bur snang |.

60. *PTT* chu rlung la dang.

61. *PTT, DG, Co* 'byung ba bzhi'i.

62. *PTT* 'byung bzhi'i rlung mnyam rgyu dang lha mo sna tshogs dang dri ro | nam mkha'; *DG, Co* lha mo sna tshogs kyis gar mchod dang dri ro | 'byung ba bzhi'i rlung mnyam rgyu dang lha mo sna tshogs nam mkha'.

63. *DG, Co, rGyud kun* lus.

64. *DG, Co* omit de.

65. *DNg, rGyud kun* phran.

66. *PTT* thig phan.

67. *DNg* nyams nga.

68. *DNg* mchil ma'i.

69. *PTT* nyams lta bu khams kun tu snang ngo |.

70. *PTT, Bo dong* A la; *DNg, DG, Co, rGyud kun* A las.

71. *Bo dong* pho brang du rlung sems mnyams par 'dus na.

72. *PTT* bzung 'dzin.

73. *DNg* yangs la.

74. *PTT, Co* rang 'byung.

75. *rGyud kun* rlung so for rlung po throughout; *Bo dong* dpyid kyi added before rlung po in a different hand, justified in Bo-dong's commentary, *Encyclopaedia Tibetica* vol 105.141.5.

76. *Co, Bo dong* gzugs.

77. *DG, Co* dri.

78. *DNg* long ba.

79. *DNg, Bo dong, rGyud kun* phyi.

80. *rGyud kun* logs.

81. *PTT, DG* mkha' 'gro ma lnga; *Bo dong* mkha' 'gro lnga dang.

82. *DG, Co* la.

83. *PTT, DG, Co* omit shes pas.

84. *PTT* sol ba'i.

85. *DNg* las.

86. *DNg*, *Bo dong*, *rGyud kun* skye bas drod; *DG*, skye ba'i dod; *Co* skyed ba'i dod.

87. *PTT*, *Co* du gtang |; *DNg*, *rGyud kun* du bskyang |; *Bo dong* du gtad do |.

88. *PTT* 'ongs bas.

89. *DG* 'cher ba'i.

90. *DNg*, *Bo dong*, *rGyud kun* yul 'gags pa na.

91. *DG*, *Co*, *Bo dong* bsnyams pas.

92. *DG* rlung pa lag cha dral bas rtsa bral|; *Co* dral bas rtsa bral |.

93. *PTT*, *DNg*, *DG*, *Co*, *Bo dong*, *rGyud kun* rjes las.

94. *DG*, *Co* byung ba'i.

95. *DNg* rjes; *Bo dong* dges.

96. *DNg* kundar; *PTT* kun dhar.

97. *Bo dong* sna rtser dkyil 'khor rgyu.

98. *DNg* rig pas; *PTT*, *DG*, *Co* rig pa; *Bo dong* rigs pa.

99. *PTT*, *Co* lus ngag yid gsum rdo rje'i; *DG* lus ngag yid gsum rdo rje.

100. *DNg* bca'; *Bo dong* dkyil dkrungs bca'.

101. *DG*, *Co* thig le.

102. *DNg* chom pa'o |; *PTT*, *DG*, *Co*, *rGyud kun* choms pa'o |.

103. *PTT* nang gis.

104. *Bo dong* sngar ma skyes pa'i.

105. *PTT*, *Co* omit par; *DG* bzod dka'.

106. *PTT*, *DG*, *Co* bzod pa'o |.

107. *PTT* 'phros na.

108. *PTT*, *DG*, *Co* omit yongs su.

109. *DNg* nang nas; *Bo dong* chos kyi nang na.

110. *PTT*, *Co* omit dang.

111. *DNg*, *DG*, *Co*, *PTT*, *rGyud kun* A nas; *Bo dong* corrected to A nas.

112. *PTT*, *DG*, *Co* rang mtshan nyid do ||.

113. *DNg*, *rGyud kun* phyi nang gi rten.

114. *PTT*, *DNg*, *DG*, *Co*, *rGyud kun* thob par byed pa throughout.

115. *PTT* omit entire phrase: bskyed . . . nas |; *DG* spyod pa'i rim pa'i.

116. *PTT*, *DG*, *Co* dag par byed pa.

117. *PTT*, *Co* gtso bo.

118. *Bo dong* mthong na.

119. *PTT*, *DG*, *Co* mthong bas | rtog pa'i; *PS* rtogs pa'i.

120. *PTT* sgul zhing nyams.

121. *DNg*, *Co* 'chad |; *Bo dong* mar brgya 'gyed followed by small correction to mar brgya 'ched.

122. *PTT* du ma'i rten mthong nas; *DNg*, *rGyud kun* khyad par mi'i rten mthong na; *DG*, *Co* mthong nas.

123. *DNg*, *rGyud kun* dga' zhing.

124. *DNg*, *rGyud kun* dus su bstan pa'i; *PTT* dus na brtan pa'i; *Bo dong* dus su stan pa'i.

125. *PTT*, *DG* de tsa na for de tsam na throughout; *DG*, *Co* rtog |.

126. *Bo dong* mchi ma lhung.

127. *DNg* rdog bro *Bo dong* rgod bro.

128. *Bo dong* ska cig mas.

129. *DNg*, *rGyud kun* rdo rje'i rtse.

130. *Bo dong* rdo rje lan cig corrected to rdo rje'i lan ga cig.

131. *PTT* ltas.

132. *DNg*, *rGyud kun* lus sems bde bas myong zhing brgyal; *Co* myong shing brgyal.

133. *rGyud kun* 'gags.

134. *PTT*, *DG*, *Co* omit mthong lam.

135. *DNg* la.

136. *DG*, *Co* dbang bzhi | *Bo dong* dbang bzhi ni.

137. *PTT*, *DNg*, *DG*, *Co* sa gnyis pa nas.

138. *DG*, *Co* sprul pa'i sku'i.

139. *DG* bskul ba; *Co* bsgul ba.

140. *PTT*, *DG*, *Co*, *rGyud kun* 'gags.

141. *PTT* lte ba'i snying.

142. *DG* sgom lam sa drug go |.

143. *PTT* brlabs; *rGyud kun* brlab.

144. *DNg* gyi.

145. *PTT*, *DG*, *Co* ngag dag pa gsan ba'i.

146. *PTT*, *NTh*, *Co* dangs ma'i rlung lnga la; *DG* dangs ma'i rlang lnga la; *Bo dong*, *rGyud kun*, *PS* omitt lnga after rlung, yet this is included in *Sras don ma*, 399.4, *sGa theng ma*, 447.2.

147. *DG* lta stang sa rnams.

148. *Bo dong* bha gha'i dkyil du.

149. *PTT* gis.

150. *PTT* phyi me.

151. *DG*, *Co*, *DNg*, *Bo dong*, *rGyud kun* A LI KA LI mthong nas.

152. *DG* yig 'bru ces pa; *Co* illegible, but insufficient room for 'bru zhes stsogs; *Bo dong* yid 'bru ces pa sogs.

153. *PS*, *rGyud kun*, *DNg* sa bdun yan chad 'khor bzhi'i brgya longs sku'i zhing khams dung phyur; *Sras don ma*, 403.2, sa bdun yan chad 'khor lo bzhi rgyal ba longs sku'i zhing khams dung phyur. *sGa theng ma*, 450.5, and other commentaries as printed.

154. *DG*, *Co* bsgul ba.

155. *DNg*, *PTT*, *DG*, *Co*, *rGyud kun* 'gags.

156. *rGyud kun* mgrin pa.

157. *Co* sa bcu'o ||.

158. *PTT*, *DG*, *Co* omit chos sku las.

159. *Bo dong* corrected to sems 'dag pa.

160. *PTT* sems dag pa dkyil 'khor 'khor lo thabs; *DG* sems dag la dkyil 'khor 'khor lo thabs.

161. *DG, Co* gyi.

162. *DNg, rGyud kun* byed pa | yid dag par byed pa shes rab ye shes; *Bo dong* byed pa | yid 'dag par byed pa shes rab dang | ye shes; *PTT, DG, Co* shes rab dang ye shes.

163. *DNg, PTT, DG, Co, rGyud kun* ni for dang; *Bo dong* rtags stobs dang|.

164. *DNg, Bo dong, rGyud kun* omit kyi.

165. *DNg, PTT, DG, Co, Bo dong, rGyud kun* bskyod pa'i.

166. *DNg* omit rtags bstan pa.

167. *DNg* sogs kyi dbang.

168. *PTT, Bo dong* 'du [omit ba]; *DG, Co* bdud rtsi lnga gar 'du mthong nas.

169. *PTT, DG, Co* omit du.

170. *PTT, DG, Co* 'dus pa.

171. *PTT, DG, Co* sku'i.

172. *DNg, rGyud kun* dpa' rnams la; *Bo dong* sems pa la.

173. *Bo dong* omit la.

174. *DNg, PTT, DG, Co, Bo dong, rGyud kun* slar spos na.

175. *PTT, DG, Co, rGyud kun* 'gags.

176. *DG* HRI la thig les brtan.

177. *PTT, DG, Co* omit sgom lam.

178. *Bo dong* yang dbang bzhi ni.

179. *DNg, rGyud kun* mthar phyin pa'i lam nas.

180. *PTT* mthar thug 'da' ba |; *DG, Co* mthar thug rten 'brel mthar thug 'da' ba |.

181. *PTT, DG* rdo rje'i rba rlabs kyi lam gyis; *Co* rdo rje'i dpa' rlabs kyi lam gyis.

182. *DG, Co* rang bzhin gyi.

183. *DNg, rGyud kun* lus ngag yid gsum gyi.

184. *PTT* 'dag dkar 'bras bu gnyis 'thob ste|.

185. *DG, Co* omit 'di ni.

186. *PTT, DG, Co* g.yo |.

187. *PTT, DG, Co* mkha' 'gro ma rnams.

188. *DG, Co* A WA DHU TIr 'jug; *Bo-dong* A BA DHU TIr 'du.

189. *PTT, DG* 'bras bu phyogs gcig 'thob ste |; *Co* 'bras bu'i phogs gcig 'thob ste.

190. *DNg, PTT, DG, Co, rGyud kun, Bo dong* longs sku'i.

191. *Co* bsgul ba.

192. *DNg, rGyud kun* bde gshegs bcud bsdus yin |; *DG, Co, Bo dong* bde gshegs bcud 'dus yin|.

193. *DNg, PTT, DG, Co, Bo dong, rGyud kun* dbyer med la.

194. *rGyud kun* lha gar |.

195. *DG, Co* rang bzhin gyi; *rGyud kun* rnam par dag | rang bzhing gyis.

196. *Bo dong* rnam par dag pa lhun grub kyi ska.

197. Between notes 197, *PTT* reads: 'bras bu longs sku'i zhing khams; *DNg, rGyud kun* as printed but with . . . longs sku'i zhing khams; *DG, Co* 'bras bu mthar phyin de kho na nyid kyi rtags longs sku'i zhing khams.

198. *PTT, DG, Co* bsgul ba; *DNg, rGyud kun* ma lus pa sgul ba, omitting la sogs pa.

199. *Bo dong* sgul nus.

200. *PTT*, *DNg*, *rGyud kun* 'gags; *DG*, *Co* A WA DHU TI'i 'gags.

201. *DG* HRI la thig les brtan |.

202. *PTT*, *DG*, *Co* omit dang.

203. *Co* 'bros bzhi.

204. *DG*, *Co* nyams kyis.

205. *DNg*, *PTT* pa.

206. *DG*, *Co*, *rGyud kun* [omit sa] bcu gsum pa'o |.

207. *DNg* 'dzin par.

208. *PTT* 'grig pa lhar snang; *DG*, *Co* 'grig pa.

209. *DNg* 'tshang rgya gar 'khor tshom bu gcig dang bcas nas 'tshang rgya |; *DG*, *Co* 'tshang rgya kar 'khor tshom bu cig dang bcas te 'tshang rgya'o |; *rGyud kun* 'tshang rgya khar 'khor tshom bu gcig dang bcas nas 'tshang rgya; *Bo dong* as printed but with 'tshangs rgya khar.

210. *PTT* rdo rje'i theg pa ni.

211. *DNg* rtogs pas brtags kyang rtogs med rtogs; *PTT*, *DG*, *Co* rtogs pas brtags pas rtog med rtogs; *Bo dong* rtogs pas rtags dang rtog med rtogs.

212. *DNg* dang.

Abbreviations

*Indicates a hypothetical reconstruction.

BEFEO	*Bulletin de l'École française d'Extrême Orient*
CAJ	*Central Asiatic Journal*
CIHTS	Central Institute of Higher Tibetan Studies
GOS	Gaekwad's Oriental Series
HJAS	*Harvard Journal of Asiatic Studies*
ISMEO	Istituto italiano per il Medio ed Estremo Oriente
IA	*Indian Antiquary*
IIJ	*Indo-Iranian Journal*
JA	*Journal asiatique*
JIABS	*Journal of the International Association of Buddhist Studies*
JIP	*Journal of Indian Philosophy*
JRAS	*Journal of the Royal Asiatic Society*
JTS	*Journal of the Tibet Society*
LL	*Lam 'bras slob bshad*
Pe.	Peking canon (+ numbers), ed. Suzuki, 1957
SKB	*Sa skya bka' 'bum*, ed. Bsod Nams Rgya Mtsho, 1969
SOR	Serie orientale Roma
T.	*Taishō shinshū daizōkyō* (+ number), ed. Takakusu and Watanabe, 1924-34
TJ	*Tibet Journal* (Dharamsala)
To.	sDe-dge canon (+ numbers), Ui et al., 1934

Bibliography

The bibliography is in the following order: Indic and Ostensibly Indic Sources, Chinese Sources, Indigenous Tibetan Sources, and Western-Language Sources. I have separated the Chinese canonical materials from the Indic and Ostensibly Indic Sources because they cannot easily be put into the order of the Indic alphabet.

INDIC AND OSTENSIBLY INDIC SOURCES

Acintyādvayakramopadeśa.

Ascribed to Kuddālapāda. Edited with *Guhyasiddhi*, pp. 195–208. Translated by Ratnavajra and 'Brog-mi Shakya ye-shes, *LL* XI.347–62. Translated by *Sukhankura and 'Gos [Khug-pa lhas-btsas]; To. 2228. *bsTan 'gyur*, rgyud, wi, fols. 99b5–104b6.

Advayavajrasaṁgraha.

Edited by Haraprasad Shastri, 1927. GOS no. 40. Baroda: Oriental Institute.

Anāvilatantrarāja.

To. 414. *bKa' 'gyur*, rgyud 'bum, ga, fols. 259b3–61b3.

Abhidharmakośabhāṣya.

Edited by Pralhad Pradhan, 1975. *Abhidharmakośabhāṣyam of Vasubandhu.* Tibetan Sanskrit Works Series, vol. 8, 2nd rev. ed. Patna: K. P. Jayaswal Research Institute.

Abhidharmasamuccaya.

Edited by Pradhan Pralhad, 1950. *Abhidharma Samuccaya of Asanga*. Santiniketan: Visvabharati. To. 4049; T. 1605.

Abhidhānottara-tantra.

To. 369. *bKa' 'gyur*, rgyud 'bum, ka, fols. 247a1–370a7.

Abhisamayālaṁkāra.

Asc. Maitreya. Edited by Theodore Stcherbatsky and Eugene Obermiller, 1929. *Abhisamayālaṁkāra-Prajñāpāramitā-upadeśaśāstra*. Bibliotheca Buddhica 23. St. Petersburg: Academy of Sciences of USSR.

Abhisamayālaṁkārāloka.

Asc. Haribhadra. Edited with *Aṣṭasāhasrikā-prajñāpāramitā*, pp. 267–558.

Amṛtasiddhimūla.

Asc. Virūpa. To. 2285. *bsTan 'gyur*, rgyud, zhi, fols. 142b7–45a1.

Amṛtādhiṣṭhāna.

Asc. Virūpa. To. 2044. *bsTan 'gyur*, rgyud, tsi, fols. 143a2–44a2.

Arthaśāstra.

Edited and translated by R. P. Kangle, 1960. *The Kautilīya Arthaśāstra.* University of Bombay Studies in Sanskrit, Prakrit, and Pali, nos. 1–3. Bombay: University of Bombay.

Avataṁsaka-sūtra.

T. 278. To. 44. *bKa' 'gyur*, phal chen, vols. ka-ga.

Aṣṭasāhasrikā-prajñāpāramitā-sūtra.

Edited by P. L. Vaidya, 1960. *Aṣṭasāhasrikā Prajñāpāramitā with Haribhadra's Commentary Called Āloka.* Buddhist Sanskrit Texts no. 4. Darbhanga: Mithila Institute.

Ārya-tathāgatoṣṇīṣasitātapatrāparājita-mahāpratyaṅgirāparamasiddha-nāma-dhāraṇī.

To. 591. *bKa' 'gyur*, rgyud 'bum, pha, fols. 212b7–19a7.

Ā li kā li gsang ba bsam gyis myi khyab pa chu klung chen po'i rgyud.

In *Dam chos snying po zhi byed las rgyud kyi snyan rgyud zab ched ma*, vol. 1, pp. 6–114; 3 chaps. in *gDams ngag mdzod*, vol. 9, pp. 2–16.

Ārya-Tārāmaṇḍalavidhi-sādhana.

Asc. *Sahajavilāsa. To. 1705. *bsTan 'gyur*, rgyud, sha, fols. 62a2–63b3.

Uḍḍiyānaśrīyogayoginīsvabhūtasambhoga-śmaśānakalpa.

Asc. Birba-pa. To. 1744. *bsTan 'gyur*, rgyud, sha, fols. 111b6–13b2.

'Od gsal 'char ba'i rim pa.

Asc. Virūpa. To. 2019. *bsTan 'gyur*, rgyud, tsi, fols. 80b5–81a6.

Olapaticatuṣṭaya.

Asc. Kāṇha. To. 1451. *bsTan 'gyur*, rgyud, wa, fols. 355b7–58b7.

Karmacaṇḍālikā-dohakoṣa-gīti.

Asc. Virūpa. To. 2344. *bsTan 'gyur*, rgyud, zi, fols. 2b7–3a5.

Kāṇhapādasya dohākoṣa.

Edited and translated by M. Shahidullah, 1928. *Les Chants mystiques de Kāṇha et de Saraha—Les Dohā-Koṣa.* Paris: Adrien-Maisonneuve. Edited by Prabodh Chandra Bagchi, 1935. Dohakoṣa. University of Calcutta Journal of the Department of Letters, vol. 28.

Kāyavākcittatrayādhiṣṭhānoddeśa.

Asc. Buddhajñānapāda. To. 2085. *bsTan 'gyur*, rgyud, tsi, fol. 161a6–b5.

Kālacakra-tantra.

Edited by Biswanath Banerjee, 1985. *A Critical Edition of Śrī Kālacakratantra-Rāja* (collated with the Tibetan version). Calcutta: Asiatic Society.

Kurukullesādhana.
To. 1319. *bsTan 'gyur*, rgyud, ta, fols. 245a6–47a5.

Kṛṣṇayamāri-tantra.
Edited by Samdhong Rinpoche and Vrajvallabh Dvivedi, 1992. *Kṛṣṇayamāri-tantram with Ratnāvali Pañjikā of Kumāracandra.* Rare Buddhist Text Series, no. 9. Sarnath: CIHTS.

Kṛṣṇayamāritantrapañjikā.
Asc. Padmapāṇi. To. 1922. *bsTan 'gyur*, rgyud, bi, fols. 312b5–337a7.

Kaumudīpañjikā.
Durjayacandra. To. 1185. *bsTan 'gyur*, rgyud, ga, fols. 1b1–58b4.

bsKyed rim zab pa'i tshul dgus brgyan pa.
Asc. Padmavajra but written by Grags-pa rgyal-mtshan. *Pod ser LL* XI.419–41.

Khasama-tantrarāja.
To. 386. *bKa' 'gyur*, rgyud 'bum, ga, fols. 199a7–202a1.

Khrodhavijayakalpaguhyatantra.
T. 1217. To. 604. *bKa' 'gyur*, rgyud 'bum, vol. pha, fols. 269a3–87a7; vol. ba, fols. 1b1–35b7.

Gaṇḍavyūha.
Edited by Daisetsu Teitarō Suzuki and Hokei Itsumi, 1949. *The Gaṇḍavyūha Sūtra.* 2nd rev. ed. Tokyo: Society for the Publication of Sacred Books of the World.

Guhyagarbha. Śrī-Guhyagarbha-tattvaviniścaya.
To. 832. *bKa' 'gyur*, rnying rgyud, kha, fols. 110b1–132a7; Kaneko 1982, no. 187.

Guhyatattvaprakāśa.
Asc. Kāṇha. To. 1450. *bsTan 'gyur*, rgyud, wa, fols. 349a3–55b7.

Guhyamaṇi-tilaka-sūtra.
To. 493. *bKa' 'gyur*, rgyud 'bum, kha, fols. 119b5–51b1.

Guhyaratna.
Ascribed to Paṇḍita Akṣobhya. To. 1525. *bsTan 'gyur,* rgyud, za, fols. 82b6–83b2.

Guhyasamāja-tantra.
Edited by Matsunaga Yukei, 1978. *Guhyasamāja Tantra.* Osaka: Toho shuppan.

Guhyasiddhi.
Asc. Padmavajra. Edited by Samdhong Rinpoche and Vrajvallabh Dwivedi, 1987. *Guhyādi-Aṣṭasiddhi-Saṅgraha.* Rare Buddhist Text Series, no. 1, pp. 5–62. Sarnath: CIHTS.

Gopālarājavaṁśāvalī.
Edited and translated by Dhanavajra Vajrācārya and Kamal P. Malla, 1985. *Gopālarājavaṁśāvalī.* Nepal Research Centre Publications, no. 9. Wiesbaden: Franz Steiner Verlag.

dGongs 'dus. Sangs rgyas kun gyi dgongs pa 'dus pa'i mdo chen po.
Kaneko 1982, no. 160.

sGra thal 'gyur chen po rgyud.
Kaneko 1982, no. 155.

Cakrasaṁvara-tantra. Tantrarāja-śrīlaghusaṁvara.
Edited by Janardan Shastri Pandey, 2002. *Śrīherukābhidhānaṁ Cakrasamvaratantram.* 2 vols. Sarnath: CIHTS. To. 368. *bKa' 'gyur,* rgyud 'bum, ka, fols. 213b1–46b7.

**Catuḥkrama.*
Asc. Kāṇha. To. 1451. *bsTan 'gyur,* rgyud, wa, fols. 355b7–58b7.

Catuḥpīṭha-mahāyoginī-tantrarāja.
To. 428. *bKa' 'gyur,* rgyud 'bum, nga, fols. 181a1–231b5.

**Caturaśītisiddhapravṛtti.*
Asc. Abhayadattaśrī. Pe. 5091. Edited and translated by James B. Robinson, 1979.

Candraguhya-tilaka-mahātantrarāja.
To. 477. *bKa' 'gyur,* rgyud 'bum, ja, fols. 247b4–303a7.

Caryāgītikośa.
Edited and translated by Per Kværne, 1977. *An Anthology of Buddhist Tantric Songs: A Study of the Caryāgīti.* Det Norske Videnskaps-Akademi II Hist.-Filos. Klasse Skrifter Ny Serie, no. 14. Oslo: Universitetsforlaget. Edited by Nilratan Sen, 1977. *Caryāgītikoṣa* facsimile ed. Simla: Indian Institute of Advanced Study.

Caryāmelāpakapradīpa.
Asc. Āryadeva. Edited by Janardan Shastri Pandey, 2000. *Caryāmelāpakapradīpam of Ācārya Āryadeva.* Sarnath: CIHTS.

Cittaguhyadohā.
Asc. *Ḍākinī. To. 2443. *bsTan 'gyur,* rgyud, zi, fols. 67a3–71a7.

Chinnamuṇḍasādhana.
Asc. Birwa. To. 1555. *bsTan 'gyur,* rgyud, za, fols. 206a1–8a4. See Nihom 1992.

mChod rten drung thob.
Asc. Nāgārjuna but written by Grags-pa rgyal-mtshan. *Pod ser LL* XI.400–6.

Jñānatilaka-yoginītantrarāja-paramamahādbhuta.
To. 422. *bKa' 'gyur,* nga, fols. 96b6–136a4.

Jñānaprasthāna.
T. 1543, 1544.

Jñānavajrasamuccaya.
To. 450. *bKa' 'gyur,* rgyud 'bum, cha, fols. 1b1–35b7.

Jñānasiddhi.
Asc. Indrabhūti. Edited with *Guhyasiddhi,* pp. 93–157. Edited by Benoytosh

Bhattacharya, 1929. *Two Vajrayāna Works*. GOS no. 44. Baroda: Oriental Institute.

Jñānodaya-tantra.
Edited by Samdhong Rinpoche and Vrajvallabh Dwivedi, 1988. *Jñānodaya Tantram.* Rare Buddhist Text Series, no. 2. Sarnath: CIHTS.

Jñānodayopadeśa.
Asc. Kāyastha Gayādhara. To. 1514. *bsTan 'gyur*, rgyud, zha, fols. 363b4–74b4.

Jñānolka-dhāraṇī-sarvagatipariśodhanī.
To. 522. *bKa' 'gyur*, rgyud 'bum, na, fols. 59a7–60b4. T. 1397, 1398.

rJe btsun ma 'phags pa sgrol ma'i sgrub thabs nyi shu rtsa gcig pa'i las kyi yan lag dang bcas pa mdo bsdus pa.
Asc. *Sūryagupta [Nyi-ma sbas-pa]. To. 1686. *bsTan 'gyur*, rgyud, sha, fols. 10a7–24b6.

rNying ma rgyud 'bum.
mTshams-brag manuscript. 1981. *The mTshams-Brag Manuscript of the rNying-ma rgyud 'bum*. 46 vols. Thimphu, Bhutan: National Library. gTing-skyes manuscript. 1973/74. *rNying ma rgyud 'bum, The Collected Tantras of the Ancient School of Tibetan Buddhism*. 36 vols. Thimbu, Bhutan: Dil mgo mkhyen brtse. See Kaneko 1982.

Ḍākārṇava. Ḍākārṇava-mahāyoginītantrarāja.
To. 372. *bKa' 'gyur*, rgyud 'bum, kha, fols. 137a1–264b7.

Ḍākinyupadeśaśrotraparamparapīḍācchedanāvavāda.
Anon. To. 2286. *bsTan 'gyur*, rgyud zhi, fols. 145a1–50a2.

Tattvaratnāvaloka.
Asc. Vāgīśvarakīrti. Edited by Janardan Pandey, 1997. *Bauddhalaghugrantha Saṃgraha*, pp. 81–142. Rare Buddhist Text Series, no. 14. Sarnath: CIHTS. To. 1889.

Tattvasaṁgraha.
See *Sarvatathāgatatattvasaṁgraha.*

Tantrārthāvatāra.
Asc. Buddhaguhya. To. 2501. *bsTan 'gyur*, rgyud, 'i, fols. 1b1–91b6.

Tantrārthāvatāra-vyākhyāna.
Asc. Padmavajra. To. 2502. *bsTan 'gyur*, rgyud, 'i, fols. 91b6–351a7.

Tarka-jvālā. Madhyamakahṛdayavṛtti-tarkajvālā.
Asc. Bhavya. To. 2856. *bsTan 'gyur*, dbu-ma, dza, fols. 40b7–329b4.

Tripratyayabhāṣya.
To. 4432. *bsTan 'gyur*, sna-tshogs, no, fols. 141b7–49a7.

Trisattvasamādhisamāpatti.
Asc. Buddhajñānapāda. To. 2086. *bsTan 'gyur*, rgyud, tsi, fols. 161b5–62b5.

gTum mos lam yongs su rdzogs pa.
Asc. *Mahācārya-cīrṇavrata-Kāṇha but written by Grags-pa rgyal-mtshan. *Pod ser LL* XI.445–57.

Daśabhūmika.
Edited by Kondo Ryuko, 1936. *Daśabhūmīśvaro Nāma Mahāyānasūtraṁ.* Rinsen Buddhist Text Series, no. 2. Reprint, Kyoto: Rinsen Book, 1983.

Divyāvadāna.
Edited by P. L. Vaidya, 1959. BST, no. 20. Darbhanga: Mithila Institute.

Dohakoṣa.
Asc. Birba-pa. To. 2280. *bsTan 'gyur,* rgyud, zhi, fols. 134a1–36a4.

Dravva-saṁgaha.
Asc. Nemicandra Siddhānta-cakravarttī. Edited and translated by Sarat Chandra Ghoshal, 1917. *Dravya-saṁgraha.* The Sacred Books of the Jainas, vol. 1. Arrah: Central Jaina Publishing House.

rDo rje sems dpa' nam mkha' che bram ze rgyas pa'i rgyud.
Kaneko 1982, no. 19.

brDa nges par gzung ba.
To. 1214. *bsTan 'gyur,* rgyud, ja, fols. 314b1–16a4.

Nikāyabhedavibhaṅga-vyākhyāna.
Asc. Bhavya. To. 4139. *bsTan 'gyur,* 'dul-ba, su, fols. 147a3–54b2.

Nīlamatapurāṇa.
Edited by K. de Vreese, 1936. *Nīlamata or Teachings of Nīla—Sanskrit Text with Critical Notes.* Leiden: Brill. See Ikari 1994.

Nepālavaṁśāvalī.
Edited by Kamal P. Malla, 1985. "Nepālavaṁśāvalī: A Complete Version of the Kaisher Vaṁśāvalī." *Contributions to Nepalese Studies* 12(2): 75–110.

Nairātmyayoginīsādhana.
Asc. Ḍombiheruka. To. 1305. *bsTan 'gyur,* rgyud, ta, fols. 212b7–15a7.

rNal 'byor pa thams cad kyi de kho na nyid snang zhes bya ba grub pa rnams kyi rdo rje'i mgur.
Pseudo-Indic title: *Yogasarvatattvāumutriāloka-vikalavajragīti.* To. 2453. *bsTan 'gyur,* rgyud, zi, fols. 92b1–115b3.

Pañcakrama.
Asc. Siddha Nāgārjuna. Edited by Mimaki Katsumi and Tomabechi Toru, 1994. *Pañcakrama—Sanskrit and Tibetan Texts Critically Edited with Verse Index and Facsimile Edition of the Sanskrit Manuscripts.* 2 parts. Bibliotheca Codicum Asiaticorum 8. Tokyo: Centre for East Asian Cultural Studies for UNESCO.

Pramāṇavārttika.
Edited by Shastri Dharmakīrti and Swami Dwarikadas, 1968. *Pramāṇavārttika of Ācārya Dharmakīrtti.* Bauddha Bharati Series, no. 3. Varanasi: Bauddha Bharati.

Pramāṇaviniścaya.
Dharmakīrti. To. 4211. *bsTan 'gyur*, tshad-ma, ce, fols. 152b1–230a7. See Steinkellner 1973.

Pramāṇasamuccaya.
Dignāga. To. 4203. *bsTan 'gyur*, tshad-ma, ce, fols. 1b1–13a7. See Hattori 1968.

Phyag rgya chen po yi ge med pa.
Asc. Vāgīśvarakīrti but written by Grags-pa rgyal-mtshan. *Pod ser LL* XI.406–19.

Phyag rgya'i lam skor.
Asc. Indrabhūti. *Pod ser LL* XI.461–79.

**Biruvajragīti.*
Asc. Virūpa. To. 2356. *bsTan 'gyur*, rgyud, zi, fol. 6b4–7.

Buddhakapāla-tantra. Śrī-Buddhakapāla-yoginī-tantra-rāja.
To. 424. *bKa' 'gyur*, rgyud 'bum, nga, fols. 143a1–67a5; Peking 63. *bKa' 'gyur*, rgyud 'bum, da, fols. 126b4–53a6.

Buddhakapālatantrapañjikā Tattvacandrikā.
Asc. Padmavajra. To. 1653 *bsTan 'gyur*, rgyud, ra, fols. 150a3–66a7.

Bodhicaryāvatāra.
Edited by P. L. Vaidya, 1960. *Bodhicaryāvatāra of Śāntideva, with the Commentary Pañjikā of Prajñākaramati.* Buddhist Sanskrit Texts, no. 12. Darbhanga: Mithila Institute.

Bodhicittabhāvanā.
Asc. Mañjuśrīmitra. To. 2591. Edited and translated by Norbu and Lipman, 1986.

Bodhicittavivaraṇa.
Asc. Nāgārjuna. To. 1800. Edited and translated by Lindtner, 1982.

Bodhipathapradīpa.
Asc. Atiśa Dīpaṁkaraśrījñāna. Edited by Helmut Eimer, 1978. See Davidson 1995.

Bodhisattvabhūmi.
Edited by Unrai Wogihara, 1930–36. *Bodhisattvabhūmi: A Statement of Whole Course of the Bodhisattva (Being Fifteenth Section of Yogācārabhūmi).* Reprint, Tokyo: Sankibo Buddhist Book Store, 1971. To. 4037; T. 1579.

Bhikṣāvṛtti-nāma.
Asc. Ḍombipa. To. 1234. *bsTan 'gyur*, rgyud, nya, fols. 67b7–70a5.

Bhikṣuvarṣāgrapṛcchā.
To. 4133. *bsTan 'gyur*, 'dul-ba, su, fols. 66a1–70b3.

Bhoṭasvāmidāsalekha.
Buddhaguhya. To. 4194. Dietz 1984, pp. 360–65.

Mañjuśrīmūlakalpa.
T. Ganapati Sastri, 1920. *Āryamañjuśrīmūlakalpa.* Reprint, Trivandrum: C B H Publications, 1992. To. 543.

Mañjuśrīnāmasaṁgīti.
See Davidson 1981.

Madhyamakālaṁkāra.
Asc. Śāntarakṣita. To. 3884. *bsTan 'gyur*, dbu-ma, sa, fols. 53a1–56b3.

Madhyamakāloka.
Asc. Kamalaśīla. To. 3887. *bsTan 'gyur*, dbu-ma, sa, fols. 133b4–244a7.

Madhyamakāvatāra.
Edited by Louis de la Vallée Poussin, 1907–12. *Madhyamakāvatāra par Candrakīrti.* Bibliotheca Buddhica, no. 9. St. Petersburg: L'Académie impériale des sciences. See Huntington 1989.

Madhyamakopadeśa.
Asc. Atiśa Dīpaṁkara. To. 3929. To. *bsTan 'gyur*, dbu-ma, ki, fols. 95b1–96a7.

Madhyāntavibhāga-ṭīkā.
Sthiramati. Edited by Ramachandra Pandeya, 1971. *Madhyāntavibhāga-śāstra.* Delhi: Motalal Banarsidass.

Mayamata.
Edited and translated by Bruno Dagens, 1970–76. *Mayamata—Traité sanskrit d'architecture.* Publications de l'Institut français d'indologie no. 40–I and II. Pondichéry: Institut français d'indologie.

——. 1985. *Mayamata—An Indian Treatise on Housing Architecture and Iconography.*
New Delhi: Sitaram Bhartia Institute of Science & Research.

Mahākāla-tantrarāja.
To. 440. *bKa' 'gyur*, rgyud 'bum, ca, fols. 45b6–86a7.

Mahāmāyātantra.
Edited by Samdhong Rinpoche and Vrajavallabh Dwivedi, 1992. *Mahāmāyātantram with Guṇavatī by Ratnākaraśānti.* Rare Buddhist Text Series, no. 10. Sarnath: CIHTS.

Mahāmudrātilaka. Śrī-Mahāmudrātilaka-mahāyoginī-tantrarājādhipati.
To. 420. *bKa' 'gyur*, rgyud 'bum, nga, fols. 66a1–90b7.

Mahāyāna-sūtrālaṁkāra.
Asc. Maitreya. T. 1604. To. 4020. Edited by Levi 1907.

Mahāvairocanābhisambodhitantra.
Extended title: *Mahāvairocanābhisambodhi-vikurvitādhiṣṭhāna-vaipulyasūtrendrarāja-nāma-dharmaparyāya.* To. 494. *bKa' 'gyur*, rgyud 'bum, tha, fols. 151b2–260a7; T.848.18.1a-55a.

Mahāvyutpatti.
Edited by Sasaki Ryōzaburō, 1916–25. *Mahāvyutpatti: Bonzo Kanwa shigaku taiko Mahāwyuttpattei.* 2 vols. Kyoto.

Mahāsāṁghika-vinaya.
T. 1425.

Mūlamadhyamakakārikā.
Edited by Louis de la Vallée Poussin, 1903–13. *Mūlamadhyamakakārikās de Nāgārjuna avec la Prasannapadā commentaire de Candrakīrti.* Bibliotheca Buddhica, no. 4. St. Petersburg: L'Académie impériale des sciences.

Mūlasarvāstivāda Vinaya.
To. 1–7. Edited by Nalinaksha Dutt, 1947–50. *Gilgit Manuscripts.* Vol. 3, parts 1–4. Srinagar: Research Department. Edited by Raniero Gnoli, 1977. *The Gilgit Manuscript of the Saṅghabhedavastu.* SOR, vol. 49, 2 parts. Rome: ISMEO. Edited by Raniero Gnoli, 1978. *The Gilgit Manuscript of the Śayanāsanavastu and the Adhikaraṇavastu.* SOR, vol. 50. Rome: ISMEO.

Mṛcchakaṭika.
Edited by M. R. Kale, 1924. *The Mrichchhakatika of Sudraka.* Reprint, Delhi: Motilal Banarsidass, 1988.

Mṛtyuvañcanopadeśa.
Asc. Vāgīśvarakīrti. To. 1748. *bsTan 'gyur*, rgyud, sha, fols. 118b7–33b3.

rDzogs pa chen po lta ba'i yang snying | sangs rgyas thams cad kyi dgongs pa | nam mkha' klong yangs kyi rgyud.
Kaneko 1982, no. 114.

Yamāntakavajraprabheda-nāma-mūlamantrārtha.
Asc. *Vilāsavajra. To. 2014. *bsTan 'gyur*, rgyud, tsi, fols. 1b1–69a7.

Yamāriyantrāvalī.
Asc. Virūpa. To. 2022. *bsTan 'gyur*, rgyud, tsi, fols. 85a1–88a4.

Ye shes kyi mkha' 'gro ma sum cu rtsa lnga'i rtogs pa brjod pa.
Anon. To. 2450. *bsTan 'gyur*, rgyud, zi, fols. 85b6–88a1.

Yogācārabhūmi.
Partially edited by Vidhushekhara Bhattacharya, 1957. *The Yogācārabhūmi of Ācārya Asaṅga.* Calcutta: University of Calcutta. See *Bodhisattvabhūmi* and *Śrāvakabhūmi.* To. 4035–4042. T. 1579.

Yoginīsañcāratantra.
Edited by Janardan Shastri Pandey, 1998. *Yoginīsañcāratantram with Nibandha of Tathāgataraksita and Upadeśānusāriṇīvyākhyā of Alakakalaśa.* Rare Buddhist Texts Series, no. 21. Sarnath: CIHTS.

Yon po bsrang ba'i gdams ngag.
Asc. Acyuta-Kāṇha but written at Sa-skya. *Pod ser LL* XI.457–61.

Raktayamāntakasādhana.
Asc. Virūpa. To. 2017. *bsTan 'gyur*, rgyud, tsi, fols. 76b3–77b7.

Raktayamārisādhana.
Asc. Śrīvirūpa. To. 2018. *bsTan 'gyur*, rgyud, tsi, fols. 78a1–80b5.

Raktayamārisādhana.
Asc. Buddhajñānapāda. To. 2084. *bsTan 'gyur*, rgyud, tsi, fols. 160a6–161a5.

Ratnakūṭa.
T. 310. To. 45–93.

Ratnagotravibhāga.
Edited by E. H. Johnston, 1950. *Ratnagotravibhāga Mahāyānottaratantraśāstra.* Patna: Bihar Research Society. See Takasaki 1966.

Ratnajvalasādhana.
Asc. Prajñedraruci. To. 1251. *bsTan 'gyur*, rgyud, nya, fols. 214a3–41b2.

Rahasyānandatilaka.
Asc. Mahāmati. To. 1345. *bsTan 'gyur*, rgyud, ta, fols. 359b6–66a7.

Rājataraṅgiṇī.
Edited and translated by Marc Aurel Stein, 1892. *Kalhaṇa's Rājataraṅgiṇī or the Chronicle of the Kings of Kashmir.* Bombay. M. A. Stein, 1900. *Kalhaṇa's Rājataraṅgiṇī, a Chronicle of the Kings of Kashmir.* 2 vols. Westminster.

Rig pa rang shar chen po'i rgyud.
A-'dzom chos-gar xylographic ed. *rNying-ma'i rgyud bcu bdun.* Vol. 1, pp. 389–855. New Delhi: Sanje Dorje, 1977. *rNying ma rgyud 'bum*, gTing-skyes manuscript, vol. 10, pp. 2–334; Kaneko 1982, no. 153; mTshams-brag manuscript, vol. 11, pp. 323–699.

Re ma ti srog sngags kyi rgyud kyis rgyal po.
Samten 1992, Phug-brag no. 772.

Laṅkāvatāra-sūtra.
Edited by Nanjio Bunyiu, 1923. Reprint, Bibliotheca Otaniensis, vol. 1. Kyoto: Otani University Press, 1956.

Lam 'bras bu dang bcas pa'i gdams ngag dang man ngag tu bcas pa.
Asc. Virūpa. To. 2284. *bsTan-`gyur*, rgyud, zhi, fols. 139a6–42b7. See app. 2.

Lalitavistara.
Edited by P. L. Vaidya, 1958. *Lalita-Vistara.* Buddhist Sanskrit Texts, no. 1. Darbhanga: Mithila Institute.

Vajraḍāka-mahātantrarāja.
To. 370. *bKa' 'gyur*, rgyud 'bum, kha, fols. 1b1–125a7.

Vajrapañjara. Ārya-Ḍākinīvajrapañjara-mahātantrarājakalpa.
To. 419. *bKa' 'gyur*, rgyud 'bum, nga, fols. 30a4–65b7.

Vajrapāṇy-abhiṣeka-mahātantra.
To. 496. *bKa' 'gyur*, rgyud 'bum, da, fols. 1b1–156b7.

Vajrabhairavasādhanakarmopacāra-sattvasaṁgraha.
*Amoghavajra. To. 1982. *bsTan 'gyur*, rgyud, mi, fols. 159b5–66a7.

Vajramaṇḍalavidhipuṣṭi-sādhana.
Asc. *Vilāsavajra. *Rong zom chos bzang gi gsung 'bum*, vol. 1, pp. 355–67.

Vajrayānasthūlāpatti.
Attributed to Nāgārjuna. To. 2482. *bsTan 'gyur*, rgyud, zi, fols. 180a2–b3.

**Vajrayānamūlāpattiṭīkā*, [*rDo rje theg pa'i rtsa ba'i ltung ba'i rgya cher 'grel pa*]. To. 2486. *bsTan 'gyur*, rgyud, zi, fols. 185a7–92b6.

Vajrayānamūlāpattiṭīkā-mārgapradīpa.
Mañjuśrīkīrti. To. 2488. *bsTan 'gyur*, rgyud, zi, fols. 197b7–231b7.

Vajravidāraṇā-dhāraṇī.
To. 750. Edited by Iwamoto Yukata, 1937. *Kleinere Dhāraṇī Texte.* Vol. 2, pp. 7–9. Kyoto.

Vajraśekhara-mahāguhyayogatantra.
To. 480. *bKa' 'gyur*, rgyud 'bum, nya, fols. 142b1–274a5.

Vasantatilakā.
Asc Kṛṣṇacārya. Edited by Samdhong Rinpoche and Vrajavallabh Dwivedi, 1990. Sarnath: CIHTS.

Vidyādharīkelī-śrīvajravārāhī-sādhana.
Asc. Advayavajra. *SKB* IV.28.4.3–29.2.3.

Vinaya-sūtra.
Asc. Guṇaprabha. To. 4117. Partially edited by P. V. Bapat and V. V. Gokhale, 1982. *Vinaya-sūtra and Auto-commentary on the Same.* Patna: K. P. Jayaswal Research Institute.

Vimalaprabhā.
Edited by Jagannatha Upadhyaya, 1986. Bibliotheca Indo-Tibetica Series, no. 11. Edited by Vrajavallabh Dwivedi and S. S. Bahulkar, 1994. Rare Buddhist Texts Series, nos. 12, 13. 3 vols. Sarnath: CIHTS.

Virūapādacaurāsi.
Asc. Virūpa. To. 2283. *bsTan 'gyur*, rgyud, zhi, fols. 138a4–39a6.

**Virūpagīti. Bir rū pa'i glu.*
To. 2369. *bsTan 'gyur*, rgyud, zi , fols. 9a5–9b1; Pe. 3197. rgyud-'grel vol. tshi 11a5–11b1.

Vairocanābhisambodhitantrapiṇḍārtha.
Buddhaguhya. To. 2662. *bsTan 'gyur*, rgyud, nyu, fols. 1–65a.

Śrāvakabhūmi.
Edited by Karunesha Shukla, 1973. *Śrāvakabhūmi of Ācārya Asaṅga.* Tibetan Sanskrit Works Series, vol. 14. Patna: K. P. Jayaswal Research Institute.

Śrī-Agnimālātantrarāja.
To. 407. *bKa' 'gyur*, rgyud 'bum, ga, fols. 244b1–45b6.

Śrī-Guhyasamājasādhana-siddhasambhava-nidhi.
Asc. Vitapāda. To. 1874. *bsTan 'gyur*, rgyud, pi, fols. 1b1–69b6.

Śrī-Cakrasaṁvaraguhyācintyatantrarāja.
To. 385. *bKa' 'gyur*, rgyud 'bum, ga, fols. 196a1–99a1.

Śrī-Jñānajvala-tantrarāja.
To. 394. *bKa' 'gyur*, rgyud 'bum, ga, fols. 222a1–23a7.

Śrī-Jñānarājatantra.
To. 398. *bKa' 'gyur*, rgyud 'bum, ga, fols. 229a2–30a2.

Śrī-Jñānāśayatantrarāja.
To. 404. *bKa' 'gyur*, rgyud 'bum, ga, fols. 239a1–39b7.

Śrī-Jvalāgniguhyatantrarāja.
To. 400. *bKa' 'gyur*, rgyud 'bum, ga, fols. 231b4–33a5.

Śrī-Ḍākārṇava-mahāyoginītantrarāja-vāhikaṭīkā.
Asc. Padmavajra. To. 1419. *bsTan 'gyur*, rgyud, dza, fols. 1b1–318a7.

Śrī-Ḍākinīsaṁvaratantra.
To. 406. *bKa' 'gyur*, rgyud 'bum, ga, fols. 242b7–44a7.

Śrī-Mahākhatantrarāja.
To. 387. *bKa' 'gyur*, rgyud 'bum, ga, fols. 202a2–3b1.

Śrī-Mahāsamayatantra.
To. 390. *bKa' 'gyur*, rgyud 'bum, ga, fols. 213b4–16a3.

Śrī-Ratnajvalatantrarāja.
To. 396. *bKa' 'gyur*, rgyud 'bum, ga, fols. 224b4–27b2.

Śrī-Vajraḍākinīgītā.
Ascribed to *Dhātujyeṣṭhā (dbyings kyi gtso mo). To. 2442. *bsTan 'gyur*, rgyud, zi, fols. 64b7–67a2.

Śrī-Vajrabhairavavidāraṇatantrarāja.
To. 409. *bKa' 'gyur*, rgyud 'bum, ga, fols.247a4–48a1.

Śrī-Śmaśānālaṁkāratantrarāja.
To. 402. *bKa' 'gyur*, rgyud 'bum, ga, fols. 235a5–37a5.

Śrī-Sahajapradīpa-pañjikā.
Ascribed to *Vajragupta. To. 1202. *bsTan 'gyur*, rgyud, ja, fols. 160a1–208b1.

Śrī-Sūryacakratantrarāja.
To. 397. *bKa' 'gyur*, rgyud 'bum, ga, fols. 227b3–29a2.

Śrī-Hevajrapañjikā muktikāvalī.
Asc. Ratnākaraśānti. To. 1189. Edited by Ram Shankar Tripathi and Thakur Sain Negi, 2001. *Hevajratantram with Muktāvalīpañjikā of Mahāpaṇḍitācārya Ratnākaraśānti.* Bibliotheca Indo-Tibetica Series, no. 68. Sarnath: CIHTS.

Śrī-Hevajrapradīpaśūlopamāvavādaka.
Asc. *Saroruhavajra. To. 1220. *bsTan 'gyur*, rgyud, nya, fols. 19a7–20b6.

Śrī-Hevajrasādhana. Asc. Ḍombi-pa. To. 1232. *bsTan 'gyur*, rgyud, nya, fols. 45a4–48a1.

Śrī-Hevajrābhisamayatilaka.
Asc. Śākya srung-ba. To. 1277. *bsTan 'gyur*, rgyud, ta, fols. 105a6–30a6.

gShin rje gshed kyi yid bzhin gyi nor bu'i phreng ba zhe bya ba'i sgrub thabs.
Anon. To. 2083. *bsTan 'gyur*, rgyud, tsi, 159a7–60a6.

Ṣaḍaṅgasādhana.
Asc. *Durjayacandra. To. 1239. *bsTan 'gyur*, rgyud, nya, fols. 126b2–30a3.

Ṣaḍdharmopadeśa.
Asc. Tillipa. To. 2330. *bsTan 'gyur*, rgyud, zhi, fols. 270a7–71a3. Also in *gDams ngag mdzod*, vol. 5, pp. 106–7.

Saṃvaravyākhyā.
Asc. Kāṇha. To. 1460. *bsTan 'gyur*, rgyud, zha, fols. 6a3–10b7.

Saṃvarodaya-tantra.
To. 373. *bKa' 'gyur*, rgyud 'bum, kha, fols. 265a1–311a6. Edited and translated by Shinichi Tsuda, 1974. *The Saṁvarodaya-Tantra—Selected Chapters.* Tokyo: Hokuseido Press.

Satyadvayavibhaṅga.
Edited and translated by Malcolm David Eckel, 1987. *Jñānagarbha's Commentary on the Distinction Between the Two Truths.* Albany: State University of New York Press.

Sandhivyākaraṇa-tantra.
To. 444. *bKa' 'gyur*, rgyud 'bum, ca, fols. 158a1–207b7.

Saptāṇga.
Attributed to Vāgīśvarakīrti. To. 1889. *bsTan 'gyur*, rgyud pi, fols. 203a3–4b4.

Samādhirāja-sūtra.
Edited by P. L. Vaidya, 1961. Buddhist Sanskrit Texts, no. 2. Darbhanga: Mithila Institute.

Sampuṭa-tantra. Sampuṭodbhava.
To. 381. *bKa' 'gyur*, rgyud 'bum, ga, fols. 73b1–158b7; Pe. 26. *bKa' 'gyur*, rgyud 'bum, ga, fols. 244a2–330a5. Partially edited by Tadeusz Skorupski, 1996.

Sampuṭa-tilaka.
To. 382. *bKa' 'gyur*, rgyud 'bum, ga, fols. 158b7–84a7; Pe. 27. *bKa' 'gyur* rgyud 'bum, ga, fols. 330a5–57a6.

Sarahapādasya dohākoṣa.
P. C. Bagchi, 1935; M. Shahidullah, 1928; see *Kāṇhapādasya dohākoṣa.*

Sarvatathāgatatattvasaṁgraha.
Edited by Yamada Isshi, 1980. *Sarva-tathāgata-Tattvasaṅgraha: A Critical Edition Based on a Sanskrit Manuscript and Chinese and Tibetan Translations.* New Delhi: International Academy of Indian Culture. Reprinted with errors by Chandra Lokesh, ed., 1987. *Sarva-Tathāgata-Tattva-Saṅgraha.* Delhi: Motilal Banarsidass, 1987. To. 479; T. 882.

Sarvadurgatipariśodhana-tantra.
Edited and translated by Tadeusz Skorupski, 1983. *The Sarvadurgatipariśodhana Tantra—Elimination of All Evil Destinies.* Delhi: Motilal Banarsidass.

Sarvabuddhasamāyoga, or *Sarvabuddhasamāyoga-ḍākinījāla-sambara-nāma-uttara-tantra.* (longer recension)
To. 366. *bKa' 'gyur*, rgyud 'bum, ka, fols. 151b1–93a6.

Sarvabuddhasamāyoga-gaṇavidhi.
Asc. Indrabhūti. To. 1672. *bsTan 'gyur*, rgyud, la, fols. 195a7–99a4.

Sarvabuddhasamāyoga-tantrarāja. (shorter recension)
rNying ma rgyud 'bum, mTshams-brag ms., vol. tsha, fols. 1b1–26a7. Kaneko 1982, no. 207.

Sahajasiddhi.
Asc. Indrabhūti. To. 2210. *bsTan 'gyur*, rgyud, zhi, fols. 1b1–4a3; Pe. 3107. *bsTan 'gyur* rgyud-'grel, tsi, fols. 1b1–4b7.

Sahajasiddhi.
Asc. Ḍombiheruka. In Malati J. Shendge, ed. and trans., 1967. "Śrīsahajasiddhi," *IIJ* 10 (1967):126–49. Edited with the *Guhyasiddhi*, pp. 181–91.

Sahajasiddhi.
Asc. Ḍombiheruka. *Pod ser LL* XI.387–95.

Sahajasiddhipaddhati.
Asc. Lha-lcam rje-btsun-ma dpal-mo (? = *Devībhaṭṭārikāśrī). To. 2211. *bsTan 'gyur*, rgyud, zhi, fols. 4a3–25a1; Pe. 3108. *bsTan 'gyur*, rgyud-'grel, tsi, fols. 4b8–29a7.

Sādhanamālā.
Edited by Benoytosh Bhattacharya, 1925. GOS nos. 26, 41. 2 vols. Baroda: Oriental Institute.

Sunisprapañcatattvopadeśa.
Asc. Virūpa. To. 2020. *bsTan 'gyur*, rgyud, tsi, fols. 81a7–84a6.

Suparigraha-maṇḍalavidhi-sādhana.
Asc. Durjayacandra. To. 1240. *bsTan 'gyur*, rgyud, nya, fols. 130a3–54a7.

Sekaprakriyā.
To. 365. *bKa' 'gyur*, rgyud 'bum, ka, fols. 146a7–50a7.

Hevajra-tantra.
Edited and translated David L. Snellgrove, 1959. *The Hevajra Tantra: A Critical Study.* 2 vols. London Oriental Series, vol. 6. Oxford: Oxford University Press. Includes the *Yogaratnamālā* of Kāṇhapāda.

Hevajrasādhana.
Asc. Mañjuśrījñāna. To. 1301. *bsTan 'gyur*, rgyud, ta, fols. 199b6–205b2.

CHINESE SOURCES

Datang xiyu ji.
Xuan-zang. T.2087.51. See Beal 1869.

Datang xiyu qiufa gaoseng zhuan.
Yijing. T.2066.51.1a-12b. See Lahiri 1986.

TIBETAN SOURCES

Kaḥ thog si tu'i dbus gtsang gnas yig.
Si-tu-pa Chos kyi rgya-mtsho. Lhasa: Bod ljongs bod yig dpe rnying dpe skrun khang, 1999.

Kun rig gi cho ga gzhan phan 'od zer.
Grags-pa rgyal-mtshan. *SKB* IV.199.1.1–228.1.6.

Kye rdo rje'i 'grel ba'i dkar chag.
Ngor-chen Kun-dga' bzang-po. *SKB* IX.284.4.1–85.1.2.

Kye rdo rje'i byung tshul.
Ngor-chen Kun-dga' bzang-po. *rGyud kyi rgyal po dpal kye rdo rje'i byung tshul dang brgyud pa'i bla ma dam pa rnams kyi rnam par thar pa ngo mtshar rgya mtsho. SKB* IX.278.1.1–84.3.3.

Kye rdo rje'i rtsa rgyud brtag gnyis kyi dka' 'grel.
Sa-chen Kun-dga' snying-po. *SKB* I.78.4.1–122.4.6.

Kye rdor lus dkyil gyi dbang gi bya ba mdor bsdus pa.
Attributed to bLa-ma Sa-chen-pa. *Sa skya'i rje btsun gong ma rnam lnga'i gsung ma phyi gsar rnyed*, vol. 1, pp. 7–20.

kLog skya ma.
Sa-chen Kun-dga' snying-po. *gZhung rdo rje'i tshig rkang gi 'grel pa rnal 'byor dbang phyug dpal sa skya pa chen po la klog skya dbang phyug grags kyis zhus pa. LL* XXVII.191–395. MS. facsimile published in *gŹuṅ bsad Klog skya ma and Other Related Esoteric Sa-skya-pa Texts*, pp. 1–345. See app. 3.

kLong chen chos 'byung.
Lhasa: Bod ljongs bod yig dpe snying dpe skrung khang, 1991.

dKar brgyud gser 'phreng.
rGyal-thang-pa bDe-chen rdo-rje. *Dkar-brgyud Gser-'phreṅ: A Thirteenth-Century Collection of Verse Hagiographies of the Succession of Eminent Masters of the 'Brug-pa Dkar-brgyud-pa Tradition.* Tashijong: Tibetan Craft Community, 1973.

dKar chag ldan dkar ma. Pho brang stod thang ldan dkar gyi chos 'gyur ro cog gi dka' chag.
To. 4364. See Lalou 1953.

bKa' 'chems ka khol ma.
Edited by sMon-lam rgya-mtsho. Lanzhou: Kan su'i mi rigs dep skrun khang, 1989.

bKa' thang sde lnga.
U-rgyan gling-pa. Edited by rDo-rje rgyal-po, 1986. Beijing: Mi rigs dpe skrun khang.

bKa' gdams chos 'byung.
A-mes Zhabs. *dGe ba'i bshes gnyen bka' gdams pa rnams kyi dam pa'i chos byung ba'i tshul legs par bshad pa ngo mtshar rgya mtsho.* Xining: Mtsho sngon mi rigs dpe skrun khang, 1995.

bKa' gdams rin po che'i chos 'byung.
bSod-nam lha'i dbang-po. In Gonpo Tseten, ed., *Two Histories of the Bka'-gdams-pa Tradition from the Library of Burmiok Athing*, pp. 207–393. Gangtok: Palace Monastery, 1977.

bKa' gdams gsar rnying gi chos 'byung.
Paṇ-chen bSod-nams grags-pa. Edited with *bKa' gdams rin po che'i chos 'byung*, in Tseten, ed., *Two Histories*, pp. 1–205.

bsKyed rim gnad kyi zla zer.
Ngor-chen Kun-dga' bzang-po. *SKB* IX.173.4–277.

bsKyed rim gnad kyi zla zer la rtsod pa spong ba gnad kyi gsal byed.
Go-rams bSod-nams seng-ge. *Go rams bka' 'bum*, vol. 12, pp. 557–693.

Kha rag gnyos kyi rgyud pa byon tshul mdor bsdus.
Edited by Khedup Gyatso, 1978. *The History of the Gños Lineage of Kha-Rag*, pp. 1–96. Dolanji: Tibetan Bonpo Monastic Centre.

Khams bde dri ba'i nyams dbyangs.
Grags-pa rgyal-mtshan. *SKB* IV.347.1.1–3.6.

mKhas grub khyung po rnal 'byor gyi rnam thar.
Edited by bSod nams tshe brtan, 1996. *Shangs pa bka' brgyud pa bla rabs kyi rnam thar*, pp 3–62. Lhasa: Bod ljongs bod yig dpe rnying dpe skrun khang.

mKhas pa lde'u chos 'byung.
Edited by Chab-spel tshe-brtan phun-tshogs and Nor-brang o-rgyan, 1987. *mKhas pa lde'us mdzad pa'i rgya bod kyi chos 'byung rgyas pa.* Lhasa: Bod ljongs mi rigs dpe skrun khang.

mKhas pa'i dga' ston.
dPa' bo gtsug lang phreng ba. *Dam pa'i chos kyi 'khor lo bsgyur ba rnams kyi byung ba gsal bar byed pa mkhas pa'i dga' ston.* 2 vols. Beijing: Mi rigs dpe skrun khang, 1986.

'Khor 'das dbyer med tshig byas rin chen snang ba.
Grags-pa rgyal-mtshan. *Pod ser*, pp. 191–94.

Ga ring rgyal po la rtsis bsdur du btang ba'i yi ge.
Grags-pa rgyal-mtshan. *SKB* IV.104.1.6–4.6.

Gang zag gzhung ji lta ba bzhin du dkri ba'i gzhung shing.
Sa-chen Kun-dga' snying-po. *Pod ser*, pp. 300–14.

Gu bkra'i chos 'byung.

Gu-ru bKra-shis. Edited by rDo-rje rGyal-po, 1990. *bsTan pa'i snying po gsang chen snga 'gyur nges don zab mo'i chos kyi byung ba gsal bar byed pa'i legs bshad mkhas pa dga' bnyed ngo mtshar gtam gyi rol mtsho.* Beijing: Krung go'i bod kyi shes rig dpe skrun khang.

Go rams bka' 'bum.

The Collected Works of Kun-Mkhyen Go-Rams-pa Bsod-Nams-Seng-Ge. 13 vols. Rajpur: Sakya College, 1979.

Gong tu ma bstan pa'i rdo rje slob dpon gyi dbang gi tho.

Anonymous but probably by Sa-chen Kun-dga' snying-po. *Sa skya'i rje btsun gong ma rnam lnga'i gsung ma phyi gsar rnyed*, vol. 1, pp. 21–25.

Grub chen bcu.

Asc. Sa-skya Paṇḍita. *SKB* V.349.3.6–53.2.1.

gLegs bam gyi dkar chags.

Grags-pa rgyal-mtshan. *gSung ngag rin po che lam 'bras bu dang bcas pa'i don gsal bar byed pa glegs bam gyi dkar chags. LL* XI.1–8.

dGag lan nges don 'brug sgra.

Sog-zlog-pa bLo-gros rgyal-mtshan. *gSang sngags snga 'gyur la bod du rtsod pa snga phyir byung ba rnams kyi lan du brjod pa nges pa don gyi 'brug sgra.* Chengdu: Si khron mi rigs dpe skrun khang, 1997.

dGa' ston la spring yig.

Grags-pa rgyal-mtshan. *SKB* III.272.3.6–74.3.2.

rGya sgom tshul khrims grags la spring ba.

bSod-nam rtse-mo. *SKB* II.39.2.4–4.4.

rGya bod kyi sde pa'i gyes mdo.

Grags-pa rgyal-mtshan. *SKB* IV.296.4.2–98.3.3.

rGya bod yig tshang chen mo.

sTag-sthang rdzong-pa. Cheng-du: Si chuan min zu chu ban she, 1985.

rGyal po bka'i thang yig.

In *bKa' thang sde lnga*, pp. 85–227.

rGyal po go pe la sras dang btsun mor bcas la shing mo yos sogs la gnang ba'i bkra shis kyi tshigs bcad rnams.

Asc. 'Phags-pa bLo-gros rgyal-mtshan. *SKB* VII.300.2.5–10.2.5.

rGyal po la gdams pa'i rab tu byed pa'i rnam par bshad pa gsung rab gsal ba'i rgyan.

By Shes-rab bzhon-nu under the direction of 'Phags-pa bLo-gros rgyal-mtshan. *SKB* VII.90.4.1–108.4.6.

rGyal bu byang chub sems dpa' la gnang ba'i bka' yig.

Asc. 'Phags-pa bLo-gros rgyal-mtshan. *SKB* VII.238.2.3–4.4.

rGyal rabs gsal ba'i me long.

bLa-ma dam-pa bSod-nams rgyal-mtshan. In B. I. Kuznetsov, ed., 1966. *Rgyal*

Rabs Gsal Ba'i Me Long (*The Clear Mirror of Royal Genealogies*). Scripta Tibetana, no. 1. Leiden: Brill. Beijing: Mi rigs dpe skrun khang, 1981. See Sørensen 1994.

rGyud kyi rgyal po chen po saṁ pu ṭa zhe bya ba dpal ldan sa skya paṇḍi ta'i mchan dang bcas pa.
Sa-skya Paṇḍita Kun-dga' rgyal-mtshan. *Sa skya'i rje btsun gong ma rnam lnga'i gsung ma phyi gsar rnyed*, vol. 2, pp. 69–669.

rGyud kyi mngon par rtogs pa rin po che'i ljon shing.
Grags-pa rgyal-mtshan. *SKB* III.1–70.1.

rGyud rgyal gsang ba snying po'i 'grel pa rong zom chos bzang gis mdzad pa.
Asc. Rong-zom Chos-kyi bzang-po. *rNying ma bka' ma rgyas pa*, vol. 25.

rGyud sde kun btus.
Compiled by 'Jam-dbyangs bLo-gter dbang-po. Delhi: N. Lungtok & N. Gyaltshan, 1971.

rGyud sde spyi'i rnam par gzhag pa.
bSod-nams rtse-mo. *SKB* II.1–37.

rGyud sde spyi'i rnam gzhag chung ngu.
Sa-chen Kun-dga' snying-po. *SKB* I.2.3.4–7.4.6.

rGyud sde spyi'i rnam gzhag dang rgyud kyi mngon par rtogs pa'i stong thun sa bcad.
Grags-pa rgyal-mtshan. *SKB* III.70.2.1–81.2.6.

rGyud bzhi'i bka' bsgrub nges don snying po.
In *Sog bzlog pa gsung 'bum*, vol. 2, pp. 213–41.

rGyud lugs rnam 'grel. rTsa ba rdo rje'i tshig rkang rgyud lugs kyi rnam par 'grel pa bshad pa.
Asc. Bo-dong Phyogs-las rnam-rgyal. In *Bo dong gsung 'bum*, vols. 104.2.1–105.414.4.

sGa theng ma.
Sa-chen Kun-dga' snying-po. *gZhung rdo rje'i tshig rkang gi 'grel pa rnal 'byor dbang phyug dpal sa skya pa chen po la khams pa sga theng gis zhus pa. LL* XXVIII.149–491.

sGam po pa gsung 'bum.
The Collected Works (*Gsuṅ 'Bum*) *of Sgam-Po-Pa Bsod-Nams-Rin-Chen.* 2 parts. Shashin Learned Works Library and Publishing House Series, vol. 5. Manali: Khasdub Gyatsho Shashin, 1975.

sGam po pa gsung 'bum yid bzhin nor bu.
Edited by Khen po shedup Tenzin and Lama Thinley Namgyal, 2000. 4 vols. Kathmandu: Shri Gautam Buddha Vihara.

sGra sbyor bam po gnyis pa.
To. 4347. *bsTan 'gyur* sna-tshogs, co, fols. 131b1–60a7.

sGrub thabs rgya rtsa.
Compiled by Amoghavajra and Ba-ri lo-tsā-ba. To. 3306–399.

sGrub thabs so so'i yig sna.
Grags-pa rgyal-mtshan. *SKB* IV.148.1.1–70.1.6.

brGyud pa dang bcas pa la gsol ba 'debs pa.
bSod-nams rtse-mo. *SKB* II.38.3.4–39.2.4.

Nges brjod bla ma'i 'khrul 'khor bri thabs.
Grags-pa rgyal-mtshan. *SKB* IV.43.1.1–45.4.5.

Ngor chos 'byung.
dKon-mchog lhun-grub, completed by Sangs-rgyas phun-tshogs. New Delhi: Ngawang Topgay, 1973.

sNgags log sun 'byin gyi skor.
Thimphu: Kunsang Topgyel and Mani Dorji, 1979.

sNgon gyi gtam me tog phreng ba.
Ascribed Ne'u (Nel-pa) Paṇḍita. Edited and translated in Uebach, 1987. Chab-spel tshe-brtan phun-tshog and lDan-lhun sangs-rgyas chos-'phel, eds., 1990. *Bod kyi lo rgyus deb ther khag lnga,* pp. 1–54. Lhasa: Bod ljongs bod yig dpe rnying dpe skrun khang.

bsNgags par 'os pa'i rab tu byed pa.
'Phags-pa bLo-gros rgyal-mtshan. *SKB* VII.285.2.2–286.1.1.

Chag lo tsā ba'i rnam thar.
By 'Ju-ba Chos-dar. Edited and translated by G. N. Roerich, 1959. *Biography of Dharmasvamin* (*Chag lo-tsa-ba Chos-rje-dpal*). Historical Researches Series, vol. 2. Patna: K. P. Jayaswal Research Institute.

Chos spyod rin chen phreng ba.
Grags-pa rgyal-mtshan. *SKB* IV.312.2.1–20.2.6.

Chos 'byung grub mtha' chen po.
Rog Bande Shes-rab-'od. *Grub mtha' so so'i bźed tshul gŹuṅ gsal bar ston pa chos 'byuṅ grub mtha' chen po bstan pa'i sgron me.* Leh: Tshul Khrims-Jam dbyang, 1971.

Chos 'byung bstan pa'i sgron me.
Ratna gling-pa. *The Nyingmapa Apology of Rin-Chen-Dpal-Bzang-Po.* Tashijong: Sungrab Nyamso Gyunphel Parkhang, 1972.

Chos 'byung dpag bsam ljon bzang.
Sum-pa mkhan-po ye-shes dpal-'byor. Lanzhou: Kan su'i mi rigs dpe skrun khang, 1992.

Chos 'byung me tog snying po sbrang rtsi'i bcud.
Asc. Nyang Nyi-ma 'od-zer. Gangs can rig mdzod, vol. 5. Lhasa: Bod ljongs mi dmangs dpe skrun khang, 1988.

Chos la 'jug pa'i sgo.
bSod-nams rtse-mo. *SKB* II.318.3.1–45.3.6.

rJe dus gsum mkhyen pa'i rnam thar.
rGwa-lo rNam-rgyal rdo-rje. In *Dus gsum mkhyen pa'i bka' 'bum*, vol. 1, pp. 47–139.

rJe btsun pa'i mnal lam.
Grags-pa rgyal-mtshan. *SKB* IV.98.2.6–100.1.6; *LL* I.57–64.

rJe btsun sa skya pa gong ma gsum gyi rnam par thar pa dpag bsam ljon pa.
Anonymous. Included in *Sa skya pa lam 'bras bla brgyud kyi rnam thar*, pp. 57–107. Dehra Dun: Sakya Centre, 1985.

rJe sa chen la bstod pa.
bSod-nam rtse-mo. *SKB* II.37.4.1–38.3.4.

Nyang ral rnam thar. sPrul sku mnga' bdag chen po'i skyes rab rnam thar dri ma med pa'i bka' rgya can.
In *Bka' brgyad bde gśegs 'dus pa'i chos skor.* 13 vols. Ngagyur Nyingmay Sungrab Series, no. 75, vol. 1, pp. 1–163. Gangtok: Sonam Topgay Kazi, 1978.

Nye brgyud gcod kyi khrid yig gsal bar bkod pa legs bshad bdud rtsi'i rol mtsho.
Pad-ma lung-rtogs rgya-mtsho. Thimphu: Kunsang Topgay, 1978.

gNyags ma.
Sa-chen Kun-dga' snying-po. *gZhung bshad gnyags ma. LL* XI.21–128.

mNyam med sgam po pa'i rnam thar.
sGam-po sPyan-snga bSod-nams lhun-grub zla-'od rgyal-mtshan. Xining: mTsho sngon mi rigs dpe skrun khang, 1993.

rNying ma bka' ma rgyas pa.
Various authors. Edited by bDud-'joms 'Jigs-bras ye-shes rdo-rje, 1982. 55 vols. Kalimpong: Dubjung Lama.

sNying thig ya bzhi.
Asc. kLong-chen-pa Dri-med 'od-zer. 11 vols. New Delhi: Trulku Tsewang, Jamyang, and L. Tashi,1970.

sNying thig lo rgyus chen mo.
In *sNying thig ya bzhi*, vol. 9, pp. 1–179. In *rNying ma bka' ma rgyas pa,* vol. 45, pp. 503–657.

Tun hong nas thon pa'i bod kyi lo rgyus yig cha.
Edited by dBang-rgyal and bSod-nams, 1992. Beijing: Mi rigs dpe skrun khang.

gTam gyi tshogs theg pa'i rgya mtsho.
'Jigs-med gling-pa. Edited by bSod-nams tshe-brtan, 1991. *'Jigs med gling pa'i gtam tshogs.* Lhasa: Bod ljongs bod yig dpe rnying dpe skrun khang.

gTer ston brgya rtsa'i rnam thar.
Kong-sprul blo-gros mtha'-yas. In *Rin chen gter mdzod chen mo*, vol. ka, pp. 291–759.

gTer 'byung chen mo.
Gu-ru Chos-kyi dbang-phyug. *The Autobiography and Instructions of Gu-ru Chos-kyi dbaṅ-phyug*, vol. 2, pp. 75–193. Paro: Ugyen Tempai Gyaltsen, 1979.

gTer 'byung chen mo gsal ba'i sgron me.
Ratna gling-pa. In Tseten Dorji, ed., 1973. *Selected Works of Ratna-Gliṅ-pa*, vol. 1, pp. 1–215. Tezu, Arunachal Pradesh: Tibetan Nyingmapa Monastery.

sTag lung chos 'byung.
sTag-lung zhabs-drung Ngag-dbang rnam-rgyal, supplemented by sTag-lung Khris-'dzin Ngag-dbang bstan-pa'i nyi-ma. Gang can rig mdzod Series, vol. 22. Lhasa: Bod ljongs bod yig dpe rnying dpe skrun khang, 1992.

brTag gnyis rnam 'grel dag ldan.
Grags-pa rgyal-mtshan. *SKB* III.96.3.1–162.3.6.

bsTan bcos lung gi nyi 'od.
In *sGam po pa gsung 'bum yid bzhin nor bu*, vol. 4, pp. 91–184.

bsTan rtsis gsal ba'i nyin byed.
Mang-thos klu-sgrub rgya-mtsho. Lhasa: Bod yig dpe rnying dpe skrun khang, 1987.

bsTod pa rnam dag gi phreng ba.
Asc. 'Phags-pa bLo-gros rgyal-mtshan. *SKB* VI.142.4.1–43.3.3.

Theg chen tshul 'jug.
Rong-zom Chos kyi bzang-po. *Commentaries on the Guhyagarbha and Other Rare Nyingmapa Texts from the Library of Dudjom Rimpoche*, pp. 223–431. New Delhi: Sanje Dorje, 1974.

Theg chen rgyud bla'i don bsdus pa.
Dharamsala: Library of Tibetan Works and Achives, 1993.

Theg pa chen po'i rnal 'byor 'jug pa'i thabs.
A-ro Ye-shes 'byung-gnas. *sNga 'gyur bka' ma'i chos sde*, vol. 59, pp. 5–47. Chengdu: Kaḥ thog mKhan po 'Jam-dbyangs, 1999. Copy provided courtesy of David Germano.

Thos yig rgya mtsho.
Ngor-chen Kun-dga' bzang-po. *SKB* IX.44.4.1–108.2.6.

Dang po'i las can gyi bya ba'i rim pa dang lam rim bgrod tshul.
bSod-nams rtse-mo. *SKB* II.143.2.1–47.2.1.

Dam chos snying po zhi byed las rgyud kyi snyan rgyud zab ched ma.
Edited by Barbara Nimri Aziz, 1979. *The Tradition of Pha Dam-pa Saṅs-rgyas: A Treasured Collection of His Teachings Transmitted by Thugs-sras Kun-dga'.* 5 vols. Thimphu: Druk Sherik Parkhang.

Dam chos dgongs pa gcig pa'i yig cha.
dbOn-po Shes-rab 'byung-gnas. Thimphu: Kunsang Topgey, 1976.

Dus gsum mkhyen pa'i bka' 'bum.
Selected Writings of the First Źwa-Nag Karma-pa Dus-Gsum-Mkhyen-pa. 2 vols. Gangtok: Dzongsar Chhentse Labrang, 1980.

Deb ther sngon po.
'Gos lo-tsā-ba gZhon-nu dpal. 2 vols. Chengdu: Si khron mi rigs dpe skrun khang, 1984. See Roerich 1949.

Deb ther dmar po.
Tshal-pa Kun-dga' rdo-rje. Beijing: Mi rigs dpe skrun khang, 1981.

Deb ther dmar po gsar ma.
Edited and translated by Giuseppe Tucci, 1971. *Deb T'er Dmar Po Gsar Ma: Tibetan Chronicles.* SOR 24. Rome: ISMEO.

gDams ngag byung tshul gyi zin bris gsang chen bstan pa rgyas byed.
'Jam-dbyangs mKhyen-brtse'i dbang-phyug. *LL* XIV.2–154.

gDams ngag mdzod.
Kong-sprul bLo-gros mtha'-yas. 14 vols. Paro: Lama Ngodrup and Sherab Drimay, 1979.

gDung rabs chen mo.
'Jam-mgon A-mes-zhabs. *'Dzam gling byang phyogs kyi thub pa'i rgyal tshab chen po dpal ldan sa skya pa'i gdung rabs rin po che ji ltar byon pa'i tshul gyi rnam par thar pa ngo mtshar rin po che'i bang mdzod dgos 'dod kun 'byung.* Beijing: Mi rigs dpe skrun khang, 1986.

bDag med ma'i dbang gi tho yig.
bSod-nams rtse-mo. *SKB* II.404.1.4–3.6.

bDag med lha mo bco lnga'i mngon rtogs.
Grags-pa rgyal-mtshan. *SKB* III.222.1.1–26.3.6.

bDag med lha mo bco lnga'i bstod pa dri ma med pa'i rgyan and *bDag med bstod pa'i bsdus don.*
Grags-pa rgyal-mtshan. *SKB* III.291.3.2–93.1.6.

bDud rtsi 'khyil pa sgrub thabs las sbyor dang bcas pa.
Grags-pa rgyal-mtshan. *SKB* IV.65.4.5–67.2.6.

bDe mchog kun tu spyod pa'i rgyud kyi gsal byed.
Grags-pa rgyal-mtshan. *SKB* IV.48.4.6–55.2.6.

bDe mchog nag po pa'i dkyil chog lag tu blang ba'i rim pa.
Grags-pa rgyal-mtshan. *SKB* III.326.4.1–44.4.6.

bDe mchog lu hi pa'i lugs kyi bla ma brgyud pa'i lo rgyus.
Grags-pa rgyal-mtshan. *SKB* III.293.2–98.4.

rDo rje phur pa'i chos 'byung ngor mtshar rgya mtsho'i rba rlabs.
In *Sog bzlog pa gsung 'bum*, vol. 1, pp. 111–201.

rDo rje 'byung ba'i yig sna.
Grags-pa rgyal-mtshan. *SKB* IV.112.2.1–47.4.6.

lDan bu ma.
Sa-chen Kun-dga' snying-po. *gZhung rdo rje'i tshig rkang gi 'grel pa rnal 'byor dbang phyug dpal sa skya pa chen po la jo gdan ldan bu mas zhus pa. LL* XXIX.297–496.

lDe'u chos 'byung.
Asc. lDe'u jo-sras. *Chos 'byung chen mo bstan pa'i rgyal mtshan lde'u jo sras kyi mdzad pa.* Lhasa: Mi dmangs dpe skrun khang, 1987.

sDom gsum rab dbye.
Sa-skya Paṇḍita. *SKB* V.297.1.1–320.4.5.

Nag po dkyil chog gi bshad sbyar.
Grags-pa rgyal-mtshan. *SKB* III.304.3.2–26.3.6.

gNas bstod kyi nyams dbyangs.
Grags-pa rgyal-mtshan. *SKB* IV.347.3.6–48.2.6.

gNas yig phyogs bsgrigs.
Edited by dGe-'dun chos-'phel et al., 1998. Chengdu: Si khron mi rigs dpe skrun khang.

gNa' rabs bod kyi chang pa'i lam srol.
Bar-shi Phun-tshogs Dbang-rgyal. Dharamsala: Library of Tibetan Works & Archives, 1979.

rNam thar rgyas pa.
Edited by Helmut Eimer, 1979.

rNam thar yongs grags.
mChims Nam-mkha'-grags. In *Pha chos*, pp. 44–228.

rNam thar lam yig.
Asc. 'Brom-ston rGyal-ba'i 'byung-gnas. In *Pha chos*, pp. 229–90.

rNal 'byor byang chub seng ge'i dris lan.
Grags-pa rgyal-mtshan. *SKB* III.276.4.1–78.2.7.

Padma bka' thang.
Orgyan gling-pa. Chengdu: Si khron mi rigs dpe skrun khang, 1987.

Pusti dmar chung. Lam 'bras gzhung bshad pod dmar ma.
First compiled by Kun-dga' dbang-phyug with later additions. LL XIII.

Pod nag. Lam 'bras bzhung bshad pod nag.
bLa-ma dam-pa bSod-nams rgyal-mtshan. *LL* XVI.

Pod ser.
First compiled by Grags-pa rgyal-mtshan, with many additions. *LL* XI.

dPal kye rdo rje rtsa ba'i rgyud brtag pa gnyis pa'i bsdus don.
bSod-nams rtse-mo. *SKB* II.168.3.1–76.1.6.

dPal kye rdo rje'i sgrub thabs mtsho skyes kyi ṭī ka.
bSod-nams rtse-mo. *SKB* II.116.3.1–31.2.1.

dPal kye rdo rje'i rnam par bshad pa nyi ma'i 'od zer.
bSod-nams rtse-mo. *SKB* II.41.3.1–109.3.6.

dPal kye rdo rje'i rtsa ba'i rgyud brtag pa gnyis pa'i dka' 'grel man ngag don gsal.
Asc. sGyi-chu-ba. *SKB* I.66.1–78.3.

dPal ldan Bi ru pa la bstod pa.
Sa-chen Kun-dga' snying-po with additions. *SKB* I.1.1.1–2.2.4.

dPal ldan sa skya paṇḍi ta chen po'i rnam par thar pa.
Gung-thang gi btsun-pa Zhang rgyal-ba-dpal. *SKB* V.433.2.1–38.4.6.

dPal Nā ro pa'i rnam par thar pa.
dBang-phyug rgyal-mtshan. *The Biographies of Tilopa and Naropa by Dbaṅ-phyug-rgyal-mtshan.* Darjeeling: Kargyud Sungrab Nyamso Khang, 1976.

dPal sa skya pa'i man ngag gces btus pa rin po che'i phreng ba.
Asc. Sa-chen Kun-dga' snying-po. *SKB* I.268.2.1–81.2.6.

dPal gsang ba 'dus pa'i dam pa'i chos byung ba'i tshul legs par bshad pa gsang 'dus chos kun gsal pa'i nyin byed.
A-mes-zhabs Ngag-dbang kun-dga' bsod-nams. Rajpur: Sakya Centre, 1985.

dPe chos rin chen spungs pa.
Asc. Po-to-ba Rin-chen-gsal. *Dharma upama ratna sangrah*. Sarnath: Mongolian Lama Guru Deva, 1965. Includes the commentary *dPe chos rin po che spungs pa'i 'bum 'grel* by bTsun-pa Shes-rab rdo-rje.

sPyod pa'i rgyud spyi'i rnam par gzhags pa legs par bshad pa'i sgron me.
Ngor-chen Kun-dga' bzang-po. *SKB* X.248.3.1–65.4.2.

Pha chos.
Asc. 'Brom-ston rGyal-ba'i 'byung-gnas. *Jo bo rje dpal ldan a ti sha'i rnam thar bka' gdam pha chos*. Xining: Mtsho sngon mi rigs dpe skrun khang, 1993.

Pha dam pa'i rnam thar.
Chos kyi seng ge. In *Pha dam pa dang ma cig lab sgron kyi rnam thar*, pp. 3–242. Xining: Mtsho sngon mi rigs dpe skrun khang, 1992.

Phag mo gru pa'i bka' 'bum.
Photocopy in possession of University of Hamburg. 5 vols. Provided courtesy of Jan-Ulrich Sobisch.

Phag mo gru pa'i gsung 'bum.
Edited by Gompo Tseten, 1976. *The Collected works (Gsuṅ 'Bum) of Phag-Mo-Gru-Pa Rdo-Rje-Rgyal-Po.* Gangtok: Palace Monastery.

Phag mo gru pa'i rnam thar rin po che'i phreng ba.
dPal-chen Chos-kyi ye-shes. In *Phag mo gru pa'i gsung 'bum*, pp. 5–62.

Phag mo las bcu'i gsal byed.
Grags-pa rgyal-mtshan. *SKB* IV.23.2.5–28.2.5.

Phyag rgya chen po gces pa btus pa'i man ngag.
Grags-pa rgyal-mtshan. *SKB* IV.302.3.1–11.4.5.

Phra mo brgyad kyi man ngag.
Asc. Sa-skya Paṇḍita. *SKB* V.353.2.1–54.3.1.

'Phags pa don yod zhags pa'i lo rgyus.
bSod-nams rtse-mo. *SKB* II.436.2.1–38.2.3.

'Phags pa rdo rje gur gyi rgyan.
Grags-pa rgyal-mtshan, written 1210. *SKB* III.175.1.1–211.1.6.

Bande ma.
Asc. Sa-chen Kun-dga' snying-po. *gZhung rdo rje'i tshig rkang gi 'grel pa rnal 'byor dbang phyug dpal sa skya pa chen po la bande gshing rje mas zhus pa. LL* XXVIII.1–148.

Ba ri be'u bum.
Be'u bum of Ba ri Lo tsa ba Rin chen grags. Delhi: Lama Jurme Drakpa, 1974.

Bu chos.
sBrom ston rgyal ba'i 'byung gnas kyi skyes rabs bka' gdams bu chos. Xining: mTsho sngon mi rigs dpe skrun khang, 1993.

Bu ston bka' 'bum.
Edited by Chandra Lokesh, 1971. *The Collected Works of Bu-ston.* Śata-Piṭaka Series, no. 68. 28 vols. New Delhi: International Academy of Indian Culture.

Bu ston chos 'byung.
Edited by rDo-rje rgyal-po, 1988. *Chos 'byung gsung rab rin po che'i mdzod.* Beijing: Krung go bod kyi shes rig dpe skrun khang. Partially edited by Szerb 1990.

Baiḍūrya sngon po.
Sangs-rgyas rgya-mtsho. *Aryaveda in Tibet: A Survey of the History and Literature of Lamaist Medicine.* Leh: Tashi Yangphel Tashigang, 1970.

Bo dong gsung 'bum.
Encyclopedia Tibetica: The Collected Works of Bo-Don Pan-Chen Phyogs-Las-Rnam-Rgyal. New Delhi: Tibet House, 1973.

Bod kyi rgyal rabs.
Grags-pa rgyal-mtshan. *SKB* IV.295.1.6–96.4.2.

Bod kyi gnas yig bdams bsgrigs. Edited by Tshe ring dpal 'byor, 1995. Lhasa: Bod ljongs bod yig dpe rnying dpe skrun khang.

Bod kyi gdung rus zhib 'jug.
lDong-ka-tsang dGe-bshes chos-grags et al. Beijing: Mi rigs dpe skrun khang, 2001.

Bod rje lha btsan po'i gdung rabs tshig nyung don gsal.
Kaḥ-thog mkhan-po Tshe-dbang nor-bu. In *Bod kyi lo rgyus deb ther khag lnga,* pp. 55–86. Lhasa: Bod ljongs bod yig dpe rnying dpe skrun khang, 1990.

Bod sil bu'i byung ba brjod pa shel dkar phreng ba.
Nor-brang O-rgyan. Lhasa: Bod ljongs mi dmangs dpe skrun khang, 1991.

Bhir ba pa'i lo rgyus.
In *gŹuṅ bsad Klog skya ma and Other Related Esoteric Texts,* pp. 347–404.

Bya rgyud spyi'i rnam par bshad pa legs par bshad pa'i rgya mtsho.
Ngor-chen Kun-dag' bzang-po. *SKB* X.265.4.2–319.1.6.

Bya spyod rigs gsum spyi'i rig gtad kyi cho ga.
Grags-pa rgyal-mtshan. *SKB* IV.252.4.1–55.1.5.

Byang chub sems dpa'i spyod pa la 'jug pa'i 'grel pa.
bSod-nams rtse-mo. *SKB* II.457.4.1–515.2.6.

Byin rlabs tshar gsum khug pa.
Grags-pa rgyal-mtshan. *SKB* III.94.2.3–95.3.4.

bLa ma rgya gar ba'i lo rgyus.
Grags-pa rgyal-mtshan. *SKB* III.170.1.1–73.1.6; *LL* I.2–14; *LL* XI.581–94.

bLa ma brgyud pa bod kyi lo rgyus.
Grags-pa rgyal-mtshan. *SKB* III.173.1.7–74.1.7; *LL* I.14–18; *LL* XI.594–99.

bLa ma brgyud pa'i rnam par thar pa ngo mtshar snang ba.
Asc. bLa-ma Dam-pa bSod-nams rgyal-mtshan. *LL* XVI.2–121.

bLa ma mnga' ris pas mdzad pa'i brtag gnyis kyi tshig 'grel.
Asc. mNga'-ris-pa gSal-ba'i snying-po. *SKB* I.13.4–65.4.

bLa ma rje btsun chen po'i rnam thar.
Sa-skya Paṇḍita Kun-dga' rgyal-mtshan. *SKB* V.143.1.1–48.3.4.

bLa ma dam pa chos kyi rgyal po rin po che'i rnam par thar pa rin po che'i phreng ba.
Asc. Ye-shes rgyal-mtshan. *LL* I.290–338.

bLa ma rnam thar bstod pa khyod nyi ma.
Grags-pa rgyal-mtshan. *SKB* III.82.4.5–83.3.6.

bLa ma ba ri lo tsā ba rin chen grags kyi rnam thar.
bSod-nams rtse-mo. *Sa skya'i rje btsun gong ma rnam lnga'i gsung ma phyi gsar rnyed*, vol. 1, pp. 255–66.

bLa ma sa skya pa chen po'i rnam thar.
Grags-pa rgyal-mtshan. *SKB* III.83.3.6–87.3.5.

dBa' bzhed.
Edited and translated by Pasang Wangdu and Hildegard Diemberger, 2000. *dBa' bzhed: The Royal Narrative Concerning the Bringing of the Buddha's Doctrine to Tibet.* Vienna: Österreichischen Akademie der Wissenschaften.

'Bri gung chos rje 'Jig rten mgon po bka' 'bum.
The Collected Writings (Gsuṅ-'Bum) of 'Bri-Gung Chos-Rje 'Jig-rten-Mgon-po Rin-Chen-Dpal. 5 vols. New Delhi: Khangsar Talku, 1969.

'Bri gung gdan rabs gser phreng.
'Bri-gung bsTan-'dzin pad-ma'i rgyal-mtshan. Lhasa: Bod ljongs bod yig dpe rnying dpe skrun khang, 1989.

'Brug pa'i chos 'byung.
'Brug-pa Padma dKar-po. Gangs-cen rig-mdzod Series, no. 19. Lhasa: Bod ljongs bod yig dpe rnying dpe skrun khang, 1992.

sBa bzhed.
Edited by mGon-po rgyal-mtshan, 1980. Beijing: Mi rigs dpe skrun khang.

sBa bzhed zhabs btags ma.
Edited by Rolf A. Stein, 1961. *Une chronique ancienne de bSam-yas: sBa-bžed.* Publications de l'Institut des hautes études chinoises, textes et documents, no. 1. Paris: Institut de hautes études chinoises.

Maṇi bka' 'bum.
Maṇi Bka' 'Bum: A Collection of Rediscovered Teachings Focusing upon the Tutelary Deity Avalokiteśvara (Mahākaruṇika). 2 vols. New Delhi: Trayang and Jamyang Samten, 1975.

Man ngag gces pa btus pa.
Asc. Sa-chen Kun-dga' snying-po. *dPal sa skya pa'i man ngag gces pa btus pa rin po che'i phreng ba. SKB* I.268.2.1–81.2.6.

Man ngag lta phreng.
Rong zom gsung thor bu, pp. 1–18. See Karmay 1988, pp. 163–71.

Man ngag lta ba'i phreng ba zhes bya ba'i 'grel pa.
Rong zom gsung thor bu, pp. 19–124.

Mar pa lo tsā'i rnam thar.
Asc. Khrag-'thung rgyal-po (gTsang-smyong he-ru-ka). Chengdu: Si khron mi rigs dpe skrun khang, 1983. See Nalanda Translation Committee 1982.

Mi la rnam thar. Edited by J.W. de Jong, 1959. *Mi la ras pa'i rnam thar: Texte tibétain de la vie de Milarépa.* Indo-Iranian Mongraphs, no. 4. The Hague: Mouton.

Myang chos 'byung. Apocryphally asc. Jo-nang Tāranātha. Edited by Lhag-pa tshe-ring, 1983. *Myang yul stod smad bar gsum gyi ngo mtshar gtam legs bshad mkhas pa'i 'jug ngogs.* Lhasa: Bod ljongs mi dmangs dpe skrun khang. See Martin 1997, no. 190.

sMon lam dbang bzhi'i bshad par sbyar ba.
Anonymous but possibly by Sa-chen Kun-dga' snying-po. *Sa skya'i rje btsun gong ma rnam lnga'i gsung ma phyi gsar rnyed,* vol. 1, pp. 81–84.

sMra sgo mtshon cha. sMra ba'i sgo mtshon cha lta bu.
To. 4295. *bsTan 'gyur,* sgra-mdo, she, fols. 277b1–281b7.

sMra sgo'i mtshon cha'i mchan rje btsun grags pa rgyal mtshan gyis mdzad pa.
Asc. Grags-pa rgyal-mtshan. *Sa skya'i rje btsun gong ma rnam lnga'i gsung ma phyi gsar rnyed,* vol. 1, pp. 767–94.

rTsa ba'i ltung ba bcu bzhi pa'i 'grel pa gsal byed 'khrul spong.
Grags-pa rgyal-mtshan. *SKB* III.235.1.1–65.3.6.

rTsa dbu ma'i khrid yig.
Grags-pa rgyal-mtshan. *SKB* IV.36.2.5–42.4.2.

Tshar chen rnam thar.
Ngag-dbang blo-bzang rgya-mtsho (Dalai Lama V). *Rigs dang dkyil 'khor kun*

gyi khyab bdag rdo rje 'chang blo gsal rgya mtsho grags pa rgyal mtshan dpal bzang po'i rnam par thar pa slob bshad bstan pa'i nyi 'od. LL II.399–637.

Tshig mdzod chen mo. Bod rgya tshig mdzod chen mo.
Edited by Krang dbyis sun et al., 1985. 3 vols. Beijing: Mi rigs dpe skrun khang.

mDzod nag ma.
Karma-pa III Rang-byung rdo-rje. *The Life and Songs of Mi-La-Ras-Pa.* 2 vols. Dalhousie: Damchoe Sangpo, 1978.

Zhang ston la bstod pa.
Sa-chen Kun-dga' snying-po. *SKB* I.2.2.4–2.3.4.

Zhi byed snga phyi bar gsum gyi khrid yig rnams phyogs gcig tu bsdebs pa bdud rtsi'i nying khu.
Lo-chen Dharma-Shrī. *gDams ngag mdzod*, vol. 9, pp. 308–404.

Zhi byed dang gcod yul gyi chos 'byung rin po che'i phreng ba.
Khams-smyon Dharma seng-ge. In *Gcod Kyi Chos Skor*, pp. 411–597. New Delhi: Tibet House, 1974.

Zhib mo rdo rje.
dMar-ston Chos-kyi rgyal-po. *bLa ma bod kyi brgyud pa'i rnam thar zhib mo rdo rje.* See Stearns 2001.

Zhu byas ma.
Sa-chen Kun-dga' snying-po. *gZhung rdo rje'i tshig rkang gi 'grel pa rnal 'byor dbang phyug dpal sa skya pa chen po la zhu byas dngos grub kyis zhus pa. LL* XXVII.1–189.

Zhu lan nor bu'i phreng ba.
'Brom-ston gZhon-nu blo-gros. In *Pha chos*, pp. 299–504.

gŹuṅ bsad Klog skya ma and Other Related Esoteric Sa-skya-pa Texts.
Edited by Tashi Dorje, 1975. Dolanji: Tibetan Bompo Monastic Centre.

gZhan phan nyer mkho.
Grags-pa rgyal-mtshan. *SKB* IV.228.2.1–37.2.6.

Zangs gling ma.
Nyang-ral Nyi-ma 'Od-zer. *sLob dpon padma'i rnam thar zangs gling ma.* Chengdu: Si khron mi rigs dpe skrun khang, 1989.

Zab don gnad kyi sgron me.
Go-rams bSod-nams seng-ge. *Go ram bka' 'bum*, vol. 12, pp. 1–29.

Zla rgyal ma.
Sa-chen Kun-dga' snying-po. *gZhung rdo rje'i tshig rkang gi 'grel pa rnal 'byor dbang phyug dpal sa skya pa chen po la byang chub sems dpa' zla ba rgyal mtshan kyis zhus pa. LL* XXVII.397–529.

'A 'u ma.
Sa-chen Kun-dga' snying-po. *gZhung rdo rje'i tshig rkang gi 'grel pa rnal 'byor dbang phyug dpal sa skya pa chen po la jo mo 'a 'u mas zhus pa. LL* XXIX.161–295.

Yar lung jo bo'i chos 'byung.
Shakya rin-chen sde. Edited by Ngag dbang, 1988. Lhasa: Bod ljongs mi dmangs dpe skrun khang.

Yi ge'i bklag thab byis pa bde blag tu 'jug pa.
bSod-nams rtse-mo. *SKB* II.345.4.1–49.4.6.

Yum don ma.
Sa-chen Kun-dga' snying-po. *gZhung rdo rje'i tshig rkang gi 'grel pa rnal 'byor dbang phyug dpal sa skya pa chen po la yum ma gcig zhang mo'i don du mdzad pa. LL* XXIX.1–159.

Rin chen gter mdzod chen mo.
Kong-sprul bLo-gros mtha'-yas. 111 vols. Paro: Ngodrub and Sherab Drimay, 1976–80.

Rin chen snang ba shlo ka nyi shu pa'i rnam par 'grel pa.
Pod ser, pp. 194–243.

Rong zom chos bzang gi gsung 'bum. 2 vols.
Chengdu: Si khron mi rigs dpe skrun khang, 2001.

Rong zom gsung thor bu.
Rong-zom Chos-kyi bzang-po. *Selected Writings (Gsuṅ Thor Bu) of Roṅ-zom Chos-kyi-bzaṅ-po.* Leh: 'Khor-gdoṅ Gter-sprul 'Chi-med-rig-'dzin, 1974.

Rwa sgreng dgon pa'i dkar chag.
Lhun-grub chos-'phel. Chengdu: Si khron mi rigs dpe skrun khang, 1994.

Rwa lo tsā ba'i rnam thar.
Attributed to Rwa ye-shes seng-ge. *mThu stobs dbang phyug rje btsun rwa lo tsā ba'i rnam par thar pa kun khyab snyan pa'i snga sgra.* Xining: mTsho sngon mi rigs dpe skrun khang, 1989.

rLangs kyi po ti bse ru rgyas pa.
Asc. Si-tu Byang-chub rgyal-mtshan, but with later additions. Lhasa: Bod ljongs mi dmangs dpe skrun khang, 1986.

Lam 'jug pa dang ldogs pa.
Sa-chen Kun-dga' snying-po. *Pod ser,* pp. 323–25.

Lam 'bras khog phub.
A-mes-zhab Ngag-dbang kun-dga' bsod-nams. *Yongs rdzogs bstan pa rin po che'i nyam len gyi man ngag gsung ngag rin po che'i byon tshul khog phub dang bcas pa rgyas par bshad pa legs bshad 'dus pa'i rgya mtsho. LL* XXII.1–314.

Lam 'bras rgyud pa'i gsol 'debs.
Grags-pa rgyal-mtshan. *SKB* III.81.3.1–82.4.5.

Lam 'bras snyan brgyud.
In *gŹuṅ bsad Klog skya ma and Other Related Esoteric Texts,* pp. 405–590.

Lam 'bras byung tshul.
Ngor-chen Kun-dga' bzang-po, supplemented by Gung-ru Shes-rab bzang-po.

Lam 'bras bu dang bcas pa'i man ngag gi byung tshul gsung ngag rin po che bstan pa rgyas pa'i nyi 'od. SKB IX.108–26.

Lam 'bras lam skor sogs kyi gsan yig.
'Phags-pa bLo-gros rgyal-mtshan. *SKB* VI.32.4.1–35.1.4.

Lam 'bras slob bshad.
Edited by Sa-skya Khri-'dzin Ngag gi dbang phyug, 1983/84. 31 vols. Dehra Dun: Sakya Centre.

Lam zab mo bla ma'i rnal 'byor.
Asc. Sa-skya Paṇḍita. *SKB* V.339.3.1–43.4.1.

Lus kyi dkyi 'khor.
Sa-chen Kun-dga' snying-po. *Pod ser*, pp. 135–38.

Lo tsā ba chen po'i bsdus don.
rNgog bLo-ldan shes-rab. Dharamsala: Library of Tibetan Works and Archives, 1993.

Sa skya bka' 'bum.
Edited by Bsod Nams Rgya Mtsho, 1968. *The Complete Works of the Great Masters of the Sa Skya Sect of the Tibetan Buddhism.* 14 vols. Tokyo: Toyo Bunko.

Sa skya gsung rab dkar chag. dPal ldan sa skya'i rje btsun gong ma lnga'i gsung rab rin po che'i par gyi sgo 'phar 'byed pa'i dkar chag 'phrul gyi lde'u mig.
By dGe-slong bKra-shis lhun-grub. *SKB* VII.310.3.1–43.1.6.

Sa skya legs bshad gter.
Sa-skya Paṇḍita. *SKB* V.50.2.1–61.32.6. See Bosson 1969.

Sa skya'i gdung rabs.
sGra-tshad-pa Rin-chen rnam-rgyal. In *Bu ston bka' 'bum,* vol. 28, pp. 309–14.

Sa skya'i rje btsun gong ma rnam lnga'i gsung ma phyi gsar rnyed.
Edited by bSod-nams tshe-'phel et al. 3 vols. n.p. (Lhasa?): n.d. (late 1980s?). Copy provided courtesy of E. Gene Smith and the Tibetan Buddhist Resource Center, Cambridge, Mass.

Saṁ pu ṭa'i ṭī ka gnad kyi gsal byed.
bSod-nams rtse-mo. *SKB* II.188.1.1–307.1.6.

Sems kyi mtshan nyid gab pa mngon du phyung ba.
sGam-po-pa bSod-nams rin-chen. *sGam po pa gsung 'bum,* part 2, pp. 24–32.

Sog bzlog pa gsung 'bum. Collected Writings of Sog-Bzlog-Pa Blo-Gros-Rgyal-Mtshan. 2 vols. New Delhi: Sanji Dorji, 1975.

Sras don ma.
Sa-chen Kun-dga' snying-po. *Lam 'bras gzhung bshad sras don ma. LL* XII.11–446.

sLob dpon dga' rab rdo rje nas brgyud pa'i rdzogs pa chen po sems sde'i phra khrid kyi man ngag.
sGya-sman-pa Nam-mkha' rdo-rje. *rNying ma bka' ma rgyas pa*, vol. 17, pp. 435–517.

sLob dpon rdo rje dril bu pa'i lo rgyus.
Grags-pa rgyal-mtshan. *SKB* III.345.1.1–46.1.4.

sLob dpon Phya pa la bstod pa.
bSod-nams rtse-mo. *SKB* II.39.4.4–41.2.5.

sLob dpon mtsho skyes kyi lo rgyus.
Sa-chen Kun-dga' snying-po. *SKB* I.380.4.1–81.4.3.

gSang 'dus stong thun.
Asc. 'Gos-lo Khug-pa lhas-btsas. New Delhi: Trayang, 1973.

gSung sgros ma.
dMar Chos kyi rgyal po. *gZhung rdo rje'i tshig rkang gi 'grel pa 'jam dbyangs bla ma'i gsung sgros ma. LL* XXX.1–295.

gSung ngag rin po che lam 'bras bu dang bcas pa ngor lugs thun min slob bshad dang | thun mong tshogs bshad tha dad kyi smin grol yan lang dang bcas pa'i brgyud yig gser gyi phreng ba byin zab 'od brgya 'bar ba.
'Jam-dbyang bLo-gter dbang-po. *LL* XX.417–511.

gSung ngag slob bshad khob phub gnad kyi be'u bum.
Mang-thos kLu-sgrub rgya-mtsho. *LL* XVIII.161–241.

gSo dpyad rgyal po'i dkor mdzod.
Grags-pa rgyal-mtshan. *SKB* IV.354.3.1–96.1.6.

bSam gtan mig sgron.
Asc. gNubs-chen sangs-rgyas ye-shes. *Rnal 'Byor Mig Gi Bsam Gtan or Bsam Gtan Mig Sgron.* Leh: Khor-gdoṅ Gter-sprul Chi-med-rig-'dzin, 1974.

Lho rong chos 'byung.
Ri-bo-che dpon-tshang. Gang can rig mdzod Series, vol. 26. Lhasa: Bod ljongs bod yig dpe rnying dpe skrun khang, 1994.

Arga'i cho ga dang rab tu gnas pa don gsal.
Grags-pa rgyal-mtshan. *SKB* IV.237.3.1–52.3.6.

Aṣṭa'i gzhi bshad.
Asc. Sa-skya Paṇḍita. *SKB* V.355.2.1–58.4.4.

A seng ma.
Sa-chen Kun-dga' snying-po. *Thams cad kyi don bsdus pa'i tshigs su bcad pa. LL* XI.188–91; *gDams ngag mdzod* vol. 4, pp.12–15; *rGyud sde kun btus* vol. 26, pp.104–6.

MODERN STUDIES

Almogi, Orna. 2002. "Sources on the Life and Works of the Eleventh-Century Tibetan Scholar Rong Zom Chos Kyi Bzang Po: A Brief Survey." In *Tibet, Past and Present*, edited by Henk Blezer, vol. 1, pp. 67–80. Leiden: Brill.

Arènes, Pierre. 1998. "Herméneutique des *tantra*: Étude de quelques usages du 'sens caché.'" *JIABS* 21 & 22: 173–226.

Aris, Michael. 1979. *Bhutan: The Early History of a Himalayan Kingdom.* Warminster: Aris & Phillips.

Arya, Pasang Yonten. 1998. *Dictionary of Tibetan Materia Medica*, translated and edited by Dr. Yonten Gyatso. Delhi: Motilal Banarsidass.

Backus, Charles. 1981. *The Nan-chao Kingdom and T'ang China's Southestern Frontier.* Cambridge: Cambridge University Press.

Bacot, J., F. W. Thomas, and C. Toussaint. 1940–46. *Documents de Touen-houang relatifs a l'histoire du Tibet.* Annales du Musée Guimet, Bibliothèque d'études, vol. 51. Paris: Librairie orientaliste Paul Geuthner.

Bajracharya, Purna Harsha. 1979. "Than Bahil, an Ancient Centre for Sanskrit Study." *Indologica Taurinensia* 7: 61–64.

Baldissera, Gabrizia. 2001. "The Satire of Tantric Figures in Some Works of Kṣemendra." In *Le Parole e i marmi: Studi in onore di Raniero Gnoli nel suo 70° compleanno*, edited by Raffaele Torella. SOR 92, vol. 1, pp. 13–35. Rome: Istituto italiano per L'Africa e L'Oriente.

Bandyopadhyay, Nandity. 1979. "The Buddhist Theory of Relation Between Pramā and Pramāṇa." *JIP* 7: 43–78.

Banerji, R. D. 1919–20. "Neulpur Grant of Subhakara: The 8th year." *Epigraphia Indica* 15: 1–8.

Barrett, David V., ed. 2001. *The New Believers: A Survey of Sects, Cults and Alternative Religions.* London: Cassell.

Beal, Samuel, trans. 1869. *Si-yu-ki: Buddhist Records of the Western World.* London: Kegan Paul, Trench, Trübner.

Beckwith, Christopher I. 1977. "Tibet and the Early Medieval *Florissance* in Eurasia: A Preliminary Note on the Economic History of the Tibetan Empire." *CAJ* 21: 89–104.

——. 1987. *The Tibetan Empire in Central Asia.* Princeton, N.J.: Princeton University Press.

Benson, Robert L. 1982. "Political *Renovatio:* Two Models from Roman Antiquity." In *Renaissance and Renewal in the Twelfth Century*, edited by Robert L. Benson et. al., pp. 339–86. Cambridge, Mass.: Harvard University Press.

Beyer, Steven. 1973. *The Cult of Tārā: Magic and Ritual in Tibet.* Berkeley: University of California Press.

Blackburn, Anne M. 2001. *Buddhist Learning and Textual Practice in Eighteenth-Century Lankan Monastic Culture.* Princeton, N.J.: Princeton University Press.

Blezer, Henk, ed. 2002. *Tibet, Past and Present.* 2 vols. PIATS 2000: Tibetan

Studies: Proceedings of the Ninth Seminar of the International Association for Tibetan Studies, Leiden 2000. Leiden: Brill.

Blondeau, Anne-Marie, and Ernst Steinkellner, eds. 1996. *Reflections of the Mountain: Essays on the History and Social Meaning of the Mountain Cult in Tibet and the Himalayas.* Vienna: Österreichischen Akademie der Wissenschaften.

Bosson, James. 1969. *A Treasury of Aphoristic Jewels: The Subhāṣitaratnanidhi of Sa Skya Paṇḍita in Tibetan and Mongolian.* Uralic and Altaic Series, vol. 92. Bloomington: Indiana University Press.

Bouillier, Véronique. 1997. *Ascètes et rois: Uni monastère de Kanphata Yogis au Népal.* Paris: CNRS Ethnologie.

Boyer, A. M., E. J. Rapson, and E. Senart. 1920–29. *Kharoṣṭhī Inscriptions Discovered by Sir Aurel Stein in Chinese Turkestan.* 3 vols. Oxford: Clarendon Press. Reprint, New Delhi: Cosmo Publications, 1997 (1 vol.).

Boyle, J. A., ed. 1968. *The Cambridge History of Iran.* Vol. 5, *The Saljuq and Mongol Periods.* Cambridge: Cambridge University Press.

Broido, Michael. 1982. "Does Tibetan Hermeneutics Throw Any Light on *Sandhābhāṣā.*" *JTS* 2: 5–39.

———. 1983. "*Bshad-thabs:* Some Tibetan Methods of Explaining the Tantras." In *Contributions on Tibetan Language, History and Culture,* edited by Ernst Steinkellner and Helmut Tauscher, vol. 2, pp. 15–45. Proceedings of the Csoma de Körös Symposium, Velm-Vienna, September 13–19, 1981. Vienna: Arbeitskreis für Tibetische und Buddhistische Studien Universität Wien.

———. 1984. "Abhiprāya and Implication in Tibetan Linguistics." *JIP* 12: 1–33.

Broughton, Jeffrey. 1983. "Early Ch'an Schools in Tibet." In *Studies in Ch'an and Hua-yen,* edited by Robert M. Gimello and Peter N. Gregory, pp. 1–68. Honolulu: University of Hawai'i Press.

Burke, Peter. 1986. *The Italian Renaissance—Culture and Society in Italy.* Princeton, N.J.: Princeton University Press.

Cabezón, José Ignacio, and Roger R. Jackson, eds. 1996. *Tibetan Literature: Studies in Genre.* Ithaca, N.Y.: Snow Lion.

Carrasco, Pedro. 1959. *Land and Polity in Tibet.* American Ethnological Society, monograph 32. Seattle: University of Washington Press.

Cassinelli, C. W., and Robert B. Ekvall. 1969. *A Tibetan Principality—The Political System of Sa sKya.* Ithaca, N.Y.: Cornell University Press.

Chang, Kun. 1959–60. "An Analysis of the Tun-Huang Tibetan Annals." *Journal of Oriental Studies* 5: 122–73.

Chattopadhyaya, Alaka. 1967. *Atīśa and Tibet.* Calcutta: Motilal Banarsidass.

Chattopadhyaya, Brajadulal. 1994. *The Making of Early Medieval India.* Delhi: Oxford University Press.

Childs, Geoff H. 1997. "Householder Lamas and the Persistence of Tradition: Animal Sacrifice in Himalayan Buddhist Communities." In *Tibetan Studies: Proceedings of the 7th Seminar of the International Association for Tibetan Studies,*

Graz 1995, edited by Helmut Krasser et al., vol. 1, pp. 141–57. Österreichische Akademie der Wissenschaften Philosophisch-Historische Klasse Denkschriften, 256 Band. Vienna: Österreichischen Akademie Der Wissenschaften.

Cleaves, Francis W. 1967. "Teb Tenggeri." *Ural-Altaische Jahrbücher* 39: 248–60.

Cochrane, Eric. 1981. *Historians and Historiography in the Italian Renaissance.* Chicago: University of Chicago Press.

Conze, Edward. 1957. "Marginal Notes to the Abhisamayālaṁkāra." *Sino-Indian Studies* 5/3–4: 21–35.

Cuevas, Bryan J. 2003. *The Hidden History of The Tibetan Book of the Dead.* Oxford: Oxford University Press.

Cüppers, Christoph. 1997. "A Ban on Animal Slaughter at Buddhist Shrines in Nepal." In Karmay and Sagant 1997, pp. 677–87.

Dargyay, Eva K. 1991. "Sangha and State in Imperial Tibet." In *Tibetan History and Language: Studies Dedicated to Uray Géza on his Seventieth Birthday*, edited by Ernst Steinkellner, pp. 111–27. Wiener Studien zur Tibetologie und Buddhismuskunde Heft 26. Vienna: Arbeitskreis für Tibetische und Buddhistische Studien Universität Wien.

Davidson, Ronald M. 1981. "The *Litany of Names of Mañjuśrī:* Text and Translation of the *Mañjuśrīnāmasaṁgīti.*" In *Tantric and Taoist Studies in Honour of R. A. Stein*, edited by Michel Strickmann. *Mélanges chinois et bouddhiques* 20: 1–69.

——. 1985. "Buddhist Systems of Transformation: *Āśraya-parivṛtti / parāvṛtti* Among the Yogācāra." Ph.D. diss., University of California, Berkeley.

——. 1990. "An Introduction to the Standards of Scriptural Authenticity in Indian Buddhism." In *Chinese Buddhist Apocrypha*, edited by Robert E. Buswell, pp. 291–325. Honolulu: University of Hawai'i Press.

——. 1991. "Reflections on the Maheśvara Subjugation Myth: Indic Materials, Sa-skya-pa Apologetics, and the Birth of Heruka." *JIABS* 14/2: 197–235.

——. 1992. "Preliminary Studies on Hevajra's *Abhisamaya* and the *Lam-'bras Tshogs-bshad.*" In *Tibetan Buddhism: Reason and Revelation*, edited by Steven D. Goodman and Ronald M. Davidson, pp. 107–32, 176–84. Albany: State University of New York Press.

——. 1995. "Atiśa's *A Lamp for the Path to Awakening.*" In *Buddhism: In Practice*, edited by Donald Lopez, pp. 290–301. New Readings Series. Princeton, N.J.: Princeton University Press.

———. 1999. "Masquerading as Pramāṇa: Esoteric Buddhism and Epistemological Nomenclature." In *Dharmakīrti's Thought and Its Impact on Indian and Tibetan Plilosophy—Proceedings of the Third International Conference on Dharmakīrti and Pramāṇa*, edited by Katsura Shoryu, pp. 25–35. Vienna: Österreichischen Akademie der Wissenschaften.

——. 2002a. "Gsar-ma Apocrypha: Gray Texts, Oral Traditions, and the Creation of Orthodoxy." In *The Many Canons of Tibetan Buddhism*, edited by Helmut Eimer and David Germano, pp. 203–24. Leiden: Brill.

——. 2002b. "Hidden Realms and Pure Abodes: Central Asian Buddhism as

Frontier Religion in the Literature of India, Nepal and Tibet." *Pacific World: Journal of the Institute of Buddhist Studies*, 3rd ser., 4: 153–81.
——. 2002c. *Indian Esoteric Buddhism: A Social History of the Tantric Movement.* New York: Columbia University Press.
——. 2002d. "Reframing *Sahaja:* Genre, Representation, Ritual and Lineage." *JIP* 30: 45–83.
——. 2003. "The Kingly Cosmogonic Narrative and Tibetan Histories: Indian Origins, Tibetan Space, and the *bKa' 'chems ka khol ma* Synthesis." In Roberto Vitali, ed., *Lungta: Cosmogony and the Origins* 16:64–83.
——. forthcoming a. "Imperial Agency in the Gsar-ma Treasure Texts During the Tibetan Renaissance: The *Rgyal po bla gter* and Related Literature." In *Studies in Tibetan Buddhist Literature and Praxis*, edited by Ronald M. Davidson and Christian Wedemeyer. Leiden: Brill.
——. forthcoming b. "Vajras at Thirty Paces: Authority, Lineage, and Religious Conflict in gSar-'gyur Central Tibet." In *Proceedings of the Eighth Seminar of the International Association for Tibetan Studies*, edited by Elliot Sperling. Bloomington: Indiana University Press.
Davidson, Ronald M., and Christian K. Wedemeyer, eds., forthcoming. *Studies in Tibetan Buddhist Literature and Praxis.* Leiden: Brill.
Dawson, Lorne L. 2001. "The Cultural Significance of New Religious Movements: The Case of Soka Gakkai." *Sociology of Religion* 62, no. 2: 337–64.
Dayal, Har. 1932. *The Bodhisattva Doctrine in Sanskrit Buddhist Literature.* Reprint, Delhi: Motilal Banarsidass, 1970.
Decleer, Hubert. 1992. "The Melodious Drumsound All-Pervading—Sacred Biography of Rwa Lotsâwa: About Early Lotsâwa *rnam thar* and *chos 'byung.*" In *Tibetan Studies: Proceedings of the 5th Seminar of the International Association for Tibetan Studies: Narita 1989*, edited by Ihara Shoren and Zuiho Yamaguchi, vol. 1, pp. 13–28. Narita: Naritasan shinshoji.
——. 1994–95. "Bajracharya Transmission in XIth Century Chobar." *Buddhist Himalaya* 6: 9–20.
——. 1996. "Master Atiśa in Nepal: The Tham Bahīl and Five Stūpas' Foundations According to the *'Brom ston Itinerary.*" *Journal of the Nepal Research Centre* 10: 27–54.
Demiéville, Paul. 1952. *Le Concile de Lhasa.* Vol. 7. Bibliothéque de l'institut des hautes études chinoises. Paris: Presses Universitaires de France.
——. 1973. *Choix d'études bouddhiques (1929–1970).* Leiden: Brill.
Denjongpa, Anna Balikci. 2002. "Kangchendzönga: Secular and Buddhist Perceptions of the Mountain Deity of Sikkim Among the Lhopos." *Bulletin of Tibetology* 38, no. 2: 5–37.
Diemberger, Hildegard, and Guntram Hazod. 1997. "Animal Sacrifices and Mountain Deities in Southern Tibet." In Karmay and Sagant 1997, pp. 261–79.
——. 1999. "Machig Zhama's Recovery: Traces of Ancient History and Myth in

the South Tibetan Landscape of Khata and Phadrug." In *Sacred Spaces and Powerful Places in Tibetan Culture—A Collection of Essays*, edited by Toni Huber, pp. 34–51. Dharamsala: Library of Tibetan Works and Archives.

Dietz, Siglinde. 1984. *Die Buddhistische Briefliteratur Indiens—Nach dem tibetischen Tanjur herausgegeben, übersetzt und erläutert.* Asiatische Forschungen Band 84. Wiesbaden: Otto Harrassowitz.

Dotson, Brandon. Forthcoming. "At the Behest of the Mountain." In *Proceedings of the Xth Seminar of IATS*, edited by Charles Ramble. Leiden: Brill.

Dubois, Abbé J. A. 1897. *Hindu Manners, Customs and Ceremonies.* Translated by Henry K. Beauchamp. Oxford: Clarendon Press.

Dunnel, Ruth. 1992. "The Hsia Origins of the Yüan Institution of Imperial Preceptor." *Asia Major* ser. 3, vol. 5: 85–111.

——. 1994. "The Hsi Hsia." In *The Cambridge History of China*. Vol. 6, *Alien Regimes and Border States, 907–1368*, edited by Herbert Franke and Denis Twitchett, pp. 154–214. Cambridge: Cambridge University Press.

——. 1996. *The Great State of White and High: Buddhism and State Formation in Eleventh-Century Xia.* Honolulu: University of Hawai'i Press.

Eckel, Malcolm David, ed. and trans. 1987. *Jñānagarbha's Commentary on the Distinction Between the Two Truths.* Albany: State University of New York Press.

Edou, Jérôme. 1996. *Machig Labdrön and the Foundations of Chöd.* Ithaca, N.Y.: Snow Lion.

Ehrhard, Franz-Karl. 1997. "Recently Discovered Manuscripts of the Rnying Ma Rgyud 'Bum from Nepal." In *Tibetan Studies: Proceedings of the 7th Seminar of the International Association for Tibetan Studies, Graz 1995*, edited by Helmut Krasser et al., vol. 1, pp. 253–77. Österreichische Akademie der Wissenschaften Philosophisch-Historische Klasse Denkschriften, 256 Band. Vienna: Österreichischen Akademie Der Wissenschaften.

——. 2002. "The Transmission of the *Thig-le Bcu-drug* and the *Bka' Gdams Glegs Bam*." In *The Many Canons of Tibetan Buddhism*, edited by Helmut Eimer and David Germano, pp. 29–56. Leiden: Brill.

Eimer, Helmut, ed. and trans. 1978. *Bodhipathapradīpa: Ein Lehrgedicht de Atiśa (Dīpaṁkaraśrījñāna) in der Tibetischen Überlieferung.* Asiatische Forschungen 59. Wiesbaden: Otto Harrassowitz.

——. 1979. *Rnam Thar Rgyas Pa: Materialien zu einer Biographie des Atiśa (Dīpaṁkaraśrījñāna).* Asiatische Forschungen, Band 67. Wiesbaden: Otto Harrassowitz.

——. 1997. "A Source for the First Narthang Kanjur: Two Early Sa skya pa Catalogues of the Tantras." In *Transmission of the Tibetan Canon*, edited by Helmut Eimer. Vienna: Österreichischen Akademie der Wissenschaften.

Eimer, Helmut, and David Germano, eds. 2002. *The Many Canons of Tibetan Buddhism.* Leiden: Brill.

Ekvall, Robert B. 1968. *Fields on the Hoof: Nexus of Tibetan Nomadic Pastoralism.* Reprint, Prospect Heights, Ill.: Waveland Press, 1983.

Epstein, Lawrence, and Richard F. Sherburne, eds. 1990. *Reflections on Tibetan Culture—Essays in Memory of Turrell V. Wylie.* Studies in Asian Thought and Religion, vol. 12. Lewiston, N.Y.: Edwin Mellen Press.

Everding, Karl-Heinz. 2000. *Das Königreich Mang yul Gung thang.* 2 vols. Bonn: VGH Wissenschaftsverlag GmbH.

Ferrari, Alfonsa. 1958. *Mk'yen Brtse's Guide to the Holy Places of Central Tibet.* Edited and completed by Luciano Petech. SOR 16. Rome: ISMEO.

Finke, Roger, and Rodney Stark. 2001. "The New Holy Clubs: Testing Church-to-Sect Proposition." *Sociology of Religion* 62/2: 175–89.

Francke, A. H. 1914–26. *Antiquities of Indian Tibet.* Archaeological Survey of India, Monograph Series, vols. 38, 50. Calcutta: Superintendent Government Printing.

Franke, H. 1978. *From Tribal Chieftain to Universal Emperor and God: The Legitimation of the Yüan Dynasty.* Munich: Verlag der Bayerischen Akademie der Wissenschaften.

——. 1981. "Tibetans in Yüan China." In *China Under Mongol Rule*, edited by J. D. Langlois, pp. 296–328. Princeton, N.J.: Princeton University Press.

Gellner, David N. 1992. *Monk, Householder, and Tantric Priest.* Cambridge: Cambridge University Press.

Germano, David. 2002. "The Seven Descents and the Early History of Rnying ma Transmissions." In *The Many Canons of Tibetan Buddhism*, edited by Helmut Eimer and David Germano, pp. 225–63. Leiden: Brill.

Gethin, R. M. L. 1992. *The Buddhist Path to Awakening: A Study of the Bodhi-Pakkhiyā Dhammā.* Leiden: Brill.

Gimello, Robert M., and Peter N. Gregory, eds. 1983. *Studies in Ch'an and Hua-yen.* Honolulu: University of Hawai'i Press.

Goepper, Roger. 1996. *Alchi: Ladakh's Hidden Buddhist Sanctuary—The Sumtsek.* London: Serindia Publications.

Gómez, Luis O. 1983. "The Direct and the Gradual Approaches of Zen Master Mahāyāna: Fragments of the Teachings of Mo-ho-yen." In *Studies in Ch'an and Hua-yen*, edited by Robert M. Gimello and Peter N. Gregory, pp. 69–167. Honolulu: University of Hawai'i Press.

Gould, Stephen Jay. 2002. *The Structure of Evolutionary Theory.* Cambridge, Mass.: Belknap Press.

Green, Thomas M. 1982. *The Light in Troy: Imitation and Discovery in Renaissance Poetry.* New Haven, Conn.: Yale University Press.

——. 1988. "Petrarch and the Humanist Hermeneutic." In *Petrarch*, edited by Harold Bloom, pp. 103–23. New York: Chelsea House.

Grupper, Samuel Martin. 1980. "The Manchu Imperial Cult of the Early Ch'ing Dynasty: Texts and Studies on the Tantric Sanctuary of Mahākāla at Mukden." Ph.D. diss., Indiana University.

Guenther, Herbert V. 1959. *Jewel Ornament of Liberation.* London: Rider.

——. 1963. *The Life and Teaching of Nāropa.* Oxford: Clarendon Press.

Gupta, Chitrarekha. 1996. *The Kāyasthas: A Study in the Formation and Early History of a Caste.* Calcutta: K. P. Bagchi.

Gyalbo, Tsering, et al. 2000. *Civilization at the Foot of Mount Sham-po: The Royal House of lHa Bug-pa-can and the History of g.Ya'-bzang.* Vienna: Österreichischen Akademie der Wissenschaften.

Gyatso, Geshe Kelsang. 1982. *Clear Light of Bliss: Mahamudra in Vajrayana Buddhism.* London: Wisdom Publications.

Gyatso, Janet. 1985. "The Development of the Gcod Tradition." In *Soundings in Tibetan Civilization*, edited by Barbara Nimri Aziz and Matthew Kapstein, pp. 320–41. New Delhi: Manohar.

——. 1987. "Down with the Demoness: Reflections on the Feminine Ground in Tibet." *TJ* 12: 33–53.

——. 1994. "Guru Chos-dbang's *Gter 'Byung Chen Mo:* An Early Survey of the Treasure Tradition and Its Strategies in Discussing Bon Treasure." In *Tibetan Studies: Proceedings of the 6th Seminar of the International Association for Tibetan Studies*, edited by Per Kværne, vol. 1, pp. 275–87. Oslo: Institute for Comparative Research in Human Culture.

——. 1996. "Drawn from the Tibetan Treasury: The *gTer ma* Literature." In *Tibetan Literature: Studies in Genre*, edited by José Ignacio Cabezón and Roger R. Jackson, pp. 147–69. Ithaca, N.Y.: Snow Lion.

——. 1998. *Apparitions of the Self: The Secret Autobiographies of a Tibetan Visionary.* Princeton, N.J.: Princeton University Press.

Haarh, Erik. 1969. *The Yar-Luṅ Dynasty: A Study with Particular Regard to the Contribution by Myths and Legends to the History of Ancient Tibet and the Origin and Nature of Its Kings.* Copenhagen: G. E. C. Gad's Forlag.

Hackin, Joseph. 1924. *Formulaire sanscrit-tibétain du X*[e] siècle. Mission Pelliot en Asie Centrale, Série Petit in Octavo, vol. 2. Paris: Librarie orientaliste Paul Geuthner.

Hattori, Masaaki. 1968. *Dignāga, on Perception.* Harvard Oriental Series, vol. 47. Cambridge, Mass.: Harvard University Press.

Hazod, Guntram. 2000a. "The Nine Royal Heirlooms." In *Civilization at the Foot of Mount Sham-po: The Royal House of lHa Bug-pa-can and the History of g.Ya'-bzang*, edited by Tsering Gyalbo et al., pp. 192–97. Vienna: Österreichischen Akademie der Wissenschaften.

——. 2000b. "The Yum-brtan Lineage." In *Civilization at the Foot of Mount Sham-po: The Royal House of lHa Bug-pa-can and the History of g.Ya'-bzang*, edited by Tsering Gyalbo et al., pp. 177–91. Vienna: Österreichischen Akademie der Wissenschaften.

Heissig, Walther. 1980. *The Religions of Mongolia.* Translated by Geoffrey Samuel. Berkeley and Los Angeles: University of California Press.

Herrmann-Pfandt, Adelheid. 1992. *Ḍākinīs: Zur Stellung und Symbolik des Weiblichen im Tantrischen Buddhismus.* Indica et Tibetica 20. Bonn: Indica et Tibetica Verlag.

——. 2002. "The *Lhan Kar Ma* as a Source for the History of Tantric Buddhism." In *The Many Canons of Tibetan Buddhism*, edited by Helmut Eimer and David Germano, pp. 129–49. Leiden: Brill.

Huber, Toni. 1990. "Where Exactly Are Cāritra, Devikoṭa and Himavat? A Sacred Geography Controversy and the Development of Tantric Buddhist Pilgrimage Sites in Tibet." *Kailash: A Journal of Himalayan Studies* 16, nos. 3–4: 121–64.

——, ed. 1999. *Sacred Spaces and Powerful Places in Tibetan Culture—A Collection of Essays.* Dharamsala: Library of Tibetan Works and Archives.

Huntington, C. W., trans. 1989. *The Emptiness of Emptiness: An Introduction to Early Indian Mādhyamika.* Honolulu: University of Hawai'i Press.

Ikari, Yasuke, ed. 1994. *A Study of the Nīlamata: Aspects of Hinduism in Ancient Kashmir.* Kyoto: Institute for Research in Humanities, Kyoto University.

Irvine, Martin. 1994. *The Making of Textual Culture: 'Grammatica' and Literary Theory, 350–1000.* Cambridge: Cambridge University Press.

Isaacson, Harunaga. 2001. "Ratnākaraśānti's *Hevajrasahajasadyoga*." In *Le Parole e i marmi: Studi in onore di Raniero Gnoli nel suo 70° compleanno*, edited by Raffaele Torella. SOR 92, vol. 1, pp. 457–81. Rome: Istituto italiano per L'Africa e L'Oriente.

Iwasaki, Tsutomu. 1993. "The Tibetan Tribes of Ho-hsi and Buddhism During the Northern Sung Period." *Acta asiatica* 64: 17–37.

Jackson, David P. 1983. "Commentaries on the Writings of Sa-skya Pandita: A Bibliographical Sketch." *TJ* 8, no. 3: 3–23.

——. 1985. "Madhyamaka Studies Among the Early Sa-skya-pas." *TJ* 10, no. 2: 20–34.

——. 1986. "Sa-skya Paṇḍita's Letter to the Tibetans: A Late and Dubious Addition to His Collected Works." *JTS* 6: 17–23.

——. 1987. *The Entrance Gate for the Wise* (*Section III*). Wiener Studien zur Tibetologie und Buddhismuskunde Heft 17, 1–2. 2 vols. Vienna: Arbeitskreis für Tibetische und Buddhistische Studien Universität Wien.

——. 1990. "Sa-skya Paṇḍita the 'Polemicist': Ancient Debates and Modern Interpretations." *JIABS* 13: 17–116.

——. 1993a. Foreword to "rNgog Lo-tsā-ba's Commentary on the *Abhisamayālaṁkāra*." *Lo tsā ba chen po'i bsdus don*, pp. 1–31.

——. 1993b. Foreword to "rNgog Lo-tsā-ba's Commentary on the *Ratnagotravibhāga*." *Theg chen rgyud bla'i don bsdus pa*, pp. 1–49.

——. 1994a. "An Early Biography of rNgog Lo-tsā-ba Blo-ldan-shes-rab." In *Tibetan Studies: Proceedings of the 6th Seminar of the International Association for Tibetan Studies*, edited by Per Kværne, vol 1, pp. 372–92. Oslo: Institute for Comparative Research in Human Culture.

——. 1994b. *Enlightenment by a Single Means.* Vienna: Österreichischen Akademie der Wissenschaften.

——. 1996. "The *bsTan rim* ('Stages of the Doctrine') and Similar Graded Expositions of the Bodhisattva's Path." In *Tibetan Literature: Studies in Genre*, edited by José Ignacio Cabezón and Roger R. Jackson, pp. 229–43. Ithaca, N.Y.: Snow Lion.

Jackson, Roger R. 1996. "'Poetry' in Tibet: *Glu, mGur, sNyan ngag* and 'Songs of Experience.'" In *Tibetan Literature: Studies in Genre*, edited by José Ignacio Cabezón and Roger R. Jackson, eds., 368–96. Ithaca, N.Y.: Snow Lion.

Jagchid, Sechin. 1970. "Why the Mongolian Khans Adopted Tibetan Buddhism as Their Faith." In *Proceedings of the Third East Asian Altaistic Conference*, edited by Ch'en Chieh-hsien and Sechin Jagchid, pp. 108–28. Taibei.

——. 1980. "Chinese Buddhism and Taoism During the Mongolian Rule of China." *Mongolian Studies* 6: 61–98.

Jagchid, Sechin, and Paul Hyer. 1979. *Mongolia's Culture and Society*. Boulder, Colo.: Westview Press.

de Jong, J. W. 1972. "Notes à propos des colophons du Kanjur." *Zentralasiatische Studien* 6: 505–59.

Kajiyama, Yuichi. 1968/69. "Bhāvaviveka, Sthiramati and Dharmapāla." *Wiener Zeitschrift für die Kunde Süd- und Ost-Asiens* 12–13: 193–203.

Kaneko, Eiichi. 1982. *Ko-tantora zenshū kaidai mokuroku.* Tokyo: Kokusho kankōkai.

Kapstein, Matthew T. 1980. "The Shangs-pa Bka'-brgyud: An Unknown Tradition of Tibetan Buddhism." In *Tibetan Studies in Honour of Hugh Richardson,* edited by Michael Aris and Aung San Suu Kyi, pp. 138–44. Warminster: Philips and Aris.

——. 1992. "The Illusion of Spiritual Progress: Remarks on Indo-Tibetan Buddhist Soteriology." In *Paths to Liberation: The Mārga and Its Transformations in Buddhist Thought*, edited by Robert E. Buswell and Robert M. Gimello, pp. 193–224. Honolulu: University of Hawai'i Press.

——. 2000. *The Tibetan Assimilation of Buddhism: Conversion, Contestation, and Memory.* Oxford: Oxford University Press.

Karmay, Samten Gyaltsen. 1972. *The Treasury of Good Sayings: A Tibetan History of Bon.* London Oriental Series, vol. 26. Oxford: Oxford University Press.

——. 1988. *The Great Perfection: A Philosophical and Meditative Teaching of Tibetan Buddhism.* Leiden: Brill.

——. 1991. "L'homme et le bœuf: le rituel de glud (rançon)." *JA* 279: 327–81. Translated in Karmay 1998, pp. 339–79.

——. 1998. *The Arrow and the Spindle: Studies in History, Myths, Rituals and Beliefs in Tibet.* Kathmandu: Mandala Book Point.

Karmay, Samten Gyaltsen, and Philippe Sagant, eds. 1997. *Les habitants du toit du monde.* Nanterre, France: Société d'ethnologie.

Karmay, Samten Gyaltsen, and Yasuhiko Nagano, eds. 2000. *New Horizons in Bon Studies.* Osaka: National Museum of Ethnology.

Kielhorn, F. 1886. "The Sasbahu Temple Inscription of Mahipala, of Vikrama-Samvat 1150." *IA* 15: 33–46.

Klimburg-Salter, Deborah E. 1987. "Reformation and Renaissance: A Study of Indo-Tibetan Monasteries in the Eleventh Century." In *Orientalia Iosephi Tucci Memoriae Dicta*, edited by Edenda Curaverunt et al., vol. 2, pp. 683–702, plates I-VII. Rome: ISMEO.

——. 1997. *Tabo: A Lamp for the Kingdom.* New York: Thames & Hudson.

Kollmar-Paulenz, Karénina. 1993. *Der Schmuck der Befreiung. Die Geschichte der Zhi byed- und gCod-Schule des tibetischen Buddhismus.* Wiesbaden: Harrassowitz.

——. 1998. "Ma gcig lab sgron ma—The Life of a Tibetan Woman Mystic Between Adaptation and Rebellion." *TJ* 23/2: 11–32.

Kölver, Bernhard, and Hemrāj Śākya. 1985. *Documents from the Rudravarṇa-Mahāvihāra, Pāṭan.* Vol. 1, *Sales and Mortgages.* Sankt Augustin: VGH Wissenschaftsverlag.

Kossak, Steven M., and Singer, Jane Casey. 1998. *Sacred Visions: Early Paintings from Central Tibet.* New York: Metropolitan Museum of Art.

Kramer, Ralf. 1997. "rNgog Blo-ldan-shes-rab (1059–1109): The Life and Works of the Great Translator." Master's thesis, University of Hamburg.

Krasser, Helmut, et al., eds. 1997. *Tibetan Studies: Proceedings of the 7th Seminar of the International Association for Tibetan Studies, Graz 1995.* 2 vols. Österreichische Akademie der Wissenschaften Philosophisch-Historische Klasse Denkschriften, 256 Band. Vienna: Österreichischen Akademie Der Wissenschaften.

van der Kuijp, Leonard W. J. 1978. "Phya-pa Chos-kyi seng-ge's Impact on Tibetan Epistemological Theory." *JIP* 5: 355–69.

——. 1983. *Contributions to the Development of Tibetan Buddhist Epistemology.* Alt- und Neu-Indische Studien 26. Wiesbaden: Franz Steiner Verlag.

——. 1985. "A Text-Historical Note on *Hevajratantra* II:v:1–2." *JIABS* 8: 83–89.

——. 1987. "The Monastery of Gsang-phu ne'u-thog and Its Abbatial Succession from ca. 1073 to 1250." *Berliner indologische Studien* 3: 103–27.

——. 1993. "Jayānanda: A Twelfth Century *Guoshi* from Kashmir Among the Tangut." *CAJ* 37: 188–97.

——. 1994. "Apropos of Some Recently Recovered Texts Belonging to the *Lam 'bras* Teachings of the Sa skya pa and Ko brag pa." *JIABS* 17:175–201.

——. 1996. "Tibetan Historiography." In *Tibetan Literature: Studies in Genre*, edited by José Ignacio Cabezón and Roger R. Jackson, pp. 39–56. Ithaca, N.Y.: Snow Lion.

Kumar, Nita. 1988. *Artisans of Banaras: Popular Culture and Identity, 1880–1986.* Princeton, N.J.: Princeton University Press.

Kværne, Per. 1971. "A Chronological Table of the Bon po: The Bstan Rcis of Ñi Ma Bstan 'Jin." *Acta orientalia* 33: 205–48.

——. 1975. "On the Concept of Sahaja in Indian Buddhist Tantric Literature." *Tememos* 11: 88–135.

——, ed. 1994. *Tibetan Studies: Proceedings of the 6th Seminar of the International Association for Tibetan Studies.* 2 vols. Oslo: Institute for Comparative Research in Human Culture.

Kychanov, E. J. 1978. "Tibetans and Tibetan Culture in the Tangut State Hsi Hsia (982–1227)." In *Proceedings of the Csoma de Körös Memorial Symposium*, edited by Louis Ligeti, pp. 205–11. Budapest: Akadémiai Kiadó.

Lahiri, Latika, trans. 1986. *Chinese Monks in India.* Reprint, Delhi: Motilal Banarsidass, 1995.

Lalou, Marcelle. 1938. "Le Culte des Naga et la thérapeutique." *JA* 230: 1–19.

——. 1949. "Les Chemins du mort dans les croyances de haute Asie." *Revue de l'histoire des religions* 135: 42–48.

——. 1952. "Rituel Bon-po des funérailles royales." *JA* 240: 339–61.

——. 1953. "Les Textes bouddhiques au temps du Roi Khri-sroṅ-lde-bcan." *JA* 241, no. 3: 313–53.

Lang, Karen Christina. 1990. "Spa-tshab Nyi-ma-grags and the Introduction of Prāsaṅgika Madhyamaka into Tibet." In *Reflections on Tibetan Culture—Essays in Memory of Turrell V. Wylie*, edited by Lawrence Epstein and Richard F. Sherburne. Studies in Asian Thought and Religion, vol. 12, pp. 127–41. Lewiston, N.Y.: Edwin Mellen Press.

Leonard, Karen Isaksen. 1978. *Social History of an Indian Caste: The Kayasths of Hyderabad.* Berkeley and Los Angeles: University of California Press.

Lessing, Ferdinand D., and Alex Wayman. 1968. *Mkhas Grub Rje'i Fundamentals of the Buddhist Tantras.* Indo-Iranian Monographs, vol. 8. The Hague: Mouton.

Lévi, Sylvain. 1907. *Mahāyāna-Sūtrālamkāra: Exposé de la doctrine du grand véhicule.* Paris: Libraire honoré champion.

Levinson, Jules B. 1996. "The Metaphors of Liberation: Tibetan Treatises on Grounds and Paths." In *Tibetan Literature: Studies in Genre*, edited by José Ignacio Cabezón and Roger R. Jackson, pp. 261–74. Ithaca, N.Y.: Snow Lion.

Lewis, Todd T. 1993. "Newar-Tibetan Trade and the Domestication of *Siṁhala-sārthabāhu Avadāna.*" *History of Religions* 33: 135–60.

Lewis, Todd T., and Lozang Jamspal. 1988. "Newars and Tibetans in the Kathmandu Valley: Three New Translations from Tibetan Sources." *Journal of Asian and African Studies* 36: 187–211.

Lhagyal, Dondrup. 2000. "Bonpo Family Lineages in Central Tibet." In *New Horizons in Bon Studies*, edited by Samten Gyaltsen Karmay and Yasuhiko Nagano, pp. 429–508. Osaka: National Museum of Ethnology.

Lienhard, Siegfried. 1993. "Avalokiteśvara in the Wick of the Night-Lamp." *IIJ* 36: 93–104.

Ligeti, Louis, ed. 1978. *Proceedings of the Csoma de Körös Memorial Symposium.* Bibliotheca orientalis hungarica, vol. 23. Budapest: Akadémiai Kiadó.

——. 1984. *Tibetan and Buddhist Studies, Commemorating the 200th* Anniversary of the Birth of Alexander Csoma de Körös. 2 vols. Bibliotheca orientalis hungarica, vol. 29, no. 2. Budapest: Akadémiai Kiadó.

Lin, Meicun. 1990. "A New Kharoṣṭhī Wooden Tablet from China." *Bulletin of the School of Oriental and African Studies* 53: 283–91.

Lindtner, Christian. 1982. *Nagarjuniana: Studies in the Writings and Philosophy of Nāgārjuna.* Indiske Studier 4. Copenhagen: Akademisk Forlag.

Lo Bue, Erberto. 1994. "A Case of Mistaken Identity: Ma-gcig Labs-sgron and Ma-gcig Zha-ma." In *Tibetan Studies: Proceedings of the 6th Seminar of the International Association for Tibetan Studies*, edited by Per Kværne, vol. 1, pp. 482–90. Oslo: Institute for Comparative Research in Human Culture.

——. 1997. "The Role of Newar Scholars in Transmitting Buddhist Heritage to Tibet (c. 750–c. 1200)." In Karmay and Sagant 1997, pp. 629–58.

Locke, John K. 1985. *Buddhist Monasteries of Nepal: A Survey of the Bāhās and Bahīs of the Kathmandu Valley.* Kathmandu: Sahayogi Press.

Macdonald, Ariane, ed. 1971a. *Études tibétaines dédiées à la mémoire de Marcelle Lalou.* Paris: Adrien Maisonneuve.

——. 1971b. "Une lecture des Pelliot Tibétain 1286, 1287, 1038, 1047, et 1290." In *Études tibétaines dédiées à la mémoire de Marcelle Lalou*, edited by Ariane Macdonald, pp. 190–391. Paris: Adrien Maisonneuve.

Mala, Guilaine, and Ryūtoku Kimura. 1988. *Un traité tibétain de Dhyāna chinois.* Tokyo: Maison Franco-Japonaise.

Malla, Kamal P. 1985. Review of *Mediaeval History of Nepal c. 750–1482. Contributions to Nepalese Studies* 12, no. 2: 121–35.

Martin, Dan. 1982. "The Early Education of Milarepa." *JTS* 2: 53–76.

——. 1992. "A Twelfth-Century Tibetan Classic of Mahamudra, *The Path of Ultimate Profundity: The Great Seal Instructions of Zhang.*" *JIABS* 15: 243–319.

——. 1996a. "Lay Religious Movements in 11th- and 12th-Century Tibet: A Survey of Sources." *Kailash* 18, nos. 3–4: 23–56.

——. 1996b. "On the Cultural Ecology of Sky Burial on the Himalayan Plateau." *East and West* 46: 353–70.

——. 1996c. "The Star King and the Four Children of Pehar: Popular Religious Movements of the 11th- to 12th-Century Tibet." *Acta orientalia academiae scientiarum hungarica* 49, nos. 1–2: 171–95.

——. 1997. *Tibetan Histories: A Bibliography of Tibetan-Language Historical Works.* London: Serindia Publications.

——. 2001a. "Meditation Is Action Taken: On Zhang Rinpoche, a Meditation-Based Activist in Twelfth-Century Tibet." *Lungta (Dharamsala)* 14: 45–56.

——. 2001b. *Unearthing Bon Treasures: Life and Contested Legacy of a Tibetan Scripture Revealer.* Leiden: Brill.

Martines, Lauro. 1988. *Power and Imagination: City-States in Renaissance Italy.* Rev. ed. Baltimore: Johns Hopkins University Press.

Mather, Richard B. 1959. *Biography of Lü Kuang.* Chinese Dynastic Histories Translations, no. 7. Berkeley and Los Angeles: University of California Press.

Mathes, Klaus-Dieter. forthcoming. "Blending the Sūtras with the Tantras: The Influence of Maitrīpa and His Circle on the Formation of *Sūtra Mahāmudrā* in the Kagyu Schools." In *Studies in Tibetan Buddhist Literature and Praxis*, edited by Ronald M. Davidson and Christian Wedemeyer. Leiden: Brill.

Mayer, Robert. 1994. "Scriptural Revelation in India and Tibet." In *Tibetan Stud-*

ies: Proceedings of the 6th Seminar of the International Association for Tibetan Studies, edited by Per Kværne, vol. 1, pp. 533–44. Oslo: Institute for Comparative Research in Human Culture.

——. 1996. *A Scripture of the Ancient Tantra Collection: The Phur-pa bcu-gnyis.* Oxford: Kiscadale Publications.

——. 1997a. "The Sa-skya Paṇḍita, the White Panacea, and Clerical Buddhism's Current Credibility Crisis." *TJ* (*Dharamsala*) 22, no. 3: 79–105.

——. 1997b. "Were the gSar-ma Polemicists Justified in Rejecting Some rNying-ma-pa Tantras?" In *Tibetan Studies: Proceedings of the 7th Seminar of the International Association for Tibetan Studies, Graz 1995*, edited by Helmut Krasser et al., vol. 2, pp. 619–32. Österreichische Akademie der Wissenschaften Philosophisch-Historische Klasse Denkschriften, 256 Band. Vienna: Österreichischen Akademie Der Wissenschaften.

——. 1998. "The Figure of Maheśvara/Rudra in the rÑiṅ-ma-pa Tantric Tradition." *JIABS* 21: 271–310.

McRae, John. 1986. *The Northern School and the Formation of Early Ch'an Buddhism*. Honolulu: University of Hawai'i Press.

Meinert, Carmen. 2002. "Chinese *Chan* and Tibetan *Rdzogs Chen:* Preliminary Remarks on Two Tibetan Dunhuang Manuscripts." In *Tibet, Past and Present*, edited by Henk Blezer, vol. 2, pp. 289–307. Leiden: Brill.

——. 2003."Structural Analysis of the *bSam gtan mig sgron.* A Comparison of the Fourfold Correct Practice in the *Āryāvikalpapraveśanāmadhāraṇī* and the Contents of the Four Main Chapters of the *bSam gtan mig sgron.*" *JIABS* 26: 175–95.

——. forthcoming. "The Legend of Cig car ba Criticism in Tibet: A List of Six Cig car ba Titles in the *Chos 'byung me tog snying po* of Nyang Nyi ma 'od zer (12th century)." In *Studies in Tibetan Buddhist Literature and Praxis*, edited by Ronald M. Davidson and Christian Wedemeyer. Leiden: Brill.

Meyvaert, Paul. 1980. "An Unknown letter of Hulagu, Il-Khan of Persia, to King Louis IX of France." *Viator* 11: 245–59.

Nagano, Yasuhiko. 1979. "An Analysis of Tibetan Colour Terminology." *Tibetano-Burman Studies* 1: 1–83.

——. 2000. "Sacrifice and *lha pa* in the glu rol Festival of Reb-skong." In *New Horizons in Bon Studies*, edited by Samten Gyaltsen Karmay and Yasuhiko Nagano, pp. 567–649. Osaka: National Museum of Ethnology.

Nalanda Translation Committee, trans. 1982. *The Life of Marpa the Translator.* Boston: Shambhala.

Namai, Chishō Mamoru. 1997. "On *bodhicittabhavana* in the Esoteric Buddhist Tradition." In *Tibetan Studies: Proceedings of the 7th Seminar of the International Association for Tibetan Studies, Graz 1995*, edited by Helmut Krasser et al., vol. 2, pp. 657–68. Österreichische Akademie der Wissenschaften Philosophisch-Historische Klasse Denkschriften, 256 Band. Vienna: Österreichischen Akademie Der Wissenschaften.

Nath, Vijay. 2001. *Purāṇas and Acculturation: A Historioco-Anthropological Perspective.* New Delhi: Munshiram Monoharlal Publishers.

de Nebesky-Wojkowitz, Réne. 1956. *Oracles and Demons of Tibet—The Cult and Iconography of the Tibetan Protective Deities.* s'Gravenhage: Mouton. Reprinted with introduction by Per Kværne. Graz: Akademische Druk-u.Verlagsanstalt, 1975.

Newman, John. 1985. "A Brief History of the Kālacakra." In *The Wheel of Time*, edited by Geshe Lhundup Sopa, pp. 51–90. Madison, Wisc.: Deer Park Books.

——. 1998. "Islam in the Kālacakra Tantra." *JIABS* 21, no. 2: 311–71.

Nihom, Max. 1992. "The Goddess with the Severed Head: A Recension of Sādhanamālā 232, 234, and 238 Attributed to the Siddhācārya Virūpā." In *Ritual, State and History in South Asia: Essays in Honour of J. C. Heesterman*, edited by A. W. van den Hoek et al., pp. 222–43. Leiden: Brill.

——. 1995. "On Attracting Women and Tantric Initiation: Tilottamā and *Hevajratantra* II, v. 38–47 and I, vii. 8–9. *Bulletin of the School of Oriental and African Studies* 58, no. 3: 521–31.

Norbu, Namkhai, and Kennard Lipman. 1986. *Primordial Experience: An Introduction to rDzogs-chen Meditation.* Boston: Shambhala.

Oberniller, E. 1931. *History of Buddhism (Chos-hbyung) by Bu-ston.* Materialien zur Kunde des Buddhismus 18 Heft. 2 vols. Heidelberg: O. Harrassowitz.

Orofino, Giacomella. 1997. "Apropos of Some Foreign Elements in the Kālacakratantra." In *Tibetan Studies: Proceedings of the 7th Seminar of the International Association for Tibetan Studies, Graz 1995*, edited by Helmut Krasser et al., vol. 2, pp. 717–24. Österreichische Akademie der Wissenschaften Philosophisch-Historische Klasse Denkschriften, 256 Band. Vienna: Österreichischen Akademie Der Wissenschaften.

——. 2001. "Notes on the Early Phases of Indo-Tibetan Buddhism." In *Le Parole e i marmi: Studi in onore di Raniero Gnoli nel suo 70° compleanno*, edited by Raffaele Torella. SOR 92, vol. 2, pp. 541–64. Rome: Istituto italiano per L'Africa e L'Oriente.

Owens, Bruce McCoy. 1993. "Blood and Bodhisattvas: Sacrifice Among the Newar Buddhists of Nepal." In *Proceedings of the International Seminar on the Anthropology of Tibet and the Himalaya*, edited by Charles Ramble and Martin Brauen, pp. 249–60. Zurich: Ethnological Museum of the University of Zurich.

Pagel, Ulrich. 1995. *The Bodhisattvapiṭaka.* Tring: Institute of Buddhist Studies.

Paludan, Ann. 1991. *The Chinese Spirit Road: The Classical Tradition of Stone Tomb Statuary.* New Haven, Conn.: Yale University Press.

Pelliot, Paul. 1961. *Histoire ancienne du Tibet.* Paris: Maisonneuve.

Petech, Luciano. 1983. "Tibetan Relations with Sung China and with the Mongols." In *China Among Equals: The Middle Kingdom and Its Neighbors, 10th–14th Centuries*, edited by Morris Rossabi, pp. 173–203. Berkeley and

Los Angeles: University of California Press.
——. 1984. *Mediaeval History of Nepal (c. 750–1482)*. SOR 54. Rome: ISMEO.
——. 1990. *Central Tibet and the Mongols.* Rome: ISMEO.
——. 1994. "The Disintegration of the Tibetan Kingdom." In *Tibetan Studies: Proceedings of the 6th Seminar of the International Association for Tibetan Studies*, edited by Per Kværne, vol. 2, pp. 649–59. Oslo: Institute for Comparative Research in Human Culture.
——. 1997. "Western Tibet: Historical Introduction." In *Tabo: A Lamp for the Kingdom*, Deborah E. Klimburg-Salter, pp. 229–55. New York: Thames & Hudson.
Pommaret, Françoise. 1999. "The Mon-pa Revisited: In Search of Mon." In *Sacred Spaces and Powerful Places in Tibetan Culture—A Collection of Essays*, edited by Toni Huber, pp. 52–73. Dharamsala: Library of Tibetan Works and Archives.
Prasâda, Râma. 1912. *Patanjali's Yoga Sutras, with the Commentary of Vyâsa and the Gloss of Vâchaspati Miśra.* Reprint, New Delhi: Oriental Books Reprint Corporation, 1978.
Rabil, Albert, ed. 1988. *Renaissance Humanism: Foundations, Forms, and Legacy.* 3 vols. Philadelphia: University of Pennsylvania Press.
Rajaguru, Satyanarayan. 1955–76. *Inscriptions of Orissa.* 5 vols. Bhubaneswar: Orissa State Muesum.
Ramble, Charles. 1997. "Se: Preliminary Notes on the Distribution of an Ethnonym in Tibet and Nepal." In Karmay and Sagant 1997, pp. 485–513.
Ratchnevsky, Paul. 1991. *Genghis Khan: His Life and Legacy.* Translated and edited by Thomas Nivison Haining. Oxford: Blackwell.
Regmi, D. R. 1983. *Inscriptions of Ancient Nepal.* 3 vols. New Delhi: Abhinav Publications.
rGya-mtsho, bSod-nams. 1981. "Go-ram bSod-nams seṅ-ge's Commentary on the *Źen pa bźi bral.*" In *Wind Horse—Proceedings of the North American Tibetological Society*, edited by Ronald M. Davidson, pp. 23–39. Berkeley, Calif.: Asian Humanities Press.
Richardson, Hugh. 1957. "A Tibetan Inscription from Rgyal Lha-khaṅ; and a Note on Tibetan Chronology from A.D. 841 to A.D. 1042." *JRAS*, 57–78.
——. 1985. *A Corpus of Early Tibetan Inscriptions.* London: Royal Asiatic Society.
——. 1995. "The Tibetan Inscription Attributed to Ye-shes-'od: A Note." *JRAS*, 3rd ser., vol. 5: 403–4.
——. 1998. *High Peaks, Pure Earth: Collected Writings on Tibetan History and Culture.* London: Serindia Publications.
Robinson, James B. 1979. *Buddha's Lions: The Lives of the Eighty-Four Siddhas.* Berkeley, Calif.: Dharma Publishing.
Robinson, Richard H. 1967. *Early Mādhyamika In India and China.* Madison: University of Wisconsin Press.
Rocher, Ludo. 1986. *A History of Indian Literature.* Vol. 2, fasc. 3, *The Purāṇas.* Wiesbaden: Otto Harrassowitz.

Roerich, George N., trans. 1949. *The Blue Annals*. 2 vols. Calcutta: Royal Asiatic Society of Bengal.

Róna-Tas, A. 1978. "On a Term of Taxation in the Old Tibetan Royal Annals." In *Proceedings of the Csoma de Körös Memorial Symposium*, edited by Louis Ligeti, pp. 357–63. Budapest: Akadémiai Kiadó.

Rossabi, Morris. 1988. *Khubilai Khan: His Life and Times*. Berkeley and Los Angeles: University of California Press.

Rosser, Colin. 1978. "Social Mobility in the Newar Caste System." In *Caste and Kin in Nepal, India and Ceylon*, edited by Christoph von Fürer-Haimendorf, pp. 68–139. New Delhi: Sterling Publishers.

de Rossi-Filibeck, E. 1983. "The Transmission Lineage of the *Gcod* According to the 2nd Dalai-Lama." In *Contributions on Tibetan Language, History and Culture*, edited by Ernst Steinkellner and Helmut Tauscher, vol. 2, pp. 47–57. Proceedings of the Csoma de Körös Symposium, Velm-Vienna, September 13–19, 1981. Vienna: Arbeitskreis für Tibetische und Buddhistische Studien Universität Wien.

Ruegg, David Seyfort. 1966. *The Life of Bu Ston Rin po Che*. SOR 34. Rome: ISMEO.

——. 1971. "Le *Dharmadhātusthava* de Nāgārjuna." In *Études tibétaines dédiées à la mémoire de Marcelle Lalou*, edited by Ariane Macdonald, pp. 448–71. Paris: Adrien Maisonneuve.

——. 1973. *Le Traité du Tathāgatagarbha de Bu Ston Rin Chen Grub*. Publications de l'École française d'extrême-orient, vol. 88. Paris: École française d'extrême-orient.

——. 1981. "Deux problèmes d'exégèse et de pratique tantriques." In *Tantric and Taoist Studies in Honour of R. A. Stein*, edited by Michel Strickmann. *Mélanges chinois et bouddhiques* 20: 212–26.

——. 1989. *Buddha-nature, Mind and the Problem of Gradualism in a Comparative Perspective: On the Transmission and Reception of Buddhism in India and Tibet*. London: School of Oriental and African Studies.

——. 1995. *Ordre spirituel et ordre temporel dans la pensée bouddhique de l'Inde et du Tibet*. Publications de l'Institute de civilisation indienne, fasc. 64. Paris: Collège de France.

——. 1997. "The Preceptor-Donor (*yon mchod*) Relation in Thirteenth Century Tibetan Society and Polity, Its Inner Asian Precursors and Indian Models." In *Tibetan Studies: Proceedings of the 7th Seminar of the International Association for Tibetan Studies, Graz 1995*, edited by Helmut Krasser et al., vol. 2, pp. 857–72. Österreichische Akademie der Wissenschaften Philosophisch-Historische Klasse Denkschriften, 256 Band. Vienna: Österreichischen Akademie Der Wissenschaften.

——. 2000. *Three Studies in the History of Indian and Tibetan Madhyamaka Philosophy*. Vienna: Arbeitskreis für Tibetische unde Buddhistische Studien, Universität Wien.

Russell, R. V. 1916. *The Tribes and Castes of Central Provinces of India.* Assisted by Rai Bahadur Hira Lal. Reprint, Oosterhout: Anthropological Publications, 1969. 4 vols.

Sachau, Edward C. 1910. *Alberuni's India—An Account of the Religion, Philosophy, Literature, Geography, Chronology, Astronomy, Customs, Laws and Astrology of India About A.D. 1030.* 2 vols. London: Kegan Pual, Trench, Trubner.

Sakurai, Munenobu. 1996. *Indo mikkyōgirei kenkyū.* Kyoto: Hōzōgan.

Salomon, Richard. 1990. "New Evidence for a Gāndhārī Origin of the Arapacana Syllabary." *JAOS* 110: 255–73.

——. 1999. *Ancient Buddhist Scrolls from Gandhāra: The British Library Kharoṣṭhī Fragments.* Seattle: University of Washington Press.

Samten, Jampa. 1992. *A Catalogue of the Phug-brag Manuscript Kanjur.* Dharamsala: Library of Tibetan Works & Archives.

Schaeffer, Kurtis R. 2002. "*The Attainment of Immortality:* From Nāthas in India to Buddhists in Tibet." *JIP* 30: 515–33.

van Schaik, Sam. 2004. "The Early Days of the Great Perfection." *JIABS* 27:165–206.

Scherrer-Schaub, Christina A. 2002. "Enacting Words. A Diplomatic Analysis of Imperial Decrees (*bkas bcad*) and Their Application in the *sGra sbyor bam po gñis pa* Tradition." *JIABS* 25: 263–340.

Schoening, Jeffrey D. 1990. "The Religious Structures at Sa-skya." In *Reflections on Tibetan Culture—Essays in Memory of Turrell V. Wylie*, edited by Lawrence Epstein and Richard F. Sherburne. Studies in Asian Thought and Religion, vol. 12, pp. 11–47. Lewiston, N.Y.: Edwin Mellen Press.

Schopen, Gregory. 1985. "The Bodhigarbhālaṅkāralakṣa and Vimaloṣṇīṣa Dhāraṇīs in Indian Inscriptions." *Wiener Zeitschrift für die Kunde Südasiens* 29: 119–49.

——. 1992. "On Avoiding Ghosts and Social Censure: Monastic Funerals in the Mūlasarvāstivāda-Vinaya." *JIP* 20: 1–39.

——. 1994a. "Doing Business for the Lord: Lending on Interest and Written Loan Contracts in the *Mūlasarvāstivāda-vinaya.*" *JAOS* 114:527–54.

——. 1994b. "Ritual Rights and Bones of Contention: More on Monastic Funerals and Relics in the *Mūlasarvāstivāda-vinaya.*" *JIP* 22: 31–80.

——. 1995. "Monastic Law Meets the Real World: A Monk's Continuing Right to Inherit Family Property in Classical India." *History of Religions* 35: 101–23.

Schram, Louis M. J. 1961. *The Mongours of the Kansu-Tibetan Frontier.* Part 3, Records of the Mongour Clans, *Transactions of the American Philosophical Society*, n.s. 51, no. 3.

Sharma, R. C. 1989. "New Inscriptions from Mathurā." In *Mathurā—The Cultural Heritage*, edited by Doris M. Srinivasan, pp. 308–15. New Delhi: American Institute of Indian Studies.

Sharma, Ram Sharan. 1965. *Indian Feudalism—c. 300–1200.* Reprint, Calcutta: University of Calcutta, 1987.

——. 2001. *Early Medieval Indian Society: A Study in Feudalisation.* Hyderabad: Orient Longman.

Shastri, Lobsang. 1994. "The Marriage Customs of Ru-thog (Mnga'-ris)." In *Tibetan Studies: Proceedings of the 6th Seminar of the International Association for Tibetan Studies*, edited by Per Kværne, vol. 2, pp. 755–77. Oslo: Institute for Comparative Research in Human Culture.

——. 1997. "The Fire Dragon *Chos 'Khor* (1076 A.D.)." In *Tibetan Studies: Proceedings of the 7th Seminar of the International Association for Tibetan Studies, Graz 1995*, edited by Helmut Krasser et al., vol. 2, pp. 873–82. Österreichische Akademie der Wissenschaften Philosophisch-Historische Klasse Denkschriften, 256 Band. Vienna: Österreichischen Akademie Der Wissenschaften.

Siklós, Bulcsu. 1996. *The Vajrabhairava Tantras: Tibetan and Mongolian Versions, English Translation and Annotations.* Buddhica Britannica Series Continua 7. Tring: Institute of Buddhist Studies.

Slusser, Mary Shepherd. 1982. *Nepal Mandala—A Cultural Study of the Kathmandu Valley.* 2 vols. Princeton, N.J.: Princeton University Press.

Smith, E. Gene. 2001. *Among Tibetan Texts: History and Literature of the Himalayan Plateau.* Boston: Wisdom Publications.

Snellgrove, David L. 1967. *The Nine Ways of Bon: Exerpts from* gZi-brjid *Edited and Translated.* London Oriental Series, vol. 18. Oxford: Oxford University Press.

——. 1987. *Indo-Tibetan Buddhism: Indian Buddhists & Their Tibetan Successors.* 2 vols. Boston: Shambhala.

Snellgrove, David L., and Tadeusz Skorupski. 1977–80. *The Cultural Heritage of Ladakh.* 2 vols. New Delhi: Vikas.

Sobisch, Jan-Ulrich. 2002. *Three-Vow Theories in Tibetan Buddhism: A Comparative Study of Major Traditions from the Twelfth Through Nineteenth Centuries.* Wiesbaden: Dr. Ludwig Reichert Verlag.

Somers, Robert M. 1979. "The End of the T'ang." In *The Cambridge History of China.* Vol. 3, *Sui and T'ang China, 589–906*, edited by Denis Twitchett, part 1, pp. 682–789. Cambridge: Cambridge University Press.

Sørensen, Per, trans. 1994. *Tibetan Buddhist Historiography: The Mirror Illuminating the Royal Genealogies: An Annotated Translation of the XIVth Century Tibetan Chronicle: rGyal-rabs gsal-ba'i me-long.* Asiatische Forschungen series, band 128. Wiesbaden: Harrassowitz.

Sperling, Elliot. 1987. "Lama to the King of Hsia." *JTS* 7: 31–50.

——. 1991. "Some Remarks on sGa A-gnyan dam-pa and the Origins of the Hor-pa Lineage of the dKar-mdzes Region." In *Tibetan History and Language: Studies Dedicated to Uray Géza on his Seventieth Birthday*, edited by Ernst Steinkellner, pp. 455–65. Wiener Studien zur Tibetologie un Buddhismuskunde Heft 26. Vienna: Universität Wien.

——. 1994. "Rtsa-mi Lo-tsā-ba Sangs-rgyas grags-pa and the Tangut Background to Early Mongol-Tibetan Relations. In *Tibetan Studies: Proceedings of the 6th Seminar of the International Association for Tibetan Studies*, edited by Per Kværne, vol. 2, pp. 803–24. Oslo: Institute for Comparative Research in Human Culture.

Spitz, Lewis W. 1987. *The Renaissance and Reformation Movements.* Vol. 1, *The Renaissance*. Rev. ed. St. Louis: Concordia.

Stark, Rodney, and William Sims Bainbridge. 1985. *The Future of Religion: Secularization, Revival, and Cult Formation.* Berkeley and Los Angeles: University of California Press.

Stearns, Cyrus. 1996. "The Life and Tibetan Legacy of the Indian *Mahāpaṇḍita* Vibhūticandra." *JIABS* 19: 127–71.

——. 1997. "A Quest for 'The Path and Result.'" In *Religions of Tibet—In Practice*, edited by Donald S. Lopez, pp. 188–99. Princeton, N.J.: Princeton University Press.

——. 1999. *The Buddha from Dolpo: A Study of the Life and Thought of the Tibetan Master Dolpopa Sherab Gyaltsen.* Albany: State University of New York Press.

——. 2001. *Luminous Lives: The Story of the Early Masters of the Lam 'Bras Tradition in Tibet.* Boston: Wisdom Publications.

Stein, Burton. 1991. "The Segmentary State: Interim Reflections." *Puruṣārtha* 13: 217–37.

Stein, Rolf A. 1951. "Mi-ñag et Si-hia, géographie historique et légendes ancestrales." *BEFEO* 44: 223–65.

——. 1959. *Recherches sur l'épopée et le barde au Tibet.* Bibliothèque de l'Institute des hautes études chinoises, vol. 13. Paris: Presses universitaires de France.

——. 1961. *Les Tribus anciennes des marches sino-tibétaines.* Bibliothèque de l'Institut des hautes études chinoises, vol. 15. Paris: Presses universitaires de France.

——. 1962. "Une source ancienne por l'histoire de l'épopée tibétaine, le *Rlaṅs Po-ti bse-ru*." *JA* 250: 77–106.

—— 1966. "Nouveaux Documents tibétains sur le Mi-Ñag/Si-hia." *Mélanges de sinologie offerts à Monsieur Paul Demiéville*, pp. 281–89. Bibliothèque de l'Institut des hautes études chinoises, vol. 20. Paris: Presses universitaires de France.

——. 1978. "À Propos des documents anciens relatifs au *Phur-Bu* (*Kīla*)." In *Proceedings of the Csoma de Körös Memorial Symposium*, edited by Louis Ligeti, pp. 427–44. Budapest: Akadémiai Kiadó.

——. 1984. "Tibetica antiqua II: L'Usage de métaphores pour des distinctions honorifiques à l'époque des rois tibétains." *BEFEO* 73: 257–72.

——. 1985. "Tibetica antiqua III: À Propos du mot *gcug-lag* et de la religion indigène." *BEFEO* 74: 83–133.

——. 1986. "Tibetica antiqua IV: La Tradition relative au début du bouddhism au Tibet." *BEFEO* 75: 169–96.

——. 1995. "La Soumission de Rudra et autres contes tantriques." *JA* 283:121–60.

Steinkellner, Ernst. 1973. *Dharmakīrti's Pramāṇaviniścayaḥ, 2. Kapitel: Svārthānumānam.* 2 vols. Vienna: Österreichische Akademi der Wissenschaften.

——. 1978. "Remarks on Tantristic Hermeneutics." In *Proceedings of the Csoma de Körös Memorial Symposium*, edited by Louis Ligeti, pp. 445–58. Budapest: Akadémiai Kiadó.

——. 1991. *Tibetan History and Language: Studies Dedicated to Uray Géza on His Seventieth Birthday.* Wiener Studien zur Tibetologie und Buddhismuskunde Heft 26. Vienna: Arbeitskreis für Tibetische und Buddhistische Studien Universität Wien.

Steinkellner, Ernst, and Helmut Tauscher, eds. 1983. *Contributions on Tibetan Language, History and Culture.* Proceedings of the Csoma de Körös Symposium, Velm-Vienna, September 13–19, 1981. 2 vols. Vienna: Arbeitskreis für Tibetische und Buddhistische Studien Universität Wien.

Stock, Brian. 1990. *Listening for the Text.* Baltimore: Johns Hopkins University Press.

Sutherland, Gail Hinich. 1991. *Disguises of the Demon: The Development of the Yakṣa in Hinduism and Buddhism.* Albany: State University of New York Press.

Sweet, Michael J. 1996. "Mental Purification (*Blo sbyong*): A Native Tibetan Genre of Religious Literature." In *Tibetan Literature: Studies in Genre*, edited by José Ignacio Cabezón and Roger R. Jackson, pp. 244–60. Ithaca, N.Y.: Snow Lion.

Szerb, János. 1980. "Glosses on the Oeuvre of Bla-ma 'phags-pa. I on the Activity of Sa-skya Paṇḍita." In *Tibetan Studies in Honour of Hugh Richardson*, edited by Michael Aris and Aung San Suu Kyi, pp. 290–300. Warminster: Aris and Phillips.

——. 1985. "Glosses on the Oeuvre of Bla-ma 'Phags-pa: III. The 'Patron-Patronized' Relationship." In *Soundings in Tibetan Civilization*, edited by Barbara Nimri Aziz and Matthew Kapstein, pp. 165–73. New Delhi: Manohar.

——. 1990. *Bu ston's History of Buddhism in Tibet, Critically Edited with a Comprehensive Index.* Beiträge zur Kultur- und Geistesgeschichte Asiens, no. 5. Vienna: Österreichischen Akademie der Wissenschaften.

Tachikawa, Musashi. 1975. "The Tantric Doctrine of the Sa skya pa According to the *Śel gyi me loṅ.*" *Acta asiatica* 29: 95–106.

Takasaki, Jikido. 1966. *A Study on the Ratnagotravibhāga.* SOR 33. Rome: ISMEO.

Tatz, Mark. 1986. *Asanga's Chapter on Ethics with the Commentary of Tsong-Kha-pa,* The Basic Path to Awakening, *the Complete Bodhisattva.* Studies in Asian Thought and Religion, vol. 4. Lewiston, N.Y.: Edwin Mellen Press.

——. 1987. "The Life of the Siddha-Philosopher Maitrīgupta." *JAOS* 107:695–711.

Templeman, David. 1999. "Internal and External Geography in Spiritual Biography." In *Sacred Spaces and Powerful Places in Tibetan Culture—A Collection of Essays*, edited by Toni Huber, pp. 187–97. Dharamsala: Library of Tibetan Works and Archives.

Thakur, Laxman S. 1994. "A Tibetan Inscription by lHa Bla-ma Ye-shes-'od from dKor (sPu) rediscovered." *JRAS* 3rd. ser., vol. 4: 369–75.

Thapar, Romila. 2004. *Somanatha: The Many Voices of a History*. New Delhi: Viking Penguin.

Thargyal, Rinzin. 1988. "The Applicability of the Concept of Feudalism to Traditional Tibetan Society." In *Tibetan Studies: Proceedings of the 4th Seminar of the International Association for Tibetan Studies*, edited by Helga Uebach and Jampa L. Panglung, pp. 391–95. Munich: Bayerische Akademie der Wissenschaften.

Thomas, F. W. 1903. "Deux collections sanscrites et tibétaines de sādhanas." *Le Muséon* n.s. 4: 1–42.

——. 1935–55. *Tibetan Literary Texts and Documents Concerning Chinese Turkestan.* Oriental Translation Fund, n.s. vols. 32, 37, 40. London: Luzac.

——. 1957. *Ancient Folk-Literature from North-Eastern Tibet.* Berlin: Akademie Verlag.

Thondup, Tulku. 1986. *Hidden Teachings of Tibet: An Explanation of the Terma Tradition of the Nyingma School of Buddhism.* London: Wisdom Publications.

Torella, Raffaele, ed. 2001. *Le Parole e i marmi: Studi in onore di Raniero Gnoli nel suo 70° compleanno.* SOR 92. 2 vols. Rome: Istituto italiano per L'Africa e L'Oriente.

Tsering, Pema. 1978. *"Rñiṅ Ma Pa* Lamas am Yüan-Kaiserhof." In *Proceedings of the Csoma de Körös Memorial Symposium*, edited by Louis Ligeti, pp. 511–40. Budapest: Akadémiai Kiadó.

Tucci, Giuseppe. 1930a. "Animadversiones Indicae." *Journal of the Asiatic Society of Bengal* 26:125–60.

——. 1930b. *The Nyayamukha of Dignāga.* Materialien zur Kunde des Buddhismus, vol. 15. Heidelberg: O. Harrassowitz.

——. 1947. "The Validity of Tibetan Historical Tradition." Reprint, *Opera minora.* Rome: Rome University, 1971.

——. 1949. *Tibetan Painted Scrolls.* 3 vols. Rome: La Libreria dello stato. Reprint, Bangkok: SDI Publications, 1999.

——. 1950.*The Tombs of the Tibetan Kings.* SOR 1. Rome: ISMEO.

——. 1956a. *Preliminary Report on Two Scientific Expeditions in Nepal.* SOR 10. Rome: ISMEO.

——. 1956b. *To Lhasa and Beyond.* Rome: Istituto poligrafico dello stato.

——. 1958. *Minor Buddhist Texts.* SOR 9. 2 vols. Rome: ISMEO.

——. 1980. *The Religions of Tibet.* Translated from the German and Italian by Geoffrey Samuel. Berkeley and Los Angeles: University of California Press.

Uebach, Helga, ed. and trans. 1987. *Nel-pa Paṇḍita's Chronik Me-Tog Phreṅ-ba: Handschrift der Library of Tibetan works and Archives, Tibetischer Text in Faksimile, Transkription und Übersetzung.* Studia Tibetica Band I. Munich: Bayerische Akademie der Wissenschaften.

——. 1990. "On Dharma-Colleges and Their Teachers in the Ninth Century

Tibetan Empire." In *Indo-Sino-Tibetica: Studi in onore di Luciano Petech*, edited by Paolo Daffina, pp. 393–417. Studi Orientali, vol. 9. Rome: Universita di Roma.

Ueyama, Daishun. 1983. "The Study of Tibetan Ch'an Manuscripts Recovered from Tun-huang: A Review of the Field and Its Prospects." In *Early Ch'an in China and Tibet*, edited by Whalen Lai and Lewis R. Lancaster, pp. 327–49. Berkeley, Calif.: Asian Humanities Press.

Ui, Hakuju, et al., eds. 1934. *A Complete Catalogue of the Tibetan Buddhist Canons (BKaḫ-ḫgyur and Bstan-ḫgyur)*. Sendai: Tōhoku Imperial University.

Uray, Géza. 1982. "Notes on the Thousand-Districts of the Tibetan Empire in the First Half of the Ninth Century." *Acta orientalia academiae scientiarum hungaricae* 36, nos. 1–3: 545–48.

de la Vallée Poussin, Louis, trans. 1971. *L'Abhidharmakośa de Vasubandhu.* 2nd. ed. *Mélanges chinois et bouddhiques* 16. 6 parts.

van der Veer, Peter. 1988. *Gods on Earth: The Management of Religious Experience and Identity in a North Indian Pilgrimage Centre.* London: Athlone Press.

Verhagen, Pieter C. 1994. *A History of Sanskrit Grammatical Literature in Tibet.* Vol. 1, *Transmission of the Canonical Literature.* Leiden: Brill.

———. 1995. "Studies in Tibetan Indigenous Gammar (2): Tibetan Phonology and Phonetics in the *Byis-pa-bde-blog-tu-'jug-pa* by Bsod-nams-rtse-mo (1142–1182)." *Asiatische studien* 49, no. 4: 943–68.

———. 2001. *A History of Sanskrit Grammatical Literature in Tibet*, Vol. 2, *Assimilation into Indigenous Scholarship.* Leiden: Brill.

Vitali, Roberto. 1990. *Early Temples of Central Tibet.* London: Serindia Publications.

———. 1996. *The Kingdoms of Gu-.ge Pu.hrang.* Dharamsala: Tho.ling gtsug.lag.khang lo.gcig.stong 'khor.ba'i rjes.dran.mdzad sgo'i go.sgrig tshogs.chung.

———. 2001. "Sa skya and the mNga' ris skor gsum legacy: the case of Rin chen bzang po's flying mask." *Lungta* 14: 5–44.

———. 2002. "The History of the Lineages of Gnas Rnying Summarised as Its 'Ten Greatnesses.'" In *Tibet, Past and Present*, edited by Henk Blezer, vol. 1, pp. 81–107. Leiden: Brill.

———. forthcoming. "The Transmission of *bsnyung gnas* in India, the Kathmandu Valley and Tibet (10th-12th Centuries)." In *Studies in Tibetan Buddhist Literature and Praxis*, edited by Ronald M. Davidson and Christian Wedemeyer. Leiden: Brill.

Vogel, Jean Phillippe. 1926. *Indian Serpent Lore; or the Nāgas of Hindu Legend and Art.* London: A. Probsthain.

Vostrikov, A. I. 1970. *Tibetan Historical Literature.* Translated from the Russian by Harish Chandra Gupta. Soviet Indology Series, no. 4. Calcutta: Indian Studies Past & Present.

Wang, Gungwu. 1963. *The Structure of Power in North China During the Five Dynasties.* Stanford, Calif.: Stanford University Press.

Wayman, Alex. 1977. *Yoga of the Guhyasamājatantra: The Arcane Lore of Forty Verses.* Delhi: Motilal Banarsidass.

Wedemeyer, Christian K. forthcoming. "Tantalizing Traces of the Labors of the Lotsāwas: Alternative Translations of Sanskrit Sources in the Writings of Rje Tsong Kha pa." In *Studies in Tibetan Buddhist Literature and Praxis,* edited by Ronald M. Davidson and Christian K. Wedemeyer. Leiden: Brill.

Weinstein, Stanley. 1987. *Buddhism Under the T'ang.* Cambridge: Cambridge University Press.

Willson, Martin. 1986. *In Praise of Tārā: Songs to the Savioress.* Boston: Wisdom Publications.

Witzel, Michael. 1994. "Kashmiri Manuscripts and Pronunciation." In *A Study of the Nīlamata: Aspects of Hinduism in Ancient Kashmir*, edited by Yasuke Ikari, pp. 1–53. Kyoto: Institute for Research in Humanities, Kyoto University.

Wright, Arthur F. 1990. *Studies in Chinese Buddhism.* New Haven, Conn.: Yale University Press.

Wylie, Turrell V. 1977. "The First Mongol Conquest of Tibet Reinterpreted." *Harvard Journal of Asian Studies* 1: 103–33.

——. 1982. "Dating the Death of Nāropa." In *Indological and Buddhist Studies—Volume in Honour of Professor J. W. de Jong on His Sixtieth Birthday*, edited by L. A. Hercus et al., pp. 687–92. Bibliotheca Indo-Buddhica, no. 27. Delhi: Sri Satguru Publications.

Yamaguchi, Zuiho. 1984. "Methods of Chronological Calculation in Tibetan Historical Sources." In *Tibetan and Buddhist Studies, Commemorating the 200th* Anniversary of the Birth of Alexander Csoma de Körös, edited by Louis Ligeti, vol. 2, pp. 405–24. Bibliotheca orientalis hungarica, vol. 29, no. 2. Budapest: Akadémiai Kiadó.

Index

PERSONAL NAMES

BUDDHAS, BODHISATTVAS, DEITIES

PLACE NAMES

TEXTS

GENERAL INDEX